Remedial and Clinical Reading Instruction

Remedial and Clinical Reading Instruction

SANDRA McCORMICK
The Ohio State University

Merrill Publishing Company
A Bell & Howell Information Company
Columbus   Toronto   London   Melbourne

Published by Merrill Publishing Company
A Bell and Howell Information Company
Columbus, Ohio 43216

This book was set in Usherwood.

Administrative Editor: Jeff Johnston
Production Coordinator: Anne Daly
Cover Designer: Cathy Watterson

Photo credits: All photos copyrighted by individuals or companies listed. Merrill Publishing/photographs by Tim Cairns, pp. 248, 348, 374, 385; Celia Drake, p.137; Jean Greenwald, pp. 226, 293, 338; Mary Hagler, p. 441; Bruce Johnson, pp. 35, 85, 120, 307; Kevin Fitzsimmons, p. 5; Lloyd Lemmerman, p. 407; and Doug Martin, p. 152. Other photos by Dick Garrett/Columbus Citizen Journal, p. 173; Vivienne della Grotta, p. 63; Harvey Phillips/Phillips Photo Illustrators, pp. 263, 435; and David Strickler/Strix Pix, pp. 27, 189, 423.

Library of Congress Catalog Card Number: 86—62387
International Standard Book Number: 0—675—20284—1
Printed in the United States of America

1 2 3 4 5 6 7 8 9 — 91 90 89 88 87

To the memory of
ROBERT EDGAR HASTINGS
who helped me learn to love
both reading and writing

Preface

The principles for diagnosis and instruction of reading disabled individuals presented in this book are based on an interactive model of the reading process. Suggested techniques have been drawn from the best in traditional and contemporary approaches to remediation. Information was selected on the basis of its consistency with the interactive view of reading and was obtained from results of psycholinguistic research, authoritative opinion about holistic approaches to reading, and techniques and findings from research and practice proven important and useful throughout the traditional subskill approach to remedial and clinical reading instruction.

This book is intended for upper level undergraduates and graduate students in their first course on remedial and clinical reading instruction. Although it presents background information (for example, on the complexity of the reading process), it also provides students with specific, practical diagnostic and remedial strategies for helping reading disabled individuals learn to read. Upper level students should be familiar with research in the field. In this book, the intention has been to present an integrated and understandable discussion of remedial and clinical reading in which research evidence is included and interpreted for the reader along with helpful recommendations based on the findings. Although it relates suggestions to sound theory and research, it also serves the practicing teacher's need for specificity in regard to program planning and instructional techniques.

Many available texts on remedial and clinical reading deal primarily with the elementary school child. Few colleges and universities offer separate courses in remedial and clinical reading instruction for elementary and secondary teachers. As a result, secondary teachers enrolled in these courses frequently complain that the text they must use gives little attention to their specific problems in working with the disabled older reader. Although this book discusses the needs of elementary school children extensively, it also presents information for the secondary teacher in every chapter. In addition, an entire chapter deals with illiterate and functionally illiterate adults.

The entire text reflects an emphasis on comprehension based on the points of view that the only purpose of reading is to gain meaning, that all instructional procedures in reading have one purpose—to facilitate comprehension, and that emphasizing meaning aids remediation in all areas. These viewpoints are stressed in the discussion of all topics. In addition, two separate chapters on comprehension provide research findings and current understandings of the process. Implications of this information for reading comprehension development in the remedial classroom and clinic are emphasized. Numerous specific examples of instructional strategies for this vitally important area are presented for teachers at all levels.

Advising teachers what not to do as well as what to do is important. Reading instruction, like much of education, has fallen prey to cyclical movements during which old ideas are resurrected and proven to be as unsuccessful the second or third times around as they were the first. Then too, it is common for many years to pass before research findings reach the field and affect practice; therefore teachers use valuable instructional time having students engage in diagnostic and instructional tasks that provide no assistance in increasing reading achievement. For these reasons, in relation to most topics in the text, ill advised practices of the past and present are pointed out. Procedures highlighted in this fashion were chosen based on research findings, not because they were antithetical to personal biases of the author. When lack of efficacy of tactics or materials are discussed, research-supported procedures are suggested as preferable alternatives.

This book has been organized to facilitate the learning of students for whom this is a first course in remedial and clinical reading instruction. Unit I presents important background information including understandings about the field of reading, current theories about the reading process, and information about causes and correlates of reading disability. Unit II treats diagnosis. Since some colleges offer a separate course on diagnosis of reading problems and another on remedial techniques, students who have had a previous course on diagnostic issues may review this unit briefly or omit it altogether. Other universities incorporate diagnosis and remediation into the same course; in that case all units of the book should be studied carefully. Units III through VI offer suggestions for many aspects of remediation, while Unit VII provides ideas for two important ancillary roles with which reading teachers are usually involved.

My thanks go to my many professional colleagues across the country who reviewed this work and whose helpful criticisms guided me in preparing the final version of the manuscript: Bernard Hayes (Utah State University), Albert J. Shannon (Rider College), Ann Marshall Huston (Lynchburg College), Steven Stahl (Western Illinois University), James Jackson (Southern Illinois University), Barbara J. Walker (Eastern Montana College), John Savage (Boston College), J. Richard Chambers (Boston University) and Alden J. Moe (Louisiana State University). I look forward to receiving comments, questions, and suggestions from the students and teachers who use this book.

Sandra McCormick

Contents

UNIT III
Planning for Instructional Intervention

UNIT IV
Remedial Procedures for Students Having Difficulty
Learning to Read

UNIT V
Remedial Procedures for Students Having Difficulty
Reading to Learn

Remedial and Clinical Reading Instruction

Foundations of Remedial and Clinical Reading Instruction

1

Important Background Information

Literacy is critical in our society. Reading provides access to employment, increases educational opportunities, promotes social adjustment, offers entertainment, and serves as a source for life-long learning. In addition, reading generates ideas that lead to social change and improvement. Thus reading is an indispensable skill for both the individual and society. See Table 1–1. Nevertheless, many elementary and secondary schools have large numbers of students who are disabled readers despite years of reading instruction. Though most students *do* attain reading skill, poor readers persist. Why is this so, and what can you do about it? You can serve as a superior teacher of reading in one of several types of programs.

TYPES OF PROGRAMS

Developmental Reading Programs

A *developmental reading program* is a regular classroom program designed for most school-aged students.[1] A developmental program should be well-balanced and include many varied opportunities to read stories and informational material as well as specific activities to develop word identification, comprehension, and other reading strategies. The eight major components of developmental reading programs are

1. Promoting readiness. Activities facilitate the initial stages of reading acquisition and prepare the student for each new step in learning.
2. Developing a sight vocabulary. Procedures help students enlarge the number of words they recognize instantly.

---

[1] Most definitions in this text conform to those given in *A Dictionary of Reading and Related Terms* (Harris & Hodges, 1981), commissioned by the International Reading Association to bring consistency to meanings of terms used in the field of reading. In the past, lack of consistency has been prevalent (for example, see the numerous conflicting definitions for the term "dyslexia" listed later in this chapter) and has prevented clear communication. This text supports the effort to agree on meanings for reading terminology.

Table 1–1
Reading levels of a sampling of items and materials encountered in adult life

Items and Materials	Approximate Grade Level of Reading Ability Needed
Help-wanted ads in newspapers	6–7
Front-page stories in newspapers	9–12+
Dosage and symptom information on aspirin bottle labels	10
Preparation directions on boxes of frozen dinners	8
Directions for filling out the 1040 income tax forms	9–10
Training materials for military cooks	7–8
Articles in *Reader's Digest, Saturday Evening Post, Ladies' Home Journal, Popular Mechanics,* and *Harper's*	12+
Articles in romance, TV, and movie magazines	8
Recent presidential inaugural addresses	9
Information on financial statements	11–16+
Life insurance policies	12
Apartment leases	College

Sources: Bargantz and Dulin (1970), Bittner and Shamo (1976), Bormuth (1973–74), Felton and Felton (1973), Hirshoren, Hunt, and Davis (1974), Hoskins (1973), Kilty (1976), Kwolek (1973), Pyrczak (1976), Razik (1969), Sticht (1975), Worthington (1977).

3. Developing word identification strategies. Students learn several strategies to use alone or in combination when they encounter unknown words.
4. Enlarging the student's meaning vocabulary. Students are helped to increase their knowledge of word meanings.
5. Increasing comprehension. Many different strategies help students comprehend material effectively. Since the only reason to read is to comprehend, this is the most important component of any program. All other components assist comprehension.
6. Reading orally. Adequate oral reading is sometimes needed for good communication. More often it is used as an informal assessment tool so the teacher can determine if a student is employing good reading strategies.
7. Promoting appropriate rates of reading. Students learn to read at a rate appropri-

ate to the specific purpose and material.
8. Developing study skills and content area reading skills. Because all reading material is not narrative (story-type) material, students learn to deal with the special types of language and reading skills that they must confront in content area materials and other types of informative writing.

A developmental program that inadequately or inappropriately treats any of these eight components or does not provide large amounts of time for reading to practice strategies may lead to mild to moderate reading disabilities in some students. Developmental reading programs exist through the end of sixth grade in some school systems; however, more districts are including developmental reading as a regular part of the curriculum in their middle schools and high schools. These

A developmental reading program should include many opportunities to read narrative and informational materials, to learn strategies, and to practice study skills.

secondary level developmental reading programs are for average, and even above average readers, and are designed to help students continue to perfect and refine advanced reading skills.

Corrective Reading Programs

A *corrective reading program* is carried out in a regular classroom by the regular classroom teacher. It is designed to help a student with a mild reading disability who needs special attention in one or more of the eight major reading components. Despite the need to provide a general developmental reading program for the class, the classroom teacher can still provide appropriate and adequate remediation for the student with a mild disability. A corrective reading program has been described as "more specific than developmental instruc-

tion, but less intensive than remedial reading instruction" (Harris & Hodges, 1981, p. 71). Some students who need corrective reading do not have a specific weakness. Rather, their scores on a battery of tests indicate a general, slight weakness in all areas.

Remedial Reading Programs

A *remedial reading program* is one in which students with moderate to severe reading disabilities leave their regular classrooms for a portion of the school day for special instruction by a specially trained reading teacher. This instruction is carried out in small groups of about 5 to 8 students. More comprehensive assessment of students' reading problems is conducted than in most developmental or corrective programs to determine students' weaknesses and the reasons for these weaknesses as well as the strengths that may help alleviate their problems. The teacher adjusts instruction to the special needs of the students, and the students are usually grouped according to common needs to attend the remedial class at the same time. At the end of a class period (usually about 45 minutes) students return to their regular classrooms and another group of students with reading problems comes to the reading room for special instruction. Since students are grouped according to common needs, some instruction may be carried out with all members of the small group participating. At other times students may work alone or in a one-to-one situation with the teacher. The special training of the teacher and the small size of each class make possible in-depth assessment, more frequent ongoing assessment, and flexibility in adapting instructional techniques to individual differences.

Clinical Reading Programs

A *clinical reading program* is designed for students with severe reading disabilities, and the clinician only works with one student at a time. Assessment may be more extensive than in other programs and often includes referrals to other professionals or agencies, such as physicians, speech and hearing specialists, and psychologists, for evaluation. Diagnostic procedures include formal testing and informal observation. Remediation is specialized, intensive, and highly individualized. A case study report is usually developed for the student and includes not only the results of assessment but also her responses to various instructional techniques. Some school systems have centrally located reading clinics to which transportation is provided for students from schools within the district. Universities and colleges frequently have educational clinics that serve severely reading disabled students. Hospitals and other social agencies may also sponsor reading clinics.

Other Reading Programs

Other programs in which you may work as a teacher of reading are learning disability programs and programs for the developmentally handicapped (also called educable mentally retarded). In 1982, 73 percent of students in learning disability (LD) programs in the United States were in those programs because they had reading problems. The Learning Disability Clinic of the Children's Hospital Medical Center in Boston reported that about 75 percent of their referrals involved students with reading disabilities (Chall, 1978). A major task of teachers of developmentally handicapped (DH) students is dealing with their difficulties in attaining an acceptable degree of literacy.

The school psychologist may also deal with reading disabled individuals. When the school psychologist is requested to assess students, it is often because of a suspected learning disorder. In most cases the possible learning problem is first noted because students are not progressing as they should in reading. School psychologists need to understand the reading process so they can assess students

according to current thinking in the field and make appropriate recommendations to teachers.

Although there may be some differences between developmental, corrective, remedial, clinical, LD, and DH reading programs in degree of individualization, intensity, and pace of instruction, they are all based on the same basic principles of learning and learning to read, and all deal with the eight major components of reading instruction listed previously. Finally, all must deal with the *affective domain,* defined as "the psychological field of emotional activity" (Harris & Hodges, 1981, p. 9). This includes both students' feelings and attitudes. Teachers often positively affect learning by capitalizing on students' interests derived from these feelings and attitudes. But feelings and attitudes can also have a negative influence on learning. Infused throughout the chapters of this book are discussions of the role reading problems play in a student's emotional outlook, the influence emotional distress has on reading disability, ways to observe interests and attitudes, and suggestions for promoting self-esteem among poor readers. Attention to the affective domain is important for all students, but it is crucial for students with learning problems.

So, although there are some differences among the various types of programs, there are more similarities. Most techniques suggested in this text are equally useful in all programs, and teachers in all programs need to know how to deal with reading problems.

ROLES OF READING TEACHERS

An individual trained in reading may serve several roles depending on the amount and focus of that training. A *reading teacher* can be loosely defined as anyone whose work includes reading instruction, but more often the term means a teacher with special training who works with students who have reading problems and teaches in a setting other than the regular classroom. The term *reading specialist* is used synonymously with the designation reading teacher. Many reading teachers work with classroom teachers as well as students. They help classroom teachers improve their developmental reading programs and offer suggestions about corrective reading techniques for students with mild reading problems. A *reading clinician* is a reading teacher who works with students in a clinical setting.

The titles *reading consultant* and *reading resource teacher* define the same role. These are specialists who use their skills and knowledge to work with other teachers; they do not usually serve students directly, but devote their time to providing inservice training programs, classroom consultation, demonstrations, and other services designed to improve reading instruction in all types of programs within a school district. An LD *resource room teacher* serves a different function. Although some teachers in LD programs have self-contained classrooms where students remain with them most of the day, more LD teachers have a role similar to the reading teacher's. They serve small groups of students with moderate or severe problems in a setting other than the regular classroom for designated times each day. However, the LD teacher works with other learning disorders as well as reading problems. Although most students enrolled in LD programs receive special instruction because they have reading disabilities, they may also have problems with math or other language arts, such as spelling or writing. LD teachers must also work with classroom teachers to coordinate students' regular class programs and the resource room program, and to help classroom teachers deal with the LD students' special needs in the regular classroom.

The designations *reading coordinator* and *reading supervisor* are also used synonymously. Both may oversee and coordinate all the reading programs within a school system or may be in charge of one specific program and the teachers within it. For example, one person may be the supervisor of the district's remedial reading program, and another may be the supervisor of the district's reading clinic.

OTHER IMPORTANT DEFINITIONS

Reading teachers, LD teachers, DH teachers, reading consultants, or reading supervisors should be able to define and differentiate certain important terms used often in the profession. Some are more useful than others, but all appear in professional journals, textbooks, and lay press articles dealing with reading. Many are used incorrectly by nonprofessionals. Teachers of reading should understand their meanings and correct uses.

Disabled Reader

Who is a disabled reader? A *disabled reader* is anyone reading significantly below her *own potential*. Although students are sometimes labeled disabled readers because they are not reading at grade level, grade level achievement is an inappropriate criterion for determining reading disability. Reading specialists recognize that there is a wide range of differences in reading ability within a single grade. In a typical classroom you will probably find good, average, and poor readers and great variations in skills, word knowledge, and comprehension.

A student's potential is determined not by assigned grade level, but by a number of factors working in combination such as chronological age and mental age or intelligence. Students with very high IQs should be reading above grade level; if not, they are not reading up to their potential. Conversely, students with a significantly lower than average IQ may be reading below their assigned grade levels, but still be reading up to their potentials.

Another term for an individual's potential is *learning expectancy level* (LEL). Some authors refer to this as *reading expectancy*. A student's approximate LEL may be assessed in different ways. Sometimes there is a discrepancy between the score a student attains when answering questions after reading material and the score she attains when answering questions after listening to material read. For example, a student may attain a reading instructional level of only 4.0 (fourth grade) on a standardized test she reads by herself, but if she attains a score of 6.0 (sixth grade) on a test of listening comprehension, it is said that her reading potential is sixth grade level.

A more common method of determining a student's LEL is to use one of several mathematical formulas for computing reading potential (discussed in Chapter 5). For now, let us suppose you have computed the LEL for Terrence, a boy referred to you as a candidate for your remedial reading class. You have determined that Terrence's LEL is 9.5, that is, when several factors have been considered (such as mental age and chronological age) it is determined that Terrence should be reading at approximately the middle of ninth grade level. Your next step is to determine his present reading achievement. You administer a standardized reading test or an informal reading inventory and find that Terrence's present reading level is 6.2, or approximately the reading level of the average student in the second month of sixth grade. A difference of 3 years and 3 months exists between the level at which Terrence should be reading according to his LEL and the level of his present reading achievement. This difference is sometimes called *capacity-achievement difference,* or *CAD.* With a CAD of 3.3, Terrence would be considered a disabled reader and should receive special reading instruction.

Learning Disability

The term *learning disability* was adopted in 1963 as a generic description to replace the many different labels applied to students who had difficulty in listening, mathematics, reading, speaking, spelling, thinking, or writing. In most states today, eligibility for services in LD programs is determined in the same way that eligibility for remedial or clinical reading programs is determined. The levels at which students should be achieving are compared to the levels at which they are achieving. If the difference is significant, students are considered learning disabled and may receive remedial instruction from an LD teacher or an LD tutor.

During the early years of the LD movement, students designated as learning disabled were believed to be perceptually handicapped or brain injured or to have processing dysfunctions in their central nervous systems. Even today the term learning disability is used differently by individuals with different theoretical biases. For students labeled as learning disabled, just as for those labeled as reading disabled, there may indeed be a number of different underlying causes for the learning difficulty, but many LD students have no discernible brain injury or other neurological problem. The current literature assumes the learning problem may have occurred for any number of reasons (discussed in Chapters 3 and 4), and whatever the origin of the problem, a student may be considered learning disabled if she manifests significant discrepancy between estimated academic potential and actual academic performance.

A general assumption is that the reading teacher works with students with less severe reading problems, and the LD teacher works with students who require more intensive and specialized instruction. In fact, the original intent of the law that requires services for LD students was to provide services only to those with the most severe disabilities (an estimated 2 to 3 percent of the student population). In practice this has not held true: both the reading teacher and the LD teacher work with students who have moderate and severe reading disabilities. For this reason, and because criteria for assigning the labels learning disabled and reading disabled are the same in most programs today, the label the student receives and the program she enters may be largely a matter of chance: the school psychologist who tests the student is more familiar with reading programs than LD programs and so suggests placement in the remedial reading class; or the reading class is full, but there is room in the LD program so the principal suggests that the student be tested to determine if she is eligible for LD services.

In contemporary LD programs the instruction a student receives in reading is no different from instruction received in remedial and clinical reading programs. This was not true in the early days of the LD movement. Because early work in this field was conducted by professionals who had worked with brain damaged and severely mentally retarded persons, their theories of what caused difficulty in learning to read had a neurological or physiological orientation. Many methods employed with students labeled learning disabled were far removed from techniques shown to improve reading ability. Students were required to engage in body management activities (such as walking on balance beams), complete perceptual exercises, and undergo training meant to improve defective brain processing functions.

Professionals in the LD field became disillusioned with perceptual-motor techniques and assessment during the early 1970s when numerous studies began to show that direct teaching of reading was effective for students with learning disorders while treating "underlying psychological processes," such as visual-perceptual, visual-motor, and auditory-perceptual problems, was not (Batemen, 1971; Black, 1974; Bryan, 1974; Hammill & Larsen, 1974b; Masland & Cratty, 1971; Saphier, 1973). Although a few LD programs still display this early process training orientation, most now employ direct teaching, that is, teaching directly what students need to learn rather than hoping their disabilities will be remediated in some roundabout fashion such as perceptual or motor activities. For example, if a student has a reading disability, instruction should involve reading activities, not physical activities; if a student has a math disability, instruction should employ math activities, not perceptual activities. A reading teacher and an LD teacher teaching reading in programs based on current research would use no significantly different methods in their classes.

Dyslexia

The term *dyslexia* elicits many conflicting definitions and contrary suggestions regarding its causes and symptoms. Some, for example, define dyslexia as a reading disability of unknown origin:

> [Dyslexia is] an inability to read when no specific causes are evident. (Hittleman, 1978, p. 407)

> Originally the word [dyslexia] was used to identify a form of brain damage that deprives the patient of his ability to recall words, letters, and symbols. By extension, it has come to refer simply to a disorder of reading, without specific regard to what might lie behind that disorder and how it should be treated. (Calkins, 1972, cited in Evans, 1982, p. 576)

> [Dyslexia describes one] whose reading ability is grossly impaired and in whom no difficulty of basic visual or auditory receptive apparatus, amentia, dementia, neurological disease or injury, or serious psychiatric illness exists. (Drew, 1955, p. 247)

Certain definitions retain aspects of the original definition used in the late 1800s by Hinshelwood (1896) in which the cause is specified as a brain defect or of other neurological origin:

> [Dyslexia is] a rare but definable and diagnosable form of primary reading retardation with some form of central nervous system dysfunction. (Abrahms, 1980, cited in Harris & Hodges, 1981, p. 95)

Other definitions refer to brain and neurological disorders but include other causes as well:

> Among the causes suggested for dyslexia are brain damage and inherited neurological abnormalities not associated with brain damage. Environmental factors, such as poor teaching, are also regarded as possible causes. (Cohen, 1969, p. 516)

Some deny that defects of a neurological origin contribute in any important way but do agree that dyslexia has a constitutional origin:

> Sometimes it [dyslexia] implies a constitutionally based reading disability in an individual who is free from mental defect, serious neurotic traits, and gross neurological deficits. (Harris & Sipay, 1980, p. 137)

Certain definitions indicate that dyslexia may be genetically determined rather than caused by damage to the brain or central nervous system:

> [Dyslexia is] a constitutional and often genetically determined deficit in written language skills such as reading, writing, and spelling. (Ekwall & Shanker, 1983, p. 316)

Others not only deny the association of brain damage with dyslexia, but specify that perceptual difficulties are also unrelated:

> To . . . criteria [for dyslexia] may be added: the absence of serious brain damage or of perceptual defects. (Critchley, 1970, p. 11)

While for some, perceptual deficiencies are central to the definition:

> [A dyslexic is] the kind of child who cannot unscramble auditory and/or written symbols which reach the brain so that they have the same order-pattern and meaning which they have for others. (Zedler, 1969, cited in Evans, 1982, p. 577)

Many definitions include the criterion that the reading disability must be serious:

> [Dyslexia is] a severe reading disability of unspecified origin. (Harris & Hodges, 1981, p. 95)

Others use the term to indicate any type of reading problem:

> [Dyslexia is] a popular term for any difficulty in reading of any intensity and from any cause(s). (Harris & Hodges, 1981, p. 95)

> [Dyslexia is] a synonym for reading disability. (Money, 1962, & Klasen, 1972, cited in Harris & Sipay, 1980, p. 137)

One of the oldest definitions of dyslexia even suggested substance abuse as a cause; Hinshelwood (1896) described a form of dyslexia which he claimed to be of a "toxic origin" after he studied an alcoholic who could not read, but whose reading disability gradually improved when alcohol was withheld from him.

In addition several terms that have been used synonymously with dyslexia include congenital word blindness, dyssymbolia, word amblyopia, specific reading disability, and primary reading retardation. These terms simply compound the prevailing confusion.

Professionals in education, genetics, neurology, ophthalmology, psychiatry, and psychology often define dyslexia differently; even specialists in reading define the term in many different ways; and the lay press uses many uninformed definitions of the term. One writer makes this suggestion: "Put all the definitions in a line and then pick every 73rd word. This would be *your* definition. It couldn't be any worse than what we have now" (Inouye, 1981, p. 3).

The term dyslexia has so many different meanings that most professionals today simply avoid its use and substitute the term *severe reading disability*. Harris and Hodges (1981) make the following observation:

> Due to all the differing assumptions about the process and nature of possible reading problems, dyslexia has come to have so many incompatible connotations that it has lost any real value for educators, except as a fancy word for a reading problem. . . . Thus, in referring to a specific student, it is probably better that the teacher describe the actual reading difficulties, and make suggestions for teaching related to the specific difficulties, not apply a label which may create misleading assumptions by all. (p. 95)

Additional Definitions

Some other definitions with which you should be familiar are

Reading deficiency. A mild reading disability in which the individual lacks a specific skill necessary for effective reading.

Reading retardation. Reading below grade level. (*A Dictionary of Reading and Related Terms* prefers the term *reading disability* because reading achievement below grade level is an inappropriate criterion for assigning students to remedial programs.)

Reluctant reader. An individual who can read but does not like to.

Underachiever. An individual whose achievement is below the level expected according to intelligence tests.

Slow learner. An individual with an IQ between 76 and 89. (While these individuals may have an intellectual functioning level below the average range of 90 to 110, they are not considered retarded.)

Developmentally handicapped. An individual with an IQ between 50 and 75[2] who also manifests deficits in adaptive behavior. (The term *educable mentally retarded* is used synonymously.)

Nonreader. An individual who has been unable to read despite reading instruction.

Illiterate. An individual who is unable to read and/or write; the illiterate person may have had little or no instruction or may not have learned from the instruction she received.

Functional illiterate. An individual who can read, but in such a limited way that she cannot read basic information needed to function in daily life.

Preliterate. A person who is not yet reading simply because she has had no reading instruction; for example, a preschool child.

THE INCIDENCE OF READING DISABILITY

Estimates of the number of reading-disabled individuals are difficult to obtain, largely because of variation in the amount of capacity-achievement difference (CAD) used to determine if a student should receive remedial or clinical reading services. Some programs include any student whose CAD is 1 year. Other programs alter the requirements according to grade level. For example, a program may

---

[2]The IQ range for this designation may vary somewhat depending on the organization making the designation, the state or individual school district providing services, and even the IQ test administered (e.g., the American Association of Mental Deficiency specifies the IQ range for mild mental retardation at 68 to 52 on the Stanford-Binet Intelligence Test but 69 to 55 on the Revised Wechsler Intelligence Scale for Children).

require a six-month CAD for primary grade students, a one-year CAD for intermediate grades, a one and a half-year CAD for middle or junior high school students, and a two-year CAD for high school students. To be eligible for remedial instruction in federally funded Chapter I programs, students must score in the lower third (by percentile) on tests of reading achievement. Because of this and similar variations, reports of the number of disabled readers differ from school district to school district and from program to program.

Spache (1981), and others have shown that the most useful and valid discrepancies for determining if a student has a reading disability serious enough to warrant instruction in a remedial or clinical program are

Primary grades	1 year CAD
Intermediate grades	2 years CAD
Secondary level	3 years CAD

Using these criteria, about 15 percent of students in the United States need remedial and clinical reading services; about 3 percent of all students have severe problems. Many more may require corrective reading programs, but because their problems are mild, instruction can be carried out effectively within regular classrooms if their teachers have sufficient training and if they can take the time to plan special instruction. Training and time are critical factors at all grade levels, but particularly at the secondary level where many teachers have little or no background in reading instruction and work with large numbers of students. For these reasons students with CADs of less than those cited are often included in remedial reading programs in actual practice, even though a corrective program would be sufficient.

The problem of reading disabilities does not end when students complete high school. Chall (1978) states that there are many college students "who are having extreme dif-

ficulty keeping up with their assignments, and who are falling short in achieving on a level equal to their intellectual potential" (p. 39). While the severity of their problems may vary, it is estimated that 1 to 2 percent of college students have reading problems for which special remediation is warranted. In the U.S. adult population the most reasonable estimates of functional illiteracy have ranged from 18 million (Peck & Kling, 1977) to 31 million (Cook, 1977). The world rate of illiteracy dropped between 1960 and 1980 from 39.3 percent to 28.9 percent, according to a report at the International Conference on Education in 1981, but the absolute number of illiterates had actually risen to 814 million persons due to increases in world population.

There have been large increases in the number of students designated as learning disabled recently. In the sixth annual report to Congress on the implemention of Public Law 94–142, the Education for All Handicapped Children Act ("Executive Summary," 1984), it was reported that there has been an 11.9 percent increase in the population served in LD programs since the first nationwide count in 1976–77. However, many states are now taking steps to ensure that students are not being classified LD erroneously and, therefore, the rate of increase is beginning to slow.

MILESTONES IN THE HISTORY OF REMEDIAL AND CLINICAL READING INSTRUCTION[3]

As a teacher who will be working with reading instruction, you need to have perspective about why we are doing what we are today in the field of reading. Present practice is based on years of investigation and practice by our

---

[3]Before his death, Dr. Edgar Dale critiqued this section summarizing the history of this field—a large part of which he lived through and contributed to. The author is grateful for his assistance.

professional predecessors. Reading instruction, like much of education, has fallen prey to cyclical movements. The prospective teacher needs to be familiar with these points of view so that when they reappear he can recognize them as ideas or procedures that have been suggested before. Many old ideas still have validity. Many do not. Certain concepts that seem nonsensical today were once accepted as genuinely useful. Old ideas resurface and often prove to be as unsuccessful the second or third time around as they were the first. Being familiar with the history of the field can help teachers examine questionable notions that arise today.

Then, too, theories of reading tend to swing from one extreme to another. For example, after the exclusive emphasis on oral reading was criticized, many teachers employed only silent reading techniques instead of using the method appropriate to the specific instructional objectives. Either/or positions usually deny students adequate instruction. Understanding the past helps us avoid such extremes.

We have moved forward in our understanding of how to help disabled readers, but at times it appears as if for every three steps forward, we move one backward. We must be careful not to repeat the mistakes of the past but to capitalize on what was good and what we have learned. Table 1–2 provides an overview of some important milestones that have affected or still do influence our field.

Table 1–2 draws upon numerous sources. Some of the most useful are listed here:

- *American Reading Instruction* by N.B. Smith
- *Teaching to Read, Historically Considered* by M.M. Matthews
- "Teaching Reading Fifty Years Ago" by J.K. Ribovich in *The Reading Teacher,* January 1978
- "Experience Related Reading for School Beginners" by G. Hildreth in *Elementary English,* March 1965

- *Adult Literacy Education in the United States* by W.D. Cook
- *The Dyslexic Child* by M. Critchley
- *Reading Disability: Developmental Dyslexia* by L.J. Thompson
- "Five Decades of Remedial Reading" by A.J. Harris, in *Forging Ahead in Reading,* J.A. Figurel, Ed.
- "Ten Years of Progress in Remedial Reading" by A.J. Harris, in *The Journal of Reading,* October 1977
- *Reading: Seventy-five Years of Progress,* edited by H. Alan Robinson
- *Teaching Reading as a Language Experience* by M.A. Hall
- *Dyslexia,* edited by M.M. Evans
- "What History Says About Teaching Reading" by R. Schreiner and L.R. Tanner in *The Reading Teacher,* February 1976
- "What Is New in Remedial Reading?" by A.J. Harris in *The Reading Teacher,* January 1981

CONCLUDING STATEMENT

This chapter presented important background information for prospective teachers of reading. In addition, reading teachers must have knowledge and skill related to the reading process, causes of reading problems, diagnosis, remedial techniques, organizing and managing programs, materials, and ancillary roles (such as consultation). To use just one job role as an example of this, let's suppose you chose to work as a reading clinician. Bader & Wiesendanger (1986) reported the following methods and materials plus their frequency of use in U.S. reading clinics: the language experience approach, 87 percent; linguistic patterning, 52 prcent; the Fernald approach, 37 percent; DRTA, 31 percent; basal readers, 6 percent. In addition, they found clinics provided sight word instruction, word identification strategies that stressed analytic phonics, emphasized silent reading with a focus on comprehension, and taught study skills and content area reading to clients in the 10 year through 17 year age group. Teachers preparing to be reading clinicians would, of course, need to be familiar with all these. Bates (1984) reported that diagnostic services provided by clinics included, among others, assessment of silent and oral reading proficiency, word recognition, intellectual development, study skills and general achievement. He also found that 66 percent of clinics offered consultant services to schools. There is diversity in organizational patterns and materials used in clinics and, in addition, many consider securing parental involvement necessary to achieving their purposes (Bader & Wiesendanger, 1986).

As can be seen, the reading clinician needs a broad perspective of knowledge and some specialized competencies. The same is true for reading teachers, consultants, resource teachers, coordinators, and supervisors, as well as for LD and DH teachers. Throughout the remainder of this book these and other important areas are discussed, accompanied by research data to support suggestions and practical ideas for applying them.

Table 1–2
Some trends and issues in remedial and clinical reading instruction

Time Period	Instructional Approaches	Suggested Causes of Reading Disability	Prevalent Assessment Techniques and Tools	Milestones
Prior to the 1800s	• The alphabetic method of reading instruction is used almost exclusively until the 1700s; students spell out words letter by letter and reading is mainly oral. • The whole-word method is introduced in the 1700s.			
1800s	• Phonics methods become popular.	• Kussmaul suggests "word blindness" as a cause of reading disability.		• Research in reading has its beginnings in Europe with Valentius' work on perceptual processes.
1900–1909		• Perinatal difficulties, such as injuries during birth, are postulated by Bronner as causal factors.		

Table 1–2, continued

Time Period	Instructional Approaches	Suggested Causes of Reading Disability	Prevalent Assessment Techniques and Tools	Milestones
1910–1919	• The "Non-Oral" method, consisting of an exaggerated emphasis on silent reading, is introduced. • Russell and Schmitt suggest a method for teaching nonreaders consisting of elaborate phonics stories and the acting out of action words.	• "Congenital word-blindness" is popularized as *the* cause of reading disability.	• The first edition of the Gray Standardized Oral Reading Paragraphs is published; it provides teachers with the opportunity to observe and analyze students' reading errors. • The first standardized reading achievement tests are used.	• The first journal article on reading disabilities is published (Uhl, W.L. [1916]. "The use of the results of reading tests as bases for planning remedial work." *Elementary School Journal, 17,* 266–275).
1920–1929	• The kinesthetic method is introduced. • A swing away from phonics and an emphasis on the whole word approach re-emerges. • An emphasis on silent reading is prevalent.	• Lack of cerebral dominance is believed by some to be the major etiological factor in reading disability. • Inappropriate eye movements are postulated as a cause.	• The first Informal Reading Inventory is developed. • Diagnosis usually involves compiling a case history.	• The first reading clinic is begun at UCLA. • The first remedial reading textbook is published in the United States (Gray, C. T. [1922]. *Deficiencies in reading ability: Their diagnosis and remedies.* Boston: D.C. Heath.)

Table 1–2, *continued*

Time Period	Instructional Approaches	Suggested Causes of Reading Disability	Prevalent Assessment Techniques and Tools	Milestones
1930–1939	• The Language Experience Approach (LEA) is developed.	• Emotional disturbance is suggested as a cause. • The concept of *multiple causation* is introduced.	• Machines begin to be used in diagnosis (e.g., eye-movement cameras).	• Monroe writes *Children Who Cannot Read,* a classic book advocating a phonic-kinesthetic approach to remediation.
1940–1949	• Both oral and silent reading are advocated. • Interest in LEA subsides.	• Much emphasis is given to emotional disturbance as a cause. • Interest in eye defects (myopia, astigmatism, etc.) as causes of reading disabilities is seen. • The concept of multiple causation gains popularity after Robinson publishes *Why Pupils Fail in Reading,* a classic interdisciplinary study which examines etiology of reading disability.	• Use of Informal Reading Inventories is popularized by Betts. • The notion of independent, instructional, and frustration levels of reading is introduced.	• The work of Strauss and Lehtinen forms the roots of the LD movement.
1950–1959	• Interest in LEA revives. • There is a trend away from the whole word method and back toward phonics again.	• Emotional disturbance as a cause continues to receive attention in the beginning part of the decade; reading problems begin to be attributed to neurological impairments and brain processing deficiencies in the latter part. • The concept of multiple causation is considered to be most viable by many.		• Many universities begin programs to train reading specialists.

Table 1–2, continued

Time Period	Instructional Approaches	Suggested Causes of Reading Disability	Prevalent Assessment Techniques and Tools	Milestones
1960–1969	• Body management activities (e.g., walking balance beams) are suggested as remedial activities. • The linguistic approach gains some popularity. • The training of students' visual perception skills is advocated. • Interest in teaching to the "strongest modality" emerges.	• Brain damage is thought by many to be a major causal factor. • Belief in multiple causation continues.	• The Illinois Test of Psycholinguistic Abilities (ITPA) is introduced and influences the focus of instructional interventions in many reading and LD programs for the next decade. • Prediction of reading failure before it occurs (called "early identification") is advocated.	• Title 1 (now Chapter I) programs begin. • Goodman's Model of the Reading Process is introduced. • Certification of reading teachers begins in many states. • The term *learning disability* is suggested to replace many diverse labels for the same general condition. • Research begins on differences in mental processes in the left and right brain hemispheres.

Table 1–2, continued

Time Period	Instructional Approaches	Suggested Causes of Reading Disability	Prevalent Assessment Techniques and Tools	Milestones
1970–1979	• There is strong interest in reading instruction based on psycholinguistic research, with an accompanying emphasis on LEA. • Another major interest is diagnostic/prescriptive teaching. • There is a movement away from training visual, auditory, and motor processes.	• Inappropriate diet is purported to be a causal factor in lay press articles. • An interest in the role of defective memory processes as etiology in reading disabilities is seen. • There is a de-emphasis on brain damage as a cause. • The concept of multiple causation continues to be supported by most authorities.	• Criterion-referenced tests are widely used. • The Reading Miscue Inventory (RMI), devised to promote qualitative as well as quantitative judgments about reading errors, receives much attention and use. • The cloze procedure is considered an important diagnostic technique.	• The National Right-to-Read Effort is begun. • The Education for All Handicapped Children Act is passed; this increases the number of LD classes in public schools. • An interactive model of the reading process is proposed by Rumelhart.
1980–present	• There is presently a heavy emphasis on techniques for improving comprehension. • Computer-based instruction is being used and its value being debated. • There is interest in how reading and writing are linked.	• The concept of multiple causation continues to be the causal theory most widely accepted.	• Investigations into improved ways to assess comprehension are being undertaken. • The RMI and cloze technique continue to be used.	• There is a growing closeness of the reading disability and learning disabilities fields.

2

The Nature of the Reading Process: Practical Implications for Remedial Instruction

How do good reading teachers know what to do? Even though they may not be aware of it, they do have beliefs and assumptions about how people learn to read. Because they have their own beliefs they are able to make sound judgments about whether to use, modify, or reject ideas from other sources, such as teacher's manuals, traditional practice, or how-to books of reading activities. Good reading teachers are critical thinkers who make decisions based on research, the opinions of authorities, and their own knowledge of the world. "Either/or" thinking, that is, complete reliance on either authority or personal knowledge alone, does not make a good teacher.

Where do teachers of reading obtain knowledge of the world? From working with students in real world classroom settings and engaging in a lot of good, hard thinking about what is helpful and what isn't. Sometimes crit-

ical thinking results in instructional procedures that contradict common practice—and may be better.

Most researchers and reading authorities have also done a lot of good, hard thinking about the reading process and have had experience working with students. Being aware of their conclusions helps us develop our own ideas, saves us time, and helps us accept new ideas. It prevents us from having to re-invent the wheel. Good theories and good practice go hand in hand.

During the early part of this century, many reading professionals attempted to find out just what our brains must do to recognize words, combine them into sentences and paragraphs, and understand the meanings of the written language. They also attempted to identify which skills must be learned to read proficiently and which objectives are important to meet all of our lifelong demands for reading. Those early twentieth-century educators proposed theories and conducted research to determine if their theories were correct. After a time, however, the interests of reading professionals began to move in another direction; researchers tried to determine which methods of instruction were best. Their research has helped us identify and weed out many spurious techniques, but numerous other important questions about how to promote reading achievement have remained unanswered. Recently, interest has returned to studying the act of reading, and many believe we will not be able to solve the persistent problem of poor reading until we understand that process.

As researchers have studied reading, they have developed *models* to explain their conclusions. In this context *model* means "a structure or design intended to show how something is formed, or how it functions, by analyzing the relationships of its various parts to each other and to the whole. A reading model is a theoretical representation of reading processes" (Harris & Hodges, 1981, p. 200). The phrases *reading model* or *model of reading* can mean either verbal explanation presented to explain a conception of reading or a diagram prepared to accompany and clarify the verbal explanation.

Even now we do not yet entirely understand the complex act of reading. However, in recent years some progress has been made. Since 1953, many different models or explanations of reading have been proposed. Some of the most important ones, and their practical implications, are presented in this chapter. These models are of two kinds. Some models describe *skill* (that is, what a person must learn to be a proficient reader) and *goals* (what we want people to be able to do to read as well as they need to in our society). Other models describe the reading *process* (that is, the functions that must occur in our brains, eyes, ears, and so on for us to read printed symbols).

SKILLS MODELS

The Holmes Substrata Factor Theory

In 1953 Jack Holmes presented a model of reading that enumerated factors related to what he believed to be the two major components of reading: the *power of reading*, consisting of integration of ideas, interpretation, understanding main ideas, understanding directly stated details, and drawing inferences, and the *speed of reading*. Using statistical techniques Holmes attempted to identify subcomponents (which he called substrata factors) that contributed to each of these components. He tested 37 factors to determine how much each promoted power or speed. Twelve were especially important (see Table 2–1).

Holmes's model was based on research conducted with college-level disabled readers and provided suggestions for planning remedial programs. Later, Harry Singer extended the research to high school and elementary school levels. Singer (1969) found many of the

Table 2–1
Holmes's substrata factors

Power of Reading	Speed of Reading
Recognition of vocabulary in context	Recognition of vocabulary in context
Word discrimination ability	Word discrimination ability
Knowledge of phonics	Knowledge of phonics
Intelligence	Intelligence
Understanding of relationships among words	Understanding of individual word meanings
Knowledge of general information	Eye span
Recognition of vocabulary in isolation	
Knowledge of prefixes	
Knowledge of suffixes	
Number of eye fixations	

same factors were important at these lower levels, but were important to a different degree. For example, word recognition contributes more to power of reading at the lower levels, while knowledge of word meanings contributes more at the higher levels.

Holmes's model has since been criticized because of deficiencies in his statistical technique. Factor analysis is a limited technique because no factor can be identified that the researcher does not put into the analysis. Also, many professionals believe that power and speed do not fully define all reading behaviors.

Practical Implications. A variety of word identification abilities contribute to both power and speed of reading. Teachers should encourage flexibility in use of word identification strategies. Reading is more than pronouncing words correctly. Teachers must help students learn word meanings, see relationships among words, and use their knowledge of general information to comprehend printed material.

The Gray/Robinson Models

Through 30 years of research and practice, William S. Gray developed, revised, and finally, in 1960, presented a model he believed described the four major aspects of reading (see Figure 2–1):

1. *word perception,* both identifying and understanding the meaning of words
2. *comprehension,* understanding literal meanings (reading the lines) and implied meanings (reading between and beyond the lines)
3. *reaction,* responding intellectually and emotionally to what is comprehended (for example, judging the validity of ideas, detecting propaganda, or appreciating humor or beauty)
4. *fusion,* combining old ideas with new ones from the materials read to change concepts or develop new insights.

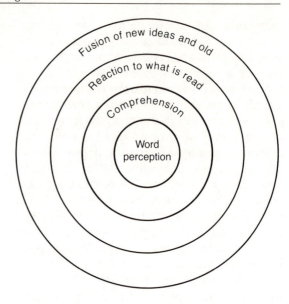

Figure 2–1
Gray's model of the major components of reading. (*Source:* From "The Major Aspects of Reading" by W. S. Gray in *Sequential Development of Reading Abilities* [pp. 8–24], ed. by H. M. Robinson, 1960, Chicago: University of Chicago Press. Reprinted by permission.)

Although Gray's model depicts each of the four aspects separately, they are closely related. For example, comprehension, reaction, and fusion cannot exist without word perception, and reaction or fusion cannot exist without comprehension.

Influenced by Holmes's model, Helen M. Robinson revised Gray's model in 1966 to include *rates of reading,* which she said developed concurrently with the other aspects and was dependent on them (see Figure 2–2).

Practical Implications. It is important to have a well-balanced program that treats all major aspects of reading. Because areas are related, a deficiency in one can affect the others. Teachers need to emphasize word meanings as well as word identification.

Higher level comprehension as well as literal level comprehension is important. The

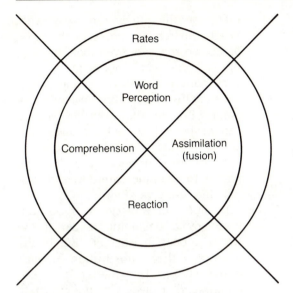

Figure 2–2
Robinson's revision of Gray's model. (*Source:*
From *Reading: Seventy-Five Years of Progress*
[pp. 28–29], ed. by H. M. Robinson, 1966,
Chicago: University of Chicago Press.
Copyright 1966 by The University of Chicago.
Reprinted by permission.)

teachers' questions and group discussions should include attention to drawing inferences, seeing cause and effect relationships, and making generalizations, and should not be limited to dealing with directly stated information.

Critical reading is important. Students must learn to detect propaganda, recognize authors' biases, and make value judgments. This is particularly important with poor readers (adults as well as children), many of whom believe that anything that appears in print is true. (For example, one parent brought an article to a reading supervisor. The article claimed fluorescent lights cause cancer and reading disabilities. The supervisor was unable to convince him that many of the article's arguments were invalid.)

The rate at which people read is dependent on where they are directing their at-

tention, but rate can also influence their ability to deal with the other factors. Teachers should help students develop flexible reading rates. For some purposes and with some material, reading should be relatively fast; for others, relatively slow.

PROCESS MODELS

The Goodman and Smith Models
Although Kenneth Goodman calls his explanation of the reading process a *psycholinguistic model* and Frank Smith calls his an *information-processing model*, and although their diagrams depicting the process vary in complexity, their models are based on the same basic principles and have the same basic implications. Goodman presented his model in 1967 and Smith proposed his in 1971. Both attempt to explain how we use various brain and language processes when we read. They base their conclusions on psycholinguistic research and information processing theory.

According to these models, two types of information are used in reading: nonvisual information and visual information. *Nonvisual information* is knowledge we already have about language and the world when we look at a page of print. *Visual information* comprises all the letters and words on the page and is taken in through our senses (the eyes of sighted individuals or the fingers of a blind person reading braille). Next, our memory systems process the visual information and then relate it to the nonvisual (background) information about language and the world already stored in our brains; we react to the printed page (read it) according to the interaction between nonvisual and visual information. Finally, some of the new visual information may be stored in the brain for future use.

If readers try to use too much visual information, reading is laboriously slow and they cannot comprehend the meaning of the material. For example, if to read the previous sentence you had to examine the *I* in the first word and decide it was an *I*, then examine the *f* and decide it was an *f*, then consciously decide that *i* and *f* together means *if*, and if you had to follow the same process for every letter and every word, you would not be able to remember the beginning of the sentence by the time you got to the end. Reading would be impossible! The same holds true if you had to sound out every letter in every word and string each sound together to read each word. As marvelous as the mind may be, certain of its memory systems are limited.

Because some memory systems of the brain are limited, they can take in only a certain amount of visual information at a time and still attend to meaning. To get around this problem, readers must do two things. They must *chunk* visual information so the brain can process whole words or phrases rather than individual bits of information. And they must rely heavily on nonvisual information already stored to reduce the amount of visual information needed. (About 90% of the information used in reading by a proficient reader is nonvisual; only about 10 percent is visual.)

It is not only impossible to use all of the visual information on a page, it is also unnecessary. Good readers pick out the most helpful visual information and use only that (this is called *sampling*); they can sample visual information and still read (comprehend) what is written because of the *redundancy* of language. Redundancy means that a written message can be picked up in a variety of ways— through spelling pattern cues, sentence pattern cues, and meaning cues. Consider an example:

The dogs ran away with the chicken bones I put out for my cat.

A spelling pattern cue. There is an *s* on the word *dog*, so there must be more than one. If more than one dog ran away with something, there must be more than one thing they ran away with. When the reader comes to the word *bones*, he may not even look at the *s*, but still read *bones*, not *bone*.

A sentence pattern cue. A beginning reader may confuse *away* and *always* in isolation. But in the example, *always* cannot be substituted for *away* and still sound like a sensible sentence. It is therefore unnecessary for the reader to examine carefully each visual clue in the word *away*.

A meaning cue. *Cat* and *car* may be confused by a beginning reader if the words appear in isolation. But in the example, that substitution doesn't make sense. The reader can use meaning (knowledge of the world: a car would have no use for chicken bones) to identify the word without having to scan the word carefully for every visual clue.

A proficient reader uses a cycle of sampling, predicting (guessing), and confirming. First, he *samples* (somewhat unconsciously) visual information while moving his eyes across a line of print. Since the brain anticipates what the eyes will see, he next *predicts* (again, somewhat unconsciously) what will be coming (based on what he already knows about language and the world). Finally, if what has been predicted makes sense, the reader *confirms* (unconsciously) that what was predicted was right and reads on; if it does not make sense, he circles back, gathers more cues, and rereads.

The process of reading is an interaction between thinking and reacting to the language depicted by ink marks on a page. Goodman's illustration of the reading process may be seen in Figure 2–3. Smith's models (Figures 2–4 and 2–5) illustrate the differences between what the reader does when the material is easy and what he does when it is difficult. Sometimes a reader can go directly from

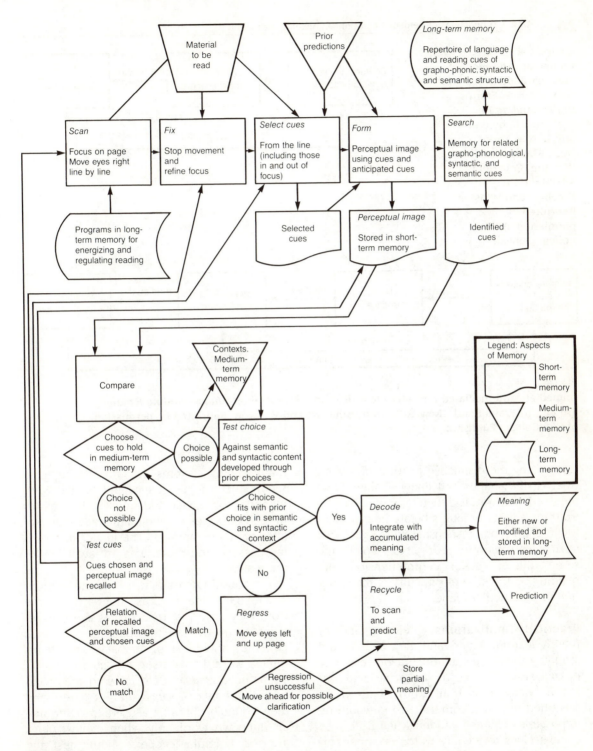

Figure 2–3

Goodman's model of the reading process. (*Source:* From *Reading: Process and Program* [pp. 30–31] by K. Goodman and O. Niles, 1970, Urbana, IL: National Council of Teachers of English. Reprinted by permission of the NCTE.)

Figure 2–4
Immediate and mediated word identification. (*Source:* From *Understanding Reading,* 3rd ed., by Frank Smith. New York: Holt, Rinehart and Winston. Copyright © 1978 by Holt, Rinehart and Winston. Reprinted by permission of CBS College Publishing.)

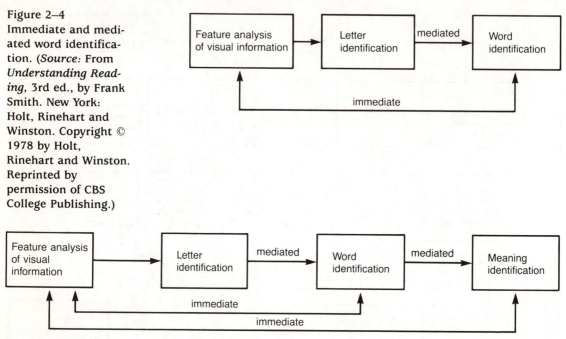

Figure 2–5
Immediate and mediated meaning identification. (*Source:* From *Understanding Reading,* 3rd ed., by Frank Smith. New York: Holt, Rinehart and Winston. Reprinted by permission of CBS College Publishing.)

recognizing the distinctive features of a word (that is, the shapes and lines) to identifying the word. If a word is difficult, he may have to examine a letter or letters before he can identify it. This second response is called *mediated word identification.* Figure 2–5 depicts the same differences for comprehension, depending on the ease or difficulty of the material for a particular reader.

Practical Implications. Reading is not merely learning letters and their sounds and stringing them together. Such a process may be necessary to decode an occasional unknown word, but if all words had to be identified this way, comprehension would be impossible. Helping students learn to use context clues to identify words is important. Context clues allow students to use the

many cueing systems available through the redundancy of language and make word identification easier and quicker. It is easier to read passages of whole language than isolated words or phrases. The longer the reading passage, the more cues are available for the reader.

Meaning aids word identification. Teach your students to ask themselves if the word they have just read makes sense in relation to the rest of the material. If it does not, they should stop, go back, and determine a word that is a sensible choice. This is often the quickest route to word identification. *Graphophonic cues* (that is, letters and their sounds) should be used to determine an unknown word only when context clues are not helpful. Teachers should test the ability of students to read passages of whole language. Whole language provides cues to the reader that do not exist in language fragments, such as lists of words. If we want to know how well a student reads, we need to know what that student does when he reads real material.

Not only does meaning aid reading, it is also the only valid goal of reading. Word perfect oral reading is not an important goal. If a student substitutes one word that means the same as another, the substitution is not significant. What *is* significant is that the student had to understand the meaning of the first word to substitute a synonym. Such substitutions should be ignored. The implication of this for the nonstandard dialect speaker/reader is that miscues resulting from a reader's oral language dialect are not considered reading errors.

Minimize the teaching of subskills. The advocates of this model believe that skills such as the use of letter/sound correspondences should be learned intuitively from reading full passages of text, not taught directly. Students do not learn to read simply by knowing names and sounds of letters and memorizing phonics rules for using these. In the first place, English has too many exceptions to the rules. Second, nonvisual information must be used for proficient reading. The best way to improve reading ability is to do a great deal of reading.

The LaBerge and Samuels Model

In 1974 David LaBerge and Jay Samuels proposed a reading model that Samuels revised somewhat in 1977. Their model emphasizes the need for automatic information processing, or as they put it, the need for "automaticity." They describe the steps a reader must go through to transform written language into meaning. First, the brain uses *visual memory* to detect the features of the ink marks that allow the reader to identify letters. The visual memory system then identifies in sequence

The best way to improve reading ability is to do a great deal of reading.

letters, then spelling patterns, and then a word. Identification of a word activates the *phonological memory* system. For example, when visual memory identifies a word such as *pretty,* the phonological memory system becomes conscious of its sound equivalent; however, if visual memory does not identify a word, the phonological system scans the word by letters or syllables then blends these sounds to identify the new word. Finally, identification of a word activates the *semantic memory* system that attaches a meaning to a word. Semantic memory can also employ attention to comprehend longer passages by combining word meanings, organizing words into grammatical units, and determining relationships in meanings. These steps occur sequentially, with the information being processed in one stage before it moves on to the next.

A proficient reader or an individual reading easy material may skip one or more of the stages. Nonetheless, according to this model, all readers must go through several stages of information processing. On the other hand, if a reader must spend too much time on every step the memory and attention limits of the brain will be exceeded. Therefore, LaBerge and Samuels suggest it is important for responses to many subcomponents of reading to become automatic. If responses to all or most words in a passage are automatic then the reader can focus his attention on understanding the message conveyed by those words. Conversely, if a reader places too much attention on decoding words, his comprehension suffers. Or, if he must consciously attend to the meanings of many individual words then his understanding and recall of the overall information will be adversely affected.

Practical Implications. Learning all types of decoding subskills is necessary, but advocates of this model believe that teachers should emphasize letter/sound correspondences and other decoding subskills early in a reading program and that teachers must teach reading subskills directly, especially to poor readers. They believe that students need practice so their responses are automatic and quick.

However, practice should not be confined to the letter and word identification level only. Students also need frequent exposure to meaningful arrangements of material so their responses to phrases become automatic. Students must resort to mere "word calling" rather than comprehension when word identification and knowledge or word meanings is not automatic.

Developing automaticity depends on practicing correct responses. The teacher must provide feedback so the student does not practice incorrect responses.

In a study used to test their model, LaBerge and Samuels found that *distributed practice* promotes automaticity in identifying letters and sounds while *massed practice* is better for meaningful material.

The Rumelhart Model

David Rumelhart proposed an interactive model of the reading process in 1976. He contends that most other process models explain reading as separate, sequential steps with no interaction. He cites research evidence that supports his view that this is an incorrect assumption. In contrast to other models, Rumelhart's model shows how processes also work simultaneously when a person reads. This is called *parallel processing.* Since the processes also work *with* each other, this model is designated as *interactive.* Models that describe processing as occurring one step at a time (or *sequential processing*) are called *serial models.*

Serial models are divided into two types: bottom-up and top-down. Bottom-up models suggest that the reader goes from small pieces of language (such as letters and words) to whole language and meaning. Top-down models suggest that the reader first predicts meaning and then identifies words. Rumelhart's interactive model proposes that reading occurs as the reader simultaneously initiates word identification and predicts meaning; the lower level processes (word identification) and higher level processes (meaning) help each other at the same time. The reader may rely more or less on the lower or higher level process depending on the difficulty of the material, using more low-level cues if the material is difficult and more high-level cues if the material is easy.

Rumelhart illustrated the interactive nature of the reading process in the diagram seen in Figure 2–6. In this model ink marks on the page *(graphemic input)* are registered in the brain's *visual information store* and are acted on to determine the features that will identify them by the *feature extraction device.* The *pattern synthesizer* (the model's most important feature) then uses *syntactical knowledge* (knowledge of sentence patterns), *semantic knowledge* (knowledge of meaning), *orthographic knowledge* (knowledge of letters, spelling patterns, and sounds), and *lexical knowledge* (knowledge of words) to extract the message (that is, the most probable interpretation) from these distinguishing features. The reader can use the four types of knowledge to hypothesize, seek information, confirm or reject predictions, add new hypotheses, and reach decisions because of information stored in what Rumelhart calls the "message center" of the brain. Hypotheses and predictions can be confirmed or rejected by any one of the knowledge sources. Diehl (1978) gives an example of this process in action:

A reader picks up a book and begins to read. Immediately, the syntactic knowledge source hypothesizes that the first meaning unit will be a noun phrase (since most sentences begin with a noun phrase). The lexical level knowledge source might hypothesize that the first word is "the". The feature level, detecting certain lines, might hypothesize that the first letter is *t,* and this hypothesis would be carried on to the letter-level knowledge source. All the various hypotheses generated—whether or not they are in agreement—are entered in the message center. Each of the knowledge sources continually scans this message center for hypotheses relevant to its own sphere of knowledge. (For example, once the letter-level source has hypothesized that the first letters are *t, h, e,* the lexical level knowledge source reviews the hypothesis to confirm that such letters do form a known word.) (p. 17)

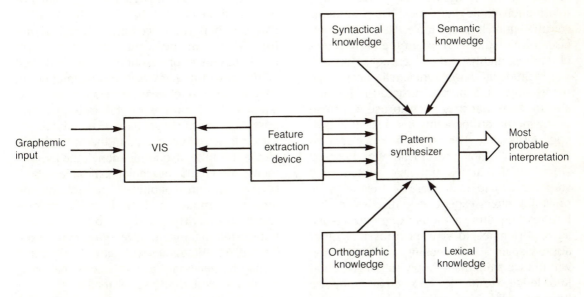

Figure 2–6
A stage representation of an interactive model of reading. (*Source:* From *Theoretical Models and Processes of Reading* [p. 736], 3rd ed., by D. E. Rumelhart. Newark, DL: International Reading Association. Reprinted by permission of D. E. Rumelhart and the International Reading Association.)

Many reading professionals agree with Rumelhart that bottom-up and top-down models do not explain many things we know to be true about the reading process, and certain experimental findings seem to confirm that the process is interactive.

Practical Implications. Instructional programs should emphasize both word identification and meaning since lower level processes aid higher level processes and vice versa. The interactive model not only shows that the reader uses many kinds of information, but also indicates that the reader must be flexible in use of strategies. Teaching just one strategy—for example, to use in word identification—is inappropriate. Students should have not only the opportunity to learn a variety of strategies, but also the opportunity to practice them. If one strategy doesn't work, have your students ask themselves, "What could I try next?" "What other information could help me?" Help students see that print is predictable. Use cloze exercises (see Chapter 13), or, in the early stages of reading, highly predictable books.

Students have syntactical knowledge (knowledge of sentence structure). Emphasize to them that they need to use it instead of relying on orthographic and lexical knowledge exclusively. For semantic knowledge to be accessible for use, meanings must be stored in the brain's message center. Help students add to their store of meanings by providing direct experiences, discussions before reading, and vicarious experiences, such as opportunities to view pictures and other audio-visuals. Use teaching strategies that will induce students to apply the background knowledge (semantic knowledge) they do have when they are reading.

Although there are more similarities than differences, written syntactic structures do vary from oral language patterns. Increase your students' knowledge of written language patterns by reading aloud to them. Since some decisions are made based on prior knowledge of print structures, students need to read themselves as much as possible. The more students read, the more efficient their predictions will be.

CONCLUDING STATEMENT

This chapter presented two types of models. Skills models attempt to explain what it is we want students to be able to do in reading; process models attempt to explain just how our brains can accomplish these complex tasks. Though there are some similarities in the theories and practical implications, it is also evident that model-makers hold some opposing views. (See Table 2–2 for a summary of some features of process models.) Other models have not been presented; although most could be broadly classified as skills or process models, they have also been designated as behavioral, cognitive, linguistic, information processing, psychometric, psycholinguistic or taxonomic models based on the model-maker's view and the manner in which the model was developed and explained. Dechant (1976), for example, proposes a primarily psycholinguistic model, but says it is actually "eclectic in that it has some elements of the taxonomic model, the psychometric model, the psychological models (both behavioral and cognitive), the information processing model, and the linguistic models (both the early formulations and the transformational-generative grammar models)" (p. 53). He agrees with Singer (1969) that it may be necessary to use a combination of models to explain the act of reading.

For now, the skills and process models will give you, the prospective reading teacher, an orientation to the current concepts of how we read.

Table 2–2
Contrasting features of process models

Nature of the Models	Goodman/ Smith	LaBerge & Samuels	Rumelhart
Information is processed sequentially.	X	X	
Information is processed in parallel steps.			X
The process is always interactive.			X
The process is interactive when reader encounters difficulty.	X	X	
The reader goes from print to meaning.		X	
The reader goes from meaning to print.	X		
The reader simultaneously uses meaning and identification of print.			X
Unskilled and skilled readers process materials differently.	X	X	X
Background information already stored in the reader's brain is important for obtaining meaning from print.	X	X	X
The reader uses as little printed information as possible to obtain meaning.	X		sometimes
Accurate identification of small printed units (letters, words) is necessary to obtain meaning.		X	sometimes

Implications of the Models	Goodman/ Smith	LaBerge & Samuels	Rumelhart
Direct and intensive practice on subskills of reading is important.		X	
Whole language activities are important; readers internalize subskills through exposure to regular connected reading material.	X		X
Some attention to subskills of reading is helpful.			X
All word identification errors should be corrected.		X	
Only word identification errors that affect meaning should be corrected.	X		X
Beginning reading instruction should emphasize word identification.		X	
Beginning reading instruction should emphasize meaning.	X		
Beginning reading instruction should treat both word identification and meaning.			X
Proficiency in word identification helps the reader obtain meaning.		X	X
Meaning helps the reader identify words.	X		X

3

Causes and Correlates of Reading Disability: Part I

A common question asked of the reading teacher or the learning disabilities teacher is "What *causes* a student to have reading problems?" Parents frequently worry that retarded reading development is due to a child's lack of intellectual ability. Some parents believe a simple intervention such as getting glasses for a child will solve a reading problem. Teachers often tell parents that a child is simply not ready to read, and that as a child develops socially and emotionally she will begin to read as well as other students. Frustrated parents may place the blame on poor teaching or other educational inadequacies. Popular magazines and newspapers frequently feature articles that attribute reading or learning disabilities to diet, emotional disorders, allergies, brain damage, hyperactivity, lack of sensory integration, or other factors.

What does cause reading disabilities? How much truth is there in the commonly held beliefs about causal factors? To answer these questions, one must first understand the difference between correlation and causation. Although two events may be correlated, one does not necessarily cause the other. For example, suppose a particularly silly researcher decided to undertake a study to determine the relationship between reading achievement and facial hairiness in school-aged boys. The researcher probably would find a higher degree of reading achievement in those males with more facial hair because of course, in general, the very students who have more facial hair are also older and normally have had more reading experience. Although a correlation between hairiness and reading achievement could be shown, it certainly would not mean that hairiness increases reading ability. Nor does it mean that if lack of hairiness could be "corrected" (for example, by giving hormonal treatments to all fourth-grade boys in remedial reading classes) reading achievement could be increased. Misunderstanding the difference between causation and correlation has led many teachers to incorrect interpretations of research on the causes of reading disabilities and to many fruitless teaching procedures.

Another important concept for the reading specialist is the principle of *multiple causation,* which states that not only are there many different possible causes of a reading disability, but also that, except in the mildest of cases, a reading disability is caused by interactions of more than one factor. In addition, there may be many different combinations of contributing factors and these combinations can vary from individual to individual. Finally, certain factors that are often direct causal factors may be present but may not contribute to the disability in a particular person. (See Figure 3–1 for hypothetical examples of multiple factors contributing to a reading disability.) The problem of causation is complex; simple answers, as often presented in the popular press, are seldom adequate.

Some educators believe that understanding the causes of a student's disability is not important. They say, for example, that if a fifth-grade boy uses inefficient word identification strategies, one must simply teach him efficient strategies. They contend that knowing the student's problem began because of slightly below average intelligence and an undetected auditory acuity problem is not an important issue for the teacher. If our concern as reading specialists were only remediation,

---

Ginger (8 years old)
Reading Level—2nd preprimer
- emotional immaturity
- hyperactive behavior
- inadequate preschool experience with books and reading

Monica (9 years old)
Reading Level—1st preprimer
- retarded language development
- recurring illness resulting in excessive absence from school
- hyperopia (farsightedness)
- poor auditory acuity

Richard (7 years old)
Reading Level—1st preprimer
- exposed to faulty teaching procedures in first grade (insufficient stress on reading for meaning, excessive drill on words out of context, overemphasis on work on isolated subskills of reading with little practice in reading contextual material)
- intelligence quotient of 85—in the "slow learner" range

Ernest (16 years old)
Reading Level—4th grade
- visual difficulty: binocular incoordination
- oral language vocabulary unusually limited for his age
- dislike of reading

Figure 3–1
Hypothetical examples of multiple factors contributing to a reading disability

then this point of view might have some validity. However, we must also be concerned with prevention. If the same fifth grader had been tested at the first sign of reading difficulties to determine possible causes, his teachers could have made adaptations in his instructional program and his hearing problem might have been corrected. For many students, early accommodations to individual differences prevent reading problems from becoming severe or may even eliminate the problems entirely.

Prevention has another dimension. In other fields research into the etiology (that is, causes) of disabilities has led to an almost complete elimination of certain contributing factors and thus to a lower incidence of a particular disability. As a result of extensive research into the etiology of mental retardation, certain conditions can now be successfully controlled. For instance, when a woman contracts rubella (German measles) during the first month of pregnancy, the fetus she carries has as much as a 50 percent risk of being born with abnormalities in intelligence (Suran & Rizzo, 1979). Extensive programs of immunization against rubella are effectively eliminating this cause of retardation. Environmental causes of retardation can also be eliminated. For example, a deficiency of protein in the diets of pregnant women or infants can cause retardation. Knowledge about the relationship between intelligence and nutrition has permitted physicians to launch awareness campaigns and to direct their patients. These examples point out the potential of research in our own field. Research and expanded knowledge may suggest preventative and corrective treatments for eliminating some potential and existing reading disability cases.

Understanding causes of reading disabilities also helps teachers employ the two-pronged approach necessary for remediating reading problems. This two-pronged approach consists of first treating the immediate problem (that is, teaching what the student doesn't know) and secondly providing treatment, when possible, for other problems that are blocking learning or, when not possible, adapting the instructional program to account for the existing condition. Consider three of the students described in Figure 3–1. The teacher dealing with Monica has no control, of course, over her recurring illness but could encourage the parents to obtain glasses to correct Monica's hyperopia; having that condition corrected would make the reading task easier when Monica is at school. Richard's problem seems to have an educational basis. The reading instruction he received would be poor for any student, but has been particularly detrimental for him; his teacher can easily provide adjustments for Richard by furnishing appropriate instruction and adjusting instruction to his intellectual ability. Ginger has entered school with little or no preschool experience with books, and obviously her teacher cannot change the past. Nonetheless, her teacher can provide a readiness program rich in experiences to help compensate for earlier deficiencies. Understanding the many causes of reading disabilities is important and helps teachers provide the best, individualized educational programs for disabled readers.

A final general consideration in understanding causes and correlates of reading disabilities is the teacher's knowledge of research methodology. Teachers who wish to help students with learning disorders should have coursework that provides information about research methodology as well as opportunities to critique existing research. Much research about the causes of reading disabilities is so poorly constructed that the results are simply not credible. Many worthless treatment programs are based on "research" that really is not research at all. Learning to identify faulty research procedures will help teachers avoid fallacious notions and identify, instead, programs that will help their students. This text will point out instances when faulty research has been the only support for a procedure, or when no evidence at all supports a hypothesis. But since no text can provide all the information a remedial teacher needs, teachers must learn to evaluate research and proposed programs critically themselves.

The remainder of this chapter and all of Chapter 4 will present information about factors which are and are not causes or correlates of reading disabilities. Seven general areas will be discussed:

1. physiological factors
2. hereditary factors
3. cognitive factors
4. educational factors
5. emotional factors
6. sociocultural factors, and
7. language factors.

The first two topics are discussed in Chapter 3; the remaining five are discussed in Chapter 4.

PHYSIOLOGICAL FACTORS

Sensory Impairment
A slight sensory impairment may have no effect on a student's reading achievement, but certain more severe impairments may contribute to a reading disability.

Vision.[1]   Some of the many types of visual problems are briefly outlined here.

Refractive errors (faulty focus of light rays entering the eyes)

1. *Hyperopia.* Farsightedness, resulting in poor *nearpoint acuity,* that is, difficulty in seeing images at the typical reading range (about 14 inches from the eye)

One contributing cause of a mild reading disability may be a lack of experience with books.

2. *Myopia.* Nearsightedness, resulting in poor *farpoint acuity,* which is usually measured by determining the clarity of an image at a distance of 20 feet
3. *Astigmatism.* Lack of a clear focus of light rays in one or more axes of the retina, causing blurred vision

Fusion difficulties (an impairment in the use of the two eyes together)

1. *Aniseikonia.* The images of an object as formed by each eye appear unequal in shape or size.
2. *Strabismus.* The eyes do not align correctly and one of several conditions results, namely,
   Esotropia. The eyes have a tendency to turn inward. (Persons with this form of strabismus are often called "crosseyed.")

[1]The author wishes to thank John W. Highbee, M.D., F.A.C.S., a practicing ophthalmologist, for his assistance in the preparation of the *Vision* section.

Exotropia. The eyes have a tendency to turn outward.

Hypertropia. One eye has a tendency to turn higher than the other.

3. *Amblyopia.* The image from one eye is not transmitted to the brain. Amblyopia eventually produces decreased vision in the affected eye if the image is continually suppressed with no corrective treatment.

Researchers disagree about the effects of visual defects on reading ability. For example, Edson, Bond, and Cook (1953) found no association between fusion difficulties and reading disability, while Park and Burri (1943), Spache and Tillman (1962), and others found a significant relationship. For certain visual abnormalities a preponderance of the research does show a relationship with reading difficulties, while for other defects the majority of the research shows no relationship. (See Table 3–1, which summarizes research on visual defects and provides a reference to one study or review supporting each conclusion. Most visual defects have been the subjects of many studies; reviews by Robinson and Huelsman (1953) and Eames (1948) provide the interested reader with more information.)

Sometimes finding no relationship between a visual defect and reading disabilities is the result of the research design. When large groups of students are compared, indi-vidual differences are lost because a mean, or average, is taken for the group. Even though the research may indicate that students with reading disabilities show no more evidence of a particular eye dysfunction than average readers, that dysfunction may be one factor contributing to the problem of a specific reading-disabled student.

Some visual abnormalities that have been related to reading disability interfere more directly with reading than others. Some defects may make it difficult for specific readers to identify written symbols, while others may simply lead to discomfort, such as fatigue and headaches, when they engage in any intensive visual activity. However, this discomfort may decrease the amount of time these individuals can or will read; their eye defects may then become an indirect cause of their reading problems.

The most prevalent visual problem among school-age individuals, that is, myopia (nearsightedness), has shown no positive relationship to reading difficulties. This is important information for teachers counseling parents of children with reading problems. Simply obtaining glasses for the most common eye problems, such as myopia or astigmatism, will not solve a child's reading problem. This is also true in relation to those problems that have been associated with reading disability. Reading takes place in the brain, not in the eye. Correcting visual problems may make it possible for students to

Table 3–1
Refractive errors and fusion difficulties and their relationship to reading disabilities

Possible Relationship	No Relationship
Hyperopia (Eames, 1951)	Myopia (Taylor, 1937)
Aniseikonia (Dearborn & Anderson, 1938)	Astigmatism (Robinson, 1946)
Asteriopsis (Robinson & Huelsman, 1953)	Esotropia (Smith & Dechant, 1961)
	Hypertropia (Smith & Dechant, 1961)
Exotropia (Eames, 1932)	Amblyopia (Harris & Sipay, 1980)

see the printed information on the page better or stay on task longer, but once the visual problem is corrected instruction is still necessary to help students learn new reading strategies.

Teachers who will be counseling parents also need to know about the effects of visual training exercises on improving reading ability. Many ophthalmologists and optometrists hold opposing views on the value of such training. (*Ophthalmologists* are medical doctors who specialize in the diagnosis and treatment of eye diseases and abnormalities and have passed the examinations of the American Board of Ophthalmology; *optometrists* are nonmedical vision specialists trained to diagnose vision defects and prescribe glasses.) Many optometrists advocate visual training as a corrective measure in treating reading problems, while many ophthalmologists believe the training has no value.

Recently a joint statement was prepared by the American Association of Ophthalmology, the American Academy of Pediatrics, and the American Academy of Ophthalmology and Otolaryngology stating their position on the relationship between learning and visual function. This statement is reproduced in Box 3–1 and should be read in its entirety. The third point in the statement indicates that these three groups of specialists do not support visual training procedures; most educators would agree with this position. A review of the research on the effects of visual training in remediating reading difficulties shows that the research methodology used in these studies was inadequate. Consequently, no conclusions can be drawn about the value of visual training (Keogh, 1974).

Visual Perception. The role of visual perception problems in contributing to reading has been much discussed in the past few years. Individuals who have good visual perception perceive an object or a printed word as it actually is, and allegedly, students with poor visual perception are plagued by confusions and distortions when they look at visual symbols. Some supposed symptoms are listed here.

1. A word appears as a meaningless mixture of letters. The word *music,* for example, appears as *msuci.*
2. Letters and words are reversed. For example, *b* appears as *d,* or *was* as *saw.*
3. If the type of print or size of a word is changed, students may not be able to identify it.
4. A word may appear as its mirror image.
5. Students who pronounce, for example, *where* as *when* may be unable to see a word as a whole, so they guess at the parts they cannot perceive.
6. Students may respond to small details of a letter, such as the curve in a lower case *r,* to the detriment of seeing the letter as a whole.
7. They may attend to the white spaces between letters in a word instead of the letters themselves.
8. They may see a sentence such as *Marie likes to ski* as *Ma ri eli kest os ki.*
9. They may perceive spots or flaws in the paper as parts of words and respond to these.

There is disagreement as to whether different instances of alleged misperceptions are a result of a neurological dysfunction or of a developmental lag. There is also disagreement about whether the supposed abnormal perceptions result from aberrations of the eye or aberrations of the brain. Some optometrists claim to be able to alleviate visual perception problems by visual training exercises. Others believe these alleged difficul-

Box 3–1
The Eye and Learning Disabilities

The problem of learning disability has become a matter of increasing public concern, which has led to exploitation by some practitioners of the normal concern of parents for the welfare of their children. A child's inability to read with understanding as a result of defects in processing visual symbols, a condition which has been called dyslexia, is a major obstacle to school learning and has far-reaching social and economic implications. The significance and magnitude of the problem have generated a proliferation of diagnostic and remedial procedures, many of which imply a relationship between visual function and learning.

The eye and visual training in the treatment of dyslexia and associated learning disabilities have recently been reviewed with the following conclusions by the American Academy of Pediatrics, the American Academy of Ophthalmology and Otolaryngology, and the American Association of Ophthalmology:

1. Learning disability and dyslexia, as well as other forms of school underachievement, require a multi-disciplinary approach from medicine, education, and psychology in diagnosis and treatment. *Eye care should never be instituted in isolation when a patient has a reading problem.* Children with learning disabilities have the same incidence of ocular abnormalities, e.g., refractive errors and muscle imbalance, as children who are normal achievers and reading at grade level. These abnormalities should be corrected.
2. Since clues in word recognition are transmitted through the eyes to the brain, it has become common practice to attribute reading difficulties to subtle ocular abnormalities presumed to cause faulty visual perception. Studies have shown that *there is no peripheral eye defect which produces dyslexia and associated learning disabilities.* Eye defects do not cause reversals of letters, words, or numbers.
3. No known scientific evidence supports claims for improving the academic abilities of learning-disabled or dyslexic children with treatment based solely on visual training such as muscle exercises, ocular pursuit and glasses, or neurological organizational training such as laterality training, balance board or perceptual training. Furthermore, such training has frequently resulted in uwarranted expense and has delayed proper instruction for the child.
4. Excluding correctable ocular defects, glasses have no value in the specific treatment of dyslexia or other learning problems. In fact, unnecessarily prescribed glasses may create a false sense of security that may delay needed treatment.
5. The teaching of learning-disabled and dyslexic children is a problem of educational science. No one approach is applicable to all children. A change in any variable may result in increased motivation of the child and reduced frustration. Parents should be made aware that mental level and psychological implications are contributing factors to a child's success or failure. Ophthalmologists and other medical specialists should offer their knowledge. This may consist of the identification of specific defects, or simply early recognition. The precursors of learning disabilities can often be detected by three years of age. Since remediation may be more effective during the early years, it is important for the physician to recognize the child with this problem and refer him to the appropriate service, if available, before he is of school age. Medical specialists may assist in bringing the child's potential to the best level, but the actual remedial educational procedures remain the responsibility of educators.

This statement was prepared by an ad hoc committee of the American Academy of Pediatrics, the American Academy of Ophthalmology and Otolaryngology, and the American Association of Ophthalmology with the assistance of the President and the Past President of the Division for Children with Learning Disabilities. Reprinted by permission of the American Academy of Pediatrics.

ties are of a neurological origin and, therefore, retraining of brain processing is necessary.

In looking at the list of symptoms ascribed to students who purportedly have visual perception problems, teachers might ask how they can know the student is responding to the printed page in this manner. What behavior would students exhibit if they were reading the white spaces between the words? What would they say? What response would students make if they were reading only the curve in the lower case *r*? How can teachers treat these responses? When students read *where* as *when,* how can teachers know they do so because they are unable to perceive a word of that length? If a student reads *I don't know where you are* as *I don't know when you are,* is it not more likely that the student has failed to learn to read for meaning?

While it is true that some reading-disabled students do reverse letters and words, research also indicates that many average readers make letter and word reversals, at least at a certain period. Ilg and Ames (1950) found that in normal readers word reversals commonly persist until about age 9, and letter reversals persist until about age 7. Spache (1976) examined 35 studies related to reversals and found that 80 percent of these showed no difference in the occurrence of reversals in good readers and poor readers. Brown (1982) makes an important point:

Although the perceptual centers in the brain invert the scene reported to it by the optic nerve . . ., they cannot invert some small portion of that scene. If, for example, a person looks out the window onto a beautiful panorama of mountains, trees, and greenery, it is not possible for him to see one tree in an inverted position while all the rest of the landscape is right side up. . . . Although the optic nerve reports everything to the perceptual centers upside down and back-

ward to what is actually there, the entire scene is interpreted right side up and in proper left and right relationship based on the perceptual center's past experience of what is real. The perceptual center cannot interpret all of a page as right side up but leave one small word such as *was* or *saw* upside down and backward. It would be even further beyond belief to imagine that the perceptual center of the brain would interpret sensations received from the optic nerve right side up with the exception of the word *was* which it would interpret in reversed right-to-left order but not inverted. Such perception would be completely incredible. (pp. 63–64)

When students continue to make reversals beyond the primary years, it is because they fail to use directionality in making discriminations (Moyer & Newcomer, 1977) or fail to read for meaning (Smith, 1978), not because they have problems with visual perception. Chapter 11 presents information on appropriate ways of dealing with reversal problems in disabled readers.

Very little that has been suggested about problems of visual perception is observable or measurable. Most is merely conjecture. A "visual perception problem" is one of the current scapegoats used to explain a problem that seems to defy explanation. In one period everything from reading difficulties to discipline problems may be blamed on a student's "minimal brain damage." A few years later the scapegoat in vogue may be "neurological handicap" or "lack of sensory integration." Similarly, reading disabilities are blamed on visual perception problems on a cyclical basis.

A variety of educational programs have been proposed for training students with alleged visual perception problems. Most have been devised with the best of intentions from theories and beliefs that indicate such training would benefit students with reading or learning disabilities. Nevertheless, both research and practice have shown that visual perception training does not increase reading ability or remediate other learning disabilities.

One well-known program designed to improve students' visual perceptual skills is the Frostig program, which requires students to match shapes, draw lines within printed lines from one picture to another, and engage in other similar activities. Buckland's (1970) investigation of the influence of this program on the word recognition ability, visual perception skills, and reading readiness of low achieving first graders failed to prove its usefulness. In Buckland's study half of the students participated in the Frostig training, while the control group listened to taped stories; the Frostig program did not produce any change in word recognition skills, and at the end of the study the untrained group scored as well as the trained group on The Frostig Developmental Test of Visual Perception (1966). There was a difference in reading readiness: the students in the control group scored higher than the students in the Frostig group. Other studies (e.g., Cohen, 1969; Jacobs,

Wirthlin, & Miller, 1968; Rosen, 1966) have confirmed the findings of Buckland's research.

Another type of training advocated for remediating visual perception difficulties is visual tracking exercises. (An example appears in Figure 3–2). Students learn to focus their eyes on one of the circles. Using their eyes only, they follow the line from that circle to its end point, which they indicate to the teacher. Such exercises have been shown to have no value in increasing reading skills of any kind. Cohen (1972) investigated the use of the *Visual Tracking and Word Tracking* workbooks of the Michigan Tracking Program with 75 remedial readers. It was concluded that including such exercises in remedial programs did not increase reading achievement.

Visual perception is indeed involved in reading, but there are no specialized kinds of perceptual skills required for reading. As Smith (1978) states

There is, in fact, nothing unique about reading. There is nothing in reading as far as vision is

Figure 3–2
A visual tracking exercise. (Source: From "Visual Tracking" by Charles B. Huelsman, Jr., 1967, *Academic Therapy Quarterly,* **2 (3), Spring, pp. 145–148. Reprinted by permission.**

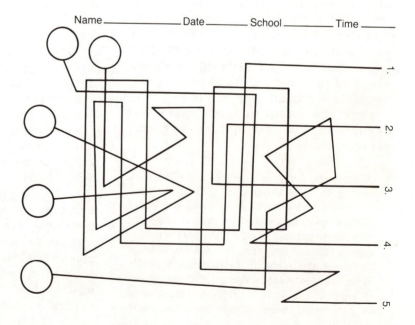

concerned that is not involved in such mundane perceptual activities as distinguishing tables from chairs or dogs from cats. (p. 2)

Based on available research evidence, it is logical to conclude that visual perception "difficulties" do not contribute to reading disabilities.

Hearing. Students who are either severely hearing handicapped or deaf frequently have pronounced difficulties learning to read. These students have an extreme loss of *auditory acuity*, the sensitivity to hear various frequencies at various intensities. *Frequency* refers to the pitch of sounds and is measured in cycles per second (cps). *Intensity* refers to the loudness of sound and is measured in decibels (db).

The degree of hearing loss individuals experience varies greatly, and so do the educational effects of this loss. Because of the trend to mainstream handicapped students into regular classrooms, other classroom teachers and reading specialists need some understanding of these effects. In regard to frequency, a student may have a hearing loss at certain frequencies, but have normal hearing at others. Individuals may be seriously handicapped if they cannot hear sound in the frequency range from 500 cps to 2,000 cps (the range of normal speech). In regard to intensity, an individual's hearing is considered to be in the normal range if the loss is no greater than 25 db. With greater losses the educational effects vary according to the loss. A slight hearing loss in the range of 26 to 40 db may necessitate special attention to vocabulary development and require special seating that places the student in a better position to hear. Students with a 41 to 55db loss may miss much of class discussion, have limited vocabularies, and need special instruction in reading. A marked loss

of 56 to 70db may result in deficient language production and understanding; these students will need special help in reading and all language skills. Students with a 71 to 90 db loss may be able to discriminate vowel sounds but unable to discriminate consonant sounds; since speech does not develop spontaneously, hearing handicapped students may need a special program designed for developing language skills. Students suffering the most extreme losses (91db or more) have defective speech and require special training in oral communication, concept development, and all reading and language skills.

Reading is a language-based activity, and students with severe problems in auditory acuity usually have a delay in normal language development. These students usually develop conventional sentence structures much later than others, if at all. In reading we rely heavily, though relatively unconsciously, on a knowledge of sentence structure that helps us make predictions about words on a printed page. Since normal oral language development is less advanced in hearing handicapped or deaf students, one piece of information critical to proficient reading is less available to them, and not surprisingly their reading scores are depressed. It should be noted, however, that there is some evidence that deaf students have a different language base—rather than a deficient one—from which to process written language (Ewoldt, 1981). Their depressed reading scores may also result from the conventional reading instruction methods that require them to use the same types of language processing that hearing readers use.

Experience, or knowledge of the world, is also highly important to vocabulary development, comprehension, and word identification in reading. We gain experiences through all our senses. Students with severe auditory acuity problems have one less avenue through which to gain experiences easily.

Because of the possible effects of a hearing handicap on language and concept development, it is important to determine the age of onset of a hearing loss. If a serious loss occurs before the child develops language—as with a congenital loss—the effects on learning are more detrimental than if the loss occurs later.

Although some deaf individuals reach a high level of educational attainment, many do not even though they may have normal intelligence. In general deaf students have more difficulty in learning to read and progressing in reading than any other group. Since the reading skills of deaf students are often atypical, special national norms have been developed for interpreting their reading scores on certain tests.

Even students with a mild hearing loss may be handicapped in some instructional tasks related to reading, especially if they cannot hear sounds in the high frequency range, and consequently certain consonant sounds. These students may also have less advanced oral language development than their hearing peers and be unable to learn as much from class discussions. When a student has a mild hearing loss, the teacher needs to make instructional adaptations. If these adaptations are made, a mild hearing loss should not contribute to a student's reading disability.

Only a low incidence of hearing problems occurs in the school-age population. In fact, only about 0.075 percent of students are deaf and about 0.5 percent have a severe to profound hearing loss (Davis & Silverman, 1970). Approximately 4.5 percent may have a mild hearing loss. Impairing defects in auditory acuity are a possible cause of a reading disability in only a small number of cases.

Auditory Perception. While auditory acuity refers to the ability of the sensory organs to receive sounds, *auditory perception* is "the extraction of information from sounds" (Harris & Hodges, 1981, p. 26). Deficits in several types of auditory perceptual processes (including auditory discrimination, auditory segmentation, auditory blending, and auditory memory) have been considered in relation to reading disabilities. These processes have a cognitive as well as a physiological base. That is, although the sensory organs allow the auditory input, cognition must also operate to select and discriminate the information.

Auditory discrimination is the ability to distinguish differences or likenesses in individual sounds or words, such as the differences between /f/ and /v/[2] or *tip* and *dip*. Although training in auditory discrimination has been a part of remedial reading programs for many years, the current consensus is that it has only a minor impact on learning to read. Several reasons prompt this change in position. First, research investigating the relationship between success in reading and auditory discrimination has shown the correlation to be low. For example, Dykstra (1966) examined the performances of beginning readers on seven tests of auditory discrimination used in common reading readiness tests and found that high or low scores on these tests were not very useful in predicting students' reading achievement at the end of first grade. Robinson (1946) reported that less than 4 percent of the severely disabled readers in her study showed evidence that inadequate auditory discrimination was a possible

---

[2] A convention that has been adopted in the field of reading, as well as in other fields, is to indicate the *sounds* of letters by placing the letter between two parallel lines like this: / /.

contributing factor to their reading disabilities. Some of the auditory discrimination skills that have been considered important to train, apparently are not; for example Gates (1940) found a correlation of only 0.28 between reading achievement and the ability to identify rhyming words.

A second reason why less emphasis is now placed on auditory discrimination as a factor in reading disabilities is that it is a developmental skill. Individuals have an innate ability to distinguish sounds. This skill is important when preschool children learn to understand speech and then learn to speak themselves. It is generally accepted today that if individuals can understand speech, they can discriminate auditorily. While children (or adults) may need a somewhat greater degree of discrimination when learning letter and sound associations during reading instruction, they come to school with the ability to auditorily discriminate. If students understand language when they are spoken to, they do not have a deficit in auditory discrimination. They may simply need instruction in further developing this ability for some of the specific tasks related to reading instruction.

The third reason for less concern about auditory discrimination problems is the changing nature of instructional programs. As we gain more understanding of the reading process, there are fewer strictly phonic programs. Today programs are more likely to teach students to use a combination of word identification strategies instead of the single approach of sounding out all unknown words letter by letter. Using the entire context of a sentence or passage in conjunction with one or two phonic clues in an unknown word is stressed. This procedure is more consistent with how discrimination skills are used in understanding oral language.

Although some research has seemed to show a relationship between auditory discrimination and other variables often related to educational attainment, this relationship holds true only in specific types of cases. In the late 1960s much discussion and some inadequately constructed research indicated that disadvantaged students had particularly poor auditory discrimination. Their reading failure was attributed to this purported lack of skill. However, these studies used auditory discrimination tests that did not take into account students' dialect differences. In other studies that employed sounder procedures the data did not justify this assumption. Sardy (1970), for example, found that the best "auditory discriminators" in her study were not middle-class students but urban, lower-class students whose teachers were giving them some training in auditory discrimination.

Other studies that have found a moderate relationship between auditory discrimination and reading achievement have also shown that the relationship exists only when the instructional approach places a heavy stress on phonics. In addition, the results of some research on auditory discrimination are doubtful because of many confounding variables that prevent definitive conclusions. In these studies it is impossible to determine if "poor auditory discrimination" is really lack of attention, a mild auditory acuity loss, a memory deficit, low mental age, or a disparity between the dialects of the test-taker and the test-giver or test-designer.

Auditory segmentation, also called phonemic segmentation, is considered to be the next step after auditory discrimination training in some programs. *Auditory segmentation* consists of breaking words into each of their individual sounds—for example, when given the word *clock,* the student is expected to be able to produce appropriate sounds for *c,* then *l,* then *o,* and so forth. The inability to do so is thought by some to hinder auditory blending, but exercises to develop this skill are usually included only in programs that later use a synthetic approach to phonics. Reasons for lack of widespread use of the technique are several. First of all, as Harris and Sipay (1980) state, "phonemic segmentation, segmenting syllables into their sounds, is very difficult for young children" (p. 385). Studies by Gibson and Levin (1975), Leong and Haines (1978), and Roberts (1975), support this assertion, although Fox and Routh (1984) did find that students learn to auditorily segment words more easily if they are taught to do so at the same time they are learning to blend letter sounds into syllables and words. Secondly, the alphabetic system of English is only partially phonetic. The aim of a reading program should be to teach only the most regular and most important grapheme/phoneme relationships. Since there is not a one-to-one correspondence between all letter/sound relationships in English, a method of word identification that relies on attacking all individual sounds in a word—some of which do not translate to the sound given in speech production—is of dubious value. Third, Bond, Tinker, and Wasson (1979) point out that in actual reading "word parts are neither thoroughly sounded nor auditorily blended" (p. 261).

Auditory blending, sometimes called sound blending, is the combining of separate sounds of letters to blend them into recognizable words. This skill, also called *auditory synthesis,* is the opposite of auditory segmentation. Some instructional programs stress auditory blending while others do not. Certain theories have suggested that a major contributing factor to reading retardation is lack of this ability. For example, Boder (1973), described individuals she called "dysphonetic" because they purportedly were

unable to sound and blend to produce words. The value of blending is questionable, however. While the studies of Haddock (1976) and others have shown that blending instruction aids word identification, Hammill and Larsen's (1974b) review of research at both the elementary and secondary levels leads to the opposite conclusion. In selecting a criterion for usefulness in the analysis of studies in their review, Hammill and Larsen adopted .35 as the cutoff point for coefficients below which the practical value would not be considered useful. In studies that did not control for mental ability the median coefficient associated with sound blending and general reading ability was .40. However, since one proposition of Hammill and Larsen's review was that the value of the procedures must be shown through the results of "carefully designed research" (p. 40), they also looked at studies that did control for mental ability; in these cases the coefficients were not significant. Based on their finding, one explanation for the differences in findings of studies on blending may lie in the degree of control exercised in conducting and analyzing the research. Another possible reason for the conflicting results may be the differences in instructional programs with which the results of blending practice are associated. If the reading program places a heavy stress on phonics—particularly a synthetic approach to phonics—the contribution of auditory blending skills may be greater than when the program uses a whole language approach or emphasizes a combination of word identification strategies.

Auditory memory is the ability to store in the brain what is heard and then to later recall this (Lerner, 1981). Sometimes auditory memory is called *auditory sequencing.* This second term is based on the manner in which auditory memory is customarily tested. In both IQ tests and reading tests, assessment of auditory memory is usually conducted by having students repeat the order of a series of numerals, nonsense syllables, words, or sentences after they have been stated orally to the students. The Detroit Tests of Learning Aptitude, which is used in some reading programs, includes such a subtest. Well-known intelligence tests such as the Stanford-Binet Intelligence Scale, the Wechsler Intelligence Scale for Children, Revised (commonly called the WISC-R), and the Wechsler Adult Intelligence Scale (commonly called the WAIS), also employ such tasks and refer to them as tests of digit span or auditory memory span. Most research investigating the relationship between these subtests and reading ability has shown that the correlations between scores on these tests and reading ability are usually low or nonexistent. In Bond and Fay's (1950) study poor readers performed better than good readers on the memory subtests of the Stanford-Binet, and disabled readers in grades 3 to 8 scored *high* on the WISC-R digit span test in Altus's (1956) research. Although some research has shown a correlation between auditory memory and poor reading (e.g., McClean, 1968), attempts to improve the auditory memory of students who perform poorly on such tests have resulted in improved scores on the auditory memory tests but with no accompanying improvement in reading ability. The supposition that auditory memory, as measured on common reading and IQ tests, is related to reading skill is based on a fallacious notion about what we do when we read. We do not recognize words by remembering all the letters in a word or all the sounds of these letters and the sequence in which they occur. Nor do we remember the exact sequence of words in a sentence in order to comprehend it. Rather, we remember the meaning that a string of words conveys. The requirements of these tests of auditory memory are not consistent with the memory tasks of reading. Al-

though specific disabled readers may score low on such tests, their reading disabilities cannot be attributed to poor auditory memory. This is clearly a case of correlation, not causation.

In conclusion, although some reading disabled students score poorly on tests of various types of auditory perception (auditory discrimination, auditory segmentation, auditory blending, or auditory memory), many average readers also score poorly on these tests. Reviews of the research of auditory perceptual skills show that reading failure is not due to deficits in this area. In an article in the *Journal of Speech and Hearing Disorders,* Rees (1973) agrees that auditory processing problems do not contribute to reading or other learning disabilities and states that, in those studies that suggest a relationship, procedures have been used and conclusions drawn that are inconsistent with recent research findings in speech perception.

Speech. The causes of a speech disorder (such as distortions of sounds, stuttering, problems of pitch, spastic speech, and others) include emotional problems, developmental delay, inadequate hearing, imperfectly developed vocal cords, cleft palate, and brain damage.

When defective speech results from a brain lesion, it is not unusual to find that the affected individual also has a reading disability. One of the several areas of the brain involved in reading is located near the language center. Injury to the language center may also affect the reading area. An individual may exhibit both speech and reading disorders, but the speech disorder does not cause the reading problem. Rather, both result from a common cause.

Most speech problems, such as poor articulation (which accounts for about three-fourths of all speech disorders), stuttering, lisping, and problems of pitch, have no direct relationship to reading disabilities. However, if a teacher evaluates reading ability inappropriately then an apparent, though incorrect, association may be perceived. That is, if reading ability is evaluated on the ability to pronounce sounds of letters in a manner consistent with correct speech, or on the basis of "good" oral reading ability, then it may appear that students' speech disorders are hindering their reading progress. Sometimes checklists that help teachers evaluate students' reading ability include items that have nothing to do with ability to read. For example, they may include such questions as

> Does the student enunciate distinctly?
> Does the student have a pleasant voice quality?
> Does the student use a suitable voice pitch?
> Does the student lisp?
> Does the student have a pronounced accent?
> Does the student stutter?

In contrast, when reading ability is evaluated appropriately (that is, based on whether or not the student is obtaining meaning), no direct relationship between speech and reading ability is evident. Speech defects are no more prevalent among disabled readers than among average readers.

Some indirect causes of reading disabilities related to the effect the disorder has on the students' personal lives, may result from defective speech. When students have difficulty making themselves understood, their speech defects can have a general handicapping influence on all aspects of their education. They may engage in avoidance tactics when speaking or when oral reading is required. If they must concentrate on how to say something rather than what

they are saying, this can be detrimental to learning and to performance of many school-related tasks. The speech defect then presents an indirect obstacle to learning to read. Although a speech disorder per se does not cause a reading disability, students should be referred to a speech therapist as soon as they are noted to have defective speech.

Neurological Difficulties

Neurology is the study of the nervous system. The human nervous system comprises the brain, spinal cord, nerves, ganglia (masses of nerve tissue) and parts of receptor organs. Several types of neurological difficulties may be associated with reading disabilities. Most of these have been suggested in relation to the brain. See Box 3–2 for a brief description of the workings of the human brain.

Some general terms used synonymously with *neurological difficulty* are *neurological involvement, neurological impairment, neurological disorder,* and *deviations in brain functioning.*

Brain Damage. Brain damage can result from injuries, disease, or the introduction of toxic substances into the body. Complications during pregnancy can cause some types of neurological damage. Brain damage may also occur at birth. Neurological difficulties related to pregnancy and birth are called *perinatal neurological disorders.* High and prolonged fevers or poisoning (for example, lead poisoning) can also damage brain tissue. Stroke is the most common cause of brain damage in adults. These various injuries, diseases, or toxins may cause a *lesion,* an abnormal change in the structure of the brain. Lesions may be mild, moderate, or severe and may occur in areas of the brain that do not affect learning to read.

Some educators have attempted to distinguish between diagnosed brain damage and what they call "minimal brain

Box 3–2
Our Brain—How It Works

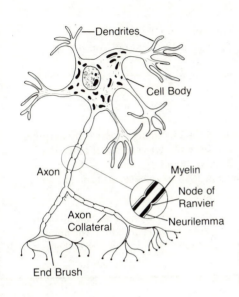

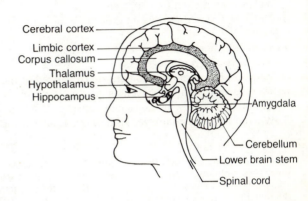

Terms

1. *Neuron.* A cell consisting of a cell body, dendrites, and an axon.
2. *Dendrites.* Many wispy, finger-like parts surrounding the neuron cell body.
3. *Axon.* A single, tail-like portion attached to each neuron cell body.
4. *Neurotransmitter.* A chemical that carries a message from one neuron to another.
5. *Synapse.* A gap between neurons.

Parts and Processes

This is a simplified version of what is presently known about how the brain works.

1. Sensory receptors all over the body (e.g., in the eyes, ears, and so on) send messages to the brain.
2. When the initial message reaches the brain, *neurons* further process it. To do this:
   a. *dendrites* receive the message and expel an electrical impulse;
   b. this impulse is moved to the axon, which releases a chemical called a neurotransmitter;
   c. the neurotransmitter moves across a *synapse* to the dendrite of the next neuron;
   d. this process is repeated over and over through many of the 5 to 25 billion neurons in the brain, each of which is as complicated as a computer.

The brain comprises many areas including the cerebral cortex, limbic cortex, corpus callosum, thalamus, hypothalamus, hippocampus, amygdala, and cerebellum, plus the lower brain stem, which is connected to the spinal cord. Specific sections specialize in specific activities, but often more than one brain area is involved in functions and behaviors. Scientists still do not understand the neural codes that translate sensory perceptions into the processes used throughout the sections of the brain.

(Continued next page)

Box 3–2 (Continued)

Interesting Facts

1. An adult brain weighs about 3 pounds and has the consistency of gelatin.
2. The outer covering, the *cerebral cortex,* is only about ⅒ of an inch thick, but controls all higher level mental functions.
3. Memory is stored in cells all over the brain, although in the long run it may end up in the cortex.
4. There are more than 50 chemical substances that make up the different neurotransmitters that carry different messages.
5. When an electroencephalogram (EEG) is used, it measures the electricity expelled by neurons.
6. There is white matter as well as gray matter in the brain. Gray matter consists of clusters of neuron cell bodies. White matter consists of bundles of nerve fibers.
7. When a neuron is damaged, a new one does not replace it; it simply ceases to function.

Schematic of a neuron from *Human Communications Disorders,* 2nd ed. (p. 120), by G. H. Shames and E. H. Wiig, 1986, Columbus, OH: Merrill. Used by permission. Cross-section of a brain adapted from *The Brain Changes* by Maya Pines, 1973, Orlando, FL: Harcourt Brace Jovanovich. Copyright © 1973 by Maya Pines. Reprinted by permission of Harcourt Brace Jovanovich, Inc.

damage." A neurological examination by a medical doctor, including an electroencephalogram (an EEG), can often determine the existence of brain damage. An EEG records the electrical activity of the brain. This record is displayed by showing a tracing of the brain waves. But even when an EEG is accompanied by a careful study of the perinatal and developmental history of the individual, the diagnosis of brain damage may be indefinite. Physicians admit that findings from an EEG are not always conclusive. In addition, the distinction must be made between major abnormalities in the EEG and those which, even though they vary from the normal readings, have no significance. Schain (1971–72) explains that some variants are common and of dubious significance. He contends that "a statement that an EEG is 'abnormal' without further detail is of almost no value to the clinician" (p. 142). Nonetheless, if a diagnosis of brain damage is made after correct procedures are followed, it is said that there are "hard signs" that brain damage does exist.

In some cases when brain damage is not indicated by an EEG and a person's developmental history, educators insist that "minimal brain damage" (MBD) exists as evidenced by certain "soft signs." They infer from behavioral patterns and certain tests administered by psychologists that brain damage is present. Some behavioral patterns believed to be indicative of minimal brain damage are inattention, poor motor coordination, difficulty in left-right discriminations, overactivity, underactivity, and distractibility. Actually over 100 symptoms have been described as indications of MBD. Poor performance on the Bender-Gestalt test, certain subtests of the Wechsler Intelligence Tests, the Draw-A-Person test, and others administered by psychologists have also resulted in labeling students as minimally brain damaged. Strang, McCullough, and Traxler (1967) state that these assumptions are misleading. Poor motor coordination, hyperactivity, lack of left-right discrimination, and other alleged symptoms may have many causes other than the assumed medically undetectable brain damage. When psychometric tests are administered the so-called signs of MBD vary with the test. Reed, Rabe, and Mankinen (1970) warn that

> results from psychological tests cannot be accepted as evidence of brain damage in the present state of knowledge. . . . To report distortions in Bender-Gestalt drawings as evidence for brain damage is naive and reveals a lack of appreciation of the complexities of obtaining neurological criterion information. (p. 398)

Irwin (1969, May) calls MBD a catchall term used to refer to widely differing problems. There is danger in labeling a student without a medical examination. The concept of "soft signs" as an indication of brain damage is not helpful to educators.

The consequences of medically diagnosed brain damage vary. Although some students with diagnosed brain damage may have reading disabilities, most have no difficulty at all in learning to read. Byers and Lord (1943) reported a study of 13 students with medically determined brain damage caused by lead poisoning; all were making adequate progress in reading. Balow, Rubin, and Rosen (1975-76) found a statistically significant, but low, correlation between perinatal neurological disorders and reading disabilities. The consensus holds that only in severe cases of reading disability is brain damage a possible factor, and even in these cases an infrequent one.

Although in some cases a neurologist may diagnose brain damage in reading-disabled students, the diagnosis of mild or moderate brain damage provides little useful information for the teacher. In the past special instructional techniques such as training in perceptual/motor coordination, manipulation of visual-spatial configurations, left/right discrimination, and memory for designs were used with these students. It has since been found that these activities have no positive influence on learning to read for brain-damaged or any other students. After reviewing the research on teaching these students, Reed, Rabe, and Mankinen (1970) found little evidence to indicate that students require or benefit from teaching procedures different from those useful for remedial readers without brain damage.

In the rare cases where brain damage has been severe there may be some implications for educators from recent studies in neurology. From studying the brain damage of previously unaffected adults, scientists have learned that different parts of the brain control different cognitive activities, even activities that seem closely related. Gardner (1975) described brain-damaged adults who cannot read, but nevertheless can write—even the same words they cannot read. These patients may be able to recognize numerals, such as *192*, but not letters such as *R T Z*. In regard to brain functions he concluded that writing ability can be separated from reading ability and ability to recognize numbers from ability to recognize letters. Many teachers of learning-disabled students or of severely reading-disabled clients have noticed in their students the latter of these two syndromes in particular. Because of the similarities in behaviors of brain-damaged adults and these students, some educators use techniques employed with adults for young people with learning disorders who also have indications of severe brain damage. They may have their students use their sense of touch (for example, by feeling three-dimensional letters) as an aid to recognizing letters. This technique has been employed successfully to help adult stroke victims regain reading skill. While a multisensory approach may be more useful for most students, a reading or learning disabilities teacher may want to try this technique in the rare cases where severe brain damage may be a causal factor in a reading disability.

Some cautions should be noted, however, before the educational community advocates a wholesale adoption or techniques used with adults with *alexia* (the loss of established reading ability). The brain of the young child differs from the brain of the adult in some respects. When damage occurs in the brains of very young children, undamaged portions of the brain may take over the functions of the damaged portions—even though these functions may not normally be linked to those parts of the brain. Older children and adults do not respond in this same manner. Therefore, some techniques useful with brain-injured adults may or may not be necessary or helpful with severely brain-damaged younger people. The age at which brain damage occurs may be an important key, but experimental evidence of this hypothesis is still needed. Meanwhile teachers may try these techniques and discard them if they do not prove helpful for specific students.

Neurological Dysfunction. Other neurological difficulties studied in relation to reading disabilities are dysfunctions resulting from causes other than brain damage. Some of these may result from atypical maturation of the brain (one area may develop more slowly than others) or from a congenital brain defect (an individual is born with an underdeveloped area of the brain) (Hinshelwood, 1917). Individuals with such abnormalities are very rare, however, and in addition, these abnormalities may not always cause a reading disability. Ackerly and Benton (1947) reported the case of a man who had very good reading skills, despite a serious congenital defect—part of a brain lobe was missing.

Abrahms (1968) believes that one of three situations may exist in regard to brain dysfunction and severe reading disability: the reading disabled student has no brain dysfunction; there is specific brain damage, that is, a lesion in the occipital-parietal areas of the brain; or there is a general defect in the central nervous system. He states that although individuals are born with the capacity to develop the basic perceptual and associative processes needed for learning, these processes develop in the central nervous system. If there is a central nervous system defect, learning may not occur as it should or when it should. But he also points out that not all individuals with a central nervous system disorder have reading or other learning disabilities.

One unfortunate notion related to neurological dysfunction is that of "lack of neurological organization." Delacato (1963) and others have proposed a theory based on the premise that development of neurological functions progresses from lower to higher levels. They theorize that the central nervous system may sometimes bypass certain normal developmental stages and a lack of neurological organization results. To remediate irregular neurological organization Delacato institutes a series of motor and other sensory stimulation activities purportedly based on the evolutionary stages of motor development in humans. His clients engage in such activities as cross-pattern creeping and walking (extending the right foot while pointing to it with the left hand and vice versa), one-sided crawling, visual pursuit activities, and sleep patterning. (Sleep patterning requires a child to sleep in specific positions; parents check throughout the night and readjust the child's position if necessary.) Delacato contends that these motor activities will cause proper neural connections to occur in the central nervous system because of the stimulation to the sensory system. This program is allegedly useful in treating reading and other learning disabilities, assisting brain damaged individuals, and increasing IQ. In four separate studies (Anderson, 1965; Foster, 1966; O'Donnell, 1969; Robbins, 1966) the results for increasing reading achievement have been negative. In addition, there is no evidence that any type of stimulation activities can remediate neurological deficits that have already occurred (Cohen, Birch, & Taft, 1970). Educational research has refuted the effectiveness of Delacato's system and disclaimed his theory of the relationship between lack of neurological organization and reading disability. His claims have been censured by major educational organizations such as the International Reading Association and the National Association of Retarded Children. Medical and health organizations such as the American Academies of Neurology, Orthopedics, Pediatrics, Physical Medicine and Rehabilitation, and Cerebral Palsy have accused Delacato of making undocumented claims of cures. Interest in Delacato's theory had begun to diminish, but recently commercial clinics employing methods similar to Delacato's have opened. These should not be recommended to parents of reading-disabled, learning-disabled, or retarded children.

Before leaving the topic of brain dysfunction, it is important to clarify the term *word blindness*. *Word blindness* is an acquired condition in adults often caused by stroke; this loss of the ability to read may be temporary. With slow and patient retraining an individual may be able to recover the ability to read. In the late 1800s and early 1900s, however, the term *word blindness* began to be applied to individuals who had never learned to read despite a great deal of instruction. In many cases this inability to read was labeled *congenital word blindness* since it was believed that a congenital brain defect made them unable to recognize words. The term *word blindness* still occasionally appears, incorrectly, in relation to young nonreaders. Word blindness is a rare defect that may be acquired by adult stroke victims; it is *not* a congenital defect.

Mixed Cerebral Dominance. In 1928 Samuel Orton proposed a theory of reading disabilities based on the premise that individuals who have difficulty in learning to read have mixed cerebral dominance. Orton proposed that normal readers have an established dominance of one side of the brain which can be determined by the side of the body the individual prefers for hand, eye, ear, and foot use. That is, if individuals are right-handed and also show clear preferences for use of the right eye and right foot this is an indication that *lateral dominance* has been established for one side of the body, in this case, the right side. Eye preference is measured in various ways such as asking students to look through a kaleidoscope or rolled piece of paper, then noting whether they consistently place the object to the same eye. Foot preference might be determined by placing students in front of a staircase on several occasions and noting if they consistently begin their ascent by raising the same foot first each time.

Orton proposed that reading-disabled students have not established cerebral dominance, which is indicated if they are right-handed and left-eyed, or left-handed, right-eyed, and left-footed, and so forth. His premise was that this resulted in a condition he called *strephosymbolia,* which means "twisted symbols." Since allegedly neither side of the brain was dominant, Orton believed that students perceived words or letters appropriately on one side of the brain and at the same time perceived them as their mirror images on the other side of the brain. According to this theory, readers with this mixed cerebral dominance would have a difficult time reading since they would sometimes respond to the appropriate image and sometimes to the mirror image. Orton (1928) believed that when they responded to the mirror image they would make reversals of letters or words, for example, calling the letter *b* the letter *d* or calling the word *on* the word *no.*

Although more than 50 years have passed since Orton's theory was proposed, and although research during the intervening period has discredited his theory, some professionals in reading and learning disabilities still subscribe to his beliefs. Much research with young beginning readers, adolescents, students with reading and other learning disabilities, and mentally retarded students has shown that lack of established lateral dominance has nothing to do with reading ability. (e.g., Balow & Balow, 1964; Belmont & Birch, 1965; Benton & McCann, 1969; Capobianco, 1967; Coleman & Deutsch, 1964; Gates & Bennett, 1933; Silver & Hagin, 1960).

Hyperactivity. Hyperactive individuals exhibit an unusual degree of motor activity that may be accompanied by chronic distractibility, impulsiveness, and a low tolerance for frustration. *Hyperactivity* (or *hyperkinesis*) has many different causes that sometimes operate singly and sometimes in combination. Neurological difficulties may be one source of hyperactivity (Keogh, 1971).

The hyperactivity and the reading or other learning disabilities of some students may have the same underlying cause. In addition, the hyperactivity itself may be an indirect cause of a reading problem because the behaviors associated with hyperactivity prevent the student from spending enough time on the tasks needed to learn to read. That is, because of lack of attention, inappropriate out-of-seat behaviors, and distractibility the student simply does not spend as much time processing the printed word as needed to progress normally. Impulsivity may also contribute to excessive incorrect responses.

Contrary to certain notions, however, not all learning-disabled students are also hyperactive. Some students are indeed both hyperactive and learning-disabled. But a majority of learning-disabled students are not hyperactive. The common misconception that the learning disability teacher must daily face a classroom full of hyperkinetic children is probably based on the practice of sometimes labeling such classrooms as LBD classes, that is, classes of learning- and behaviorally disordered students. Students who are merely discipline problems have sometimes been shunted into these classes as an easy solution by those who do not wish to deal with them—even, in some cases, when the students have no learning problems. In many states today students in these two categories are being separated. Students with learning problems are being placed in LD or remedial reading classes, and students with behavioral problems are being placed in classes for students with mild behavioral disorders.

The proper identification of hyperactivity is also an issue. Sometimes students enter reading clinics accompanied by reports of hyperactivity. Yet when the same students are tutored on a one-to-one basis in the clinic, no signs of hyperactivity (distractibility, excessive movement, lack of attention, etc.) are present. In these cases it must be concluded that either the normal behaviors of young children (short attention spans, inability to sit still for long periods, etc.) are being labeled as hyperactive behavior, or that the classroom teacher does not have good management or behavior-change skills. Berber and Romanczyk (1980) reported a study of the methods used to identify hyperactive students for inclusion in special programs. They found inconsistent the criteria for selection and also a selection usually based on subjective indices; they called for more standardized assessment procedures for reliable identification of hyperactive students. All students with "discipline" problems are not hyperactive and in need of drug or other therapy; many may simply be taking advantage of a teacher who has poor control in the classroom.

One interesting aspect of the Berber and Romanczyk (1980) study was the finding that only 3 percent of students determined to be hyperactive were given achievement tests as part of the identification process. Since academic deficiencies are frequently associated with hyperactivity, measures of achievement levels are certainly called for. The lack of adequate testing may be one reason learning disability teachers have complained that their classrooms have sometimes been dumping grounds for students who are discipline problems but who have no learning disorders.

Controlling true hyperactivity so learning can take place is a concern of teachers, and three types of dietary controls have been suggested: elimination of foods containing certain additives, megavitamin therapy, and elimination of refined sugar from the diet. The National Advisory Committee on Hyperkinesis and Food Additives (1975) and the Committee on Nutrition of the American Academy of Pediatrics (1975) have found claims for the efficacy of treatments using megavitamins or eliminating additives to lack objective evidence. They have discounted the effectiveness of these therapies in reducing hyperactivity.

The suggestion that refined sugars be eliminated from diets of hyperactive or learning-disabled students is based on the notion that after eating large amounts of sugar learning-disabled or hyperactive individuals secrete too much insulin which consequently induces hypoglycemia; this hypoglycemia supposedly interferes with the functioning of the brain. A number of arguments refute this theory. For one, Sieban (1977) points out that no research has been conducted to determine if abnormal amounts of insulin are secreted in hyperactive or learning-disabled students. In addition, Sieben says that "since the body sees to it that the brain has first claim to whatever sugar is available, a truly hypoglycemic person would not be able to sustain the muscular effort required to be hyperactive" (p. 138). In sum, controlling hyperactivity through dietary control has not been effective.

Drug therapy and behavior modification techniques are helpful in controlling behaviors associated with hyperactivity. But because drugs have been overused with some students, there has been some reaction against using them at all. Using certain drugs, such as dilantin and phenobarbital, discriminately is helpful, however, and can effectively eliminate hyperactive behaviors that prevent learning. Behavior modification techniques provide a particularly promising avenue for working with hyperactive students. For example, Patterson (1965) reduced the hyperactive behavior of a third grade boy by rewarding him for on-task behavior—and by rewarding his classmates for not encouraging his off-task behavior. This combination procedure deprived him of reinforcement he had been receiving from peers for inappropriate behaviors and substituted reinforcement for behaviors conducive to learning. That hyperactivity can be controlled in this fashion indicates that, regardless of its original source, many of its associated behaviors are learned and increased by environmental conditions.

Motor Coordination.   Some educators have proposed that poor motor coordination is linked to reading disability (e.g., Cruickshank, 1966). Although poor coordination and reading difficulty in some few cases may stem from a common neurological difficulty, coordination difficulties themselves do not cause a reading disability, nor does training to improve motor development assist in eliminating reading or other learning disabilities.

Many programs have been proposed to promote sensory-motor development with the belief that they will increase academic achievement. A widely known example is Kephart's (1960) program of motor activities and body management. Kephart advocated such activities as balance beam walking, performing "angels in the snow" routines on the classroom floor, jumping on trampolines to get a feeling for the body's "position in space," and tracing circles on the board to practice crossing the body's "midline."

Hammill, Goodman, and Wiederholt (1974) reviewed 76 studies pertaining to the Kephart and Frostig procedures. They concluded that the effect of this training on achievement in academic skills or on intelligence was not demonstrated. In addition they found that the training did not produce favorable results for perceptual-motor performance itself. This second point is also important; though some teachers may be convinced that walking balance beams and engaging in other motor activities do not help their students' academic success, they sometimes continue to include these activities in their programs because they believe the activities will improve their students' coordination. Their reasoning goes like this: If Kenny is more coordinated, he may have

more experiences of success in gym class and on the playground; therefore, he will feel better about himself, and this improved self-concept may cause him to do better in reading, spelling, and so forth. However, since research has indicated that these motor and body management activities do not aid motor performance itself, this reasoning is not valid. Class time spent on perceptual-motor activities is wasted time that would better be spent on reading activities. Balow (1971), after an extensive review of the research, stated that

> in numerous searches of the literature . . . no experimental study conforming to accepted tenets of research design has been found that demonstrates special effectiveness for any of the physical, motor, or perceptual programs claimed to be useful in the prevention or correction of reading or other learning disabilities. (p. 523)

Sensory Integration.   Most neurological difficulties suggested as possible causes of reading disability have involved the brain itself; however, alleged problems of sensory integration purportedly originate in the brain stem. Ayres (1972) has theorized that learning disorders result from deficient integrative functions located there. Her program for treating learning problems is to stimulate the position awareness and balancing systems of the body, which supposedly will help the brain stem make better neurological connections. Sieban (1977) points out several flaws in her theory. First, medical researchers have contended that such stimulations cannot do this. Secondly, there is no evidence that the brain stems of learning-disordered students malfunction in any way. Finally, although coordinated eye movements are certainly helpful in making reading easier, it is difficult to see how good balance can aid reading ability.

Hyperlexia. One rare condition that may be a result of a neurological difficulty is hyperlexia. First described by Parker in 1917, *hyperlexia* is a syndrome in which individuals have a significant delay in both oral language and cognitive development, yet begin to recognize written words even though they have had no reading instruction. A similar syndrome has also been reported in cases in Great Britain and in Scandinavia (Hallgren, 1950).

The reading behaviors of hyperlexic students include extremely proficient word recognition coupled with unusually deficient comprehension. Healy (1982), for example, reported the performances of 12 hyperlexic students on the Reading Miscue Inventory (Goodman & Burke, 1972). Although the mean chronological age of the students in her study was 8 years, 2 months, the students made so few word recognition errors (even on passages as high as twelfth-grade level) that the assessment could not be scored properly. Even so, they understood almost nothing of the story content even at the simplest level.

Because hyperlexia is rare, little attention has been given to understanding it. Hyperlexic students have, however, been described by Huttenlocher and Huttenlocher (1973), Mehegan and Dreifus (1972), Silberberg and Silberberg (1967), and Healy (1982). Even though investigations of hyperlexic students have been few, a number of consistencies, summarized here, in their behaviors have been identified.

1. There is an unusually early and dominating preoccupation with words to the exclusion of other activities.
2. Recognition of written words begins between ages 2 and 4.
3. Sometimes single words are read before they are used in oral language.
4. There is rapid development in the recognition of written words advancing to the pronunciation of complex words even though there may be little understanding of their meanings.
5. When comprehension necessitates abstract thinking, the child's understanding of the material is extremely deficient, nonexistent, or bizarre.
6. In some cases "good expression" in oral reading incorrectly suggests that the student is understanding the material. In other cases the oral reading, although word perfect, has a monotonous and stereotypic tone indicating attention to the graphophonic features of words rather than to the content of the material.

A broad range of studies has uncovered some other interesting and significant findings about the behaviors and characteristics of hyperlexic children.

Great similarity in social and psychometric factors has been found in hyperlexic children, independent of intellectual level and age (Hartlage & Hartlage, 1973).

The IQs of students identified as hyperlexic have ranged from those with intelligence quotients designated as within the retarded range to those with above average intelligence. Hyperlexics perform poorly on the verbal section of the WISC-R (DeHirsch, 1971). In the Silberberg and Silberberg study (1967), presumably because of their unusual behaviors, over one-half of the students had been previously diagnosed as autistic, as having some form of neurological dysfunction, or as retarded.

Severely delayed oral language development is exhibited. In some cases, hyperlexic children have a total lack of speech but can respond to written materials.

Hyperlexic individuals have good memories for unrelated and nonmeaningful material, such as sequences of shapes and nonsense words. These students are often unusually good at memorizing long passages of written material, but, as Healy (1982) points out, have great difficulty when they must organize written material in a meaningful way.

Many hyperlexic students have exhibited autistic-like behaviors, engaging in prolonged and repetitive body movements such as bouncing up and down for excessively long periods of time or going through extended periods of arm movement. Huttenlocher and Huttenlocher (1973), Healy (1982), and Mehegan and Dreifus (1972) all reported autistic-like symptoms in the hyperlexic students they studied.

In at least two cases this rare condition was found in sets of brothers, one set of which were twins (Silberberg & Silberberg, 1967).

Some behaviors exhibited by hyperlexic students appear similar to those of adults with alexia (Gardner, 1975) or children with neurological dysfunctions attributed to atypical maturation of the brain. As yet, no one has identified the underlying cause.

Teachers are cautioned not to apply the term *hyperlexic* to all students whose comprehension abilities are significantly below their word identification abilities. Hyperlexia is rare, and students should be referred for diagnosis for hyperlexia only when reading and language, cognitive, and social-emotional behaviors appear to be consistent with the patterns described in this section.

New Frontiers. Attention to neurological correlates of reading disabilities began to subside in the late 1970s. By the mid 1980s interest had resumed because of work investigating abnormal brain structures, cerebral blood flow during reading, and mapping of electrical activity in the brain. New and unusual techniques are being used in these studies, such as analyses of brains of se-

verely reading-disabled individuals during autopsies and computerized topographic (CT) scans of the brain (Hynd, 1986). While this research appears to support the existence of neuroanatomical abnormalities in severe reading cases (Hynd & Hynd, 1984), many authorities consider the work controversial (e.g., Otto, 1986; Smith, 1982). At this time more data is needed to resolve the conflict.

HEREDITARY FACTORS

Some studies have suggested that reading disability is inherited, and a number of these have compared the differences in reading ability between identical twins and fraternal twins. Identical twins often share almost identical personal characteristics; fraternal twins, on the other hand, do not necessarily share similar personal characteristics. Bakwin (1973) believes his research with reading-disabled twins supports the theory of the genetic origin of reading disabilities since his study showed a significantly higher proportion of both twins exhibiting a reading disability when they were identical twins. The research of Matheny, Dolan, and Wilson (1976) supports these findings. However, most educators have long believed that both biological and environmental influences affect academic learning, and since one fraternal twin may be male and one female each may be subjected to quite different environmental influences.

Other studies that have attempted to show that reading disabilities are genetically linked have identified family groups in which there is a high incidence of reading disability. One group of researchers investigated the reading abilities of the family members of 20 problem readers and found that siblings and parents of these students also had a high percentage of reading problems (Finucci, Gutherie, Childs, Abbey, & Childs, 1976). In Hallgren's study (1950), only 1 percent of his 122 reading-disabled subjects did not come from homes where there was a family history of reading difficulties; he calls inherited reading difficulties *primary disabilities* and all those attributed to other causes *secondary disabilities*. Results of studies by Bettman, Stern, and Gofman (1967), the Institute of Behavioral Genetics and others seem to support the genetic interpretation of reading problems. However, Coles (1980) has provided an extensive critique of many of these studies and has pointed out major procedural problems in many of them.

However, there does seem to be a genetic predisposition to certain aptitudes. For example, musical ability seems to run in some families, or unusual mathematical facility may be found in a student whose parent has a similar, strong aptitude. It may be that parents transmit a stronger or weaker aptitude for learning to read just as they transmit other characteristics to their children. A student who has inherited a strong aptitude for learning music, reading, or any other skill, will likely become quite proficient in that area despite inadequate instruction or other debilitating factors. But of course, because some individuals do not have a strong aptitude for music, for example, does not mean that they cannot learn music at all. The same holds true for reading. Nonetheless, a student with a weak aptitude for learning a skill may face greater difficulties in learning a skill and not be able to overcome the effects of the other negative factors that also impinge upon his learning.

Some families do seem to have a higher incidence of reading disorders. The genetic transmission of an aptitude or lack of aptitude may indeed be a tenable explanation for the success or failure of some individuals in acquiring a skill. However, teachers should remember the concept of multiple causation. Except in the mildest of cases, a reading disability results from an interaction of more than one factor. In addition, what may appear to be a hereditary cause may be an environmental one. Individuals growing up in the same family system are exposed to many of the same environmental influences. Some of the best predictors of success in reading are the parents' academic guidance of their child, intellectuality in the home, parental aspirations for their child, parental language models, praise, and work habits. While some of these may possibly have a genetic origin, others, such as aspirations and work habits, more likely have an environmental base. Finally, some of the "research" that has investigated the degree to which reading disabilities are genetically determined (particularly that research that has attempted to identify family groups with reading disorders) has been unscientific and, therefore, does not provide a confirmation of this hypothesis. Although an explanation of a genetic predisposition for aptitudes in reading may certainly be reasonable in a few cases, it is unlikely that it is the sole contributing cause of a reading disability, and in the majority of cases an individual's reading disability is not linked to inheritance.

CONCLUDING STATEMENT

Chapter 3 has provided information about the prevailing thought related to hereditary and physiological causes of reading retardation. In one chapter it is not possible to discuss all theories or all important research findings pertinent to the topic; in addition, new hypotheses are constantly being offered as explanations for this difficult problem. Some of these hypotheses have merit, but some are spurious indeed. Teachers who deal with reading-disabled students need to be critical readers and thinkers when they confront these issues. Coles (1980) offers the following warning:

> An examination of the response to ideas in their historical context reveals that it is frequently difficult to judge the merit of social and scientific theories in one's own time. For example, the late

19th- and early 20th-century theory of craniology, with its guiding technique, the "cephalic index," claimed that humans could be classified as roundheads (brachycephalics), longheads (dolichocephalics), and in-between heads (mesocephalics), and that these physical classifications correlated with fundamental social and intellectual characteristics (Chase, 1977, pp. 94–97, 181–188). From this theory came illuminating conclusions, such as the tendency of urban residents to be more long-headed because they "showed a stronger inclination to city life and a greater aptitude for success" (p. 95) than did roundheads. Craniology remained part of the prevailing wisdom of anthropology for decades, even after Franz Boas conclusively repudiated it. Analogous examples may be found in the theory of witch-pricking (Szasz, 1970, pp. 37–39), masturbational insanity (Comfort, 1967, pp. 76–77, 102–106), criminal atavism (Nassi & Abramo-witz, 1976, pp. 591–594), inherited pellagra (Chase, 1977, pp. 201–225), and immigrant intelligence (Kamin, 1974, pp. 5–32). In each instance we look back on the simplistic, reductionist explanations of a problem that is sociological in origin and are appalled, angered, and perhaps amused by the investigations, conclusions, and statements made under the guise of "scientific thought." Yet at the time, these ideas were presented and received largely as credible and worthy of consideration. (p. 379)

To continue to learn about the topic of causation teachers must read their professional journals, but they must also carefully evaluate what they find there. Most of all they must be careful to evaluate critically what they read in the popular press.

4

Causes and Correlates of Reading Disability: Part II

Chapter 3 provides information about two general areas—physiology and heredity—that have been studied to determine linkages with disabilities in reading. This chapter discusses five other areas of concern: cognitive factors, educational factors, emotional factors, sociocultural factors, and language factors.

COGNITIVE FACTORS

Cognitive factors sometimes linked to reading disabilities include intelligence, cognitive style, memory, and left and right hemispheric functions.

Intelligence

There *is* a relationship between intelligence and reading achievement. Since reading is a learned skill, the laws of learning apply to reading. Generally, less practice is needed to learn anything by an individual whose intelli-

gence quotient, or IQ, is greater than an individual whose IQ is less. In addition, proficient reading requires anticipation of meaning, association of ideas, and perception of relationships—all of which require some degree of abstract thinking. Students with lower mental ages, or MAs, have more specific, or concrete, reactions to words and written text.

The relationship between intelligence and reading ability is variable, however. For instance, the correlations between reading ability and IQ vary at differing grade levels. These correlations are relatively low for children in the primary grades but become higher in intermediate grades and at secondary school and adult levels. This is undoubtedly due to the increasing complexity of reading tasks at these higher levels. In addition, although higher intelligence is generally associated with higher reading achievement, this is most true when we are considering a fairly wide difference in intelligence. For instance, if all other factors are equal, we would expect a student with an IQ of 108 to be a better reader than a student with an IQ of 79. If, however, we are comparing two individuals with IQs of 108 and 99, and all other factors are equal, there should be little significant difference in reading ability.

Does low intelligence cause a reading disability? While a student of low intelligence may be expected to have a lower reading achievement than a student of average intelligence, lower intellectual functioning level does not necessarily cause a reading disability. Today, expectations of reading achievement are based on individual potentials, not on grade level expectancies. A student with a significantly lower than average IQ is not expected to read "on grade level," as might be expected of the student's intellectually average peers. For example, let us consider Jamie, who has a chronological age (CA) of 13.5, but an MA of only 10.9. Using an appropriate formula for determining a student's individual learning expectancy level, we might find that Jamie should be reading at approximately a 6 grade 6 month (6.6) reading level. Although at age 13.5, Jamie may be in an eighth grade class, she would not be expected to be reading at eighth grade level and would not be considered a disabled reader, if her reading achievement was at or near 6.6.

Sometimes less intelligent students do become reading disability cases, usually when appropriate adaptations are not made in their instructional programs. Students of less than average intelligence need more opportunities to practice, as well as new material to be introduced at a slower pace. If the adjustments are not made, these students' reading achievement levels may not reach even their own individual potentials. In such cases the contributing cause to the reading disability is an educational one and is not due to intelligence. Almost all students can learn to read, even educable mentally retarded individuals. Today, even some institutionalized retarded persons are being taught functional reading skills.

Samuels and Dahl (1975) contend that the correlation between intelligence and achievement can be reduced by simplifying learning tasks; they cite a study by Stolurow (1964) to substantiate this point. Stolurow developed two programs for teaching the same sequence of information about fractions. One was an easy program and one was difficult. After instruction through the easy program, achievement differed very little between students of low intelligence and students of high intelligence; however after instruction through the difficult program the high ability group received significantly higher achievement scores than the low ability group. Samuels and Dahl (1975) point out that, "In this study one finds that in the easy program the correlation between IQ and achievement was reduced, but in the more difficult program the usual correlation between IQ and achievement was found" (p. 33). This is a particularly important point to remember when planning programs to prevent students with low IQs from becoming reading disability cases.

That there is not a simple cause and effect relationship between intelligence and reading is evident from the number of students of normal intelligence who have difficulty learning to read. Monroe (1932) found an IQ range from 60 to 150 in reading disability cases she studied. A student or researcher examining a population of clients enrolled in a reading clinic can expect to find that the subjects' IQs conform fairly closely to a standard bell-shaped curve, with the largest number of students having IQs in the average range, a smaller and approximately equal number with IQs slightly above and slightly below average, and a very small and approximately equal number with very high and very low IQs. (See Figure 4–1).

While there are undoubtedly more disabled readers with very low IQs than are typically enrolled in a reading clinic, the reason for the fairly small size of the enrollment of this population is that these students are usu-

Figure 4–1
Bell-shaped curve
indicating the
approximate number
of disabled readers at
various IQ ranges
typically enrolled in a
reading clinic

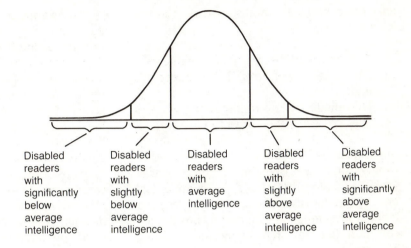

Disabled readers with significantly below average intelligence

Disabled readers with slightly below average intelligence

Disabled readers with average intelligence

Disabled readers with slightly above average intelligence

Disabled readers with significantly above average intelligence

ally receiving services through other special programs (such as classes for the educable or trainable mentally retarded). An additional confirmation that no simple cause and effect relationship between intelligence and reading achievement exists is that the correlation between IQ and reading improvement gains for students enrolled in remedial reading programs and clinics is not high—in other words, IQ scores are not good predictors of the amount and rate of progress a student enrolled in such programs will make.

Cognitive Styles

Recently there has been much interest in the effects of individual cognitive styles on learning. Sawyer (1974) defines *cognitive styles* as styles of coping, which she says, ". . . simply means a way of processing and organizing one's perceptions and conceptions of the world that is related to one's personal makeup" (p. 557). Sometimes cognitive styles are called *learning styles*. Various cognitive styles have been described and contrasted. Some of these include:

Constricted versus flexible

Field independent versus field dependent

Reflective versus impulsive

Descriptive versus relational

Inductive versus deductive

Analytic versus synthetic

Subjective versus objective

Research related to some cognitive styles has been undertaken to determine the effects on reading achievement. There has, for example, been research on constricted and flexible cognitive styles in relation to reading ability. A student with a constricted learning style supposedly attends equally to all information presented in written text, while a student with a flexible learning style selectively ignores some information while attending to other information. Presumably, based on psycholinguistic models of the reading process, a flexible style would facilitate effective reading. In a study conducted by Santostefano, Rutledge, and Randall (1965) poor readers had more constricted cognitive styles than did good readers.

Stein and Prindaville (1976), Kagan (1965), and Hood and Kendall (1975) all examined the reading behaviors of students with reflective or impulsive learning styles. Results of these studies indicated that reflective readers were superior to impulsive readers in the following ways:

1. They acquired discriminations earlier.
2. They made fewer errors in word recognition.
3. They made fewer errors in oral reading.
4. They corrected their errors more often.

In contrast good readers and poor readers in Denny's study (1974) and in a study by Hayes, Prinz, and Siders (1976) showed no differences in reflectivity and impulsivity. These two latter studies failed to confirm any positive association between reflectivity and reading achievement.

Field independence is defined as the ability to distinguish relationships when analyzing material; while *field dependence* is the inability to do so. Keogh and Donlon (1972) found learning-disabled boys to be highly field dependent and Cohen (1968) found field independence to have a significant positive relationship to the ability to comprehend material that had been read. Newsome (1986) conducted two experiments that measured effect of field dependence on remembering information from text; in one there was evidence of effect, but in the other there was none. Harris and Sipay (1980) have stated that not enough evidence is presently available to establish a direct relationship between field independence/dependence and reading disabilities.

In contrast to the opinion of Harris and Sipay (1980), which is related to one specific pair of contrasting cognitive styles (field independence/dependence), other authorities believe that cognitive style is important in learning to read. Spache (1981) contends that cognitive style is as important a variable in affecting learning rate as IQ, and Sawyer (1974) believes that severely disabled readers should have assessments of their cognitive styles included in their diagnostic workups.

As apparent from these few brief examples, presently available information does not provide teachers with definitive answers about the importance of the relationship of cognitive styles to reading achievement or reading disability. Some ideas about types of cognitive styles and how they affect an individual's reading behavior do seem to have more validity than others, but research is meager and inconclusive; even authorities have contradictory opinions. More research is needed before educators can determine the degree of importance of cognitive style as a cause of reading disability. Some important questions remain to be answered. Are there discrete, definable cognitive styles? Do present tests provide valid identification of defined cognitive styles? Do cognitive styles really affect reading behavior, or is an interaction of a number of variables producing the effect? Can students be taught more effective cognitive styles? Does matching the type of instruction to a student's cognitive style have any effect in producing greater reading achievement?

Preferred Learning Modality. The concept of a *preferred learning modality* is a subarea of the concept of differences in cognitive styles. "A modality is any sensory channel through which an individual receives and retains information" (Barbe & Swassing, 1979, p. 1). Some educators have hypothesized that individuals have a specific sensory channel through which they learn best; they benefit most from a visual, auditory, kinesthetic, or tactile presentation of material. This idea seems to be accepted as common wisdom as well. It is not unusual to hear a person say, "Don't read that to me. Let me read it myself. I'm a visual learner." Other individuals may want to hear how a written piece of material sounds when read aloud before they evaluate the degree to which it communicates information adequately. You may be feeling now that one of these descriptions fits your own mode for learning material most easily.

Despite this, there is still a question about whether most individuals do indeed have a sensory mode through which they learn best, or whether most individuals learn best through a multisensory approach. A *multisensory presentation* of materials is one that uses a combination of several senses. As with the whole area related to cognitive styles, research results regarding learning modalities are contradictory. In Robinson's study (1972) most beginning readers were either high in both visual and auditory aptitudes or low in both; only about 11 percent

had a strength in a specific modality. Barbe and Swassing (1979), however, have found some clear-cut differences, with about 30 percent of their subjects being visual learners, approximately 20 percent auditory learners, approximately 10 percent kinesthetic learners, and another 10 percent with a mixed pattern of strengths. The remaining 30 percent of the subjects had no preference and showed equal strength in all three modalities.

Differences in research findings may be due in part to the test used to determine modality preference. Many such tests exist. Some of these are The Barsch Learning Style Inventory, The New York University Learning Modality Test, The Swassing-Barbe Modality Index, The Learning Methods Test, The Inventory of Learning Processes, and the Learning Style Inventory. These tests use different methods to identify an individual's preferred modality, and some are designed to assess other aspects of an individual's cognitive style as well as modality preference. The fact that different studies assess different modalities and that researchers employ different definitions is another reason for the conflicting data. Barbe and Swassing (1979), for example, define the term *kinesthetic* so that it includes the sense of touch as well as muscle movements, while other researchers differentiate the sense of touch and call it the *tactile* modality.

If individuals do indeed have preferred learning modalities, it has been postulated that matching the type of instruction to an individual's preferred modality will enhance learning. This is called *aptitude-treatment interaction*. A summary of a study by Ringler and Smith (1973) shows how aptitude-treatment interaction research is often carried out. (The procedures used in aptitude-treatment interaction programs do differ, but those described here are fairly typical of ones used in both research studies

Many authorities believe a multisensory approach is best in which presentation of materials uses a combination of several senses.

and instructional programs.) In the Ringler and Smith study the New York University Learning Modality Test (Smith, Ringler, & Cullinan, 1968) was administered to 128 first graders. Based on test results it was determined that 33 children had visual aptitudes, 30 had auditory aptitudes, 28 had kinesthetic aptitudes, and 37 had no preference. Children were randomly assigned to treatment groups to learn recognition of words. Children in the visual treatment group matched words to models or words to pictures, selected one word from among others, and pointed out salient characteristics of words printed on overhead projector transparencies. Children in the auditory treatment group compared and contrasted word parts, listened to words in context and isolation as presented orally by the teacher and by audiotape, associated graphemes with phonemes, matched sounds of words, and selected a written word when it was spoken. The children in the kinesthetic treatment group traced words outlined in pipe cleaners or cut from sandpaper and wrote words on newsprint with crayons. The children with no preference pointed out salient visual characteristics of words, associated pictures with words, compared and contrasted word parts, listened to words in context, and traced words. The results of this study showed that matching the reading treatment to children's assessed modality preferences made no difference in increasing their reading achievement. Sabatino, Ysseldyke, and Woolston (1973) conducted a similar study with mentally retarded students; again, when instruction was matched to the students' stronger modality, no significant differences were found in their reading scores and those of a control group for which instruction using the preferred modality was not provided.

Tarver and Dawson (1978) reviewed 15 studies that examined the effects of aptitude-treatment interaction. Twelve showed no positive effects on reading achievement when the instructional methods were matched to the preferred learning modality; three studies showed a positive effect. Tarver and Dawson did point out, however, that many of the studies reviewed (whether they found positive or negative effects) had major shortcomings in the use of correct research procedures.

In light of our present knowledge about modality preference, no definitive conclusions can be drawn about the effects on reading ability. It may be best at this time to provide instructional programs based on a multisensory approach for a number of reasons. It is difficult to make a valid determination of an individual's modality preference. Then too, results of matching modality preference to instructional procedures are contradictory, but most show that matching preference and instruction makes no difference in a student's reading achievement. Programs designed to match modality preference to instruction are not always successful in controlling the degree of match. Vandever and Neville (1974b) reported that the second-graders in their study had to be constantly reminded to use certain cues since otherwise they often chose cues "inappropriate" to the method being used. Although there may be differences among students, reading materials also differ. In some cases visual cues may be a more appropriate aid in word identification; in other cases auditory cues may be more helpful; and in many cases, a combination of cues is the most efficient. In addition, reading does require some visual input, at least for a sighted person. It would be impossible to provide an instructional program that is entirely auditory or kinesthetic/tactile. It has also been shown that some auditory input is used and apparently needed by all readers since implicit speech (in the form of miniscule vibrations in the throat) is always present, even during silent reading (Gray & Reesi, 1957). Finally, it should not be forgotten that only about 10 percent of the information used by an individual when reading comes from the printed page. About 90 percent is nonvisual, that is, it comes from the reader's previous knowledge and experience of the world (Smith, 1978). Modality preference, then, is related to only a small part of what is necessary to read proficiently; it is unlikely that a mismatch between a student's preferred modality and the instruction provided is a major contributing cause to the individual's reading disability.

Memory

A question being asked today by educational psychologists and reading educators is whether the problem of the reading-disabled student is one of storage or one of retrieval. Is the difficulty in getting information into the brain and retaining it, or is the difficulty in retrieving (remembering) the information that is stored?

Many psychologists postulate the existence of three stages in acquiring information. First, information is contained in a perceptual stage, called *sensory store;* after the eye picks it up, information theoretically remains in sensory store for one or two seconds while the brain makes some decisions about it. Next, information from sensory store is selected and stored in *short-term memory,* which is also called *working memory;* the working memory processes information, holds it until it is stored in long-term memory, or sometimes loses information—because it is not important enough to store in long-term memory, or because short-term memory is overloaded. Finally, information is transferred from short-term memory to *long-term memory* by being associated with previously stored information. The information in long-term memory is our continuous knowledge of the world (Smith, 1982; Travers, 1967).

Many authorities believe that aberrations in memory processes may be a cause of difficulty in learning to read. Daneman and Carpenter (1980), for example, suggest that differences in reading comprehension abilities may stem from differences in facility to use short term memory. Their research showed that poor readers' short-term memories were less efficient than good readers'; the poor readers processed and stored less information.

Most psychologists believe that once information *is* stored in long-term memory, it is there forever. The task then becomes gaining access to it. Teachers recognize this problem of accessing information and are often heard to say something like, "Todd knows this one day, but can't remember it the next." Or, "Some days Alyssa seems to know this and some days she doesn't." One difference between good and poor readers is apparently the speed with which they can remember graphic information. In Jackson's (1980) study with young adults, better readers had better memory reaction times than poor readers. LaBerge and Samuels (1974) believe that quick or automatic responses to written words are necessary so a reader can focus attention on the meaning of the material. Since Jackson's (1980) research indicates that good readers come to the task with faster memory reaction times rather than learn to remember quickly through practice, what distinguishes good readers from poor readers may be their quick recall of stored information.

Developmental immaturity may also cause apparent difficulties in memory. Keister's (1941) study demonstrated the differences between memory in 5- and 6-year-old children; the younger students learned to read first grade material as well as the older students, but forgot more over the 3-month summer vacation. The lower a student's mental age, the less able is the student to handle the memory tasks required in reading. Of course, a low mental age may simply be correlated to a low chronological age—an average 7-year-old is expected to have an MA of 7, not 9 or 10. If classroom expectations are not reasonably matched to students' MAs, they may have difficulties remembering what is taught.

Students with lower than average IQs will have MAs lower than their chronological ages; basing reading requirements for these students on those generally expected of students of a certain chronological age may result in their failure. In addition, many researchers (e.g., Ellis, 1970; Scott & Scott, 1968) have shown that short term memory facility varies with intelligence. Students with lower than average IQs need to be taught how to use rehearsal strategies, such as verbal association and labeling, to help them retain information in short term memory long enough to process it for long term memory. Interestingly, long term memory facility appears to be less affected by intelligence; if teaching is geared to students' abilities students with lower than average intelligence will forget no more than their average peers (Klausmeier, Feldhusen, & Check, 1959).

A major hindrance for the practitioner in determining if a student's reading disability is caused by faulty memory is that many tests purporting to assess various facets of memory are only partially related to the memory requirements of reading. Test batteries available to reading specialists and school psychologists assess only short term auditory and visual memory. Short term memory may be important to reading, and some believe it is the short term memory that stores words or information just read while the reader gathers additional words or information to understand the material. (A reader who cannot remember the words at the beginning of a sentence by the time he or she reaches the end is not likely to comprehend the whole sentence.) But long term memory is of even greater importance in reading, and commonly used published tests do not provide any insight into problems of storage and retrieval in a disabled reader's long term memory.

Much of the research that discusses the role of memory in reading is based on a *stage model* of cognitive processing, a model in which the brain (mind) processes information through several stages from the time of input to the time of output or storage. Analyzing the acquisition of information into sensory store, short-term memory, and long-term memory is an example of a stage model. Others might diagram the stages in this way: (1) feature analysis, (2) short term memory mechanism, (3) additional processing, such as determining underlying meaning, (4) decision-making, and (5) response (Norman, 1984). According to this theory, information stays in one stage until processing is complete and only then moves into the next stage. But psychologists, like reading educators, hold many opposing views, and other models of memory have recently emerged. These are based on criticisms of the stage model and on new theories of information processing. Criticisms of the stage model include the manner in which information is allegedly encoded (Kroll, Parks, Parkinson, Bieber, Johnson, 1970), the view of effects of recent learning and retention (Bjork & Whitten, 1974), and assumptions about the storage capacity of short-term memory store (Craik & Lockhart, 1972). The new theories of information processing include the schema model and the interactive model. Some of the newer memory theories seem to have important applications to reading, such as the levels of processing concept proposed by Craik & Lockhart (1972). Other researchers will probably continue to explore these areas.

Left and Right Brain Hemispheric Functioning

For many years reading specialists were interested in the influence of *lateral dominance* (the preference for use of one side of the body) on reading problems. As discussed in Chapter 3, research has shown that lateral dominance is not related to reading ability. Not to be confused with this familiar concept, however, is a new idea interesting many educators that involves hemispheric dominance and is based on recent work of neuroscientists exploring the functions of the left and right hemispheres of the brain. Their research indicates that each side of the brain has discrete functions. As a result they hypothesize that some individuals appear to be more "left-brained" and others more "right-brained" and consequently have different aptitudes and skills.

Until the late 1940s neuroscientists believed that the brain was highly plastic and that many parts had interchangeable functions. Nerve circuits were thought to be shaped entirely by experience rather than by predetermined roles. Based on more recent experimental evidence, however, contemporary scientists have taken a different view—they now believe the function of each neural connection is determined at conception and is part of "an enormously complex, preprogrammed biochemically controlled system" (Sperry, 1975, p. 31). And although brain research is far from being complete, the functions of the left hemisphere of the brain apparently include

1. dealing with complex verbal ideas and complex or abstract uses of words,
2. dealing with difficult mathematical calculations,
3. engaging in inductive reasoning, that is, determining whole principles based on observation of parts,
4. dealing with fine motor coordination,
5. segmenting patterns,
6. carrying out analytical thinking, sequential thinking, and symbolic thinking, and
7. perceiving conceptual relationships.

The evidence presently indicates that the right hemisphere's functions include:

1. dealing with nonverbal ideas,
2. dealing with spatial concepts, including depth perception and sensitivity to geometric forms,
3. dealing with simple uses of words and simple mathematical concepts,
4. visualizing,
5. engaging in deductive reasoning, that is, inferring specific instances based on known general principles,
6. engaging in holistic thinking,
7. dealing with gross motor coordination,
8. making sensory discriminations, such as recognizing environmental sounds and detecting tactile patterns,
9. performing mechanical types of information processing, and
10. perceiving perceptual relationships.

Some educators have looked at these findings to determine if there are implications for instructing students. They have speculated that some aspects of school performance may be related to whether an individual's right or left brain hemisphere is dominant. Based on the functions of each hemisphere as described above, they have postulated that a "left-brained" person would be more academic and well-organized and that a "right-brained" individual would be more successful in creative endeavors and more physically oriented. They have even raised the question whether reading or other learning disabilities may be the result of teaching students with a dominant right hemisphere in ways inconsistent with the way they learn best. These educators are more concerned about "right-brained" students because they believe that typical instruction favors the types of learning in which a "left-brained" individual is more proficient.

Although neuroscientists have made major advances in understanding brain functions, complete and definitive evidence about many neurological functions does not exist, and many scientists hold contrasting views. Furthermore, understanding the implications these findings have for education is little more than speculation. Even though it may eventually be established that certain functions do indeed occur in one hemisphere or the other, the notion that one hemisphere works more efficiently than the other in some individuals has only been inferred from behavior. For example, a teacher might say, "Heidi is a poor reader, but she's good in art; therefore, she might be 'right-brained.'" (That is, she doesn't deal well with complex and abstract uses of words, but she does deal well with spatial concepts; therefore, her right hemisphere must be dominant.)

While this is an interesting idea to pursue, well constructed, well controlled neural research is needed to support the hypothesis that certain individuals have one hemisphere that operates more efficiently than the other. Neuroscientists have postulated that various combinations of genes genetically determine the degree to which the left or right hemisphere may be dominant, but this idea is still a hypothesis. Further, if research does show that certain individuals have a strong hemispheric dominance, then well constructed, well controlled educational research findings, confirmed by many replications of the research, are needed to determine if specific types of educational experiences enhance learning for individuals with a specific hemispheric dominance. Some suggestions made for teaching "right-brained" students are:

1. Provide many exposures to the material to be learned.
2. Teach in a one-to-one situation so the student can focus attention on the task at hand.
3. Use dramatization to aid learning.
4. Use stories, puppets, and poetry.
5. Use audiotapes, films, and pictures.
6. Teach students to finish a task.
7. Allow students to manipulate materials.
8. Use peer modeling.
9. Have students deal with real situations.
10. Provide many opportunities for correct responses; do not let students practice incorrect responses.

As can be seen these suggestions would enhance the learning of any student and simply reflect good teaching practice. Left and right brain hemispheric functioning is a provocative area deserving further exploration. However, teachers should not look upon these notions as providing *the* answer to the question of what is causing a student's reading disability; nor should they regard these unresearched suggestions for matching teaching activities to an inferred hemispheric preference as representing a panacea for reading problems. Indeed, many reading educators believe that reading is a "whole brain" activity. For example, Zutell (1985) states

> Reading is primarily a means of communicating through written language. As such, it is best understood as a "whole brain" activity. While disconnection of particular cortical regions may disrupt reading ability in some cases. . ., effective reading requires the integration of both sequential and parallel, holistic processes. . . . Consequently, fluent reading and learning to read are activities which depend on perceptual and conceptual relationships. (p. 37)

Neuroscientists also agree that many activities require an integration of hemispheric functions. That is, each hemisphere must use part of the other side's knowledge to solve certain types of problems.

EDUCATIONAL FACTORS

Educational factors may contribute to a mild or moderate reading disability, but are not usually an initial cause of a severe disability. Many people believe that poor teaching is the predominant educational factor contributing to these problems. Sometimes the teacher is at fault, but sometimes not.

Lack of Research Information

We do not yet entirely understand the reading process, and until we do, all the answers teachers need to help students learn best are not available. Instead, teachers must rely on existing research and their own judgments in making instructional decisions. Teachers can also make use of recommended procedures based on presently available information. Nonetheless as we come to understand more about the reading process, and as more well constructed research becomes available, procedures based on teacher judgments that seemed entirely appropriate at the time as well as procedures suggested by authorities sometimes, though certainly not always, prove to be wrong. This dilemma occurs in many fields.

We do have some research evidence about the behaviors and skills of teachers that seem to lead to good reading achievement. This body of research has come to be known as the "teacher-effectiveness literature" and deals with such topics as time on task, management skills, grouping, pacing, and other related topics (Allington, 1984; Brophy, 1983; Gambrell, 1984; Rosenshine and Stevens, 1984). Among other findings, these studies show that direct instruction is important for low-achieving students; effective teachers avoid wasting time; students learn more when instruction is paced so their success rates are high; and teachers who spend larger amounts of time on reading produce greater gains. Although we do not know all of the teacher behaviors necessary to help students increase achievement, these findings can guide teachers in structuring their attitudes and developing their own skills. Teachers can also con-

tinually increase their learning by subscribing to professional journals. Box 4–1 lists some journals that can help teachers of reading.

Lack of Time on Task

Sometimes administrative policies prevent good teaching. Teachers may be required to carry out so many tasks unrelated to the academic needs of students that they do not have enough time to treat academic areas as comprehensively as necessary. Many studies show that the amount of time students spend directly engaged in the actual skill the teacher wishes them to learn is significantly related to their achievement. For example, Kiesling (1977–78) found that the amount of instructional time was positively related to reading gains whether or not the teacher employed small or large group instruction; in addition, this relationship was strongest for students reading below or at grade level.

The time teachers spend on nonacademic tasks can mean that students do not have enough time to learn. Some nonacademic tasks required of teachers are unnecessary. Administrators should carefully examine the things they ask teachers to do and eliminate those not directly related to students' learning or not absolutely necessary. Of course, some nonacademic tasks *are* necessary. Teachers with good management skills can structure the time needed to carry out these tasks so they impinge on students' learning as little as possible. For example, an elementary teacher who is required to collect students' lunch, milk, and snack money each morning might plan to have students engage in sustained silent reading during the 15 or 20 minutes it takes to collect money. While one student at a time comes quietly to the teacher's desk to deposit money, the other students read. By eliminating what is usually educationally dead time a teacher can add 1 to 1½ hours of learning time during a school week. Perceptive teachers at all levels can turn

---

Box 4–1
Selected Journals with Articles on Reading Instruction

Subscribing to journals and reading an article or two in each monthly issue can help teachers stay abreast of new teaching developments. These journals also contain ideas for classroom teaching activities.

Two journals for elementary teachers

The Reading Teacher
International Reading Association
800 Barksdale Rd.
P.O. Box 8139
Newark, Delaware 19711

Language Arts
National Council of Teachers of English
1111 Kenyon Rd.
Urbana, Illinois 61801

A journal for secondary teachers and teachers of adults

Journal of Reading
800 Barksdale Rd.
P.O. Box 8139
Newark, Delaware 19711

Some journals for both elementary and secondary teachers

Teaching Exceptional Children
The Council for Exceptional Children
1920 Association Dr.
Reston, Virginia 22091

Reading Horizons
Reading Center and Clinic
Western Michigan University
Kalamazoo, Michigan 49008

Reading World
Strine Printing Co., Inc.
1–83 Industrial Park
York, Pennsylvania 17402

Learning Disability Quarterly
c/o The Council for Learning Disabilities
P.O. Box 40303
Overland Park, Kansas 66204

---

nonlearning time (such as homeroom in junior and senior high schools) into times of academic engagement. Stallings (1986) promotes a self-analytic approach for teachers to determine if they are using time effectively. She encourages the use of a checklist to carefully analyze duration of activities, nature of interactions between pupils and teacher, on-task rate, intrusions from outside, type of activities, and who took part. Teachers are to examine the results and use problem-solving skills to make thoughtful adjustments in programs for low-achieving students.

Another administrative policy that causes problems of time is the continually increasing number of subjects teachers must cover in a school day. In the 1800s more than 90 percent of the school day was devoted to

reading, writing, and arithmetic. Time allotments for these subjects have decreased markedly; not only basic academic areas but also driver's education, consumer education, sex education, values clarification, productive use of leisure time, and other worthwhile, but time-consuming topics are subjects included in today's school curriculum. Since a school day has only a specified number of minutes, each new area added to the curriculum means additional minutes must be taken from existing subjects. Judicious decisions must be made about the value of each proposed new program in relation to existing programs. The value of different school programs may also vary with the individual. Although the quality of life may be enhanced by learning ways to use leisure time, a nonreader or functionally illiterate individual's quality of life may be more critically affected by lack of reading skill. Teachers must set priorities in regard to what they teach and how much time they devote to each subject, and these priorities may be different for each student they teach.

Sometimes the teacher is at fault when school time is not used for instruction. Durkin (1978–79) reported a study she conducted to determine the amount of instruction in reading comprehension received by students in grades three to six. She found that almost no instruction occurred; what little time was spent on comprehension was primarily used for assessment, that is, students were tested over material to determine *if* they had comprehended the material they had read but had no direct instruction beforehand on how to comprehend it. In addition, large portions of instructional time were spent giving and checking assignments rather than helping students learn strategies for comprehending the material. Many teachers need to rethink how they organize and use time during a school day.

Inappropriate Instructional Materials and Techniques

Administrative policy may also be the culprit when teachers are required to use out-of-date materials and nonproductive techniques. Occasionally when administrators do not have in-depth understanding of or familiarity with current practice of an area where they establish instructional policy, teachers are forced to use methods or engage in activities that are not as productive as they should be. In regard to this problem the role of reading specialists is important; teachers with special training in reading must help inform administrators about effective reading instruction techniques through inservice training sessions and one-to-one discussions.

Another educationally caused problem can occur when teachers uncritically follow

the dictates of publishing companies. Many reputable companies that publish reading materials use editors who are reading authorities and who screen materials and evaluate the value of suggested activities to be published. Other publishers do not follow this policy and often end up publishing outdated or unsupported suggestions and methods based on a layperson's ideas about what is helpful in reading instruction. When teachers follow these programs uncritically, they waste a lot of student learning time. Teachers try to instruct students not to believe everything they read, and teachers need to adopt the same healthy skepticism. Because a suggestion is made in a teacher's manual or an activity is found in a workbook does not mean the suggestion or activity is always useful in helping students learn to read. Teachers should question every procedure they carry out and every activity they assign. Teachers need to ask, "What does this activity really do to help increase this student's learning?" "Is this an activity that recent evidence says is not very helpful?" "Is this an activity used for many years to increase this skill, but do we now know better ways to accomplish this goal?" "Is this an activity leading to learning of such minor importance that I should substitute an activity that will be of greater value to this reading-disabled student?" "Is this activity designed correctly? Does it really teach rather than test? Is it just a time filler rather than a learning experience?" These and other questions will help a teacher plan lessons so learning can occur. Using many hours and days of valuable instructional time to have students engage in nonuseful activities prevents them from using the time to learn. Over the weeks and months this inefficient use of time can contribute to a student's reading problem. The decisions teachers make about instructional planning do affect student learning.

Teachers sometimes feel that if they could find just the right method, or just the right set of materials, or adopt just the right classroom organization their students would learn more. Methods do not teach; materials do not teach; classroom organizations do not teach. Teachers teach. Good teaching is the major key to eliminating educational causes of reading disabilities. Harris, Morrison, Serwer, and Gold (1968) reported a study of minority, disadvantaged, inner-city students who, unlike many such students, were reading at grade level. The key to this accomplishment was that their teachers had been given more than the usual amount of training and supervision to ensure they used appropriate procedures in carrying out reading instruction.

Features of Successful Reading Programs

After a review of successful reading programs, Samuels (1981) reported that these educational factors were found in exemplary programs:

Administrative Factors in Successful Programs

1. Exemplary programs had administrators who provided time for teachers to plan and carry out instruction.
2. Teachers were allowed to participate in making decisions.
3. Teachers' instructional behaviors were supervised.
4. Regular inservice sessions were part of the program and focused on real problems.
5. Teachers were allowed to observe other successful teachers to use them as role models.

Characteristics of Teachers in Successful Programs

1. Teachers devoted large amounts of energy and time carrying out the program.
2. Teachers had had practical training.

3. Teachers employed direct instruction, that is, when the goal was to have students learn to read, they gave them the opportunity to practice reading strategies. They did not ask students to walk balance beams, match shapes, or engage in other activities not directly related to the goal.
4. Teachers provided large amounts of instructional time and used time efficiently.
5. The level of complexity of instruction was kept low.
6. Teachers used ongoing evaluation to measure student progress frequently and determine immediate needs.
7. Classes were structured, but teachers maintained a friendly atmosphere.

Support Services in Successful Programs

1. Teacher's aides were employed and used in direct instruction with students.
2. Reading specialists were responsible for not only working with students but also providing guidance to classroom teachers and aides.

These characteristics offer some specific clues for establishing educational programs that will not contribute to students' reading failure.

EMOTIONAL FACTORS

The 1940s and 1950s witnessed great interest in the effects of emotional disturbances on reading disability. Despite the cautions of leading educators (e.g., Gates, 1941) to the contrary, emotional maladjustment was considered by many at the time to be a frequent cause of students' reading problems. During the same period research designed to verify this hypothesis was common. Results of the research show, however, that rather than emotional disturbances being a contributing factor to reading disabilities, in most cases, the converse is true.

Admittedly a small number of students have emotional problems so severe that their problems have a debilitating effect on their social behaviors and, consequently, on all aspects of their academic learning, including learning to read. But for most students who are both reading disabled and emotionally disturbed, the reading problem is at the root of the emotional disturbance rather than the other way around. These students come to school with emotionally healthy outlooks but when they have difficulties in learning to read while their peers are progressing normally, mild to moderate emotional problems begin to appear. A circular effect usually occurs, that

is, emotional problems stemming from difficulties in learning to read, in turn, contribute to lack of further progress in reading. For these students once the reading problem is remediated, the emotional disturbance disappears. A case that illustrates this phenomenon is Brian. (See Box 4–2.)

In those rare cases where a student's emotional problems are the initial underlying cause of the reading disability, therapy or psychological counseling is called for. For example, if the student comes from a home environment characterized by stress, conflict, and lack of security, neurotic symptoms that block learning may occur. In these cases an integrated effort such as the combined project of the Family Therapy Program and the Reading Clinic at Lehigh University (Garrigan, Kender & Heydenberk, 1980) may be needed. Such

---

Box 4–2
Brian—A brief case study

Brian, a fourth-grade boy labeled as learning- and behaviorally-disordered, was able to read almost nothing when he was enrolled in a university reading clinic. When Brian's tutors attempted to engage him in any type of reading-related activity, he would spend only a few minutes on task. Then he would engage in a variety of avoidance behaviors such as putting his head down, saying he was too tired to read, stating that his eyes hurt (although no visual problems of any kind existed), attempting to climb on the desk (even though he was quite large) to peer at students being tutored in other carrels, talking in a loud voice about off-the-subject topics, making abusive comments to his tutor, crawling on the floor, hiding under the desk and grabbing his tutor's legs when she came in, and simply refusing to engage in any planned activity. After 5 months of patient work during which many instructional techniques were tried and even the smallest bit of progress was praised and visually demonstrated to him, Brian began to read. An almost immediate change in his behavior was seen. He remained on task for the entire one-hour tutoring session; he asked to engage in specific reading activities; he became eager to demonstrate his reading skill to other clinic personnel; he was quiet, attentive, and pleasant in dealings with his tutor; and before and after tutoring sessions he wandered about the clinic attempting to read everything in sight. On the day Brian came into the clinic wearing a badge he had received at school that day, a cheer went up in the clinic—the badge said that he had been chosen as the good citizen of the month for his entire elementary school. As soon as Brian began to read, his other inappropriate behaviors disappeared. When these behaviors disappeared he was able to focus on tasks necessary in learning to read, and his progress in reading increased rapidly.

programs recognize the need for total family involvement in treating the student's emotional problems and recognize that this is best carried out in conjunction with reading remediation efforts.

SOCIOCULTURAL FACTORS

Sociological factors are those related to human social behaviors and their origins. Cultural factors are those that influence the transmission of these behaviors so patterns of behavior and values become characteristic of a population or community. In 1932 Bartlett conducted a classic study that showed how beliefs or values can affect learning. Some sociocultural factors that may have an impact on a student's reading ability are socioeconomic status, ethnic identification, and culturally determined sex roles.

Socioeconomic Status

There are differences in reading achievement when comparing students from high, middle, and low socioeconomic status (SES) backgrounds. Students from low SES homes tend to do less well in school generally and many studies have shown the incidence of reading disability increases as SES decreases (e.g., Abelson, Zigler, & Deblasi, 1974; Thorndike, 1973; Weber, 1973).

Many Americans tend to associate low socioeconomic status with race or ethnicity although in many cases this association does not hold true. For this reason, it should be emphasized that low school achievement is linked with low socioeconomic status only, not with race or ethnic background.

Wachs, Uzgiris, and Hunt (1971) found intellectual deficiencies among black and Caucasian low SES children in the U.S. as early as 7 months of age. They believed this to be the result of several aspects of home environ-

ment, such as lack of intellectual stimulation. Other causes of poor reading achievement related to home environments may be disorganized life styles, family environmental patterns that are unresponsive to school-dictated requirements such as homework, and social behaviors and values of self-discipline different from the mainstream culture. Because of low verbal and educational levels of parents, there may be a lack of abstract language use in the home; children may not be encouraged to deal with conceptual problems; and since parents usually read less they provide a poor model for a child learning to read. Low SES preschool children usually have less access to opportunities that lead to school readiness. Their homes have fewer books, and no one purposely stimulates their interest in reading; therefore, they do not come to school eager to learn to read. Fewer books are read to them at home so they lack the familiarity with book language and the larger, higher quality oral language vocabularies of children who have been read to regularly. Students from low SES homes often have poor health care and inadequate diets that may lead to health problems and poor school attendance.

Some school-related factors can also cause poor reading achievement in students from low socioeconomic backgrounds. Lower teacher expectations seems to be a variable leading to lack of success. Cooper, Baron, and Love (1975) reported a study of college-age elementary education and psychology majors' reactions to descriptions of Caucasian and black middle-class students in contrast to Caucasian and black low SES students; they expected low SES children to do less well. It has been suggested that teachers must be trained to assess students' abilities independent of their socioeconomic status. Hoover (1978) and Anderson, Hiebert, Scott, and Wilkinson (1985) have reported on successful schools in low-income neighborhoods where the reading levels of students were equal to those of students from middle-class backgrounds. Classrooms were described as quiet and conducive to learning, there was a high degree of teacher-directed instruction, teachers had high expectations, and a wide variety of library books were available to students.

Administrative regulations may be another contributor to lack of reading success for low SES students. Governmental programs, such as Chapter I, designed to provide remedial instruction for low-income students, have required that these special services be provided only to students in the lowest 33rd percentile. Students who are eligible one year may not be eligible the next since, because of effective instruction, they are no longer in the lowest 33rd percentile of their school population. Although they may not yet be reading up to their potentials or to the grade norm, and although they both need and have shown they can benefit from special instruction, they are no longer allowed services in the program.

Another school-related factor thought to be a possible contributor to low achievement is the apparent mismatch between the cultural and linguistic experiences of low SES students and the language, settings, and activities in standard reading materials. Several pieces of research have shown that this mismatch does not affect reading achievement. Ratekin (1978), for example, compared reading abilities of white, black, and Spanish-surnamed children instructed in identical reading materials—a standard basal reader series. All children in the study were from low socioeconomic backgrounds and were at similar reading levels at the beginning of the study. There were, however, linguistic differences among the groups; the black children spoke an inner-city black dialect, and the majority of the Spanish-surnamed children were bilingual and spoke Spanish widely in their communities and homes. But although these linguistic differences existed, there were no differences among the groups on an achievement test

given at the end of the year. In addition, the cultural experiences conveyed in the stories were for the most part representative of middle-class life and did not reflect the lifestyle of any of the groups. Despite these differences, however, all groups of children had made equal and excellent gains when beginning-of-the-year pretests and end-of-the-year posttests were compared. Ratekin believed that an important factor in these gains was that their teachers were prepared to accept and understand language and cultural differences. The results of this and other studies indicate that a mismatch between the cultural experiences and the language of students and their textbooks does not contribute to reading disability if teachers are sensitive to and handle the mismatch appropriately. A later chapter of this text suggests ways to accommodate linguistic and cultural differences.

Ethnic Identification

The culture of a student when shaped by ethnic origins apparently can have an effect on ways the student learns best. For example, Au and Mason (1981) reported that verbal interactions in a school setting that were similar to those of the cultural life of Hawaiian children produced more achievement-related behaviors than dissimilar interactions. In one classroom children were required to wait to be called on by the teacher before speaking in reading group and were required to speak one at a time—behaviors typical in classrooms of the mainstream culture. In another classroom, reading group verbal interactions were allowed to assume the characteristics of a Hawaiian talk story—students took turns responding to the same question or engaged in joint responses. Children allowed to respond in the second manner had more academic engaged time and made more reading-related responses during group time.

Similar studies have been reported with Native American populations. Children at the Warm Springs Indian Reservation were less willing to participate in school activities if they were directed at individuals and more willing if group activities were involved (Phillips, 1972). Many Indian cultures are family- or group-centered and students from these cultures are often uncomfortable if required to compete. This culturally determined trait contrasts with the requirements of mainstream culture classrooms where individuals are singled out to exhibit their understanding of a topic. Many Indian students respond to this singling out by remaining silent rather than excel over their peers; their silence as a response to a question may be incorrectly interpreted by a teacher as lack of knowledge.

Thonis (1976) and others have described certain culturally determined factors that may lead to school failure of Spanish-surnamed students. These include:

1. lack of experiences with concepts specific to the mainstream culture,
2. lack of understanding of rules of mainstream schools,
3. lack of understanding of mainstream cultural values involving time concepts,
4. appearance of timidity, which is really a display of good judgment in uncertain situations,
5. a cooperative attitude that results in putting aside one's own needs in deference to others,
6. and, if bilingual, a language system that though previously helpful in controlling the child's world, is not useful in the school setting.

Bicultural students often appear to lack competence and intelligence in school settings, while more than adequately demonstrating these traits in their own communities and homes. Good teachers adapt instruction to the ethnic experiences and values of their students and at the same time help them adjust to the mainstream culture. When teachers fail to adapt, their students may not achieve their potential.

Culturally Determined Sex Roles

Sex differences have been demonstrated in relation to reading achievement. In the United States, girls have better reading readiness scores than boys and superior attainment in early reading progress. Although in the general school population these differences tend to disappear by age 10, more boys than girls have reading difficulties that necessitate a remedial or clinical program. Males enrolled in university-based reading clinics outnumbered females 3:1 in a recent national survey (Bader & Wiesendanger, 1986).

Although these differences may be partially explained by biological reasons, they may also have a sociocultural base. One premise has been that the content of stories used in reading instruction reflects interests consistent with the culturally determined sex roles of girls rather than boys—and that this in turn affects boys' motivation and achievement. Blom, Waite, and Zimet (1970) examined all the stories in the 12 most widely used basal reader series and found this assumption to be untrue. Stories did not favor girls' interests over boys, nor did they more frequently describe activities thought of as feminine.

A second premise has been that boys' achievement is adversely affected because schools have predominantly female staffs. Some have suggested that women teachers provide instruction that requires learning styles unnatural for boys, and that they have lower expectations for boys. A review of 22 studies by Lahaderne (1976) has laid this myth to rest. What Lahaderne did find was that both men and women teachers seem to operate from the same cultural biases. There were no differences between the perceptions of male and female teachers—they both perceived boys as having more problems than girls; there were also no differences in the grades they assigned for academic performance. There were no differences between male and female teachers in regard to their treatment of boys and girls: boys received more interactions of all types (approval and disapproval) from both groups, and both groups were more directive with boys. Finally, there were no differences in pupil outcomes between the boys or girls who had male teachers and the boys and girls who had female teachers: no differences in pupil adjustments, no differences in reading or math achievement, and no differences in self-concept.

A third premise is that general cultural expectations related to sex roles exist that are reflections of larger societal norms. These expectations come from parents, peers, and society as a whole. Johnson's (1973–74) study supports this cultural explanation. He compared reading achievement of males and females in four countries. In England and Nigeria boys' achievement was higher; in Canada and the United States girls' achievement was higher. Specific factors that can affect perceptions of sex roles vary from cultural group to cultural group. In North America, preschool boys and girls view reading as a masculine activity (May & Ollila, 1981), but school-aged boys and girls view reading and books as feminine. Culturally determined appropriateness of reading in relation to sex roles may influence the amount of reading done by boys and girls as well as their motivation to become good readers. In certain cases, then, these sex-related expectations may be a contributing cause to a mild reading disability.

LANGUAGE FACTORS

Reading is a language-based activity. Proficient readers rely heavily, though rather unconsciously, on their knowledge of oral language when they read. The three major aspects of oral language are phonemes (sounds), syntax (sentence structure), and semantics (meaning). In written language a fourth is added, namely, graphemes (letters).

Readers use knowledge of oral language in two main ways. First, they determine if what they have just read "sounds right." If what a good reader has read does not sound right, that is, if it is not syntactically or semantically correct, the good reader usually rereads and self-corrects. Secondly, good readers use oral language to make predictions (in other words, good guesses) about words. For example, read the following sentence:

I bought a loaf _____ bread.

Everyone reading this textbook can read the sentence—including the word that was left out. Knowing English sentence structures allows a reader to guess correctly that the omitted word is *of*. Being able to make predictions helps readers read text without really looking at every single word; since they have knowledge of English syntax, good readers often unconsciously guess which word is going to come up next and focus their attention only on some of the more significant or unfamiliar words. Because they don't have to focus on every word, good readers—whether reading orally or silently—read more fluently and obtain meaning more easily. Making predictions is also helpful because readers do not have to laboriously decode each unknown word letter by letter. By using knowledge of sentence structure and perhaps, one or two initial letters of a word, they can often correctly guess a word that is not part of their reading recognition vocabulary. Suppose for example, a young reader had not yet learned to recognize the word *was*. This student would still probably be able to guess and read that word as it appears in the example here because knowing oral language helps a reader anticipate.

> The boy wanted a brown dog, but this dog w_____ black and white.

Though all readers can use oral language knowledge, many poor readers do not. Students who lack the intuitive use of this strategy or who have received no direct instruction to make up for this lack may often be reading-disabled to some degree. Grammatical sensitivity (both syntactic and semantic) has been found to be significantly related to reading skill (Willows & Ryan, 1986).

There are more similarities than differences between oral and written language. If this were not so, a reader would not be aided by knowledge of oral language in the ways just described. But there are also some important differences that have implications for teaching reading. Written language is not simply "talk written down," as some teachers have told their students. Certain types of sentence patterns encountered in written language are seldom, if ever, used in oral language. McCormick and Moe (1982) give some examples of dialogue structures.

> "There's a hole in my pocket," laughed Joey.
> "In the morning," Pete yelled up to his brother, "I'll show you how to throw a fast ball." (p. 49)

Because these types of patterns and others are not employed in oral language, students are less able to use their language knowledge to make predictions about upcoming words or to use syntax to aid in self-correction. Vocabulary use and intonation, which also play an important part in conveying a message in oral language, may differ too. To deal with the problems caused by the incongruency between oral and written language, students must gain as much familiarity with written language as they have with oral language. This is best ac-

complished by reading aloud to children. Young children who have had books read aloud to them frequently and regularly during the preschool years come to school able to respond to written language structures as well as to oral language. Students who have not been exposed to the more elaborate formal code of written language lack an important readiness experience that may contribute to a reading disability.

A previously cited study (Ratekin, 1978) indicated that a difference between the oral language dialect of students and standard English does not affect reading achievement. Other studies have also shown this to be true. At one time there was much interest in writing reading materials in the nonstandard dialects of the students who were to use them and a number of publishers developed materials of this type. In the end, they proved not to be useful in increasing the reading achievement of nonstandard dialect speakers. Weber (1970) pointed out that many reading materials contain language that is divergent from the oral language of any speaker. For example:

> See me. See me go. See me go up.
> Dan, the big man, has a fan.

Divergencies between oral and written language will always exist whether a speaker's dialect is standard or nonstandard.

A student's nonstandard dialect may not contribute to a reading disability if language differences are handled appropriately by teachers. Too often, however, teachers mistake a language difference for a reading error. Cunningham (1976–77) studied the degree to which teachers made students correct reading miscues that did not change the meaning of the text. When these unimportant miscues were not caused by use of nonstandard dialect, the students were required to correct them only 27 percent of the time, but when use of nonstandard dialect was the root of the miscue, teachers required corrections for 78 percent of them—even though the miscues caused no change in meaning. Hunt (1974–75) scored students' performances on an oral reading test, first scoring them according to the directions given in the test manual. Then they were rescored leaving out all "errors" that simply reflected a dialect difference. On the rescoring, students' scores were significantly higher; some students received scores a year or more above their original scores. Teachers' misperceptions of what constitutes reading skill plus traditional scoring of reading tests can lead to erroneous evaluations of students' true abilities when they do not take into account language differences versus reading errors. Students may be falsely labeled as reading-disabled.

Some researchers have attempted to change the language of students rather than the language of materials to correct the mismatch between their oral language and the language of reading texts. Rystrom (1970), for example, conducted an intensive program in use of standard English with black dialect speakers; the program did not bring about an increase in their reading achievement. Some commercial language development programs are designed to teach students to speak only in complete sentences. These programs assume that the failure of students, particularly low SES students, to do so makes it difficult for them to contend with the more formal sentence structures they encounter in written material. Teaching students to use written language structures in oral language is unnecessary, since, for all speakers, oral language patterns are more informal. Short phrases or even single words often, and appropriately, serve as complete sentences in oral language. For example, a friend might say, "What did you have for lunch today?" and you might simply respond, "Chili." It is unnecessary to say, "I had chili for lunch today." Incomplete sentences occur frequently in oral language, even the language of well-educated adults. Oral and written language patterns are well suited to their special purposes, and it is unnatural and inappropriate to train students to speak in atypical ways since to do so does not help their reading ability. Using oral speech patterns that do not conform to written language will not cause a student's reading disability. Rosen and Ortega (1969) reviewed the research on programs designed to remediate "deficit" oral language and concluded that they were not useful in promoting reading success.

Other myths have developed about the relationship of language problems and their effect on reading ability. One myth is that low SES students are poor readers because they are less verbal. Sometimes low SES students do appear to be less verbal in formal testing situations because they are unfamiliar with the examiner and the testing environment; but when they are tested in more familiar settings, low SES students are found to be highly verbal (Labov, Cohen, Robbins, & Lewis, 1968). Another myth is that low SES students have deficient oral vocabularies that interfere with their learning to read in the early grades. Although research does indicate that low SES children have more limited vocabularies than middle-class children, it is believed that this research may be an underestimate of students' true abilities. However, even assuming these underestimates to be correct, it has been shown that low SES students do have the oral vocabulary knowledge necessary to deal with the words found in the most widely used beginning books (Cohen & Kornfeld, 1970).

CONCLUDING STATEMENT

Chapters 3 and 4 have discussed possible causes and correlates of reading disabilities and the need for teachers to be aware of possible causes. These chapters have also pointed out, however, the necessity of using a two-pronged approach to understand and then help correct a student's reading problem. That is, while it is important to determine the causes of a student's difficulties so they may be eliminated or lessened if possible, the major role of the teacher is to assess specific reading areas and provide excellent reading instruction.

UNIT TWO

Diagnostic Procedures

5

Assessment for Identification

Assessment is the total process of collecting information to make instructional decisions; testing is one part of assessment. *Formal assessment* uses *standardized tests* (also called *norm-referenced tests*), which are published tests for which norms based on the performances of many students have been developed. These norms allow teachers to compare the performances of students with those of the group used in norming the test. *Informal assessment* employs many types of nonstandardized measures, such as teacher-prepared tests; daily, ongoing observations; published informal inventories; other nonstandardized tests; checklists that evaluate the whole child; interest inventories; measurements of attitudes or habits; interviews; and student self-evaluations. See Table 5–1, which shows the general characteristics of formal and informal assessments. Examples of formal and informal assessment procedures are interspersed throughout all the chapters in Unit Two. This placement reflects the pattern and sequence teachers in real school or clinic settings generally use. Introducing the assessment procedures in order of need seemed to be more useful than discussing formal and in-

formal tests in separate sections (as is often done). The organization in this book provides both a scope and a sequence for diagnosis. Unit Two consists of the following:

This chapter discusses assessment techniques that are often used *before* students enter a special reading program. These techniques are employed to determine eligibility for placement in a Chapter I or other remedial reading class, LD programs, or reading clinic.

Chapter 6—This chapter discusses the *first type of assessment usually conducted once students are enrolled* in a program—assessment to determine or confirm reading level.

Chapters 7 and 8—Chapters 7 and 8 present a large number of tests that are often *used next in the assessment process.* These are used to determine specific strengths and weaknesses. Chapters 7 and 8 also discuss measures of interest and attitude so that teachers can structure affective environments which facilitate learning.

Teachers using assessment procedures must realize that scores are generally approximations. For example, students who receive an IQ score of 94 on a specific test probably

Table 5–1
Types of reading assessment

Formal assessment/ standardized tests	Informal assessment/ nonstandardized procedures
A. Group tests 1. Used for determining reading levels 2. Used for determining specific strengths and weaknesses in strategies, knowledge, and skills	A. Group procedures 1. Used for determining reading levels 2. Used for determining specific strengths and weaknesses in strategies, knowledge, and skills
B. Individual tests 1. Used for determining reading levels 2. Used for determining specific strengths and weaknesses in strategies, knowledge, and skills	B. Individual procedures 1. Used for determining reading levels 2. Used for determining specific strengths and weaknesses in strategies, knowledge, and skills

have intelligence quotients quite close to 94, ranging a few points above or below this obtained score. When the learning expectancy level (also called reading expectancy) for a student is determined to be 6.0, this means it is approximately sixth-grade level, and so forth. Assigning numerical scores to human abilities is not an exact science by any means. A score derived from an assessment instrument represents a good ballpark figure and is helpful because it gives us a place to begin when making instructional or placement decisions. It should never be interpreted as definitive.

In addition, sometimes scores obtained from a single test may simply be wrong (Farr & Carey, 1986; Harris, 1967; Johnston, 1983). When Stephanie receives a score of 75 on an IQ test, but all her academic behaviors indicate she is functioning above the mildly retarded range, it is likely that factors other than intelligence have depressed her test score. Perhaps she was feeling ill the day she was tested, or perhaps the examiner was not skillful in administering the test. Sometimes teachers will say something like, "Juan's stan-

dardized test score indicated he is reading at fourth-grade level, but he is having no difficulty handling fifth-grade material in my class." They seem reluctant to rely on their own observations if these do not agree with the results of formal testing. Tests are helpful starting places when selected and administered properly, but their scores should be interpreted in light of other available evidence (Croft, 1951).

Furthermore, assessment should be carried out over a period of time, conducted in various settings and social contexts, and undertaken while students are reading for various purposes. It is especially important that students' behaviors be assessed while they are engaged in real reading, and not just when they are taking tests.

ISSUES RELATED TO FORMAL ASSESSMENT

The first assessment task of a reading teacher is to identify those students who warrant remedial services. This is called *assessment for*

Assessment should be carried out over time, in various settings and social contexts, and while students are reading for different purposes.

identification. Not only must teachers be aware of the general limitations of testing and assessment, but, since a good deal of assessment for identification involves use of formal assessment (that is, use of standardized tests) they should also be aware of the important issues raised about the limitations of reading tests in particular, as well as the advantages of testing and other types of assessment when the measures are properly selected, administered, and interpreted.

Judging the Merits of Test Quality

Two types of standardized tests are frequently administered to students with reading problems. *Survey tests* are designed to determine students' general reading levels. *Diagnostic tests* (sometimes called analytical tests) are used to analyze a student's specific strengths and weaknesses in reading strategies, knowledge, and skills.

Teachers need to consider many factors when they choose a standardized survey or diagnostic test. Some involve practical matters. For example, a teacher may ask, "Is the time needed for administration reasonable since I have many other students to assess?" Other factors related to the technical acceptability of the test are crucial. If a test has not been properly devised, the results may be meaningless, and consequently, valuable time may be wasted, and a student's instructional program may be based on incorrect information.

The technical acceptability of a test is based on three factors: norms, validity, and reliability.

Norms. Norms are scores that represent an average and are used for comparing one student with other students. Test makers develop norms by administering their test to a large sample of students. To develop adequate norms, they need to have a sample group that includes students who are similar in age, IQ range, and general characteristics to the group with whom the published test is to be used. Most test publishers also try to select their sample of students from urban, suburban, and rural areas—and if they are attempting to develop *national norms,* that is, norms based on a nationwide sample, from all regions of the country. (*Local norms,* based on data from certain schools or certain areas, are occasionally used instead of national norms.) Based on the performances of the students in the sample, *grade norms,* that is, the average score of students from a given grade level, are determined. Test manuals should report the characteristics of the sample on which the test was normed so teachers can determine if the test is appropriate for their students. In addition, norms must be revised at least every 15 years to remain current.

Validity. The *validity* of a test is the degree to which it measures what it claims to measure. *Content validity* is the degree to which a test assesses the whole class of subject matter about which conclusions will be made.[1] An example of a test used in reading diagnosis that lacks content validity is one that is a mere list of words students read orally and which purportedly can specify a student's instructional level based on this performance. These tests claim to measure general reading ability, but do not measure all the factors involved in real reading (Mavrogenes, Winkley, Hanson, & Vacca, 1974). Some other types of validity are *construct validity* (the degree to which performance on a test actually predicts the degree to which an individual possesses a trait), *concurrent validity* (the degree to which performance on a test predicts performance on a criterion external to that test), and *predictive validity* (the degree to which a test predicts future performance in an area). Test manuals should report evidence of validity.

Reliability. The reliability of a test relates to the degree of consistency of its scores. In other words, if a student took the same test more than once, would she make approximately the same score every time? Test makers can determine a reliability coefficient for a test by such methods as computing a coefficient of correlation between two alternate forms of the test or between scores obtained from repeated administration of the same test. Adequate reliability coefficients for a test used to compare groups should be above 0.60, but should be above 0.90 if used for diagnostic purposes with individual students (Salvia & Ysseldyke, 1981). Reliability coefficients should be reported in test manuals.

Before administering a test, teachers should examine the accompanying manual for information on norming procedures, validity, and reliability. Buros, who edited the *Mental Measurements Yearbooks* for 40 years, stated that one of his goals was "to make test users aware of the importance of being suspicious of all tests—even those produced by well-known authors and publishers—which are not accompanied by detailed data on their construction, validation, uses, and limitations" (Mitchell, 1985, p. xiv). Table 5–2 details some of the flaws in well known published reading tests.

Advantages of Standardized Tests
Generally, standardized tests save time since they may be administered to many students simultaneously. Group tests may also be used with individual students if this is more appropriate to the teacher's purpose. In addition, if a test has been properly devised, the test passages and questions have been tried out with numerous students. Some items are discarded in the process, and new items are tested until a final group of suitable items is chosen. Most teachers do not have the time to prepare tests they devise themselves with such thoroughness. Some test makers monitor *passage dependency;* they take care to ensure that a student must actually read a passage to

---

[1]Definitions obtained from Farr (1986).

5

When Susan first stepped into the living room, she could not tell what had happened. The lamp was lying on the floor, and the paper was scattered about. But when she saw the chewed slipper, she knew who the culprit was.

A. How did the living room look?

⬭ the same   ⬭ bare

⬭ bright   ⬭ messy

B. Who was the culprit?

⬭ Susan   ⬭ a burglar

⬭ the wind   ⬭ a puppy

6

Henry wanted to go bike riding. "Come on, Kevin," he said. "Today is the first day it hasn't rained in a week."

"Then it's too muddy outside," Kevin said.

Henry looked out the window. "No," he said, "I don't see any puddles. It's sunny."

"Well, I want to read this new book," Kevin answered.

A. What did Henry see when he looked out?

⬭ sunshine   ⬭ puddles

⬭ rain   ⬭ bike riders

B. Kevin's real reason for not wanting to go out was that he

⬭ was tired   ⬭ wanted to read

⬭ had no bike   ⬭ saw the mud

7

The children were trying out for the play. They were all excited.

John wanted to be the hero. "I'm the strongest," he said.

"But I beat you in the race yesterday," said Bill. "Which is more important, being fast or strong?"

The teacher said, "Both are important for some things. But for the play we need someone who can speak loudly and clearly."

A. The children were excited because

⬭ of a race   ⬭ Bill had won

⬭ of a play   ⬭ John was a hero

B. The teacher said the hero should

⬭ speak clearly   ⬭ be fast

⬭ be strong   ⬭ try hard

8

Mary likes living in her apartment building. Her uncle lives just below her on the second floor. Her friend Lynn lives right above her on the fourth floor.

A. On which floor does Mary live?

⬭ the second   ⬭ the fourth

⬭ the third   ⬭ the fifth

B. Who lives on the second floor?

⬭ Lynn   ⬭ Lynn and Mary

⬭ Lynn's uncle   ⬭ Mary's uncle

GO ON ➜

Figure 5–1

Page from a published standardized reading test designed for the third grade. Reproduced from Gates-MacGinitie Reading Tests, Form 2, Level C copyright © 1978. Reprinted with permission of the Publisher, The Riverside Publishing Company, 8420 W. Bryn Mawr Avenue, Chicago, Ill. 60631. All rights reserved.

Table 5–2
Technical inadequacies of some published reading tests

Norms inappropriately developed or information on norming group inadequately reported	Lack of validity or evidence of validity inadequately reported	Low reliability or reliability inadequately reported
Frostig Developmental Test of Visual Perception	Frostig Developmental Test of Visual Perception	Frostig Developmental Test of Visual Perception
Slosson Oral Reading Test	Slosson Oral Reading Test	Slosson Oral Reading Test
Illinois Test of Psycholinguistic Abilities	Illinois Test of Psycholinguistic Abilities	Illinois Test of Psycholinguistic Abilities
Diagnostic Reading Scales	Gates-McKillop-Horowitz Reading Diagnostic Tests	Gilmore Oral Reading Test
Gates-McKillop-Horowitz Reading Diagnostic Tests	Gilmore Oral Reading Test	Gray Oral Reading Test
Silent Reading Diagnostic Test	Gray Oral Reading Test	Durrell Analysis of Reading Difficulty
Gilmore Oral Reading Test	Wide Range Achievement Test	
Gray Oral Reading Test	Durrell Analysis of Reading Difficulty	
Wide Range Achievement Test		
Wepman Auditory Discrimination Test		
Durrell Analysis of Reading Difficulty		

Source: Adapted from *Assessment in special and remedial education,* 2nd ed., J. Salvia & J. E. Ysseldyke, 1982. Boston: Houghton Mifflin. Reprinted by permission.

answer the questions, rather than answer the questions based on previous knowledge. Finally, standardized tests are usually available in two or more equivalent forms so students can be retested to measure growth.

Survey Tests.   The general reading achievement levels obtained on survey tests can be used for comparative purposes. Some reasons for comparing students' reading performances with others' are to evaluate the effectiveness of specific instructional procedures and to compare and evaluate programs from different school systems. Group standardized tests can also be used to select students who require remedial programs by comparing their performances with the performances of other students. In fact, administration of a standardized test is re-

quired for determining eligibility for most LD programs and Chapter I remedial reading programs.

Diagnostic Tests.   If the grade scores from standardized diagnostic tests are ignored and substituted with an analysis of student performance on specific reading tasks, some helpful diagnostic information may be obtained.

Disadvantages of Standardized Tests

There has been an increase in use of standardized tests every decade since the 1950s (Resnick, 1981). Although there are some disadvantages in using them, certain standardized tests provide useful information if they are applied to the appropriate purpose.

Survey Tests.   Survey tests provide some information about how well a student is performing in reading but do not provide an analysis of why she is performing well or poorly (Salmon-Cox, 1981). Although these tests are usually divided into subtests, the subtests are not appropriate for diagnosing specific strengths and weaknesses in strategies, knowledge, and skills and should not be used for this purpose (Farr, 1969; Schell, 1984a). Nor should diagnostic profiles be developed from students' performance on types of items (e.g., inferential comprehension questions or questions that require recognizing directly stated main ideas) (Hunt, 1957). Survey tests cannot be used diagnostically because not enough items of each type are provided to make adequate judgments. In addition, since test passages become increasingly more difficult as one moves from the beginning to the end of a section, students may miss items simply because the overall passage difficulty is above their reading levels, not because they have a specific skill deficiency related to the types of items answered incorrectly. Furthermore, standardized survey tests cannot measure all understandings a student needs to perform well on all reading tasks, for example, the special skills necessary for reading content area texts, appreciating an author's style, or conducting a plot analysis (Anderson, Hiebert, Scott, & Wilkinson, 1985). Finally, using the grade level scores obtained on survey tests alone for planning instruction is of somewhat questionable value since both research and practice has shown that these scores are often an overestimate of the reading level at which a student can actually function in instructional material (Ransom, 1968).

Diagnostic Tests.   Grade level scores obtained on many of the standardized diagnostic tests commonly used in remedial programs vary from test to test (Eller & Attea, 1966) and do not provide an accurate index of reading level. One reason for this variance is that criteria for evaluating students' errors differ from test to test (Farr, 1969; Schell, 1984b).

Using Standardized Tests with Students Who Speak Nonstandard Dialects

Another issue about which there has been much concern is the degree to which standardized reading tests are suitable for students who speak nonstandard dialects. Some argue that students should not have to take tests in a dialect they do not speak. These authorities emphasize that the disharmony between the sound (phonological systems) of standard English and nonstandard dialects puts some students at a disadvantage. For example, some sound discrimination items found on primary grade standardized tests are not differentiated in the oral language of certain nonstandard dialect speakers (Hutchinson, 1972). It should be noted, however, that this argument is applicable only to primary-level standardized tests. Above this level, these tests usually do not include items designed to measure how well students can identify letter sounds. Rather, they typically include items that require whole word recognition and passage comprehension.

Those who favor use of standardized tests with these students assert that students from nonmainstream cultures are really bidialectal, that is, although they speak a nonstandard form of English, they understand standard English when they hear it, as evidenced by their responses to television, their teachers, and so forth (MacGinitie, 1973b). These students obviously understand standard English sentence structures (the syntactical system) and standard English vocabulary (the semantic system), because they can obtain meaning from standard English utterances in these situations.

Ideally, standardized tests should not require students to recognize isolated words, which places a heavy emphasis on using the sounds in a word. Instead, test items should require contextual reading where the nonstandard dialect speaker's ability to comprehend standard English sentence structures and vocabulary aids in determining meaning, and therefore, in recognition of words and comprehension of the material.

A further point to consider is the objective of reading tests and reading programs. The material students must read in school, and later throughout life, is written in standard English. Therefore, it seems reasonable to test students in standard English to determine just how well they can handle this task and to plan instruction if tests show they do not handle it very well (MacGinitie, 1973b).

Finally, a substantial amount of research has now shown that in reading testing, as in reading instruction, dialect differences do not play a major role in affecting performance. For example, Hochman (1973) compared black and white third-, fourth-, and fifth-graders' performances on two forms of the California Reading Test. One form was written in standard English; one was written in a black vernacular dialect. No differences were found in the test scores of black or white students on either form; if students did well on one form they did well on the other, and if they did poorly on one they did poorly on the other.

STEPS IN ASSESSMENT FOR IDENTIFICATION

In Chapter 1 you learned that the most common method for identifying students who need corrective, remedial, or clinical reading services (or placement in an LD program) is to assess students' present achievement and compare this with their potentials to determine the degree of discrepancy between the two. You will remember that this discrepancy is called *capacity-achievement difference,* or CAD. To substantiate CAD, you must determine the student's potential, more commonly called *learning expectancy level,* or LEL, and assess the student's present reading achievement.

Determining Learning Expectancy Level

Three steps in determining a student's LEL include obtaining IQ or mental age scores, verifying exact chronological age, and using an appropriate LEL formula.

Obtaining IQ or Mental Age Scores. To determine a student's IQ and mental age (MA) an intelligence test must be administered. The best type of IQ test is one individually administered by a trained examiner, such as the Wechsler Intelligence Scale for Children-Revised (WISC-R), the Stanford-Binet Intelligence Scale, or the Wechsler Adult Intelligence Scale-Revised (WAIS-R). A new intelligence test, the Kaufman Assessment Battery for Children (KABC), holds promise for use with students having learning problems because it separates items related to school learning from those that measure more general aspects of intelligence. All of these tests are valid and reliable and their standard error of measurement is small. The *standard error of measurement,* or SEM, is the degree to which a student's true score probably deviates from the score specified by a test. For example, if an IQ test has a SEM of 3 and Patrick receives an IQ score of 111, this means his true IQ could be up to three points above or below 111. His "true" IQ score probably falls somewhere in the range between 108 and 114. Obviously, the larger the SEM the less helpful a test score is. The best IQ tests have an SEM of no greater than 3.

Because the WISC-R, Stanford-Binet, WAIS-R, and KABC are administered individually the student must do very little reading, a crucial factor for students suspected of having a reading disability, and who, if faced with reading test items, may receive depressed scores simply because they cannot read the words.

Most reading teachers do not have the special training to administer and interpret the WISC-R, Stanford-Binet, WAIS-R, or KABC; therefore, students with possible reading disabilities should be referred to a school psychologist for assessment. Since school psychologists often have a heavy case load of students, however, and may be unable to assess students promptly, reasonably current IQ and MA scores available from a previous assessment may be used.

The second best alternative to acquire IQ and MA scores is to administer an individual IQ test designed to be given by an examiner without extensive training in administering and interpreting intelligence tests. The best such test presently available is the Slosson Intelligence Test (SIT), whose developers used the Stanford-Binet as a criterion for determining validity of the SIT and adapted many specific items from the Stanford-Binet. A second edition of the test was published in 1981 with new norms that create a deviational IQ for the SIT and correspond with those on the 1972 renormed version of the Stanford-Binet. The SIT has a high reliability coefficient of .97 and an acceptable SEM of about 4. The population used for norming the SIT was diverse, including preschool through high school-aged students from public and private, rural and urban schools, white, black, and native Americans as well as adults, and gifted and retarded persons. The SIT incorporates a wide variety of types of test items and has several practical advantages. First, because it is' administered individually, the teacher

reads the questions to the student. Since the student is not required to read, it is particularly useful for students suspected of having reading problems. Then too, it takes only a short time to administer—approximately 15 minutes, and scoring procedures are easy and quick. Finally, it can be used with anyone over 4.

The SIT is available in a booklet that includes lists of questions arranged by chronological age level, recording sheets, and directions for administering and scoring. Ordinarily a student suspected of having learning problems is first tested with items two years below her actual age. Without allowing the student to see the test page, the teacher asks questions. The correct answer appears on the test page immediately following each question. If the student's answer is correct, the teacher records a (+) on the record sheet; if it is incorrect, he records a (−). Testing continues until the student gives 10 incorrect answers in a row. These and several other easy to follow directions are provided in the teacher's section of the test booklet. After testing, the student's raw score is easily converted to IQ and MA scores.

Teachers who use the SIT need to remember that its purpose is to provide a global IQ and MA score, not a diagnosis. Occasionally a teacher will re-examine the test after computing scores to determine specific items the student missed so he can plan instruction to alleviate weaknesses. For example, after finding a student was unable to repeat a series of numbers in two items, the teacher may believe that activities for practicing this task should be provided. Or, a teacher will say, "I think LeAnn's IQ is higher than the score obtained here. She had trouble with all the meaning vocabulary items. If she had a larger knowledge of word meanings, she would have scored higher." The point is that the test covers many types of items for the very purpose of measuring the wide variety of abilities that make up the complex trait of intelligence. An inner analysis of individual test items to develop a diagnostic profile or provide practice on specific item types is inappropriate.

An unacceptable choice for obtaining IQ and MA scores of students with reading problems is a group-administered intelligence test that requires the student to read in order to make correct responses. Obviously if students cannot read the passages, questions, or possible answer statements, they may give incorrect responses. IQ and MA scores will then appear to be lower than they actually are.

Verifying Exact Chronological Age.   To determine LEL, you must know a student's exact chronological age in years and months. Since young or less intelligent students may not know their exact birth dates, especially the year, obtain this information from school records.

Using an Appropriate LEL Formula.   An appropriate LEL formula provides an estimate of a student's potential functioning ability. The most widely used LEL formula is the Bond and Tinker formula (Bond & Tinker, 1957). This formula has several disadvantages. It is appropriate for use only with students of average intelligence and tends to overestimate the LEL of students with lower than average IQs. In addition, the mathematical model on which the Bond and Tinker formula is based is statistically inadequate (Burns, 1982). Other commonly used formulas (such as those proposed by Cleland, Monroe, and Myklebust) and other procedures (such as the so-called Mental Age Method in which you simply subtract 5.0 from a student's MA) all have features or outcomes that make them less than appro-

priate (Hoffman, 1980; Simmons & Shapiro, 1968).

The most conceptually and technically adequate method for determining LEL is through use of the Horn formulas (Torgerson & Adams, 1954), a series of formulas that provides the most accurate estimate for students of any intellectual level. These formulas are based on an MA/CA weighting procedure that is a simplified form of the linear regression model recommended for research purposes (Burns, 1982). The Horn formulas were based on the premise that, while CA and MA are equally important in determining the learning potential of young students, MA is increasingly important for older students. For this reason a different formula is used at each of four chronological age ranges.

For chronological ages 6.0 to 8.5

$$\frac{MA + CA}{2} - 5.0$$

For chronological ages 8.6 to 9.9

$$\frac{3MA + 2CA}{5} - 5.0$$

For chronological ages 10.0 to 12.0

$$\frac{2MA + CA}{3} - 5.0$$

For chronological ages above 12.0

$$\frac{3MA + CA}{4} - 5.0$$

Assessing Present Reading Achievement

After recording all information obtained to this point on a record sheet, such as the hypothetical one shown in Figure 5–2, the teacher must determine the student's present reading

---

Diagnostic Information Sheet

Student's Name: David Adams

Grade Level: 4th

Intelligence Quotient:
   1)   Name of test   WISC-R

   2)   IQ   106

   3)   MA   9.6

Chronological Age:
   1)   Birthdate   February 19, 19—

   2)   Age   9.0

Learning Expectancy Level: $\dfrac{3MA + 2CA}{5}$ = 5.0
   1)   Method of determination   Horn Formula:

   2)   LEL   4.4

Figure 5–2
A partially completed record sheet of diagnostic information for a hypothetical student

achievement. Informal procedures are usually unacceptable for designating present achievement level when the purpose is to verify eligibility for programs. Federal or state regulations frequently require that a standardized test be administered for this purpose.

Entry Level Assessment. It is becoming common practice to administer out-of-level standardized tests to students with reading problems. An *out-of-level* standardized test is one designed for students at the grade level equivalent to a student's suspected reading level rather than actual grade level. For example, if we suspect Donna, a 5th grader, is reading at about 3rd-grade level, we would administer the test that the publishers have

specified for 3rd graders rather than the one specified for 5th graders. Fisher's (1962) study of over 1,000 students showed that, for both poor and gifted readers, this procedure provided a more accurate measure of reading achievement. Long, Schaffran, and Kellog (1977) refer to use of out-of-level tests as *instructional-level testing.*

If the purpose of administering a standardized test is to determine a student's reading achievement level, how can we decide her level beforehand to administer an appropriate out-of-level test? *Entry level tests,* quick screening devices that provide a rough approximation of a student's reading ability, are used for this purpose. However, an entry level test should never be used as the definitive specification of a student's reading level (Marzano, Larson, Tish, & Vodehnal, 1978). If an entry level test specifies that a student is reading at 5th-grade level, we can feel fairly certain she isn't reading at 7th-grade level or above, or 3rd-grade level or below, but not much more.

With such a very rough estimate, then, how can entry level tests be helpful? They are useful because even with such a broad estimate they usually pinpoint the level of test to be administered closely enough to prevent students from possible demoralizing experiences, prevent wasted time, and provide an accurate estimate of reading. Consider this example: Joseph, a 16-year-old, is enrolled in a reading clinic by his parents. They are quite unsure of his present reading level and only know he is behind the level needed to perform adequately in his 10th-grade class. A call to Joe's school by the clinician, Mr. Doughty, results in the same information—Joe is apparently behind the other students in reading because he's having difficulty with all assignments involving reading, but neither the counselor nor the classroom teachers whom the clinician is able to reach have an idea about what his approximate reading level might be. What should the clinician do? Should he choose a test designed for 7th- or 8th-grade students since there is at least agreement that Joe is behind the average readers in his classes? Let's suppose this is the choice. Joe sits down to begin this test only to find he cannot read the first passage. Embarrassed, he tries to hide this deficiency from the clinician and begins putting on a fair imitation of a student reading and marking the answers, although he is marking them randomly since he cannot read the question items nor the passages. As passages become successively more difficult and Joe begins to see many more words in a passage that he doesn't know, frustration

takes over and he gives up any pretense of reading. He pushes the test a bit to the side, takes the answer sheet in front of him and marks any square on which his pencil happens to fall. As a result, he completes a 27-minute section of the test in 8 minutes. The clinician, who has been observing Joe from the corner of his eye, realizes that any score obtained from this test is obviously worthless in specifying an accurate reading level. He decides that the next day he will have Joe take the form of this standardized test designed for 4th- to 6th-graders since he is sure from Joe's behavior that the previous test was too difficult for him and that his test-taking performance was not because of laziness or perverseness. When Joe sees the test being handed to him, it looks very little different from the one with which he had such a frustrating experience the day before. He becomes tense, and makes up an excuse for what he expects will be his similarly poor performance today ("I've got a terrible headache, Mr. Doughty.") But, because he's a cooperative student he reluctantly and with feelings of great distress tries again. This time he is able to read the first passage, can handle the second passage somewhat, but after that it is all uphill again. Today he makes no pretense of reading. When passage three turns out to be totally undecipherable to him, he uses yesterday's strategy. He pushes the test away and marks answers randomly—without having set eyes on passages four through nine. The result is that a 24-minute section of the test is completed in 10 minutes. Having again observed Joe surreptitiously, the clinician, also feeling frustrated, decides he must administer a primary level test so Joe can read the test, and so he can get some meaningful measure of Joe's ability. On the third day, Joe is given the 2nd grade form of the same standardized test. The clinician has to provide many words of comfort and encouragement to get

Joe to begin, but when he does, he finds he can read and answer almost all parts of the test. He works thoughtfully and when Mr. Doughty calls "time" at the end of 20 minutes, he has completed all but the last question. If Mr. Doughty had administered an entry level test before choosing the first form of the standardized test much wasted time and much frustration on both their parts could have been eliminated.

The developers of the 3-R's Test: Achievement have provided directions in their teacher's manual for out-of-level testing with their test battery. Other publishers have established special norms for using out-of-level testing; for example, this has been done with one of the more widely used series of standardized tests, the Gates-MacGinitie Reading Tests (2nd edition). In addition, the 1981 edition of the Comprehensive Tests of Basic Skills (CTBS) provides entry level tests called "locator tests" and overlapping levels (e.g., 2.6–3.9 and 3.6–4.9) to facilitate out-of-level testing.

Entry level tests usually consist of graded word lists. Students read the lists orally, and teachers estimate reading levels from their performances. Many published informal reading inventories contain such a list. Box 5–1 shows the teacher's copy of the list from the Houghton Mifflin Pupil Placement Test. To use this specific list the student is asked to read words until he misses four to six in a section. The grade level specified for that section is considered the student's entry level. If our hypothetical student David Adams missed 4 to 6 words in the 2nd grade section, we would specify 2nd grade as his entry level and select a 2nd grade form of a standardized test to administer to him. Specific directions for obtaining an estimated level vary according to the graded word list used. Other sources of graded word lists are the published informal inventories listed in Chapter 6.

Administering a Standardized Test. A teacher needs to select a standardized test with care and, before tests are purchased, request a specimen set from the publishers. A specimen set usually includes one copy of each level of a test, plus a teacher's manual and technical manual. The technical manual should be examined carefully for information on the norming population, reliability, and validity. Most teachers do not relish the thought of carefully reading a test's technical manual, but doing so is a necessary and important part of a reading teacher's job. When considering test selection for the purpose presently being discussed—determining a student's eligibility for a special program—a teacher should select a survey test; a survey test provides information about students' general reading levels, rather than specific information about strengths and weaknesses in strategies and skills. Some standardized reading survey tests are the Iowa Tests of Basic Skills, the Metropolitan Achievement Tests, the Iowa Silent Reading Tests, the Nelson-Denny Reading Test, the Stanford Achievement Test, the Gates-MacGinitie Reading Tests, the Comprehensive Tests of Basic Skills, the California Achievement Tests, and the Nelson Reading Skills Test. The Curriculum Referenced Tests of Mastery is a standardized instrument which provides grade levels based on national norming, as well as an evaluation of mastery of specific skills. The content of different survey tests varies, but most include a section on vocabulary and on comprehension. Most survey tests also have alternate forms at the same level so that one form may be used as a pretest and another as a posttest to measure growth at the end of an instructional program.

A special caution is in order about certain tests which purport to measure general reading achievement level, but which, in fact, do not. These tests usually consist en-

---

Box 5–1
Word Recognition Test (Teacher's Copy)

A *(Preprimer)*

mother	the	ball	see
play	come	will	is
big	funny	I	little
here	go	and	no
a	good	father	to

B *(Primer)*

are	for	called	we
said	home	have	away
boy	at	like	did
he	run	get	can
with	some	they	in

C *(First Reader)*

very	baby	please	our
when	again	would	many
pretty	give	how	could
way	be	morning	took
friends	other	must	day

From *Houghton Mifflin Reading Program: Pupil Placement Tests* by Hollander-Reisman. Reprinted by permission.

---

tirely of lists of isolated words which are read orally by the student. Two such tests frequently used are the Slosson Oral Reading Test (not to be confused with the Slosson Intelligence Test) and the Wide Range Achievement Tests (WRAT). These tests cannot be used to determine general reading achievement level, even though they claim to do so, because of the limited type of reading behavior they measure—the ability to pronounce words in isolation. They include no assessment of a student's understanding of the meanings of the words, no measure of general comprehension ability, no measure of the ability to read words in context (as found in normal reading situations), nor

measures of any other type of reading ability. Spache (1981) has criticized the Slosson Oral Reading Test (SORT) on other grounds. He points out that the test is culturally biased because of a scoring procedure that accepts only standard English pronunciations, that concurrent validity for the SORT was based on the Gray Oral Reading Test (also an incomplete measure of the reading act), and that scores obtained appear to be correlated with intelligence and consequently do not reflect reading ability independent of IQ (as should be done). A number of studies have been conducted to determine if there is any congruency between the grade level scores obtained on these tests of limited measures and student's reading ability as seen in actual classroom performance. The results of many of these have not been favorable. Bradley (1976), for example, found that 90 percent of the 150 students in his study were given incorrect instructional placement by the WRAT. Many standardized tests tend to overestimate the reading achievement level of students, but overestimates by the WRAT in this study were extreme—the reading levels of approximately 38 percent of the students were overestimated by three or more grade levels. If these tests measure only a limited type of reading behavior and the scores obtained are often widely divergent from students' actual functioning levels, why are they used? Primarily because they are quick and simple to administer. Spache (1981) has said "Judging from such tests as the WRAT or the Slosson, which require about 3 to 5 minutes, it appears that school personnel want the shortest, most superficial measures they can find" (p. 288). Time is a major problem for teachers, but, since these tests have been inappropriately devised to measure general reading achievement and since the results are often questionable, clearly they should not be used.

Administering a survey test correctly is essential. If a teacher does not follow directions in the teacher's manual exactly, the norms will not be applicable, because the test was standardized using these directions. Directions include exact specifications for the length of time a student may work on each section of a test. Allowing more or less time, even by a minute or two, invalidates the results. At times teachers feel they should allow a student with learning problems to have more time than specified in the manual, but this is inappropriate and should in no case be allowed. However, other strategies might ease the test-taking task for a poor reader. It is often possible to allow the student to have a break between sections of

the test, that is, after the teacher has called "time" on one section, to engage in some other activity for a while before beginning the next timed section. The poor reader might also be allowed to mark answers directly on the test rather than on an answer sheet. This can eliminate a possible source of errors since some students have difficulty finding the correct answer space when they must look back and forth between the test and a separate answer sheet. Most sections of survey tests involve silent reading. Even though teacher involvement is unnecessary while the student reads and responds to questions, the teacher should remain close at hand to unobtrusively observe the student's reading and test-taking behaviors, and to quietly prompt if the student should give up or lapse into periods of daydreaming. Survey tests are designed to be administered to groups of students during the same time period. In a remedial situation tests can be administered this way if several students need to take the same level tests. If not, tests must be administered individually.

Scoring a standardized test is easy since an answer key is provided for the teacher. The raw scores for each section (which are simply the number of correct responses) are combined to obtain a total raw score. The teacher then consults a table in the teacher's manual that indicates the grade level equivalent of the total raw score. For example, after combining the numbers of correct answers for all sections of a test, the teacher may find that David Adams' total raw score is 24; the table indicates this is equivalent to 3.1 or 3rd grade, first month.

Standardized Test Scores: To Convert or Not to Convert? Once a teacher has obtained a grade level score from a standardized test, what should he do with it before using it in the CAD equation? Since the grade level score is the average score made by all students at that level on whom the test was normed, if Robert receives a raw score of 52 and the test manual tells us this is equivalent to 6.0 grade level, this means that the average raw score of all students at the 6.0 grade level who took this test during the norming procedure was 52. This helps us to compare Robert's performance with that of other students. It does not necessarily tell us what level of instructional materials Robert is able to handle in real classroom situations. Sometimes this standardized test grade level score is a fair estimation of a student's instructional level, but sometimes it is not. The *instructional level* is the level at which a student can handle material in an instructional situation with normal teacher guidance, that is, the typical amount of assistance with new vocabulary, help with small comprehension difficulties, and so forth.

Because teachers have often noticed that the scores on a standardized test overestimate the instructional level of many students, a number of studies have been undertaken to determine how valid these scores are for specifying the level of functioning in actual classroom materials. The data are conflicting. In research with students in grades four through seven, several investigators have found that these scores do overestimate the actual instructional levels of students by about a year, with the overestimations particularly seen with poor readers (Betts, 1940; Glaser, 1965; Killgallon, 1942; McCracken, 1962). William's (1964) study with fourth, fifth, and sixth graders, however, found standardized test scores to be relatively close to students' instructional levels, and Sipay (1964) found that whether these test scores provided a good estimate depended on which standardized test the teacher used and the criteria used to determine actual classroom functioning level.

Teachers who work with poor readers find that standardized test scores do indeed provide an overestimate of instructional levels for the majority of students, although not for all. For this reason, it has become common practice to consider the score obtained from a standardized test to represent a student's frustration level. *Frustration level* is the level at which the material becomes too difficult for a student. For example, if 4.0 is specified as Elaine's frustration level, material at 4th grade level and above should not be selected for her. To determine the student's instructional level based on a standardized test score, common practice is to subtract 1 year from that score; e.g., if Elaine's standardized test score is 4.0, her approximate instructional level would be 3.0. Further, the student's independent level is estimated by subtracting an additional year. The *independent level* is the level at which a student can easily handle material without teacher guidance; this material is easy enough for the student to read independently. If Elaine's instructional level is 3.0, her approximate independent level is 2.0. (One standardized test, The Metropolitan Achievement Tests, provides a table for converting grade level equivalents to instructional levels.)

There is some argument, however, against subtracting a constant of 1.0 (1 year) from the obtained standardized test score to derive an estimate of instructional level. MacGinitie (1973a) argues that the practice is statistically incorrect. Also, as noted above, the standardized test score is not an overestimate of actual functioning levels for all students. In fact, it may be an underestimate for those students whose reading ability is adequate but whose test-taking skills are poor. Thus, there are two choices when using a standardized test score in a CAD equation.

1. *Do not convert the score.* That is, do

not subtract a constant of 1 year from the standardized score, but rather, use the score exactly as obtained. Some program regulations may require this approach, because administrators are unaware that these scores overestimate the actual functioning level of most students, MacGinitie's (1973a) objections are cited, or, since the scores are relatively accurate estimates for some poor readers, subtracting a year from the score will result in an underestimate of instructional level for a few poor readers.

2. *Do convert the scores.* That is, subtract a constant of 1 year from the standardized test score. The author of this text prefers this practice since it provides a better estimate for most students with less than average reading abilities.

Although either choice can result in error, the first choice may result in many students' being denied eligibility for programs they need, while the second choice can result in a few students being placed in special programs they do not need. The second choice seems to be the lesser of two evils. If students in a program are found not to require special help, it is easy enough to report this happy finding and dismiss them from the program. On the other hand, if a student is denied placement it may be a long time before she is considered for eligibility again—time during which she may slip even further behind. Because of this difficulty with grade equivalent scores, some programs require use of a percentile rank instead. If a student scores at the 63rd percentile, this means the score is better than 63 percent of the students at that grade level who have taken the test. It is common practice in many Chapter I programs to enroll only students who score below the 33rd percentile.

In considering our hypothetical student David Adams, whose partial diagnostic information sheet is seen in Figure 5–3,

choice 2 will be employed. We will assume that David received a grade equivalent score of 3.1 on a standardized test and we have computed his present reading achievement level to be approximately 2.1.

Computing Capacity-Achievement Difference (CAD)

This step is easy. Using the CAD equation introduced in Chapter 1, the result for David Adams is

$$
\begin{array}{r}
4.4 \text{ (LEL)} \\
-\ 2.1 \text{ (Present reading achievement)} \\
\hline
2.3 \text{ (CAD)}
\end{array}
$$

David's CAD indicates he is approximately 2 years behind the level at which he should be reading according to his estimated potential. Using the criteria specified in Chapter 1 (1 year CAD in primary grades; 2 years CAD in intermediate grades; 3 years CAD at the secondary level) we can see that David, an intermediate-grade-level student, does warrant special remedial services.

Additional information can now be added to David Adams' diagnostic information sheet. See Figure 5–3.

CONCLUDING STATEMENT

Although the most common practice for determining eligibility for special programs is to compute capacity-achievement difference, other factors should also be kept in mind.

1. Does the CAD indicate that remedial reading or LD services are required, yet the student has made very little progress in such programs previously? A clinical reading program should then be considered.

2. Is classroom functioning level well above or below test performance level? Remember, there can be error in even the best

Diagnostic Information Sheet

Student's Name: David Adams

Grade Level: 4th

Intelligence Quotient:
  1) Name of test   WISC-R

  2) IQ   106

  3) MA   9.6

Chronological Age:
  1) Birthdate   February 19, 19—

  2) Age   9.0

Learning Expectancy Level:
  1) Method of determination   Horn Formula: $\dfrac{3MA + 2CA}{5} = 5.0$

  2) LEL   4.4

Entry Level Assessment Results: 2nd grade

Standardized Survey Test:
  1) Name of test   Gates-MacGinitie Reading Tests, Primary B, Form 1

  2) Grade score obtained   3.1

Present Reading Achievement Level (based on standardized test results):   approximately 2.1

Capacity-Achievement Difference: 2.3

Figure 5–3
A continuation of a partially completed record sheet of diagnostic information for a hypothetical student

test estimates. All available information should be considered before placement in a special program is accepted or denied.

3. If a corrective reading program in the regular classroom is deemed sufficient to meet a student's needs, does the classroom teacher have the skills and the time to provide a special program for the student?

4. If more students are eligible for a special program than can be accommodated, have you considered all students' needs

before making the final selection so that first priority may be given to students with the greatest need?

Determining capacity-achievement difference is an important, and often required, first step in assessment for identification, but good teacher judgment must also enter into the decision-making process. Table 5–3 suggests some questions a teacher might ask when conducting an assessment for identification.

Table 5–3
A teacher checklist for conducting assessment for identification

	Yes	No
1. Has an intelligence test been administered, and IQ and MA scores obtained?		
2. Have school records been examined to verify the student's exact chronological age in years and months?		
3. Has an LEL been determined?		
4. Has an entry level assessment been administered?		
5. Has a standardized group survey test, at the appropriate level, been administered?		
6. Has the constant of 1.0 been subtracted from the grade equivalent score obtained from the standardized test?		
7. Has CAD been computed?		
8. Have other factors been considered before a final placement decision is made?		

6

Assessment for Verifying General Reading Level

After completing the assessment procedures described in Chapter 5, some students will be assigned to a remedial program. Their teachers will already have certain diagnostic information from their assessments. Refer to Figure 5–3 and note the types of information already recorded for David Adams.

Now it is up to the teacher to make the most important assessments—the ones that will help her obtain information for planning an excellent remedial program for each student. Two major types of assessment must be made: determining the student's general reading level (or, at this point, verifying the level obtained on the standardized test), and determining the student's strengths and weaknesses in reading strategies, knowledge, and skills. This chapter will describe procedures for verifying students' general reading levels.

Determining a reading level for a student is an important instructional consideration. Some deny this and say that the only task of importance is determining the specific skills students lack so these can be taught. This point may be valid in relation to spelling or math; it certainly does not make much

sense to determine a spelling level since different words are presented at various levels in different programs. The same is true for math. A level in these areas can only represent some comparison with the scores of a norm group and does not help the teacher to decide what to do to help a student who is performing poorly. But, this is decidedly not the case in reading.

An essential activity in helping students increase their reading achievement is to have them read a great deal in regular connected reading material, that is, whole stories, chapters, articles, books, and so forth. To assign or help a student select material to read, teachers must know the student's instructional reading level and independent reading level. They need to use material at the student's approximate instructional level when they plan to provide some assistance as the student reads the material. Teachers should assign material at the independent level if the student is going to read the material independently at home, in study hall, or in any situation where there will be no assistance. Placing students in material that is too difficult is a major hindrance to progress and should be carefully avoided. Determining students' functioning levels is a key step in reading diagnosis.

As previously noted, there is a question about the accuracy of instructional level scores obtained from some standardized tests. Even when teachers subtract one year from the grade equivalent score, although in many cases the resulting instructional level will be accurate, in some it may be an over- or underestimate. In addition research has shown that using several measures of achievement provides the best estimate of actual reading level (Farr, 1969; Johnston, 1983). Therefore, it is common diagnostic practice to first use an informal reading inventory or a cloze procedure to verify general reading achievement level. (Some programs use an informal reading inventory or a cloze test in place of a standardized test, rather than in combination with it.)

INFORMAL READING INVENTORIES

An informal reading inventory (IRI) is a series of graded passages, each of which is followed by a comprehension check. One of two types of IRIs may be used: one based on the specific instructional material the student will be using or a published IRI designed for general use.

IRIs Based on Specific Instructional Materials

IRIs based on the actual material students will be using provide the most valid measure of the level of the material appropriate for instruction if these IRIs have been carefully developed and are correctly administered and scored.

IRIs Furnished by Basal Reader Publishers. Teachers using a basal reading series as the principal material of instruction may find that the publishers have already pro-

duced an IRI based on these materials. Although it is important to determine if appropriate steps (described later) have been used in developing the IRI, properly developed published IRIs can save teachers preparation time.

Teacher-Prepared IRIs. When teachers choose to use materials that have no accompanying IRI, they may develop their own. These assessment instruments can be highly valid because they are based on the material of instruction, but preparing an IRI properly is also quite time-consuming. Time devoted to preparing an IRI is well worthwhile, however, if the teacher plans to use the same basic materials over a period of time with many students. Also, this instrument can be re-used with students throughout the year for periodic, ongoing assessment. Since this test must be carefully developed and since the information it is to provide is of critical importance, it is often helpful for two or more teachers to work together to develop an IRI available for all teachers using the same materials. Listed here are recommended procedures for preparing, administering, and scoring a teacher-made IRI.

The steps necessary for *preparing* an IRI are:

1. For every book in the series of reading materials, select five passages. The length of each passage should vary according to the grade level of the book as follows.

preprimer-primer	=	100 words
1st grade	=	125 words
2nd-3rd grade	=	150 words
4th-6th grade	=	175 words
above 6th grade	=	200 words

   When selecting passages do not stop in the middle of a sentence since a few words over the specified number will cause no problem. If whole stories in books at the lowest levels (for example, in preprimers) do not contain 100 words, use two or more stories. Keep each story separate and develop separate questions for each.

2. Use a readability formula to check the reading level of each of the five passages from each book. (Readability formulas are discussed in Chapter 18.) Choose two of the five passages that are most representative of the reading level of the stories in that book. Include these passages in your completed IRI, one to be read orally and one to be read silently at each level.

3. Label the passages in the following manner: The first passage from the easiest book should be designated "Level A-Oral." The second passage from the easiest book should be designated "Level A-Silent." The first passage from the second book should be designated "Level B-Oral," and so forth.

4. Type each passage on a separate page, and label each page ("Level A-Oral" and so forth). Use a primary typewriter, if available, for typing passages for the first preprimer through second grade levels. Spacing between lines should be 1½ spaces. For the remaining levels, use pica type and double spacing. Here is a sample of how a portion of two pages might look.

Level G-Oral

The stork had made a nest on the roof of the farmer's house. Everyone in the family had . . . .

Level G-Silent

Mr. Pott was the dog's name. We thought that was the silliest name we . . . .

---

5. Make copies of the stories. Students will use one set; the teacher uses copies for marking errors.

6. Place the pages to be used by students in a sequence from easiest to most difficult, with the passage for oral reading preceding the passage for silent reading at each level. Store the teacher's sets so that multiple copies of each story are placed in separate file folders.

7. To assemble the IRI from which the students will read, first type a cover sheet like the one shown here. Place the cover sheet on top of the sequenced pages. Staple these inside a manila folder.

Informal Reading Inventory

Based on: [Which series?]

Date this series was published _____

Level A = 1st preprimer
Level B = 2nd preprimer

[etc.]

---

8. Next, devise ten questions about each passage. Try to include factual questions, main idea questions, inference questions, vocabulary questions, and sequence questions. Write the same number of specific types of questions for both the oral and silent passages at any given level. By doing so, you will be able to make comparisons between a student's oral and silent reading. Type the questions for each passage on a file card, and title the file card (for example: Level C-Silent). State the type of question in front of each question. Then type the answer to the question. Here is a brief example.

```
┌─────────────────────────────────────────┐
│              Level D-Oral                 │
│  (factual)   1.  Why was the dog sad?     │
│                  (He was going to be      │
│                  sold.)                    │
│  (inference) 2.  Why do you think the     │
│                  rabbits wanted to help?  │
│                  (He was the only dog who │
│                  did not chase them.)     │
└─────────────────────────────────────────┘
```

Instead of asking specific types of questions, a teacher may choose to have students retell the information they have just read. If you prefer this alternative, prepare a retelling outline listing the major points to be retold.

9. Using masking tape and a piece of another manila folder, make a pocket inside the front cover of the manila folder in which you have stapled the selected passages. Place the questions on file cards or the retelling outline in this pocket.

10. With a marking pen, print "Informal Reading Inventory" on the outside front cover.

11. A word about pictures. Some stories in the lowest level books make little sense unless the pictures appear in conjunction with the text to help students follow the story line. A comprehension check over such a passage read without the accompanying pictures will not provide accurate information. If this is the case, make some provision for students to use the pictures with the passage as they read by drawing the pictures on the IRI page containing that passage, by photocopying (with permission) necessary pictures and affixing them to the page, or by allowing students to read that passage directly from the textbook.

Authorities do not agree on all procedures for *administering* an IRI, but research and the majority of authority opinion suggest the following steps.

1. To prepare for the test,
   a. select a place where no other students can overhear the reading or responses to the questions;
   b. plan about 30 minutes of testing time for each student;
   c. set up a tape recorder to record students' responses; and
   d. select the first passage by using the entry level score obtained during assessment for identification.

2. When the student joins you for the test,
   a. allow him to play with the tape recorder for a minute or two (by talking into it, listening, turning it off and on, and so forth, he will begin to feel comfortable with its presence);
   b. begin with a motivating statement, saying something like, "Read this passage to find out what funny thing a girl's pet raccoon did";
   c. be certain to tell the student ahead of time that you will ask questions after he has read the passage; and
   d. if the passage is to be read orally, do not allow it to be preread silently.

3. While the student is reading,
   a. if the student cannot pronounce a word, tell him to do anything he can to figure out the word and, if he still cannot pronounce it, to skip it and continue reading;
   b. do not mark the student's oral reading errors, or miscues;[1] instead follow along and keep a mental count of these.

4. After the student has read each passage,

---

[1]The term *miscue* is being used with increasing frequency instead of the term *error*. The term *error* applied to a student's deviation when reading orally seems to imply that the deviation was a random response. As we learn more about the reading process, we have come to understand that these deviations are cued by the language and thought processes of readers as they interact with the printed text and are not random at all (Goodman & Burke, 1972). When the oral response cued is not the one the author intended it is therefore called a *miscue*.

a. remove the test before checking comprehension;

b. allow the tape recorder to continue to run and ask the questions previously prepared or ask the student to retell the information in the passage;

c. provide careful prompting if the student is having difficulty with a question (taking care not to divulge the answer to the question at hand or subsequent questions); if using the retelling procedure, use the retelling outline to prompt the student if important information has been omitted (the retelling outline is for teacher use and is not shown to the student);

d. note the number of questions the student answers correctly; Rupley and Blair (1979) suggest that the maximum number of allowable miscues for word identification and errors in comprehension be listed directly on the IRI for each passage so the teacher can quickly determine if a student's reading behaviors suggest that he is at his frustration level; (A good place for making these notations is on the file cards listing the comprehension questions or on the retelling outline); and

e. have the student read passages until you identify his frustration level.

Score an IRI when the student is not present. Use the duplicate sets of passages and mark word identification miscues as you listen to the tape recording of the student reading. Some commonly used types of marking procedures appear in Table 6–1 and Table 6–2. Next, determine comprehension of each passage based on responses to the questions or during the retelling. Finally, determine if each passage is at the student's independent, instructional, or frustration level based on percentages of correct word identification and correct comprehension. To determine percentage of correct word identification, note the difference between the miscue types listed in Table 6–1 and those shown in Table 6–2. Miscues of the type described in Table 6–1 are recorded and scored; that is, the teacher marks these on the duplicate copies of the passages while listening to the tape and considers them when determining percentage of correct word identification. Miscues shown in Table 6–2 are recorded but not scored; that is, the teacher marks them on the duplicate passages to analyze later for the student's reading stategies, skills, and knowledge but does not include them when scoring passages to determine percentages of correct word identification.

To score word identification miscues, count each miscue that causes a change in meaning as one miscue; if a miscue does not cause a change in meaning do not count it at all. For example, the miscue in the first sentence would be counted when scoring the student's responses, but the one in the second sentence would not be counted:

1. One morning Tommy and Ann came
sitting
skipping into the kitchen.

2. Around the doors and windows his
dad
father nailed thin pieces of wood.

If the student repeatedly makes a miscue on the same word, count it only the first time. Pronunciations that differ from the expected response due to a student's oral language dialect should not be counted as miscues.

Authorities have suggested various criteria for determining whether a passage is at a student's independent, instructional, or frustration level. Some have also suggested different criteria for different grade levels. Research has been undertaken to determine which of these criteria provides the most accurate estimates. For example, Fuchs, Fuchs, and Deno (1982) reported that their analyses support the criterion of 95 percent accuracy in word identification as a standard for determining instructional level. Powell's (1971) research, on the other hand, suggested the following range of criterion levels for determining instructional level based on word identification miscues:

Table 6–1
Marking procedures commonly used with IRIs for miscues that are both recorded and scored

Type	Example	Marking Procedure
1. Substitutions	The student says *when* although the text word is *where*.	Write the word the student said above the text word: *when* "I don't know where the cat went."
2. Omissions	The student leaves out a word that is in the text.	Circle the word: "The tall, (old) man was sitting on the bench."
3. Insertions	The student adds a word that is not in the text.	Insert the word with a caret: *big* "That ∧ black dog bit the boy."
4. Use of nonwords	The student substitutes a nonsense word for a real word.	Phonetically write the nonword above the text word for which it was substituted: *pauk* "He sat on the back porch."
5. Word reversals	The student pronounces the word *no* as the word *on*.	Code this as a substitution.

Table 6–2
Marking procedures commonly used with IRIs for miscues that are recorded but not scored

Type	Example	Marking Procedure
1. Repetitions	The student repeats the same word or phrase one or more times.	Draw a wavy line under the text portion the student repeated: "We saw an elephant at the zoo."
2. Self-corrections	The student makes an error, but then corrects it.	Code the original error in the usual manner, but then place a "C" above it: C *sit* "His chemistry set is going to get him in trouble."
3. Hesitations	The student hesitates for a long time before pronouncing a word.	Place a slash in front of the word: "Please hand me my / glasses."
4. Ignoring punctuation	The student appears not to have noticed a period, comma, or other punctuation mark.	Code as an omission, i.e., circle the omitted punctuation mark.

preprimer through 2nd grade (87% to 94%): 3rd through 5th grades (92% to 96%); 6th grade and above (approximately 96%).

Both word identification and comprehension accuracy must be taken into account to determine a student's reading levels. Based on the best available research evidence and the opinions of authorities, the following criterion levels are suggested:

Level	Word Identification	Comprehension
Independent	100%–96%	100%–90%
Instructional	95%–90%	89%–70%
Frustration	below 90%	below 70%

Published IRIs Designed for General Use

The best choice for many remedial teachers selecting an informal reading inventory is a commercially published IRI designed for general use. In most remedial reading programs, reading clinics, LD classrooms, and other similar programs, more than one basic set of reading materials is used. Teachers use a variety of materials such as easy-to-read, high-interest level books, experience stories dictated by students, stories selected from a number of different reading books to meet the students' interests, books from a variety of kits designed especially for remedial programs, and so forth. For teachers to prepare an IRI specifically related to each of these materials is not practical, and to prepare an IRI based on only one set loses the advantage of the test being directly related to all instructional materials used. A published IRI designed for general use is a satisfactory alternative.

There are many commercially prepared IRIs from which to select. Most contain graded word lists to determine the level at which testing should begin and for assessing word knowledge as well as a series of graded passages (to be read orally and silently) designed to help the teacher assess word knowledge, word identification strategies, and comprehension and determine a student's independent, instructional, and frustration levels.

Some commercially prepared IRIs include the Analytical Reading Inventory (ARI), the Basic Reading Inventory (BRI), the Classroom Reading Inventory (CRI), the Contemporary Classroom Reading Inventory (CCRI), the Diagnostic Reading Inventory (DRI), the Diagnostic Reading Scales (DRS), the Edwards' Reading Test (ERT), the Ekwall Reading Inventory (ERI), the Informal Reading Assessment (IRA), the Standard Reading Inventory (SRI), and the Sucher-Allred Reading Placement Inventory (SARPI). Some of these include additional supplementary tests for diagnosis, and some are standardized (e.g., the 1981 revision of the Diagnostic Reading Scales). An IRI of interest to secondary teachers is the Advanced Reading Inventory, which is designed for grade 7 through college. See Table 6–3 (p. 109) for important characteristics of some of these tests.

Now let us return to David Adams, the hypothetical student for whom we have been gradually completing a diagnostic information sheet. To verify general reading levels, let us suppose you have chosen to use a published IRI, and that David's performance on this test indicates his functional reading levels to be:

Frustration Level   approximately 2.5 and above
Instructional Level   approximately 2.0
Independent Level   approximately 1.0

If we compare his present reading achievement level based on the results of the previously administered standardized test with the instructional level obtained from this IRI, we find they are similar indeed. This means we can feel confident that placing David in material at approximately the beginning of second grade level will be appropriate for beginning his instruction. Scores obtained on an IRI to verify general reading levels should be recorded on the student's diagnostic information sheet, as was done for David Adams in Figure 6–1.

Diagnostic Information Sheet

Student's Name: David Adams

Grade Level: 4th

Intelligence Quotient:
    1)   Name of test   WISC-R

    2)   IQ   106

    3)   MA   9.6

Chronological Age:
    1)   Birthdate   February 19, 19—

    2)   Age   9.0

Learning Expectancy Level:
    1)   Method of determination   Horn Formula: $\dfrac{3MA + 2CA}{5} - 5.0$

    2)   LEL   4.4

Entry Level Assessment Results: 2nd grade

Standardized Survey Test:
    1)   Name of test   Gates-MacGinitie Reading Tests, Primary B, Form 1

    2)   Grade score obtained   3.1

Present Reading Achievement Level (based on standardized test results):   approximately 2.1

Capacity-Achievement Difference: 2.3

Verification of General Reading Levels:
    1)   Name of test   Analytical Reading Inventory

    2)   Grade scores obtained   Frustration level—approximately 2.5 and above

                                            Instructional level—approximately 2.0

                                          Independent level—approximately 1.0

Figure 6–1
A continuation of a partially completed record sheet of diagnostic information for a hypo-thetical student

Table 6–3

Important features of 11 published IRIs

Informal Reading Inventories

Features	ARI	BRI	CRI	CCRI	DRI	DRS	ERI	ERT	IRA	SARPI	SRI
Contents											
No. of forms	3	3	3	3	1	2	4	2	4	1	2
Range of passages	P–9	PP–8	PP–8	P–9	1–8	1–8	PP–9	6–13 yrs.	PP–12	P–9	PP–7
	P–6	PP–8	PP–6	P–7	1–8	1–6	PP–9	6–13 yrs.	PP–12	P–9	PP–7
Graded word lists	Yes	Yes	Yes	Yes	Yes	Yes	Yes	Yes	Yes	Yes	Yes
Separate student passages	Yes	Yes	Yes	Yes	No	No	Yes	Yes	Yes	Yes	Yes
Student summary sheet	Yes	Yes	Yes	No	No	No	No	No	No	Yes	Yes
Class summary sheet	Yes	Yes	No	No	No	No	No	No	No	No	No
Pictures/illustrations	No	No	Yes	Yes	Yes	No	No	No	No	No	No
Motivation/purpose statement for each passage	Yes	No	Yes	Yes	Yes	No	No	No	Yes	Yes	Yes
Supplementary features[1]	B	B	ST	B, ST	ST	CL, ST	ST	B, ST	B	TT	CL, RS
Passages											
Length (words)	50–339	50–100	24–174	47–316	224–361	29–221	31–202	25–100	61–217	51–191	47–151
Content[2]	N, E	N, E	N, E	N, E	N	N, E	N, E	N, E	N, E	N, E	N, E
Readability estimates given	Yes	Yes	No	Yes	No	No	No	Yes	No	Yes	No
Readability formulas used[3]	HJ, SP	DC, FR, SP	DC, FL, SP	BG, DC, FR, HJ, SP	NI	DC, SP	DC, HJ	E, SM	FR, SP	DC, SP	DC, SP
Same format student/teacher copies	No	Yes	No	No	No	No	No	Yes	No	No	Yes
Questions											
No. per passages	PP–2:6	PP:4	5	P–1:5	1–3:12	1–2:7	PP:5	4–10	PP–2:8	5	PP:5
	3–9:8	P–8:10		2:6	4–8:20	3–8:8	1–9:10		3–12:10		P–7:13–15
	3–9:8			3:7							
				4–9:8							
Types of questions[4]	L, I, CE, MI, V	L, CE, MI, V	L, I, V	L, I CE, MI, S, V	L, I, CE, V	NI	L, I, V	NI	L, I, CE, MI, S, V	L, I, CE, MI, V	L, I, V
Suggested answers given	Yes	Yes	Yes	Yes	No	Yes	Yes	Yes	Yes	Yes	Yes
Administering											
Require											
Oral	Yes	Yes	Yes	Yes	Yes	Yes	Yes	Yes	Yes	Yes	Yes
Silent	Optional	Optional	Optional	Yes	Yes	Yes	Yes	Yes	Optional	No	Yes
Listening Comprehension	Yes	Optional	Optional	Optional	Yes	Yes	Optional	Yes	Optional	No	Optional
Directions given for											
Starting/stopping	Yes	Yes	Yes	Yes	Yes	Yes	Yes	Yes	Yes	Yes	Yes
Marking miscues/errors	Yes	Yes	Yes	Yes	Yes	Yes	Yes	Yes	Yes	Yes	Yes
Aid given in oral reading	Yes	No	Yes	Yes	Yes	Yes	Yes	NI	Yes	Yes	Yes
Probing of comprehension recommended	NI	Yes	NI	Yes	No	Yes	Yes	NI	Yes	NI	Yes
Timing of rate	NI	Optional	Optional	NI	NI	Yes	NI	Yes	Optional	NI	Yes

Table 6–3, continued

Features	ARI	BRI	CRI	CCRI	DRI	DRS	ERI	ERT	IRA	SARPI	SRI
Scoring											
Types of miscues/errors counted[5]	A,I,I/R, O,R,S	"Sig. Miscues"	A,I,O,R, S	A,I,I/R, M,O,R,S	A,I,O,S	A,I,I/R, M,O,R,S	A,I,I/R, M,O,R,S	I,O,S	A,I,I/R, M,O,R,S	A,I,M,O, R,S	A,I,M,O, P,R,S,SC
Partial credit for Comprehension questions	NI	Yes	Yes	Yes	No	Yes	Yes	Yes	NI	Yes	Yes
Criteria for levels											
Independent WR	99/more	99/more		97/more	98/more	NI	99/more	95/more	99/more	97/more	
Comp.	90/more	90/more	NI	80/more	90/more	60/more	90/more	70/more	90/more	80/more	NI
Instructional WR	95/more	95/more	95/more	92/more	92/more	NI	95/more	90/more	85-95/more	92/more	
Comp.	75/more	75/more	75/more	60/more	60/more	60/more	60/more	70/more	75/more	60/more	NI
Frustrational WR	90/less	90/less		91/less	90/less		90/less	90/less	90/less	92/less	
Comp.	50/less	50/less	NI	60/less	50/less	NI	50/less	70/less	50/less	60/less	NI
Listening comprehension	75/more	75/more	75/more	60-75/more	60/more	60/more	70/more	70/more	75/more	NI	40 unaided 70 aided
Interpreting											
Suggestions for diagnostic interpretation	No	Yes	Yes	Yes	Yes	Yes	Yes	No	Yes	No	Yes
Sample cases demonstrated	No	Yes	Yes	Yes	Yes	No	Yes	No	Yes	Yes	No
Teaching suggestions offered	No	Yes	No	No	No	No	No	No	No	No	No
Guidance for handling discrepancies in performance	Yes	Yes	Yes	Yes	Yes	Yes	Yes	No	Yes	Yes	Yes

KEY:

NI = Not Indicated

[1] Supplementary Features: B, Bibliographies; CL, Checklists; CS, Case Studies; RS, Rating Scales; ST, Additional Student Tests; TT, Teacher Test

[2] Content: N, Narration; E, Exposition

[3] Readability Formulas: BG, Botel-Granowsky; DC, Dale-Chall; E, Edwards; FL, Flesch; FR, Fry; HJ, Harris-Jacobsen; SM, SMOG; SP, Spache

[4] Types of Questions: CE, Critical-Evaluative; I, Interpretive-Inferential; L, Literal-Factual; MI, Main Ideas; S, Sequence; V, Vocabulary

[5] Types of Miscues/Errors: A, Aid; I, Insertions; I/R, Inversions/Reversals; M, Mispronunciations; O, Omissions; P, Punctuation; R, Repetitions; S, Substitutions; SC, Self-Corrections

(*Source:* From "Test Review: Commercial Informal Reading Inventories" by K. Jongsma and E. Jongsma, 1981. *The Reading Teacher* (March), pp. 700–702. Reprinted by permission of K. Jongsma and the International Reading Association.)

However, suppose instead that you see a great discrepancy between the results of two tests; for example, a student's present achievement level according to a standardized test is 4.2, but the instructional level according to an IRI is 5.5. In this case, you should carefully review any circumstances during the administration of the tests that might have resulted in a score not accurately reflecting the student's reading level. For example, did the student work conscientiously only during the first part of the standardized test then appear to become bored and rush through questions during the last part? Did you tend to be more lenient in scoring comprehension checks on the IRI when there was question about the correctness of a student's response? After answering questions such as these, and if the discrepancies cannot be resolved, you would do best to place the student in materials at a level consistent with the lower of the two scores. Follow placement with careful daily monitoring and if it appears the lower test score was indeed too low, move the student up through successively more difficult material until you find an appropriate level for instruction. It is better to place the student in material that is too easy at the beginning rather than too difficult.

Using an Informal Reading Inventory to Analyze Specific Strengths and Weaknesses

Although the major purpose of this chapter is to describe procedures for verifying students' general reading levels, some information about a student's specific strengths and weaknesses may be gained from IRIs if miscues and behaviors are analyzed, as well as counted to obtain a score. Let us suppose a teacher is now going to go back through David Adams' IRI and do just that. First, she takes the teacher's copy of each passage from the IRI on which his miscues were marked and some blank paper and begins to analyze his performance on each passage. (See Figure 6–2)

Based on her analysis, the teacher can already reach some conclusions about what is needed in his instructional program and make some decisions about further testing that should be conducted. Finally, she adds these conclusions in a summary statement at the end of her analysis and attaches her analysis of David's IRI performance and her summary of the analysis to the student's diagnostic information sheet. (See Figure 6–3, pp. 116–117.)

Issues Related to Informal Assessment Using IRIs

For determining both actual reading levels and specific strengths and weaknesses in reading, informal procedures can often provide more reliable information than standardized tests because they may be carried out more frequently and, therefore, provide a larger sampling of the same behaviors for the teacher to use in instructional planning (Farr, 1969). IRIs are the most frequently used of the many types of informal assessments. (See Figure 6–4, p. 119, for an example.)

Advantages of Informal Inventories. An IRI may serve the functions of both a survey test and a diagnostic test. IRIs are often used as substitutes for or in conjunction with standardized survey tests to determine a student's reading level. They may also be used to analyze specific strengths and weaknesses in reading strategies, knowledge, and skills. Then too, research shows that grade scores obtained on IRIs are often closer to the actual classroom performance of students than scores from standardized survey tests. Informal reading inventories are probably the most useful type of assessment for planning instruction when the graded reading passages are taken directly from the actual materials a student will be reading. Tests developed in this way have high content validity. Finally, since IRIs are individually administered the teacher is able to observe students directly while they are responding to reading tasks.

Disadvantages of Informal Inventories.
Accurate results on an IRI depend on the competence of the teacher administering the test. Scoring these tests requires more skill than scoring standardized tests. Also, despite a teacher's efforts to be objective, evaluating a student's performance on an IRI always involves some degree of subjectivity. For example, when a student's response to a comprehension question is questionable, one teacher may decide the answer is more right than wrong and score it correct; another teacher might apply more stringent criteria to the same answer and score it wrong. The type of comprehension check used affects the results; in teacher-prepared IRIs, questions must be planned carefully ahead of time. Accuracy of results depends on careful selection of the passages to be read. For example, if the "sixth grade" passage in an inventory is actually easier or more difficult than typical sixth grade material, the teacher may incorrectly evaluate a student's performance. In published IRIs the criteria used for measuring performance varies; when tests employing different criteria are used, different results may be obtained. Since IRIs must be administered individually, they are more time-consuming than group-administered standardized tests. Alternate forms of many published IRIs are not equivalent; therefore, these IRIs cannot be used as pre- and posttests to measure student growth. Nonetheless, despite some disadvantages, IRIs are an excellent assessment tool, if used for appropriate reasons and if prepared, administered, and interpreted correctly.

CLOZE TESTS

The cloze procedure has recently become popular for three purposes: first, to determine readability levels of text materials; second, to instruct students in the use of context clues and to help them predict and infer; and finally, to test students to determine placement. This third use of the cloze procedure is called a cloze test, which can be used as an alternative to an IRI for verifying general reading levels obtained on a group, standardized survey test. A *cloze test* consists of a passage from which words have been systematically deleted; the student is asked to supply the missing words. Based on the student's performance an estimate of reading levels can be obtained.

To Prepare a Cloze Test

Select two passages from each book in a series for which the reading levels are known. The passages should be material that students have not previously read, and each passage should be about 300 words in length. The first sentence in the paragraph should be left intact. Beginning with any of the first five words in the second sentence, delete every fifth word until 50 words have been omitted. Fifty words must be deleted to have a reliable measure. Include one additional sentence after the 50 deletions; keep this last sentence intact as well.

Always delete every fifth word, even if you think a specific word deletion may be difficult for students to supply. (The criteria of deleting every fifth word is not applied when the cloze procedure is used for instructional proposes; rather, specific key words are omitted to fit the objective of that lesson.) If numerals appear in a passage and are to be deleted, consider the whole numeral as one word. For example in the sentence, "Indians lived in this area 350 years ago", *350* would be considered one word. When typing the passages, leave all blanks the same length.

To Administer a Cloze Test

Ask students to write responses in the blanks or to respond orally. Specify the following directions to the students:

Analysis of David Adams' IRI Performance

Preprimer Level

Oral Reading

Word Identification: One sight word confusion (<u>there</u>/<u>where</u>); even though the resulting sentence did not make sense when he made this miscue, David read on with no attempt to self-correct.

Comprehension: All responses were correct.

Silent Reading
Comprehension: All responses were correct.

Primer Level

Oral Reading
Word Identification: 1. One sight word confusion (<u>get</u>/<u>got</u>); David did not self-correct although resulting sentence did not sound like normal language.
2. There was one basic word David could not read at all (<u>first</u>). He immediately attempted to "sound it out" when he could not recognize it rather than first attempting to identify the word through context clues. He was unsuccessful, repeatedly producing the sound of the first letter of the word, but then giving up, omitting the word, and reading on.

Comprehension: All responses were correct.

Silent Reading
Comprehension: All responses were correct.

First Reader Level

Oral Reading
Word Identification: 1. Four confusions of basic words (<u>of</u>/<u>off</u>; <u>this</u>/<u>these</u>; <u>black</u>/<u>back</u>; <u>soon</u>/<u>some</u>). No attempts at self-correction although in no case did the resulting sentence make sense or sound like normal language.
2. Did not know one basic word (<u>are</u>) at all; again attempted to sound it out, saying /ă/ several times then abandoning attempt and reading on. No attempt to use context, which would have cued the word in this passage.

Comprehension: Missed 1 question out of 10 (a question that required the reader to draw a conclusion).

Silent Reading
Comprehension: All responses were correct.

Figure 6–2
An analysis of David Adams' IRI performance

2₁ Level[1] (First Semester of Second Grade)

Oral Reading

Word Identification: 1. Five confusions of basic words (everything/everyone; came/come; that/what; eat/ate; because/become). No attempts to self-correct although the resulting sentences made no sense.

2. Two basic words he did not know at all (were; show). Attempted to sound them out by using first one or two letters, but did not use context along with these cues. Omitted both words after unsuccessful attempts.

3. After a brief hesitation before the word doesn't, omitted it with no obvious attempts to work it out using any word identification strategy.

Comprehension: Missed 2 out of 10 questions (one requiring him to identify the main idea of the passage; the other requiring him to make an inference).

Silent Reading

Comprehension: Missed 1 out of 10 (a question requiring him to draw a conclusion).

2₂ Level[2] (Second Semester of Second Grade)

Oral Reading

Word Identification: 1. Confusions of 11 words (have/had; their/they; stay/start; slid/slide;/ skin/sky; which/with; something/someone; like/let; soup/soap; when/then; I'll/It's). No attempts at self-correction.

2. After hesitations before chipmunk and remember, omitted these with no obvious attempts to use any word identification strategy.

3. On eight other words (people, smart, stood, birds, waiting, knows, rider, seeds), he attempted unsuccessfully to sound them out, only producing sounds of the first one or two letters of the word before abandoning attempt; no attempts to use context clues.

4. Two words were pronounced as nonsense words (gravel/"gratel"; wheels/"we-les").

Comprehension: Missed 5 out of 10 questions (two of those missed were literal level questions; one required him to make an inference; one required him to follow a sequence of events; and one required him to draw a conclusion).

Silent reading

Comprehension: Missed 4 out of 10 (one literal level question; one required him to draw a conclusion; one required him to select main idea of passage; and one required him to make an inference.[2]

---

[1]Numbers with subscripts are used conventionally to denote grade and semester. 2₁, for example, denotes first semester of second grade.

[2]As you will remember from the report of David Adams' IRI performance earlier in this chapter, material at the 2₂ level was determined to be at his frustration level. Normally, miscues made at a student's frustration level are not analyzed because they frequently represent atypical responses by that student. (For example, students will often misread words they usually know when material is at a level of difficulty beyond that which they can handle with a reasonable degree of success.) In this analysis, David's performance is being noted for the passages at his frustration level so readers of this text who may be learning how to use IRIs may compare a student's reading behaviors on materials at the independent, instructional, and frustration levels.

Summary of David Adams' IRI Performance

Implications for Instruction

David must be taught to use a variety of word identification strategies rather than attempt to sound out each unknown word he encounters. He needs special help learning to use context clues (a skill he lacks) along with use of the beginning letter(s)/sound(s) of a word (a strategy he already employs). He must be taught to read for meaning and, most important, to self-correct when what he reads does not make sense or sound like normal language. His heavy use of graphic clues in word identification is also causing many sight word confusions; he substitutes words that look similar (e.g., of/off; because/become) even when they make no sense in that passage. He must be taught to use meaning as an aid in word identification.

David appears to need more work in higher level comprehension tasks rather than in literal level ones. On this test he had difficulty with literal level questions only when he reached his frustration level. He also had slightly more difficulty with comprehension after oral rather than silent reading. Since oral reading requires more attention to word identification than silent reading, increasing his efficiency in word identification strategies also appears to be important for the purpose of allowing him to attend more to comprehension of the material.

Figure 6–3
A summary of David Adams' IRI performance

1. Read over the whole passage, then go back and fill in words.
2. Try to use the exact word you think the author would have used.
3. Write one word on each line, or tell me one word.
4. If you have trouble guessing a word, skip it, and go back after you have finished the whole passage and try again.

Begin by completing a practice passage with the students to be sure they understand the task. Give students as much time as they need—a cloze test is untimed.

To Score a Cloze Test
Score as correct only the exact words deleted from the text. (This scoring specification is not used when the cloze procedure is employed for instructional purposes; instead, any word that conveys the same meaning intended by the passages is accepted as correct.) Do not score misspellings of correct words as incorrect responses. To determine the percentage

Implications for Further Testing

A test of knowledge of basic sight vocabulary should be administered to determine specific words David does not know. The IRI indicated that he needs work in this area but more comprehensive and specific information is needed.

A test of knowledge and use of word identification strategies is also needed. The IRI indicated that David employed only one strategy and that this one strategy was not well developed. Does he know other strategies but fails to use them in contextual reading? Are other strategies unknown to him? More definitive information is needed.

David should take a Reading Miscue Inventory. Since this test requires the student to read a whole story or informational selection, rather than shorter passages as found on an IRI, it will be helpful in discovering the strategies he uses when reading longer pieces of connected material that approximate more closely material found in real reading situations. Does he employ meaning and oral language knowledge as an aid to word identification when more meaning and language are available because of the longer length of the material? Is his higher level comprehension affected positively when more meaning clues are available because of the length of the material?

More in-depth assessment of David's comprehension strategies should be undertaken. An individually administered assessment is needed to obtain additional information about how he approaches comprehension tasks and to permit the teacher to determine the cues and thinking processes he uses or fails to use.

---

of correct words for each passage, divide the number of correct responses for that passage by 50 (the number of deletions). For example, if Dale had 32 correct responses on one 4th-grade passage, his percentage of correct responses is 64 percent (32.00 ÷ 50 = .64). Average the student's percentage of correct responses for the two passages selected for each reading level. If, for example, Brian scored 58 percent correct on one 3rd-grade passage and 50 percent on the second 3rd-grade passage, his average percentage of correct responses at the 3rd-grade level is 54 percent. The following criteria are used to determine a student's reading levels (Bormuth, 1968):

Independent Level	over 57%
Instructional Level	44% to 56%
Frustration Level	43% or less

These criteria are based on the deletion of every fifth word from the text, and on accepting as correct only responses identical to the deleted word. If these specifications are not followed, these criteria are not valid for determining reading levels.

Advantages. Cloze tests are easier to prepare, administer, and score than IRIs. Cloze tests also measure a student's ability to use knowledge of language and the world to fol-

**Examiner's Introduction
(Student Booklet page 33):**

Imagine how you would feel if you were up to bat and this was your team's last chance to win the game! Please read this story.

Whiz! The baseball went right by me, and I

struck at the air!

"Strike one," called the man. I could feel my

legs begin to shake!

Whiz! The ball went by me again, and I began

to feel bad. "Strike two," screamed the man.

I held the bat back because this time I would

kill the ball! I would hit it right out of the park! I

was so scared that I bit down on my lip. My knees

shook and my hands grew wet.

Swish! The ball came right over the plate.

Crack! I hit it a good one! Then I ran like the wind.

Everyone was yelling for me because I was now a

baseball star!

**Comprehension Questions
and Possible Answers**

(mi) 1. What is this story about?
(a baseball game, someone who gets two strikes and finally gets a hit, etc.)

(f) 2. After the second strike, what did the batter plan to do?
(hit the ball right out of the park)

(inf) 3. Who was the "man" in this story who called the strikes?
(the umpire)

(t)   4. In this story, what was meant when the batter said, "I would kill the ball"?
(hit it very hard)

(ce) 5. Why was the last pitch a good one?
(because it went right over the plate)

(ce) 6. What did the batter do after the last pitch?
(The batter hit it a good one and ran like the wind.)

Miscue Count:

O___ I___ S___ A___ REP___ REV___

Scoring Guide	
Word Rec.	Comp.
IND 1	IND 0
INST 6	INST 1–2
FRUST 12 +	FRUST 3 +

Figure 6–4
An example of a typical IRI. (Source: From *Analytical Reading Inventories,* 3rd edition
(p. 49), by M. L. Woods and A. J. Moe, 1985, Columbus, Ohio: Charles E. Merrill. Reprinted
by permission.)

low the sense of a passage and, on that basis, have been shown to be valid and reliable measures for determining a student's reading levels (Jones & Pikulski, 1974; Paradis, Tierney, & Peterson, 1975; Rankin, 1978; Ransom, 1968; Warwick, 1978).

Disadvantages.   One disadvantage of cloze tests is that they provide only a global measure of comprehension. They do not provide specific information about students' use of strategies and skills. This disadvantage can be ameliorated if the teacher has the student orally describe why he selected words for deletions. But though understanding a student's thinking provides some diagnostic information, a teacher will obtain less information about specific strengths and weaknesses from a cloze test than she will from analyzing IRI responses.

A second disadvantage is that cloze tests provide a reliable and valid measure only for students reading at the third-grade level or above. A modified cloze procedure that can be used with students reading below third-grade level is called a *maze test*. Suggested by Gutherie, Seifert, Burnham, and Caplan (1974) as an easier task for younger children and poorer readers, the maze test provides the student with three alternatives for each deleted word. In a maze test every fifth word is omitted from a passage of about 125 words so that there are 20 deletions. The first and last sentence remain intact. The three alternatives always include the correct word, one incorrect alternative that has the same grammatical function as the deleted word (e.g., if the deleted word is a verb, this alternative is also a verb), and one incorrect alternative that has a different grammatical function. See the example in Figure 6–5.

Criteria for determining reading levels based on percentage of correct responses on a maze test are:

Independent Level	over 85%
Instructional Level	50% to 84%
Frustration Level	49% or less

All other procedures for preparing, administering, and scoring maze tests are the same as those for cloze tests.

DAILY ONGOING OBSERVATIONS

One of the most powerful forms of informal assessment is daily observation, which provides teachers with a chance to diagnose what students can and cannot do in real reading. Most teachers make judgments about the ability of students to handle material in daily work and note areas where more instruction should oc-

---

The queen told her _____ to go
                        (servants, friends, sleeping)

into the _____ and pick all vegetables
          (woods, dark, fields)

_____ saw lying above the _____.
     (they, that, he)   (clouds, ground, wet)

Figure 6–5
Example of maze procedure

cur, but many feel hesitant to assume that this is a legitimate form of assessment.

Johns (1982) proposed the name innerocular technique, or IOT, be used for observations during daily lessons. His tongue-in-cheek suggestion of this pseudoscientific term is an attempt to legitimize an important diagnostic procedure. Teachers sometimes believe their own judgments lack the value of real tests. This is simply not true. Careful and thoughtful decisions based on daily work provide a highly useful form of evaluation that can help the teacher verify (or disprove) test results, note when growth has occurred, and provide clues for changing instructional procedures when daily performance does not conform to test performance. The "IOT" can be used to confirm or reject results of intellectual assessment, refine decisions about students' reading levels, and identify strengths and weaknesses in reading strategies, knowledge, and skills. Keeping graphs and charts provides a permanent record of daily performance that lends credence to the decisions based on this type of informal assessment.

It is false to assume that the only assessment information that should be used in planning remedial instruction comes from formal or informal tests. Observing responses during instruction is important, and behaviors noted should be included in the written diagnostic workups of students if these behaviors conflict with those exhibited on tests.

Ethnographic Observation

Recently there has been a resurgence of interest in a slightly more organized type of observation than Johns' IOT called *ethnographic observation,* and defined as "onsite, naturalistic studies of classroom teaching/learning situa-

Daily, on-going observation while the student is reading is an important part of informal assessment.

tions" (Harris & Hodges, 1981). In other words, the teacher directly observes students' natural behaviors in their natural environment and records, then describes the behavior. Ethnographic observation is based on the premise that a teacher cannot really understand all facets of a student's academic or social performances unless the individual is studied holistically.

Through keen observation and interpretation of classroom events, the teacher can learn. This learning may promote students' academic development for several reasons. In the first place, the teacher can formulate questions directly related to difficulties a particular student is having and structure observation to answer those questions. Secondly, this type of assessment may be more valid than conventional assessments because students are behaving and responding naturally in real-life situations. (E.g., a student may respond one way during a formal test and quite differently when reading a funny passage to a friend during a free period.) Finally, observing a student may help teachers generate new ideas about why a student is having difficulty—ideas that

do not fit into the typical pattern of the assessment data usually gathered.

Irwin and Bushnell (1980, p. 64) offer these guidelines for ethnographic observation:

1. Make a clear distinction between your observation and your interpretation of the event (although ultimately both are important).
2. When appropriate, take down exact words and behaviors, including the type of body language exhibited.
3. Make an attempt to interpret what was observed from the student's point of view (or in other words, ask *Why?*).

Some tools teachers use during ethnographic observation are checklists, participation charts, and rating scales. Checklists consist of statements used to record specific behaviors. The teacher simply checks off or writes "Yes" or "No" to indicate their presence or absence during a particular observation. (See the example in Figure 6–6.) Cartwright and Cartwright (1984) suggest a variation of a checklist called a participation chart, which

Figure 6–6
Example of checklist used in ethnographic observation

Reading Participation Chart

Situation: *Teacher-directed group of four students; expository passage*

Date: *Oct. 11*

	Karen	Marc	Bob	Al
1. Participated in prereading discussion	✓	✓		✓
2. Made attempt to predict story or passage events	✓			✓
3. Began reading when directed to do so	✓	✓		✓
4. Read attentively without obvious mind-wandering	✓	✓	✓	✓
5. Volunteered information in follow-up discussion	✓	✓		✓
6. Appeared uncomfortable when asked to answer questions			✓	

Figure 6–7
Example of participation chart used in ethnographic observation

can be used when several students are being observed. (See Figure 6–7.) Unlike a simple checklist, rating scales (like the one in Figure 6–8) allows the teacher to record quality or frequency of behavior. Because observing students in natural settings allows a teacher to say more about real world behaviors, some reading educators favor ethnographic observation over formal testing. This type of assessment also generally focuses on qualitative, and not mere quantitative, information.

Oral Reading

Since daily observation has frequently meant observing students during oral reading, a few words about oral reading performance are in order. Consider this quote, which illustrates the ideas about reading instruction that prevailed until the 1920s—reading instruction was primarily oral.

Articulation
Suggestions to Teachers. Thorough and frequent drills on the elementary sounds are useful in correcting vicious habits of pronunciation and in strengthening the vocal organs. (*McGuffey's Second Eclectic Reader*, Revised Edition. New York; American Book Company, 1896, p. 7)

Stress was placed not only on reading every word correctly but also on expressiveness and

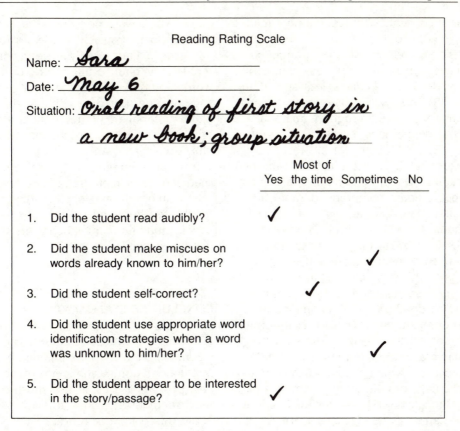

Figure 6–8
Example of a rating scale used in ethnographic observation

correct enunciation of each sound within words according to what was considered to be contemporary standard English. Then in 1917 Thorndike published a classic study that showed that although many students could pronounce the words in their reading texts, their comprehension was poor. Thorndike blamed this lack of understanding on the excessive emphasis on good oral reading, and his study led to a shift in the opposite direction. During the early 1920s many teachers employed the *non-oral method* of reading instruction in which all reading was silent. Today reading educators recognize the need for both oral and silent reading and avoid using one method to the exclusion of the other.

Oral reading does have a place in remedial and clinical programs, but major emphasis on oral reading ability is not appropriate. There are several reasons why silent reading should be given attention equal to, if not greater than, the attention given to oral reading when working with disabled readers. First, in most real-life situations and in many school settings students must read material silently. Poor readers need practice in sustaining attention and gaining ideas during silent reading. Second, many students of low reading ability comprehend better after reading silently because they can concentrate on the message rather than pronunciation. This is particularly true when the task involves understanding higher level concepts. Third, some poor readers, especially older students, are self-conscious about reading aloud in front of others; because they are nervous their oral reading performance reflects less skill than they actually possess. Finally, students reading silently may move through the material at their own pace, perhaps regressing if an idea or word presents difficulty; for this reason disabled readers often feel less pressure during silent reading. On the other hand, although many poor readers comprehend more adequately after silent reading, some have greater understanding of the material after reading orally (Swalm, 1972); many of these students seem to need to hear the language they are reading since this additional input provides a link between spoken and written language. Others try harder during oral reading because they are demonstrating their abilities to someone else; some have less difficulty sustaining attention in oral reading (during silent reading they are on their own to choose whether to attend to the page or not). Finally, some simply prefer oral to silent reading—it is fun because they have captured the teacher's attention.

When oral reading is used in remedial programs, the teacher should understand the appropriate (or inappropriate) objectives for its use. Figure 6–9 shows an exercise from McGuffey's Fifth Reader designed to provide practice in correct expression for young readers at the turn of the century. Even today, some teachers worry about lack of expressiveness in poor readers' oral reading. However, recent understandings of the reading process indicate that good expression is a reflection of students' understanding of the material and is not an important objective in itself. When students comprehend material (and no longer have to laboriously concentrate on word identification), good expression follows naturally as the student absorbs the message rather than attends consciously to the ink marks on the page.

Nor is word perfect oral reading an important goal. Proficient readers seldom read all words in a text exactly as printed in the material; they often omit, insert, or substitute words and still understand the author's message. Miscues that do not change the meaning of the material are unimportant and should be ignored. Those that do change meaning are clues to where instruction is needed. In other words, the main purpose for oral reading in remedial or clinical programs is to serve as a frequent, informal, and ongoing diagnostic tool for the teacher. Oral reading provides a window to students' reading behaviors so teachers can stress needed strategies.

CONCLUDING STATEMENT

It is common practice to assess the progress students have made after a period of remedial instruction. Comparing performance on pre and post measures is the most commonly used method of making this assessment. To make this comparison, the teacher uses the same form or an alternate form of the group, standardized survey test for both assessment and a posttest or asks the student to read a form of an IRI that contains passages not read during the initial assessment. She then compares the student's original test to the posttest to determine the student's progress after instruction. For example, if Tom's instructional level derived from a standardized test was 4.0 before instruction and 4.8 after instruction, he would be said to have made an 8 month gain.

There is some question as to whether using the same form of a test is appropriate for measuring progress. If the same test is used, some believe that the "practice effect" will cause students to receive higher scores even if they have not progressed. On the other hand, others have noted that test results will sometimes indicate a student has made no progress

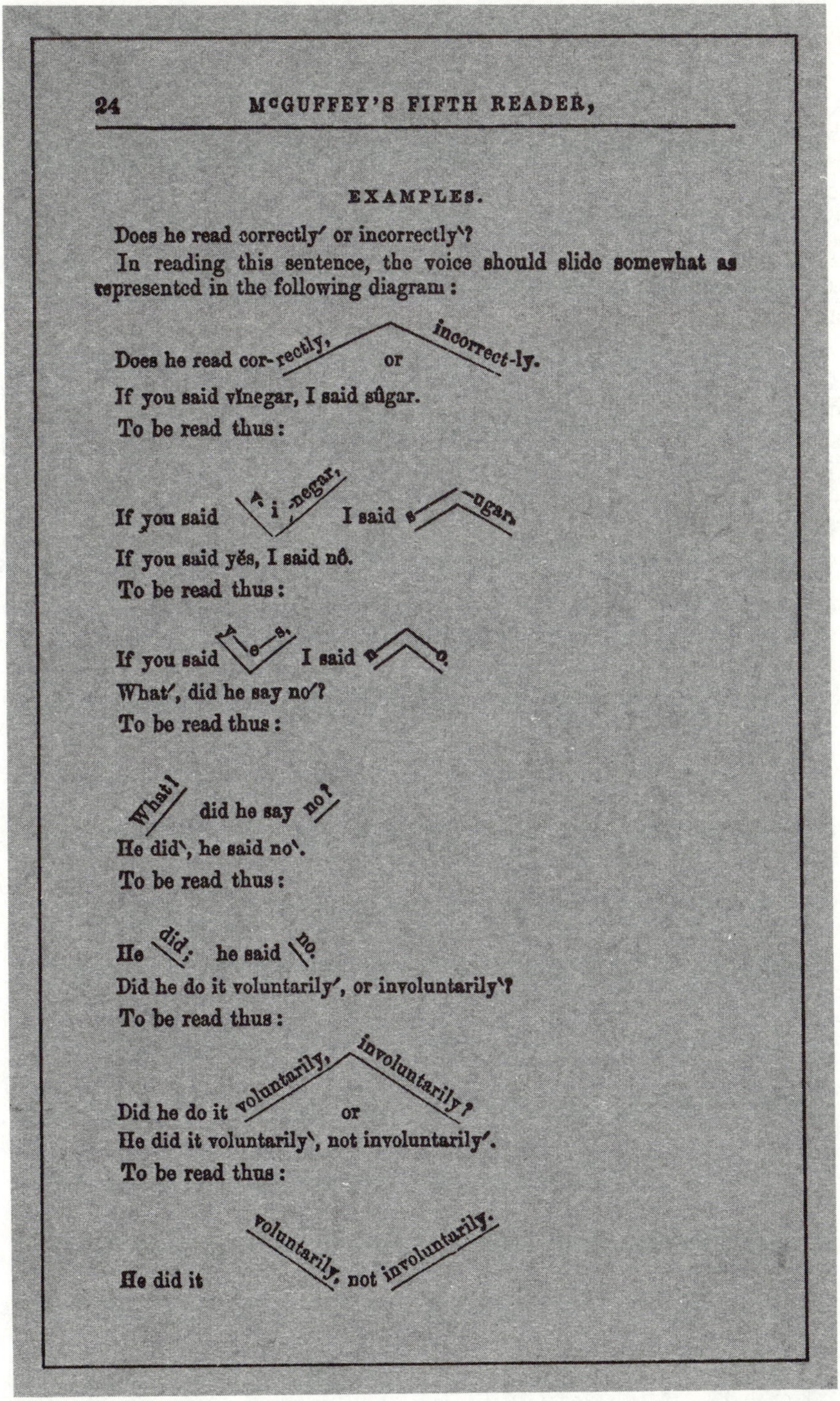

24 McGUFFEY'S FIFTH READER,

EXAMPLES.

Does he read correctly′ or incorrectly‵?

In reading this sentence, the voice should slide somewhat as represented in the following diagram:

Does he read cor-rectly, or incorrect-ly.

If you said vĭnegar, I said sûgar.

To be read thus:

If you said vi-negar, I said s-ugar.

If you said yĕs, I said nô.

To be read thus:

If you said y-e-s, I said n-o.

What′, did he say no′?

To be read thus:

What! did he say no?

He did‵, he said no‵.

To be read thus:

He did; he said no.

Did he do it voluntarily′, or involuntarily‵?

To be read thus:

Did he do it voluntarily, or involuntarily?

He did it voluntarily‵, not involuntarily′.

To be read thus:

He did it voluntarily, not involuntarily.

Figure 6–9
Good expression was itself an important goal in the early 1900s. Now we realize that good expression follows naturally from good comprehension. (Source: From *Early American School Books* (p. 24) by Myron Johnson, 1960, Scotia, N.Y.: American Review. Reprinted by permission.)

even when growth is obvious; this may occur because the student remembers answers he gave on the original test and marks them again, rather than applying the new skills and strategies he has developed in the remedial program.

There are also some problems with using an alternate form of a standardized test or IRI. Although the authors of some tests may be able to claim statistical equivalency of alternate forms, it is doubtful that real equivalency exists between all of the many factors that make up the test. For alternate forms of a test to be exactly equivalent the authors of the test would have to control a large number of variables including the content of test passages, the length and complexity of all sentences, word length, vocabulary difficulty, and many other factors (Farr, 1969). Although they may attempt to control some of these it is impossible to control every factor. Of the two procedures—using the same form of the test versus using an alternate form—it is probably best to use the alternate form but in doing so, teachers need to remember the previous admonition that all test scores are approximate. In addition, pre and post measures should be coupled with teacher observation in assessing growth. Finally, to obtain an accurate picture of student growth and to determine if the student has maintained the gain, teachers should conduct posttest measures not only at the end of a remedial program but also after 3 to 6 months.

7

Assessment for Identifying Specific Strengths and Weaknesses in Reading: Part I

After verifying approximate instructional level, the teacher must next determine a student's specific strengths and weaknesses in reading strategies, knowledge, and skills. Some indications of the tests that should be used to determine a student's strengths and weaknesses can be obtained from her IRI performance, as illustrated in Chapter 6. The assessment tools and procedures will vary according to the instructional level of the student; for example, assessing the dictionary skills of a student reading at the preprimer level would usually be a waste of time. Likewise, a student reading at sixth-grade level almost certainly has a knowledge of basic sight vocabulary or she could not be reading at that level; testing basic sight vocabulary would usually be unnecessary.

The diagnostic process should include necessary assessment only. Although diagnosis should be thorough, it should also be completed as quickly as possible so instruction to alleviate problems can begin. The time

needed to conduct a thorough diagnosis will vary from student to student, and some students may require tests not typically necessary for students reading at that level. Box 7–1 lists a general outline of basic tests to administer at each reading level; it provides teachers with a starting point, but adjustments should be made for individual students. This chapter and Chapter 8 describe some tests that may help a teacher assess a student's specific needs.

THE CONCEPTS ABOUT PRINT TEST

The Concepts About Print Test is used with both nonreaders and beginning readers. For a student whose standardized test or IRI score indicates that preprimer material is at the student's frustration level, Concepts About Print is a good test with which to begin. For this test booklets titled *Sand* or *Stones* are read to students. The teacher asks questions to assess

Box 7-1

A General Outline of Basic Tests to Administer at Each Reading Level

For students whose scores on a standardized test or IRI indicate that material at the preprimer level is at the student's frustration level:

1. administer the Concepts About Print Test
2. use the student's own dictated story for assessment
3. administer tests of knowledge of basic sight vocabulary
4. administer a test of knowledge and use of word identification strategies
5. assess listening comprehension
6. orally administer an interest inventory

For students whose instructional levels are at the preprimer level:

1. use an informal test to determine if the student's approximate instructional level is first, second, or third preprimer level
2. use the student's own dictated story for assessment
3. administer tests of knowledge of basic sight vocabulary
4. administer a test of knowledge and use of word identification strategies
5. assess comprehension
6. orally administer an interest inventory

For students whose instructional levels are at the primer level:

1. use the student's own dictated story for assessment
2. administer tests of knowledge of basic sight vocabulary
3. administer a test of knowledge and use of word identification strategies
4. assess comprehension
5. orally administer a measure of attitudes toward reading
6. orally administer an interest inventory

For students whose instructional levels are at first, second or third grade levels:

1. administer tests of knowledge of basic sight vocabulary
2. administer a test of knowledge and use of word identification strategies
3. administer the Reading Miscue Inventory
4. assess comprehension
5. orally administer a measure of attitudes toward reading
6. orally administer an interest inventory

For students whose instructional levels are at fourth, fifth, or sixth grade levels:

1. administer selected portions of a test of knowledge and use of word identification strategies
2. administer the Reading Miscue Inventory
3. assess knowledge of word meanings
4. assess comprehension
5. administer an attitude scale
6. administer an interest inventory

For students whose instructional levels are above the sixth grade level:

1. administer the Reading Miscue Inventory
2. assess knowledge of word meanings
3. assess comprehension
4. assess reading rate
5. administer an attitude scale
6. administer an interest inventory

the student's knowledge of several concepts such as where the front of a book is found; words, not pictures, tell the message; where to begin reading on a page; it is necessary to move from one line to another; what a "letter" is; what a "word" is; the left page should be read before the right; and other concepts about printed language.

USING THE STUDENT'S OWN DICTATED STORY FOR ASSESSMENT

It is difficult to test beginning readers in normal, contextual reading because they can read so little. By using a student's own dictated story for assessment, a teacher can examine reading behaviors and knowledge while the student is reading connected text, rather than measure isolated behavior. Directions for using student-dictated stories for this purpose appear in Box 7–2.

One helpful suggestion is to tape students reading their own stories or published materials several times throughout the year and keep these on file for comparison and reports to parents (Anderson, Hiebert, Scott, & Wilkinson, 1985).

ASSESSING KNOWLEDGE OF BASIC SIGHT VOCABULARY

The term *sight vocabulary* (or *sight words*) is used three ways. Sometimes it is used synonymously with the term *instant words* to mean words a student recognizes instantly. It is also used to mean *irregular words,* that is, phonetically irregular words that some believe must be recognized at sight rather than identified through use of word identification strategies. The term is also often used synonymously with the phrase *core vocabulary,* that is, those

words that occur frequently in written material (Hood, 1977).

In the following section the term *sight vocabulary* is used to mean core vocabulary. A good sight vocabulary is important to fluent reading because these basic words appear so often in anything a student reads. A student who has to focus on each individual word or identify each word with a word identification strategy usually loses the sense of the material. Immediate recognition allows students to focus on meaning. Also, because they appear often, these words provide much of the context for other words. Students need to master basic sight words so they can use context clues to identify less frequently occurring unknown words.

Lists of high frequency words, or core vocabulary, have been compiled for teacher reference. Some of these include the *Dolch Basic Sight Word List* (Dolch, 1936), the Durr list of high frequency words in primary level library books (Durr, 1973), the *Harris-Jacobson Core Lists* (Harris & Jacobson, 1972), *A Basic Vocabulary for Beginners* (Johnson, 1971), the Ekwall list (Ekwall, 1975), and *The New Instant Word List* (Fry, 1980). The first couple of hundred words on all of these lists are just about the same because they are basic function words such as *the, and, of, but, for, in, a, that, be, is, to, are, so, it, this,* and so forth. (See how many and how often each of these basic function words occur on the page you are reading right now.)

A test of knowledge of basic sight vocabulary, that is, core vocabulary, should always be individually administered with the student reading to the teacher. Some published tests of sight word knowledge have been devised so that three or four words are printed by each item number, the teacher pronounces one of these, and the student circles the word. This procedure does not provide an accurate measure because a student can often recognize a word when it is pronounced for

Box 7–2
Using Student Dictated Stories for Assessment

1. Materials needed:
   a. tape recorder with microphone
   b. blank tape
   c. object or picture to stimulate discussion
   d. paper and pencil
   e. index cards
2. Initiating Procedures
   a. At the beginning of the session, allow the student to talk into the tape recorder, listen to the tape, turn the recorder on and off, and engage in any other activity that will help the student feel at ease with the subsequent taping procedures. Temporarily put the tape recorder aside.
   b. Use an object or picture to stimulate discussion.
   c. Have the student dictate a short "story" based on the previous discussion. For some students the story may consist of no more than two or three sentences. Other students will dictate a longer narrative. Write down the story for the student exactly as it has been dictated.
3. First Taping Procedure:
   a. Turn on the tape recorder.
   b. Have the student read the dictated story.
   c. If the student has difficulty, encourage him/her to:
      1) use any procedure known to figure out the unknown word,
      2) guess what word would "sound right there" or,
      3) skip the word and go on.
      Student success during the first taping procedure must be assessed subjectively by the teacher. In general, success can be judged by the student being able to read back the sentences within the dictated story in a reasonably meaningful manner. The successful student may not be able to pronounce correctly every word as was originally dictated, but the majority of each sentence will remain intact.
      The behaviors of unsuccessful students may consist of any of the following: the student simply cannot read back any of the dictated story; or, the student will focus on isolated words in the story, pointing out only those few which are known; or, the student may attempt to scan sentences in correct left to right progression, but can only pronounce an occasional word; thus rendering the story meaningless.
   d. Turn off the tape recorder. Write each word from the story on an individual card. Shuffle the cards and present the words to the student in a *random* order. Record the student's responses by placing a check or an *X* on the back of each word card to indicate a correct or incorrect response. When one word is substituted for another, write the substitution on the back of the card.
4. Second Taping Procedure:
   a. If the student had relative success during the first taping procedure, repeat the taping procedure after a short interval (approximately 30-60 minutes) using the *same* story.
   b. If the student has been decidedly unsuccessful during the first taping procedure, do not engage in the second and third taping procedures.
5. Third Taping Procedure:
   a. If the student has had relative success during the second taping procedure, repeat the procedure *the next day* using the *same* story.
   b. If the student has been decidedly unsuccessful during the second taping procedure, do not engage in the third taping procedure.

(Continued next page)

Box 7–2 (Continued)

6. Analysis:

Make one, two, or three copies of the story, depending on the number of taped readings you have obtained. On these copies of the story write information as you listen to the tapes. As you listen, write down words the student substitutes for other words and whether the student subsequently corrects the substituted words. Indicate words that are omitted or added.

Analyze the student's reading behaviors by responding to the following questions, and by making other observations and statements that are applicable to a specific student's performance.

a. How does the student's performance in reading the story compare with his/her performance in reading the isolated words printed on the card? Are there differences between these two performances during the first, second, and third sessions?

b. Does the student seem to understand correct directional movements in reading connected printed material, *i.e.,* does s/he attempt to read from left to right across a line of print?

c. When the student has substituted words in reading the story, do the words:
   1) look similar?
   2) mean about the same thing?

d. Did the student's behavior in substituting words in the story differ from any substitutions s/he made when reading the isolated words from cards? What differences were seen?

e. Each time the student omitted or added words within the story, did the sentence:
   1) still make sense?
   2) retain its general meaning?

f. When the student has read aloud a rendition that changes the meaning of the original text, does the student self-correct? If so, how did the student determine that a correction should be made?

g. When reading the story, what strategies did the student employ when faced with an unknown word? Did s/he attempt to sound out the word, letter by letter? Did s/he use the first one or two letters of the word only, then pronounce any word that begins with those letters? Did the student pronounce any word that has a general configuration similar to the text word? Guess wildly? Use context to make a meaningful choice?

h. What reading knowledge did the student's performance indicate s/he possessed at the time of the first taping procedure?

i. What differences were noted in the student's reading behaviors and knowledge when comparing the results of the first, second, and third taping? (McCormick, 1981)

(*Source:* From "Using Student Dictated Stories for Assessment" by S. McCormick, 1981, *Reading World* (Oct.), 31–34. Reprinted by permission of the author and the College Reading Association.)

him, but is unable to identify it when he must read it for himself. These types of published tests should not be used.

There is some controversy over whether words should be read in context or in isolation on a test of sight vocabulary knowledge. Those who argue for a contextual presentation correctly point out that in most reading tasks words do not occur in isolation, and other words in the sentence or passage provide con-textual clues that aid in word identification. While some words in real-life do appear in isolation (such as the word STOP on traffic signs or *Men* and *Women* on restroom doors), there is an environmental context that aids identification in these cases. Certainly many high frequency words, such as *of* or *that* and so forth, do not occur in isolation in real reading tasks. Have you ever found a sign with the single word *of* printed on it, or found the single word *that* printed all by itself on a door, or wall, or book page? In addition, some research has shown that reading words in context is an easier task. Goodman (1965), for example, found that the majority of first-grade students in his study could read correctly in context more than ⅔ of the same words they had missed in isolation; second-graders could read more than ¾ of the words they had missed; and third-graders could read more than ⅘ of the words they had originally missed.

Those who argue for presenting words in isolation during assessment of sight vocabulary point out, also correctly, that although context often aids word identification, it does not do so in all cases. For example, suppose Don is often confused by the words *was* and *saw;* in the following example, context would not provide any clue to eliminate his confusion.

I _____ a witch on Halloween.
(was, saw)

Although the longer the selection, the more likely that context will provide clues, it does not always do so. Since instant and accurate recognition of these frequently occurring basic words is so important, proponents of an isolated presentation of words during assessment contend that we must determine a student's ability to recognize these words in any situation, including those where context does not help.

Testing Sight Vocabulary in Context

The best resolution to this problem is to test these basic words both ways. Poor readers often have particular difficulty with the high frequency words because many are function words such as prepositions and conjunctions. Function words are more abstract than content words such as nouns. Can you define the word *of,* for example? Other than saying it is a preposition, probably not. Function words are

more difficult for poor readers to learn initially because they lack concrete meaning; at the same time they are easier to confuse with similar words for the same reason. Therefore, these words should initially be tested in context. Words the student is unable to read, even in context, should have the first priority for instruction. Once a student's basic core vocabulary has been assessed in context, it can be tested in isolation. Words recognized in context but not in isolation should be taught after the first priority words are learned.

To *develop* a contextual test of basic sight vocabulary:

1. Use all words from one of the lists of basic high frequency words or select all words from the first preprimer of the material to be used for instruction to compose section 1 of your test; then do the same for the second preprimer to compose section 2 of your test; and so forth.
2. Write sentences that include each word; other words in the sentences should be words the student can identify so they provide a context for the target word you are testing. In constructing these sentences, you will probably use some of the basic high frequency sight words several times; that is, they will probably occur not only as a target word but also in the context of sentences for other target words. In this way you will have several opportunities to observe the student's response to the same word.

To *administer* a contextual test of basic sight vocabulary:

1. Have the student orally read the sentences into a tape recorder.
2. If a word is not known, tell the student to do anything she can to figure it out; if she still cannot identify it, she should skip it and continue reading.

3. If a student begins to exhibit great difficulty as the test progresses, discontinue testing. Plan to provide instruction for those words missed up to the point when you stopped testing. After the student has mastered these words, you can administer the test again to identify further words to be learned.

To *score* a contextual test of basic sight vocabulary:

1. When the student is not present, listen to the tape and mark miscues on a duplicate copy of the test.
2. Do not mark words only as right or wrong; rather, write down what the student said when a word was mispronounced. For example, if *when* is read as *then,* write *then* above the word *when.*
3. Circle any word the student is unable to pronounce at all.
4. Consider correct only those words for which there was "instant" recognition. If there is a long pause before the student can say a word or if a word identification strategy must be used, then there is not instant recognition.
5. Prepare a list of words the student cannot recognize at all and another list of words confused with similar words (such as *on* for *no, here* for *there,* and so forth). On the second list note the test word and the similar word.
6. No grade score is obtained from this type of assessment. Instead, it is used to determine if the student does or does not need instruction on basic sight vocabulary and how much instruction is required. A contextual test also informs the teacher about the kind of instruction needed: is initial instruction needed with most words because the student cannot identify them at all, or is the main problem that the student is confusing words with other graph-

ically similar words? A contextual test provides lists of specific words for which instruction is needed.

Testing Sight Vocabulary in Isolation

Testing basic sight vocabulary in context should be followed by a test of recognition of these words when context provides no clue to their identification; that is, sight words should also be tested in isolation. It is preferable to have each word printed on a separate index card rather than on one long list. A long list of words can overwhelm some poor readers and they may feel defeated even before they begin the task.

To *develop* a test of basic sight vocabulary in isolation:

1. Use a typewriter that has large or primary type; type one word per card. Alternatively you may simply print each word on a card, using correct manuscript writing. If you are using a popular word list such as the Dolch list, you may also purchase sets of preprinted flashcards.
2. Divide the word cards into sets of 10. In each set, number the cards on the back from 1 to 10.
3. Make duplicate copies of sheets to be used during scoring, with each word in each set listed on the sheet. One example of such a sheet is shown in Figure 7–1.

To *administer* the test of sight vocabulary in isolation have students read from one set of word cards at a time, following the three procedures for administering a contextual assessment of sight vocabulary. Always present the words within a set in the same order (card 1 first, card 2 second, and so forth) so they will conform to the sheets you have prepared for scoring.

To *score* the test of sight vocabulary in isolation use scoring sheets and follow the

Student's Name _____ Date _____

1. on _____	1. have _____	1. is _____
2. of _____	2. go _____	2. go _____
3. the _____	3. if _____	3. now _____
4. for _____	4. and _____	4. know _____
5. with _____	5. red _____	5. never _____
6. some _____	6. so _____	6. no _____
7. where _____	7. every _____	7. from _____
8. because _____	8. a _____	8. off _____
9. to _____	9. have _____	9. which _____
10. it _____	10. had _____	10. said _____

Figure 7–1
Example of scoring sheet

same procedures described for administering the contextual test of sight vocabulary.

ASSESSING KNOWLEDGE OF WORD IDENTIFICATION STRATEGIES

Although we hope that students will eventually recognize most words instantly, they will undoubtedly encounter some words they do not know during the developmental stages of acquiring reading proficiency. Even skilled adult readers occasionally find unknown words as they read. Therefore, readers must learn strategies to identify words they do not recognize on sight. An assessment of a student's knowledge of word identification strategies should include tests of phonic analysis, structural analysis, and use of context clues. Analysis of student performance on an IRI provides some incidental information in these areas, but there are several ways to obtain more in-depth information. See Figure 7–2 for a diagram that summarizes several approaches.

Published Tests

The published tests discussed in this section provide diagnostic information, rather than a reading level as is the case with the survey tests discussed in Chapter 5. *Diagnostic tests* assess specific strengths and weaknesses in reading. There is no perfectly adequate published diagnostic test, and a variety of problems may occur. They don't test all important areas, or they test areas that research has shown to be unimportant for reading achievement. Some only sample sets of knowledge; for example, they may test only a few consonant sounds instead of them all. Some tests measure skills and strategies inappropriately. For example, many test designers use nonsense words to test word identification strategies because they believe that students may recognize real words at sight and their performance on the test would not be a true reflection of their knowledge of word identification strategies. Using nonsense words is nonetheless inappropriate for several reasons. Even though students may be told that the "word" they are to pronounce is a nonsense word, many will attempt to pronounce a real word and, therefore, incorrectly pronounce the sounds of the nonsense word as intended by the test. This is, of course, an indication that they are attempting to use knowledge of the world and language to identify words, a strategy we in fact want them to employ. In addi-

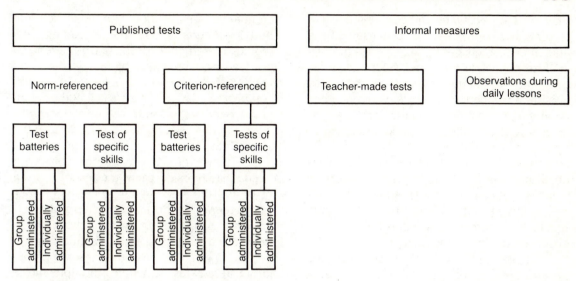

Figure 7–2
Methods of assessing knowledge of word identification strategies

tion, research has shown that pronouncing a nonsense word requires greater skill than pronouncing a real word (Cunningham, 1977), and is, therefore, an inappropriate test of what a student needs to know in real reading tasks.

Some tests don't measure what they say they do. For example, one test of ability to use letter-sound correspondences presents a picture instead of a word and the student is to circle a letter representing the sound heard at the beginning. This is a test of auditory discrimination rather than the ability to produce and use the sound to identify the unknown words.

To be fair to test designers, it must be said that some of these problems are difficult to resolve. For example, those who employ nonsense words to test word identification strategies are correct in saying that using real words presents the possibility that a student will know the word at sight and selecting real words that no student will know is a difficult task. Today many teachers attempt to get around the problems of assessing knowledge of letter sounds by having students write

words from the teacher's dictation. When doing so, the teacher is not concerned with misspellings, but only with the use of letters that do represent the sounds heard. For example, if the student is asked to write *hammer* and writes *hamer* the teacher knows she can correctly match the sounds heard in the word with letters or letter combinations that commonly represent those sounds. If the student is asked to write *can* and writes *kan,* again she has correctly matched sounds with common letter representations and the teacher can extend the assessment by saying "Yes, that's one way you can write the sound heard at the beginning of *can*; now do you know another way?" When using this procedure, however, the teacher must remember that if the student already knows how to spell the word, this method is not a test of the ability to match sounds with letters. In addition, it does not test whether the student uses this knowledge when reading.

There are no simple solutions to some of these problems in preparing published or teacher-made tests, and sometimes a teacher may need to select a test procedure that is the lesser of two (or more) evils. Because of these and other problems it is necessary to carefully analyze published tests and select the most adequate. In some cases a teacher may choose to use certain subtests within one test battery and reject others in the same battery. In many circumstances it will be necessary for parts of several different published tests to be combined, and used along with some teacher-developed subtests to appropriately assess all word identification strategies. Even after following this procedure, teachers need to verify results of all formal assessments through daily observations during instruction.

Some published, diagnostic tests are *norm-referenced* (i.e., standardized). However, providing grade scores is not very important information on a diagnostic test since grade levels do not tell the teacher specifically what a student needs to learn. In addition grade scores obtained from various published diagnostic tests are generally not comparable (Farr, 1969). Grade level scores obtained on norm-referenced diagnostic tests should be ignored. Diagnostic tests should be used only for determining a student's specific strengths and weaknesses in various areas related to reading.

Some norm-referenced published assessment instruments are test batteries. A *test battery* consists of many subtests that assess different skills. Most test batteries provide better tests of word identification strategies than of comprehension.

A few norm-referenced test batteries may be group-administered. One such battery is the Basic Skills Inventory. Another is the Stanford Diagnostic Reading Test designed for levels 1.5 to 3.5, 2.5 to 5.5, and 4.5 to 9.5. Subtests for the first level of the Stanford include auditory vocabulary, auditory discrimination, phonic analysis, word recognition, and comprehension; the second level also includes a test of structural analysis and measures inferential as well as literal comprehension; the third level adds a measure of reading rate. Another commonly used norm-referenced, group-administered test battery is the Botel Reading Inventory. The problem with *group-administered* diagnostic tests is that they often do not require the same type of performance needed in real reading tasks. For example, the student's test paper may include a list of numbered items with three or four consonant blends listed beside each, the teacher says a word, and the students circle the blend they hear in the word. This task is easier, and different, than encountering an unknown word in reading and producing a blend sound to aid in identifying the word. In addition, some group-administered tests include multiple-choice items so the student may score a correct response by guessing. As a result, group-administered diagnostic tests provide only a ballpark notion of the student's needs. As such they are usually more suitable for planning corrective reading instruction; the information gained is not specific enough for remedial or clinical reading or LD programs.

Other norm-referenced test batteries are *individually administered*. Some of these are the Diagnostic Reading Scales and the Durrell Analysis of Reading Difficulty; both of these tests have undergone recent revisions. If they have met other standards for test construction, most individually administered diagnostic tests provide a more accurate assessment than a group-administered test because the student can be required to perform tasks that are closer to those necessary in the real act of reading. For example, students can be asked to read a response to you rather than circling a letter or item number in a multiple-choice question.

In addition to norm-referenced test batteries there are also norm-referenced tests of specific skills. These tests assess detailed information about one area. Some norm-referenced tests of specific skills may be

Individually administered tests often provide a more accurate assessment than group-administered tests.

group-administered. Two tests that assess word identification strategies are the Primary Reading Profiles and the Silent Reading Diagnostic Tests. One norm-referenced test of specific skills that may be *group- or individually administered* is the McCullough Word Analysis Test. Designed for grades 4 to 6, this test assesses eight phonic and structural analysis skills, namely, initial consonant blends, initial consonant digraphs, phonetic discrimination of vowels, matching letters to vowel sounds, sounding out whole words, interpreting phonetic symbols, dividing words into syllables, and identifying root words and affixes. This test provides an adequate sampling of items in most categories and requires about 65 minutes to administer.

Some published diagnostic tests are *criterion-referenced.* Criterion-referenced tests do not compare students' performances with a norm group, but are designed only to provide information about whether students have mastered certain knowledge, strategies, or skills. They often give more specific and comprehensive information about a student's strengths and weaknesses than norm-referenced tests. There are some problems with published criterion-referenced tests, however. For example, enormous numbers of different skills are often tested. One criterion-referenced test has 302 separate objectives, another 343, another 367, and another 518. Many skills tested are unnecessary; they represent rules and principles of low utility. In other cases basic word identification strategies are fractionated into tiny splinter skills, while other skills tested are overlapping. Needless to say, an entire test would be very time-consuming and, for some skills tested, simply a waste of time, since no information of significant relevance for instruction would be obtained. Some criterion-referenced tests do not include enough items for each skill. For example, the Reading Yardsticks test uses only three to five items to measure each skill. Reliability of tests with so few items per skill is usually very low. Criterion levels set for supposed mastery of a skill are subjective and questionable on some tests (Hittleman, 1983). For important word identification knowledge, 100 percent mastery may be necessary if the student is to be proficient in using that knowledge when encountering an unknown word. Yet, many criterion-referenced tests specify levels of only 80 percent to 90 percent to indicate mastery. If a student knows 80 percent of the consonant sounds, this is a problem when encountering unknown words with the other 20 percent.

As with all published tests, the teacher should carefully analyze criterion-referenced tests to determine which are worth purchasing. In many cases the teacher may choose to use only certain subtests and may adapt mastery levels set by publishers to more appropriate standards.

Published criterion-referenced tests, like norm-referenced tests, include test batteries. One which may be either *group- or individually administered* is the Reading Diagnosis test. A *group-administered* criterion-referenced test battery is the PRI/Reading Systems. Examples of those that must be individually administered are the Assessment of Basic Competencies, the Diagnostic Reading Test Battery, and the Brigance Diagnostic Inventory of Basic Skills. The Brigance has sections for spelling, handwriting, math, and English usage, as well as reading. The reading section includes 19 subtests of word identification skills, plus subtests in other reading areas. This test is designed for grades K to 6. When students score at or above grade level, this means they should be able to perform successfully at the next level. Time needed for testing varies according to the number of subtests administered.

Certain criterion-referenced tests are tests of specific skills. One example which is primarily *group-administered* is the Cooper-

McGuire Diagnostic Word-Analysis Test. This test has a section on readiness for word analysis plus 17 subtests of phonic analysis and 10 subtests of structural analysis. Two other tests of this type which are group-administered are the Doren Diagnostic Reading Test of Word Recognition Skills and the Group Phonics Analysis test.

Criterion-referenced tests of specific skills that are *individually administered* are the Decoding Inventory and the Sipay Word Analysis Tests. The Sipay Word Analysis Tests, commonly called the SWAT, has 17 subtests to measure word identification skills, each of which requires 10 to 15 minutes to administer. Students respond to all items orally. Teacher materials for each subtest of the SWAT include a "Mini-Manual," a group of test cards, an answer sheet, and a report form for recording the student's correct and incorrect answers.

Bench Mark Measures is a criterion-referenced test of specific skills that has some individually administered and some group-administered parts. It tests general phonic knowledge and has some useful sections; one unfortunate feature, however, is that certain portions require producing sounds in non-sense words, which, as one reviewer says, means "the student is asked to exemplify his knowledge of phonetics in reading words that he cannot possibly have any understanding of" (Carroll, 1985, p. 1981).

In conclusion, then, there are some problems with published diagnostic tests of word identification strategies; however, they can be helpful if used judiciously.

Informal Measures

Many teachers find developing their own test of word identification strategies preferable to using published tests. To develop a teacher-made test for this purpose:

1. list the areas to be assessed within the broader areas of phonic analysis, structural analysis, and use of context clues;

2. carefully consider the problems of published diagnostic tests to avoid those faults in your own teacher-made instrument;
3. examine published tests for appropriate ways of assessing various strategies you can adapt and improve upon in your test;
4. carefully develop items for each subarea within your test;
5. divide the test into logical sections so you have the choice of administering the entire test or only selected sections if that is more appropriate;
6. prepare typed copies of the test for your pupils, a typed set of directions for the teacher for consistency in administration, and duplicate copies of pupil record sheets for indicating students' responses to each item;
7. be prepared to revise and improve sections if you note inadequacies in the original version when you actually administer and interpret the test.

Since few published diagnostic tests include an adequate assessment of use of context clues, even the teacher who chooses to use published tests to assess phonic analysis and structural analysis knowledge may wish to prepare a test of this most important word identification strategy.[1] There are two major ways to assess a student's use of context clues. The first procedure requires the teacher to select several paragraphs or one longer passage for all reading levels. (Since students must be tested at their instructional levels, develop test passages for all levels so you have a passage suitable for any student you test.) Leave the first sentence of the passage intact; thereafter, periodically omit words that can be determined from the context of the passage. (Some words can be identified from the syntactic context of material; sentence structure clues help the reader identify unknown words. Other words are identified from semantic clues; information related to meaning that is provided in the passage is used in conjunction with information in a reader's background knowledge to provide clues to the unknown word.) Finally, when omitting words, retain the first letter (or letters, if the word begins with a consonant blend or consonant digraph) since the most efficient strategy to employ when using context clues is to combine the graphic clue provided by the first letter(s) of the unknown word with context to aid identification. Figure 7–3 is a brief example of a fourth-grade level test passage using this first procedure for assessing use of context clues.

A second procedure for assessing use of context clues has been described by Timian and Santeusanio (1974). First, compile a list of words believed to be in the student's oral language vocabulary, but not in the student's reading sight vocabulary. In the first session, test the student's sight recognition of these words when they are presented in isolation; discard those words the student is able to recognize at sight. Following the first test session, write sentences using the words the student did not recognize in isolation, being certain that the other words in each sentence (the context) do indeed provide clues to the unknown word; for example, if the student does not know the word *audience,* you might write the following sentence.

Henry thought he'd like being in the school play, but he got scared when he stepped out on the stage and saw how many people were in the audience.

In the second session have the student read each sentence to determine if context can be used to identify each word that was unknown when presented in isolation; if the student does not readily pronounce the word with use

---

[1]The Biemiller Test of Reading Processes includes one subtest that assesses how quickly a student uses context to facilitate word identification. The Decoding Inventory also has a test of use of context clues.

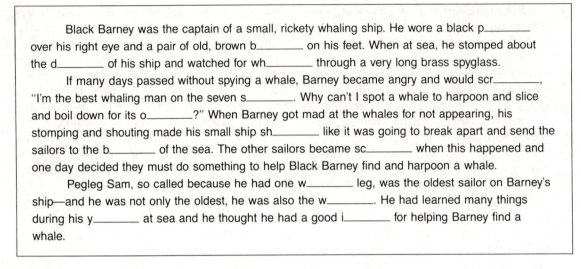

Figure 7–3
A sample text passage for assessing use of context clues

of the available context, say "Use the other words in the sentence to decide what it is."

Tests, whether published or teacher-made, provide a guide for instructional programs designed to eliminate weaknesses in word identification strategies. Although there are no perfect tests, it is more efficient to administer tests and use the results of these for initial program planning then to rely exclusively on incidental information. Ongoing daily observations are important for verifying and extending these test findings. At times students perform better during instruction than they did during assessment. In addition, weaknesses not identified through administration of diagnostic tests may become evident as daily instruction progresses. In these cases, modifications of original instructional goals are necessary.

USING THE READING MISCUE INVENTORY

The Reading Miscue Inventory, commonly called the RMI, is an important assessment in-strument for students with reading problems. The RMI provides information about two basic areas. It helps the teacher determine if a student's reading miscues prevent her from obtaining meaning from a passage, and it helps the teacher decide if a student is using knowledge of language and the world as an aid in reading. The RMI assessment procedures are based on the following ideas:

1. The purpose of reading is to gain meaning.
2. Some miscues are "better" than others. Compare, for example, these two student responses to the same sentence.

Ralph ran *wiggling* wildly about the room trying to catch his pet mouse before his mother found it was loose.

Ralph ran *madly* wildly about the room trying to catch his pet mouse before his mother found it was loose.

The miscue in the second sentence does not change the essential meaning of the sentence as the first one does, and therefore, is considered a better miscue.

3. Reading is not an exact process. Even proficient readers change words, omit words, and insert words, with no change in the author's intended meaning.

4. Teachers should not treat all miscues the same way. Miscues should be evaluated according to how much they change meaning; that is, an analysis of student's reading performance should be qualitative as well as quantitative.

The RMI is different from an IRI in several ways. No reading level is obtained from an RMI, but rather, it provides information about strengths and weaknesses in use of specific reading strategies. During administration of an RMI, the student reads a complete selection, that is, a whole story or a complete selection of informational material. In comparison to an IRI, which uses relatively short passages, the RMI presents more opportunities for the teacher to see how a student interacts with text when more language and meaning clues are available. Additionally, in contrast to an IRI, an RMI bases analysis on oral reading performance only.

Although modifications of the basic RMI procedures are sometimes used, the procedure described here is based on the original assessment instrument, the Reading Miscue Inventory developed by Goodman and Burke (1972). Seven items are needed to administer this test: a test manual, a book titled *Readings for Taping,* a worksheet copy of a story that you have selected for the student to read from *Readings for Taping,* a Coding Sheet, a Profile Sheet, a tape recorder, and a blank tape.

To administer the RMI the teacher first selects a story from *Readings for Taping* that is difficult enough so the student will make at least 25 miscues but not so difficult that it cannot be handled at all. Next, the student reads the story into the tape recorder, and then, while the tape recorder is still running, retells

what has been read. Later, the teacher asks additional questions, being careful not to cue answers that do not reflect actual comprehension and recall. A retelling outline is provided at the end of the worksheet copy of the story for the teacher to use in guiding the retelling. Later, when the student is not present, the teacher listens to the tape and marks the student's miscues on the worksheet copy of the story and determines the student's retelling score. Then the teacher codes 25 of the student's miscues on the Coding Sheet and transfers a summary of the information on the Coding Sheet to the Profile Sheet. Finally, the teacher plans instruction based on an analysis of the student's performance. Clear and specific directions for marking and coding miscues, for determining a retelling score, and for all other necessary procedures are found in the test manual. (See the sample Coding Sheet in Figure 7–4.) Instead of using the stories available in *Readings for Taping,* teachers may choose a story or informational selection from another source. However, when doing so, they must also prepare their own worksheet copy of the selection and their own retelling outline; directions for preparing these materials appear in the test manual. No stories available in the *Readings for Taping* book are suitable for students reading below first reader level or above eighth-grade level. It takes approximately 15 minutes to administer the RMI and about 1 hour to analyze it.

ASSESSING KNOWLEDGE OF WORD MEANINGS

Knowledge of the meanings of words is one indication of the background knowledge a student can use to understand reading material. As such, vocabulary knowledge is an important aspect of comprehension. Although most group survey standardized tests administered during assessment for identification contain subsections on meaning vocabulary, these subsections do not provide an adequate meas-

READING MISCUE INVENTORY CODING SHEET

Column headers (rotated):
GRAMMATICAL RELATIONSHIPS — Overcorrection, Weakness, Partial Strength, Strength
COMPREHENSION — Loss, Partial Loss, No Loss
9 MEANING CHANGE
8 SEMANTIC ACCEPTABILITY
7 GRAMMATICAL ACCEPTABILITY
6 CORRECTION
5 GRAMMATICAL FUNCTION
4 SOUND SIMILARITY
3 GRAPHIC SIMILARITY
2 INTONATION
1 DIALECT
Text — Reader — Miscue Number

142

Figure 7–4

Example of a completed reading miscue inventory coding sheet. (*Source:* From *Reading Miscue Inventory Manual* [pp. 82–83] by Y. Goodman and C. L. Burke, 1982, New York: Richard C. Owen. Reprinted by permission.)

ure of knowledge of word meanings for diagnostic purposes for several reasons. First, because time limits are used, a teacher cannot always determine whether a student who scores poorly lacks vocabulary knowledge or is merely reading slowly and methodically. In addition, because of poor sight vocabulary knowledge or inadequate word identification strategies, the student may not be able to identify many words in written form even though she knows their meanings when she hears them spoken. Then, too, most of these tests measure only common meanings of words, and ignore knowledge of multiple meanings of the same word. Finally, vocabulary items tested represent only a very small sample of words.

Even though a student's performance on these tests is not definitive enough for diagnostic purposes, it can provide clues about the necessity of administering a diagnostic test of knowledge of word meanings. If the student has performed poorly on a group, standardized survey test, the teacher may wish to read words from this test to the student and informally check her knowledge of their meanings. If under these conditions the student performs well, the original poor performance probably has a different basis (for example, lack of adequate word identification strategies, or inability to work well when speed is required). However, if the student performs poorly during this oral probe, more in-depth assessment is advisable.

Some published diagnostic tests of specific skills are available for assessing knowledge of word meanings. One is the Test of Reading Comprehension (TORC). This test is suitable for use with grades 2 through 12 and tests vocabulary related to common concepts, vocabulary related to several content areas (science, social studies, and math), and vocabulary necessary for reading directions for school work. The Nelson Reading Skills Test assesses some of the vocabulary words in its

three levels in context; this is an unusual and positive feature for a standardized test.

Teacher-made tests of knowledge of word meanings can also be devised. To do so, the teachers may compile a file of test forms for each grade level. To develop such a file, the first step is deciding on the content for every level. The general content of word meaning tests should involve assessment of:

1. knowledge of synonyms;
2. use of precision when encountering words with similar meanings (for example, one man *saved* money but another *hoarded* it —what is the difference?); and
3. knowledge of multiple meanings of words (Johnson and Pearson, 1978).

Decisions about the specific content involves selecting the words to be tested. Obviously you cannot devise a test of all possible words. A sample of words may be obtained from one or more of the following sources:

1. A book titled *The Living Word Vocabulary* (Dale & O'Rourke, 1976) that provides a listing of about 44,000 words with a grade level specified for each indicating the level at which the meaning of that word is known by most students.
2. Word lists from basal readers beginning at grade 4. (Words introduced in basal readers prior to grade 4 are generally selected because they are words that are in the oral language meaning vocabularies of most children; the task in these early years is one of getting students to recognize these known words in printed form. Beginning at grade 4, an additional objective is to introduce words for which meanings must also be learned.)
3. Lists of frequently occurring affixes and roots. One such source is Stauffer's (1969) list of the 15 most frequently occurring prefixes in the English language.
4. Lists of content area words, such as the

Carroll, Davies, Richman list for grades 3 through 9 (Carroll, Davies, & Richman, 1971).

The next step is to choose a method of assessing the words. Kelley and Krey (p. 103 cited in Farr, 1969, p. 34) suggested one or more of the following methods:

1. Unaided recall
   A. Checking for familiarity
   B. Using words in a sentence
   C. Explaining the meaning
   D. Giving a synonym
   E. Giving an opposite
2. Aided recall
   A. Recall aided by recognition
      1. Matching tests
      2. Classification tests
      3. Multiple-choice tests
         a. Choosing the opposite
         b. Choosing the best synonym
         c. Choosing the best definition
         d. Choosing the best use in sentences
      4. Same-opposite tests
      5. Same-opposite-neither tests
      6. Same-different tests
   B. Recall aided by association
      1. Completion tests
      2. Analogy tests
   C. Recall aided by recognition and association
      1. Multiple-choice completion tests
      2. Multiple-choice substitution tests

Published or teacher-made tests should be supplemented with observations during daily work to determine a student's need for remediation in the area of meaning vocabulary.

CONCLUDING STATEMENT

This chapter has discussed several procedures for determining a student's specific strengths and weaknesses in reading. Some of these involve using published tests and others teacher-constructed instruments. In either case, assessment procedures should be evaluated with the checklist found in Figure 7–5 before use. This checklist should also be kept in mind as you read about additional diagnostic procedures in the next chapter.

	Yes	No

1. Is the test valid?
2. Is the test reliable?
3. Are all important areas covered?
4. Does the test do more than merely sample a few items within a skill or knowledge area?
5. Does the test refrain from assessing areas that research has shown to be unimportant to reading achievement?
6. Does the test or each subtest within the test assess what it purports to test?
7. If information is needed to plan programs for moderately or severely disabled readers, is the test individually administered?
8. As much as is possible, is the required performance on the test like the performance required during the real act of reading?
9. Does the test provide detailed, comprehensive information about a student's knowledge and skills rather than merely a ballpark notion of needs?

Figure 7–5
A checklist of adequacy for diagnostic tests

8

Assessment for Identifying Specific Strengths and Weaknesses in Reading: Part II

This chapter further describes assessment procedures for determining specific strengths and weaknesses in reading.

ASSESSING COMPREHENSION

Comprehension assessment can be conducted by use of either conventional tests or teacher-constructed instruments and procedures. Each approach has advantages and disadvantages.

Using Conventional Tests

Conventional tests typically used are survey tests, group-administered diagnostic tests, individually administered diagnostic tests, IRIs, and the RMI.

The comprehension section of the standardized group survey test employed during assessment for identification is often used to determine whether a student's poor reading performance results from comprehension difficulties. These tests are designed to measure comprehension after silent reading—the type required in most "real-life" reading tasks.

Sometimes the group survey tests have been criticized because they are timed; some researchers question whether they measure speed of comprehension rather than power of comprehension. However, if other diagnostic tests have indicated that the student has no difficulty with word recognition and word identification strategies, then the time limits of these tests are sufficient; if the student cannot complete the comprehension section, this indicates comprehension difficulty. If a student has poor word recognition and identification skills, after completion of the group survey test an alternate form of the same test at the same level can be employed for diagnostic purposes. This time the student is asked to orally read the test and answer the questions. The teacher can then determine whether poor performance results from word recognition and identification difficulties, from comprehension problems, or from both. Additional insights into the student's thinking process and background knowledge can be obtained if students are asked *how* they arrived at each correct and incorrect answer.

Another criticism of group survey tests is that they do not measure retention. Because during these tests students can refer to a relevant passage to find an answer, the tests are said to measure immediate recall. Retention of comprehended material is important, especially in schoolwork, and the ideal test probably would include some sections where students could refer to a passage and some where they could not. Yet Vernon's (1962) study showed that performance on test passages where students *can* look back to find answers more accurately measures reading achievement.

Other criticisms of group survey tests for determining comprehension ability are:

1. although they claim to measure higher-level as well as literal comprehension, examination of some items on some tests indicates they do not;
2. because answers are often written in a multiple-choice format, this allows for guessing, and may provide clues that are not available when students must resort to unaided recall;
3. most measure comprehension of only short selections of material (for example, single paragraphs), which is not representative of most real reading tasks.

Standardized group survey tests are only the beginning point in diagnosis since the results provide no more than an overall measure of understanding.

Some published group-administered diagnostic tests are available for assessing comprehension. Most of these are subtests in larger *test batteries*. Some test batteries that include comprehension subtests are the Sequential Tests of Educational Progress, the Basic Skills Assessment test, and the Stanford Diagnostic Reading Test. Comprehension subtests of test batteries should be examined before being selected to determine if they measure what they say they do. For example, the "comprehension" subtest of the Botel Reading Inventory tests only a student's ability to recognize word opposites. An example of a group-administered diagnostic *test of specific skills* that does assess comprehension is the Test of Reading Comprehension (TORC) for grades 2–12. In addition to paragraph comprehension, the TORC also includes subsections on sequencing sentences and determining whether sentences are similar although syntactically different. Because standardized, group-administered diagnostic tests are usually timed and read silently, the follow-up procedure of having students orally reread the test or an alternate form of it, as suggested earlier, can provide more specific diagnostic information.

Some individually administered diagnostic test batteries that include subtests of comprehension are the Brigance Diagnostic Inventory of Basic Skills, the Diagnostic Reading Scales, the Basic Achievement Skills Individual Screener, the Durrell Analysis of Reading Difficulty, and the Diagnostic Achievement Battery.

An advantage of individually administered tests is that students can be observed while they are responding. Some of these tests assess comprehension only after silent reading, some only after oral, but some assess after both. However, most such tests specify an oral response to specific questions or a retelling of the passage, rather than a written response. This method is advantageous when assessing students with poor academic skills. Remember, however, that subtests of test batteries do a better job of assessing word identification strategies than of assessing comprehension. The comprehension subtests often contain flaws that make them less than useful unless the teacher makes adaptations. In addition, basic information on norming, reliability, and validity should be obtained by checking the test's technical manual to assure that the test is suitable for the intended purpose and group. For example, the validity of the Basic Achievement Skills Individual Screener has been questioned for students beyond 8th grade (Conley, 1986), although the test may be useful for younger children. The questions found in Figure 7–5 (p. 144) for critiquing diagnostic tests should also be used before selecting a test for reading comprehension.

The IRI, usually administered to verify students' general reading levels, also provides some information about comprehension ability, if the teacher goes beyond merely counting the number of correct and incorrect responses and looks at the types of questions with which a student had difficulty. An IRI also enables the teacher to analyze the degree to which comprehension is affected by word recognition and word identification difficulties. In addition, the teacher can compare comprehension levels after oral versus silent reading. Often, assessment is conducted following oral reading only, because some authorities believe that oral reading behaviors accurately reflect how students process words during silent reading. If comprehension levels differ after oral versus silent reading, however, this belief may not hold true for a given student. If a student's comprehension is better after oral reading, for example, this result may mean one of several things. Students with lower than average IQs often comprehend better after oral reading, perhaps because oral responses keep the student's attention focused on the material. This characteristic is also observed in some severely disabled readers as well as in some students with specific learning disorders who otherwise may have average or above average intelligence. The need to hear what they are reading is also typical of average beginning readers, but this need usually disappears with experience.

If comprehension is better after silent reading, this finding may mean that during oral reading the student is focusing on word pronunciation rather than meaning. If comprehension after both oral and silent reading is substantially lower than the student's word identification performance on the IRI, remediation is almost certainly needed. Another advantage in using an IRI to assess comprehension is that the test is untimed. The teacher can thus feel confident that power of comprehension is being assessed rather than speed of comprehension.

The results of a Reading Miscue Inventory (RMI) also help to assess comprehension. Because complete selections (whole stories, whole articles, and so forth) are read, the RMI enables the teacher to measure student comprehension of longer passages than those found in survey tests, diagnostic tests, or IRIs. In addition, the analysis of individual miscues provides information about the degree to which students use sentence structure and background knowledge to gain meaning, and the degree to which oral miscues may affect comprehension of the material. This analysis also provides a look at student self-correction.

Use of self-correction is a metacognitive skill. *Metacognitive skills* are skills readers use to monitor their own progress through the reading task. This self-monitoring is necessary for good comprehension. Analysis of students' self-corrections provides information about the intent to read for understanding. It also indicates what clues they are using to comprehend material.

Let's suppose, for example, that a student initially reads:

pleasant

Long ago, a peasant boy who lived with his family in a poor hut went sullenly every day to work in the king's fields.

Suppose the student then self-corrects the word *peasant* immediately after reading the word *sullenly.* This self-correction may be prompted because the word *sullenly* seems to conflict with the word *pleasant.* In this case the student is using a meaning clue at the word level as a prompt to re-examine the original response to the word *peasant*. On the other hand, suppose the student self-corrects after reading the whole sentence. In this case, background information may have been used to cue the more appropriate response—for example, familiarity with other stories or history material may cause the student to think that it would be logical to find a *peasant* boy in a poor hut working in the fields of a king. An analysis of many self-corrections furnishes some information about cues a student does or does not use, and this review is helpful in planning instruction. A disadvantage to the use of self-correction data in assessing comprehension strategies is that some students mentally self-correct a miscue but do not do so orally. Performance during the retelling of a *story selection* for the RMI demonstrates the student's proficiency in literal recall of characters and events, understanding of character development, grasp of overall plot of the selection, and the ability to infer a theme. Performance during retelling of an *informational selection* assesses recall of specific details, ability to form generalizations based on specific facts in the text, and ability to infer major concepts abstracted from the text. The RMI supplies a measure of the degree to which a reader uses three cue systems to comprehend material: graphophonic, syntactic, and semantic. There are, however, other cue systems that a reader might use to comprehend better. Johnston (1983) suggests that test procedures are needed to determine whether a reader is using the following types to vary his comprehension strategies: cues about the type of text (e.g., informational as opposed to narrative); cues about the task demands (e.g., reading for pleasure in contrast to reading to learn); and cues about the content area of the material and what the reader already knows about the topic. Different comprehension strategies may be needed to understand material in these

varying contexts. The RMI does not provide a measure of the use of these types of cues.

Developing Teacher-Prepared Instruments and Procedures

Obviously, preparing tests is more time-consuming than using published tests, but has the advantage of allowing the teacher to devise assessment processes that do not contain some of the flaws found in conventional tests. Teachers can improve upon traditional comprehension tests by doing the following:

1. make multiple-choice questions more diagnostically relevant,
2. determine the types of prompts a student needs to comprehend material,
3. design questions that assess higher-level comprehension of many types,
4. use free recall measures followed by probes.

There are two important ways to improve on traditional comprehension tests using multiple-choice questions. One of these is to write multiple-choice questions over story or informational passages so that each alternative answer reflects a certain type of response behavior. For example, in a series of multiple-choice questions one of the incorrect alternatives could always be written so that it reflects an answer for which the inference drawn is too broad or too narrow; another alternative answer could always be written so that it is a literal response to an inference question; and so forth. Because many alternatives of the same type would appear through the series of multiple-choice questions, a pattern of student response strategies should emerge to provide suggestions for future instruction. The second way to strengthen the diagnostic value of multiple-choice questions is to ask students to rate each alternative answer on its probability of correctness rather than having them select *only* the best answer

(Pugh & Brunza, 1975). For example, students could use a rating scale of 1 through 4, with *1* indicating the answer that is most likely correct and *4* indicating the answer that is least likely correct. Here is an example of a question in which both multiple-choice procedures have been used:

The reason the fairy let Pinocchio cry about his nose was that

4 A. The fairy let Pinocchio cry for an hour about his nose.

2 B. She didn't notice he was crying because she was thinking about his lies.

1 C. She wanted to teach him a lesson.

3 D. She liked to hear people cry.

Note that alternative *A* is simply a literal statement taken directly from the test. It is somewhat related to the question but does not answer it. A student who consistently selects an alternative of this type as the most probable correct response needs a different type of instruction than does the student who usually chooses alternatives like *D*. Alternative *D* was written so that its choice indicates a student who is not integrating important text information with background information in order to draw an inference. Examination of the ratings a student gives to each alternative allows the teacher to note the thinking processes and the test-taking skills a student employs. This test helps determine why students miss answers, and whether they get them right for the right reason. By thus analyzing the thinking and test-taking strategies a student uses, the teacher can better plan instruction.

Teachers may want to know the types of prompts a student needs in order to correctly answer comprehension questions. To test for this, a series of selections is chosen for which

questions are written in a multiple-choice format. Students are asked to read some selections orally and others silently. After reading, they orally read the alternative answers and attempt to select the correct one. On those passages where an incorrect answer is selected, the teacher asks questions and provides prompts as would be done in an instructional situation (until a correct response is obtained). The student's responses and the teacher's questions and prompts are tape-recorded for later analysis. The analysis is then used to determine areas of weakness in background knowledge or thinking strategies and the type of prompts needed to enable the student to figure out the correct answer.

Let's look at an example of this technique. The student is asked to read the passage and then to choose the most appropriate response to the multiple-choice item.

In 1849 when gold was discovered in California, many men in other parts of the country left their jobs and families to travel there. The journey to California was often long and hard, but they thought it was worth it. They believed they would strike it rich once they reached California. When these men, called *forty-niners,* arrived in California one of the first things they did was buy supplies needed for mining gold. The most important of these was a mining pan. The miners would take this pan when they went out to try their luck at finding gold in stream beds. They would put water from the stream and sand from the stream bed into the mining pan and shake it. Gold can be found in this way because it is heavier than sand and settles to the bottom of the pan while the sand still floats in the water. If the miners did find gold it was usually in the form of fine particles called *gold dust,* but sometimes they found a larger piece that was called a *nugget*. Many miners stayed in California for years and years before returning to their families. Some of these determined men did find gold, but only a few found enough to become very rich.

What is the main point of this paragraph?

A. It is written to tell you some things about the forty-niners.

B. It is written to tell you why gold settles to the bottom of a pan.

C. It is written to tell you the year gold was discovered in California.

D. It is written to tell you two forms in which gold can be found.

Here is a typescript of a student's responses after reading this passage and a teacher's prompts and questions.

STUDENT: I think the answer's *B*.

TEACHER: Why do you think so?

STUDENT: It says it in the story.

TEACHER: It does say that, but I want you to read the question to me again.

STUDENT: "What is the main point of this paragraph?"

TEACHER: When you read the question the first time, did you notice the word *main*?

STUDENT: (Pause) Not really.

TEACHER: *Main* is a key word in the question. Often when you have to answer questions about what you've read, there's a key word that helps you get the correct answer. Did you know that, Tommy?

STUDENT: (Laughter) No.

TEACHER: In this question *main* is the key word. Do you know what the question is asking you when it asks for the *main* point?

STUDENT: (Pause) Important?

TEACHER: Right. *Main* can mean important. So what are they asking you to tell if they ask you for the main point?

STUDENT: The important point?

TEACHER: Right! Or another way to say it is the major point.

STUDENT: But it says that right here about the gold settling.

TEACHER: You're right. It does. That *is* one thing they told you in the passage, but there are many other things the author told you, aren't there?

STUDENT: Yes.

TEACHER: That's just one small point that was made. When the question asks you for the main point it wants you to figure out what the whole thing was about. Or, in other words, you could ask yourself "What was the *main* reason the author wrote this? What was the overall idea he wanted me to learn from this?" What do you think it was?

STUDENT: About those men, I guess, about what they did.

TEACHER: Great! Now you've got it. Okay, read the answers to yourself again. Now which one do you think is right?

STUDENT: None of them say anything about the men.

TEACHER: Well, let's work on each answer together. Maybe I can help you. Read the first answer out loud to me.

STUDENT: "It is written to tell you some things about the forty-niners."

TEACHER: Do you understand that answer, Tommy?

STUDENT: I guess so.

TEACHER: Do you remember the paragraph saying anything about the forty-niners?

STUDENT: (Pause) Yes . . .

TEACHER: Well, let's find the part in the paragraph that mentions the forty-niners and you read it out loud to me.

STUDENT: "When these men, called forty-niners, arrived in California one of the first things they did was buy supplies needed for mining gold."

TEACHER: What does the term *forty-niners* mean in that sentence?

STUDENT: (Long pause) The men!

TEACHER: Right! When you read the sentence the first time, did you realize the sentence was telling you the men were called forty-niners?

STUDENT: No.

TEACHER: What did you think it meant when it said, ". . . these men, called forty-niners, . . ."?

STUDENT: They called it. They said it.

TEACHER: You mean you thought the men called something out? They called out, "Forty-niners"?

STUDENT: Yeah.

TEACHER: Okay, I tell you what, let me write a sentence for you that's almost like that, but is about something you're more familiar with. Watch what I write. (Teacher writes sentence on paper.) Read that to me.

STUDENT: (Reads sentence teacher just wrote.) "Our school football team, called the Tigers, is the best team in town."

TEACHER: What does *called* mean in this sentence?

STUDENT: (Rereads sentence silently.) Named!

TEACHER: Right! Look back at the sentence about forty-niners. Could *called* mean the same thing there?

STUDENT: (Reads sentence silently.) Yeah. It does.

TEACHER: Okay, let's look at answer *A* again. What do you think? Is it the right or wrong answer?

STUDENT: (Reads alternative *A* silently.) Yeah. It's the right one 'cause the story's about the men.

TEACHER: It seems to me you're right, but let's look at the other answers just to be sure there's not a better one. We've already decided *B* is not correct. Read *C* out loud to me.

STUDENT: "It is written to tell you the year gold was discovered in California."

TEACHER: What do you think? Right or wrong?

STUDENT: Wrong, 'cause . . . (Long pause)

TEACHER: Why?

STUDENT: Well, it's just a small point.

TEACHER: Super. It *does* tell when gold was discovered, doesn't it? But you're right. It's not the overall or major idea the author wanted you to learn about in this paragraph. What about *D*? Read that one to me.

STUDENT: "It is written to tell you two forms in which gold is found."

TEACHER: What do you think?

STUDENT: It tells you those and I think that's important, but it tells more than that and it's mostly about the men and what they did. (Rereads alternative *D* silently.) So *D* isn't the right answer.

TEACHER: Excellent. And what happened to them? What did it say happened to the men in the end?

STUDENT: Some got rich and some didn't.

TEACHER: Right. Did more of them get rich or more not get rich?

STUDENT: (Has to reread last sentence of passage.) More didn't.

TEACHER: Super. Okay, now read this next passage silently and when you get done I'll ask you to answer a question about it.

When a teacher uses questions and prompts in this fashion it is possible to learn much about the students: their approaches to the comprehension task, their test-taking skills, the background knowledge they do or do not possess, the types of prompting necessary to help them understand material, their skills in dealing with written language structures, their abilities to generalize from familiar knowledge to the unfamiliar, and how readily they pick up on instructional cues provided by the teacher. In short, the teacher can determine rather specifically what is preventing comprehension.

What is a solution to the failure of many published tests to measure higher-level thinking processes involved in comprehension, or at best to measure only a limited number of them? Spache (1981) suggests that teachers develop a series of questions based on the question categories proposed by Sanders (1966) and apply these to a series of graded passages. Sanders' categories were derived from Bloom's *Taxonomy of Educational Objectives* (1956, p. 3) and are listed here.

1. *Memory:* Recognizing and recalling information directly stated in the passage
2. *Translation:* Paraphrasing ideas

3. *Interpretation:* Seeing relationships among facts or generalizations
4. *Application:* Solving a problem that requires the use of facts or generalizations
5. *Analysis:* Recognizing and applying logic to a problem; analyzing an example of reasoning
6. *Synthesis:* Using original, creative thinking to solve a problem
7. *Evaluation:* Making judgments

Using Sanders' question categories extends the measurement of comprehension beyond responses to literal questions.

Use of free recalls, sometimes called *retelling,* is another method for assessing comprehension. To use this method, the teacher prepares an outline of important information about a selection. This outline is used by the teacher, not by the students. After stu-

Having students simply retell what they have read can measure comprehension, especially if the retelling is followed by probes.

dents have read the selection, they are simply asked to retell what has just been read. When asking for a free recall, the teacher should carefully specify the task demand, that is, students should be asked to tell everything remembered. Failure to do this often results in superficial retellings during which students do not relate all the information gained. To further minimize the problem of superficial retelling, the teacher can use the retelling outline to follow up a student's retelling by asking about material neglected by the student. These follow-up questions are called *probes.* The student's free recall and answers to the probes are tape-recorded. Later, when the student is not present the retelling outline is used to analyze the student's taped performance. There are several advantages to using free recall measures. They help the teacher determine whether students have noted important information in a selection, whether they can reproduce it in a manner that makes sense, and whether their background knowledge had an effect on the way they interpret the material.

These procedures also provide some information about a student's short-term retention. In addition, if there is a delay between the time when students read some selections and the time when they are asked to retell, a measure of long-term retention can also be obtained. Another advantage is that the teacher's preparation is minimal.

One disadvantage is that sometimes students who do understand the material they have read nevertheless have difficulty adequately retelling the selection: they don't know where to begin or what sequence to follow. This results in a disorganized retelling in which important information is overlooked, conveying the false impression that the student did not comprehend or recall the material. This problem usually can be overcome with practice and some training in retelling. Production problems can also result if students are asked to write their responses during a free recall. Although they may understand the material, they may have trouble producing the information in written form. When assessing students with poor academic skills, asking for oral responses is preferable.

A second disadvantage is that relying on free recalls without probes often does not enable assessment of higher-level comprehension. Students tend to report only facts and information directly stated in the selection. For example, it would be highly unusual for students during their retellings to say, "Oh, by the way, the theme of this story is _____," or, "Incidentally, an important generalization I drew from the information in this article is that _____." Therefore, using probes to follow up student retellings is important so that higher-level comprehension can be assessed. Another problem is that greater demand on memory is required of the student during free recall than with multiple-choice questions, which provide some clues for remembering the material. Because of this problem, students should always be told prior to reading a selection that they will be asked to retell it afterward. Four published tests that employ free recalls are The Reading Miscue Inventory (RMI), the Basic Reading Inventory, the Bader Reading and Language Inventory, and the Durrell Analysis of Reading Difficulty. However, it is suggested here that teachers extend free recall procedures in their teacher-devised comprehension assessment programs to:

1. include assessment after silent reading, as well as after oral reading as done on the RMI;
2. assess after reading *any* selection—not only after those selections for which oral reading miscues have been analyzed; and
3. include methods for measuring long-term retention as well as short-term recall.

It also is useful to try using free recalls, instead of asking specific questions after students have read any selection.

As with other areas, the best measure of a student's comprehension is gained through a combination of assessments. Johnston (1983) says

> The object of much past development of reading comprehension assessment has been a single test which will tell us all we want to know. It is my contention that pursuing this objective in the current manner is futile, given the complexity of the reading task and the number of variables to be assessed and/or taken into account. I believe that a potentially more reasonable approach would be to refine and use the variety of approaches to measurement which we have available already, in the light of our knowledge of the skills and abilities involved in each, though we might want to add some supplementary approaches. By appropriately selecting combinations of these measures, we may gain a clearer picture of what and how a reader comprehends under a given set of circumstances. (p. 54)

ASSESSING LISTENING COMPREHENSION

A measure of students' comprehension after they have listened to material read to them can be used with nonreaders or those who read so poorly that they cannot read connected material of a length sufficient to provide meaningful assessment. A measure of listening comprehension tells us the level of material students could understand if they could read the material themselves.

Assessing listening comprehension is quite simple. The teacher reads a series of graded passages to each student, beginning with the easiest. Questions are asked upon completion of each passage and the process continues until the students are able to answer so few questions that it is evident that their frustration levels have been reached. Graded passages in an IRI may be used for this purpose, and the scoring criteria employed for IRIs to determine frustration level based on comprehension may be used. Other published tests that include subtests for listening comprehension are the Basic Reading Inventory (2nd edition), Durrell Analysis of Reading Difficulty, the Diagnostic Achievement Battery, the Stanford Achievement Test: Listening Comprehension Tests, and the Analytical Reading Inventory.

ASSESSING READING RATE

An unusually slow rate of reading or an excessively rapid one can hinder comprehension. If it is suspected that an inappropriate reading rate is compounding a student's reading problems, an assessment of reading rate may be included in the diagnostic procedures.

Beginning at the fourth-grade level many group survey tests include a test of reading rate along with the usual vocabulary and comprehension subtests. Some IRIs also contain a rate measurement, such as the Informal Reading Assessment test and the Houghton Mifflin Pupil Placement Test. These tests require students to answer comprehension questions after reading passages so that rate of comprehension is determined. Checking comprehension is important since any measure of rate is useless without information on whether students understand what they read at that rate. Rapid word recognition is not helpful if the student does not comprehend the information.

Informal tests of reading rate also may be used. To do this the teacher asks the student to silently read a story or informational selection of appropriate instructional level. At the end of a specified time—for example, 5 minutes—the teacher calls "stop" and the student places a slash mark after the last word read. Rate (words per minute) is determined by dividing the total number of words read by the number of minutes:

$$\text{Number of minutes} \begin{array}{|c} \text{Words per minute} \\ \hline \text{Total Number of words read} \end{array}$$

Comprehension should also be checked.

Because good reading requires that students vary their rates of reading according to the material and purpose, informal rate assessments should be conducted with different types of material, and when giving readers different purposes for reading. For example, 5-minute rate samples could be taken when the student is asked to read narrative material, read various selections from content area materials such as history or science texts, skim an article to determine its overall purpose, or read to answer several factual questions.

ASSESSING ATTITUDES AND INTERESTS

Conducting a brief assessment of students' attitudes about reading and their interests in general can help in planning instruction.

Measuring Attitudes toward Reading

An important principle for helping students increase their reading proficiency is to have them engage in a great deal of reading. Teachers should schedule time to include this critical component in their programs. Students who do additional reading outside of class usually improve in reading performance more rapidly than those who do not. But some poor readers do not like to read and will not voluntarily do so on their own time. Measuring attitudes toward reading helps to identify when to act to change attitudes toward reading.

Several attitude scales are available. The Estes Attitude Scale (Estes, 1971), which has been validated for students in grades 3 through 12, employs a format in which students rank a list of statements from A to E to indicate attitudes ranging from "strongly agree" to "strongly disagree" about each statement. (See Figure 8–1.)

A = Strongly agree   C = Undecided   E = Strongly disagree
B = Agree   D = Disagree

1. Reading is for learning but not for enjoyment.
2. Money spent on books is well-spent.
3. There is nothing to be gained from reading books.
4. Books are a bore.
5. Reading is a good way to spend spare time.
6. Sharing books in class is a waste of time.
7. Reading turns me on.
8. Reading is only for grade grubbers.
9. Books aren't usually good enough to finish.
10. Reading is rewarding to me.
11. Reading becomes boring after about an hour.
12. Most books are too long and dull.
13. Free reading doesn't teach anything.
14. There should be more time for free reading during the school day.
15. There are many books which I hope to read.
16. Books should not be read except for class requirements.
17. Reading is something I can do without.
18. A certain amount of summer vacation should be set aside for reading.
19. Books make good presents.
20. Reading is dull.

Items	Response Values				
---	A	B	C	D	E
The negative items: Nos. 1, 3, 4, 6, 8, 9, 11, 12, 13, 16, 17, 20	1	2	3	4	5
The positive items: Nos. 2, 5, 7, 10, 14, 15, 18, 19	5	4	3	2	1

Figure 8–1
The Estes Attitude Scale. (*Source:*   From "A Scale to Measure Attitudes Toward Reading" by Thomas H. Estes, 1971. *Journal of Reading,* November 1971. Reprinted with permission of Thomas H. Estes and the International Reading Association.)

This scale may be re-administered after a period of remediation to determine if a change in attitudes has occurred. (☺) (☹)

For students reading at third-grade level and below, Johns (1982) suggests that statements be read orally to them and that they mark their responses on an answer sheet by circling the appropriate face
Statements he suggests for use with primary students are

I can read as fast as the good readers.
I like to read.
I like to read long stories.
The books I read in school are too hard.
I need more help in reading.
I worry quite a bit about my reading in school.
I read at home.
I would rather read than watch television.
I am a poor reader.
I like my parents to read to me. (p. 5)

These two procedures measure attitudes by having students rank statements. Attitudes can also be measured by direct observation by the teacher. Heathington and Alexander (1978) and Rowell (1972) have presented checklists that may be used in this method.

Measuring General Interests

Knowing areas of student interest can help teachers select material that they will enjoy reading. *Interest inventories* consist of statements for students to complete or questions to answer so that students can express their likes and dislikes. Sample questions for an interest inventory might include

What do you like to do most after school and on the weekends?

What things do you think you do well?

What do you like best in school?

What do you like least in school?

What is your favorite TV program?

Do you have any hobbies?

What do you like to do with your family?

What is your favorite sport?

Are there any kinds of animals you like?

Do you have any pets?

Do you belong to any clubs?

What is your favorite activity during recess?

What do you and your best friend do together?

If you could have anything you wanted for Christmas, what would it be?

If someone granted you three wishes, what would you wish?

Has your family ever taken a vacation? Where did you go?

Have you traveled to any other states? Where?

What do you like most to read about?

What do you like least to read about?

An interest inventory is an excellent way to break the ice between teacher and student.

Questions and responses should be given orally. Using a tape recorder and simulating a radio or TV interview can be fun.

At this point let us assume that initial diagnostic procedures with our hypothetical student, David Adams, have been completed using some of the assessment processes described in Chapters 7 and 8. Examine the additional notations placed on his Diagnostic Information Sheet, illustrated in Figure 8–2.

ASSESSMENT PROCEDURES THAT ARE NOT USEFUL

As has been noted, there are no perfect assessment instruments or procedures. Even the best available have shortcomings. But when employed judiciously and in combination with other measures, most of these do provide helpful information.

However, there are other tests and assessment procedures that, although suggested for reading diagnosis, simply are not useful.

One reason that these tests lack value is that they are based on faulty ideas or theories about reading and the reading process; therefore, their procedures and interpretations are in conflict with research evidence. Another reason is that they are so poorly constructed that they do not provide valid information.

In previous sections of this text, some tests have been discussed that should be avoided. Other tests to avoid are listed in Table 8–1 (p. 160), with reasons for their inadequacies.

MEASURING GROWTH IN SPECIFIC STRATEGIES, KNOWLEDGE, AND SKILLS

Measurement of students' growth in specific strategies, knowledge, and skills may occur at various times after a remedial program has

Diagnostic Information Sheet

Student's Name: David Adams

Grade Level: 4th

Intelligence Quotient:
  1) Name of test   WISC-R

  2) IQ   106

  3) MA   9.6

Chronological Age:
  1) Birthdate   February 19, 19———

  2) Age   9.0

Learning Expectancy Level:
  1) Method of determination   Horn Formula: $\dfrac{3MA + 2CA}{5} = 5.0$

  2) LEL   4.4

Entry Level Assessment Results: 2nd grade

Standardized Survey Test:
  1) Name of test   Gates-MacGinitie Reading Tests, Primary B, Form 1

  2) Grade score obtained   3.1

Present Reading Achievement Level (based on standardized test results):   approximately 2.1

Capacity-Achievement Difference: 2.3

Verification of General Reading Levels:
  1) Name of test   Analytical Reading Inventory

  2) Grade score obtained   Frustration level—approximately 2.5
                                                                and above
                                           Instructional level—approximately 2.0
                                           Independent level—approximately 1.0

Figure 8–2
A record sheet of diagnostic information for a hypothetical student

Figure 8–2 (Continued)

Specific Strengths and Weaknesses in Reading Knowledge, Strategies, and Skills:

A. An analysis of strengths and weaknesses determined from David's IRI performance is attached to this Diagnostic Information Sheet, along with implications for instruction.

B. Knowledge of basic sight vocabulary
1. On a contextual inventory, David confused 24 words with similar words
2. On a test of words in isolation, David was unable to pronounce 5 words and confused 37 others with similar words
3. Specific words from both tests which David did not know and those he confused with others are listed on a form attached to the back of this Diagnostic Information Sheet

C. Knowledge and use of word identification strategies
1. An informal assessment confirmed the finding from the IRI that David does not use context clues to identify unknown words, nor does he seem to have any concept of this strategy
2. On a teacher-prepared instrument, strengths in phonetic analysis knowledge were seen for:
   a. consonant sounds
   b. blends (clusters)
   c. consonant digraphs
   d. naming of vowels
   e. long vowel sounds

   Weaknesses were seen for:
   a. short vowel sounds
   b. sounds of *r*-controlled vowels
   c. combinations with silent letters
   d. use of consonant substitution in combination with phonograms
   e. special vowel combinations
3. On a teacher-prepared instrument, strengths in structural analysis were seen for:
   a. use of inflectional endings
   b. reading contractions and recognizing their derived forms

   Weaknesses were seen for:
   a. identifying compound words
   b. identifying words when their spelling was changed before adding an inflectional ending
   c. dividing words into syllables
   d. recognizing prefixes
   e. recognizing suffixes

Specific phonetic and structural analysis information David did and did not know is listed on a form attached to this Diagnostic Information Sheet.

D. Performance on the Reading Miscue Inventory
1. Most of David's miscues resulted from substituting a graphically similar word for the text word. In many of these cases, words were used that did not have the same grammatical function as the text word and, therefore, syntactically and semantically unacceptable sentences were produced.
2. David self-corrected only 2 of the 25 miscues that were analyzed, even though 15 of these resulted in a loss or partial loss of the intended meaning.
3. Percentage scores for comprehension were
   a. No loss—40%
      Partial loss—14%
      Loss—46%

4. Percentage scores for use of grammatical relationships were
   Strength—24%
   Partial strength—30%
   Weaknesses—46%
   Overcorrection—0%
5. Retelling
   a. Score 59
   b. Strengths were seen in recall of characters and remembering events
   c. Weaknesses were seen in stating the overall plot of the story and identifying the theme
   d. He had some difficulty stating information related to character development because of two miscues he made throughout the story, which caused a misinterpretation of important information

E. Comprehension assessment
   In addition to analysis of comprehension performance on the IRI and RMI, two additional assessments were carried out.
   1. David was asked to orally read passages and answer questions from the comprehension subtest of the group standardized survey test that had been used during assessment for identification. This oral assessment showed that the majority of his difficulties on this test stemmed from word recognition and identification problems. Questions were answered incorrectly because he confused words or could not identify many of them. When the teacher told him the correct word, he was usually able to answer the question. On a few questions requiring higher-level comprehension strategies, particularly inference questions, he was unable to respond correctly, even with this assistance. When asked why he responded as he did on these questions, he appeared confused by the task of being asked to draw an inference and was attempting to find the answer directly stated in the passage.
   2. David was asked to read silently a story selected from a basal reader at his instructional level and then retell it. His retelling was followed by probes. This assessment was used to compare his performance with his retelling after oral reading on the RMI. His performance was somewhat better after silent reading, but only slightly.

F. Measures of attitudes and interests
   1. An informal measure of reading attitudes was conducted. David believes he is a poor reader and needs more help in reading, but still says he likes reading and being read to.
   2. An interest inventory revealed that
      a. David loves anything having to do with football—playing it, reading about it, watching it on TV. He hopes to be a football player, like his brother, when he gets to middle school.
      b. He likes animals of all kinds. He owns two cats (Scruffy and Stripes) and two ducks (Sally and Ronald). He says he likes to write stories about his animals and likes to look at books that have pictures of animals from Africa.
      c. If he could have three wishes they would be
         1) to get a 10-speed bike,
         2) for his sister to leave his stuff alone, and
         3) to have muscles.
   3. On Saturday mornings he loves to watch cartoons on TV.
   4. In school he likes math, gym, music, and studying about "people of long ago" best.
   5. His family takes summer vacations and he loves going to the beach and going fishing.

been instituted, including at the end of the program. If formal tests are used for this purpose, care should be taken to select tests that measure the same areas treated in the instructional program. For instance, if stress has been placed on developing higher-level comprehension strategies, a test that predominantly assesses literal-level comprehension would be an inappropriate choice.

More often, informal procedures are used to assess growth in these areas. Teacher-made tests of strategies, knowledge, and skills similar to those used during the initial diagnostic procedures are appropriate and should be combined with judgments made during daily teacher observations.

Finally, an attempt should be made to determine whether students are employing newly gained strategies, skills, and knowledge

in regular classroom settings. There is little value to limiting these to the remedial class only. If newly gained learning has not generalized to other settings and is not serving to bring about overall academic improvement, efforts to assist the student in generalization of these skills should be undertaken by the remedial teacher.

CONCLUDING STATEMENT

Since many diagnostic procedures incorporate at least one published test, a valuable resource for the teacher is the *Mental Measurements Yearbook (MMY)*. This important reference book provides descriptions of reading and other tests currently in print, addresses of the publishers, and critiques of the tests. The

Table 8–1
Some tests and their inadequacies

Published Tests	Inadequacies
Visual Motor Gestalt Test (Bender)	1. Ability to copy designs is not related to reading. 2. Scores do not differentiate learning-disabled, reading-disabled, and average readers. (See studies by Robinson & Schwartz, 1973, and Chang & Chang, 1967).
Motor-free Visual Perception Test	Ability to visually discriminate geometric figures does not transfer to visual discrimination of letters and words.
Developmental Test of Visual-Motor Integration (Beery-Buktenica)	Ability to copy geometric designs is not related to reading. (See also the review of this test in Bush and Waugh, 1982.)
Frostig Developmental Test of Visual Perception	1. Visual perceptual factors measured by this test are not related to reading. 2. Scores do not discriminate between good and poor readers. 3. Inadequate norming procedures 4. Inadequate reliability (See Robinson & Swartz, 1973; Ysseldyke & Algozzine, 1982).
Illinois Test of Psycholinguistic Abilities (ITPA)	1. All subtests but one are uncorrelated with reading ability 2. Scores are correlated with intelligence

	3. Scores do not distinguish between good and poor readers
	4. Norms are based only on middle-class students
	5. There is questionable retest reliability
	6. Students who speak a nonstandard dialect may be penalized. (See a review of this test in Newcomer & Hammell, 1975).
Peabody Individual Achievement Test (PIAT)	1. Reading Recognition subtest involves only letter knowledge and word pronunciation in isolation; therefore, lacks content validity
	2. Reading comprehension subtest consists only of reading *single sentences;* therefore, lacks content validity
	3. Questionable reliability obtained on Reading Recognition subtest; low reliability obtained on Reading Comprehension subtest (See also the review of this test in Mangrum and Strichart, 1984.)
Woodcock Reading Mastery Tests	1. Word Identification subtest only assesses words in isolation
	2. Word Attack subtest employs only nonsense words
	3. Word Comprehension subtest uses word analogies, which is really an inference skill
	4. In the Passage Comprehension subtest, each of the first 24 "passages" consists of only one sentence; the remaining 60 "passages" contain only one or two sentences each
	5. Reliability is questionable for making diagnostic decisions
Test of Nonverbal Auditory Discrimination (pitch, timbre, duration, loudness, rhythm)	Nonverbal auditory discrimination is not related to the auditory discrimination demands of reading

Observational Tests	*Inadequacies*
Tests of visual tracking of a moving object	Ability to visually track a moving object is unrelated to reading ability
Tests of balance	Balance is unrelated to reading ability
Tests of eye-hand coordination	Eye-hand coordination is not related to reading ability.
Tests of left-right discrimination	Ability to distinguish between left and right is unrelated to reading ability
Tests of lateral dominance	Lateral dominance is not related to reading

critiques are especially helpful in selecting tests for a remedial program. Because a test has been published, or because it is widely used, does not necessarily mean it is a good test. The *MMY* lists strengths and, if any, major weaknesses of specific tests. The usefulness and adequacy of many tests were discussed in the chapters of Unit II, but because there is an extensive number of tests from which a teacher may choose, it is impossible to describe them all. The *MMY* can provide information about other tests of concern. This reference book is found in most college and university libraries. All school systems should purchase at least one copy of the most recent edition for use by teachers and administrators. The most recent edition is *The Ninth Mental Measurements Yearbook,* published in 1985 by the Buros Institute of Mental Measurements

and distributed by The University of Nebraska Press. (See Box 8–1 for an example of a typical entry in the *MMY.*)

This institute also publishes a volume called *Tests in Print III (TIP).* Inclusion of a test in *MMY* is based on whether the test is new or has been revised since the last edition (there are 97 reading tests reviewed in the latest edition), while *TIP* includes all tests currently available for purchase. *TIP* does not provide critiques of tests, as does *MMY,* but only a listing and description; therefore, *TIP* cannot be used when questioning whether a test is good or bad—only to determine if it is still published. Another helpful resource produced by the same institute is *Reading Tests and Reviews II,* which contains lists, references, and critiques of reading tests that have appeared in *all* Institute publications since 1938.

Box 8–1
Typical Entry in the *MMY*[1]

Assessment of Reading Growth. Grades 3, 7, 11; 1979–1980; tests of reading comprehension based on National Assessment of Educational Progress; no data on reliability and validity; 3 levels; Level (Age) 9/Grade 3 ('79, 6 pages), Level (Age) 13/Grade 7 ('79, 8 pages), Level (Age) 17/Grade 11 ('80, 8 pages); manual ('80, 4 pages); 1984 price data: $8 per 30 tests and manual; Jamestown Publishers.*

   a) LEVEL 9. Grade 3: 1979; 3 scores: literal comprehension, inferential comprehension, total; 1 form; (50) minutes.

   b) LEVEL 13. Grade 7; 1979; 3 scores: literal comprehension, inferential comprehension, total; 1 form; (50) minutes.

   c) LEVEL 17. Grade 11; 1980; 3 scores: literal comprehension, inferential comprehension, total; 1 form; (42) minutes.

Review of Assessment of Reading Growth by DARRELL L. SABERS, Professor of Educational Psychology, The University of Arizona, Tucson, AZ:

   The Assessment of Reading Growth (ARG) consists of three tests of reading comprehension, each having 18 items on literal comprehension and 18 items on inferential comprehension. Although the manual says the ARG tests may be administered to any student of any age, they are compilations of released items from the 1971 National Assessment of Educational Progress and thus have norms only for ages 9, 13, and 17.

   The ARG items share the advantages and disadvantages of the NAEP items. The major advantage is that the items are clearly written and are relatively free from technical flaws. A positive aspect of ARG, not shared by all reading comprehension tests, is that a student must be able to comprehend the reading passage in order to answer the items.

Two problems associated with the compilation of the released items are evident in the ARG. The first is the inefficiency of having to read an entire passage in order to answer a single item. In the level nine test, a reading passage is repeated four or five times with only one item asked after each presentation. The effect of this repetition on the item norms is not addressed in the manual.

The second problem with these items is the use of "I don't know" as an option with all the choice-type items. Data from NAEP indicate a systematic bias resulting from use of this distractor. There are two examples at level nine where the DK distractor is especially unjustified. One test item (no. 14) asks the student what happened first in a story. Because there is no way for the reader to know which of two options (a or d) is correct, the actual answer should be "don't know." Naturally, the DK distractor is not keyed even though in this case it is correct. Another item (no. 34) asks the student for his/her opinion.

The effort to preserve the integrity of the NAEP items is evident. Even minor changes, such as reordering the options within an item, were not made. As a result, although there are four or five options (in addition to DK) for each of the 104 multiple choice items, option a is keyed only 10 times.

The directions have four obvious flaws. First, there is not a complete congruence between the directions the teacher reads to the students and the directions the students are to read at the same time. Although the differences in these directions are slight, students attending to the directions may be distracted. Students should be reading the same words that the teacher is reading. Second, the directions indicate that all the items will be multiple choice when in fact there are items (one at level 13 and three at level 17) that are not multiple choice. Third, no mention is made that there is a DK distractor included in the items, and from reading the directions one could not discern that such an option existed. Last, there are no guidelines for the teacher to follow when the students ask how much time is allowed or how much is remaining. The students are told only "Don't rush, but don't waste time" with regard to time limits.

The manual is inadequate in more than directions for administering the test. Reliability is completely ignored. Validity information is meager, and found only in the table of specifications that indicate how each item is categorized. Validity appears to be assumed in the one sentence that says "Each test covers most of the reading comprehension skills tested in the National Assessment of Educational Progress and found on most standardized reading comprehension tests."

---

[1]From the *Ninth Mental Measurements Yearbook,* ed. by James V. Mitchell, 1985, p. 101. © 1985 by the Buros Institute of Mental Measurements. Reprinted with permission.

UNIT THREE

Planning for Instructional Intervention

9

Organizing and Managing Remedial and Clinical Reading Programs

This chapter discusses the logistics of organizing and managing superior remedial and clinical reading programs. It focuses on those teacher tasks, decisions, and behaviors necessary to arrange the learning environment.

SELECTING INSTRUCTIONAL MATERIALS AND EQUIPMENT

Materials can influence method of instruction and can positively or negatively affect student progress. There are hundreds of materials from which to choose. Some are described in this text. To locate others, teachers can write to publishers whose addresses are listed in Appendix B and ask for free catalogs. Many professional journals also list recommended materials and, on request, publishers' representatives can call on teachers and demonstrate their products.

Teachers should not assume, however, that commercially published materials are necessarily good or that they necessarily sug-gest sound methods or teaching activities. It is the teacher's responsibility to carefully evaluate materials before they are purchased. The checklist in Figure 9–1 is helpful in appraising the usefulness of materials designed for reading instruction.

Individual Books

Books are the most important material in any type of program for remediating reading problems. They should be available for use during direct instruction and independent work, and for students to take home to read for pleasure. A permanent selection of books should be kept in the classroom and should be supplemented by new books brought in periodically from the school or public library. The permanent collection should include informational books as well as fiction. Picture books of high literary quality can also be used; many of these are written at about 3rd-grade reading level but are still suitable for 4th or 5th graders in terms of interest. Using a special type of picture book called a *predictable book* (in which

167

	Yes	No
1. Does the material provide much opportunity for the student to read in regular, connected material?		
2. Is it based on current research and not on outdated notions?		
3. Does it really teach what it says it teaches?		
4. Does it teach anything important?		
5. Does it teach anything at all?		
6. Is the instructional level appropriate?		
7. Is the interest level suitable for students in terms of topic, pictures, and type size?		
8. Is it better for initial learning, practice, or review?		
9. Is it attractive and appealing rather than shoddy or dull?		
10. Are directions easy for students to understand?		
11. Is it well-organized rather than difficult to follow?		
12. Are lessons of an appropriate length for your students?		
13. Is it reusable rather than consumable?		
14. Is it durable?		
15. Would something less expensive do the job just as well?		

Figure 9–1
Checklist for evaluating reading materials

words or phrases are continually repeated) is excellent for students with limited sight vocabularies.

High interest/low vocabulary books are another essential material in remedial programs. These books are easy to read, but have stories and topics that appeal to students with more mature interests. One example is *Disasters!* (Jamestown), a booklet of 21 articles about famous disasters such as the Hindenburg fire, the San Francisco earthquake, Krakatoa, the Black Death, and Pompeii. This booklet is written at 6th-, 7th-, and 8th-grade levels, but designed for high school students and adults. A monograph titled *Easy Reading: Book Series and Periodicals for Less Able Readers* (IRA) lists many others. (Also see Teachers' Store in Appendix C.) Teachers may also purchase special books likely to "turn on" turned-

off readers. A good example is *Slugs* (Little, Brown), a wild and crazy book by David Greenberg describing many things you can do with slugs. With wonderful illustrations, it's the kind of book that makes readers say "Yuk-k-k. Let me read some more!" and is probably more appreciated by middle-school boys than by the teacher.

Book Series

Some series of books contain selections to read, accompanied by follow-up activities located directly in the student materials. One of these, designed for intermediate grades through high school, is *Reading for Concepts* (McGraw-Hill), in which books ranging from 1.9 through 6.4 reading levels consist of one-page informational articles followed by a page of comprehension questions. Another series is

Superstars (Steck-Vaughn), comprised of six softcover books containing 90 mini-biographies of superstars of rock, soul, and country music, plus superstars of sports, movies, and TV (some inclusions are Burt Reynolds, Stevie Wonder, and Magic Johnson). Each short biography in the *Superstars* books is followed by vocabulary and comprehension exercises; the reading levels are 4 through 6.

Other series of books consist primarily of stories, with the suggestions for activities found only in the teacher's manual. The *Monster Books* (Bowmar) and *The Best in Children's Literature* (Bowmar) contain stories highly appealing to children. *Giant First–Start Readers* (Troll) is a series in which each book is written with very few words (for example, one uses only 34 different words, another 37, and another 47). Basal reader series may also be used. Basal series today include interesting, high-quality selections and attractive formats. One of these is the *Sounds of Language Readers* (Holt, Rinehart, & Winston). In most remedial and clinical reading programs the use of basal readers is different from their use in developmental reading programs, however. In remedial programs students are not asked to read all stories in a book; instead, certain stories are selected because they complement student interests.

Kits Containing Reading Materials and/or Skills Activities

Many kits of attractive materials for poor readers are on the market. The *NFL Reading Kit* (Bowmar) appeals to students interested in football. It contains 150 cards with colorful photographs, and short articles at reading levels 2.0 through 4.0 about real National Football League players and teams. Each article is followed by a series of questions to develop vocabulary and comprehension. *Story-Plays* (Harcourt, Brace, Jovanovich) consists of a primary and an intermediate kit of play booklets. Four copies of each play are included so groups of students can work together. The *Supermarket Recall Program* (William Orr) is three kits of cards, each of which has a label for students to read taken from a real supermarket product. Reading activities related to the vocabulary found on each label also appear on the card.

(Reproduced by permission of the artist, Clem Scalzetti)

"It's a book, dear. It's what they use to make movies for TV."

Multi-Media Kits

Multi-media kits include audiovisual materials in addition to skills activities and reading selections. One kit popular with secondary students is the *Action Reading System* (Scholastic). Although stories in this kit are written at second-grade level, the books are mature-looking and appeal to teens' interests. The kit includes action stories, romance, science fiction, mysteries, and plays. Exercise pages for word identification, vocabulary, and comprehension, and cassette tapes are included in the program. The *Double-Action* kit, a part of the same series, has stories written at levels 3.0 through 5.0.

A kit suitable for students reading at primary levels is the *Breakthrough to Literacy* kit (Bowmar). Books in this program are based on stories told by children and are accompanied by audiovisuals. There are two *Interaction* kits (Houghton Mifflin), one for primary reading levels and one for reading levels 4.0 through 6.9. This program has various components such as booklets supplemented by cassette tapes, photo stories, nonsense stories, and activity cards. The *Power Reading Series* (Gamco) is highly appealing to many students because each of its seven kits is composed of ten 20-page comic books and one record on which the comic is read word for word. Written for reading levels 3.0 through 6.0, the comic books are used to develop vocabulary and comprehension skills. Kits of each of the following are available: "Beneath the Planet of the Apes," "Batman," "Captain America," "Star Trek," "Superman," "Wonder Woman," and "Spider-Man."

Workbooks

Teachers sometimes are criticized for using workbooks in reading programs. Workbooks have received a bad reputation. This is partly because teachers often have over-used them until no time remains for the most important reading activity, which is practice in reading regular, connected material. In addition, some workbooks are poorly prepared and dull. Nevertheless, workbooks can be helpful if they are thoughtfully selected and used. Thoughtful use includes using workbook pages occasionally as part of a wider variety of materials, and not requiring the student to complete every page in a book, but instead selecting only those pages directly related to a strategy or skill on which the student needs specific instruction. Careful selection of workbooks that have sound and appealing activities is also important. One interesting workbook is *Using the Want Ads* (Janus), which is designed to teach reading strategies and a survival skill at the same time; this workbook is written at the 2.5 reading level.

Activity cards may be substituted for workbook pages. These are individual cards on which a single activity is printed. Boxes of activity cards are available from various companies, such as the sets for practicing use of context clues developed by Frank Schaffer Publications.

Duplicating Masters

The same admonition concerning selection and use of workbooks applies to duplicating masters. Occasional use of well-developed activity sheets reproduced from duplicating masters is appropriate. One example of duplicating masters for reading activities is *Super Survival Skills for Reading Activity Sheets* (Kids & Co.), which includes exercises for reading bus schedules, TV guides, menus, and other practical items. Another is *Cartoon Comprehension* (Frank Schaffer), each page of which presents a 6-frame cartoon to be read and then followed by vocabulary and comprehension exercises.

Games

Games, carefully selected and appropriately used, are good materials for remedial programs. Because most students enjoy games, they attend carefully to the activity and often expend more effort to determine correct responses than during more traditional school activities. Games are most beneficial in a directed lesson with the teacher present to prevent students from practicing errors. Teachers can also model correct responses and solution-seeking behaviors by playing the games with the students, who usually enjoy this.

One caution about games: in most cases they provide little opportunity to read in connected material. Therefore, devoting a whole class period to playing games is rarely appropriate.

Whether bingo games, card games, domino-type games, puzzles, or board games, the majority of games published for school use emphasize practice with words and word identification skills. One publisher that has a series of games for comprehension practice is Learning Well Corporation. This series includes board games for practice in drawing conclusions, getting the main idea, discerning between fact and opinion, identifying cause and effect, reading for details, drawing inferences, and following written directions.

Teacher-Made Materials

Teacher-made materials can include books, strategy lessons, games, and audiovisuals.

For example, teachers may write their own classroom books or short stories stressing use of specific words with which certain students may need practice. Other books can be developed from student-dictated stories. Some teachers write or type these directly onto ditto masters as students dictate them, so the stories can be reproduced for wider distribution. When several stories have been accumulated they can be bound together with construction paper or other inexpensive materials and placed in the class library.

Teachers can also compose their own strategy lessons. These can take the form of reading-activity sheets designed to provide practice using a single word identification or comprehension strategy. A strategy lesson that has demonstrated success in helping one student can be easily duplicated and placed in a file for future use with students displaying the same need.

Many teachers enjoy constructing their own learning games and activities for students. For independent use, games should be designed to be self-correcting so that students can discover immediately whether they are responding correctly. One helpful source of materials for teachers who like to make their own games is Marie's Educational Materials, which markets inexpensive items such as blank bingo boards, spinners, and game markers to be used with teacher-prepared activities. Another useful booklet is the *Classroom Reading Games Activities Kit* (Center for Applied Research in Education). Hints for successful game making also can be found in "A Potpourri of Game-Making Ideas for the Reading Teacher" (McCormick & Collins, 1981). This article provides down-to-earth suggestions such as how to prevent air blisters when applying clear plastic contact paper to games, where to obtain pens that will write on laminated materials, a trick for quickly drawing neat squares for "tracks" on game boards, and other helpful ideas.

Teachers can also make their own audiovisuals. For example, making filmstrips is a simple task if outdated commercial filmstrips are available. These old filmstrips are dipped in common household bleach, which quickly removes all photographed and printed material. On the now-clear filmstrip, new frames can be drawn using a ruler and marking pen. Sight words, contractions, consonant letters, or similar brief materials can be written in the frames for use in a filmstrip lesson. Kits for creating filmstrips from clear film are available from Barry Instrument Corporation. Professional books with directions for creating several other types of audiovisuals include *Making and Using Inexpensive Classroom Media* (Professional Educators Publications).

Magazines and Newspapers

Some students find magazines or newspapers more appealing and less intimidating than books. This may be because the selections usually are shorter, or because, unlike books, they may not be associated with failure and frustration in the classroom. One newspaper written especially for lower-achieving secondary readers is *Know Your World, Extra* (Weekly Reader Secondary Periodicals). With a subscription, multiple copies of this newspaper can be received weekly in the classroom. A magazine popular in elementary classes is *Ranger Rick* (National Wildlife Federation). The monograph (cited in the previous section titled *Individual Books)* lists many periodicals suitable for remedial classes.

And almost any community's daily or weekly newspaper can be used as a learning tool. An inexpensive booklet, *Teaching Reading Skills Through the Newspaper* (IRA), has many suggestions for using newspapers in a reading class.

Mechanical Equipment

A cassette tape recorder and sets of headphones are important equipment in the modern remedial program. Students can listen and read along silently or orally with books, follow prerecorded teacher directions for completing an activity sheet, or use recording and playback equipment in many other productive ways. A Language Master (Bell & Howell) is another helpful teaching aid. This machine is accompanied by cards with an audiotape running along the bottom of each. Teachers can write words, sentences, and so forth, on each Language Master card, then record in audio on each card what has been written. Students

attempt to read each card, then place the card in the machine, and press a button to hear what the teacher recorded. Thus, students can determine if their own responses are correct or incorrect. This device provides the immediate feedback so important during the independent work of low-achieving readers.

A filmstrip projector and phonograph are also useful additions to remedial classes.

Computers. Microcomputers are the latest major advance in equipment to assist the teacher of reading. They are the most recent outgrowth of a technology that began with large mainframe computers, such as PLATO, which was used in early attempts at Computer Assisted Instruction (CAI). As early as 1965, Stanford University and a few other educational institutions were experimenting with CAI in the teaching of reading. Most early computer programs were designed for primary students and emphasized decoding skills. Initially, CAI was almost exclusively self-directed, but it was soon extended to other educational uses.

Microcomputers were introduced commercially around 1975 and were being widely used by the mid-1980s in American as well as European schools. Microcomputer programs are available to assist the teacher with management of classroom instruction or to provide students with drill and practice, instructional games, simulation learning, or tutorial experiences. Because several publishers have devised programs useful in assessment, microcomputers can now provide valuable assistance in dealing with reading and learning disability problems in regular classrooms. Mangrum and Strichart (1984) discuss the use of microcomputers at Hofstra University for bright students with learning difficulties; they believe microcomputers will be very important for reading- and learning-disabled college students in the near future. Another source predicts that before the end

Computer programs can assist the reading teacher with management of classroom instruction and assessment as well as provide students with drill and practice, instructional games, simulation learning, or tutorial experiences.

of this decade, there will be 2 million computers in use in American schools ("Two Million Micros," 1983).

The introduction of this new technology requires students to obtain nontraditional skills in order to learn. Because—even as early as kindergarten—students must have at least a rudimentary knowledge of typing, young children are mastering the keyboard through games and activities. They must also know components and accessories of the computer such as the video monitor, space bar, modem, or printer. In addition, specialized terminology must be learned for computer literacy. Of interest to the reading teacher is the list of words Dreyer, Futtersak, and Boehm (1985) suggest students must read to use computers (see Box 9–1). If students are taught to program, as many are, they must also learn programming languages. In other words, to be able to take advantage of microcomputers in reading or other classrooms, teachers must incorporate several new teaching/learning activities into daily class work.

Of course, the computer itself must be accompanied by *software.* Software is the informational component comprising the in-

dividual lessons used in the microcomputer. Educational software is often categorized in the following ways.

1. Programs for instructional management: These help teachers track student progress and monitor tasks accomplished.
2. Drill and practice programs: The purpose of these is to reinforce basic skills and strategies through independent practice.
3. Instructional games: These are designed to provide drill and practice in a more interesting manner.
4. Simulation learning: These programs simulate real experiences and allow students to role-play hypothetical situations.
5. Tutorial experiences: The purpose of these is to provide more instruction than is found in drill and practice programs; for example, detailed explanations of how to accomplish an exercise, or explanations of why an answer is incorrect. Tutorials often feature *branching,* a technique allowing learners to bypass some instruction or spend additional time when appropriate.

Box 9–1

Essential Words for Computer-Assisted Instruction in the Elementary Grades, Based on a Sample of 35 Programs

activity	complete	end	lesson	play	selection
adjust	command	* enter	letter	player	* sound
again	computer	erase	level	* please	* spacebar
another	* continue	* escape or \<esc\>	list	point	speed
answer	control or \<cntrl\>	exit	load	practice	start
any	copy	find	* loading	* press	team
* arrow	correct	finished	match	print	text
audio	correctly	follow	memory	problems	then
bar	cursor	format	* menu	* program	try
before	delete	* game	[module]	quit	turn
begin	demonstration	good	monitor	rate	* type
bold	description	help	move	ready	up
button	different	hit	* name	regular	use
[cartridge]	directions	hold	need	remove	video
[cassette]	disk	incorrect	no	repeat	wait
catalog	diskette	incorrectly	* number	* return	want
change	display	indicate	off	[rewind]	which
choice	document	insert	on	rules	win
* choose	down	instructions	options	save	word
colors	drive	joystick	paddle	score	work
column	edit	* key	password	screen	yes
compete	effects	keyboard	picture	select	your

*Words present in at least 10 of the 35 programs
[ ] Additions—not in any of the 35 programs

Source: From "Sight Words for the Computer Age: An Essential Word List," by Lois G. Dreyer, Karen F. Futtersak, and Ann E. Boehm, October 1985, *The Reading Teacher*, pp. 14–15. Reprinted with permission of the authors and the International Reading Association.

Blanchard and Mason (1985) use the following alternative classifications:

1. story architecture programs: students build their own stories with the micro-computer's assistance
2. telecommunication programs: these use a modem and telephone line to access data from other computers
3. utility programs: in these the teacher is able to select the information to be taught; for example, by entering a different set of spelling words into the program each week
4. word-processing programs: these can help young writers write, edit, read, and print text material.

Here is a typical sequence found in an educational software program:

- Display of the title page and program identification information.
- Display of the program menu, after which the user is asked to select an option.
- The chosen part of the program is loaded while a message such as "Loading . . . please wait" appears.

- The user's name is requested so that the program can be personalized.
- Decisions about other choices are requested such as: "Do you want sound effects?" and "Do you want instructions?" If the user requests instructions or help, explanatory statements then follow.
- In some programs the user may also select a level of difficulty and a rate of item presentation.
- Procedural statements such as "Press return to begin" and "Press spacebar to continue" are incorporated within the program at appropriate points.
- When the chosen part of the program is completed, the user may then select another option from the program menu or stop (*exit* or *quit*). (Dreyer, Futtersak, & Boehm, 1985, pp. 14–15)

There are many new computer programs in reading. In fact, about 9% of all software is for reading/language arts instruction (Chan, 1985). While many older programs were not highly recommended, better-quality software is becoming increasingly available. Two well-designed programs that provide exciting practice are the *Playwriter* series (Woodbury Software) for elementary school students, and *Reading Around Words* (Instructional/Communications Technology), usually used at the secondary level. For other software that has been positively reviewed by reading educators, see the Teacher's Store in the Appendix. In addition, several programs are cited throughout this text in relation to a variety of topics. Finally, there are several resource books and lists of available programs, such as *The Educational Software Selector* (EPIE Institute), or *Computers and Reading Instruction* (Addison-Wesley), which specifies commercial and public-domain programs (public-domain software may be copied legally by anyone, usually for the price of a computer disc).

A number of pros and cons have been voiced about reading programs designed for microcomputers. Some criticisms are that certain software is no more than a set of very expensive workbook pages that are electronically displayed; that drill and practice programs, especially, provide no more than an electronic flashcard; and that uninspired program development leads to an inferior educational experience. On the other hand, some high quality software is now valued for supplementary instruction: it provides good practice; allows for instant feedback; serves as an effective tool for review; allows students to control the rate of presentation of material; and enables highly individualized teaching.

Most reading teachers believe that computers can teach students thinking skills by engaging them in programming tasks, for example, using simulation programs, or employing word-processing programs to compose and edit. Drill and practice programs are viewed less favorably, however, even though they are by far the most widely available type of reading software. To make the best use of software programs, teachers should *not* view computers as a panacea. They should preview software before purchasing it, and they should integrate microcomputer teaching programs with teacher-directed instruction. Maddux (1986) proposes two classifications of computer-use: Type I, or passive, that is, rote teaching in the traditional way things have always been taught, such as drilling students on word recognition; and Type II, or active, involving students in new and better ways of learning, such as working on improving cognitive skills or engaging in vicarious experiences through simulations. Maddux admonishes that computers should not be used in trivial ways.

Teachers need to learn four major things about computers. First of all, they need to master the same skills their students must acquire with the component parts, operation, and special vocabulary of micros. Second, to use computers efficiently, they need to recognize those times when less-expensive alternatives can serve the educational task just as well. Third, they need to learn how to manage a classroom program that integrates computer use. And fourth, teachers should be taught to develop their own software so they can mold it to the specific needs of their students. Many books, magazines, and computer programs are available that can provide a form of inservice education to help educators stay abreast of the explosion of new developments in computer uses and technology. One such computer program is *The Computer Connection for Teachers* (Instructional Software); this one is for teachers who know nothing about computers. A helpful magazine is *Teaching and Computers* (Scholastic). And many professional journals now feature columns that give suggestions for teacher-created lessons, new uses for microcomputers, and lists of recommended software.

Media

Films and filmstrips add variety to reading lessons. Films can be obtained from many sources, including public or school libraries. Three excellent films for encouraging writing and vocabulary development are *Let's Write A Story* (Churchill Films), for grades 3 through 6, *Poems We Write* (Grover Films Productions), also for grades 3 through 6, and *The Red Balloon* (Brandon Films) for grades 1 through 12 (even the teacher will enjoy this last one). Filmstrips are relatively inexpensive, so teachers may wish to start their own classroom collections. Many publishers have catalogs of filmstrips suitable for reading instruction.

Professional Books and Journals

Carefully selected professional books and journal articles can provide a wealth of good ideas for teachers to use in their own teaching. Here's a brief sampling of some with practical suggestions:

For Teachers of All Grades

- "Jingles, Jokes, Limericks, Poems, Proverbs, Puns, Puzzles, and Riddles: Fast Reading for Reluctant Readers" (*Language Arts*, Nov./Dec., 1978)
- "Sources of Free and Inexpensive Materials" (*Language Arts*, May, 1978)

For Elementary and Junior High Teachers

- *The Reading Idea Book* (Education Today)

For Intermediate and Junior High Teachers

- *Look It Up! 101 Dictionary Activities* (Pittman Learning)

For Secondary Teachers

- "Games, Games, Games—and Reading Class" (*Journal of Reading*, May, 1971)
- "Twenty-two Sets of Methods and Materials for Stimulating Teenage Reading" (*Journal of Reading*, May, 1978)

There should be a place on the classroom shelves for professional books, and folders in file drawers for keeping articles from journals that have good teaching ideas.

The brief review of selected materials and equipment in this section is provided to indicate the variety of materials available to enhance reading instruction. Many other excellent choices are available at both higher and lower reading levels.

ORGANIZING THE CLASSROOM OR CLINIC TO TEACH

A *well-organized* classroom facilitates the use of a variety of materials, permits both individualized and group activities, and encourages on-task behavior of students. It also helps the teacher carry out various functions efficiently.

Occasionally a remedial education teacher is assigned a funny little room in which to conduct classes, perhaps the janitor's former supply room, or the abandoned bell tower above the school attic. The reasoning seems to be that since these teachers don't work with a regular-sized class group all at one time, they don't need a regular-size classroom. Teachers forced to work in such facilities must take the attitude that good teaching can occur anywhere—which is true—and that students can receive an excellent program even if space is scarce and the room is an architectural mongrel. Nevertheless, the following description assumes the more nearly ideal condition of a regular-size classroom; teachers with less space can, with ingenuity, make the necessary adaptations to have a well-organized room.

Physical Organization

Arrange desks so that some students can work individually while other students are working elsewhere in a small group with the teacher. Arrange desks for small-group instruction near a chalkboard so it can be used for teaching. If you have been assigned a room with no chalkboard, ask for a good portable one. Teachers also need a place to neatly display all the many books they should have in a remedial classroom. If there are no bookshelves, some can be made with boards and bricks. A revolving metal rack for storing and displaying paperbacks, magazines, and newspapers is an excellent addition to the reading class; one source for bookracks is Scholastic. If possible, create a comfortable reading area perhaps equipped with a small rug and a beanbag chair or two, near the bookshelves.

Use a table or desk for a *listening station area*. Place a tape recorder and earphones on the table and several chairs around it. Find a place to store games neatly so they are con-

venient for use. Ask that a pull-down screen be installed in the room for showing filmstrips, or that a portable one be made available. Find a place for neatly storing kits and mechanical devices so they are accessible. Obtain a teacher's file cabinet and file folders for efficiently organizing tests, strategy lessons, information on teaching ideas, forms, and student records.

Devise attractive, organized ways to store supplies. For example, cover round potato chip cans for storing game pieces, or after removing the labels, cut plastic detergent bottles in half for storing pencils or felt tip pens. Make supplies accessible to students who are working independently. This minimizes interruptions when the teacher is working with other students.

Learning Centers

Find a place in your classroom for one or more learning centers. A *learning center* is a designated area where students can work independently on activities designed to help them concentrate on a specific knowledge, strategy, or skill area. Here are some points for developing learning centers.

- To begin, select a single skill, strategy, or knowledge area (for example, learning to use context clues as a word identification strategy, or reading to predict outcomes). Develop or locate materials and media related to this area. These materials could include books, game-like activities, worksheets, teacher-made or commercial audiotapes, a tape recorder and earphones, a filmstrip, a table-top filmstrip projector, activity cards, newspapers, a flannel board, a magnet board, and so forth. (A cookie sheet makes a good, inexpensive magnet board.)
- Include a variety of learning activities such as reading, manipulating, observing, writ-

ing, creating, comparing, researching, orally answering questions into a tape recorder, or typing.

- Whenever possible, devise activities so they are self-correcting.
- Organize materials at a table or desk maintained permanently for their access. Provide space on that table for students to work. Usually, only one chair should be placed at the table since work in a learning center is usually carried out individually.
- Post clear and simple instructions at the learning center so students can complete their activities with a minimum of teacher assistance.
- Devise a system for keeping records of what students accomplish during work at the learning center. Maintain a scheduling calendar for assigning students to the learning center.

The design and construction of a learning center requires much thought and effort on the part of the teacher. Because this process takes time and often requires trial and error solutions to unique problems, it is best to develop a single, successful learning center before attempting to start another. Many books are available to assist the teacher in this challenging task. One of these is *Center Stuff for Nooks, Crannies, and Corners* (Incentive Publications).

Bulletin Boards

Devise bulletin boards that teach. There are three functional levels of bulletin boards. The least useful are those that merely provide a colorful visual display in the room, for example, the one that says "It's Spring!" accompanied by cut paper flowers. The second type presents information, for example, pictures about the American Southwest with labels beneath them giving facts. The third and most productive type of bulletin board is the one around which a learning activity can take

place. This third type enables the teacher to teach small groups of students lessons related to the materials displayed. In addition, the bulletin board can serve as a kind of learning center: students can use it independently to manipulate materials or otherwise engage in activities that have been arranged there. This is a good solution for teachers who would like to have a learning center in their classrooms but cannot because of space limitations.

A Pleasant Place to Learn

Make the classroom attractive. A bright and pleasant atmosphere is certainly more conducive to learning than is a dreary room. When students or visitors come to the classroom, their response should be, "It is certainly evident that reading is taught here!" and, "This would be a nice place in which to learn!"

The basic organizational procedures, equipment, and supplies apply to reading clinics as well as classrooms. Clinics, however, should include more areas reserved for one-to-one instruction, because most teaching in the clinic setting is carried out in this manner. Individual study carrels are generally used for this purpose, especially if more than one student will be receiving instruction from several different clinicians at the same time.

GROUPING AND INDIVIDUALIZING INSTRUCTION

In remedial reading classes the teacher sometimes works directly with groups of students; at other times the teacher works with only one student while the other students work independently. Individualized instruction can take place in either—or neither—of these instructional arrangements. Individualized instruction does not necessarily imply working with just one student at a time. Rather, *individualized instruction* is the tailoring of instruction to a student's specific needs. Where more than one student has the same instructional need, grouping these students is appropriate: individualized instruction can still occur. Conversely, a teacher could work on a one-to-one basis with a student and yet individualized instruction might not occur if the instruction simply fails to address the specific weaknesses of that student.

Deciding how and when to group students for direct instruction is based on diagnosis, not only preceding initiation of the instructional program, but also on informal, daily, ongoing evaluation of students' reading progress. This means that the decision to have a student work in a group or work individually with the teacher or work independently can vary from day to day as the needs of members of a class change because of their different learning rates.

Grouping for instruction has several advantages. One of these is efficient use of teacher time. Another is that because the teacher is directly involved with the students he can ensure high rates of academic engaged time; that is, the teacher can be sure that the students are working more of the time on academically relevant activities. This is more difficult when students have been assigned to work independently. Rosenshine (1980), for example, found rates of academic engagement to be 84 percent during teacher-led instruction as opposed to only 70 percent during independent activities. The amount of time students are actually engaged in academic tasks is an important variable in learning. The third advantage of grouping is that students often learn from each other by hearing other students' responses and by sharing in problem-solving tasks.

In addition to group work, most students require some individual work with the teacher as well as some independent work because students' needs change over time and with different content areas. An advantage of individual work is that there are increased opportunities for response. That is, an individual student is doing all of the responding during a lesson rather than sharing the responding with others in a group. Research has shown that the number of opportunities for response is correlated with achievement (e.g., Greenwood, Delquadri, & Hall, 1984). A second advantage of particular interest to secondary teachers is that students in this age group often prefer independent work rather than group activities. Secondary classes are, therefore, sometimes managed so that students work alone, with the teacher moving from student to student to provide some direct, individual instruction for part of each period.

It should be noted, however, that research has shown that independent work without teacher supervision is negatively related to academic gains. (See, e.g., Sindelar & Wilson, 1982). This implies that careful planning is necessary if students are to spend the maximum amount of time on academically relevant tasks when working alone. Independent work can be effective if

1. it immediately follows teacher-directed instruction;
2. it is at the appropriate instructional level;
3. it is engaged in for short periods of time, and interspersed with either group or individual teacher-directed instruction; and
4. students are carefully monitored to ensure that they spend a high percentage of time on task (Sindelar & Wilson, 1982).

To facilitate good use of time during independent work, the teacher can prepare individual assignment sheets (like the one in Figure 9–2) and have students check off tasks as they are completed.

Group instruction and individual instruction make maximum use of *teacher-directed* activities, while independent work does not. It appears that more teacher-directed time is necessary for remedial stu-

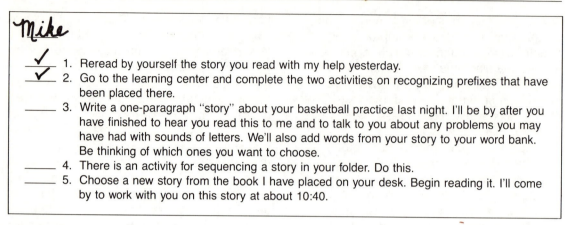

Mike

___✓___ 1. Reread by yourself the story you read with my help yesterday.

___✓___ 2. Go to the learning center and complete the two activities on recognizing prefixes that have been placed there.

_____ 3. Write a one-paragraph "story" about your basketball practice last night. I'll be by after you have finished to hear you read this to me and to talk to you about any problems you may have had with sounds of letters. We'll also add words from your story to your word bank. Be thinking of which ones you want to choose.

_____ 4. There is an activity for sequencing a story in your folder. Do this.

_____ 5. Choose a new story from the book I have placed on your desk. Begin reading it. I'll come by to work with you on this story at about 10:40.

Figure 9–2
Example of an individual assignment sheet

dents. For example, Stallings (1980) found that when low-achieving students made high achievement gains, 72 percent of their instructional time had been spent in teacher-directed activities, while average readers made high gains when only 49 percent of their time was spent in teacher-directed instruction. In addition, although the number of opportunities for student response is correlated with growth in learning, not all response opportunities have the same impact. Sindelar and Wilson (1982) reported that their studies showed that opportunities to respond during teacher-directed instruction were more likely to lead to learning than responses made during independent work. This is probably due to the lack of immediate feedback about correctness of responses when students work alone. Instructional feedback from the teacher has been found to be more consistently and strongly related to student learning than has any other teacher behavior.

Finally, in considering the value of group and individual instruction versus independent work, the differences between allocated time and engaged time must be stressed. In discussing the amount of time they have allocated for instruction, teachers will sometimes say something like, "In Nicole's daily schedule I have 20 minutes planned for sustained silent reading," or, "I'm having Scott work on higher-level comprehension skills for 25 minutes of each period." But what too often occurs is that Nicole is sent to a desk to read independently while the teacher is engaged with other students; Nicole then spends 3 minutes looking through her purse, 5 minutes looking at pictures elsewhere in her book, 4 minutes daydreaming, and only 8 minutes really reading. Or, during Scott's 25 minutes of independent work, he reads a workbook article, then watches what another student is doing, then reads and marks a few multiple-choice answers, then plays with his pencil, then reads and marks a few more answers, then draws a picture on his paper, then writes any answer without reading the remainder of the questions. Obviously, he has really spent considerably less than 25 minutes in genuine learning activities. Allocated time, then, has no impact on learning time. Engaged time does.

In remedial programs, independent work often is necessary so the teacher can meet the diverse needs of all students, but when students work independently, more care is necessary in planning and monitoring activities if there is to be adequate academic engaged time. It should be said, however, that the nature of teacher behaviors and instructional activities during teacher-directed instruction also determines the ultimate value of academic engaged time. For example, if the teacher chooses an activity of little importance to skills needed in real reading or allows students to waste instructional time with constant off-task behaviors, little reading growth will occur.

Classroom organization should be flexible, allowing the teacher to vary group instruction with individual instruction and independent work. The choice of the teaching arrangement should fit the teaching goal and thus provide for optimal learning.

PLANNING SCHEDULES FOR INSTRUCTION

In developing schedules for remedial instruction, two types of planning are necessary—the planning of an overall daily schedule and the careful planning of what will occur within each class period.

When developing a daily schedule, the teacher should try to group students with similar needs. Because of the seriousness and diversity of remedial readers' problems, some individual work with students is almost always necessary, but when students attending during any given period have some similar needs, group instruction can occur during part of the period, thus making more efficient use of teacher time. Teachers should also avoid scheduling conflicts with an activity a student considers highly enjoyable; for example, if students consider gym class their favorite activity and miss it every week because of remedial reading class, it is likely that they will be less than enthusiastic learners. Also, because poor readers should receive reading instruction

available in their regular classrooms as well as in the special class, they should be scheduled in the remedial reading program so they do not miss this additional instruction.

Working with groups of five to eight students during each class period is common practice, although some research has shown that when a group becomes larger than six, learning diminishes (Payne, Polloway, Smith, & Payne, 1981). Also, the length of each class period should be at least 40 to 45 minutes. Less time does not permit thorough teaching or allow time for all needed activities. In most cases, it is optimal to place students in the remedial reading class for at least one period per day. A program in which students attend fewer than 3 days per week simply does not produce sufficient achievement gains.

Another important consideration when planning daily schedules is students' attendance. Poor readers often have a high incidence of absenteeism. If they are not consistently present for instruction, their reading growth will be negligible. Teachers have successfully combated the poor attendance problem by talking with parents or by working regularly with the school attendance officer. After students begin experiencing success in their reading program, excessive school absences frequently disappear.

Within each class period, instruction schedules must vary from group to group and individual to individual. Remedial-reading teachers should follow certain basic guidelines to achieve this.

1. At least a third of every class period should be devoted to regular, connected reading by students. Reading in regular, connected reading material means the student's brain should be processing connected pieces of meaningful, written language with a developed beginning, middle, and end; for example, whole

chapters, stories, articles, or short books. (It does not mean reading single sentences, isolated words on flash cards, individual paragraphs on worksheets, and so forth.) Some of this time may be devoted to silent reading and some to oral. The reading time also may be allotted in smaller segments (for example, 5 minutes at the beginning of the period, 10 minutes during the middle, and 5 minutes more at the end). However it is achieved, the goal is to assure that one-third of the time students spend in remedial reading classes is spent in connected reading. The only acceptable variation to this rule is to add more reading time.

2. When planning the class period, allocate time so that all reading is followed by a comprehension check. This can be accomplished by asking specific oral or written questions, by asking the student to retell the material, or both. This time should be in addition to the time planned for the student to read regular, connected reading material.

3. Activities should be varied throughout the period. For example, a long period of concentrated effort might be followed by an academically relevant game. Also, some activities should be varied from day to day to prevent boredom.

4. Provide students the opportunity to make choices within tasks. For example, you may have decided that Charles should spend the first 10 minutes of the period reading silently, but he may choose from among three suitable stories the one which he prefers to read. Research has shown that activities are more effective when students are offered some choices within the teacher-selected structure.

5. Spend some time during each class period reading aloud to students or have them listen to taped stories. This assures student exposure to written language structures, which in turn aids prediction

of unknown words and promotes comprehension. Reviews of the research on reading aloud to students (McCormick, 1977b, 1983) show that when students have been read to on a *regular* basis they have larger quantities of vocabulary knowledge, a higher quality of vocabulary knowledge, and greater comprehension. Reading aloud to students also affects reading interests and enhances oral language development.

6. Daily lesson plans should be modified if students are not demonstrating appropriate progress. Devise a simple record-keeping system so you don't have to rely on memory. Evaluations of the success of lesson plans should occur at least monthly.

Planning instructional schedules for students enrolled in reading clinics is similar to planning schedules for students in remedial reading classes. Activities scheduled for clinical reading programs need not be of a different, unusual, or peculiar nature. Clinical reading instruction should exemplify the best of any type of reading instruction with rich and meaningful activities in abundance. Clinical programs incorporating current learning theory do not resort to materials that are different, nor to artificial instructional procedures that too often supply only meager contact with real reading tasks. The distinguishing characteristic of clinical programs is simply that a higher proportion of teaching time involves instruction on a one-to-one basis and is therefore more intensive. In Figures 9–3 and 9–4 a sample of two consecutive days' lesson plans are seen for a hypothetical student enrolled in a reading clinic.

CONCLUDING STATEMENT

Students enrolled in remedial programs usually demonstrate learning rates far exceeding their previous rates of progress. Bliesmer

Name: Jim Coyne
Age: 10
Approximate instructional level: 2.5
Date: Oct. 31, 19___

9:00–9:10 *(CRT = 5 min.)	Jim and I will orally read Chapter 1 of *Max the Monkey* (reading level, approximately 2.5). This book was chosen because of his interest inventory. Jim said he "loves monkeys" and "I wish I could go to the zoo every week to see the monkeys." Since this is his first day with this book, I'll take turns reading with him (I'll read one page, he'll read the next, etc.) to ease him into it. By my doing this, he'll hear me pronounce some of the new vocabulary. He'll also begin to get a feeling for the story line so he can make predictions when he reads the book without this assistance from me. Also, by hearing him read orally from the first chapter, I'll be able to make some determinations about whether this book is really at the appropriate level for him.
9:10–9:15	Jim will retell the chapter we have just read and at the conclusion I will ask the following inference question: "What are two things that Max's new owner did that tell us he already knew a lot about monkeys?"
9:15–9:25 *(CRT = 10 min.)	Jim will silently read Chapter 2 of *Max the Monkey*. (While he reads I will silently read a book of my own to model reading behavior.)
9:25–9:30	I will ask him to orally answer four questions I have prepared ahead of time about Chapter 2. One of these is a factual question; one is related to a new vocabulary word whose meaning is implied in the chapter but not directly stated; and two require him to draw conclusions.
9:30–9:40	Jim and I will play a game to review the work we did yesterday on consonant digraphs. He may choose between "Digraph Dominoes" or a digraph bingo game. Then he will read six sentences I have written, each of which contains a word beginning with one of the digraphs in the game.
9:40–9:45 *(CRT = 5 min.)	Jim will orally read a one-page information selection on monkeys from the easy-to-read worktext series, *Learn About Your World*. During his reading I will stress the self-correction strategies we have been working on.
9:45–9:50	He will answer the three multiple-choice questions which follow the informational selection on monkeys.
9:50–10:00	I will read aloud to him chapter 1 of *Follow My Leader,* by Garfield. This is a book of realistic, contemporary fiction of high literary quality, and is also very popular with intermediate grade students. The book is written at about 4.0 reading level, which makes it too difficult for Jim to read by himself. He should have no difficulty understanding it, however, based on what I've observed of his listening comprehension. This book was chosen not only because of its interest level, but also because *Follow My Leader* is the story of a boy who is blind; it was chosen from many other good choices because a blind student is to be mainstreamed into Jim's room beginning next week. I'll read a chapter a day to him until the book is completed.

Figure 9–3
The first of two consecutive days' lesson plans for a hypothetical student enrolled in a reading clinic. *(CRT = Amount of *connected reading time* engaged in by student)

Name: Jim Coyne
Age: 10
Approximate instructional level: 2.5
Date: Nov. 1, 19____

9:00–9:10	Jim will complete a strategy lesson on predicting and confirming. I have prepared a cloze story and he will be asked to do the following:

1. Read the whole story silently.
2. Reread it silently and tell me each word that he would supply where words have been omitted; I will write the word in the blank.
3. Orally read the story to me and make changes if any of the original words he supplied do not make sense.

9:10–9:20 *(CRT = 10 min.)	Jim will silently read chapter 3 of *Max the Monkey.* (I will read my own book as he reads.)
9:20–9:30 *(CRT = 10 min.)	He will orally read chapter 4 of *Max the Monkey.* I will help him use the word identification strategies we have been working on, but will not take turns reading with him.
9:30–9:40	As a comprehension check over chapters 3 and 4 of *Max the Monkey,* he will play a game I have devised. I have prepared 10 questions, all of which require him to draw an inference. He will have a gameboard in front of him that says "Find the Treasure." For each question he answers correctly he may move one space on the board toward the "treasure." When he reaches it, he can lift a flap where he will find something he can have: a silly-looking picture of a monkey I found in *Field and Stream* magazine.
9:40–9:50	I will read aloud to him chapter 2 of *Follow My Leader.* Afterward, I will ask Jim to orally summarize this chapter.
9:50–9:55	Jim will orally read a one-page story I wrote which contains 21 words that begin with consonant digraphs.
9:55–10:00	He will dictate a story to me about the Halloween party in his room yesterday. I will write down the story as he dictates and give it to him to take home. His parents have agreed to listen to him read any of his dictated stories which I send home and are filing them in a folder he decorated.

Figure 9–4
The second of two consecutive days' lesson plans for a hypothetical student enrolled in a reading clinic. *(CRT = Amount of *connected reading time* engaged in by student)

(1962), for example, reported that average gains made by students enrolled for 1 year in a public school reading clinic were 1½ times their previous rates of progress, while the average gains of students in a second clinic were 3 times their preclinic rates. These results are fairly typical.

Unfortunately, what is also fairly typical is that after students are dismissed from spe-cial instructional programs they do not maintain this improved rate of progress. Johnson and Platts (1962), for example, reported that learning rates of remedial readers who received individual and small-group instruction were 2 to 3 times those of students who did not receive this special help; however, in a follow-up study 2 years after these students had been dismissed from the program, they had continued to make some progress, but it was at a markedly slower rate, and they had again fallen behind their peers.

There are three implications. First, students should be retained in special programs until they have had an opportunity for horizontal growth as well as vertical growth. *Vertical growth* implies an increase in reading instructional level. *Horizontal growth* is the establishment of new reading strategies as firm patterns of behavior. Immediately dismissing students from a program as soon as they have attained a reading level commensurate with their learning expectancy levels often does not allow time for new skills to become habitual. Retaining students in the remedial reading program for an additional semester, for example, promotes maintenance of early gains as well as continued acceptable rates of progress.

Second, after students have been dismissed from intensive remedial programs into the mainstream, supportive assistance through periodic tutoring probably will be advisable. Periodic tutoring by a reading teacher or a peer tutor, supplemented by parental assistance, has been found to be helpful if students are to continue to develop beyond remedial reading classes or clinics in reading competence. Agreements can be made with parents at the conclusion of a student's intensive remedial program to listen to their child read aloud for 10 or 15 minutes each day, to have the child read silently for a period of time each evening, or to read aloud to him every day.

Third, and finally, in the cases of severely disabled readers, it cannot be expected that any brief program of remediation will be sufficient to actualize the ability of these students to sustain and continue their reading progress; long-term instructional programs will more than likely be necessary in these cases.

10

Important Principles of Remedial and Clinical Reading Instruction

The previous chapter discussed procedures for organizing and managing remedial reading programs. Good organization and management are the foundation upon which to build excellent instruction. This chapter presents the instructional principles required for success in promoting reading growth.

PRINCIPLE ONE: LET THE STUDENTS READ

Teachers who work with poor readers often are so concerned about the skills and strategies these students lack that they allocate the majority of instructional time to specific exercises related to these inadequacies. Yet, while there can be no question that instructional time must be spent in these activities, it is inappropriate to require that students spend all of their reading time on developing specific learning skills while never being given the opportunity to practice such skills in meaningful material.

It is now generally recognized that the single most helpful activity for promoting growth in reading competence is the processing of large amounts of regular, connected reading material. Harris and Serwer (1966), for example, found that one of the most important variables positively correlated with reading success was the amount of time spent "actually reading." In their study, "actually reading" did *not* mean engaging in supportive activities such as drawing a picture to accompany a language experience story, discussing objects the teachers had brought in to furnish background for a story, or engaging in other language arts activities. Although the teacher may choose to include these types of experiences in a remedial reading program, time spent on such activities should not be counted as part of actual reading time.

In those remedial and clinical programs in which maximum reading growth is seen, a large portion of each class period is devoted to reading in regular, connected reading material. In those programs in which the ma-

186

jority of time is allotted to skills and strategy practice, students do improve in these specific skills, but the degree to which these skills are generalized to real reading tasks remains limited. For example, suppose a criterion-referenced test reveals that Kimberly lacks knowledge of consonant sounds. Based on the test results, the teacher plans instruction so that most of each class session is devoted to drill, games, worksheet activities, and so forth, to help her learn these. After a time, it is very likely that when the test is readministered, Kimberly will show marked improvement in knowledge of consonant sounds. However, it is also likely that when asked to read in her regular classroom, she will not perform significantly better than she had before the remedial instruction—because she has not had sufficient opportunity to practice or transfer the new skills to a real reading situation.

Teachers should carefully determine the number of minutes any given student spends actually processing regular, connected reading material in teacher-directed activities as well as in independent work. The teaching plan should work ample time for reading into lessons every day. In addition, teachers should not forget that one of the most valuable independent or seatwork activities that can be assigned is *reading a book.*

PRINCIPLE TWO: EMPHASIZE MEANING AS AN AID TO LEARNING

Not only do we want students to get meaning *from* what they read, but we also want them to learn how to *use* meaning *to* read. An important factor related to initial learning and retention is the degree of meaningfulness of the material. Poor readers, in particular, need to be able to relate what is being taught to something that has meaning for them. There are three basic ways teachers can help students use meaning to read. Two of these are ante-

cedent conditions. An *antecedent* condition is one that comes before another; these conditions already exist or are arranged prior to a learning activity.

One antecedent condition that can be arranged by the teacher is the choice of *content* of reading material. Material should be selected for which the student already has some background information. When background is lacking the teacher must build the student's concepts about the topic through discussion, showing of pictures, using media, and so forth, prior to having the student read the selection.

The second antecedent condition is related to the type of activity chosen for instruction. When reading is fragmented so the student must focus entirely on small bits and pieces of language it often becomes meaningless and, therefore, harder to learn. To avoid this, during the initial stages of learning in particular, the teacher should turn activities and games that give practice with isolated words and skills into whole-language activities and games. A *whole-language activity or game* is one that enables the integrated use of all three cuing systems of language (the graphophonic, the syntactic, and the semantic cuing systems). When all of these are working together, the poor reader receives the most help. An example of an activity that is *not* a whole-language activity is the use of flash cards with single words on them to drill students. In this activity, students can use only graphophonic clues—the letters and/or their sounds—because neither syntactic information (sentence structure) nor semantic information (the meanings of other words in a sentence or passage) is available to aid them.

Some approaches to whole-language activities follow.

1. Don't throw away flash cards. Instead, use them for sentence-building. In sentence-building, students attempt to rearrange

several randomly placed word cards so they make grammatical sentences. This is excellent practice for students who make miscues resulting in sentences that do not sound like language. It can also give much exposure to basic sight vocabulary in a meaningful context.

2. Adapt traditional board games that students enjoy so they are required to read contextual material. These games typically consist of a series of squares on which isolated words or letters are written; students move from the first square toward the winner's square by pronouncing each item correctly. A better idea is to leave the square blank, but print sentences or paragraphs on cards with a target word underlined on each. Each student selects a card and reads the sentence. If the target word is read correctly, a number printed at the bottom of the card tells how many squares on the board the student may move.

3. Design crossword puzzles so the clues are not the usual single words or phrases. Instead, prepare paragraphs with words omitted as is done in the cloze procedure, but leaving in the initial one or two letters of each word as clues. The student then attempts to predict the omitted words by using a combination of context and graphophonic clues, then writes each word in the crossword puzzle.

There are many other ways to design or adapt activities so students can use the meaningfulness of whole language.

The third basic way to help students use meaning to learn involves the processes they are taught to employ as they read. The major strategy they should be helped to adopt is to be intolerant of nonsense. This implies that the student engage in constant self-monitoring. If what is read does not sound like language or does not make sense in terms of what the students know about the world, they

should be taught to stop and reread. Some remedial students have come to look upon reading as anything but a meaning-seeking process. Rather, "word-saying" is what they believe is expected of them. Teaching students to self-monitor and to reject any meaningless renditions helps them to minimize sight word confusions and to increase efficiency in word identification. The result is better comprehension of material.

PRINCIPLE THREE: ENCOURAGE OUTSIDE READING

The results of the 1979–80 National Assessment of Educational Progress showed that students of all ages who engaged in free-time reading every day performed significantly better in reading comprehension than those who read less frequently ("NAEP Data on Reading Comprehension Released," 1982). There is no question that poor readers who regularly spend some time outside of reading class reading books, magazines, newspapers—or anything—make more substantial and rapid progress than those who do not. The teacher should have interesting, easy-to-read materials in the classroom and encourage students to check out one of these each time they leave the class. Parents should be asked to turn off the TV and have their child read for 15 or 20 minutes daily. Working with regular classroom teachers to set up programs of sustained silent reading (SSR) in their rooms is also urged. During SSR, all students, including those from the remedial program, read anything they choose for a designated time period every day.

PRINCIPLE FOUR: PLAN FOR SUCCESS EXPERIENCES

Students selected for remedial programs have experienced much failure in their previous

Results of the National Assessment of Educational Progress have shown that students of all ages who engage in free-time reading every day perform significantly better in reading comprehension than those who read less frequently.

school careers. To reverse this negative conditioning, teachers should structure remedial programs so that many success experiences are *guaranteed*. This is particularly important during the first few sessions. To meet most objectives during the remainder of the program, students will read from material at their instructional levels. But during the first 2 or 3 days they should receive material during direct instruction that is targeted to their independent levels. This is one way to ensure success; it gives students the opportunity to perform well for a new teacher in a new program and encourages the belief that this time they will be able to learn. In addition, throughout the program the teacher should be certain that students have the prerequisite skills necessary to complete any task required of them.

PRINCIPLE FIVE: MAKE QUALITATIVE AS WELL AS QUANTITATIVE JUDGMENTS ABOUT STUDENTS' READING PERFORMANCE

The approach the teacher takes when working with students while they are reading has a major impact on their progress in the classroom as well as on the types of reading strategies they develop for independent reading.

Compare these two examples of students miscalling words in written text:

to his house

John rode his bicycle home.

bread

The old man had a black beard which covered most of his face.

Which of these two miscues results in a change in meaning? It is the one in the second sentence, of course. Since the miscue in the first sentence does not change its meaning, what should be done about it? It should be ignored! The poor readers enrolled in remedial classes generally have so many problems needing attention that teaching time should not be wasted nor energies focused on miscues that do not matter. Because the whole purpose of reading is to gain meaning, the test of whether a miscue "matters" is the answer to the question, "Does it cause a significant change in meaning?"

Suppose a sentence in the text is written as "The tall, old man sat on the bench," but the student reads it as "The old man sat on the bench." In this example the teacher must make a quick decision. Is the fact that the man is tall important to the story? If so, then the student should be helped to correct the miscue. If not, it should be ignored and the student allowed to get on with the story. Assessing the quality of each miscue keeps interruptions to a minimum.

What should be done with each of these miscues?

1. I saw footprints leading back to my house. *honz* (The student said a nonword, "honz." Because this sentence now makes no sense, the student should be helped to correct the miscue.)

2. Tom ran rapidly to the ball park. *get to* (The student added two words that were not in the text, but they do not change the meaning. Ignore this miscue.)

3. The bear caught a fish in the stream. *street* (This miscue seriously disrupts meaning. Help the student make a correction.)

PRINCIPLE SIX: FOCUS INSTRUCTION ON THE CAUSES OF PROBLEMS, NOT ON THE SYMPTOMS

When observing students during daily reading, teachers often look for patterns of miscues with the hope that these patterns will suggest remediation procedures. (Of course, teachers should also look for students' strengths as well as attempting to alleviate their weaknesses.) This is a sound process if the focus is on what is causing a given problem. When the focus is on the symptom, however, remedial procedures sometimes go awry. For example, suppose the teacher notices that a student makes many repetitions of words when reading orally. Remedial procedures suggested when the focus is on the symptom (repeating words) might be to use a controlled reader (a machine that projects words at a given speed) so that the student must keep reading forward and cannot repeat; or tape-record a story, then have students read along with the tape to prevent them from repeating. The design here seeks to eliminate the repetition itself. Perspectives based on recent reading research would suggest a different approach, however. The question should

be asked, "Why is the student making repetitions?" The focus is then on the *cause* rather than the symptom.

Phillip reads,

We saw the big, fat hippopotamus at the zoo.

He reads *fat* once, then repeats it before reading on. It is likely that Phillip repeated *fat* to give himself time to work out the word *hippopotamus* or to recall it. He used the repetition as a time-holder rather than merely saying nothing while he read silently to the end of the sentence in an effort to employ context as an aid, or to use phonic or structural analysis skills to figure out how to pronounce *hippopotamus*. There is no reason for the repetition itself to be eliminated in this case. Actually, Phillip's reading behavior is a positive one. It indicates that he is using word-identification strategies to identify unknown words, or that he is taking time to try to remember a word to which he has previously been exposed.

Another example is Ted, whose reading is impulsive, excessively rapid, and characterized by numerous omissions of words. Here is a partial typescript of a story he read.

The boy and his dog ran to play. They found their friends in the ball park. "Give me the bat," yelled Timmy. His little dog was very excited.

If the focus were on the symptom (excessive omissions) the teacher might have the student choral-read with other students, ask the student to point to each word in the story, or prevent the student from omitting words by immediately calling attention to each omission. On the other hand, if the focus is more appropriately on the cause, the teacher will first let Ted know that very fast reading is often not good reading, and then she will consider each omission in light of its unique implications for instruction. Looking at this sample of his reading, it is obvious that Ted is not applying his knowledge of language patterns to reading tasks. The sentences here exemplify more useful instructional procedures.

1. The boy and his (dog) ran to play. (The teacher should ask, "Did that make sense?")
2. They found their friends in the (ball) park. (The teacher should ask, "Did that make sense?")
3. "Give (me) the bat," yelled Timmy. (The teacher should ask, "Did that sound like language?")
4. (His) little dog was very excited. (The teacher should ignore this omission: it does not cause a significant change in meaning.)

If we examine what was done when the focus was on the cause rather than the symptom, it can be seen that these procedures were faster than setting up a program of choral reading. Also, they did not encourage bad habits, such as pointing to each word (a temporary aid that would have to be eliminated later). Finally, they can help establish self-monitoring behaviors that will remain useful when the student is reading independently (since the teacher can't follow students around and call their attention to omissions every time they read something).

Similar questions should be asked for each type of miscue: "Why did the student make this particular substitution (or omission, or insertion, and so forth)?" It is not helpful to simply count the number of various kinds of miscues and then decide that instruction is needed to eliminate the most frequent types. Teachers need to determine why the miscue was made in order to decide what to do to eliminate it—or to conclude that instruction to eliminate it is unnecessary.

PRINCIPLE SEVEN: MODEL EFFECTIVE READING BEHAVIORS

If students have difficulty accomplishing a task when told what to do, add another dimension: demonstrate how to do it. For example, during oral reading, take turns reading with them. It is surprising how quickly a student's oral reading will begin to take on characteristics of the teacher's when this is done.

Role-playing in reading situations can also help. For example, the teacher can pretend to come to an unknown word and then talk through some strategies to identify it. Or, the teacher might read several sentences and demonstrate appropriate identification strategies when she pretends not to recognize a particular word (in this example, the word *bridge*).

> On Sunday our family went for a drive. As we drove along we came to a bridge we had to cross. It went over a small river.

When she comes to the word *bridge,* the teacher might say, "I'm not sure what that word is, so I'll figure it out." She might continue reading out loud, then say, "Well, I know it's something you can cross in a car. It might be a highway or a street or a bridge. I'll look at the beginning letters of the word. They're *br-*. *Bridge* begins with the sounds of those letters, so it's probably *bridge*. I'll read on and see if I can tell if I'm right." After reading the next sentence, she might say, "Yes, I must be right because it would make sense for a bridge to be over a river." In this kind of role-playing, it is best to choose a word that is unknown to the student.

Modeling the strategies needed in comprehension tasks is also effective. If a student has difficulty responding to a question, the teacher may take over the student's role and demonstrate the thinking processes one would go through if the answer were unknown, showing how to select clues, rejecting some answers because of the text information, testing possible answers against background knowledge, and so forth. Modeling effective reading behavior shows students how to learn, not just what to learn.

PRINCIPLE EIGHT: USE ALTERNATIVE INSTRUCTIONAL MATERIALS

If students have bad vibes about books, teachers may wish to use other types of written materials for instruction, at least temporarily, until negative attitudes toward books can be overcome.

Newspapers

Readability levels of newspapers have risen in recent years, although of course these vary from newspaper to newspaper and even from section to section within newspapers. Some research has found that front-page stories range from 9th– to 12–grade levels, and that many help-wanted ads (important to many secondary students) are written at about 6th– to 7th–grade levels. This information is important to keep in mind if teachers are planning to use newspapers as an alternative instructional resource. Obviously, students who read at primary levels may have difficulty if asked to read newspaper sections without assistance. Yet the same newspaper material could be used in a listening lesson, that is, with the teacher reading to these students. Also, some of the easy-to-read newspapers mentioned in Chapter 9 could be substituted for a community's daily paper. Some low performers who read above the primary level may be able to learn from reading regular newspapers if the teacher works with them individually to provide any needed assistance; some others may be able to read some newspaper sections by themselves.

Once the teacher has determined the approximate readability levels, newspapers may serve many educational purposes, a number of which are listed here.

1. For vocabulary study, read a feature story to the students. Then ask them to change every adjective to a synonym.
2. To work on critical reading skills, read an editorial with the students. Ask them to underline facts and circle opinions.
3. Cut apart news stories and their pictures. After students have read the stories, ask them to match the pictures with their story counterparts as a comprehension check.
4. To practice evaluation skills, read newspaper stories for one week. Then as a group activity, list on the chalkboard stories that would fit under two categories, good news and bad news. Discuss why.
5. Have students cut out bar, circle, line and pictorial graphs found in newspapers. Have them describe how to read each one.
6. To work with content area vocabulary, ask students to search for math words (sales tax, square feet, metric measurements, pints, math words found in recipes, percentages, etc.). Make a group math collage with these.
7. To increase skimming skills, have a scavenger hunt. Provide a list of items found in one daily newspaper. Students must list page numbers on which items are found. First one with a complete (and correct) list is the winner.
8. For one week read and collect all articles on the President of the United States. At the end of the week, in a group activity, summarize his activities. The second week, do the same, but have students write individual summaries. Discuss and evaluate these as a group.
9. To work on inferencing skills, study editorial cartoons for one week. Discuss their

meanings. Also, discuss how one can learn from pictorial material.

10. Ask students to use the travel ads to plan a vacation. Have them list all information they can cull from the ads—climate, recreational opportunities, sports attractions, and so forth.

11. Read book reviews. Classify the books as *fiction, nonfiction, biography,* and so forth.

12. To work on word meanings, have teams develop crossword puzzles using words from the newspaper to exchange with other teams to work.

13. To practice classification skills, read the sports section. List the sports under various categories (Activities that Took Place in Our Community versus Those in Other Communities; Team Sports versus Individual Sports; Spectator Sports versus Participation Sports; etc.). Which sports may be listed under more than one category?

14. Study comic strips. Have students infer from their actions each character's personal characteristics. List vocabulary describing each one.

15. Use headlines to generate predictions about articles before they are read.

16. Select an article and have students act out what was reported.

17. Ask students to read feature and sports articles to find these types of figures of speech:

- alliteration—several words in a row beginning with the same letter
- simile—a comparison using *like* or *as*
- metaphor—a comparison that does not use *like* or *as*
- personification—giving human characteristics to something that is not human

The teacher should list two or three examples of each of these on the board before students begin.

18. White-out dialogue in a comic strip. Make photocopies to give to each pupil. Have them write their own dialogue.

19. Give students several articles to skim. Next, ask each student to make up one question for each article, using the *W* words *who, what, where, when,* and *why.* Then hold a news contest: two students are the contestants and are asked questions by the other students; when a student gives an incorrect answer, he is replaced by another student as a contestant.

Driver's License Manuals

An easy way to capture interest in reading with many older students is to use the state's driver's license manual as the instructional material in remedial classes. Obtain several copies and work through the manual section by section over a period of time. Plan lessons to highlight students' strategy and skill needs. If, for example, students need to enlarge their sight vocabularies, make a cumulative card file and select three new words for it from each day's lesson; review all the words each day. If meaning vocabulary is the need, write definitions of the words on the backs of the cards and frequently review these. If word identification strategies are deficient, select some words for preteaching before each lesson. In one lesson have students examine structural elements (prefixes, suffixes, base words); in another, ask them to divide multisyllabic words into syllables, or to guess words from the context of the sentence or paragraph in which they are embedded. Always ask comprehension questions after each section.

Table 10–1 lists readability levels of driver's license manuals for the 50 states in the United States. Some states have learning packets that can be used to make the driver's manual an instructional tool. For example, *Improving Reading Skills: A Learning Module Based on the South Carolina Driver's Handbook* (Bohac, 1976).

Table 10–1
Readability levels of driver's license manuals. (*Source:*   From "Are Drivers' Manuals Right for Reluctant Readers?" by Norman Stahl, William Itenk, and James King, 1984, *Journal of Reading,* November, p. 167. Reprinted with permission of the authors and the International Reading Association.)

| | Readability formula | | | |
State	Raygor	Fry	Flesch	Average difficulty
Alabama	12	12	10–12	Fairly difficult
Alaska	College	13	10–12	Difficult
Arizona	9	9	8–9	Moderate
Arkansas	11	11	10–12	Fairly difficult
California	9	9	8–9	Moderate
Colorado	11	11	10–12	Fairly difficult
Connecticut	6	6	6	Easy
Delaware	College	10	10–12	Fairly difficult
Florida	11	10	8–9	Moderate
Georgia	7	7	7	Fairly easy
Hawaii	11	12	13–16	Difficult
Idaho	12	11	10–12	Fairly difficult
Illinois	10	9	8–9	Moderate
Indiana	11	10	10–12	Fairly difficult
Iowa	10	10	10–12	Fairly difficult
Kansas	8	8	8–9	Moderate
Kentucky	11	11	10–12	Fairly difficult
Louisiana	7	7	7	Fairly easy
Maine	10	10	8–9	Moderate
Maryland	11	12	13–16	Difficult
Massachusetts	College	12	13–16	Difficult
Michigan	7	8	8–9	Moderate
Minnesota	12	11	10–12	Fairly difficult
Mississippi	12	12	13–16	Difficult
Missouri	11	12	13–16	Difficult
Montana	11	11	10–12	Fairly difficult
Nebraska	Professional	15	17+	Very difficult
Nevada	10	11	10–12	Fairly difficult
New Hampshire	8	9	10–12	Moderate
New Jersey	8	7	7	Fairly easy
New Mexico	11	10	10–12	Fairly difficult
New York	12	12	13–16	Difficult
North Carolina	8	9	8–9	Moderate
North Dakota	11	10	8–9	Moderate
Ohio	12	14	13–16	Very difficult
Oklahoma	College	13	13–16	Very difficult
Oregon	10	9	8–9	Moderate
Pennsylvania	9	10	8–9	Moderate
Rhode Island	10	10	10–12	Moderate
South Carolina	8	9	7	Moderate
South Dakota	11	10	10–12	Fairly difficult
Tennessee	12	11	10–12	Fairly difficult

Table 10–1, *continued*

State	Readability formula			
	Raygor	*Fry*	*Flesch*	*Average difficulty*
Texas	11	11	8–9	Moderate
Utah	8	9	8–9	Moderate
Vermont	College	13	13–16	Difficult
Virginia	8	8	8–9	Moderate
Washington	College	13	13–16	Difficult
West Virginia	10	10	10–12	Fairly difficult
Wisconsin	12	11	10–12	Fairly difficult
Wyoming	10	10	10–12	Fairly difficult
Puerto Rico	10	9	8–9	Moderate
Mean	10.5	10.2	10–12	Fairly difficult

Other Materials

There is nothing sacred about resorting to the narrative story-type material typically assigned in reading instruction. The important thing is that the student read, read, read. Use poetry, children's cookbooks, or even cartoons. Plays are popular with all age levels and provide many opportunities for engaging the mind with print: read the play silently to learn the story, silently reread your own part to prepare, orally reread your own part by yourself to practice, orally reread the play as a group activity, orally reread the play to present it to another group, and so forth. Some secondary teachers have students read the lyrics to popular music and base strategy lessons on the words and meanings. To motivate middle school students, Klasky (1979) collected a file of funny anecdotes and comedy routines; these were given to students for oral reading, for reading to prepare group skits, and for comprehension activities.

PRINCIPLE NINE: STIMULATE MOTIVATION

Motivation is learned. From infancy, children are selectively rewarded for their behaviors.

The child learns to crawl and the movement feels good. Children begin to talk and their parents reward them with responses and praise. As a result, during the preschool years a natural motivation to achieve and learn new things usually is at least to some degree established. When some children begin school, however, they fail to develop many of the skills that get rewards in the school environment. By the time many students are identified as needing special instruction and are placed in a remedial or clinical reading program (or in classes for the learning disabled or the educable retarded), their desire to participate in learning experiences has been extinguished. For many of these children, then, the teacher in the special program must make definite plans to re-establish motivation so that academic learning can occur. Plans to stimulate motivation can be classified into two types: those that are antecedent conditions, and those that are consequences.

Antecedents

Antecedents, that is, conditions planned prior to the learning experience, are important. It is not enough merely to attempt to shore up a poorly planned or dull program by rewarding students' performances after a learning experience. Here are six approaches to antecedent conditions designed to motivate students to read.

Instill a need for reading. Help students recognize how reading can assist them in achieving personal goals. If Randy is interested in playing Little League football, find an easy-to-read book on how to be a football player and use this as his material for regular, connected reading. If Harrison wants to obtain a driver's license, help him learn to read traffic signs as part of your word identification strategy lessons.

Understand that a reward for doing an activity can exist within the activity itself. Example: if the action or plot in a story is intrinsically interesting to a particular student, he will be impelled to finish it. Teachers should find out what interests their students. In nonfiction material, reading for a definite purpose gives students a reason to finish the task, or even to engage in it in the first place. Some examples are: reading and following directions to cook or to construct something, or to play a game; or reading to satisfy curiosity (sometimes fomented by the teacher). The point is to use materials and activities that are responsive to the unique or group interests of the students because learning can then become its own reward.

Use student-prepared materials. Have students dictate books about themselves. Even students who initially pretend to be interested in nothing usually find "self" to be a very interesting topic. Each day's dictation can comprise one chapter of the book. These can be used for connected reading and the focus of strategy lessons. Dictating books is made even more interesting to secondary students if a machine is involved: interview the students with a microphone and tape recorder to get stories of their lives, or have

them type their own chapters, even if a hunt-and-peck system must be used. Students also enjoy reading stories written by their peers. Establish a classroom mailbox system: a student writes a story and places it in a manila envelope addressed to someone else in the class; the student who receives the story reads it as an independent activity, then must write and mail a story to someone else.

Rewrite difficult material. If you find an article or story on a topic of interest to students, but it is too difficult for them to read, rewrite it using easier vocabulary and less complex sentence structures. Teachers who try this find that it is not very difficult to do.

Make a conscious effort to relieve student anxiety. Anxiety can block responses and the desire to engage in an activity. Tell students that making errors is a normal occurrence for everyone and that people can learn from their mistakes. Point out that you will also be learning ways to help them from errors they make. Give kind, constructive help when difficulties occur. (Few teacher behaviors can discourage motivation as quickly as comments such as, "Don't you remember that word? We had it yesterday," or, "I just showed you how to do that. How could you forget already?" Few individuals would risk the humiliation of such comments if they could really perform the task, and most slow learners have had their full share of humiliation.) When *you* make a miscue when reading to students—as all readers do—call their attention to this and point out that even good readers make mistakes. Tell them why you made the error and how you were able to correct it.

Obtain professional materials that suggest ideas for motivating reluctant readers. One of many helpful booklets is *125 Motiva-*

Box 10–1
Positive Reinforcements

Primary Reinforcers
Unconditioned reinforcers are an integral part of life and are effective without any history of specific experiences, for example, food, water, sex. Sometimes food (e.g., candy) is used as a reinforcer in academic programs, but this is usually inappropriate because students can become satiated and then the food is no longer reinforcing. There are also practical problems with using food as a reinforcer—a student may be allergic to a particular food and have an undesired reaction, or parents may object because it interferes with good nutritional habits.

Learned Reinforcers
Conditioned reinforcers acquire value as a result of experiences.

Tangibles.   The student is given tangible items as a result of desired performances. Examples of items sometimes used are inexpensive books, stickers, or collectibles.

Tokens.   The teacher prepares small cards or pieces of construction paper and gives the student one of these "tokens" for correct responses. When a specified number of tokens have been collected, they may be exchanged for a tangible item, activity reinforcer, or natural reinforcer.

Activity Reinforcers.   As a result of a change in academic performance the students are allowed extra gym time or may view a cartoon movie.

Natural Reinforcers.   A privilege is given in relation to a naturally occurring classroom event, for example, being allowed to: a) choose the story the teacher will read to the class today; b) sit at the teacher's desk during sustained silent reading time; c) have an extra turn at the class typewriter; d) write a story on the chalkboard today, instead of paper; or e) design this week's class bulletin board.

Knowledge of Progress.   Instead of merely telling students they are doing well, a visual display, such as a chart or graph, is used to demonstrate growth.

Praise.   The teacher praises effort as well as accomplishment. Praise is frequent yet conveys sincerity. *Labeled praise* is best, that is, the teacher specifies why the praise has been given. For example, instead of saying "Good job!", the teacher says "Good job! You tried to use context clues on every hard word today, instead of just guessing wildly." Praise can also be administered nonverbally, for example, with a wink, a smile, or a pat.

---

tors for Reading (Feron-Pitman). Be selective. Certain idea booklets provide some suggestions which are not directly related to reading. Be thoughtful in deciding which ideas to choose and which to reject.

When planning antecedent conditions to motivate students, the teacher should remember that the main reason the student is in the program is to learn, not just to have fun. We want learning to be enjoyable.

The principle of academic engaged time also must be kept in mind. If a possible activity is heavy on pleasure and light on learning, that activity should be abandoned. There are so many possible ways to make reading experiences enjoyable that it is unnecessary to select those that have only a cursory effect on academic gains.

Consequences

Consequences are conditions that occur after a learning experience. These may also be planned and have an important effect on learning. Consequences can be thought of as rewards—or reinforcers—of behaviors. Whenever a behavior, whether personal, academic, or social, is positively reinforced, it will probably occur again.

For some students who have never experienced the joys of reading, extrinsic rewards may serve as temporary propellants into the process. Intrinsic motivation should later supplant extrinsic rewards if the right combinations of learning experiences are selected and used. Types of reinforcers, listed from the more intrusive to the less intrusive, are shown in Box 10–1.

Reading is a hard job for many students in remedial programs and, often, in the initial stages, not considered a very pleasant one.

Providing positive reinforcement as a result of improved performance or effort can make the task more palatable ("A spoonful of sugar makes the medicine go down in the most delightful way"). It is important, however, to use the least intrusive reinforcer that is effective for a specific student. If Brian will expend more effort as a result of keeping a graph of his own progress, it is inappropriate to set up a token system to provide him with activity reinforcers. If Scott is motivated to try to learn more sight words simply by being told that for each day that he shows an improved performance, he may sit at the teacher's desk for silent reading, it is inappropriate to give him tangibles as reinforcers. Reinforcers should be gradually faded from the more intrusive to the least as the student moves toward the ultimate goal of intrinsic motivation.

Additional specific suggestions for planning positive consequences are:

Figure 10–1
A colorful bulletin board can recognize a student in a positive way

1. *Give positive recognition.* For example, incorporate a student's name into bulletin boards, papers, and so forth, as a form of praise. (For example, see Figure 10–1.) What student wouldn't love to walk into a classroom and see that he is the focus of the class bulletin board, or that one of the group activities that day is reading a short paper complimenting him?

2. *Visually demonstrate progress.* Use charts, graphs, add-to puzzles, or color-in puzzles. An add-to puzzle is made by cutting a picture into many puzzle-like shapes. A backing on which to attach the puzzle is devised so that the shapes of each piece are drawn there. For each correct answer the student may attach a puzzle piece to the backing so that after a specified number of correct responses he has a completed puzzle. A color-in puzzle uses the same idea, but a shape is embedded in the puzzle. (See Figure 10–2.) The student colors in one section for each correct response until he has a complete picture.

3. *Help students get through all the tasks of a lesson.* Even when students work directly with the teacher, concentrated effort and on-task behavior can be a problem for unmotivated, poor readers. Devise a system in which students can observe their own progress by marking off each task as

Figure 10–2
Example of a color-in puzzle

it is completed. A simple checklist may be sufficient for older students, but an attractive picture to color works well with elementary school children. See the example in Figure 10–3. The students color in each figure in the picture as each designated activity ends. They can thus see what has

Figure 10–3
An imaginative checklist for younger readers

been accomplished and where the lesson is going.

4. *Inform parents about the student's learning.* Some teachers have had success in using daily report cards to motivate students. Each day, a report is forwarded to the parents indicating the progress their

child is making. Most parents praise students when growth is evident, thus they receive reinforcement at home as well as at school. In addition, on-task behavior may be increased with daily report cards. Sulzer-Azaroff and Mayer (1977) cite the incident of a high school girl

I, _____Paul_____, agree to ___study___
    (student's name)   (what)

*the title and pictures of stories and make a prediction about each story before I read*_____, to do this for ___*1 story a day*___
               (how much)

_____, to do it ___*everyday for one week*___, and ___*not to put my head down and say I don't want to.*___
          (when)   (under what conditions)

I, _____Mrs. Daly_____, agree to ___let___
      (teacher's name)   (what)

Paul take home my tape recorder and dictate a story onto tape

_____, to do this for

___*one night*___, to do it ___*the day after*___
  (how much)   (when)

*he completes all 5 stories as agreed to above*___, and ___*to provide the tape, which he may keep.*___
                             (under what conditions)

Signed *Paul Hill*

Signed *Mrs. Daly*

Figure 10–4
Example of a contract between a student and teacher

who did not complete assignments. A card was devised on which the teacher placed a check mark for each assignment completed during a class period. The student's parents awarded her privileges at home based on the number of check marks received. As a result, there was a substantial increase in completion of assignments.

5. *Use contracts to spell out goals and rewards to the student.* A contract is a written agreement between the teacher and the student designed as both a prompt and a reminder to help the student meet an objective. The contract delineates the task very specifically and specifies the reward when the goal is accomplished. An example of a contract is seen in Figure 10–4.

CONCLUDING STATEMENT

Although individual students' needs differ when they are enrolled in remedial classes, the principles discussed in this chapter apply to all students. For example, a student who needs assistance in developing a variety of word identification strategies and one who requires help with comprehension will *both* benefit from Principle One: "Let the Students READ"; Principle Two: "Emphasize Meaning as an Aid to Learning"; Principle Three: "Encourage Outside Reading"; and so forth. It is wise for teachers to review the principles in this chapter occasionally to compare them with programs they are developing to determine if all these important ideas are being incorporated.

UNIT FOUR

Remedial Procedures
for Students Having Difficulty
Learning to Read

11

The Nonreader and the Severely Disabled Reader

The reading difficulties of students enrolled in remedial and clinical reading programs vary in severity. With skillful remediation some of these students make rapid gains. Others, with larger discrepancies between their present achievement and their potentials, nevertheless progress steadily with the specialized help they receive. A few students, however, have much more severe problems and require special considerations beyond those made for other disabled readers.

CHARACTERISTICS OF NONREADERS AND SEVERELY DISABLED READERS

A *nonreader* is an individual who is unable to read, despite much reading instruction. Taken literally, the term *nonreader* would indicate that the student can recognize *no* words. In most cases this is not true. Even extreme disability cases can usually identify a few words— perhaps their own names, or *Boys* or *Girls* on restroom doors, or words important in their everyday lives, such as McDonalds or Burger

King. As a result of instruction, some of these extreme cases may have spotty knowledge of a few words typically taught in beginning reading programs, such as a color word or two, a few function words from a high-frequency word list, or a few words learned from a readiness book or a first preprimer. The number of words known by a "nonreader" may range from about 2 to 50, but because they know so few words and because the words they do know are usually so unrelated, they cannot combine the words into any kind of meaningful reading. The fact that most of these students have learned even a few words is a hopeful sign however, and dispels the erroneous notion that these students are "word-blind" or have some neurological processing problem that will make it impossible for them to ever be able to read.

The term *nonreader* should be distinguished from the term *prereader*. *Prereaders* are individuals who cannot read simply because they have not yet been exposed to reading instruction; for example, many 5 year olds are prereaders. A nonreader, on the other hand, has been exposed to extensive instruction and still is unable to read in any meaningful sense. Older individuals who are often labeled as *illiterates,* are sometimes nonreaders, but in other cases are really prereaders; that is, they do not read because they have not had the opportunity to learn. (The term *preliterate* is often used synonymously with the term *prereader.*)

Although nonreaders are certainly subcases of the group called *severely disabled readers,* this latter term is generally used to mean individuals who have progressed further into the reading process than the nonreader, but who are still reading at a level extremely below their LELs. Severe reading disability cases, including nonreaders, comprise about 3 percent of the population. Reading teachers, learning disability (LD) teachers, and teachers of educable mentally retarded students may all work with severely disabled readers.

Some other characteristics of nonreaders and severely disabled readers are

1. Their problems result from multiple, and differing causes.
2. They are found in all IQ ranges, but most have average intelligence.
3. Some appear to be impulsive, that is, they make thoughtless guesses when attempting to read. These behaviors are usually a result of a faulty understanding of what is required in the reading task. Sometimes they result from being exposed to faulty methods of instruction.
4. Some, on the other hand, are extremely reticent about making any attempts to pronounce words if they have the least doubt about the correctness of their responses.
5. After teachers have worked with them for awhile it becomes evident that they have a desperate desire to read as well as their peers, although their initial, overt behaviors often belie that conclusion. Initially, they avoid reading, exhibit off-task behaviors, and sometimes are uncooperative.

6. They are discouraged and think they cannot learn to read. Many have been given information by well-meaning but misinformed individuals that reinforces this notion. For example, Eric, a university football player who was referred to a college of education reading clinic, said to the staff at the first meeting, "I can't learn to read. I have dyslexia." Eric was then given a short selection of material to read. After reading he was told, "You don't have dyslexia; you just don't recognize some words. We'll teach you how to figure out words you don't know." Eric's response was, "But, at the medical facility I was told that I have dyslexia." The response was simply, "We're reading specialists and they aren't. You don't have dyslexia." Later assessment determined that Eric was reading at about fifth-grade level. This is certainly an indication of a severe disability for a college student, but it also indicates that he did not have some mysterious malady that made it impossible to read. Eric, who had average intelligence and wanted to read better, was delighted to find that he wasn't "dyslexic," and cooperatively engaged in activities suggested for remediation.
7. They usually require one-to-one instruction. Frequent remedial sessions are needed, and the typical severe reading disability case must be enrolled in a program for an extended period of time.
8. They can learn to read. Commonly these students make very slow progress during the initial few weeks of the program, then a breakthrough occurs and progress is rapid for a fairly extensive period. "Plateaus" are reached periodically, however, during which progress continues but slows considerably. These plateaus are followed by periods of a return to rapid progress. Recognition of this cycle in learning rate is important. Failure to learn to read can occur when either the parents,

the teachers, or the student decides during the initial stage of slow progress that the program is not working and the student drops out before the breakthrough can occur. Failure can also occur after the initial stage of rapid progress begins, and the student leaves the program because she believes that she will now be able to progress without further specialized help. Finally, failure can occur when the first plateau period is reached if the individuals concerned become discouraged and, believing the student has reverted to her past nonlearning behaviors, they discontinue the program. The key to success is sticking with the program.

IMPORTANT PRINCIPLES FOR WORKING WITH NONREADERS AND SEVERELY DISABLED READERS

Those general principles for reading instruction that are important for disabled readers (as discussed in Chapter 10), also apply to nonreaders and severely disabled readers. There are, however, additional principles to consider for these extreme disability cases.

One: Make Reading As Easy As Possible

When working with students who are in the beginning stages of reading acquisition, and who, despite a great deal of instruction, seem unable to move ahead, the key often is to focus on the concrete before moving to the abstract. (Some beginning reading programs designed for poor readers do just the opposite.)

There are three basic orientations upon which approaches to reading instructions are based. One of these is the *grapheme/phoneme* orientation. Approaches based on this orientation generally follow three steps. First, students work with letters, first by learning to identify their written forms (graphemes), then

by learning the sounds (phonemes) attached to these. Next, they learn to identify individual words by putting letter sounds together. Finally, they put words together to read sentences and then to read connected reading material. One published program based on a grapheme/phoneme orientation is DISTAR.

The second approach, employed by most basal reader programs, is based on a *skills* orientation. This approach specifies many skills to be learned, and establishes a hierarchy for instruction in these. Skills programs strive to develop competence in a variety of word-identification strategies (as opposed to the one strategy of "sounding out" unknown words that is emphasized in grapheme/phoneme approaches). Skills programs also attempt to balance word-identification practice with instruction in other areas, such as comprehension.

The third basic orientation is called a *whole-language* orientation. Methods based on this orientation, such as the language experience approach (LEA), begin reading instruction by having students read "whole language" (for example, whole sentences or short, student-dictated stories); only later do they work with smaller language parts, such as letters and their sounds.

While reading approaches that subscribe to each of these three orientations emphasize the salient features described above, in actuality, many programs incorporate some features of all three orientations. Most students can learn to read in instructional programs that employ any of these orientations. The Cooperative Research Program, a large, nationwide, government-sponsored study that compared 27 different reading programs, found no one method superior to another for increasing students' reading achievement (Bond & Dykstra, 1967). Although this research was carried out in regular classroom settings, the same results have been found with students having learning problems. For example, reading achievement of educable retarded students has been compared for use of the language experience approach, basal readers, programmed materials, the Initial Teaching Alphabet (ITA), basals using rebus symbols, Words in Color, synthetic phonics approaches, and teaching machines. The results have been the same; no one of these methods has been found to be superior to another. (See, for example, Blackman & Capobianco, 1965; Boyle, 1959; Cegelka & Cegelka, 1970; Woodcock, 1967.)

There are two groups of students, however, for whom the method used does appear to make a difference, at least initially. These are chronic nonreaders and the severely disabled readers. When a program begins a reader with the task of letter recognition, and then adds the learning of the sounds of those letters, the student must grapple with a great many abstractions. For example, when learning the letter *r*, the student is expected to remember that a line like this |, and a line like this ⌒, placed together in just the right relationship (for example, not like this ʰ or this ⌐), together have a name that people call by the nonsense sound "ar," but which is said to make a different nonsense *sound*, /r/, as heard at the beginning of *red* or *robin*. And in addition, an "ar" has another form consisting of lines like these: | ⊃ \ . And these lines also must be put together in just the right relationship, like this **R**, and not like this **Я** or like this **Ʀ** . And even though this looks different from the first letter, it's an "ar," too. Learning to attach nonsense names and nonsense sounds to lines and squiggles requires much abstract thinking and places a higher demand on memory than does concrete, or meaningful, material. A heavy emphasis on abstract learning makes reading anything but easy.

Reading approaches based on a grapheme/phoneme orientation begin with such abstractions. Many, though not all, skills approaches also start readers with the task of working with individual letters. One basal reader series, for example, devotes the first section of the first-grade readiness book to this task. Although most students have no difficulty learning letter recognition, many poor readers have decided difficulty. In the second semester of first grade they have not progressed beyond the first section of the readiness book because this basal reader program advocates retaining students at any given level until they have mastered all skills taught at that level.

While in theory this may be a sound idea, in practice the success rate is higher when the first skills taught are easier rather than more difficult than later skills. When teachers working with these poor readers have ignored the dictates of the program and have allowed students to move on to working with whole stories, the students begin to read—even though they have not mastered letter recognition. At a later time, the teachers have the students return to the task of learning letter names and have them work gradually on this skill in combination with other reading activities.

Some skills programs and all whole-language programs begin students' initial reading instruction with concrete, meaningful material. Whole-language programs that begin by having students read their own dictated material are particularly helpful to nonreaders and severely disabled readers, who, typically, have difficulty dealing with abstractions. Suppose a student has just dictated this sentence after an experience of particular interest.

We saw an elephant at the zoo.

Think how much more meaningful this is than trying to memorize all the abstractions necessary to learn the letter *r*, or the letter *m*, or any of the other letters of the alphabet in their upper- and lower-case forms.

People who have developed programs that break the reading task down into very small components, (for example, learning letters and their sounds: e.g., /b/, /a/, /t/, /m/, then blending these to produce syllables; e.g., /ba/, /ma/, then stringing these together to make words; e.g., *bat, mat*) have done so with the good intention of making reading easier for students. The premise that the smaller the part the easier it is to learn is true to some extent with certain types of learning; for example, learning the component skills of arithmetic calculations. But the opposite is true in reading because reading is a language-based activity. In language, the smaller the component the more abstract it is. A whole story is more meaningful than a single paragraph, a paragraph is more meaningful than a single sentence, a sentence is more meaningful than a single word, and a word is more meaningful than a single letter.

The specific approach selected for reading instruction is not highly significant for most readers, including most disabled readers. However, many nonreaders and severely disabled readers learn more rapidly when their initial reading experiences are made easier by focusing on concrete, meaningful material rather than on tasks that require abstract learning.

Two: Instructional Activities Should Approximate the Real Act of Reading

This principle certainly holds true for the instruction of *all* students. Deviation from it has most often occurred with nonreaders and severely disabled readers, because remedial teachers and programs have advocated activities far removed from the act of reading. For example, some of these programs employ body management and/or perceptual training, and may include activities such as work with the Frostig (1966) perception program; visual tracking exercises; body management training (walking balance beams, crawling, jumping, climbing, and rolling on the floor); and eye-hand coordination exercises such as throwing bean bags or drawing lines. The stated purpose of this training has been to provide a prereading perceptual/motor foundation that ultimately would foster reading achievement. Yet, whatever the goal of these programs may be, research has shown that they provide no assistance to academic learning for reading disabled, learning disabled, or educable retarded students.

Certain types of visual discrimination activities often used in prereading programs also have been found to provide no readiness for reading. One such activity requires students to visually discriminate between shapes and pictures. A typical exercise of this type asks the student to look at the first shape or picture and find all others in a line that look the same or to find all the shapes or objects of one type in a picture. Research has shown that matching shapes and pictures as preliminary instruction for letter and word discrimination is useless (Barrett, 1965; Gates, 1926). If teachers want students to visually identify the distinguishing features of letters and words, the exercises should include *letters* and *words* (not non-word forms). Similar findings have resulted from research on auditory discrimination training. These studies have shown that training with nonverbal sounds does not transfer to the auditory discrimination skills needed for reading. Training with nonverbal sounds may involve having students auditorily discriminate between environmental sounds, for example, by asking them to close their eyes while the teacher taps on several objects such as a desk, the chalkboard, or a window, and guess the object being tapped; or having them listen to tape-recorded sounds such as an alarm clock, lawn mower, or bird call, and guess each sound. Such exercises simply do not help to teach reading. If it is decided that auditory discrimination training is necessary for a particular program or a specific student, the training should involve discrimination of letter or word sounds.

When choosing activities for reading instruction, the teacher should ask, "How close to the real act of reading is this?" If reading teachers are deciding between asking students to walk a balance beam and asking them to dictate and read a story, then of course they would select the story activity. If they were choosing between an exercise sheet involving discrimination of triangles and ovals versus one involving discrimination of words, they would, of course, select the latter. Making these types of decisions will prevent teachers from wasting instructional time on worthless activities so that more time will be available to carry out activities that do help students learn to read.

PREREQUISITES FOR INITIAL READING ACQUISITION AND READING PROGRESS

Because nonreaders and severely disabled readers have not learned to read as other students have, a first question might be, "What is lacking when they first come to the reading task—what knowledge or aptitudes found in most students were missed to prevent them from starting to read or making normal progress?" If we knew this, it would seem that we could plan a program of instruction to alleviate these weaknesses and thereby enable the student to begin to learn to read.

It is important that teachers understand the prerequisite knowledge and understandings helpful to the successful acquisition of reading. When considering these prerequisites, there are two areas of inquiry.

• What are those knowledge areas and understandings necessary to enable a beginning reader (or a nonreader) to be ready to learn to read?

• What are those deficiencies in prerequisite understandings that may be preventing a disabled reader (including the severely disabled reader) from advancing at a normal rate of development?

To answer these questions we must learn which understandings and knowledge *are* helpful, and we must study the research literature to identify those fallacious notions about prerequisites that can cause teachers to make incorrect assumptions, misdirect student programs, and waste instructional time.

Helpful Prerequisites

The prerequisites discussed in this section facilitate the process of learning to read and ensure a greater likelihood of success. Good readers possess these understandings and knowledge, and poor readers often do not.

Familiarity with Book Language. Almost all students, including severely disabled readers, had an unconscious understanding of the basic sentence structures of *oral* language and had sizeable oral vocabularies when they entered school. (An exception to this can be individuals with severe hearing handicaps.) This familiarity allows students, as listeners, to understand what is being said to them. Proficient reading also requires an unconscious understanding of language forms. However, book language differs somewhat from oral language, both in sentence structure and in the scope of vocabulary items used. If they are to employ for reading purposes those skills they acquired to comprehend oral language, students need as much familiarity with written language as they have with spoken language. If they come from homes where there has been little preschool exposure to books, or from regular classrooms where the instructional emphasis is on learning isolated skills, this familiarity may be limited.

The best way to acquaint students with the sentence structures found in book language is to read aloud to them. A feeling for sentence structures in written language enables students to make predictions about upcoming words in a text. These predictions aid word recognition and comprehension.

Reading aloud to students also helps them deal with the larger scope of vocabulary items found in books. As students hear stories or informational material read, they form new concepts and attach new vocabulary words to these concepts. Knowledge of multiple-meanings of words may also be developed in this way. For example, the meaning of *run* may be familiar to students from their oral language vocabulary when it means "to move your feet rapidly to get from one place to another," but it may be unfamiliar when it refers to a *salmon run* or a *ski run*. Reading aloud to students helps them increase their repertoires of word meanings.

Research has provided evidence that hearing stories read is important for all students, but is particularly helpful to students in the lowest ranges of reading achievement (D. Cohen, 1968; Fearn, 1971). Reading aloud to nonreaders and severely disabled readers provides readiness for reading and promotes reading progress by familiarizing them with the complex sentence structures and diverse vocabulary of book language.

Understanding How Language is Transformed to Print. Providing an orientation to printed matter is necessary for many extreme disability cases. If these students are in the very beginning stages of reading acquisition, their lack of understanding of certain conventions and terminology may cause confusion when they are given the task of dealing with a page of print. Understanding these conventions and terminology is called *metalinguistic awareness*—a big name for some basic concepts.

Two *conventions* for reading English are: start at the top of the page, not the bottom; and move from left to right. *Terminology* that may seem obvious to the teacher may not be obvious at all to the beginning reader, especially a student who has limited experience with books. For example, students must understand what a letter is, what a word is, what a sentence is, and what a paragraph is. These prerequisite concepts are already familiar to many beginning readers and, therefore, teachers are not always aware of the necessity to directly teach them to those students to whom they are not known. Administering the Concepts About Print Test (described in Chapter 7) or using informal questioning and observation will identify the extent of instruction needed in these prerequisite areas for certain nonreaders and severely disabled readers.

Understanding the Task Requirements of Reading. Many extreme disability cases have major misconceptions about just what it is they are supposed to do when they are given a page of print. They know that other individuals look at these pages full of ink marks and say words. As teachers observe them working with printed matter, it is obvious that they perceive the task as one of remembering combinations of lines, and letters, and word shapes. They, therefore, study the lines and squiggles and try to remember how certain ones of these when put together in a certain pattern mean a certain word. For instance, given the word *take,* the student may approach the task by thinking, "There's that word that begins with that tall letter with a line across it and there are two small round letters and a tall letter in the middle. What was that word?" Or if they are already familiar with the names of letters they may try to memorize the spellings of every word. They do this because they think this is how other people remember and recognize words. Such an approach puts too great a load on memory and reading becomes impossible.

Although reading requires some use of graphic information (the letters and words), attention to all of the graphic information on a page is not only unnecessary but actually prohibits normal responses to print. Every attempt must be made to demonstrate to these students that they should not try to memorize each small component of a word, but that instead they should use some graphic information in combination with the knowledge they already possess about language and the world. This means, of course, that when an unknown word is encountered the reader should make a guess (prediction) about what word would make sense or sound right in that context, and confirm the guess by looking at *some* graphic features of the word, perhaps just the first letter, or one or two consonants. For an occasional word the students may need to study the graphic aspects more carefully, but they must be taught that it is not necessary to examine each and every letter in each and every word. To do so makes reading so laborious that it cannot occur in any normal sense.

When students learn to use language knowledge and meaning in combination with graphic information, reading becomes markedly easier. All students are able to use this knowledge, but many nonreaders and severely disabled readers do not do so intuitively. These students must be directly taught this crucial prerequisite concept.

Using oral and written cloze procedures is helpful for demonstrating how language and meaning aid word recognition. Some useful activities are:

1. a. The teacher says a sentence, omitting the final word. The student orally supplies a word that makes sense.

The boy was wearing a yellow tee _____.

I like to read _____.

b. The teacher writes short sentences, omitting the final word. The teacher reads the partial sentence and asks the student to supply a word that would make sense. When a sensible word is offered, the teacher writes the word in the blank while pronouncing it. Then the student is told, "See, you could figure out what word went there without even seeing the letters."

2. a. The teacher says sentences in which a word is incorrect.

His mother is a nurse. She works at the (tree).
My favorite animal is a (run).

The student is asked to explain what is wrong with the sentence, then asked to orally substitute a sensible word.

b. The teacher writes short sentences in which a word is incorrect, using a word that is graphically similar to a sensible substitute.

The cowboy wanted to ride away, so he jumped on his *house*.

The teacher reads the sentence, asks what is wrong with it, and what word could make it sound right. When a meaningful word is supplied, the student is told, "You knew the right word because you know what would make sense or what would sound right. This is what good readers do to figure out words."

All of these activities are aimed at teaching the student to use context (that is, meaning and syntax), and to eliminate the habit of relying exclusively or excessively on graphic clues.

Unnecessary Prerequisites

Some skill and knowledge areas previously assumed to be important for reading readiness and normal progress are not. Some are helpful in other aspects of instruction, though not necessary prerequisites before a student can begin to read. Others are simply not related to reading in any way.

Letter Recognition. This term does not mean that the student knows the letters in their correct alphabetical sequence, nor does it mean that the sounds of the letters are known. It simply means a student is able to look at a letter, recognize it, and name it.

Many people believe that students must be able to recognize letters before reading instruction can proceed. This is simply a logical assumption for some, but for others the assumption is based on a large number of studies that have shown that knowledge of letter names is the single best predictor of success in first-grade reading

(Dykstra, 1968; Johnson, 1969; Lowell, 1971; Samuels, 1972; Venezsky, 1975; and others). The purpose of these studies to determine predictors of reading success was to identify those factors that could be used to measure reading readiness. Because knowledge of letter names has consistently been shown to be the best predictor, certain school districts are relinquishing use of standardized reading-readiness tests and are substituting a test of letter recognition.

But, some educators have gone further and said, "If letter recognition is the best predictor, let's *teach* letter names early, and let's be sure students have mastery of these before we allow them to begin reading instruction. This will ensure a greater chance for their later success." The problem here is in their interpretation of the research. It must be remembered that correlation does not necessarily mean causation; even though knowledge of letter names may be correlated with first-grade reading success, this does not mean letter recognition causes higher reading achievement. Rather, being able to recognize letters may reflect other

---

Box 11–1
Significance of Letters

Dear John,
   I just read that a ten-year study of mortality statistics at a London hospital, which was reported to the British Medical Association, showed that people whose last names begin with the letters between S and Z are twice as likely as others to develop ulcers and three times more prone to heart attacks (quoted in *Harpers,* January 1976, page 8). Does this have some significance for us in education?

Jan

Dear Jan,
   From your data, it seems to be *letters* that are giving people ulcers and heart attacks.
   I say we should get *rid* of *letters*.

John

Source: From "Significance of Letters" in *Journal of Reading,* December, 1977, p. 269. Reprinted with permission of the International Reading Association.

variables, such as preschool experiences with books, or parents who cared enough to teach letter recognition to their child during the preschool years. Any of these variables could affect reading achievement. Thus, it appears that reading success and letter knowledge may both result from common factors, rather than one causing the other.

Although letter recognition can be used with a fair degree of precision as a predictor of achievement, letter recognition is not a necessary prerequisite before students can begin to read. We know, for example, that the language experience approach (to be discussed later in this chapter) is a highly successful method of beginning reading instruction for many students, and that in this approach students often do not learn to name individual letters until after they are successfully reading whole stories, sentences, and words.

Teachers should understand that students do not have to recognize letters before they can learn to read, and that students should *not* be held back from exposure to meaningful material until they have mastered letter recognition. But, although knowledge of letter names is not a necessary prerequisite, it is helpful knowledge that can assist in other instructional objectives.

Perceptual and Motor "Processing" Skills. In 1976 Evans and Smith reported a study that has important implications for an examination of prerequisites for reading. Students participating in this research were administered several tests designed to assess certain psycholinguistic and perceptual processes often assumed to be prerequisite for normal reading. In this study, a significant number of students scored *below* average on the following tests.

1. The Illinois Test of Psycholinguistic Abilities (ITPA) subtest of "Visual Reception."

This subtest assesses the ability to see relationships between two similar visually perceived objects (for example, one item on this test assesses visual reception by determining the student's ability to note the relationship between a wastebasket and a garbage can when pictures of both are shown to the student).

2. The ITPA subtest of "Visual Closure." This subtest assesses the ability to recognize an object when that object is in different positions or when only a part of the object is visible (for example, one test item presents a scene at a construction site with many hammers lying about in such a way that only a portion of their forms is seen; the student's task is to find them all).

3. The ITPA subtest of "Grammatic Closure." This subtest assesses use of conventional oral language forms (for example, "Here is one mouse, but here are two _____.")
   (mouses, mice)

4. The Colarusso-Hammill Motor-Free Test of Visual Perception. This assesses perception of shapes.

5. The Bender-Gestalt Test. This tests visual-motor integration. Students must be able to visually perceive shapes and then reproduce them by drawing.

6. Visual tracking of a moving object. Students are required to follow a moving object with their eyes.

7. A test of lateral dominance. Such tests are designed to determine if a student has established preference for use of the eye and the hand that are on the same side of the body.

8. Hopping skill. This test determines whether a student can hop as well on one foot as on the other.

9. Left-right discrimination. This test determines whether students can distinguish

left from right, including on their own bodies.

Obtaining below average scores on these tests is supposed to indicate a reading or learning disability. However, the students who scored below average in this study had no learning difficulties. In fact, they were academically gifted kindergarten and first-grade students who were already reading at fourth-grade level! All of the areas on which these students were tested (visual closure, visual-motor integration, left-right discrimination, and so forth) involve abilities or skills that have been suggested by one group or another as important aptitudes that are necessary for success in reading. The Evans and Smith study is just one of several indicating that this is not so.

Reading readiness is not promoted by perceptual processing abilities, such as being able to see similarities in objects or being able to note that a portion of an object is related to a whole; nor by motor processing skills such as ability to draw shapes, track moving objects, hop, or discriminate left from right. None of these abilities or skills is a prerequisite for reading, nor does their absence prevent normal reading. They are not related to reading. In 1986 the Council for Learning Disabilities adopted a position statement opposing measurement or training of perceptual and perceptual motor functions as part of remedial programs; this position was based on the extensive body of research discounting the value of such assessment and instruction ("Measurement and Training," 1986).

GENERAL APPROACHES FOR TEACHING NONREADERS AND SEVERELY DISABLED READERS

Despite their past histories of failure, many nonreaders and severely disabled readers can learn through standard reading methods when these are individually applied with adaptations in technique. There are certain other specialized methods that are seldom used except with extreme disability cases. But it should be remembered that no one method, whether an adapted standard method or a specialized method, works with every nonreader and severely disabled reader. If one method does not seem to be promoting progress after a fair trial, others should be tried until one is found that works.

The Language Experience Approach

One standard reading method, the Language Experience Approach (LEA), is particularly helpful with severe disability cases because it is based on use of the student's own language and experiences, and involves concrete, meaningful reading tasks from the outset. Stauffer (1970) reported that students enrolled in the university reading clinic with which he was associated made better progress with LEA than with more typical clinical procedures such as the Fernald approach. Many extreme disability cases who did not progress well under instruction using the grapheme/phoneme or skills approaches have finally begun to read when LEA procedures were substituted. Techniques used in LEA seem to provide the entrée into the reading process that previously eluded those students. This occurs with so many students that it is probably best to try LEA first, because in doing so the odds are with you. If it proves not to be helpful, other methods may then be tried.

Sample LEA Program to Use With Any Disabled Reader in the Beginning Stages of Reading Acquisition. First, elicit the student's oral expression. This may be done by briefly discussing an experience, an object, a book, or an audiovisual. When working with a group, the teacher must stimulate interest in a common or shared experience. The teacher may, for instance, have brought a turtle into the room that day to place in the class aquarium to be the focus of a brief group discussion.

In the second step, a story is dictated by the students. For example, after they have taken a few minutes to examine and discuss the turtle, the teacher may go to the chalkboard and have them tell some of the things they noticed about it. As the students express themselves the teacher writes their statements on the chalkboard, saying each word out loud as it is printed. This results in a short "story" of about a half a dozen sentences. For example, here is a story that might be dictated collectively by a primary age group.

> Our turtle's name is Tom Turtle.
> This turtle is little.
> He has colors on his back.
> He eats turtle food.
> Turtles like to sit in water.
> I wish I had a turtle at home.

The level of sophistication of such stories will of course vary depending on the age of the students, but in the initial stage the story should be kept short.

During step three, the students read what they have expressed. First they may "read" the story by repeating sentences the teacher reads while he points briefly to the words. Next, they all read aloud together. In a short time, the students have moved from a concrete experience to a verbal experience, and then to the printed word. Upon completion of each lesson, the teacher should leave the story on the chalkboard so that it may later be copied onto an experience chart. This chart allows the story to be read again the next day.

In step four, in order to strengthen the reading experience the teacher initiates a number of related activities. For instance,

the students may be asked to draw a picture about their story. As they do so, the teacher goes to each student's desk and writes on the picture a word or sentence that the student used to describe it. The printing on the pictures may range from one word, such as *turtle,* to a complete sentence, "We have a new turtle." The teacher may also find a book about turtles and point out some of the words found there that were also used in the experience story. This session might be concluded with the teacher reading aloud from the book about turtles.

The next day, for step five, the group reads the experience chart about turtles. In this step the teacher begins to work more carefully on word identification and recognition skills. Volunteers may be asked to point to words they remember, and to pronounce them. Or, they may be asked how many times they see the word *turtle* in the story, or what other words in the story begin with the same sound, and so on. In this way the students begin building a basic sight vocabulary and some word identification strategies.

For step six, which also occurs on the second day, the teacher will have used a typewriter to reproduce the story for duplication and distribution to each student. Students silently read their individual copies and underline all the words they are not certain they know. After the stories have been read silently, each student reads a copy aloud to the group while standing beside the teacher. In this way, the teacher can see which words have been underlined and be ready to provide help. The individual copy of the story, stapled to yesterday's picture, can be taken home to be read to parents. The teacher keeps one copy of the story to be bound into a permanent class book of experience stories.

In the language experience approach, other activities take place as well as dictating and reading personal stories. In *Language*

Experiences in Reading (Allen & Allen, 1966), a teachers' resource book, a program is suggested that includes spending 40 minutes a day on dictating and reading stories. In addition, there is a continuous program of the following activities: exploratory work with manuscript handwriting using words from the story; use of a writing center; encouraging students to read and write at home; using games and activities to review words and word identification strategies; making individual word lists; making a class book of large experience charts; viewing and reading filmstrips; and writing all words from each story on individual index cards and giving a set to each student to be placed in a personal file box (these are used for sentence building, writing messages to one another, playing matching games, alphabetizing, and finishing incomplete sentences). After students spend 1 or 2 days on reading and engaging in extension activities, a new story is dictated and the process begins again.

Following a period of several weeks during which students read their own language, the next step is reading the formal written language found in classroom texts and library books. In the process of reading their own stories, students learn to recognize enough words to successfully read beginning reading materials.

An Adaptation for Some Nonreaders and Severely Disabled Readers. Many extreme disability cases can progress in reading by following the Language Experience Approach outlined above, especially if the procedures are carried out individually with maximum feedback by the teacher. Other nonreaders and severely disabled readers may need an adaptation to profit from the LEA. Adding new stories every day or two seems to overwhelm some students because of the numbers of new words they encounter. If standard procedures are not meeting with

success, then instead of having the student dictate a new story every day, use the same story each day until all words are learned. A variety of games and activities to practice each word can be employed until the student can read the story perfectly. This will instill in the severe reading cases the confidence that they can learn to read something with no mistakes. Words the student learns should be placed in a file box and reviewed daily. Each completed story can be kept in a notebook and two or three of these selected every day for rereading before work on the present story begins.

Most nonreaders move more rapidly through each succeeding story. To assist in speeding up the process of word learning, constant and immediate reinforcement is particularly helpful at this stage. Here is an example of how reinforcement may be applied. (Italicized words and phrases indicate positive reinforcements.)

1. Joan reads the three-sentence story she has just dictated. When she doesn't know a word, she is asked "What word would make sense there?" If she responds correctly, she is *praised*. If she cannot respond, she is told the word in order to allow her to continue her reading.

2. After the complete story is read, the teacher selects one sentence and asks Joan to reread it. When there is difficulty with a word, she is asked to use context ("What word would make sense there?"). A correct response is *praised*. If there is an incorrect response, she is told the word.

3. Step 2 is carried out with all sentences in the story.

4. The teacher chooses a word from the story that he thinks Joan will *be able to recognize*. If she can pronounce it, the

teacher *immediately gives her a check (or a star, etc.) on a card,* plus *praise.*

5. Step 4 is repeated for all words, with the teacher *interspersing words Joan may not remember with those he is sure she will know to ensure some success experiences with word recognition. Every* correct response is *immediately* given a *check* and *praise.*

6. After work with all words in the story, *Joan counts the total number of checks she has received.*

7. *A bar graph is begun on which Joan colors in squares for every check.*

8. Joan is told she will *receive a reward for every 10 squares that are colored in.* The number of colored squares specified to receive a reward is *set so that it is expected that she will receive a reward each day.* ("Rewards" should be *selected so the activities or items are reinforcing to that specific student.*) (See Figure 11–1 for an example of a bar graph of this type.)

9. All words Joan recognizes are written on index cards. These are filed in a box labeled *"Words I Know".*

10. Unknown words are also written on cards and filed in a separate box as "Words I Am Working On".

11. When the words filed in both boxes are reviewed each day, Joan *receives one check for correct responses on words known the previous day and two checks when words she is working on may be transferred to the box of known words.* This same technique can also be successfully applied to very easy published materials such as preprimer level, easy-to-read, high interest books.

The requirement that students learn all words in a story does not imply that the program should be one of boring drill. Good teachers vary the word practice exercises and make them fun. They also include other types of activities during a session, such as orally guessing words from context, listening and reading along with tapes of predictable books, and so on.

After the student begins to make rapid progress, repetitive work on the same story and the requirement of mastery of all words before beginning a new story should be dropped. Although a stress on word-perfect reading is inappropriate with most reading disabled students, for nonreaders it is appropriate as a temporary strategy in the initial stages of reading acquisition. Its purpose is to build a base of words, as well as confidence, to help the student get into the reading process.

The language experience approach has been used successfully with very poor readers of all ages, including older students. Edwards (1965), for example, reported its success with culturally deprived, illiterate adolescents and adults. Some topics for story dictations with such students of intermediate, middle school, or senior high school age might be sporting events, television programs, career choices, learning to drive, dating, favorite music, school lunches, funny experiences, magic tricks.

The Fernald Approach

Probably the best-known clinical procedure for nonreaders and severely disabled readers is an approach developed in 1921 by Grace Fernald and Helen B. Keller. Known as the Fernald, or VAKT, approach, the procedure is carried out in four stages that employ the *V*isual, *A*uditory, *K*inesthetic, and *T*actile senses. Since four senses are involved, it is often referred to as a *multisensory approach.* The Fernald method uses the following four stages.

Stage 1: Tracing.　The program is begun with whole words, not letters. Students choose a word to learn. This can be a short word, long word, easy word, or

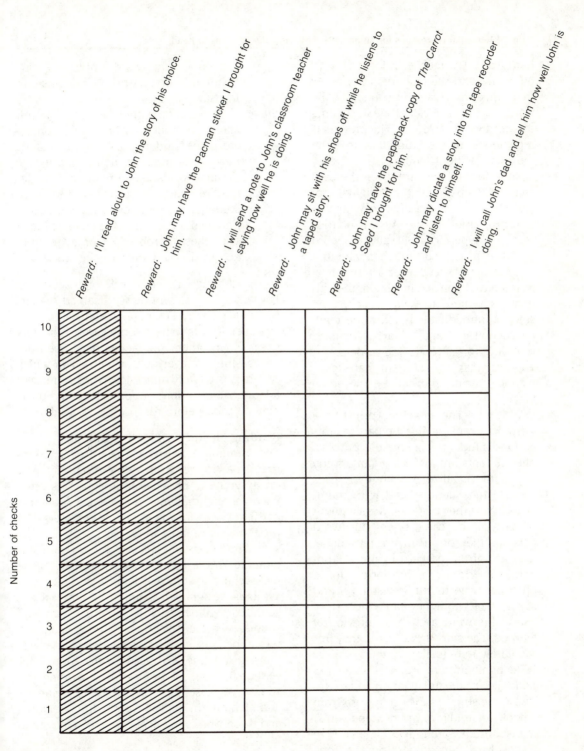

Figure 11–1
A bar graph for charting the number of words known by a student

219

hard word. The teacher prints the word on a card and the students trace it. As they trace, they say the sounds of the word *parts* (this does not mean spelling the word letter by letter). The process is repeated until the students can write the word without looking at it. If they cannot do this, they are given the card again and must repeat the original process. When they are able to write the word from memory, it is typed and they read it in typed form. Finally, the word on the card is filed alphabetically in a box for later review. After a number of words have been accumulated, the student uses these to write a story. The story is immediately typed to be read. Instruction in Stage 1 may occur for a few days or several weeks before it appears that the student can learn without tracing and can be moved to Stage 2.

Stage 2: Writing. The teacher prints the word on a card, saying the parts as this is done. Students observe the process. The students are given the card, study it, try to visualize it with their eyes closed, and silently "say" it to themselves. Next they write the word without looking at the card, saying the word parts as they do. If an error is made, they are given the card again to compare the error with the correct form. They continue to study, visualize, and say the word until they can write a story using this word and those previously learned. The story is typed and they immediately read it silently, then orally.

Stage 3: Recognition from print. The teacher no longer prints the word on a card. Instead, the students choose a word from a book, are told its pronunciation, study it, visualize it, "pronounce" it silently to themselves, then write it from memory. If they cannot do this, they study and

pronounce the word until they can. Reading in first preprimers begins during Stage 3.

Stage 4: Recognition without writing. In this stage, each new word is not written. Instead the students are taught to study new words and note their similarities to familiar words. Silent reading precedes oral reading. During oral reading, if students do not know a word it is pronounced for them. After the reading, only these "problem" words are pronounced and written by the student.

Although the research on use of the Fernald approach with most disabled readers has shown contradictory results, this approach has been known to help some severe disability cases when other approaches have been unsuccessful. However, it is a method in which progress is usually quite slow. For this reason, a language experience approach should probably be tried before resorting to this method.

Reading Mastery: DISTAR Reading

The Reading Mastery: DISTAR Reading program is a grapheme/phoneme program based on a synthetic phonics approach. It is often used in remedial reading and LD programs and in classes for the educable retarded. The program is available in two kits.

In the initial stages of the program students learn the sounds of 40 symbols. These include the lower case letters, certain letter symbols designed by joining letters that are sounded together such as *ng,* and long vowel sounds with their diacritical marks. Silent letters appear in small type. (Later in the program a transition is made to the more conventional forms of print.) After learning the sounds of these symbols, students sequence and blend them to form words. Still later, two- and three-word sentences are read. One of the first of these is

hē rēads.

Eventually the students progress to reading stories.

One advantage of the DISTAR program is that there is a great deal of instructional time for each student because, a) one requirement of the program is that students have daily lessons; if students miss one day, they must have two lessons the next day; b) the teacher carries out procedures to ensure 100 percent attention from everyone in the group; c) the procedures ensure that every student responds during every lesson; and d) the lessons are usually about 40 minutes in length—twice the length of lessons in many beginning programs. Another advantage is that there is immediate feedback to each student response.

There are also disadvantages to the DISTAR program. One is that some of the skills taught are based on older theories of the reading process and have been found unnecessary in learning to read. Time spent on mastering these skills is time that could be allotted to learning more efficient strategies. Another disadvantage is that students' instruction is begun with the abstract task of learning the sounds of letters; they do not read words until they have mastered the sounds. For some students this means that it is a long time before they are in contact with meaningful material in which more rapid progress can be made.

The Orton-Gillingham Approach

In 1966 Gillingham and Stillman developed a program for working with severely disabled readers based on theories about causes of reading disability advanced in the late 1920s by Samuel Orton. This is generally known as the Orton-Gillingham Approach. In 1976, Slingerland proposed certain adaptations to the program. The adapted program is referred to as the Gillingham-Slingerland Approach or the Orton-Slingerland Approach. Both approaches employ a grapheme/phoneme orientation and include four basic steps.

1. Students trace single letters, then learn their sounds. Many weeks are spent on working with letters and letter/sound associations.
2. Students are taught to blend consonants and short vowels into words that have a consonant-vowel-consonant pattern. They blend the first two letters, then add the last: /ma/ + /t/. Then they spell the word.
3. Sentences composed of the resulting words are read.
4. Phonetically irregular words are learned through tracing.

There are several disadvantages to these Orton-based approaches. First, daily lessons for 2 years are required to complete the basic programs. In addition, students are not allowed to actually read until they have mastered a large number of skills. Finally, these approaches teach only one word-identification strategy, "sounding out" unknown words.

Although these programs have been successful with some students, Ruppert's (1976) research showed that the Orton-Slingerland Approach produced no better reading achievement than a more flexible, eclectic method when used with learning disabled students.

Linguistic Approaches

Recently there has been much discussion about basing reading instruction on psycholinguistic research. *Psycholinguistic* processes are those that combine thinking processes with language knowledge.[1] Approaches based on psycholinguistic research emphasize meaning as a means and an end to reading

---

[1]The term *psycholinguistic* is used differently by educators and researchers in different fields. For example, in *special education,* it refers to ability training and process approaches involving body management and perceptual activities. Special educators advocate instruction that is radically different from that advocated by reading educators when the latter suggest reading instruction based on psycholinguistic research.

and generally advocate instruction based on a whole-language orientation.

The *linguistic* approaches discussed in this section are *not* the same as approaches based on psycholinguistic research, even though there is a similarity in name. There are many different types of linguistic programs. Most of these stress word recognition ability rather than comprehension of material. The rationale for this emphasis is that it is believed that comprehension will follow naturally when students recognize words. The textbooks used in most linguistic programs stress phonetically regular words, and employ the principle of minimal variation in which words introduced together are alike except for one letter. Examples are *sit, bit,* and *fit,* or *Dan, ran,* and *can.* Reading selections are written with words that fit these patterns, such as

Dan, the man, ran as fast as I can.

The stilted language patterns thus produced do not promote use of normal language clues and in many linguistic texts the resulting stories are not very interesting. Some programs also omit pictures from primary readers so students cannot rely on picture clues to identify words. Certain students have made progress in linguistic programs, but more meaningful approaches through which success is likely to occur more rapidly should be tried first.

Programmed Materials

Programming is a format through which reading material is organized; it is not an approach itself. For example, instructional material can be programmed for computer-assisted instruction, but it can also be made available through specially designed, or programmed, text-workbooks. A wide array of materials based on various teaching orientations or approaches has been programmed.

A well known set of these types of materials is the Sullivan Program (McGraw-Hill), which employs a phonic-linguistic approach.

The Sullivan workbooks are divided into short frames of instructional material through which students work individually and at their own pace. Each frame poses a question and provides a short answer. Students immediately check their answers by moving a cover sheet to expose answers printed in the margin. Two advantages of the Sullivan Program are that the frames break up tasks so they seem easy and manageable to severely disabled readers, and that the immediate correction of answers prevents practicing of errors. Two disadvantages are that some of the lessons focus on tasks that are not very important for reading regular, connected reading material, and that these materials do not emphasize those strategies that are most helpful in word identification. For both of these latter reasons, severely disabled readers who appear to be achieving in this series may experience some difficulties in other reading material.

When choosing an approach to use with extreme disability cases, the teacher should remember Special Principle Number One, which urges that reading be made as easy as possible. Some traditional methods for working with nonreaders and severely disabled readers, including certain approaches described here, seem to make reading harder by focusing on smaller, less meaningful aspects of language. Because whole-language tasks are more meaningful and therefore easier for most readers, those methods employing them are the best first choices when adopting a method to facilitate reading acquisition by extremely disabled readers. If progress is not seen within a program's planned schedule, alternative methods should be explored.

SPECIAL TECHNIQUES FOR SPECIFIC PROBLEMS

There are certain specific teaching/learning problems that often occur with extreme disability cases, regardless of the general approach used. Suggestions for remediating these follow.

Teaching Letter Recognition

Although recognition of letters is not a skill that must be mastered before students can begin to read, there are practical reasons why it is helpful for students to possess this knowledge. For example, we know that a powerful clue to word identification is the use of context clues in conjunction with the initial letters of words. Obviously, for students to use this strategy they must know what letter it is that begins the word they are attempting to identify. The naming of letters helps teachers communicate their roles in words. These descriptions of /f/ and /g/ suggest how cumbersome it would be to have to go through a student's instructional program referring to letters in ways other than by their names: "What sound does that upside-down candy cane with a line across it make?" or "Notice that this word begins with a ball with a tail."

It has been noted that nonreaders and severely disabled readers often have difficulty learning letter recognition because of the abstractions in the task. Therefore, teachers should not prevent students from starting to read merely because they have not yet mastered the naming of letters. In addition, competence in letter recognition should be one of several goals rather than the primary focus of the student reading program. For example, in a 1 hour lesson 10 minutes might be devoted to learning letter names, with the remaining time spent on other skills and reading experiences. Here are some suggestions for assisting students with letter recognition.

1. Probably the best way for students to learn the names of letters is during handwriting lessons. As they learn to form each letter, they are taught its name. Writing the letter also calls the student's attention to its distinguishing features.

2. Another technique that will help students note the distinguishing features of letters is to have them trace letters and say the name. Several variations of letter tracing that may be employed are tracing letters written on paper, tracing sandpaper letters purchased through a teacher supply catalog, and placing a light layer of sand in a cafeteria tray and having students trace letters in the sand. Using several methods provides variety in lessons. It should also be noted that there has been some misunderstanding about the purpose of tracing activities. Tracing is not used because certain students learn in some unusual manner; that is, it is not because these students learn with their fingertips instead of their brains. Tracing is used simply because it aids impulsive students who might not attend to specific details of a letter if asked merely to look at letters as they are learning them.

3. Some teachers have found it more successful to have students learn capital letters before they are taught lower-case letters. An advantage of this is that letters that are easily confused are less similar in their capital forms. Note the differences in similarity between the capital and lower-case forms of these often confused letters:

BD bd

A disadvantage is that in reading, students encounter lower-case forms much more often than capitals.

4. Relate lessons on letter recognition to other materials that are meaningful to students. For example, write Susan's name and call attention to the letter it begins with. Then have her find all the words in the day's experience story that begin with that letter.

5. Work with only a few letters at a time—

perhaps two or three—and introduce new letters only after these are learned.

Helping Students Eliminate Letter Confusions

When students confuse similar letters this is often the result of a *reversal* of the left and right directions of letters (for example, confusing lower-case *b* and lower-case *d*). At other times the confusion is an *inversion;* that is, the tops and bottoms of letters are inverted (for example, in confusing *b* and *p*).

In the past, when students mistook *b/d, n/u, d/p, M/W,* and so forth, this was often attributed to a visual perception problem, mixed lateral dominance, or a neurological processing problem, and it was an easy way to get a student labeled as "dyslexic." Research in the fields of education, neurology, and psychology has shown these views to be incorrect. In the first place, reversals and other letter confusions are found in only about 10 percent of reading disability cases (Harris, 1970). In addition, letter confusions are as common with young average readers as with poor readers. Most educators today believe that these confusions simply result from inexperience with *directionality* as a way of making discriminations (Moyer & Newcomer, 1977). When identifying concrete objects like chairs, or pipes, or birds, or cars, the direction of the object does not affect its name. A chair facing right or a chair facing left, or a chair placed upside down, is still a chair. To discriminate among many similar letters, however, direction is important. A line with a circle on its right side is a *b,* but a line with a circle on its left side is a *d,* while an "upside-down" line with a circle on its right side is a *p.* With training in the importance of directionality even preschool children have eliminated their confusions of reversible and invertible letters.

Confusion of letters is a fairly typical behavior pattern during the early stages of learning to read. It should not be presumed to be a danger signal indicating some type of imminent or unusual problem. However, such confusions need not be ignored; instructional procedures can be implemented to ensure that they do not persist. Some suggestions for helping students eliminate letter confusions follow.

Don't forget the helpfulness of context. Suppose a student frequently confuses *b* and *d.* With regular, connected reading material, if the student is reading for meaning the context frequently will not allow these confusions. For example, reading *big* as *dig* would not make sense in this sentence.

That big dog chased me.

When context does provide a clue to letter or word identification, rather than ask the students to examine the visual aspects of the letter, encourage them to use the more efficient strategy of relying on meaning; that is, have them read to the end of the sentence and ask "Did that make sense?"

If students confuse *b* and *d,* (probably the most common reversal), prepare a capital *B* and a lower case *b,* each cut from oaktag. Show students how the small *b* could fit on top of a capital *B.*

Tell them that if the letter they are looking at does not fit on top of the capital *B* correctly it is not a *b.*

Use file cards. Print *b*s on some cards and *d*s on the others, or do this with whatever letters you're working on. Mix them up. Have the students sort all the *b*s into one pile and all the *d*s into the other. When they can do this accurately, then time them to see how *quickly* they can make the discriminations in order to build up speed of recognition.

Make up worksheets containing rows of letters. Have the students circle all the *b*s, or *m*s, or whatever letters they are confusing. When they can do this accurately, time them to see how quickly they can do this correctly. For example:

w o h w n s o n u p l o n g i u l n u

p r u t u o v n k a b t z n h u j

The worksheet should contain both letters the students are confusing, for example *n* and *u*, but the students should be asked to circle only one of the two.

Have the students go over a page from a magazine and circle with a marking pen all of one of the letters in the pair they are confusing.

Improving Nonfluent, Word-by-Word Reading

Word-by-word reading is a normal behavior in beginning reading. Average readers usually progress through 4 stages.

Stage 1: Initial reading is quite fluent, and students are unaware of their miscues.

Stage 2: Students become aware of matching their speech responses to words in the text and, therefore, begin to point to individual words and read in a staccato fashion.

Stage 3: Finger pointing disappears but word-by-word reading continues as they consciously match their oral responses to each word.

Stage 4: Word-by-word reading disappears as students read in meaningful phrase units (Clay, 1967).

Only when students remain at the second or third stage of this sequence does their nonfluent reading become a concern. Excessively slow and halting oral or silent reading can adversely affect comprehension and limits the amount of reading that can be accomplished.

The first consideration when dealing with this problem is to be certain that students are not being required to read material at their frustration levels. If the student encounters an excessive number of words she does not recognize in a passage of a text, the context cannot be used efficiently to identify unknown words, and reading necessarily becomes halting and word-by-word.

When material at the appropriate level is used and the student's reading is still unusually nonfluent, the *neurological impress method* is often used. Developed by Heckleman, the neurological impress method, or NIM, is a technique in which the teacher and student read aloud simultaneously from the same material (1966). The student selects a book of interest. The teacher sits slightly behind the student in order to read directly into the student's ear. The teacher and student read orally together. As they read, the teacher slides a finger under each line being read so that the student can observe the words. At first the teacher reads in a slightly louder voice than the student, and just fast enough to try to move the student along at a reasonable pace. After the beginning stages, the student assumes the responsibility of sweeping a finger under the words being read and the teacher does not attempt to read louder or faster. If the student misses a word, no attempt is made to use word-identification strategies; instead, the teacher just keeps the student moving along by continuing to read. This program is not suitable for nonreaders since students must have at least a small sight vocabulary to read with the teacher in this way.

NIM is a supplementary technique that requires no more than 15 minutes per session. This method has been used successfully with older as well as younger severely disabled readers.

Allegedly, NIM is effective because "neurological memory traces" are developed when the student hears and sees words simultaneously. This technique was originally proposed in the 1960s, a time when there was a heavy emphasis on neurological defects as a cause of reading disability. Although this explanation of why NIM is helpful is a spurious one, the technique may have value for other reasons. To begin with, the student receives immediate feedback about whether responses are correct or incorrect by hearing the teacher's responses. Second, the brain interacts with a great deal of regular, connected reading material.

NIM is often referred to as a program of *language immersion,* that is, the student is immersed in large amounts of connected language. Another language immersion program has been developed by Chomsky (1976).

Chomsky worked with very poor readers who had beginning reading skills, but who had failed to progress beyond the beginning level. She had these students follow along in books while they listened over and over to taped stories. The students engaged in this process until they could read the story by themselves with complete ease. Most students required about 20 listenings before they could fluently read their first story; but thereafter, they were able to read each successive book smoothly, naturally, and with ease after fewer and fewer listening sessions. Not only did fluency increase, but students participating in this program acquired confidence and increased interest in reading. Chomsky reported that one parent said that her daughter, who had previously avoided reading, had begun to read all the time at home and that "She even reads to the dog and cat" (p. 291).

A *language immersion* technique is to have students follow along in books while they listen repeatedly to taped stories.

INDEPENDENT ACTIVITIES FOR NONREADERS

There are two reasons why nonreaders may be asked to work on activities independently. First of all, although instruction is best carried out individually with these students, a clinical reading program may not be available in the area where the student lives. Therefore, enrollment in a remedial program in which most instruction is carried out in a group setting may be the only recourse. Some instruction in these cases may be conducted individually, but there will be times when the student must work alone so the teacher can provide direct instruction to others. Secondly, nonreaders spend only part of the school day in the reading teacher's class; during the remainder of the day, they are in regular classrooms with 30 or so other students. Obviously, the regular classroom teacher cannot spend all of the day working on a one-to-one basis with any one student.

Appropriate independent activities are difficult to devise for nonreaders because there is so little they can read. Unfortunately, this results too often in these students being given independent work that provides no assistance to academic learning (such as coloring pictures unrelated to any reading skill or activity).

The instructionally relevant activities that follow may be especially useful to special teachers in their reading programs, but also prove successful in the regular classroom. Most teachers are especially perplexed about how to handle students who read very little (if at all), and welcome good ideas for independent student activities. Reading teachers can make copies of these or similar suggestions and give them to classroom teachers who have students in the earliest stages of reading acquisition. Used in the regular classroom, these activities provide the nonreader with reading-related experiences in addition to those provided in the special clinical or remedial program.

1. Ask a more skilled reader to read and record a story onto an audiotape. Have the nonreader listen to the story, using earphones. After the story is completed, the nonreader is to fold a piece of paper into four sections, then draw pictures about the story in a four-part sequence that follows the sequence of main occurrences in the story.

2. Place labels on objects around the room, for example, *clock, chalkboard, door, chair, desk,* and so forth. Give students index cards with the same words written on them. They are to match the word cards with the labels around the room. Next, they mix up the cards and attempt to read each one without looking at the labels. After silently reading each word, they then check it against the labels in the room. They place the cards back in their packs

and continue to practice until they feel confident that they can correctly read them all without looking at the labeled objects. A peer tutor can listen to them read the words and place those they read correctly in a file box of "Words I Know." The others are retained for more practice.

3. After hearing the teacher read a story to the whole group, nonreaders can use the tape recorder at the room's listening center and record retellings of the story. They may be given differing instructions according to their individual needs such as, "Be sure to tell something about all of the important characters," or "Tell the story exactly in the order things happened," or, "At the beginning, tell the main idea of the story, then give as many details as you can.") At a later time the teacher listens to the taped retellings and provides feedback during the next individual session with each student.

4. Write words on one half of the front side of an index card. Place an illustration of the word on the other half of the card's front side. Make a cut between the word and its illustration, jigsaw puzzle fashion. The cut should be slightly different for each card. The students are to try to read the words, but when they cannot, they match the illustration to the word by finding the jigsaw cut that fits. They read and match until they can say each word without using the illustration. Here are two examples of such word/picture cards.

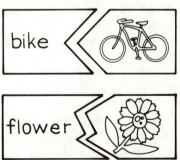

5. Have the students use a wordless picture book. A wordless picture book illustrates a story from beginning to end but contains no words. Many of these are available. A particularly delightful one is *The Chicken's Child* (Scholastic Book Services). The students should be asked to study the pictures from beginning to end and silently develop their own stories. In the next individual session with the teacher, with the book used as an aid, the student can dictate a story for the teacher to write. This story can be used as the focus of a language experience lesson for one or several days.

6. Have the student use a language master, as described in Chapter 9 under the section titled *Mechanical Equipment*.

7. Ask students to listen to a tape recording of an informational selection that the teacher or an aide has previously taped. Include questions on the tape about the selection and ask students to draw their answers (since they probably cannot write the words necessary to respond). Example: "According to what you have just heard, which of these is a reptile: a bird, a dog, or a snake? Turn off the tape recorder now and draw a picture of the right answer. When you have finished, turn on the tape recorder again to hear the next question."

8. Give the students a magazine along with an envelope labeled with a letter, such as *f*. Have them cut out all the pictures in the magazine they can find that begin with the sound of that letter and place them in an envelope to take home for their parents to check. The teacher should be sure to talk with the parents or enclose a note to them so they understand the task requirement. Also, it is important to set up a system, such as requiring a parent's signature on the envelope, for determining whether the check was made.

9. Collect old reading books that can be cut apart. In one session have a peer tutor read a story to the students from one of the books. Before the second session cut out the pictures from the story. In the second session, during which the students will work independently, give them the pictures in a mixed-up order and ask them to place them in the correct order and paste them on hole-punched notebook paper, one picture to a page. By tying yarn through the holes in the paper, they can assemble their own wordless picture books. In a third independent session the students can use this "book" to dictate the story into the tape recorder to be checked later by the teacher for accuracy in remembering details.

10. Cut pictures from old readiness books or magazines so there are pairs of pictures representing words that rhyme. Paste the pictures on colorful construction paper squares and give them to the students in random order and have them match those that rhyme.

11. Tape-record a series of word pairs, some of which begin with the same sound and some which do not. Prepare a worksheet like this:

As students listen to the tape, they circle the happy face if the paired words begin with the same sound, or they circle the unhappy face if the words do not.

12. Paste two pictures on a card side by side and draw frames around each, cartoon-style. The pictures should be related to

one another and placed in a sequence to show a logical progression of events or action. (Old reading books are a good source for these.) Leave space on the card to draw one more frame, but leave this third frame blank. To aid in story prediction, ask the students to draw a picture in this frame depicting what they think might logically occur next.

The suggestions here are only a sampling of ideas for providing reading-related independent work for nonreaders. These ideas were selected to demonstrate a variety of ways to make adaptations through various substitutes for direct teacher intervention (by use of peer tutors, taped material, self-correcting materials, and so forth), and by enabling alternative ways by which students may respond when they lack the skills to make written responses (by drawing, circling happy faces, coloring, and so forth). These suggestions were chosen to illustrate several different skill, strategy, and knowledge areas for which readi-

ness can be developed (following a sequence of events, developing a sense of story, recognizing words, relating reading activities to the real world, noting details and main ideas, relating words to concrete objects, using picture clues, recognizing the messages conveyed by books, making letter/sound correspondences, dictating stories, and gaining familiarity with the book language of narrative and expository material). Teachers should add to these suggestions and maintain a file of ideas for academically relevant, independent activities that can be used with nonreaders.

CONCLUDING STATEMENT

Working with severely disabled readers of any age can be one of the most rewarding of all tasks for the remedial teacher. To continually increase one's skill in this difficult area, professional journals should be regularly perused for new information on the topic.

12

Helping Students Develop an Extensive Sight Vocabulary

Look at all the words on this page. How many are unfamiliar to you? The answer is *none!* All of these words are part of your sight vocabulary. With only a glance, you recognize each one. This is one definition of the term *sight vocabulary* (or *sight words*), that is, words a given reader recognizes instantly. In Chapter 7, three common, and different, definitions for the term *sight vocabulary* were given. They were:

- *Instant Words:* Words the reader recognizes instantly. The reader has no need to use any word identification strategy (such as context clues or phonic analysis) to determine the word.
- *Core Words:* Words that occur with high frequency in all written language; various lists (such as the Dolch list) of high frequency words have been compiled as references for reading instruction.
- *Irregular Words:* Words that are phonetically irregular and therefore cannot be identified by applying knowledge of letter/sound correspondences and phonics rules, or, in more popular terminology, cannot be "sounded out" (Hood, 1977).

In this chapter the terms *sight vocabulary* and *sight words* are used to mean those words that an individual can recognize instantly. Sometimes the term *sight vocabulary* is confused with the term *sight method.* The sight method is a general approach to reading instruction that has been popular in certain previous eras (see the history section in Chapter 1). In general, it introduces words as "wholes" and places little or no emphasis on using phonics or other strategies to examine word parts to identify unknown words. The students are to look at the words, say them, and engage in various other experiences with each word until it can be recognized at sight. The sight method is also called the whole-word method or the look-say method.

Very few reading programs today employ a sight method exclusively. Rather, learning whole words well enough to recognize them at sight is combined with the learning of various word identification strategies that can be used when unknown words are encountered. Research and experience have taught us that relying on a method that teaches reading strictly by sight *or* by a method that is devoted exclusively to one word identification strategy (such as phonics) is ineffective with many students. Although articles appear periodically in the popular press with titles such as "Look-Say versus Phonics for Teaching Reading," these articles present debates that only attack a straw man. This debate has long been settled as an issue in the reading education profession. Contemporary reading programs, with the exception of a very few that are not widely used, do not make this dichotomy in practice. Instead, they combine the development of sight recognition of words with the development of skills in phonics, knowledge of structural analysis, and use of contextual strategies.

RATIONALE FOR DEVELOPING AN EXTENSIVE SIGHT VOCABULARY

Good readers recognize most words instantly. Since these readers do not have to pause frequently to apply phonics or some other strategy to identify unknown words, their reading is fluent and they can concentrate on the meaning of the material. Research has shown that a reader needs instant recognition of about 90 percent of the words in any given text in order to read the text independently. When readers know fewer words than this they must stop too often to try to identify the unknown words as they encounter them. Stopping to determine many words in a passage is detrimental to comprehension because it disrupts the reader's train of thought and concentration on the material.

An extensive sight vocabulary is also important if the reader is to employ the most efficient word-identification strategy, use of context clues. When employing this strategy, readers use the other words in a sentence or passage to help them figure out what the unknown word should be. For example,

Elaine and her mother had just moved to the country. Elaine was lonely and

missed her old friends. She was sitting in a chair with nothing to do one morning when suddenly someone _____ at the door.

Obviously the reader must know the words surrounding the word he is attempting to identify, otherwise this context provides no help.

Another reason why development of extensive sight vocabulary is important is that while letter-sound correspondences in English are not arbitrary, they are not always consistent with exact rules (Venezky, 1970). Readers may be able to match sounds to each letter to figure out most words, but for others they must actually know the word first before they know the sounds of the letters. For example, the word *where* would be pronounced as *were* if one common phonics rule was applied, or *we're* if another common phonics rule was used. But actually it is pronounced neither way because *where* is one of many "irregular" words in English. One must simply learn that a rule doesn't apply here, and learn by rote the correct pronunciation of the word. Only then can one say that the letters *-ere* in the word *where* make a sound like /air/, instead of /er/ or /ear/. English words that do not follow common letter-sound correspondences or phonics rules cannot be "sounded out." In many cases, context helps the reader identify such words, but sometimes it does not. Therefore, sight recognition of these words is often needed.

Finally, when readers no longer must stop often to puzzle over unknown words, they can read more. Clay (1967) reported in a study of first graders that the good readers had read approximately 20,000 words in a year's time but the poor readers had read only about 5,000 words. We know that the amount of contextual reading and the number of opportunities for response are important to reading achievement. The good readers had more opportunity to practice responding to words and therefore became even better; the poor readers had much less practice on the very task on which they needed to work. As in the old saying, "the rich get richer and the poor get poorer," in this case the good reader gets better and the poor reader remains poor. Increasing the number of words a student can instantly recognize saves the time that would be needed to apply a strategy to identify these words; reading then becomes more fluent and more rapid, and therefore more can be read.

SELECTING THE WORDS TO BE TAUGHT

Teachers of students with reading problems must decide what words to choose for instruction when helping students extend their sight vocabularies. But what words should be given priority, which should be taught first, and once these are learned which should be taught next?

Certain words have been identified as occurring frequently in all written material. They make up a large percentage of words in materials at the primary, intermediate, secondary, and even adult levels. They also occur equally often in story-type and informational material. Obviously these words are very important for students to know. Several lists of high frequency words have been compiled. The list names and the references for locating each are found in Chapter 8 in the section titled *Assessing Knowledge of Basic Sight Vocabulary.*

Some high-frequency word lists were compiled decades ago and some more recently, but examination of all of them reveals few differences between them. In other words, most words appearing on any one list are found on all the other lists. In addition, all the lists are current for today's needs. While new words constantly are being added to our language (some recent ones are *microcomputer* and *space shuttle*), the basic function words (such as *for, a, of, and, with, which, be, the,*

that, and so forth) that occur with very high frequency remain the same. For example, one of the older and better known lists, the Dolch list (1936), was analyzed by Mangieri and Kahn (1977) to see if it needed to be updated. They found that 66 percent of all words in current primer through third-grade basal readers appeared on the Dolch list. These researchers concluded that it is still of critical importance for words on the Dolch list to be acquired by students if they are going to be successful in reading experiences. Equally high percentages of the words on the Dolch list have been found at other levels and for other types of materials. It does not matter very much which high-frequency word list teachers use. But, undoubtedly, words from these lists should be given high priority in a program to increase sight words.

Many words on high frequency lists are prepositions and conjunctions, plus a few adjectives, pronouns, and verbs. Because it is quite difficult to write or read materials using just these words, many other words, such as nouns, must also be learned early in order for students to read meaningful material. Therefore, merely having students memorize the words on a high frequency list is inadequate; other words must be taught simultaneously. These other words may be "story-carrying" words—nouns and other words from stories the students will be attempting to read in the very near future. Words that represent things, or words in familiar phrases may be of special interest to students. The introduction of high-interest words stimulates secondary students in particular to learn to read material needed for their daily lives. In the process they pick up many high frequency words that can in turn enable them to read other material. Just one example of how sight vocabulary can be learned in this way can been seen in Box 12–1, which provides a list of highway signs that high school students wishing to obtain a driver's license should learn to read. This list also contains 101 exposures to words found on the Dolch list.

Box 12–1
Highway Signs Requiring Instant Recognition of Words

All Cars (Trucks) Stop

Beware of Cross Winds
Bridge Out

Caution
C.B. 13 Monitored by Police
Congested Area Ahead
Construction Ahead
Curve

Danger Ahead
Dangerous Curve
Dangerous Intersection
Dead End
Deer Crossing
Detour
Dim Lights
Dip
Divided Highway
Do Not Block Walk
Do Not Enter
Drive Slow

East
Emergency Parking Only
Emergency Vehicles Only
End Construction
Entrance
Exit
Exit Only
Exit Speed 25

Falling Rock
Feet
Fine for Littering
Flooded
Fog Area
Food
Four Way Stop
Freeway

Gasoline
Go Slow

Hill—Trucks Use Lowest Gear
Historical Marker
Hospital Zone

Maximum Speed 55
Mechanic On Duty
Men Working
Merge into Single Lane
Merge Left (Right)
Merge Left (Right)
Merging Traffic
Minimum Speed

Narrow Bridge
Next Gas 15 Miles
Next Right
No Dumping
No Left Turn
No Parking This Side
No Passing
No Passing When Solid Line Is
    Right of Center Line
No Right Turn on Red Light
North
Not a Through Street
No "U" Turn

One Way Do Not Enter
One Way Street

Parkway
Pavement Ends
Pedestrians,
    Non-Motorized Traffic,
    Motor Driven Cycles,
    Prohibited
Pedestrians Prohibited
Peding
Ped X Ing
Plant Entrance

Left Lane Ends
Left Lane Must Turn Left
Left Turn on Signal Only
Litter Barrel
Loading Zone
Local Traffic Only
Loose Gravel
Low Clearance

Police Jurisdiction
Private Road
Put on Chains

Right Turn Only
Right Turn on Red After Stop
Road Closed
Road Construction
Road Ends Ahead
Roadside Park

School Bus Crossing
School Zone When Flashing
Signal Ahead
Slide Area
Slippery When Wet
Slow
Slower Traffic Keep Right
Soft Shoulders
South
Speed Checked by Detection
    Devices/Radar
Speed Limit
Speed Limit 15 When Children
    Are Present
Speed Zone Ahead
Steep Grade
Stop
Stop Ahead
Stop for Pedestrians
Stop While School Buses Load
    or Unload

Truck Escape Ramp Unless
    Otherwise Posted
Truck Route
Trucks and Combinations
Trucks Entering Highway
Trucks Over 11'6" Height
Two Way Traffic

Unlawful to Block Intersection
Unloading Zone
Use Low Gear

Vehicles

Warning
Watch for Ice on Bridge
Watch for Loose Gravel
Wayside Park
Weigh Station
Weight Limit 8 Tons

Box 12–1 (Continued)

Ice on Bridge	Radar Checked	West
Information Center	Railroad Crossing	Winding Road
Intersection	Ramp Speed 25	Wrong Way
Interstate	Reduce Speed Ahead	
	Resume Speed	Yield
Junction	Right Lane Must Turn Right	Yield Right of Way

(Source: From "Riding and Reading" by Lana McWilliams, *Journal of Reading,* January 1979, pp. 338–339. Reprinted with permission of Lana McWilliams and the International Reading Association.)

INCREASING SIGHT VOCABULARY: FOUR PRINCIPLES

Following are some points to remember when helping students develop an extensive sight vocabulary.

One: Words Should Be Introduced in Context, But Can Be Practiced in Both Context and Isolation.

There is much controversy over whether words should be taught in the context of a sentence or in isolation. At first glance the research seems to be conflicting on this point. However, a careful examination of well-conducted studies on sight-word learning tells us that:

• Introduction of words in context produces slower initial learning than when they are introduced in isolation, but produces fewer errors in later contextual reading (Ceprano, 1981).
• Introduction of function words (for example, prepositions and conjunctions found on high-frequency word lists) should be within the context of written sentences, not spoken sentences (Ehri, 1976).
• If students are to be tested on words in isolation, practice is better on isolated words, but if students are to be tested on words in context (which is more consistent with the tasks of real reading), it doesn't matter whether they practice words in isolation or in context. Both work equally well (Ceprano, 1981).
• Practice in isolation or context are equally effective for transfer of the word knowledge to *reading* in real contextual material (Kibby, 1975).

The implication of these studies is that working with words in the context of whole language is preferable during their introduction and in the initial stages of learning. In later stages of practice, however, work with isolated words is acceptable. During the later stages many teachers find a combination of contextual and isolated practice to be the most helpful. They may therefore institute a sequence of context, then isolation, then context again. For example

Step 1: Context. Each word to be practiced during a session is read in a sentence.
Step 2: Isolation. A game is used to promote instant recognition of the words.
Step 3: Context. Students read a one- or two-paragraph "story" that the teacher has written to include all words practiced in that session.

Two: Provide Opportunities for Many Exposures to a Word.

Students learn what they practice. An important question when helping readers develop instant recognition of words is, "How much practice is needed before a word is recognized automatically?" The number of exposures needed for each word varies according to its level of abstraction and the degree to which it resembles a similar word. Nevertheless, some information is available about the average amount of practice students need for words in general. In 1931, Gates (p. 35) determined the number of repetitions needed as a function of intelligence levels.

Level of Intelligence	IQ	Required Exposures
Significantly above average	120–129	20
Above average	110–119	30
Average	90–109	35
Slow learner	80–89	40
Upper ranges of the educable mentally retarded	70–79	45
Middle ranges of the educable mentally retarded	60–69	55

These averaged results do not imply that a specific number of exposures is required in isolation; for example, 35 opportunities to say a word that is printed on a flashcard. Rather, it means total exposures of all kinds, including repeated exposures to the same word in a variety of regular, connected reading materials. The goal of the teacher should be to provide overlearning, and not just drill. Drill implies that the student must do the same thing in the same way day after day. A common example of this is the practice of limiting sight-word learning to daily flashcard exercises only. Overlearning, on the other hand, implies that the student will have practice with the word in a variety of ways and in a variety of materials, including contextual material. Overlearning facilitates generalization of word knowledge to all reading situations.

Gates' 1931 findings also are not intended to indicate the exact number of repetitions required by every student. It cannot be presumed, for example, that because Victor has an IQ of 88 that he is going to need exactly 40 exposures to every word. Some words may require more exposures, others less. In addition, Victor may learn all words more rapidly or more slowly than another student with the same IQ.

There are two general implications of Gates' findings that are important here. First, all students, including those with high intelligence, need many exposures to a word before it becomes part of their sight vocabularies; three or four opportunities to respond to a word are not enough. Second, the lower the student's intelligence quotient, the greater the likelihood that more practice will be required. For example, a student with average intelligence will probably need more opportunities to respond to new words than will a student with above average intelligence; a slow learner will probably need still more opportunities, and so on. Keeping these two main ideas in mind, teachers can avoid such statements as "I don't understand why Bob still doesn't know that word! We've worked on it for three days."

Three: Provide Review Opportunities.

Related to the principle of many exposures to a word is the principle of review. During the stages of initial learning, a single correct response to a word should not cause the teacher to assume that the word is known and will be recognized instantly in future situations. Instead, the student should be able to respond correctly and without hesitation in several trials before knowledge of the word is assumed. Even then, the teacher should periodically provide opportunities to review those words that have recently been learned.

Four: Evaluate Sight Word Miscues in Relation to the Degree to Which They Change the Meaning of the Text.

Some apparent miscues of basic sight words result when readers unconsciously change written words to match what they use in their own oral language. For example, both these sentences are typical ways of expressing the same fundamental idea:

> He went there *in* the bus.
> He went there *on* the bus.

The second sentence represents a common way by which to render the first sentence into many vernacular speech patterns, but the meaning of the whole sentence is not altered. Thus, if a student in this example reads *in* as *on* to conform to his oral speech, this should not be treated as a *reading error.* Instead, correction of this substitution should be made at those times when it is a miscue causing a change in meaning.

A GENERAL APPROACH FOR TEACHING SIGHT WORDS

A general approach for teaching sight words can be carried out in four stages.

Beginning Stage

The teacher prepares a contextual assessment of high frequency words as described in Chapter 7. Words missed by students are placed on their Priority One list of words to be learned. The teacher also administers a test of words in isolation, as described in Chapter 8, and places missed words on the student's Priority Two list. Instruction is carried out in the following manner.

1. A program of student-dictated stories is instituted, as in the language experience approach. This technique can be used with secondary as well as elementary students. Mallett (1977), for example, reported the successful use of language experience procedures with junior-high Native Americans in British Columbia; and Becker (1970) reported its use with 16- to 18-year-olds in a Job Corps reading lab. As noted in Chapter 11, the major difference is simply in the choice of topics for story dictation with elementary versus secondary students.

2. Lessons are designed to assure that students develop instant recognition of words that occur in the student-dictated stories. Some or all words from each story are written on cards, with each word written in context on one side of the card and in isolation on the other. For example, "I am a boy." may appear on one side of the card; "am" may appear on the other side. Initial work with the words on these cards is carried out in the context of the sentence. When the student is consistently recognizing the word in context, the other side of the card is used. A variety of teaching activities is employed for initial learning and practice (see the following sections for ideas).

3. Each student keeps two word banks. A word bank can be any kind of a container (for example, a metal file box, a shoebox, or a manila envelope) in which a student's personal word cards are placed. Even if instructional procedures involve a group, students should keep individual files of

words. One of the word banks can be labeled "Words I'm Working On" and the other "Words I Know."

4. When it is determined that a word can be moved from the "Words I'm Working On" to the "Words I Know" word bank, check the student's Priority One and Priority Two lists: if the word is on one of these lists, mark it off. Most high frequency words will occur in students' dictated stories because they are used so often in all oral and written language. Henderson, Estes, and Stonecash (1971–72) confirmed this in a study of word acquisition in a program that used a language experience approach. These researchers found that in one week's sample of beginning readers' dictated stories, the average number of words per story was 54. Words from the stories were then compared with the Lorge–Thorndike Word List and it was found that 45 percent of the students' dictated words were in that list's category of highest frequency.

5. Consult the student priority lists periodically. Check to see if any words on the Priority One list are failing to occur in a student's dictated stories. If so, structure a situation so the word will be used. For example, suppose the word *green* is on Bradley's list but has not come up in any of his stories. At one session the teacher might bring in several green items (a green leaf, a puppet with a green shirt, a green apple) and say to Bradley (or his group), "Today we are going to write our story about things that are green." If it is difficult to structure a story-dictation situation that will guarantee that the student will produce the desired word, the teacher can prepare a story in which the word occurs one or several times and say, "For many days we've been reading stories you've written. Today, you have a holiday. *I* wrote the story." After all Priority One

words have been learned, the Priority Two list should also be checked to see whether it contains words that have not occurred naturally in the student's stories. If so, the teacher again must structure a situation to introduce them into meaningful story material.

6. Words from student stories other than the high-frequency function words also should be included for learning (for example, nouns, verbs, and other story-carrying words). By this procedure, the student learns concrete words as well as the important, but more difficult to learn, high frequency words. This allows students to build a base of words that will enable them to read contextual material in published books.

7. If other words are learned incidentally or in other teaching situations (such as signs, labels, and so forth), these can be added to the student's word bank.

8. Throughout the beginning stage, a chart or graph showing the student's progress should be kept so there is a visual record of how many words have been learned. Figure 12–1 shows an example of such a chart. This chart or graph should be kept in a folder and be available to the teacher and student to use each day, but, except in rare situations, should not be available to other students or on public display.

9. During the same time that sight vocabulary is being developed, the student should have lessons that will help in learning word identification strategies. This knowledge is not only necessary for identifying unknown words not yet in the student's sight vocabulary, but can actually assist in the initial learning of many sight words.

Intermediate Stage A

After the student has learned enough to begin to read in published materials, use his own

Figure 12–1
Progress charts can help the student and the teacher visualize progress

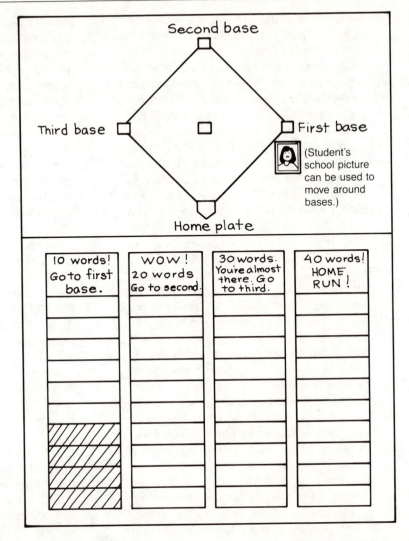

dictated stories in conjunction with published stories. First, check the words in the student's word bank labeled "Words I Know" against words in the stories found in beginning reading material. Match the word bank to the reading material (for example, a first preprimer in a basal reader series used in the student's regular classroom, or an easy-to-read, high interest book being used in the special program). When the student knows most words in the first story, have him read it. This will provide practice with newly acquired words, an entrée into published material, and a success experience with published material because the student learned the words in the story before being asked to read it. Then, follow the same procedure with the second story, third story, and so on, throughout the book. During this stage, dictated stories should be used to teach the words in published stories before the published stories are read. Finally, continue work on word identification strategies.

Intermediate Stage B

At this stage most reading should occur in published materials. Follow the sequence of procedures described here. First, select sight words to be learned by perusing published material before the student reads it. Anticipate the words that may present difficulty and preteach those first. (A good way to preteach is to present a sentence that includes the word so the student can guess the word from context.) When the student has finished reading the story, work with him on the words he found difficult even if you did not anticipate a problem with them. The following sections offer some specific teaching ideas.

Use dictated stories about once a week so that words in the student's oral language that may not occur in easy reading material but that may be of interest to the student can be added to the repertoire of sight words. Maintain the word bank system, using words from the published materials as well as from the weekly dictated stories. File words in the "Words I'm Working On" word bank and use various practice activities until students can move words into the "Words I Know" word bank. Continue work on word identification strategies.

Advanced Stage

At this stage, reading is carried out almost exclusively in published material. Sight vocabulary to be developed is selected as specified in intermediate stage B. Use an occasional dictated story to provide variety. Work on word-identification strategies continues concurrently, as in the previous stages.

SPECIFIC TECHNIQUES

Although some activities suggested in the following sections may be used for all three purposes (introduction and initial learning, practice, and elimination of word confusions), they are presented under the specific section in which they are most useful.

Introduction and Initial Learning

Helpful activities for introduction and initial learning of words include those that use the student's own dictated stories, those that employ contextual material prepared by the teacher, and those that use published contextual material.

Activities Using the Student's Own Dictated Story. Using a student's own story is advantageous because the student can feel confident that he knows the material.

1. At the completion of a student's dictation and reading of a story, the teacher points to one sentence in the story and asks the student to reread it. From the same sentence the teacher randomly points to a word and asks "What is this word?" Upon eliciting a correct response, she points to another word within the same sentence and again asks "What is this word?" This procedure continues until the student has pronounced each word in the sentence. Using index cards, the teacher now writes one of the words from the sentence in isolation on one side of a card, pronounces it, turns the card over and asks the student to make up another sentence using the same word. The teacher then incorporates the word into this new sentence on the second side of the card.

   The same procedure is used with each word from the dictated-story sentence until a pack of word cards can be assembled for the entire sentence. The cards are shuffled and the student is asked to read each sentence on the individual cards in which the words are written; if time permits during that session, other contextual activities for providing exposure to these words are used. (If it is appropriate for a particular student, words from more than one sentence may be selected from the dictated story for introduction during a single session.) At the conclusion of the session, the student files the new set of cards in a word bank labeled "Words I'm Working On." In the next session, the student reviews these words by reading them from the contextual side of the card before engaging in other activities with the words.

2. Prior to a session, the teacher writes each sentence from the previous day's dictated story on separate strips of colored construction paper.

> My brother and I played softball.
> My mother made chicken and potato salad.
> On Sunday we had a picnic.
> Our dog kept getting in our way.

During the session the student rereads yesterday's story, then is given the sentence strips in random order. He reads the sentence strips orally and then places the strips in the correct sequence. Finally, he rereads the story again from the rearranged strips.

> On Sunday we had a picnic.
> My mother made chicken and potato salad.
> My brother and I played softball.
> Our dog kept getting in our way.

Finally, word cards related to this story are taken from the student's word bank and shuffled. These are matched to words on the sentence strip story. For example, if the first word in the shuffled pack is *made,* the student finds *made* in the story, places the word card under it, and pronounces it.

3. Prior to a session the teacher copies the students' previous day's dictated stories onto another piece of paper. (Typing this copy may make it more appealing for older students.) After students have read the sentences on the index cards in their word banks, they use these index cards to find each target word in the copy of the story and underline the target word with a colored marking pen. They pronounce the word after underlining it. When all words have been found, they reread the whole story.

Activities Using Contextual Material Prepared by the Teacher. In addition to using student-dictated materials, the teacher can prepare materials for general sight vocabulary instruction or to highlight specific words. Some ideas for this are presented here.

1. The teacher prepares highly predictable material by repetitively using words and accompanying these with pictures. For example, she might assemble a small book with one sentence and one picture to a page for the student to read. (She can cut pictures from magazines or draw them herself.) The pages in one such booklet might be:

> I see a cat.   I see a hat.
> I see a boat.   I see a book.
> I see a truck.   I see a fish.

On the next day, the teacher may have a new booklet introducing an additional word.

> I see a big fish.
> I see a big truck.

2. The teacher writes cloze sentences, leaving blanks where words on which the student is presently working would fit.

Student places the word bank cards on his desk with the single words facing up. Next, he reads the first sentence and selects a word from the word cards that he thinks would fit the blank. Finally, he places that card above the sentence and uses it as a model to write the word in the blank.

Get _____ the bus.

3. The teacher introduces new words through riddles. The riddle can be read by the teacher from chart paper as the student follows along. The student supplies the word to answer the riddle and the teacher writes it on chart paper, chalkboard, or another convenient material. Afterward, these words are written on word bank cards, in context and isolation, and practiced using methods discussed earlier. Nouns are easiest to predict (guess) and provide concrete words to add to high frequency prepositions and conjunctions in the student's word bank. These nouns may be chosen from a published story soon to be read, or may be chosen to build upon a specific theme of words in the student's oral language.

Activities Using Published Contextual Material. Published materials offer the teacher a variety of formats for introducing and reinforcing basic sight vocabulary.

1. *Reading Systems* (Scott Foresman) is a basal reader program that features highly predictable stories in the first books of the series. These books may be used for the introduction and the initial learning of words.

2. The *Read-A-Part* books (Houghton Mifflin) provide students just beginning to develop a small sight vocabulary an opportunity for contextual reading. These books consist of many short stories. The teacher reads the majority of each story as students follow along. At certain points the teacher stops and students read dialogue that is printed in speech balloons. The material that students read is made up of short sentences consisting primarily of high frequency words. The reading by the teacher provides a strong context that prompts correct student responses when they read sentences. See Figure 12–2 for a sample page from these books.

3. The *Janus Career Education* series and the *Janus Survival Guides* (Janus) provide contextual material that can be used to introduce sight words needed for real-life reading. These materials provide initial learning experiences with words for reading want ads, job applications, supermarket food labels, and newspapers.

Practice
After the teacher has introduced new words and the student has progressed through the initial learning stage, the activities described here may be used for additional practice until the student recognizes the words instantly. However, remember that it is also important for the student to have many opportunities to read the words in regular, connected reading material.

1. Use sentence-building. Give the students several piles of word cards on which individual words are written. Place the cards randomly in each pile, but make sure that each pile contains words that when properly arranged can form a sentence. (For example, one set might include the words *fish, here, can, you;* another might include

"Where is the wheat?" they asked, looking at a small square package that Little Red Hen had under her wing.

Little Red Hen answered . . .

It is in a box.

Then she showed them the grains of wheat she had in the box. "This grain will grow into food. Who will help me plant it? Pig, will you help me?"

The pig turned his back and said . . .

Not I.

Then Little Red Hen asked the mouse, "How about you, Mouse? Will you help me?"

The mouse stroked its whiskers and squealed . . .

I will not.

Figure 12–2
A page from the Read-A-Part series. (*Source:* From *Read-A-Part,* ed. by J. Lewis, P. McKee, and W. E. Spaulding. Boston: Houghton Mifflin, 1974. Used with permission.)

will, go, you, where.) Put rubber bands around each pile. The student selects a pile, removes the rubber band, places the cards on his desk, reads them, and then sequences them into a sentence. This sentence remains on his desk and he selects the next pile and follows the same procedure. When all sentences are "built," the teacher comes to each desk to check for corrections and hear students read the sentences (*you can fish here* or *where will you go*).

2. Make blank bingo boards from oaktag, one for each student in the group. The squares on these cards should be drawn large enough so that an index card can be placed on each square. Each student places his individual word bank cards (single word up) on the bingo board in a random order. (See Figure 12–3.)

Before beginning the game, the teacher prints cloze sentences on individual oaktag strips. (For example: This _____ not fun.) These are prepared so there are sentences for all students' word bank words (the group of words on which each student is presently working). The teacher places one cloze sentence strip on the chalkboard tray. Any student who has a word bank card that makes sense in the sentence, raises his hand, points out to the teacher the word card on his bingo

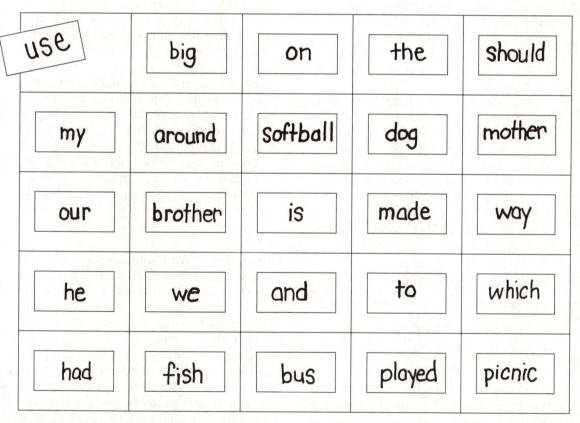

use	big	on	the	should
my	around	softball	dog	mother
our	brother	is	made	way
he	we	and	to	which
had	fish	bus	played	picnic

Figure 12–3
An example of a bingo board with sight-word cards from a student's word bank.

board that would fit, and reads the sentence pronouncing that word instead of the blank. If the student's word does make sense in the sentence, he gets to remove that word card from his bingo board. This game is played like traditional group bingo, except that the student who first gets 5 *blank* bingo squares in a row or column wins. (If an easier or quicker bingo word game seems more appropriate for a given student group, the teacher can make 16-card bingo boards or even 9-card bingo boards.)

3. If a student misses a word he should know while reading a story or expository material, encourage him to use context and/or graphophonic clues to figure it out. If a word remains unidentified, pronounce the word for the student and let him continue with the reading. Afterward, however, provide practice with that word. Following is one example of how this might be done.

Mike does not recognize the word *off* when it is encountered twice in the story he is reading orally. At the completion of the story, the teacher asks him to think of some sentences that name things that can be turned off. The teacher asks Mike to begin each sentence with "You can turn off _____." The teacher writes these sentences as Mike completes them, and underlines the word *off* each time.

You can turn off the stove.

You can turn off the air conditioner.

You can turn off the lights.

You can turn off the TV.

Mike observes as the teacher records the sentences and is then asked to read the sentences orally. This usually produces successful recognition and response to the word *off* every time. To promote gener-

alization of the correct response to other material, the teacher re-opens the lesson book to the place where Mike had missed the word *off,* and asks him to read it correctly in those sentences.

4. Group games may be used even if students are working on individual words in their personal word banks. Prior to a game, one or two words are selected from each student's group of "Words I'm Working On." Students take turns teaching their words to the group. A student begins with the contextual side of the word card, then uses the side with the word in isolation to point out important graphic features. All the words that all of the students have taught to the group are then included in a group game (a board game, rummy card game, bingo, and so forth). If a student has difficulty with another student's word during the game, the latter student assumes the role of teacher and gives instruction for identifying the word (showing the contextual side of the word card, calling attention to the beginning letters of the word, and so forth). This provides an excellent learning experience for both the "teacher" and the "student." Secondary as well as elementary teachers have used this technique successfully in their classrooms.

Elimination of Word Confusions

For many older disabled readers the problem with sight vocabulary is not one of needing initial learning experiences with words, but rather, one of confusing similar words. They do not look at a word such as *of* and simply block because they do not know it at all. Instead they confuse it with another word that looks somewhat the same, like *if* or *off.* The following activities may be used to help students eliminate sight word confusions (sometimes called *habitual grammatical associations*).

1. Encourage the student to attend to meaning. In many cases in contextual material, words frequently confused cannot be read for each other and still result in a meaningful sentence. For example,

   It is fun for u*s* to play in the park. *use*

   I can't play there o*n* a school day. *no*

   May My father is going in the car.

   Came C*o*me here and look at this.

   When a student produces miscues of this type, before calling attention to the graphic clues of the word ask, "Did that make sense?" Teaching students to use the meaning and language clues the text has to offer will eliminate many word confusions.

2. Goodman and Burke (1972) suggest placing both of two frequently confused words in a short teacher-written story in such a way that the correct choice of the two is unambiguous, that is, sentence structure and meaning clearly convey which word it is. Figure 12–4 contains such a story written for a fourth grader who had a persistent sight word confusion with the words *so* and *some*. After reading words in contextual material such as this, the student may be asked to visually discriminate between the two words he confuses. An example is an exercise in which the student circles all those words on a line that are identical to the first.

some	so	some	some	so	
so	so	so	some	so	some

   This lesson may end with another contextual activity to follow the rule of thumb of using context, isolation, and then context again in practice activities. Cloze sentences can be used for the final practice.

   Michael was so glad that it was Friday! He knew that this was the day of the school Christmas party. Some of the other boys were going to stop by his house to walk to school with him today, so he had gotten up early.

   The teacher had asked Michael and some of the boys to bring cookies from home, so they were going to go to school early so they could put the cookies on plates and put them out on tables. Some of the girls had been asked to come early so they could make a bowl of punch.

   When the other boys got to Michael's house, he went to get his cookies. Much to his surprise some little parts of some of the cookies had been eaten away! He was SO mad!

   Crumbs from the cookies were all around the plate. A small line of crumbs led to the edge of the table. Another line of crumbs led from the table to a place under some of the kitchen cabinets.

   David and some of the other boys watched as Michael followed this line of crumbs to where they led. Michael got down on his knees. He saw a small hole under one cabinet. "So, that's it," he said. "Some little mouse has already had himself a party." David and some of the other boys laughed. David said, "That's okay. Christmas is for giving, and we just gave part of our party to a mouse."

   Figure 12–4
   Example of a story that gives a student many opportunities to practice frequently confused words

   a. He wanted _____ apples.
   <u>so, some</u>

   b. She had grown _____ big that
   <u>so, some</u>
   I did not know who she was.

   c. _____ boys like to play football.
   <u>So, Some</u>

3. Use S-S-S: *Seeing, Sounding, Sensing.* When two words are consistently con-

fused, students may be asked to *see* how each one looks different from the other, to note the differences in the *sounds* of the two words, and to attend to the differences in the *sense* of each (that is, differences in meaning or grammatical function).

For example, if a student regularly confuses *on* and *in,* he is asked to name the letter he sees at the beginning of each word, to note the difference in the sounds of the two initial letters, and, in order to sense the differences in meaning, to use each word in a sentence such as "My book is *on* the table," and "I rode *in* a car to come to the clinic." The student's sentences should be discussed, and the lack of sense of each sentence should be pointed out if *in* or *on* were substituted for one another in either sentence. This procedure focuses on graphic and sound clues as well as the important clue of meaning. The ability to distinguish between the different graphic and sound clues of confused words becomes important when context (meaning) does not provide a clue to the word's identification. Some research has demonstrated that highlighting the visual characteristics of words is important whether the words are introduced in context or isolation (see, for example, Arlin, Scott, & Webster, 1978–79, and Kibby, in Ceprano, 1981).

4. Use "every-pupil-response cards" (Moe, 1972) along with cloze stories. The purpose of every-pupil-response cards is to increase opportunities for individual responding when groups of children are engaged in the same activity. Each student is given several cards on which possible answers are printed. As the need for a response occurs, instead of one student being called on to give the answer, all students select from their cards the answer they believe to be correct, and then

hold this card up. At a glance the teacher can see who needs corrective feedback. To see how to use this group technique for eliminating sight-word confusions, let's look at an example. Three students are consistently confusing *which* and *with,* so the teacher prepares a cloze story on chart paper such as the one in this example.

I don't know _____ boys I want to go _____ to the fair. No matter _____ ones I choose, I know I'll have fun. When I go with Al and Bob, though, they never know _____ thing to do first. They can't decide if they want to go see the goats or go get one of those hotdogs _____ onions and peppers on it (_____ make *me* sick!)

Each student is asked to print *which* and *with* on separate index cards and place these on his desk. The story is posted so everyone can see it and the teacher reads it out loud as the students follow along. The teacher pauses at each blank and each student quickly selects and silently holds up the word he believes to be the correct response. The teacher gives corrective feedback when necessary.

5. The first one or two letters of a word provide the most important graphic clue to that word (Goodman & Burke, 1972). Lack of attention to the initial portion of a word can result in word confusions (such as *your/our, would/could, when/then,* or *where/here*) and miscues commonly called *word reversals* (as in *was/saw, or on/no*). To eliminate habitual confusions of this type, give students activities that require them to attend to the first letters of the confused words. Thus, if a student was confusing all the words in both lists above, he could be given these to alphabetize. (Alphabetizing necessarily causes

a focus on the beginning portions of words.) Immediately after a decision is made by the student about each word's position in the alphabetical sequence, the student should be encouraged to pronounce it.

Another way to deal with word confusions is to use maze exercises in which the possible alternatives differ only in their initial one or two letters so that the student *must* attend to the beginning of the word in order to make a choice.

I like to wear this old _____.
(bat, hat)

_____ I get some new jeans,
(Then, When)

_____ I'll throw away these baggy
(then, when)
pants.

WORD RECOGNITION AND ORAL READING

Word confusions and other types of word recognition miscues are obviously more easily recognized during oral reading than during silent reading. When teachers' instructional responses to students' miscues during oral reading have been studied (Spiegel & Rogers, 1980), eight main classifications of response have been observed, as follows.

1. Tell—The teacher simply tells students the correct words when words are read incorrectly.
2. Visual—The teacher instructs the student to look at the word more carefully.
3. Visual/Context clues—The teacher repeats a few words that came before the student's error and says "What?" to indicate that the student is to use context, plus examine the word again. For example,

Text: Listen to the kitchen clock.
Student: Listen to the curtain—
Teacher: Listen to the *what?*

4. Sound—The teacher prompts students to "sound out" words they read incorrectly.
5. Spell—The teacher spells the word read incorrectly. For example,

Text: A bluebird is smaller than a robin.
Student: A bluebird is smaller then . . .
Teacher: t-h-*a*-n

6. Meaning—The teacher asks if what was read makes sense.
7. Structural analysis—The teacher breaks the word into syllables for students or tells them to do this.
8. Reference to prior use—The teacher tells the student that the word was used before, for example, saying something like, "I used that word when I gave you your math assignment after recess."

Spiegel and Rogers' study (1980) found that, more than half the time, teachers simply told students words when oral reading miscues occur. For only 5 percent of the miscues were students prompted to use meaning clues. These results indicate an unfortunate tendency among too many teachers to view the purpose of oral reading as one of correctly pronouncing each word on a page rather than as a chance to help students develop efficient and independent reading strategies. Spiegel and Rogers observe that teachers who perceive miscues as spontaneous instructional opportunities show better results. Although there are some occasions when merely telling the student the word is appropriate, used indiscriminately, this teacher response has little long-term value in aiding reading growth.

The immediateness of teacher response to miscues is another major concern when developing student reading strategies. Studies by McNaughton and Glynn (1981), and others, have compared students' behaviors when teachers correct miscues immediately as they occur, versus correcting them after the student reaches the end of a phrase or sentence. Students who were corrected immediately after they made mistakes employed fewer self-corrections and demonstrated less accurate word identification. It is likely that these students attempted fewer self-corrections because they opted to rely on the teacher's input rather than rely on self-correction strategies based on the sense of what they read. Remedial reading teachers must be sensitive to dependencies that are detrimental to reading progress. Readers must learn to correct miscues themselves if they are to read independently. Positive correlations between reading ability and use of self-corrections have been demonstrated (Clay, 1979; Recht, 1976). Likewise, less accurate word identification probably resulted from overdependence on the teacher, perhaps combined with the attitude, "If I can make a quick guess, and if I say it wrong, the teacher will tell me." Unfortunately, as Weinstein's (1976) study shows, disabled readers have their miscues immediately corrected more often than do good readers. The implication is that students need time to monitor their own reading, based on the meaning of what is being read, before being interrupted by corrections.

Another way to encourage the self-correction process is to use tape recordings of students' oral reading to create awareness of nonmeaningful miscues. To do so, first have a student read a story or informational selection independently into a tape recorder. Next, with the student, follow along in the book while listening to the tape-recorded selection. Have the student stop the tape whenever a miscue must be corrected. Tell the student which mis-

One way to encourage self-corrections is to have students mark their own miscues while listening to tapes of their oral reading.

cues are important to correct and which are not; clarifying this distinction is important in assisting students to read for meaning. The prompt, "Did that make sense?" is the key phrase the student should use to make these judgments. After some practice, the student can work through the replaying activity independently, circling corrections that should be made on a copy of the reading selection or lightly with a pencil in the book. Using this activity, even poor readers will usually find large numbers of their miscues and correct them independently.

At this point, it should be noted that some students correct their miscues internally during oral reading; that is, although they do not make a correction out loud, they have corrected it in their minds and, therefore, continue reading. This behavior is generally characteristic of more advanced rather than less advanced readers.

The major reason for employing oral reading in remedial and clinical programs is to provide on-the-spot diagnostic and remediation possibilities. In some cases a secondary purpose is to help students gain a reasonable degree of oral reading fluency. This in turn can assist the development of fluency in silent reading by giving students a feeling for the structure of language and its relationship to the spoken word.

One method for increasing oral reading fluency is to have the teacher act as a model. The student reads the first page in a new story orally. Then the teacher reads the next page orally with the student listening and following along. The teacher should read this page with normal fluency at just an average pace, not rapidly or dramatically, but approximating a nice flow of oral language that communicates with a listener. On page 3, it's the student's turn again. Usually the student's fluency begins to improve noticeably as the teacher's reading is imitated. The teacher and student should take turns throughout the story. (For some students, alternating after every paragraph instead of page by page may be more helpful.)

Other activities for increasing oral reading fluency are the use of plays, so that students can take turns reading, and can follow along as other students read their parts; read-along records and commercially published cassette tapes with their accompanying books; and captioned filmstrips. Also, see the suggestions found in Chapter 11 for working with severely disabled readers titled *Improving Nonfluent, Word-by-Word Reading*.

CONCLUDING STATEMENT

The foregoing sections suggest only a few activities for introducing and practicing recognition of sight vocabulary. Many sources are available from which additional ideas may be derived. Two resource books are *Reading Activities for Child Involvement* (Allyn & Bacon), and *Anchor* (Educational Service).

Several commercial materials have been cited that are useful for helping students develop an extensive sight vocabulary. Many others are available. A sampling of these is offered in the "Teachers' Store" (Appendix C), where some published materials for improving oral reading fluency also are listed.

13

Helping Students Develop Word Identification Strategies

There are two types of word identification, immediate and mediated (Smith, 1978). *Immediate word identification* means that a reader recognizes a word instantly. The importance of being able to recognize large numbers of words immediately and instructional procedures for facilitating instant recognition were discussed in Chapter 12. *Mediated word identification* is necessary when the reader encounters an unknown word; in these cases the reader must employ one or a combination of several strategies to identify the word.

To develop perspective about the importance of each of the several strategies that may be used in mediated word identification, and to know appropriate ways of teaching these, the teacher must consider several important understandings.

First of all, it should be remembered that there are two kinds of information used in reading. One of these, as you may recall from Chapter 2, is called *visual information*. This is the information the reader gets from the letters and words printed on the page. The other is called *nonvisual information*. This information comes from the reader's brain. It is stored

information the reader already has about language and the world.

In the past when students were having difficulty identifying unknown words, teachers usually concentrated on teaching them to make use of the visual information found on the printed page, teaching such things as the importance of noting the letters that words begin and end with, helping them learn sounds attached to those letters, teaching them to use known word parts, and so forth. Using letters and word parts and their sounds is called using *graphophonic cues*. We must still be concerned with teaching students to use these clues, but recent research has shown that another area—teaching students to use the nonvisual information that is already stored in their brains—has been neglected. Proficient readers use this information intuitively, but poor readers often do not, unless they are directly taught to do so. It is unfortunate that this area has been neglected because it is from this area that the most assistance is gained in helping a reader identify unknown words.

Let us look at some examples of the use of nonvisual information. Identify the missing words.

Today _____ Wednesday.

Three _____ us went in her car.

The class went _____ the zoo yesterday.

There is no visual information given for one word in each sentence. Yet, you can say the unknown words because of your familiarity with language structures. The information you need is already stored in your brain. Everyone who can comprehend spoken language is capable of using unconscious knowledge of language structure in this way, including even the poorest reader.

Let's look at another example.

Please turn off the _____.

In this example, there are several guesses (or predictions) that could be made that would make sense, for example, stove, light, TV, air conditioner, or radio, but knowledge of the world limits the possible choices. You would not answer with the words desk, leaf, umbrella, rose, or window, for example. One more clue can help the reader focus in on the word to be identified and that clue is the beginning letter or letters of the word. Try the example now.

Please turn off the l_____.

Of the possible choices, it is highly likely that the unknown word is *light*. The most powerful clues to word identification are the other words in the sentence plus the initial letter(s) of the word.

CONTEXT CLUES

Another term for using knowledge of language to identify unknown words is *use of syntactic cues*. Another term for using knowledge of the world is *use of semantic cues*. And another term that encompasses both of these is *use of*

context clues. When readers use "context clues" to identify an unknown word, they use the other words in the sentence or passage to help determine the word. These other words may provide syntactic cues, semantic cues, or both.

In the past we *have* thought about the necessity of teaching students to use context clues. For a long time, for example, it has been said that the three major word identification strategies are phonic analysis, structural analysis, and use of context clues. The problem has been that this list has also reflected the way priorities have been set in most instructional programs. A heavy emphasis has been placed on phonic analysis (or phonics), some emphasis has been placed on structural analysis, but very little attention has been given to the use of context clues. Recent research has shown that our priorities have been wrong. Does this mean, then, that we should ignore instruction in phonic and structural analysis strategies? No. Even proficient readers may fall back on the use of these skills when the more efficient strategy of using context fails. But the emphasis should be changed. A heavy emphasis should be placed on use of context (especially in conjunction with the initial portion of a word) and some emphasis placed on phonic and structural analysis.

General Teaching Procedures for Encouraging Use of Context Clues

To instill in students the strategy of using context, two major teaching procedures should permeate all instruction.

First, when students are reading and come to words they cannot pronounce, teachers should not automatically say "Sound it out," nor should they simply tell the student the word. Instead the teacher should quickly scan the sentence to determine whether context can convey the word. Research has shown that the context of the particular sentence in which an unknown word is found is more helpful than prior sentences (West, Stanovich,

Feeman, and Cunningham, 1983). In some cases, however, it may be helpful to scan the sentences that follow the unknown word. If context does give a clue to the word, the student should be encouraged to skip the word temporarily, read to the end of the sentence (or farther), and again attempt to guess the word from the context. If appropriate, the student should also use the beginning letter or letters of the word, and also, if appropriate, the sounds of the beginning letter(s). If the student is unable to determine the word from this combination of context plus the initial graphophonic clues, *then* the use of more extensive structural or phonic analysis skills should be encouraged.

Second, the student should be taught to self-correct. If students miscall a word when reading, it is usually best not to stop them in the middle of the sentence and give them a mini-phonics lesson. Rather, the use of context should be emphasized as an aid to self-correction by allowing the student to read to the end of the sentence, at which point it is to be hoped that she will self-correct. When students produce a miscue that results in a meaningless sentence, but read merrily on without self-correcting, the teacher should stop them and ask that most important of all questions, "Did that make sense?"

Specific Activities and Materials for Practicing Use of Context Clues

In addition to the two general procedures suggested above, teachers may also need to provide specific practice activities for poor readers. Although the cloze procedure is the most commonly used technique, other techniques are also employed.

The Cloze Procedure. As you remember, cloze sentences and passages are prepared by deleting words. For purposes of testing, or for determining the readability level of materials, there are precise specifications for choosing the words to delete, but when cloze sentences are used for instruction, the choice depends on the purpose of each activity. Valmont (1983) makes several suggestions for deleting words for instructional cloze tasks.

- In certain cases, delete a word where more than one word would make sense. Through discussion of students' varied answers, the teacher can point out that when guessing unknown words from context the reader should use only words that make sense and fit the sentence pattern.

   We had _____ bread with lunch.

- In some cases, give additional clues. Research has shown that the use of initial single letters, blends, or digraphs in combination with the context is effective, but that the exclusive use of *final* letters as clues actually hinders identification (Freeman cited in Valmont, 1983).

   They went into the drugstore to get a milkshake and found a t _____ at the back where they sat and waited to be served.

- Delete words only when the meaning is familiar to the student. As an example, it might be appropriate in the following sentence to delete *stop, off, onto, field, slowed,* or *streets,* but for many students it might not be appropriate to delete *elevated,* because that word may not yet be part of the student's meaning vocabulary.

   The train slowed to a stop and quickly the boys stepped off onto an elevated platform from which they could look down on buildings, a baseball field, and busy streets.

- Delete words at the beginning of a sentence

when you want students to practice using the context that comes *after* an unknown word.

_____ cawed loudly in the corn field.

• Delete words at the end of a sentence when students are just beginning to learn to use context clues and need much assistance from context within the sentence; research has shown that deletions of nouns at the ends of sentences is the easiest cloze task (Smith cited in Valmont, 1983).

When we asked how much it cost to take the bus to Smithville, the man said, "Just $3.00," so we bought two _____.

Here are some specific activities for using the cloze procedure.

1. With students who are very deficient in use of context, the suggestions for using oral and written cloze found in the section of Chapter 11 titled *Understanding the Task Requirements of Reading* may be used.
2. In addition to paper and pencil cloze activities, Blachowicz (1977) suggests using an overhead projector. Prior to the lesson the teacher prints sentences or paragraphs on transparencies and blocks out certain words, as shown here.

One day a _____ from the city newspaper came to take a picture of the school band. While the photographer was putting _____ into his camera, several of the students left the room. Mr. Evans, the band _____, seemed surprised at this, but asked the other students to get ready to play. Lucy was sitting in the front _____ of the band, and she saw the photographer _____ his camera right at her.

After students make guesses about an unknown word, the teacher "zips" off the masking tape so the students may confirm or correct their choices. Cunningham, Moore, Cunningham, and Moore (1983) suggest an extension of the activity in which, after guesses are made, only enough of the tape is pulled up so that the initial letter, blend, or digraph shows. Further guesses are then made before the entire word is exposed. This procedure gives practice in using that very powerful word identification strategy, the use of context plus the initial portion of the word.

3. A commercially available set of materials suitable for older students is "Word Mysteries" from the *Word Puzzles and Mysteries Scope Skills Book* (Scholastic).[1] Another is *Cloze in the Content Area* (Learning Well). This latter set of materials provides cloze practice with materials related to science, social studies, and math in booklets ranging from 2.0 through 7.9 reading levels.

Other Procedures. Techniques other than the cloze procedure are also helpful when providing practice in using context clues. Here are some specific activities that can be used.

1. The Mystery Word Game helps students see how context of a greater length than one sentence can aid identification of an unknown word. Prepare short paragraphs and type one of these on each of many index cards. Use a nonsense word in place of a real word in each paragraph.

A <u>krit</u> is something many people like to hear. <u>Krits</u> may be heard on records.

---

[1]Publishers' names are in parentheses after commercial materials cited in this and other chapters. Full names and addresses appear in Appendix B.

We like to sing <u>krits</u>. A <u>krit</u> is a _____.

A <u>delac</u> is often shiny. A <u>delac</u> can be eaten. <u>Delacs</u> swim in the sea and have fins. A <u>delac</u> is a _____.

On other cards print single words that represent answers to match with each paragraph. The game is then played like the card game, rummy. Students are dealt five cards. They attempt to match paragraphs with words by guessing the unknown words from context. Matched pairs are read to the group. If the match is correct the pair may be removed from the student's hand. When no matches remain in a student's hand, she draws from a pile of extra cards. If no match can be made with a card, she discards one card. Students draw from the extra pile or discard pile until all cards are used. The student with the most pairs wins.

2. Use word and phrase strips, like *she/ate/ the hotdog/a noise/ran*. Provide the student with a packet of sentence parts, some of which may be combined to make a sentence and some of which may not. Combining words and phrases to build sentences helps students see how other words aid in selecting the correct word to make a meaningful sentence.

3. A commercially available game to use for sentence building is *Rolling Reading* (Gamco). This game includes seven cubes with words imprinted on all faces of each cube; a small number is also printed in the corner of each face. Students roll the cubes, then try to form a sentence from the words shown before a sand timer runs out. Their scores are obtained by adding the numbers on the cubes in their sentences.

4. Play the Prediction Game. The teacher begins by writing a sentence on the board in which only every second or third word is given; lines are drawn for the remaining words. See the example in Figure 13–1.

The Prediction Game is good for students who are afraid to guess. Although remedial readers do bring experience, a sense of meaning, and knowledge of sentence structure to the reading task, they are often reluctant to predict unknown words based on this knowledge. They have become passive in the reading process. They perceive word identification to be based on mysterious skills they cannot grasp and often simply wait for the teacher to tell them unknown words. This game, and all activities that require students to make informed and reasonable guesses from context, make them take an active role in the act of reading.

PHONIC ANALYSIS

Phonic analysis is more commonly just called *phonics*. In *phonic analysis,* the reader uses sounds of individual letters or letter combinations to assist in identifying unknown words. Phonic analysis strategies are most effective when used in combination with context clues.

Research has been undertaken to determine the most helpful sequence in which to teach phonic analysis skills, but no specific sequence has been found to be more efficient than another. The sequence in which these skills are taught varies from program to program and is based on logical reasoning rather than empirical data. A typical program includes instruction in readiness activities; consonants; consonant blends; consonant digraphs; phonograms, plus consonant substitution; short vowels; long vowels; R-controlled vowels; and special vowel combinations. Each of these elements of phonic analysis will now be discussed.

A student from Team 1 guesses a word for a specific slot. If the response is right, the teacher writes that word in, gives the team a point, and asks Team 2 for a prediction for another word. If a response is wrong, the teacher writes in a graphic clue consisting of the first single consonant, vowel, initial blend, or digraph; if there is a wrong prediction no points are awarded and the other team is asked for a prediction of any word in the sentence.

_____ _gull_ _____ _____ _wings_ _____ _out_ _____ _sea_.

Team 1 "The second word is *sea*." Teacher writes in *sea*.

_____ _sea gull_ _____ _____ _wings_ _____ _out_ _____ _sea_.

Team 2 "The first word is *the*." Teacher writes in *the*.

The sea gull _____ _____ _wings_ _____ _out_ _____ _sea_.

Team 1 "The word just before wings is *its*." Teacher writes in *its*.

The sea gull _____ _its wings_ _____ _out_ _____ _sea_.

Team 2 "The word after *out* is *to*." Teacher writes in *to*.

The sea gull _____ _its wings_ _____ _out to sea_.

Team 1 "The fourth word is *spread*." Teacher responds, "*Spread* does make sense there. That's a good prediction! But this word begins this way." Teacher writes *fl* at the beginning of that line.

The sea gull fl _its wings_ _____ _out to sea_.

Team 2 "The word before *out* is *flew*." Teacher writes in *flew*.

The sea gull fl _its wings_ _flew out to sea_.

Team 1 "The word before *flew* is *and*." Teacher writes in *and*.

The sea gull fl its wings and flew out to sea.

Team 2 "The last word is *flew*." Teacher responds, "Does that sound like language? Would it make sense to say he "*flew* his wings?"

Team 1 "It's *flapped*!" Teacher writes in *flapped*.

The sea gull flapped its wings and flew out to sea.

Figure 13–1
An example of the steps in the Prediction Game

Readiness Activities

One common readiness activity is that of helping students discriminate individual sounds. At this stage students do not match sounds with their corresponding letters, but only learn to note likenesses and differences. For example, when hearing two words given by the teacher, such as *ball* and *bat*, or *horse* and *car*, the student should be able to tell if the sounds at the beginning are the same or different. Regular classroom procedures may be used for this practice. For instance, when students are lining up to go to lunch the teacher may say, "Everyone whose name starts with the sound at the beginning of *sun* may line up first. Now everyone whose name starts with the sound at the beginning of *rabbit* may line up," and so on.

A second common readiness activity is working with rhyming words. The teacher may ask students to provide a word that rhymes to complete a sentence (such as: The funny little mouse/Ran into his _____). Or students may be asked to tell the two words in a sentence that rhyme (for example: That shoe is dark blue). Working on rhymes just for the sake of identifying rhyming words is not very useful, but does provide some prerequisite knowledge for a concept used when later working with phonograms.

Consonants

Consonant sounds are taught before vowel sounds in most programs because consonants provide the framework of words. Try to read this sentence.

W__ h__ __rd h__r wh__n sh__ y__ll__d __t h__ __ br__th__r.

Although there are no vowels given, you were probably able to determine easily that the sentence says "We heard her when she yelled at her brother." Now try this one.

__e__ __ __ou__ __i__ __e__ __a__ __ __ __e __i__ __e__.

Consonants provide important graphophonic clues to words, while vowels and their sounds provide relatively little assistance, as just demonstrated. If you were unable to read the second sentence, try the same sentence now,

when you may use the consonant sounds instead:

H__lp y__ __r s__st__r w__sh th__ d__sh__s.

Using consonant clues plus context makes it easy to determine that this sentence says "Help your sister wash the dishes."

Many published games, booklets, manipulatives, kits, audiovisuals, and other materials are available to help students learn consonant sounds. A sampling of these is found in The Teachers' Store in Appendix C. But many teachers like to devise their own activities for teaching phonic analysis skills. Here are some suggestions for providing practice with consonant sounds.

Self-Correcting Matching Games. Collect plastic margarine containers. On the outside of each, print a different single consonant sound with an indelible felt-tip pen. On a large index card paste four single small pictures, each beginning with the same sound (many teachers use old readiness books or workbooks as a source of small pictures). Make a card with four pictures for every consonant sound. Turn each index card over and draw a simple picture on the back; the picture should be different on each card. Now turn the cards back over and cut the cards into four parts so each picture is separate. (See Figure 13–2.)

Mix up all the pictures from all the cards and have the students sort the pictures according to the consonant with which each one begins, then place each one in the container labeled with that consonant. Students can check their work by taking the sorted cards from the container, turning them over, and arranging them to form the picture drawn by the teacher. Mistakes are immediately apparent because the picture will not make sense.

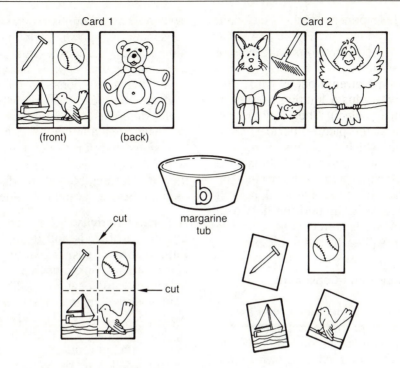

Figure 13–2
Materials for a self-correcting matching game

Using a Language Master. A Language Master (Bell & Howell) may be used to practice consonant sounds. (See Chapter 9 for a description.) The teacher orally records statements on each of several cards, such as "On your paper print the letter for the sound you hear at the beginning of *pumpkin*"; "print the letter for the sound you hear at the beginning of *magic*"; and so on. The teacher prints the correct letter on the back of each card.

The students are given a pack of these cards; sit at the Language Master; run the first card through the machine to hear the teacher's directions; print their responses on a piece of notebook paper; remove the card from the machine; and self-check their answers by turning the card over to see the answer the teacher has printed there.

Composing Alliterations. Secondary students enjoy this activity. An *alliteration* is a phrase or sentence in which all words begin with the same letter (for example, Tiny Tommy tied two toads together). As a first step, alliterative sentences may be read to the students, asking them to identify the consonant sound heard at the beginning of each word. Next, students are asked to compose their own alliterations. Older students seem to think work with alliterations is fun. This task gives practice with consonant sounds in such a way that it is not viewed as "babyish" by more mature students.

Playing Guess and Poke. Prepare flashcard-sized pieces of oaktag. Each card should have a small picture pasted or drawn at the top. Below the picture make three holes with a hole punch. Print a consonant letter above each hole. (See Figure 13–3.) On the back draw a red star around the hole of the correct answer.

Students are given a pile of cards prepared in this way, plus a knitting needle (or pencil, or similar object). They pick up the first card, look at the picture, decide on the consonant with which it begins, and poke the knitting needle through the hole labeled with that consonant. *Without* removing the knitting needle, they turn the card over. If the knitting needle is through the hole with the star, the answer is correct. They continue in this manner with each card in the pack.

Consonant Blends and Consonant Digraphs

A consonant *blend* (sometimes called a *cluster*), is two or more consonant letters that commonly appear together, but even when in this combination each retains its own sound. Some common blends are listed in Box 13–1. A consonant *digraph* (also sometimes called a cluster), is two consonant letters that commonly appear together, but do not retain their own individual sounds. For example, in the consonant digraph *sh-* (as found at the beginning of *ship*), neither the usual sound of *s*, nor the usual sound of *h* is heard; rather, the sound that corresponds to these two letters when they appear in combination is an entirely different sound. Some common digraphs are listed in Box 13–1. Teaching activities suggested for working with consonant sounds may also be used by students when they are learning blends and digraphs. In addition, here are several other ideas.

A Sorting Activity. Use word sorts to call attention to blends and digraphs during the introductory stages of learning these letter combinations. Give students a pack of cards in which words beginning with single consonant sounds are intermixed randomly with words beginning with blends and digraphs. If, for example, the digraphs *ch-* and *sh-* have been introduced, students may be given the following packs of words to sort.

Pack 1   car, champ, chair, come, chicken, cap, cut, chip, can't, chat

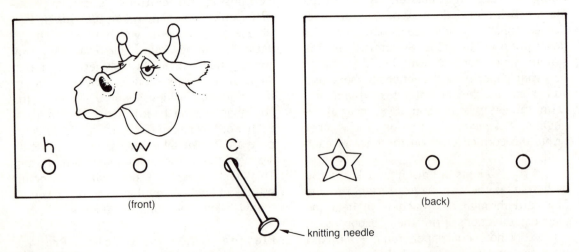

(front)   (back)

knitting needle

Figure 13–3
An example of a card used in Guess and Poke

Box 13–1

Some Common Consonant Blends and Consonant Digraphs

Consonant Blends

bl-	(blond)	gr-	(great)	sp-	(spit)
br-	(brain)	pl-	(plate)	spl-	(splash)
cl-	(clock)	pr-	(practice)	spr-	(sprain)
cr-	(crown)	sc-	(scat)	squ-	(squirrel)
dr-	(drum)	scr-	(scram)	st-	(step)
dw-	(dwarf)	sk-	(skate)	str-	(straight)
fl-	(flower)	sl-	(slide)	sw-	(swim)
fr-	(from)	sm-	(small)	tr-	(train)
gl-	(glad)	sn-	(snail)	tw-	(twin)

Consonant Digraphs

ch-	(chair)	gh-	(rough)	th-	(*unvoiced:* path *voiced:* this)
sh-	(shoot)	ph-	(phone)	wh-	(wheel)

Pack 2   ship, she, shed, some, so, shot, seem, so, shook, see

Have students sort cards into piles according to the beginning feature of the words (in other words, according to whether they begin with a single consonant or a consonant blend or digraph). Next, have students pronounce each word to the teacher and use each one orally in a sentence.

A Completion Activity. The teacher prints blends or digraphs on flash cards with a different blend or digraph on each. A line is drawn after the blend/digraph to indicate that a word is to be filled in. On the back of each card, the teacher writes several statements, each of which describes a word beginning with the blend/digraph on the front side. For example, for the *str-* blend card, some statements on the back might be:

She wore braces; now her teeth are _____.

He is not weak; he is _____.

A zebra has black and white _____.

To carry out the activity, the teacher selects one blend/digraph card, holds it up so the front side is seen by the students, reads statements from the back side, and the students call out a word that is a response to each statement and begins with the appropriate blend or digraph.

A Matching Activity. After students have read a story, give them sentences related to it in which words beginning with blends and digraphs have been omitted. On the same paper there should be pictures of each omitted word. The students are to paste the correct picture on each line. These types of activities not only help students learn, but also help them enjoy it. However, it is important to consider Durkin's admonition to "avoid getting so involved with a means (for example, attractive materials and displays)

Box 13–2
Phonograms That Occur Frequently In Common Words

-at: bat, cat, fat, hat, mat, pat, rat, sat, vat, brat, flat, scat, slat, spat, splat, chat, that

-ed: bed, fed, led, red, wed, bled, fled, sled, sped, shed

-all: ball, call, fall, hall

-in: fin, pin, sin, tin, win, grin, skin, spin, chin, shin, thin

-ap: cap, gap, lap, map, nap, rap, tap, clap, flap, scrap, slap, snap, strap, trap, chap

-est: best, nest, pest, rest

-ore: bore, core, more, pore, sore, tore, wore, score, snore, store, swore, chore, shore

-ink: link, mink, pink, rink, sink, wink, blink, drink, stink, think

-an: can, fan, man, pan, ran, tan, van, bran

-ick: kick, lick, pick, quick, sick, tick, brick, click, slick, stick, trick, chick, thick

-im: dim, him, rim, brim, grim, skim, slim, swim, trim

-op: cop, hop, mop, pop, top, crop, drop, flop, stop

-ip: dip, hip, lip, nip, rip, sip, tip, zip, clip, drip, flip, grip, skip, slip, strip, chip, ship, whip

-ake: bake, cake, fake, lake, make, quake, rake, sake, take, wake, brake, flake, snake, stake, shake

-ot: cot, dot, got, hot, lot, not, pot, rot, plot, slot, spot, trot, shot

-ice: dice, lice, mice, nice, rice, price, slice, spice, twice

-ob: bob, cob, job, mob, rob, sob, blob, slob, snob

-ack: back, hack, lack, pack, quack, rack, sack, tack, black, crack, smack, snack, stack, track, shack

-ide: hide, ride, side, tide, wide, bride, glide, pride, slide

-ight: fight, light, might, night, right, sight, tight, bright

-ade: fade, jade, made, wade, blade, grade, spade, trade, shade

-old: bold, cold, fold, gold, hold, mold, sold, told, scold

-ash: cash, dash, hash, mash, rash, crash, flash, slash, smash, splash, trash

mall
tall
wall
small
stall

-ing
king
ring
sing
wing
bring
cling
fling
sling
spring
sting
string
swing
thing

-et
bet
get
jet
let
met
net
pet
set
vet
wet
yet

---

test
vest
west
zest
blest
crest
chest

-ell
bell
cell
fell
sell
tell
well
yell
dwell
smell
spell
swell
shell

-ear
dear
fear
gear
hear
near
rear
year
clear
smear
spear

---

clan
plan
scan
than

-ay
bay
day
gay
hay
lay
may
pay
ray
say
way
clay
gray
play
pray
slay
spray
stay
stray
sway
tray

-ew
dew
few
mew
new
blew
crew
drew
flew
grew

---

chop
shop

-oke
coke
joke
poke
woke
broke
smoke
spoke
stroke
choke

-ug
bug
dug
hug
jug
mug
rug
tug
drug
plug

-ill
bill
dill
fill
hill
kill
mill
pill
will
drill
grill
skill
spill
still
chill

-it
bit
fit
hit
kit
pit
quit
sit
wit
grit
skit
slit
spit

-ate
date
gate
hate
late
mate
crate
plate
skate
slate
state

-ent
bent
cent
dent
lent
rent
sent
tent
vent
went
spent

---

flight
fright

-eam
beam
seam
team
cream
dream
gleam
scream
steam
stream

-ock
dock
hock
lock
rock
sock
block
clock
flock
stock
shock

-ank
bank
rank
sank
tank
blank
crank
drank
prank
spank
thank

-ace
face
lace
pace
race
brace
grace
place
space
trace

-ave
cave
gave
pave
rave
save
wave
brave
grave
slave
shave

-ab
cab
dab
jab
lab
tab
blab
crab
drab
flab
grab
scab
slab
stab

that the end (word practice) is forgotten."
(Durkin, 1975, p. 476.)

Phonograms, Plus Consonant Substitution

Investigations by Glass and Burton (1973) indicate the importance of helping students gain familiarity with sequences of letters called *phonograms.*[2] Phonograms are often called "word families" by teachers. These are word parts of two or three letters that appear in many different English words. For example, the phonogram *-ill* appears in *fill, hill, pill, will,* and *chill.* Box 13–2 lists common phonograms, plus several words containing each phonogram. This latter information can be helpful when teachers are preparing practice activities.

Learning phonograms should involve using them in whole words, but substituting the initial portion of the word. For example, if students know the words *sat* and *hat,* and also know consonant sounds, they can be taken through the following steps:

1. Student reads the known word *sat.*

2. Student is asked to change the *s* to *h,* and read the known word *hat.*

3. Teacher points out that words ending with the same group of letters—such as *-at* in these two words—usually rhyme, and this can be a clue to identifying unknown words.

4. Student is asked to change *h* in *hat* to *r,* to think of the sound for *r,* and to combine it with the sound for *-at* heard in the two words already known (*sat* and *hat*) to determine the unknown word *rat.*

5. Several initial consonants are substituted for one another to make various words (*b*at, *br*at, *ch*at, *c*at, *sc*at, *th*at, *f*at, *sl*at, and

so forth). This process of using various consonants in front of the same phonogram is called *consonant substitution.* Consonant blends and consonant digraphs, as well as single consonant sounds, are used when employing this word identification strategy.

Two additional activities follow.

Phonogram Tic Tac Toe.   Make many small tic-tac-toe boards from oaktag. Each board should feature a different phonogram. Laminate the boards. Give the two students who will play each game different colored, fine-point, washable marking pens. Student A thinks of a word that includes the phonogram and writes in the beginning blend, digraph, or single consonant with a *green* marking pen (which can be wiped off later

Learning phonograms should involve using them in whole words, but substituting the initial portion of the word.

---

[2]The word *phonogram* is pronounced so that the first *o* is long.

since the game is laminated). Student B makes another word by writing in the initial portion of a word with a *black* marking pen, and so on. When there are three words in the *same color* in a row, that student wins.

Create A Crazy Story.   Give students a story which has several words containing phonograms. Underline these. Tell the students to make a "crazy" story by changing the first part of the underlined words to another letter or letters. Then they can illustrate the story. Students may do this with several short paragraphs or one longer story. (See Figure 13-4.)

Vowels

As was shown in an earlier example, vowel sounds do not provide as much assistance in identifying unknown words as is provided by consonants and context, especially when an individual is engaged in normal, connected

reading. Work with vowel sounds may warrant some attention, but should have a low priority in instructional programs.

Short Vowel Sounds. The short vowel sounds are represented in the following words: ă (*at*), ĕ (*egg*), ĭ (*it*), ŏ (*on*), and ŭ (*up*). Many programs introduce short vowel sounds before long vowel sounds because the short sounds occur more frequently in words found in beginning reading materials. Students often have difficulty learning these sounds although they may have learned consonant sounds fairly quickly. Because of students' difficulties in remembering short vowel sounds, teachers sometimes place a heavy stress on practicing these, having students engage in large numbers of isolated activities, continuing this practice over a long time period, and excluding work on other word identification strategies in order to focus on learning these sounds. Such a heavy

Figure 13–4
Imaginative activities give students opportunities to practice consonant substitution in an enjoyable way.

emphasis on this difficult-to-learn skill is inappropriate, however, since more efficient strategies are available. Although some focus on these sounds may be appropriate, devoting large amounts of instructional time, especially while excluding practice on other strategies, is not justified.

Long Vowel Sounds. Long vowel sounds are those represented in the following words: ā (ate), ē (eat), ī (ice), ō (oat), and ū (use). Students seem to find it easier to learn long vowel sounds than to learn the short sounds of vowels, probably because the sound that long vowels represent is the same as the letter name. Still, because the relative amount of usefulness of vowel sounds is less than that gained from knowledge of consonants and use of context, only a small amount of attention to these is warranted.

R-controlled Vowels. Some teachers seem to think that vowel sounds are either long or short. Actually there are other sounds as well. When a vowel is followed by an r, the sound is often neither long nor short, but instead results in a special sound called an *R-controlled vowel.* R-controlled vowel sounds are those represented in the following words: ar (star), er (cover), ir (circus), or (for), and ur (fur). Note that the er, ir, and ur sounds are the same.

One reason vowel sounds are hard to learn is that the same letters have so many variations in sounds. Another is that the same sounds can be represented by so many letters. For example, the e in bead is long, but the e in bread is short, although they both contain the letter pattern ea. Or, as another example, the short /a/ sound is represented by a single a in had, by au in laugh, and by ai in plaid. R-controlled vowel sounds, on the other hand, are comparatively regular. In studies to determine how often words encountered in reading materi-

als actually conform to the rules that students are taught about sounds, three separate investigations found that in a large percentage of words the sound heard *is* the one conventionally taught for each r-controlled vowel. Clymer (1963) found that in primary material, in 78 percent of the words that contained a vowel followed by an r, the "regular" r-controlled sound was heard; Bailey's (1967) investigation of reading material through sixth grade found 86 percent of the words with these letter patterns to be regular, and Emans (1967), in a study of words selected from *The Teacher's Word Book of 30,000 Words* (Thorndike & Lorge, 1944), found that there was 82 percent regularity for r-controlled vowels in these words.

One suggested activity for helping students become familiar with these sounds is to prepare stories with many words containing r-controlled vowels. Have students circle all the words containing these, then read the story silently using the r-controlled sounds to aid in identification of the words. When students have completed these activities independently, they should be asked to read the story to the teacher. Here is an example of a teacher-prepared story containing many words with r-controlled vowel sounds.

> The worn-out old witch stirred the ugly mess in her old pot. "Heh, heh, heh," she laughed horribly. "I need just one more ingredient, and it must be a living creature!" I shivered as I sat behind a large bush watching her. Then suddenly she pointed her wrinkled finger in my direction. I was stiff with fright. She came closer . . . but she pulled a half-dead bird from off a branch of that bush and dropped it into the boiling pot. I was shocked and wanted to help the poor bird. But just then I was surprised to see the

Figure 13–5
An example of teacher
prepared materials for
an activity to help
students distinguish
among r-controlled
vowels

A second activity requires the teacher to punch holes and attach sentence strips with paper fasteners onto colored posterboard. (See Figure 13–5.) The strips should have sentences written on them which include a word that is to be completed with an r-controlled vowel. To the left of each strip, punch another hole and put in another paper fastener; attach a length of colored yarn to each of these latter fasteners. On the right side of the posterboard list r-controlled vowels with a paper fastener in front of each of these. The student is to read each sentence, then attach the yarn to the paper fastener by the r-controlled vowel that would complete the word. Since the sentence strips are at-

witch's black-furred cat spring up and pull the bird from the pot. I was glad to see that the bird was still alive. The bird flew off through the forest. The cat ran off through the field. And I fell out of bed.

tached with paper fasteners, one set may be removed and others placed there after all students have had an opportunity to participate.

Special Vowel Combinations. In reading programs of the past, students were often required to practice and learn many different diphthongs and vowel digraphs. A *diphthong* is a vowel combination that begins with one sound and moves to another sound in the same syllable, such as *oy* in *toy*.[3] Vowel digraphs are formed like consonant digraphs: they are pairs of vowels representing a single sound, such as *ea* in *heat*.

Some vowel diphthongs and digraphs taught in programs of the past are not included in most programs today because research has shown that many of these occur

---

[3]Teachers sometimes mispronounce the word *diphthong*. Notice the consonant digraph *ph* in this word. As you know, *ph* is represented by the /f/ sound, therefore, the word is pronounced /dĭf′ thŏng/.

infrequently and/or have many exceptions to the rules about their sounds. Today, diphthongs and digraphs usually are not even taught as separate categories. Instead, a small group of these, which do occur fairly frequently and have few exceptions, is selected for teaching and is given the generic label *special vowel combinations*. Studies by Bailey (1971) and others indicate that these special vowel combinations are important to teach: *au* (caught), *aw* (raw), *oi* (boil), *oy* (toy), *oo* (cool), *oo* (foot), *ou* (out), and *ow* (cow) or *ow* (snow).

One set of commercial materials that may be used to practice these sound/symbol correspondences is the duplicating-master booklet titled, *Special Vowels* (Frank Schaffer). Each lesson is illustrated with charming cartoon-like drawings, and practice is provided for special vowel combinations plus r-controlled vowels.

Phonic Generalizations

Instruction on many phonic generalizations is often included in reading programs. Large numbers of these generalizations involve "vowel rules." Some commonly taught generalizations are

1. When one vowel is between two consonants, that vowel is short, as in *cat*.
2. When there are two vowels side by side, the long sound is heard for the first and the second is silent, as in *mean*.
3. When a word ends with an *e*, the *e* is silent and the vowel preceding it is long, as in *make*.

Some others are

4. In the special vowel combination *ie*, the *i* is silent and the *e* is long, as in *shield*.
5. When the letter *g* is followed by *i* or *e*, it sounds like /j/, as in *gin*.
6. In a multisyllabic word containing the let-

ter *v*, the *v* stays with the preceding vowel to form a syllable, as in *riv/er*.
7. When *a* is preceded by *w* it has the *schwa* sound, as in *was*.
8. When *w* is preceded by *e*, the sound is the same as that represented by the special vowel combination *oo* in *shoot*, as in *lewd*.

As can be seen, many of these rules are cumbersome, and, as might be expected, students often have difficulty learning them.

Even when only a few of these generalizations are taught, although students may be able to repeat the rules to the teacher, they seldom *apply* them unless a) the teacher prompts them to do so (e.g., the student has difficulty with the word *held* and the teacher says, "Look, there is one vowel between two consonants, so what sound would the vowel make?" or b) the student is given a specific practice activity that stresses the relevant generalization (e.g., directions on a worksheet might say, "When two vowels are side by side, the first is long and the second is silent. Mark all the vowels that are long."). When reading independently in most regular, connected reading, students do not stop to consciously apply a phonic generalization if they cannot identify a word.

Another serious obstacle to teaching vowel rules is that many English words are exceptions. For example, note these exceptions to the rules just listed:

Rule 1: told	Rule 5: get
Rule 2: bread	Rule 6: over
Rule 3: gone	Rule 7: way
Rule 4: friend	Rule 8: sew

In fact, several researchers who have investigated the usefulness of the phonic generalizations often taught in primary and intermediate reading programs have found that a preponderance of these rules have so many exceptions that they have low utility. Clymer

(1963), for example, found only 45 percent utility for the generalization that "when two vowels are side by side the first is long and the second is silent." That is, 55 percent of the words in the four widely used primary reading programs he examined were exceptions to this rule. Another way to say this is that in more than half the attempts by a student to apply this rule to an unknown word, the rule would not work! When Bailey (1967) applied the same vowel rule to words found in eight basal reader series through grade six, only 34 percent utility was found. In other words, some of the rules taught in primary reading programs are even less useful when applied to more difficult words found in higher-level reading materials. The percent of utility found in Bailey's study for the commonly taught rules listed earlier in this discussion were: Rule 1: 71 percent; Rule 2: 34 percent; and Rule 3: 57 percent. Further, of the 45 generalizations taught in major reading programs and examined by Bailey, only 27 were useful at least 75 percent of the time.

Finally, Hillerich's (1967) research found that primary-grade students who were taught phonic generalizations failed to demonstrate word recognition superior to those who had not been taught these rules.

The preceding discussion indicates why teachers should reevaluate the heavy emphasis that is frequently placed on direct practice of phonic generalizations. Learning of common word patterns appears to be more productive when students are simply given much exposure to many words containing those patterns and inductively form generalizations about them.

Summary

It should be remembered that even when working on phonic analysis skills, the emphasis should be on the total context of reading. When practicing letter sounds and pronunciation of words with these sounds, lessons should include opportunities to read these words in contextual material. For example, in a session in which consonant substitution and work with the phonograms *-ake* and *-ill* have provided practice in identifying the words *bake, cake, make, take,* and *shake,* and *fill, will, spill,* and *still,* the lesson might conclude by having the student read a short passage the teacher has written, such as

> Jason has a birthday today, so his mother will bake him a big cake. She is going to fill a cup with milk and add it to some eggs and flour. Then she will take some salt and shake it in. She hopes she won't spill the sugar like she did last time. Sometimes the cakes she makes look funny, but they still taste good!

It should also be noted that phonics is not, nor should it be, considered *the* method for teaching reading. Rather, phonics is one of several cuing systems available to the reader to assist in identifying unknown words.

STRUCTURAL ANALYSIS

Structural analysis is a strategy in which attention is given to meaningful word parts so that an unknown word may be identified. In phonic analysis the focus is on *letter* sounds; in structural analysis the focus is on *larger* word parts. Instruction in structural analysis deals with inflectional endings, recognition of words when their spellings have changed because an ending has been added, contractions, compound words, prefixes, suffixes, and syllabication. Work with structural analysis should occur concurrently with instruction in phonic analysis and the use of context clues.

Inflectional Endings

Inflectional endings are word parts added to the ends of words to form plurals (cats,

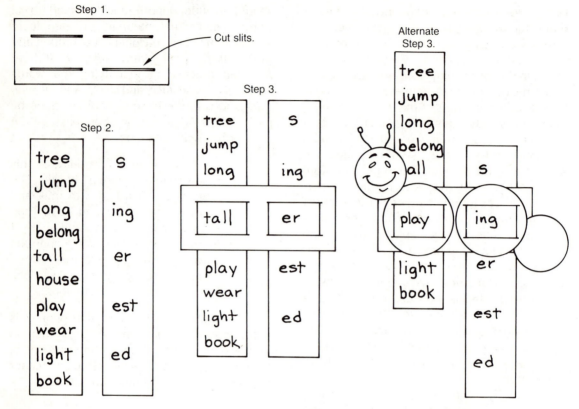

Figure 13–6
An example of a word slide with an alternate suggestion suitable for younger students

dishes), third person singular (runs, washes), past tense (jumped), present participle (talking), possessives (Mary's), and comparisons in adjectives and adverbs (smaller, smallest). To teach inflectional endings, the teacher simply presents a *known* root word[4] and the same root word in an inflected form. For example, "Here is one *duck*" and "Here are two *ducks*." The student is asked to note the word element that changes the word. Practice with many other similar examples, using known words plus inflectional endings, is given. One useful material for practicing inflectional endings is the word slide. (See Figure 13–6.)

To make a word slide, cut four slits in a colored 5″ by 8″ file card. (You may wish to laminate the card for durability.) Next, make sets of strips containing known root words and inflectional endings. The student inserts the strips into the slits and slides them through attempting to form words. She reads each pair silently. If she thinks it does form a word, she says so and pronounces the word.

For young students, pieces cut from other file cards can be added to the basic file card along with colorful drawings to make the material appealing. (See the figure.) After the word has been presented using a word slide, each inflected form should be presented in a sentence so the student may read the word in context.

---

[4]In structural analysis, the terms *root word* and *base word* are used synonymously.

Recognition of Words When Their Spellings Have Changed Because an Ending Has Been Added

Although a poor reader may recognize a root word, she may not recognize it as a known word when an inflectional ending (or suffix) is added. For example, Iris may know *run* and may know the ending *-ing* when added to other words, but because the final consonant is doubled in *run,* to make *running,* it may not be apparent to her that this is a known root word plus a familiar ending. Students often need instruction in the principles of spelling changes in combination with opportunities to match inflected forms with their roots—for example, doubling final consonants (hopping, hitter, wrapped, bigger); changing *y* to *i* before adding an ending (married, busily, dried, happily); dropping the final *e* before adding an ending (hoping, lived, releasing, freezer).

To practice recognition of known words when the spellings have been changed in front of an inflectional ending, the teacher may have students play board games such as the one in Figure 13–7.

Another group game can be easily prepared by starting with the purchase of a piece of felt or thin foam. Next, use an indelible marking pen to draw a target on this fabric and to write on root words. Also purchase a lightweight plastic golf ball. Glue a strip of velcro around the ball. Mount the target on the chalkboard, using masking tape. Beside the target write inflectional endings on the chalkboard itself. (See Figure 13–8.)

To play the game students throw the golfball at the target in the same way they would throw a dart; the velcro causes the ball to stick to the target. After the student has determined which root word the golfball has hit, she goes to the chalkboard and writes a new word by combining the root with one of the inflectional endings. This is written under the appropriate ending already on the board. To score a point for a team the student must re-member to change *y* to *i* when writing the word.

Contractions

Although contractions occur frequently in oral language, and most contemporary reading programs introduce contractions in early first grade materials, many students still find them confusing. Perhaps this is because the word form itself is unusual with its use of an apostrophe and a space within the word. Direct practice in recognizing contractions and their relationships to the words from which they derive often is needed in remedial programs. Some commonly occurring contractions are listed in Box 13–3. Activities and materials to practice recognition of contractions are also presented.

One set of self-correcting commercial materials for practicing identification of contractions is Contraction Boards (Developmental Learning Materials). These boards are designed so students can work independently. All contractions are taught in the context of simple sentences in this set of materials.

Compound Words

There are three types of compound words. The type which teachers most often describe to students are those formed when "two small words are put together to make a longer word" (e.g., *butterfly, into*). Hyphenated words are also often compounds (e.g., *self-correction*). The third type are those words not physically joined, but having a special meaning when found together that is different from the meanings of the individual words when not together. *Ice cream,* for example, means something different from just *ice* plus *cream.* In this latter example, although the words do not appear connected when conveyed by ink marks on paper (i.e., the surface structure of the language unit), they do function as one meaning unit (i.e., in deep structure) and are therefore considered to be a compound word.

Figure 13–7
A board game for practicing a structural analysis word identification strategy

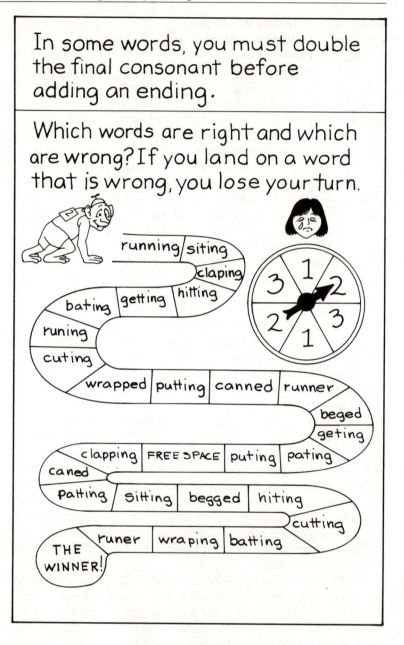

- An activity students enjoy when practicing recognition of compound words is Compound Dominoes. The teacher writes compound words on oaktag strips, drawing a line between the two word parts (e.g., bath/ line between the two word parts (e.g., bath/ house, coat/room, fly/ball, game/bird, light/house). Students try to match compound words so a new compound word is formed from the word parts of two other compounds. For example, matching *lighthouse*

Figure 13–8
Game for practicing structural analysis

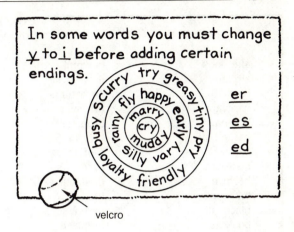

In some words you must change y to i before adding certain endings.

er

es

ed

velcro

Box 13–3
Some Commonly Occurring Contractions

he's	you've	that's	didn't
she's	we've	weren't	I'll
it's	they've	shouldn't	you'll
I'd	we're	wouldn't	he'll
you'd	you're	couldn't	she'll
he'd	they're	isn't	it'll
she'd	let's	hasn't	we'll
we'd	don't	haven't	they'll
they'd	won't	hadn't	I'm
I've			

---

with *flyball* produces the compound *housefly*, matching *flyball* with *gamebird* produces *ballgame*, and so on. The longest sequence of matches wins.

light/house   fly/ball   game/bird   bath/house   coat/room

• Play *Twister*. Use masking tape to attach oilcloth or butcher paper to the floor. Write parts of compound words on stepping stones all over this "playing field." A student from Team 1 places one foot on the beginning of a compound and the other foot on the ending.

Then she places one hand on the beginning of another compound and the other hand on its ending. If both words are correct, the student stays in this position, while a student from Team 2 does the same on the same playing field. Then another Team 1 member joins them, and so on. Soon students have to twist and turn through each other's arms and legs to reach their word parts. Points are lost if a wrong choice is made or anyone falls down in a happy pile.

Box 13–4 presents a list of some compound words that teachers can use when preparing exercises. References such as this are

---

Box 13–4
Some Compound Words

afternoon	downhill	mailbox	seaplane
airplane	downtown	mailman	shoeshine
backbone	downstairs	maybe	shoestring
barnyard	driveway	moonlight	snowball
baseball	drugstore	necktie	snowfall
basketball	everyone	neighborhood	snowflake
bathtub	everything	newspaper	sometimes
bedroom	eyebrows	nightgown	sunrise
beehive	firecracker	notebook	sunset
billboard	firefly	outlaw	sunshine
blackout	firehouse	overboard	surfboard
bookcase	fireplace	overcoat	tablecloth
bookmark	flashlight	pancake	toothbrush
bulldog	football	playground	typewriter
chalkboard	fullback	playhouse	underline
checkerboard	goldfish	piecrust	uphill
classroom	hallway	quarterback	waterfall
coffeeshop	headlight	railroad	watermelon
cookbook	highchair	rainbow	whirlpool
cowboy	highway	raincoat	wildlife
cupcake	homesick	rowboat	without
deadline	horseshoe		

---

helpful since it is often hard to think of a sufficient number of example words when designing activities and games.

Prefixes

A *prefix* is a meaningful word part affixed to the beginning of a word, for example, the *un-* in *unhappy*, or the *dis-* in *disorganized*. Work with prefixes should include *recognition* of prefixes; *identification* of words when prefixes are added to known root words; and attention to *meanings* of prefixes and the meaning changes that occur in words when prefixes are added to them.

Because prefixes are meaning units, for instructional purposes teachers often group those with like meanings. For example, introduction of prefixes might begin with *un-* and *dis-*, because these are both "negative" pre-fixes: they mean "not," as in *unhappy*, or "the opposite of," as in *untie*.

Stauffer (1942) has identified the 15 most commonly occurring English-language prefixes. These are listed in Box 13–5. Some of these prefixes are called absorbed prefixes and others active prefixes. An *absorbed prefix* is a syllable that functioned at one time in the English language as a prefix but no longer does so (Durkin, 1976). Examples are *ad-* in *adjacent* and *com-* in *combine*. An *active prefix*, on the other hand, is one that still functions as a prefix in the manner in which prefixes are generally defined, that is, they are word parts that are added to *complete* root words (such as *re-* in *repay*, or *sub-* in *subzero*). Certain of the prefixes identified by Stauffer are today adapted primarily as absorbed prefixes. At the stage of teaching at which the emphasis is on

---

Box 13—5
The Most Commonly Occurring English Prefixes

a- or *ab-atypical, amoral, abnormal*

ad- *adjoining*

be- *beside, befriend, beloved, befitting, bemoan, besiege, becalmed, bedazzled, bedeviled*

com- *compatriot, compress, commingle de-dethrone, decontaminate, degenerate, dehumanize, dehumidify, deactivate, decode, decompose, decentralize, decompress, debug, de-escalate*

dis- *disobey, disapprove, disagree, disrespectful, dishonest, disconnect, distrust, disarm, disuse, disability, disadvantage, disappear, disbelief, discomfort*

en- *encircle, enable, endanger, enforce, entangle, enslave, enclose, entwine, enrobe, enact, enfold, enthrone, encamp, encode*

ex- *ex-president, ex-wife, ex-husband, exterminate*

in- *(meaning into)* ingrown, inbreed, incoming, inlay, input, inset, intake

in- (meaning *not*) incomplete, inaccurate, invisible, informal, inconvenient, inexcusable, inexpensive, incapable, infrequent, inactive, inadequate, inaccessible, inadvisable, inconsiderate

pre- preschool, prehistoric, precooked, prepaid, prefix, prearrange, pretest, prepackaged, preview, precaution, presuppose, premature, prejudge, pre-revolutionary

pro- pro-war, pronoun, prolong, pro-American, pro-revolutionary

re- repay, retie, recook, rewrite, reread, reappear, remake, replace, reload, reopen, re-entry, review, repopulate, recall, repack, redraw, rearrange, rejoin, reactivate, react

sub- submarine, subzero, subtropical, subheading, subsoil, subdivision, substandard, subcommittee, subhuman

un- unfair, unhappy, uncooked, unlock, untie, uncover, unable, unlucky, untrue, unwrap, uninvited, undress, unfinished, uncertain, unreal, unripe, unwise, unlawful, untruthful, unconscious, unpopulated, undisturbed, unload, unwilling, unsold, unwashed, unspoken

---

the identification of words, the majority of instructional time should be devoted to those prefixes that serve as active prefixes. At later stages of reading development, when the objective is to add sophistication to the strategies that students use to determine word *meanings,* some attention to absorbed prefixes may be appropriate. Several activities that may be used when working with prefixes follow.

1. Use worksheets that help students discern word parts. The exercise shown here is an example. The students are to write the prefix and the root in the two separate columns. (See Figure 13–9.)

2. Play group games. On file cards print prefixes. Pass these out to students. Write root words on oaktag strips. Place one of the root word cards on the chalkboard tray. A student who has a prefix that will fit with the root word comes up and places it in front of the root word card. If it is correct *and* the student can pronounce the new word, the student may take the root word. The student with the most root word cards at the end of the game is the winner.

3. Find prefixes in published stories. Select a story from a sports magazine and have the students circle with a fine-point red marking pen all of the prefixes they can

	PREFIX	ROOT
1. disobey	dis	obey
2. enclose		
3. repay		
4. incomplete		
5. prehistoric		

Figure 13–9
Worksheet for students learning prefixes

find. Give points for each one found. Give additional points for correct pronunciation of each of the words containing a prefix. Then read the article together.

Suffixes

Procedures for teaching suffixes are similar to those used for teaching prefixes. Instruction should include *recognition* of suffixes; *identification* of words when suffixes are added to known root words; and attention to *meanings* of suffixes and the meaning changes that occur in words when suffixes are added to them.

Suffixes, like prefixes, can alter the meanings of words, but they also often change a word's grammatical function. For example, the suffix *-ness* serves to change adjectives to nouns, such as in *dark/darkness* and *happy/happiness*. A listing of some English suffixes can be found in Box 13–6. Activities used for instruction on prefixes can also be used for work with suffixes. Here are some additional suggestions.

Use Flip Strips. On colored strips of construction paper print root words on the front lefthand side. On the back print suffixes, so the back can be folded over to form a new word with the suffix. When introducing a new suffix, packs of flip strips can be prepared so that the same suffix is used over and over with different root words. After sev-

eral suffixes have been introduced the flip strips can be prepared with many different suffixes being added to the same root word. This demonstrates to students how their repertoires of known words have been substantially extended. Flip strips may also be used for practicing identification of words in which the spelling of the root has changed when an ending has been added. After students have read each flip strip from a set, have them read or write each word in a sentence.

Decorate a Bulletin Board With a Tree. Attach index cards labeled with root words to the roots (where else!) of the tree by stapling the ends of small strips of oaktag to the tree's roots and simply slipping the index cards behind the strips. Write suffixes on other index cards and place these in a pile face down. Students take a card from this pile and attempt to match it with a root word. If the match is correct, the root word is removed from the trunk and attached with the suffix to the leafy part of the tree.

Have Students Analyze Multisyllabic Words. After suffixes as well as prefixes have been introduced, give practice with multisyllabic words that contain both. Students can be asked to identify and write each part of the word, or form new words, as

	PREFIX	ROOT	SUFFIX
1. unbreakable	un	break	able
2. disgraceful			
3. refillable			
4. previewer			
5. dishonorable			

Figure 13–10
Worksheet for students working with multisyllabic words

in Figure 13–10. Or, they can be asked to form new words, as in this exercise.

Prefix	Root	Suffix	Word
re	+ fresh	+ ment	= refreshment
un	+ sound	+ ness	=
un	+ success	+ ful	=
re	+ settle	+ ment	=
un	+ law	+ ful	=

Have Students Build Word Trees.
When students have been introduced to both prefixes and suffixes they can also be helped to see the relationships of words that are similar to others by building word trees:

joy
enjoyable
joyful
enjoyment
joyous
rejoice

This not only highlights known word parts as assistance to word identification, but it also stresses interrelatedness of word meanings.

Syllabication
Syllabication, or dividing words into syllables, is considered a part of phonic analysis instruction in some programs, but a part of structural analysis in others. In the former, work with syllabication is believed to be crucial because the ways in which words are divided into syllables are clues to the vowel sounds in words. In these programs students are taught syllabication rules. Some commonly taught rules are:

1. When there are two like consonants, divide between them. (For example, pup/py.)
   Exception: When -ed is added to a word ending in *d* or *t,* it forms a separate syllable (add/ed).
2. When there are two unlike consonants, divide between them. (For example, wal/rus.)
   Exception: Do not divide between blends or digraphs (be/tween).
3. When a consonant is between two vowels, divide after the first vowel. (For example, si/lent.)
   Exception: When the consonant between two vowels is *x,* divide after the consonant (ex/am).
4. Prefixes, suffixes, and inflectional endings are separate syllables. (For example, re/state/ment.)
   Exception: When -ion is added to a word that ends in *t,* the *t* joins with the -ion to form the final syllable (ac/tion).
5. When a syllable ends in a vowel, the vowel is long.

Box 13–6
Some English Suffixes

-able	enjoyable, comfortable, enviable		*-ion*	suggestion, graduation, creation, discussion
-age	shortage, leakage, wreckage, breakage		*-ity*	stupidity, humidity, sincerity, productivity
-al	musical, personal, original, removal		*-ive*	productive, expensive, excessive, destructive
-ance	appearance, performance		*-ize*	alphabetize, dramatize, colonize, symbolize
-ant	contestant, attendant, informant		*-less*	spotless, sleeveless, nameless, friendless
-ary	imaginary, summary, boundary, missionary		*-ly*	consciously, quickly, friendly, officially, slowly
-ation	confirmation, information, starvation, relaxation		*-ment*	refreshment, amazement, punishment, enjoyment
-ative	informative, talkative, administrative, imaginative		*-ness*	completeness, wholeness, sickness, darkness
-ence	existence, persistence		*-or*	sailor, actor, inventor, inspector, translator
-ent	excellent, insistent, correspondent		*-ous*	joyous, famous, dangerous, nervous, courageous
-er	helper, teacher, player, farmer, miner, follower		*-th*	growth, truth, warmth, width, fourth
-ery	bakery, bravery		*-ty*	loyalty, safety, cruelty
-ful	delightful, careful, cheerful, truthful, plentiful		*-ward*	homeward, toward, westward, eastward
-fy	classify, beautify, falsify, simplify, purify		*-y*	rainy, windy, noisy, gloomy, curly, snowy

---

6. When a syllable ends in a consonant, the vowel in that syllable is short.

By applying a combination of these rules, presumably a reader would be aided in identifying vowel sounds, and, ultimately, unknown words. For example, by applying rule 3 and rule 5 this word could be identified as *sīlent,* not *sĭlent.*

However, many students have difficulty learning these rules, and even when they do, they generally reserve the use of these rules for specific workbook or teacher-directed exercises on syllabication and seldom consciously apply them independently. Also, as can be seen for even the most commonly taught generalizations, many words that students will encounter are exceptions.

On the other hand, in programs where syllabication is considered a part of the structural analysis component, the purpose of showing students how words can be divided is to demonstrate that a long and possibly intimidating word may be analyzed in terms of its smaller word parts, and thus identified. For example, when a poor reader first encounters in print such words as *enlargement* or *irreplaceable,* the first reaction may be, "I don't know that word and I'll never be able to figure out a word that big." On the other hand, the word can seem quite manageable if the student has developed the habit of dividing the word up and looking for familiar word parts. For example, if context does not help, the student might go through these steps to identify the word *enlargement:*

> "Oh, it begins with *en-*. We worked with a prefix like that. It's /en/."
> "The middle of the word is *large."*
> "The end is just that suffix, *-ment."*
> *"En-large-ment. Enlargement.* 'I'll need to make an enlargement of this picture,' the photographer said."

The emphasis in syllabication in these programs is on looking for known word parts and not on memorizing rules. In such a program the following activities would occur.

Step 1: Students are told that long words can be divided into smaller parts to aid identification. This is demonstrated by removing inflectional endings from words (e.g., entering = enter/ing; darkest = dark/est). The term and concept of "syllable" is applied to each of these smaller parts.

Step 2: Step 1 is repeated, this time with prefixes (e.g., disgrace = dis/grace; unselfish = un/selfish.)

Step 3: Step 1 is carried out again, this time with suffixes (e.g., importantly = important/ly; enrollment = enroll/ment).

Step 4: Step 1 is carried out with both prefixes and suffixes (e.g., un/rest/ful; dis/appear/ance.)

Step 5: Students are told that there are some other ways to divide long words and are given brief practice in dividing words based on frequently taught rules. The emphasis at this time remains on looking at common word parts. Memorization of the rules is not required. (Knowledge of syllabication rules is actually more helpful for writing than for reading so that correct conventions of written language usage may be applied when a word is hyphenated at the end of a line.)

CONCLUDING STATEMENT

A major problem for large numbers of students in remedial reading programs is their lack of word-identification strategies. Because of this, teachers often place too great an emphasis on any strategy they believe will solve the problem. It should be reiterated here that focus on any single strategy to the exclusion of others is detrimental to student progress. The nature of English words and English text structure requires use of a variety of strategies as unknown words are encountered.

Proficient readers, like poor readers, also encounter unknown words in their reading. Proficient readers, however, have a variety of word-identification strategies at their disposal, and intuitively select the most efficient one first. If the most efficient strategy doesn't work, they quickly and unconsciously select the next most efficient, and so forth. Proficient readers generally follow the steps listed here when they do not recognize a word. These are carried out almost instantaneously and usually with very little conscious thought about the strategies being applied. (As you read the steps, see if they apply to your own reading behaviors.)

Step 1: Context is used. When proficient readers come to an unknown word, their eyes unconsciously flit back and forth across the line to see if any other words convey the unknown word. (They do *not*, as an ordinary first step, attempt to sound out the word letter by letter.) Often, the word is identified in Step 1 and no other steps are necessary.

Step 2: If context doesn't help, these readers *look for known word parts;* that is, they use structural analysis. They may notice that the word begins with the prefix *re-*, or has the ending *-ion*, or that they recognize the root word, and so forth. This is accomplished rapidly and without much awareness that it is being done. If the word is identified at this point, no other steps are employed.

Step 3: If the word parts do not provide adequate clues, good readers may further *divide the word;* that is, they syllabicate. Again, they do this rather unconsciously: and they do not specifically apply rules (e.g., they do not say, "Let's see now. In a multisyllabic word ending with *-le,* the consonant preceding the *-le* is part of the second syllable.") Instead, they quickly chunk up the word based on their familiarity with common word elements (*he ma tol o gy; in de pen dence; neb u lous*).

Step 4: If good readers still have not identified the word by this time, it is very likely that they have skipped the word and gone on. This is not a bad strategy since the redundancy of language makes it quite possible that context will make the word's identification apparent in a later part of the passage.

If, however, they want very much to know this word (e.g., there will be a quiz over the material tomorrow, or it's in a love letter), then they may apply *phonic analysis skills.* Starting with the beginning of the word, they think of the sounds the letters usually make. (Actually they may not find it necessary to use any *but* the beginning letters since the word is in context.) In any case, their thought processes are slower and at a more conscious level at this point.

Step 5: Finally, if all else fails—and they really need to know this word—they may use a dictionary or ask someone.

These steps that proficient readers use in mediated word identification should be a clue to teachers that it is necessary to teach a variety of strategies to their students and should suggest which ones to prompt students to use first.

Finally, don't let the tail wag the dog. Remember that the real reason for work on word identification is to enable students to read and understand regular, connected reading material. Care should be taken to ensure that any emphasis on word-identification training does not consume so much of a session that students have no time left for reading. The excerpt in Box 13–7 is from an article by Du Bois (1977). It presents a reading period from a young student's point of view to emphasize this point.

Box 13–7
"I'm Sorry I Asked,"

Let me tell you what happened at school just this morning.

We were supposed to all be reading, unless it was our group's "talking time."

So I got out my book about fires.

"Emergency" is my favorite television show.

I like to look at books about firemen and fire trucks and this one had some easy words.

I could almost read it.

I started to read.

"This is a book about fire trucks."

Good, I thought, I like stories about fire trucks, so I turned the page to find out more about fire trucks.

The next page was not so easy.

"Fire *e-n-g-i-n-e-s* are red."

I've never seen that word "*e-n-g-i-n-e-s*" before.

I started to ask Elizabeth, the girl in front of me, but the teacher shook her finger at me.

I tried to think of fire *what* is red?

I couldn't think of anything so I held up my hand.

When the teacher finally nodded, I went to her desk. I took my book and I said to her in my best whisper, "What is this word?"

She likes to play guessing games:

TEACHER: "What do you think it is?" "What does it look like?"

ME: "It doesn't look like anything."

TEACHER: "Can you tell me what it starts with?"

ME: "*E*"

TEACHER: "Good, now what sound does the *E* make?"

ME: "*E* as in *elephant* or *E* as in *eel*?"

TEACHER: "The word starts like *N*."

ME: "An *E* word starts like *N*?" "That's a new one!"

TEACHER: "Now, is the *G* soft or hard?"

ME: "Let me see, a *G* is soft when it is

followed by *a, e, i, u,* or is that hard? Or does it come before?"

TEACHER: "It sounds like a *J*."

ME: "Oh. *N-J-Ine*."

TEACHER: "The *gine* is not pronounced *gine*."

ME: "But you said *c-ī-c* final *e*, then the first vowel is long."

TEACHER: "In this word it's a *schwa* pronounced *jən*."

ME: "What's a *schwa*?"

TEACHER: "You'll find out later."

ME: "Ok, but what's an engine?"

TEACHER: "Read the whole sentence."

ME: "Fire engines are red."

TEACHER: "Now look at the picture. What do you see that is red?"

ME: "Fire house, hose, truck and uniforms."

TEACHER: (looking at watch) "Engine means truck."

ME: "It does?" "Fire trucks at Station 56 are yellow."

TEACHER: (again looking at watch) "Usually, fire engines are red."

I went back to my seat.

The book didn't seem nearly as interesting as it did before.

I learned a new word.

Engine means truck—but my reading time was over.

I whispered to Elizabeth.

"Did you know this word says 'engine' and it means 'truck'?"

"Of course," she whispered back.

I wondered why I couldn't ask her in the first place, then I could have finished my book.

I've decided it has something to do with "*e's*" like in *elephant* or *eel*, or "*g's*" that sound like "*j*" and *schwa's* and final "*e*" are not always magic.

Sometimes reading is fun, but it takes so long to find out the words you don't know.

I would like to point that out to my teacher—if I dared.

(*Source:* From "I'm Sorry I Asked," by DuBois, 1977, *Language Arts, 54,* pp. 899–901. Reprinted by permission of the National Council of Teachers of English.)

14

Increasing Knowledge of Word Meanings

Apprehension of the semantic fields of morphological units is pivotal for deriving semantic content when reading. This seems to be consummately plausible and most preceptors' ripostes to this attestation would predictably be, "Inexorably so."

You may have had some difficulty in getting the gist of the previous two sentences; they were written with words whose meanings are not familiar to most people. The next two sentences say the same thing but use words more frequently found in the meaning vocabularies of the average college student. Now try it again.

Knowledge of word meanings is important for reading comprehension. This seems to be quite logical and most teachers' responses to this statement would probably be, "Of course."

However, this idea is controversial. A number of educators have believed that, because of the redundancy in language, cues within written material provide the information needed for comprehension, and that knowledge of individual word meanings therefore is not really that critical.

While it is true that redundancy in language does provide important clues to word meaning, the contrasting examples in the previous paragraph show that ease of comprehension *is* affected by knowledge of individual word meanings. Further, research has confirmed this premise (Clark, 1972; Marks, Doctorow, & Wittrock, 1974; Kameenui, Carnine, & Freschi, 1982). Since adequate meaning vocabulary is important to reading comprehension, remedial teachers must be concerned with this area of instruction.

Meaning vocabulary is defined as the number of words to which an individual can attach one or more meanings. Such knowledge must occur first in an individual's oral language and then must be extended to words in print. Dale (1965) has reported that children come to school with a meaning vocabulary of about 2,000 words and that the average student adds about 1,000 words during each school year thereafter. If poor readers have not attained this level of vocabulary acquisition, attention to the development of meaning vocabulary must occur as part of their programs.

Roelke's (1969) research showed that the most important aspects of vocabulary knowledge affecting comprehension are the following (listed in order of importance).

- The number of words a student knows meanings for;
- Knowledge of multiple meanings of words; for example, knowing that *light* can mean "not heavy" as well as a shade of color (as in "light pink"), free from worry (as in "light hearted"), a source of illumination, moderate (as in a "light meal"), or a small quantity (as in "light rain"), and so forth;
- Ability to select the correct meaning of a word having multiple meanings in order to fit a specific context.

The three major ways a teacher can help students increase their meaning vocabularies in all these areas are a) by encouraging wide reading, b) by providing opportunities for new experiences, and c) by providing specific language exercises.

ENCOURAGING WIDE READING

Knowledge of meaning vocabulary improves reading, and interestingly, the converse is also true—reading improves knowledge of meaning vocabulary. A person who reads voraciously usually has a rich vocabulary that is larger in terms of quantity of known words and broader in terms of quality than that of individuals who do not. Wide reading also increases knowledge of multiple meanings of words for which previously only the common meaning was known. An effective and practical way to help students improve their word knowledge is to get them to read lots and lots of books, magazines, articles, newspapers, and so forth. It is, therefore, legitimate for a re-medial teacher to spend a portion of each instructional period getting students interested in all types of reading material.

Ironically, those poor readers who have deficits in meaning vocabulary are often the very ones who do not like to read. Many other poor readers, when given library books, stories, and so forth, at an appropriate level so they *can* read them, are often delighted to read, and within such a context they will choose reading for pleasure over other activities. Too often this is not the case with the student who has a meager meaning vocabulary. The teacher, then, must find ways to motivate interest in reading as a worthwhile activity. The following ideas are suggested.

1. Try to discover students' interests through interviews and use of interest inventories (see Chapter 8 for sample questions to use on an interest inventory). Then start their reading programs with short, easy (for them) books targeted to their interests, or even material as short as a magazine or newspaper article written at an easy reading level.

2. Provide time for sustained silent reading (SSR). *Sustained silent reading* is an activity in which all students in a group must engage in silent reading for a period of time. They may read anything they wish, but no other activity is allowed during this time period. The teacher uses a timer (facing the teacher and not the students so the teacher doesn't have a room full of clock-watchers instead of readers) with the time period on the first day being very short, usually 5 minutes. Students read until the timer rings. Each day the amount of time is increased by a minute or two until, after several days, students are sustaining their silent reading from about 15 minutes (in elementary-level remedial classes) to 30 minutes (in secondary-level reading classes).

Box 14—1

Some Books to Read Aloud to Reluctant Readers

The Ghost Rock Mystery	Grades 4, 5, 6	Really scary. Leaves you "hanging" at the end of each chapter as something awful is about to happen. A good one to start the year with. Also available in paperback.
The Snake Who Went to School	Grades 3, 4, 5, 6	Funny. A snake gets loose in the school, isn't captured for several days, and is the cause of a number of wild happenings.
Casey, the Utterly Impossible Horse	Grades 3, 4, 5, 6	Ridiculously funny; a horse that talks. Available through Arrow Book Club. If your children order books from these book clubs the teacher gets a free children's book for each 15 books the students buy.
All Pippi Longstocking books: *Pippi Longstocking; Pippi in the South Seas; Pippi Goes on Board*	Grades 3, 4, 5, 6	Even the teacher will laugh while reading these books. Pippi's father is the king of a cannibal island and her mother is dead, so she lives alone in a house in Sweden with her horse, her monkey, and a chest full of gold. And she does *anything* she wants to do.
Julie of the Wolves	Grades 5 and 6	Newbery Award Winner. Exciting, interesting, scary. An Eskimo girl is saved from starvation when a pack of wolves allow her to share their food and shelter. Realistic.
The House of the Sixty Fathers	Grades 5 and 6	Frightening, but realistically told story that takes place during the Japanese occupation of China during World War II when a boy becomes separated from his family and attempts to find them. Runner-up for the Newbery Award.
The Matchlock Gun	Grades 3, 4, 5, 6	A picture book for older children. Very exciting story and dramatic pictures. A settler's cabin is attacked by Indians during the French and Indian Wars. A Newbery Award Winner.

SSR was first described by Hunt (1970). He and others believe the technique works best if the teacher also reads a book of his/her choice to serve as a model for students. Teachers sometimes post a DO NOT DISTURB sign on the door during SSR and students as well as teachers begin to look upon this time period as the best of the day. Very reluctant readers may at first "refuse" to read and may just sit staring at an open page. After a period of time this behavior simply becomes too boring and these students will begin to look at the pictures, and then begin to read captions under the pictures, until eventually they are seduced into the reading material. Thereafter, they begin to read as the other students do, and participate willingly in this part of the class period. SSR has been used successfully with elementary and secondary students.

3. Read aloud to groups of reluctant readers. In addition to its other positive effects, reading to students is one of the best ways to get them interested in reading for themselves. If time is short, poetry often is

---

Box 14–2
Some Books to Read Aloud to Middle School Students

Some of the books suggested here are most suitable for reading aloud to younger middle school students; some are better for use with older middle school students; others are suitable for any middle school student. Teachers should skim the first chapter of the book and read the information presented on the dust jacket to determine if a suggested book is suitable for the students in their classes.

1. *Best Short Shorts,* Eric Berger, Editor (Paperback available from Scholastic. Every story has a surprise ending. Because selections are short, this book would be good to use when there is only a little time for reading aloud to students.)
2. *How To Eat Fried Worms,* Thomas Rockwell
3. *Fifty-two Miles to Terror,* Ruth and Robert Carlson (Nine tension-packed short stories.)
4. *Encyclopedia Brown Takes a Case,* Donald Sobel
5. *Passport to Freedom,* Dorothy Bonnell
6. *Ben and Me,* Robert Lawson
7. *Out of the Sun,* Ben Bova
8. *Kareem! Basketball Great,* Arnold Hano
9. *The Wonderful Flight to the Mushroom Planet,* Eleanor Cameron
10. *New Sound,* Leslie Waller
11. *Julie of the Wolves,* Jean George
12. *Follow My Leader,* James B. Garfield
13. *Old Yeller,* Fred Gipson
14. *The Lost Ones,* Ian Cameron
15. *Island of the Blue Dolphins,* Scott O'Dell
16. *The Hornet's Nest,* Sally Watson
17. *Earthfasts,* William Mayne
18. *Trouble for the Tabors,* Barbara Goolden
19. *The House of the Sixty Fathers,* Meindert De Jong
20. *Hunger for Racing,* J. M. Douglas
21. *Incident at Hawk's Hill,* Allan Eckert
22. *Pippi Longstocking,* Astrid Lindgren
23. *Journey Outside,* Mary Q. Steele
24. *Bully of Barkham Street,* Mary Stolz
25. *The Phantom Tollbooth,* Norton Juster
26. *My Name is Pablo,* Aimee Somerfelt
27. *The Forgotten Door,* Alexander Key
28. *Escape To Witch Mountain,* Alexander Key
29. *A Wrinkle in Time,* Madeline L'Engle
30. *Funny Bananas,* Georgess McHargue
31. *The Witch of Blackbird Pond,* Elizabeth George Speare
32. *The Sound of Coaches,* Leon Garfield
33. *Eskimo Boy,* Pepaluk Fruchen
34. *The Gift,* Peter Dickinson
35. *The Yearling,* Marjorie Rawlings

---

a good choice for reading aloud, because it takes very little time to read a poem or two or three. An excellent book for this purpose is *An Invitation to Poetry* (Addison-Wesley), because it includes poems that relate to children's real life interests. The limerick section of this book is particularly popular. *Where the Side-walk Ends,* by Shel Silverstein (Harper & Row), is another poetry book enjoyed immensely by students. Some books to read aloud to students who initially may not want to be read to are listed in Box 14–1. Box 14–2 suggests books for reading aloud to middle school students.

4. Use movies of children's and adolescents'

books to stimulate interest in reading the book itself. These may be obtained from many public libraries. Also, most school districts have central audiovisual libraries from which teachers may select films. Two well-known picture books for which movies have been produced are *Andy and the Lion* and *The Camel Who Took A Walk*. The original illustrations are depicted as the stories are read in these films. A movie of interest to intermediate-grade students is "The Doughnut Machine," a funny episode from the popular book, *Homer Price*.

It is important that the teacher have one or more copies of these books available after the students have viewed the movie. Although one might think that once students have seen the movie and know the story they would not be interested in repeating the story again by reading it in a book, the opposite effect occurs. The book based on the film becomes the most popular book in the room for the next 2 or 3 weeks and even reluctant readers want to read it.

5. Filmstrips of books may be used in the same ways as movies. These are often available in the school media center.

6. Cassette/book combinations are also available (e.g., from Scholastic). Books accompanying these are usually in paperback form; since paperbacks are relatively inexpensive it is often feasible to purchase multiple copies of the books. Students may listen to the tape as a group and then the book is offered to students who wish to read it.

7. Commercial audiotapes have been prepared in which dramas of well-known books are presented, complete with sound effects. One teacher's successful experience with older remedial readers involved the group listening to a taped drama of H. G. Wells' *The Time Machine*. When easy-to-read versions of this classic

story were offered to the group afterward, almost all students chose to read the book. Check the school district's central audio-visual library or the public library for similar tapes.

8. Have the students join a book club. Scholastic and other companies sponsor such clubs from which students may order paperbacks monthly at a reasonable price. In a remedial class, a typical occurrence is for only a few students to order books the first month. To change this situation, on the day these books arrive the teacher should make a big production of opening the package, removing the books one at a time, and passing them out to each student who ordered one. This should be accompanied by enthusiastic comments about how interesting this one looks, about how that one is one of your own personal favorites, how this one really looks funny, and perhaps reading a page from one or two, or showing pictures. During that class period, students who have received new books should be allowed to just sit and read them for the duration of the session. Thereafter, larger numbers of students will usually order books monthly.

9. Have books available that can be directly used in lessons on word meaning. For example, the *Amelia Bedelia* series (Harper & Row) has funny plays on words that students can enjoy and learn from. These books can be read for the fun of it to generate interest in reading, but follow-up lessons directly related to the word concepts will be easily tolerated because they are enjoyable.

10. Fill bookshelves with books that students can check out. Teachers should select the books so reading levels appropriate for all students in the class are represented. If students are going to read them on their own, books should be available on their independent reading levels. If there are

funds for purchasing books, the Hi-Lo paperbacks (Bantam) are a good choice for adding to a bookshelf collection for very low achievers. Reading levels in this series range from second through third grade, while the subject matter is of interest to many contemporary teens. Some titles from the series are: *Village of Vampires, The Bermuda Triangle and Other Mysteries of Nature,* and *Rock Fever.*

11. Engage students in follow-up activities that will interest other students in a book they've liked. For example, several young children who have read the same book could make simple stick puppets to dramatize the story to others. Such puppets can be made easily by having students paste tongue depressors on the backs of pictures they have drawn of characters from the book. Preparation of the puppets could occur outside of reading class (a fun homework assignment) so class reading time will not be used.

Another way to gain broader interest is to have students write brief book reviews. To enable this, create a group file box for index cards on which students are to write the names of books they've read, along with two or three observations about each book. Colored file cards and white file cards should be available. If students really like a book, they "review" it on the colored file cards. If their reaction is that the book was just so-so, the information goes on the white cards. When students want to choose a new book, they can refer to the file box and read the reviews on the colored cards.

PROVIDING OPPORTUNITIES FOR NEW EXPERIENCES

A second effective and lasting way to increase meaning vocabulary is through participation in new experiences. Not only does direct participation in real and vicarious experiences increase vocabulary, but it also develops precision in word knowledge and clarifies misconceptions. In addition, experiences with concepts and the words that label them make it easier for students to select the appropriate meanings of words with multiple meanings.

Real Experiences

When teachers consider providing new experiences for students, one of the first thoughts to come to mind is probably the field trip. However, practical considerations involving time and transportation make frequent trips of the usual type less than feasible. Teachers, therefore, should rethink just what a "field trip" is. If any brief excursion away from the confines of the classroom is considered a "trip," then many practical possibilities are available. Using this expanded definition of a field trip, one teacher simply took her students outside to examine the school building in ways they had never done before. One of several things noted during this trip was the block above the front door in which a sentence had been carved: new words such as "motto" and "lintel" (the block above the door) emerged. Before each new school year, another teacher makes it a point to drive around the neighborhood of the schools in which she teaches. Her purpose is to locate places of interest within walking distance of the school. This has resulted in walking trips to a doughnut-making shop and an agency that trains guide dogs for the blind, among others. On occasion, she takes an 8mm filmloop camera and films a portion of the experience. After the steps in making doughnuts were filmed and then viewed in the classroom, lessons on vocabulary and following a sequence of events were based on the film.

A second way to capitalize on real experiences without the impracticalities of frequent or elaborate excursions is to use experiences students have had in common outside of school. For example, if many of your secondary students attend hockey or football games, their interests can be the basis of vocabulary development activities. Discuss the activity, have the group write about it together, and use synonyms for common words ("Jones moved so fast across that ice—" can be changed to "Jones moved so swiftly across that ice—").

Some real experiences teachers can organize *within* the classroom include the following.

- cooking
- food-tasting parties
- bringing in objects (e.g., a weather balloon that fell in your yard; a starfish Ken got on his vacation in Florida)
- science experiments
- displays (e.g., of clothing, artifacts, or art objects from other countries)
- inviting people to the classroom for demonstrations (e.g., of musical instruments; of origami-making)

Following all such experiences, *words* that symbolize these experiences must be used in discussion, writing, and reading. If teachers fail to take this follow-up step, students will not end up with any more useful words than before. Teachers must also remember the importance of *time on task,* and the specific purpose for providing new experiences, which is to help students expand their meaning vocabularies through development of new concepts and the acquisition of new labels (words) for old concepts. For example, if four reading-class sessions are devoted to an experience but only 20 minutes of follow up for the development of related vocabulary are provided, this would be an inappropriate division of time. Better planning would call for a briefer experiential activity (perhaps 30 minutes, or a single class session) and more time devoted to work with related words.

Vicarious Experiences

It is not possible for individuals to experience everything directly. Few people, for example, have actually seen a volcano erupt, or flown in a helicopter, or skinned a deer. Nevertheless, they can understand many things about these events and processes, can visualize them, and can use words to discuss them (e.g., lava, ash, rotary blade, altimeter, sinew, hide). They know these things because they have had vicarious experiences that have helped build concepts. A *vicarious experience* is one in which events are performed in substitution for other events, and learning or concept building is fulfilled by this substitution. A vicarious experience occurs in place of something else: it is an indirect experience. For example, although you probably have never directly seen a volcano erupt, you may know quite a lot about eruptions from viewing a film about volcanoes when you were in elementary school, reading about them in a magazine or a high school science book, or seeing TV news clips of erupting volcanoes. All these experiences are vicarious because they are indirect. Nevertheless, they can teach a great deal.

In remedial classes vicarious experiences can be provided in many ways and can be used to develop meaning vocabulary. Pictures may be shown to develop concepts before students read a story or article. If, for example, the story to be read includes a horse and mentions its "forelock," the teacher may pull from the picture file a photograph of a horse, point to its forelock so that students will see what it looks like, and talk about the meanings of "fore" and "lock" (*fore,* meaning "in front of," combined with *lock,* as in "lock of hair," equals a tuft of hair at the front of the horse's head).

Picture sets designed to help students explore and *use* new words are on the market (for example, from Bowmar). Or, teachers can make their own collections from magazine pictures. Slides can also be shown in conjunction with follow-up worksheets that require students to practice using the words that were discussed when the slides were viewed. Filmstrips, movies, and records with sound effects all can be employed in the same way. *TV programs* that students watch at home can also provide an opportunity for enhancing well-developed meanings for words. The teachers may ask students to watch a particular program (one that many students might watch anyway, or one for which it is likely that enough interest exists so that students *will* watch it); then to bring in one word from the program to share with the class. These words are listed on a chart, along with their meanings and synonyms, and examples of their uses.

It is critical that students *use* the words they have been exposed to through vicarious experiences. If the words are to become a part of their meaning vocabularies, just hearing them is not sufficient. Students should be induced to use these new words in their own oral language, in discussions, in written activities, and through reading printed text—either published material or teacher-developed selections.

SPECIFIC EXERCISES

The third way to help students increase their meaning vocabularies is through specific exercises. Hittleman (1983) reported that successful programs focusing on specific exercises as the means to vocabulary development include the following features.

A few words are taught in-depth rather than many words presented in a more cursory fashion.

Any technique is employed that calls attention to the meanings of word parts.

Context, the dictionary, and the derivations of words are studied to obtain word meanings.

The instruction is systematic and continuous. Students are exposed to the same word in many different contexts.

Game-like activities are incorporated into the schedule to stimulate students to study vocabulary.

Direct Practice

Research has shown that direct practice of vocabulary words (sometimes called "drill") can be effective; that is, if it is carried out in specific ways. In the Kameenui, Carnine, and Freschi study (1982), two techniques were found to be effective. The first instructional technique involved presenting words and their meanings written on index cards to the students and conducting the following procedures (pp. 375–376).

1. Teacher says the word (e.g., *altercations*).
2. Student says the word.
3. Student is asked to read the word's meaning from card (e.g., *fights*).
4. Teacher asks questions related to word (e.g., "Do you have *altercations* with your teacher?" "Do you have *altercations* with a tree?")
5. Teacher asks student to say meaning of word again.
6. Teacher presents a second card and instruction on second word begins employing the same five steps.
7. Instruction on third word is conducted using same steps.
8. After instruction on the third word, a review is carried out: the student is asked questions about each of the three words to determine if meanings are known. If not, the relevant card is shown again and the student is asked to respond to questions while looking at the card.

9. Following this cumulative review, all of the above steps are carried out with three additional words.

While this direct practice technique was found to facilitate comprehension of passages that included the instructed words, students who were exposed to a second technique scored even higher. Technique number two consisted of all the steps used in technique number one, but, in addition, students were taught to "integrate" the meanings of the words during passage reading. "Integration" means that their reading was halted whenever they encountered one of the instructed words in a passage and they were required to say its meaning as well as to answer a question asked by the teacher, which also required knowledge of the meaning of the word.

Direct practice also was found to be effective with LD students in a study by Pany and Jenkins (1977), in which vocabulary exercises consisted of the following procedures.

- Flashcards were made by the teacher, each containing a new word and its definitions.
- Students practiced saying the word and its definition aloud.
- Practice was conducted for a total of 2 minutes on six words over a period of several days.

Use of Context Clues

In the last chapter the importance of using context to aid *recognition* of words was emphasized. Context can also a) provide clues to *meanings* of words and b) be used as a method of word study. Gipe (1978–79) investigated four methods for teaching vocabulary.

The Context Method. The context method requires students to read a paragraph in which the target word appears in each of three sentences that provide contexts to help define the word. Students are then asked to write something that would relate the word to their own experiences. One such paragraph is:

> The barbarian kicked the dog and hit the owner in the nose. Any person who acts mean to anybody or anything is a barbarian. Barbarian means a person who is very mean. Write down something a barbarian might do at the dinner table (p. 630).

The Association Method. The association method requires students to associate new words with either a synonym for a word they already know or a short, written definition. Four such pairs are memorized each day and then students are required to write them from memory.

> wretched: unhappy
> barbarian: cruel, mean person

The Category Method. This method has two steps. In the first step words are listed by categories for students to read, then students are required to add their own words to each category. For example (Gipe, p. 630):

> *Bad People*
>   mean
>   cruel
>   barbarian
>   robber

Write your own words {

> *Things You Can Write With*
>   pencil
>   graphite
>   marker
>   chalk

Write your own words {

In step two the students are given a list of all target words in random order, plus the category titles; for example, Bad People or Things You Can Write With. Then they are required to list the target words under the right category without referring to the study sheet from step one.

The Dictionary Method. In the dictionary method the students are required to look up each word in the dictionary, write its definition, and write each word in a sentence. (This latter method is typical of the approach used for vocabulary building by large numbers of teachers.)

Of the four methods, the "context method" worked best, but the "association method" also worked. The "category method" and the "dictionary method" were *not* helpful in bringing about an increase in students' knowledge of word meanings.

Gipe's study used context as a way of presenting new target word previously selected by the teacher. However, students should also be taught how to use the context of a passage if they encounter a word with an unknown meaning when they are reading independently. Although context does not always provide a word's meaning, often it does. According to Dale and O'Rourke (1971), for example, the following types of context clues can assist in establishing the meanings of unknown words.

1. Synonyms. "A martin is a *bird.*"
2. Antonyms. "The plastic dish *won't break* but the glass one probably will shatter."
3. Apposition (use of a word or phrase set off by commas). "Florida is a peninsula, *a body of land surrounded on three sides by water,* and has many beaches."
4. Comparison. "A newsreel is *like a short motion picture* of news events."
5. Contrast. "A story that *rambles on and on is not* concise."

6. Description. "Flying lizards are *found in Asia and can spread winglike membranes out from the sides of their small bodies so they can sometimes be seen gliding through the air.*"
7. Example. "A task force is a temporary grouping of forces, *for example, a military unit that has been called up to achieve a specific objective.*"
8. Origin. "The Italian word for 'fresh' is 'fresco,' which gives us the name of a painting done on fresh plaster." (Dale & O'Rourke, 1971, p. 34)
9. Formal definition. "'Lightsome' *means buoyant, graceful, light, or nimble.*"

Students should be given specific exercises to practice using each of these types of context clues.

A teacher-made activity for practicing use of context can be made by cutting manila file folders into four folding strips. A sentence providing context for an underlined target word is written on the outside of each of the four strips. The meaning of each target word is written inside each folded strip. Students are given a pack of these, asked to read the sentence on each, guess the meaning of the underlined word from context, then open up the file folder piece to find the answer. This activity can be carried out independently and is self-correcting.

Helpful commercial materials include the *Using the Context* booklets from the Specific Skills Series (Barnell Loft). These booklets, in versions for beginning and advanced readers, provide students with practice in using context for identifying unknown words and deriving word meanings.

Synonyms and Antonyms

Gipe's (1978–79) study, cited earlier, shows that direct practice with words and their synonyms is an effective procedure. Gipe's synonym practice, called the "association method," was a *drill* procedure. A *manipulative* activity for practicing synonyms can be made from 8½" by 11" pieces of colored construction paper. Draw two sets of lines across each piece with a marking pen. Write known words on the left-hand lines of each construction paper "board" (for example, name, tight, grumpy, winding, sparkle, useless, hothouse). Cut strips of plain oaktag to a size that will fit on each of the right-hand lines. Write a synonym on each oaktag strip for one of the listed known words (for example, sinuous, designation, taut, conservatory, etc.). Place one set of these construction paper "boards" plus the accompanying synonym strips in each of several manila envelopes. Label the envelopes #1, #2, and so forth. Give each student one manila envelope set and a dictionary. Have students use their dictionaries to determine which words are synonyms and then place the oaktag strips next to the matching words on their "board."

Examining and substituting words in written materials also provides effective practice with synonyms. Three stages may be used.

1. Mark the word that would *best* substitute for the underlined word:

   Jim's *clever* story was entertaining everyone when I walked into the room.

   _____ funny

   _____ intelligent

   ✔ witty

2. Choose the word that would *best* fit the blank.

   As the wind _____ through the huge sails, all the sailors shuddered with fear.

   (howled)   blew   moved

3. Use a thesaurus to select a more effective synonym for the underlined word.

   The pirate was wild with rage and said to the prisoner, "Into chains with you!"

A commercial game for practicing synonyms as well as antonyms is *Swap* (Steck-Vaughn). Similar practice with antonyms is also helpful. Edgar Dale (personal communication, February 22, 1984) stated that when a person can specify the opposite of a word he truly understands its meaning.

Antonym cards may be prepared by the teacher for students' independent practice. Following are directions for preparing self-correcting cards. On index cards print single words. Next, print their antonyms on an equivalent set of cards, one antonym to a card. Turn pairs of antonyms over so they are placed next to one another. Paste a paper sticker on the cards so half of the sticker is on one card and half on the other. With scissors then, snip the cards apart. Do the same with all pairs. As students practice with the antonym cards they should attempt to line them up by pairs on their desks. At the completion of matching, each pair should be turned over to see if the two half pictures (forming the snipped sticker) on the backs fit together to make a whole; if not, a wrong choice has been made and the student should re-study the cards.

Multiple Meanings

The difference between the meaning vocabularies of good and poor readers is often found in the number of meanings each is able to provide for a specific word. Frequently, a poor reader can give only the most common meaning. Students in remedial programs need work with multiple meanings of words, including words that have specialized meanings in content area fields. For example, although Joe certainly knows the meaning for *mouth* when one is talking about the opening in the head used for eating and talking, he may have no understanding of its meaning when his geography book refers to the *mouth of a river.* Having students draw pictures of right and wrong meanings of such terms helps them remember less familiar definitions of words with multiple meanings.

Discussion of differences in shades of meaning when working on multiple meanings also can help develop precision in word usage. For example, questions such as the following might be asked.

What is the difference between *soft* fur and *soft* fruit?

What is the difference between *soft* light and *soft* pink?

Games, too, can be used for practice with multiple meanings. One example is the game illustrated in Figure 14–1 called "multiple meaning bingo." This game helps students become familiar with a number of meanings for the same word and gives practice in selecting the correct meaning to fit a specific context. To make this game, the teacher must first consult a dictionary to compile a list of different meanings for a single common word. Number and list these meanings as shown in the bottom portion of Figure 14–1. On a ditto-master draw a bingo board as shown in the upper portion of Figure 14–1, and write sentences conforming to each of the listed definitions, writing one sentence in each square. Students are then given a paper copy of the bingo board together with a piece of oaktag of the same size. They are to quickly cut apart each square of the paper copy so that there are 25 separate squares. These are to be glued to the piece of oaktag in random order—not in the same order as on the original paper copy—so that each student has squares in different places on the oaktag, but with five in a row horizontally and five vertically (as in typical bingo games). Students are also given 25 *numbered* markers for covering each square.

To begin the game, the teacher reads definition number one from her materials; each student then selects a marker numbered "1" and places it on the sentence whose con-

text is thought to indicate a match for the meaning given. When a student has five squares covered in a column or row he says "bingo." The teacher then uses the numbered markers to check the covered sentences against the numbers of the respective definitions on the teacher's master copy, and these must match for the student to win.

Work with Words in Material to Be Read

Kameenui, Carnine, and Freschi's (1982) study showed that students comprehend stories and expository material better if they are instructed on unfamiliar word meanings before reading these materials. Using words related to actual texts that students will be reading is a good choice for target words in a vocabulary study program because the students are able to use these words shortly after instruction. Any of the methods suggested earlier—direct practice, use of context activities, practice with multiple meanings, and work with synonyms or antonyms—may be employed.

For variety, teachers may also prepare games for practicing words before a story is read. For example, prepare a card game by printing words along with a sentence on each of several index cards. (For example, *hut* He was so poor that he lived in a small, poorly built *hut*.) Prepare a second pack of cards on which only the word appears. Put both packs together and shuffle them. Deal five cards to each student and leave the remainder on the table as an extra pile. The game is played like rummy; students must obtain pairs of matching cards (one with the word alone, and one with the word in a sentence), by drawing and discarding. Before students are allowed to keep a pair to count toward winning the game, they must tell the meaning of the word. To determine the meaning, they use the context of the sentence written on one card of the pair.

Previewing. Oral or written tasks that help students preview material can aid their vocabulary knowledge. One way to conduct an oral preview is to use a *semantic map* (Freedman & Reynolds, 1980; Johnson, 1984). Similar terms employed by some au-

(Student's materials)

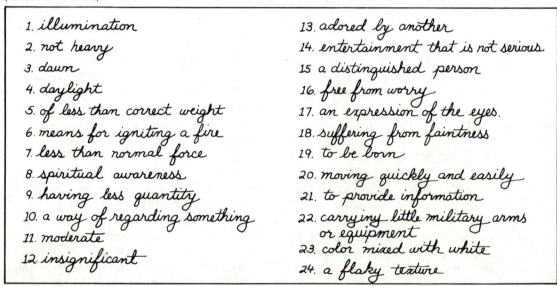

After praying the man saw the light.	It is ligh⬚1⬚ut.	He is one of the brighter lights of American literature.	Evelyn is a light eater.	He gave her a light for her cigarette.
His daughter is the light of his life.	The sweater is light blue.	We will get up at first light.	Her eyes lighted up with liveliness.	Her light movements across the ice won her the championship.
He was in the light brigade.	We got a light snow last night.	LIGHT (free space)	The ⬚ is light ⬚2⬚	The football missed the goalpost because it was a light kick.
I hate sitting in the dark; I wish it was light.	The Taming of the Shrew is light comedy.	I hope you can shed some light on the subject.	After the good news, Karen felt light at heart.	She felt light-headed.
Her piecrust is always light.	On November 1, 1918 he first saw the light of day.	She now saw things in a different light.	I think that butcher gave me a light pound.	Those women spend their lunch hours engaging in light chatter.

(Teacher's materials)

1. illumination
2. not heavy
3. dawn
4. daylight
5. of less than correct weight
6. means for igniting a fire
7. less than normal force
8. spiritual awareness
9. having less quantity
10. a way of regarding something
11. moderate
12. insignificant
13. adored by another
14. entertainment that is not serious
15. a distinguished person
16. free from worry
17. an expression of the eyes.
18. suffering from faintness
19. to be born
20. moving quickly and easily
21. to provide information
22. carrying little military arms or equipment
23. color mixed with white
24. a flaky texture

Figure 14–1
A game for practicing multiple meanings

thorities are *structured overview* (Vacca, 1981), *conceptual vocabulary map* (Haggard, 1985), *group mapping activities* (Davidson, 1982), *cognitive mapping* (Ruddell & Boyle, 1984), or *word map* (Schwartz & Raphael, 1985). All these terms refer to the same basic idea. Two types of semantic maps exist. One type is process-oriented and the other is product-oriented. Both are designed to help students understand terminology and concepts prior to reading narrative or informational material. They are, in effect, advance organizers (Ausubel, 1960).

In a process-oriented semantic map there is group discussion before a story or informational material is read. The discussion is illustrated in some graphic manner by the teacher. Here is an example of this type of semantic map.

TEACHER: The story you're going to read tells you what happens when a boy uses sarcasm and people think his remarks are serious. What do you think *sarcasm* is?

DAVID: A way of talking that's not serious.

CRAIG: Smart-alecky talk.

ALBERT: It seems to me it's being mean.

Teacher writes on board:

> Sarcasm—Talk that is:
> –Not serious
> –"Smart alecky"
> –Being mean

JANA: I had this Girl Scout leader once who would say sarcastic things to us if we didn't do things the way she tried to teach us.

TEACHER: How about you, Kimberly? What do you think *sarcasm* means?

KIMBERLY: I don't know.

MICHAEL: Sometimes kids say sarcastic things to you on the playground just to act big.

Teacher adds to information on board:

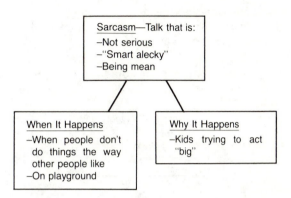

TEACHER: Who can think of other times or reasons people have been sarcastic?

DAVID: My dad has been sarcastic to me.

TEACHER: When? And why do you think he was?

DAVID: Like he gets tired of me arguing back when he tells me to do stuff, so he says, "Okay, Mr. Big Shot! No more arguing. Just do it."

Teacher writes more information on board:

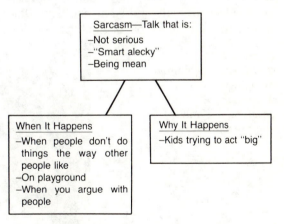

TEACHER: Why do you think David's dad said something sarcastic when David argued with him?

DAVID: It's his way of getting me to do it in a kind of joking way, but letting me know he means business.

TEACHER: Why do you think Jana's Girl Scout leader sometimes made sarcastic remarks?

ALBERT: Maybe she's mean.

JANA: She wasn't really mean to us, but my mother said she was impatient.

Teacher completes diagram on board:

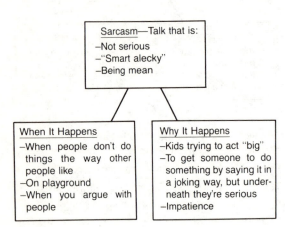

Sarcasm—Talk that is:
- Not serious
- "Smart alecky"
- Being mean

When It Happens
- When people don't do things the way other people like
- On playground
- When you argue with people

Why It Happens
- Kids trying to act "big"
- To get someone to do something by saying it in a joking way, but underneath they're serious
- Impatience

Barron (1969) calls this type of discussion a visual-verbal presentation. It is particularly effective with remedial students for whom mere explanation of concepts before

Using structured overviews or semantic mapping aids both vocabulary development and comprehension.

pupils read material may not be sufficient to enable them to relate ideas to their own backgrounds. It also allows the input of many group members, which may in turn extend students' limited notions about concepts. At the conclusion of a discussion such as this, the teacher points to each part of the diagram she has developed during the discussion, and directs students to compare what they are about to read with the ideas they have contributed. For instance, for the example just given, the students may be asked to predict whether the boy in the upcoming story will be sarcastic because he is "smart alecky" or because he is mean. The students may also be asked to note whether *when* and *why* the boy was sarcastic are similar to any of the reasons they have suggested. After reading the story, these comparisons are made in a follow-up discussion.

More teacher preparation is required in a product-oriented semantic map. Pachtman and Riley (1978) suggest that the teacher selects the concept to be emphasized, lists vocabulary related to the concept, lists ideas related to the concept, arranges vocabulary and ideas in a diagram (semantic map) that is not seen by the students, and writes vocabulary and concepts, each on many separate cards.

Next, students develop a product by working in small groups to arrange the cards into their own semantic map to show relationships (teacher monitors and makes suggestions). Finally, teacher and students engage in whole-group discussion, examining and critiquing each others' completed semantic maps and comparing them with the teacher's.

Figure 14–2 provides an example of a semantic map students used before reading a selection on the history of money. The product developed by students in this activity helps them see the interrelationships among ideas before they read the material in prose form, and also provides an introduction to vocabulary terms. In this case the product itself is referred to as a semantic map, while in a process-oriented semantic map the whole procedure is referred to as semantic mapping. Use of either type of semantic map is particu-larly helpful before reading books in which the concept load is heavy, such as science, history or other textbooks.

Work with Important Roots and Other Word Parts

Another way to select target words for a word study program is to choose a few roots and word parts to be learned that will help students determine meanings of any words in which these word parts appear. Many authorities (e.g., Dale & O'Rourke, 1971) emphasize this approach to increasing knowledge of word meanings because of its efficiency. They point out that attempting to learn many unrelated words is a great deal more time consuming than learning several carefully selected roots and word parts that may then be applied to many more words. Culyer (1978) estimates that Greek and Latin roots, for example, ap-

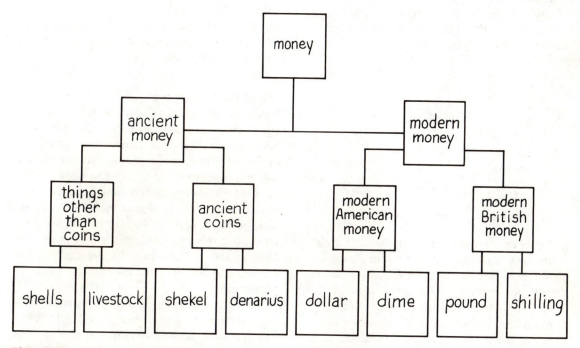

Figure 14–2
A semantic map based on concepts and vocabulary from a reading selection on the history of money

---

Box 14–3
Learning Number Prefixes

The Greek and Latin prefixes from one to ten are (1) *mono-, uni-;* (2) *bi-, di-;* (3) *tri-;* (4) *quad-, tetra-;* (5) *quint-, penta-, pent-;* (6) *sex-, hex-;* (7) *sept-, hept-;* (8) *octo-;* (9) *novem-;* (10) *dec-.* If you have learned these number prefixes, you can easily complete the prefix problems that follow.

Example: mono + uni = b _____   **Answer:** bi

1. sex + bi = o__ __ __
2. bi + di = q__ __ __
3. penta + quad = n__ __ __ __
4. tri + di = q__ __ __ __
5. quad + bi = h__ __
6. quad + uni = p__ __ __ __
7. quint + mono = s__ __
8. bi + di = t__ __ __ __
9. tri + quad = s__ __ __
10. tetra + hex = d__ __

11. penta + di = h__ __ __
12. mono + bi = t__ __
13. quad + tetra = o__ __ __
14. bi + tri = p__ __ __ __
15. octo − quad = t__ __ __ __
16. tri × tri = n__ __ __ __
17. bi ÷ di = m__ __ __
18. octo − di = h__ __
19. sex ÷ hex = u__ __
20. dec ÷ penta = b__

Source: From *The World Book Complete Word Power Library* (Volume 2) © 1981 World Book-Childcraft International Inc. Used by permission of World Book, Inc.

---

pear in about ¼ of the words in an English dictionary. One set of word parts often suggested for learning under this approach is the set of *number prefixes.* These are:

mono, uni	one
bi, di	two
tri	three
quad	four
quint, pent	five
sex, hex	six
sept	seven
oct	eight
novem	nine
dec	ten

Students may be asked to write words they already know that begin with each of these prefixes, such as monorail, bicycle, bi-monthly, tricycle, or triplets. Then, meanings of the words should be discussed and additional words added to each list. An interesting activity for working with number prefixes has been devised by Dale and O'Rourke (1971) and may be seen in Box 14–3. Point out other Latin and Greek roots that appear in many English words. The list in Box 14–4 is suggested by Voigt (1978, p. 421).

See Chapter 13 for additional ideas for working with meanings of other word parts, such as prefixes and suffixes.

Use of the Dictionary

Dale (personal communication, November 17, 1974) once conducted a survey in which students were asked what activity they liked *least* in school. The winner of this dubious honor was the looking up of a list of words in a dictionary and writing their meanings. Skill in using the dictionary is important for individuals who need to increase their meaning vocabularies, but this approach to dictionary work is tedious and, as Gipe's (1978–79) study (cited earlier) showed, it is not as effective as other procedures.

One reason students shy away from using a dictionary is that their speed in locating words is slow. Game-like activities can provide practice to increase their speed. Try this one. Prepare a list of index cards to be *used by the teacher.* On each card write one word for

---

Box 14–4
Common Greek and Latin Roots

Meaning	Root	Meaning	Root
above	super-	across	trans-
after	post-	again	re-
against	anti-	against	contra-
before	pre-	I believe	credo
between	inter-	book	liber
both	ambi	capable	-able, -ible
to carry	port-	city	urbs
study, science	logos	disease	-itis
distant	tele-	enough	satis-
for	pro-	instead	vice-
I lead, led	duco, ductus	life	bios
light	photos	I make, made	facio, factus
not	in-	out of	ex-, e-
people	demos	play, I play	ludus, ludo
power	kratia	right	dexter
ripe	maturus	ship	navis
short	brevis	single	monos
small	micros	star	aster
stone	lithos	suffering	pathos
through	per-	under	sub-
windpipe	bronchos	writing, drawing	graphe
written	scriptum	two	bi-
cycle	circle	foot	ped

which it is likely that no student in the group will know the meaning, and then write a question about the word, along with three possible answers. For example, *timbrel*

If you had a *timbrel,* would you:
1. serve soup in it,
2. plant it in your garden, or
3. play it in a band?

A dictionary should be placed on each student's desk. To begin the game, the teacher selects a card and reads it to the group. Then, students must vote. For example, the teacher would say, "How many would serve soup in it?" "How many would plant it in their gardens?" and so forth. The teacher then says, "All right. Look it up!" Because they've made a commitment to one of the choices, students

dive for their dictionaries and try to locate the word rapidly. Giggles begin to be heard from students who made choices number 1 or 2 when they find that a *timbrel* is a musical instrument like a tambourine. After all students have read the meaning, the teacher directs them to close their dictionaries and she reads from the next index card.

To give practice with the pronunciation key of a dictionary, use riddles or jokes with the answers or punch lines written in dictionary respellings. For example,

MRS. HASTINGS: Robert, I would like to go through one whole day without having to punish you.

ROBERT: yōō hăv mī pərmĭshən.

RIDDLE: One day two fathers and two sons went fishing and each one caught a fish. Only three fish were caught, however. How could this be?

ANSWER: Ā boi, hĭz fäthər, ănd grăndfäthər wər thə tōō fäthərz ănd tōō sənz, sō thâr wər ōnlē thrē fĭshərmĕn.

A unit of dictionary study should include work with a thesaurus. Many simplified thesauruses are now available for use in elementary classrooms, and abridged paperback editions can be purchased for secondary programs. Here is one activity for introducing the contents and value of a thesaurus. Choose a theme, such as Halloween or pioneers or basketball, and ask students to tell you every word they can think of related to that topic. As students contribute words, write them on the chalkboard. When they have exhausted their suggestions and the chalkboard is quite full, tell them they are each to write a short story about this topic, *but they may not use any of the words listed on the board*. The task entails using the thesaurus to locate synonyms for any words on the board they wish to use in their stories. Not only is this fun and challenging, the resulting stories are usually quite interesting.

Writing Haiku can also be a stimulus for using a thesaurus, as well as for adding new synonyms to meaning vocabularies. *Haiku* is a form of Japanese poetry that has exactly 17 syllables in each poem. The syllables must follow a prescribed pattern: in the 3-line poem there must be 5 syllables in line one, 7 in line two, and 5 in line three. If students wish to use a word in their poems to express a thought, but it doesn't have the right number of syllables, they use the thesaurus to find a word expressing the same thought but with the right number of syllables.

Computer Programs

Today, as more and more educational technology finds its way into classrooms, teachers should consider the use of the computer for enhancing word knowledge. Commercially prepared programs for vocabulary development are available. One such program is *The Game Show* (Computer Advanced Ideas). This program is based on the television program "Password" and is designed for reading levels 2 through 8. The game is used by two students at a time or by two teams, and features vocabulary on a variety of topics.

Another computer program is *Dictionary* (Microcomputers and Education). Designed for reading levels 2 through 4, this set of activities provides practice in locating words in a dictionary.

Stickybear Opposites (Weekly Reader Family Software) is a cartoon-like program in which appealing brown bears teach young children such opposite concepts as "high" and "low". This software was designed by an author and illustrator of children's books and is accompanied by a hardcover book, a poster, and stickers. (See Figure 14–3.) Teachers

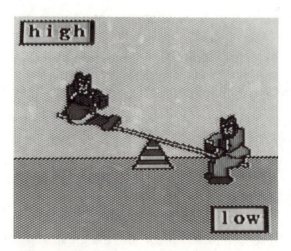

Figure 14–3
New computer software can be used in a word study program. (*Source:* From Stickybear Early Learning Program by R. Hefter, S. Worthington, and J. Worthington, 1983, Columbus, OH: Weekly Reader Family Software. Reproduced by permission.)

should investigate other computer programs to use in their word study activities.

Instilling An Interest in Words

Helping students learn to love interesting aspects of language can assist them in developing a growing awareness of words that will lead to a richer vocabulary. One excellent booklet that will help teachers instill an interest in words is *Growing from Word Play into Poetry* (Professional Educators Publications). The author of this booklet has included creative classroom activities for using words, such as word choirs, word trading cards, and poetry computers.

PHOBIA: fear, dislike, aversion

The root *phobia* is itself a complete word. Children may have "school phobia" or "ghost phobia" or "lion phobia." Their fear may be real or imagined. Likewise, adults may have a phobia of the dark, a phobia of responsibility, or a phobia of death.

Check the dictionary to determine whether phobias are rational or irrational. (Underline your choice.)

Is a phobia a mild dislike or extreme fear? (Underline your choice.)

Write a definition for *phobia:* _____

_____

Phobia is the root of each of these ten words. Use a dictionary to define them.

acrophobia   _____

agoraphobia   _____

Anglophobia   _____

claustrophobia   _____

Germanophobia   _____

hydrophobia   _____

monophobia   _____

phobia   _____

photophobia   _____

xenophobia   _____

Exercise: Complete each of the following sentences.

1. You wouldn't expect a mountain climber to have _____.

2. As we grow up, we overcome our childhood _____ of the dark.

His _____ prevented him from swallowing liquids.

Figure 14–4

Worksheets to develop meaning vocabulary can be interesting. (*Source:* From *Thinking Thursdays* (p. 40) by D. M. Cleary, 1978, Newark, DE: International Reading Association. Reprinted by permission.)

DO YOU KNOW?

anti- + Macassar = antimacassar

<u>Anti-</u> is a prefix meaning "against." Macassar was a popular hair oil made of oils from one of the islands of Indonesia. An antimacassar is a protective covering for the back of chairs and sofas to protect them from the hair oil.

Figure 14–5
Work with word origins can instill an interest in language. (*Source:* From *Emblems: Reading and Language Bonus Duplicating Masters* (p. 38), 1981, Boston: Houghton Mifflin. Reproduced by permission.)

Cleary (1978) had her secondary students engage in Phobia Day to stimulate interest in words. First, students completed a worksheet like the one shown in Figure 14–4. Next they were allowed to invent phobias based on Latin roots (one example: *barbaphobia,* meaning "a fear of whiskers"). Finally, they each chose a phobia and for an entire class period exhibited behavior that would be typical of an individual having that phobia. At the end of the class, of course, students tried to guess which phobias were being dramatized by their classmates.

Many teachers also find that introducing students to information about word origins stimulates interest in vocabulary. (See Figure 14–5, above.) A number of books are available that describe the history and origin of words, such as *The Abecedarian* (Little Brown).

CONCLUDING STATEMENT

Work on meaning vocabulary is important to high reading achievement and is a task that must pervade all of a student's school years. Therefore, teachers in addition to the remedial teacher should give attention to increasing students' knowledge of word meanings. Marlowe (cited in Culyer, 1978) conducted a study in which all students in an elementary school participated in a program that expected students to show mastery of new word meanings before they read selections that included the words. Mastery was accomplished by using specific vocabulary teaching, testing, and review exercises. At the end of the year prior to the study, the school-wide average reading gain on a vocabulary subtest of a standardized test was 2 months. A year after the program had been put in place, the average gain was 13 months.

15

Increasing Comprehension: Part 1

Everything we do in reading instruction should be aimed at helping students comprehend written material. It matters not a bit whether students can instantly recognize every word on a page if they cannot understand the message those words are conveying. Being able to read orally with "expression" has no value if the student has missed the meaning. Increasing a student's rate of reading is purposeless if comprehension suffers in the process. Knowing how to identify difficult words is important only if the resulting word identification leads to comprehension of the words, sentences, and passages a student must read.

Although few people would disagree with the premise that the purpose of reading is comprehension, there is considerable disagreement about the best way to help students increase their comprehension achievement. One reason for this disagreement is that the comprehension process is not entirely understood. Although there has been more educational research in the area of reading in general than in any other subject area, until recent years the amount of research directed specifically at the comprehension process was

sparse. Since 1970 there has been a flurry of comprehension research, yet there are still many unanswered questions. Furthermore, those findings that are available from recent research have not sifted down to teachers in the schools; much of this research is found primarily in technical reports and in journal articles read infrequently by practicing teachers. As a result, instructional procedures used by remedial specialists often are based only on "what has always been done," regardless of whether those procedures have been very effective. Although all answers are not available for how comprehension takes place and how we can help students increase their comprehension, many new ideas are known. This chapter and Chapter 16 will present some of the newer findings with the hope of updating current practice in remedial programs.

BACKGROUND INFORMATION

Theories about how comprehension takes place in the human brain and how to teach students to comprehend better are numerous.

301

However, they can be divided into two general areas that in this text will be called the *traditional* points of view and the *newer* points of view. As will be seen, the two areas are not really discrete; some overlapping ideas are found.

Traditional Points of View

There are two major traditional viewpoints on comprehension. One is that material is understood by going from the part to the whole. That is, the reader must first understand meanings of individual words, then phrases (or thought units), then sentences, then paragraphs, and then longer passages. This viewpoint is called a "bottom-up" or "text-driven" explanation of comprehension. Many authorities believe that the poorer the reader (or the less the reader knows about a topic), the more likely he or she is to engage in bottom-up processing of the material.

A second traditional point of view does not attempt to explain the comprehension *process,* but instead suggests instructional procedures for accomplishing an increase in comprehension. These suggestions involve mastering a set of specific skills. The skills considered important have often been classified and organized into lists. A summarized version of one of these, Barrett's Taxonomy (1979, pp. 63–66), is illustrated in Box 15–1.

Each skill listed in a taxonomy is not considered to be a completely separate entity, but to be interrelated with the other skills. Findings of research designed to confirm or reject the hypothesis on which this second point of view is based—that comprehension can be broken down into specific subskills—have been contradictory. Some research (e.g., Davis, 1944; Davis, 1968) has supported the subskills notion, while other research (e.g., Spearitt, 1972; Thorndike, 1974) does not. And still other research seems to indicate that there is a difference according to the proficiency of the reader. For example, Gutherie's (1973) study showed that good readers integrate skills so they appear holistic rather than separate, while poor readers seem to need to attend to specific subskills. Some authorities who do not think comprehension can be separated into identifiable subskills believe that comprehension is a global process of *reasoning.* Other authorities counter-argue that reasoning itself can be broken down into subskills, such as problem-solving or using appropriate question-answering strategies; they say that while comprehension can be broken down into separate skills, we just may have been looking at the wrong skills (Johnston, 1983). Most published instructional materials on reading are based on the subskills point of view.

Newer Points of View

Today's research focuses on understanding the comprehension process itself, and on investigating instruction to determine what really helps to improve comprehension—and what doesn't. Several interesting ideas have emerged as a result of these studies. Some of the general ideas from this research will be discussed while specific instructional procedures are presented throughout the remainder of this chapter and Chapter 16.

Schema Theory. The words *schema* and *schemata* are found frequently in professional writings. When many teachers see unfamiliar terminology such as this in information about reading instruction they choose not to read it because they believe it will be incomprehensible or that it will not relate to practical, day-to-day teaching matters. To overcome this tendency, a list of terms currently being used in the reading comprehension literature can be found in Table 15–1. Familiarity with these terms and their common meanings will help teachers understand the more recent additions to theories about reading comprehension.

Box 15–1
The Barrett Taxonomy of Cognitive and Affective Dimensions of Reading Comprehension

Learn

1.0 Literal Comprehension

1.1 Recognition

  1.11 Details
  1.12 Main ideas
  1.13 Sequence
  1.14 Comparisons
  1.15 Cause and effect relationships
  1.16 Character traits

1.2 Recall

  1.21 Details
  1.22 Main ideas
  1.23 Sequence
  1.24 Comparisons
  1.25 Cause and effect relationships
  1.26 Character traits

2.0 Inferential Comprehension

2.1 Supporting details
2.2 Main ideas
2.3 Sequence
2.4 Comparisons
2.5 Cause and effect relationships
2.6 Character traits
2.7 Predicting outcomes
2.8 Figurative language

3.0 Evaluation

3.1 Judgments of reality or fantasy
3.2 Fact or opinion
3.3 Adequacy and validity
3.4 Appropriateness
3.5 Worth, desirability, and acceptability

4.0 Appreciation

4.1 Emotional response to plot or theme
4.2 Identification with characters or incidents
4.3 Reactions to the author's use of language
4.4 Imagery

Source: From "A Taxonomy of Reading Comprehension" by T. C. Barrett in Teaching Reading in the Middle Grades, 2nd. ed., 1979, pp. 62–66. Reading, Mass.: Addison-Wesley.

As can be seen in Table 15–1, *schema* refers to background information (also sometimes called *prior knowledge*), and *schemata* is this word's plural. Many of the new ideas about comprehension have been based on *schema theory*. This theory says that what you already know or don't know about a topic can greatly influence your comprehension. This idea, developed by Anderson (1977), Rumelhart (1981), and others, suggests that when students recognize words on a printed page, they think and react based on their prior background information (or schemata). For example, suppose Sheila reads the statement, "On the first night of the camping trip, Tom sat cross-legged under a huge sycamore tree watching a small red squirrel scamper in and out of the hole at the end of the branch." The author's words may trigger a match with Sheila's prior knowledge in the following manner.

1. She has not been on a camping trip herself, but from talking with her friend,

Table 15–1
Definitions of comprehension-related terms

Terms Used in Recent Writings about Comprehension	Terms More Familiar to Teachers
bottom-up processing	comprehension based on what is in the book—not on the reader's individual experiences (at least not very much); the reader goes from the part to the whole
text-driven processing	same as bottom-up processing
data-driven processing	same as bottom-up processing
top-down processing	comprehension based on what is already in the reader's head, i.e., background information, that helps him make intelligent guesses about events, and so forth, in material, and to understand relationships about them
concept-driven processing	same as top-down processing
interactive processing	comprehension is based on both bottom-up and top-down processing—the reader and the book work together so that student gains meaning
schema	background information
schemata	background information (plural of *schema*)
prior knowledge	background information
schema availability	the familiarity of the topic to the student
surface structure	the printed words on the page and how they are arranged within sentences
deep structure	the meaning conveyed by printed words on a page
microstructure	a) as regards surface structure, the words *within* a sentence and how they are arranged; b) as regards deep structure, the details in a passage
macrostructure	a) in regard to surface structure, how ideas are arranged *among* sentences to make up the organization of a passage; b) in regard to deep structure, the main idea of a passage
text structure	how material has been organized by the author into main ideas and supporting details, how these are sequenced, and how they are interrelated

Table 15–1 (Continued)

Terms Used in Recent Writings about Comprehension	Terms More Familiar to Teachers
cohesion, or cohesiveness in text	the way parts of printed text are linked by certain words or statements within and between sentences so the text seems to "hang together" or is seen to be related by the reader
anaphora	words that refer to or provide a link to previous words; pronouns, for example, often have anaphoric relationships with nouns, such as in the sentence, "When *Tom* was asked if *he* liked to run, *he* said *he* did" (the noun—*Tom* in this case—is called a pronoun antecedent)
proposition	a phrase or sentence that asserts something; a basic unit of thought
proposition density	the number of propositions (or ideas) in a given piece of written material
concept load	the same as proposition density
density	same as proposition density
textual features	things in printed text that relate to reading ease or difficulty, such as vocabulary difficulty, cohesiveness, and density
textual analysis	analysis of the things in printed text that relate to reading ease or difficulty (see textual features)
superordinate units	sentences
subordinate units	words
lexical item	a word
new information	ideas with which the reader is unfamiliar
old information	information already in the reader's background knowledge
reconstructing the author's message	slightly modifying the author's intended meaning to conform to information already in the reader's background knowledge
explicit information	directly stated facts
implicit information	information that is not directly stated; it must be inferred since it is only implied
imagery	imagining mental pictures of what is read

Table 15–1 (Continued)

Terms Used in Recent Writings about Comprehension	Terms More Familiar to Teachers
advance organizers	material or activities (such as previewing or summarization) presented *before* students read material to help them understand it
structured overview	a type of advance organizer (see advance organizers) in which vocabulary or ideas are visually related by drawings or diagrams
hierarchical summarization study strategy	outlining
cognition	the process of reasoning
metacognitive skills	skills that help students "learn to learn"
chunk	to organize small pieces of print into larger pieces (e.g., letters into words, or words into phrases)
prediction strategy	use of knowledge of language structure and meaning to anticipate words that are upcoming in the text; also, guessing about ideas that will follow, based on prior knowledge about the topic
retrieval from long term memory	remembering
introspective reporting	students report the thought processes that occurred when they were reading material

Theresa, who has, Sheila knows that these trips are often to wooded areas away from a city.

2. She has been to a park with lots of trees, bushes, and the like, and remembers the general impression.
3. She sometimes sits cross-legged herself on her living room floor when she is watching TV, and knows the look and feeling.
4. She does not know what a sycamore tree is, but there is a huge old oak in her grandmother's back yard and she visualizes this one.
5. She has not seen a red squirrel, but there are gray squirrels all around her neighborhood and she knows what they look like when they scamper on the ground and on a tree trunk.
6. She has not seen a hole in the end of a tree branch before, but she has seen a picture in her science book of a hole in a tree trunk with owls peering out.

Sheila has thus developed several schemata that she can match with the words she has just read to comprehend them. But as can be seen, two discrepancies may arise here. First, because her schemata are not parallel to the author's, her comprehension may not be as precise as another reader's (for example, gray squirrels are larger than red squirrels; therefore, the squirrel she visualizes may be larger than what the author intended).

Second, readers interpret written words differently according to their respective background experiences. Thus, while Sheila may have visualized an oak tree when she read *sycamore,* if the only large tree Lindsey has seen is an Austrian pine, she might call up that memory from her schema for a large tree; a third reader with more sophistication about trees, meanwhile, may call upon schema of what a sycamore tree looks like and, therefore, her comprehension is more likely to agree with what the author meant to convey. The degree of "closeness" of the schema of the reader to that of the author affects the quality of comprehension as the reader "reconstructs" the author's meaning. Comprehension, therefore, is an active process involving "inference-

Wide reading increases comprehension because information is added to the reader's schemata.

making." In this context, inference-making is not meant as a specific skill (as in "drawing inferences"), but as a process that permeates all aspects of reading. Johnston (1983) points out that inference-making is necessary even when attending to single words, such as in deciding on the specific meaning of a word like *run,* which has multiple meanings.

Actually, a third process can occur when readers apply their schemata to words they read—their schemata can change. Returning to Sheila's schema for squirrels, perhaps squirrels came in only one color (gray) prior to her reading about Tom and the red squirrel. Now she knows that squirrels can also be red; thus, her schema has been altered and expanded. This process is referred to as an interactive process: Schemata allow the reader to understand material that is read, and reading new material often changes schemata.

schema

↓

comprehension of material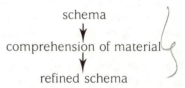

↓

refined schema

In summary, we must combine old *and* new information to be good comprehenders. The old information comes from our brains and the new information comes from the written text.

What practical implications are available from schema theory for remedial teachers? First, we can conclude that wide experiences (direct and vicarious) are important for good comprehension. If students do not have these experiences, prereading discussions become very important. Second, wide reading on any topic will increase students' comprehension about it because there will be more and more old information in their schemata to help them understand new information. Engaging in a great deal of reading will make better readers, not only in terms of word recognition, but also in terms of comprehension. Third, one reason for poor readers' failure to comprehend may well be their lack of *attempt* to use the background information they do have to comprehend what they read. Therefore, teachers must direct them to do this and show them how to do it. A number of instructional procedures suggested later in this chapter and the next are based on these premises.

Kintsch's Model of Comprehension. Kintsch (1979) has proposed a model (or explanation) of comprehension that is based on schema theory. This model says that the amount of difficulty students have in comprehending is related to how much searching of their memories they have to undertake to find a schema that closely matches the words the author has presented. If they are familiar with the topic, little searching is necessary. If they are not familiar, much searching is necessary, or they may match incoming information with the wrong schema, or they may not be able to find a match at all. In these circumstances comprehension is diminished or even absent.

According to Kintsch, readers must make two kinds of matches to understand what they read.

- schema matches with the microstructure of the text (*microstructure* means the details in a passage and the terms and relationships *within* sentences that help readers understand the details; such as the individual words or the order in which words are arranged)
- schema matches with the macrostructure of the text (*macrostructure* means the main idea, or topic, of a passage and how ideas are arranged *among* sentences to make up the organization of the passage)

If comprehension is deficient, the problem can be in the material or in the reader.

When the microstructure (words, sentence structure) is too difficult for the readers, so that they cannot find matches in their schema even though they understand the concept, then the problem is in the material. For instance, Jocelyn reads, "Don't forget to use apostrophes." Jocelyn knows what apostrophes are, has heard the word in oral language and has used them ever since first grade when she was taught to spell contractions; but she has never seen the word in print and does not recognize it. She cannot match a-p-o-s-t-r-o-p-h-e-s with anything she has stored in her schemata of known words. Therefore, she does not get the meaning of the message. As can be seen, word recognition and knowledge of word identification strategies are interactively involved with reading comprehension.

When students have no schema stored in their memories, or only a partial one, for the ideas being presented in a text, and cannot understand the message because the information is "too new" for them, then the problem is in the reader. In such a case, there is no old information or too little of it to use in comprehending what the author wrote. Read the following paragraphs and try to answer the questions.

"They were obviously Maglemosian, as was evident since the culture was Mesolithic. Given these clues any budding archaeologist can guess the area of the world in which these shards were found."

1. To what does the term *Maglemosian* refer?

2. Where were the shards found?

"A magnetron tube is of the thermionic type. Its electron beam generates microwaves that are high powered and is influenced by electromagnetic fields."

1. Write a one paragraph description of a magnetron tube using terminology

that can be understood by the general public.

2. Given the information about the obvious advantages of thermionic tubes, suggest their possible uses.

If you have some feelings of unease about the correctness of your answers to these questions, this is undoubtedly due to your lack of schema to match the topics. While an electrical engineer may be able to answer questions about the second paragraph, the same engineer might have considerable difficulty answering questions about word identification strategies in reading—a topic for which readers of this book should have, at this point, stored information (or schemata).

The two factors that Kintsch refers to as problems in the reader and problems in the material are called by Pearson and Johnson (1978) "factors inside the head" and "factors outside the head." They say that factors inside the student's head which influence comprehension (pp. 9–10) are

- what the student knows about language
- motivation
- how well the student can read (recognize words)
- interest

Factors outside the head are

- elements on the page, such as how difficult the material is and how well it is organized to help the reader (e.g., by providing subheadings, etc.)
- the quality of the reading environment, such as what the teacher does to facilitate comprehension—before the student reads, while the student is reading, and after the student reads

A Definition of Comprehension

Based on what we currently know, *comprehension* may be defined as

matching information provided by an author with a reader's background information to determine the intended meaning in a text. Comprehension involves both a *process* (recognition of words and their relationships, searching memory for stored schemata, finding a match, etc.) and a *product* (the resulting information that is understood, perhaps stored in memory, and perhaps later recalled).

INSTRUCTIONAL STRATEGIES

While it is important for teachers to understand what is known about the comprehension process so they can make on-the-spot decisions about sources of students' confusions, it is also helpful to have knowledge of some specific strategies for enhancing comprehension. The rest of this chapter is about instructional techniques and procedures useful in remedial classes and clinics.

General Strategies for Instruction and Practice

The strategies presented in this section provide a framework for, and can be infused within, all comprehension lessons—whether literal or higher level skills are required.

DRTA. The acronym DRTA stands for *Directed Reading—Thinking Activity* (Stauffer, 1969). DRTA is a carefully organized procedure directed by the teacher and designed to be a generic lesson plan format for better comprehension of any narrative or informational material. The steps for these lessons are as follows.

- Prepare and motivate students for reading by having them *preview* the material (sometimes called "surveying"); previewing can consist of reading the title and other headings, and looking at pictures.

310 Unit 4 Remedial Procedures for Students Having Difficulty Learning to Read

- Before they read, ask students to *predict* events or information in the first portion of the material (the size of the portion should vary according to the reading ability of the students). To encourage predictions, ask questions specific to the story such as, "What do you think will happen?" or, "After reading the title and looking at these two pictures, what do you think this section of the chapter is going to be about? What else?" (The majority of questions employed in DRTA are asked *before* students read and they focus on predicting and hypothesizing.)

- *Set a purpose* for reading. Tell students to check their predictions: "Read to find out if you're right," or, "Read to find out who's right."

- Have students read the first portion silently.

- Stop to *verify (or reject)* predictions through discussion.

- *Ask for new predictions* before reading the next section. In many cases, these predictions will necessarily be based on what has been previously read in the passage.

- Continue with a cycle of *predicting, reading, confirming/rejecting* through discussion until the material is completed.

After the total story or other reading selection is completed, there is often oral rereading and specific skills development.

DRTA teaches students to consider information, form hypotheses, suspend judgment, find proof, make decisions, and develop critical reading skills (Stauffer, 1975). Research has shown that the quality and quantity of students' answers are better when using the DRTA process than when using traditional questioning procedures found in basal reader manuals (Petre, 1972). Richek, List, and Lerner (1983) state that they have found DRTA especially effective with disabled readers because it is new to them and involves them

actively. DRTA can be used for listening comprehension lessons, as well.

Previewing. In Chapter 14, semantic mapping was discussed as a preview process for increasing understanding of word meanings. Semantic mapping is essentially an oral activity. However, research has shown that written previews can also increase comprehension. One such study involving written previews was conducted with reading-disabled middle-school students (Graves, Cooke, & Laberge, 1983). In that study, previews were used before students read short stories. The teaching activity consisted of the following steps.

1. The teacher gave each student a written preview of the story. (See Box 15–2 for a sample preview.)

2. The teacher read *to* the students the statements and questions found at the beginning of the preview. These were designed to a) arouse interest and b) link the story to something familiar in the students' backgrounds.

3. The teacher led a brief discussion about these statements and questions and about the topic of the story.

4. The teacher read the summary of the story, which comprised the middle portion of the preview, to the students. The summary included the setting, general statements about the characters, and a brief description of the plot up to the ending.

5. Students were asked to look at the chalkboard, where the teacher had previously listed the characters and a short statement about each of them. These were read to the students.

6. Student attention was redirected to the written preview, and the teacher read the remainder of it to them. This final portion defined three or four difficult words they would encounter in the story.

Box 15–2
A Written Preview for a Short Story

Preview for "The Signalman"

It seems sometimes that life is full of dangers! Would you agree? Nearly every day an accident or a disaster of some kind happens somewhere. A plane crashes, an earthquake occurs, or cars pile up on the freeway. Can you think of some accidents or disasters that have happened lately?

Many times before a disaster occurs a warning is given. For example, lights might blink on the instrument panel of an airplane, or instruments might pick up tremors in the earth that predict an earthquake is about to occur. Can you think of other types of warnings? Were warnings given for the disasters we just talked about?

Some people believe that they are warned of dangers in supernatural ways. They believe in spirits, or voices, or maybe even ghosts guiding them to do—or not do—something. Have you ever heard of someone being warned like this? What did that person say?

Maybe you've been warned about something. For example, have you ever awakened from a dream thinking that what you dreamed would happen? And then—did it? Have you ever had a feeling something bad was about to happen? and then—did it happen? Can you think of any examples?

The story you will read today is about a man who often gets warnings. But, the warnings this man gets don't come from dreams or his mind. The man gets warnings of bad things about to happen from a ghost, or specter. It seems that the ghost always appears before something terrible happens, as if he is trying to warn of danger.

The story takes place in a very lonely and gloomy spot, hidden away in the mountains. The man you will read about lives alone in a hut which is on a railroad line and near a tunnel. The hut has many things the man needs—such as a desk, a record book, an instrument to send telegraphs, and a bell.

The man is a signalman. His job is to signal the trains, watch for danger on the tracks, and warn passing trains of trouble ahead. The signalman works very hard at his job and is quite exact in all his duties. He is nervous, though, because he has seen many people die in train accidents near his post. He wants to be sure that he signals the trains of any danger.

You will learn about what the signalman does and says through the man who tells the story. This man visited the signalman at two different times and learned much about him. The story you will read is the story the visitor tells after meeting the signalman.

The story opens as the visitor calls "Hello! Below there!" to the signalman. He wants to know how to reach the signalman's hut from where he is at the top of a cliff. The signalman hears the man call to him but doesn't answer. He is afraid and looks down the railroad line instead of up to the man.

What does the signalman think he will see? Why is he afraid? Read to find out.

Before you read the story, I want to show you a list of some of the people in it. They don't have names and are described by who they are or what they do. The signalman is the man who lives in a hut near the railroad. The visitor is the man who visits the signalman and who tells the story. Another character is the ghost.

There are also some words I would like to define for you. The signalman is a dark, *sallow* man, with a dark beard and heavy eyebrows. *Sallow* means that he looks sickly and pale.

The signalman's hut is also called a *post* because it is where he is stationed to do his job.

The ghost is also called a *specter*.

Source: From "Effects of Previewing Difficult Short Stories on Low Ability Junior High School Students' Comprehension, Recall, and Attitudes" by M. Graves, C. Cooke, and M. LaBerge, 1983, *Reading Research Quarterly,* Spring 1983, p. 267. Reprinted with permission of the authors and the International Reading Association.

7. The previews were put away and students were asked to silently read the story on which the preview was based.

As a result of this procedure, students' literal level comprehension increased by 13 percent and inferential comprehension by 38 percent. In addition, scores on a test of recall of information, given after several days had elapsed, were significantly higher than when no written previews were used. And, important for poorly motivated remedial readers, an attitude survey showed that students liked the technique.

The use of written previews as just described is fairly easy for teachers to implement. Although the type of previewing described here is conducted in much more depth than the suggestions found in most reading material, it takes only about 10 minutes to carry out. Other studies have shown that written previews are also effective with elementary and senior high school students (Graves & Palmer, 1981; Graves & Cooke, 1980).

Promoting Familiarity With Text Structure.   "Promoting familiarity with text structure" means helping students see how material is organized by an author into key ideas and supporting statements, how these are sequenced to explain a point, and how they are interrelated. Research indicates that good readers appear able to note and use text structure either intuitively or because they generally read more (Eamon, 1978–79). Poor readers, on the other hand, do not seem to recognize how the organization of material helps them comprehend it, unless they receive direct instruction in the special ways written text is structured to convey ideas. This instruction is particularly helpful when the material being read is expository material, that is, informational writing designed to explain. Because students must read much expository material in school (science books, social studies books, etc.) and later in life (newspapers, magazine articles, etc.), practice in comprehension of expository material is important.

Taylor and Beach (1984) found that use of a *hierarchical summarization study strategy* significantly improved understanding and recall of social studies material by middle-school students. This study strategy, an adapted form of *outlining,* helps students gain familiarity with text structure. In using this strategy, the following steps are taken (Taylor & Beach, p. 139).

1. An outline is begun by drawing a line at the top of the page. (The line is not filled in at this time; a heading representing the key idea of the entire passage will be written there later.)
2. A letter is designated for each subheading found in the selection.
3. Students read each section (as designated by subheadings), decide on a main idea for the section, and write the main idea in their outlines next to the letter for that section.
4. Two or three important details about each main idea are listed across a line or two under each main idea.
5. Topic headings are selected and these are written in the left margin, along with lines connecting main ideas related to the same topic.
6. The key idea for the entire selection is chosen and written on the blank line mentioned in number 1. (See Figure 15–1 for an example of a hierarchical summary.)

(Note: During the first few sessions the teacher must work with the students as they develop their summary/outlines, but after a few sessions students can begin to work independently.)

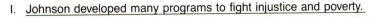

I.   Johnson developed many programs to fight injustice and poverty.

    A. *Lyndon Johnson became President of the U.S. after Kennedy was assassinated.*
       hard worker, tried to carry out some of Kennedy's programs.

    B. *Johnson fought for civil-rights law.*
Civil   purpose: to protect blacks from discrimination in hotels and restaurants, blacks had
Rights   not been allowed in some hotels or restaurants in the South.

    C. *Johnson persuaded Congress to pass a law ensuring all people the right to vote.*
       protected black people's right to vote, literacy tests now illegal.

    D. *Johnson started a "war on poverty."*
Great   job training, education for poor people, plans for a "Great Society."
Society E. *Johnson persuaded Congress to develop a medicare program.*
Programs   for people at least 65 years old, hospital bills paid, doctor's bills paid in part.

    F. *Johnson persuaded Congress to pass a law giving money to schools.*
       purpose: to improve education of children from poor families, one billion dollars in
       aid to schools.

Figure 15–1
An example of a hierarchical summary for a three-page social-studies text segment containing one heading and six subheadings. (*Source:*   From "The Effects of Text Structure Instruction on Middle-grade Students' Comprehension and Production of Expository Text" by Taylor and Beach, 1984, *Reading Research Quarterly, 19,* p. 139.)

When individual summaries have been completed, group discussion, in which the summaries are critiqued, should follow. Finally, students should work as partners, first reviewing their own summaries for 5 minutes, then telling their partners as much as they can about their summaries, as well as other information they remember from the selection. By using this study strategy for only one hour per week, the students in Taylor and Beach's (1984) study improved their comprehension of *unfamiliar* material more than a control group not having this instruction.

However, they found that if the assigned topic was familiar, this fairly complex strategy was no more productive than the more traditional procedure of simply having students write answers to questions about main ideas and details *after* reading the selection.

Asking Questions. For some teachers, a comprehension "program" hinges mainly on asking questions. Morrison (1968), for example, found that teachers ask as many as two questions per minute in a typical reading session. Is all this question-asking really useful for improving comprehension? The answer to this depends on the quality of the teacher's "asking behavior" and the types of questions asked.

"Asking behavior" refers to how teachers set the environment for question-and-answer sessions. Some good ways and poor ways to do this in remedial and clinical reading programs are listed in Table 15–2.

Table 15–2
Asking questions of students

Effective Asking Behaviors	Poor Asking Behaviors
Give students time to think before answering. Also, if they hesitate in mid-answer, be patient.	Demand immediate responses. Call on another student when an immediate response is not forthcoming. Allow other students to sit with hands raised while the first student is trying to think.
When a student gives a correct answer, take it a step further—ask the student to explain how she knows it is the correct answer.	When a correct answer is given, always move immediately to the next question.
Ask all students to respond, and to respond as often as possible, during any given session.	Only call on students who volunteer.
Require all students to pay attention during question-asking and during answering by another student. When appropriate, involve other students in the answering—for example, by saying something like, "Phillip, do you agree with Judy?" or, "How would you support the correct answer that DeMerrill has already given?"	When one student is answering a question, allow other students to be off-task (looking around the room, talking, working on something else).
If a student doesn't understand the question, rephrase, break it down into parts, or in some other way assist the student in arriving at the correct response. Researchers (e.g., Guszak, 1967) have found that wrong responses often result because teachers ask questions that are too difficult.	If a student doesn't understand the question, blame the student and call on another person.
When an incorrect answer is given, take time to *teach*: model how *you* would determine the answer; ask the student to think of a previous answer; explain; give additional information; illustrate. Teach the student *how* to answer questions.	When an incorrect answer is given, immediately call on another student.

The quality of students' comprehension performance is also influenced by the *types* of questions asked. Obviously, important rather than trivial questions should be the focus. Avoid questions such as "What color was Mary's dress?"—questions that highlight irrelevant details. Place emphasis on higher level questions. In fact, many different types of questions can be asked about any one story or informational passage. Higher level questions expand students'

meaning vocabulary, ask them to call upon their background information, encourage them to seek out the important information conveyed by a story (main ideas), and stimulate them to recall directly stated facts.

Beck, Omanson, and McKeown (1982) suggest that teachers use *story maps* to develop good questions. A story map is a sequential listing of the important elements of a story. A story usually has the following elements.

- characters
- setting
- a problem and a goal to resolve it
- events to solve the problem
- achievement of the goal

Before writing questions, teachers can use this list of story elements as a guide to determine the story map for the selection to be read by students. One or more questions can be written for each element. The questions should be sequenced in the order in which each aspect occurs in the story. This does *not* mean that only literal questions based on directly stated information are used; higher level questions should also be written about each element. In the study conducted by Beck, et al., when questions systematically focused on central story content in this way, students showed better comprehension. In fact, the less skilled readers who answered questions based on story maps did as well on comprehension performance as skilled readers who answered questions found in basal reader manuals.

Since students must learn how to recall answers (with the book closed) as well as locate answers, practice should be given in answering questions involving both types of tasks.

Finally, it should be remembered that asking specific questions is not the only way to follow up the reading of a selection. For example, having students retell the story or informational passage can be one useful alternative.

Strategies for Independent Reading

Independent reading is a fact of life, in school and through adulthood. Students are asked to read silently in their classrooms and are later called upon to answer oral questions about what they read. Students are sent to study hall to read a chapter from a geography book and to write answers to the questions found at the end of the chapter. In homework assignments, when textbooks must be read and questions must be answered, students usually receive little help from their parents.

In adult life, when reading income tax forms, reports, or other material, adults usually do not have the luxury of another person to guide and prompt them through what may at first seem incomprehensible. All comprehension strategies that are taught to students should be aimed, therefore, at enabling them to internalize those strategies so they can use them when reading on their own.

Question-answering Strategies When Reading Independently. A big difference exists between the independent reading strategies used by good comprehenders and poor ones. Poor comprehenders show they do not understand the task requirements of answering questions. "Text lookbacks" are a task requirement that demonstrates how good students and poorer ones differ. *Text lookbacks* (Garner, Wagoner, & Smith, 1983) simply mean looking back in the material when a question cannot be answered. Table 15–3 shows results from a lookback study with fourth and sixth graders by Garner et al.

The results of this study have implications for the instruction of students with poor comprehension skills. Strategies that good readers apparently use naturally when reading for meaning must be taught directly to most students in remedial programs. A three-phase approach to such instruction follows.

Phase 1: Present a short, expository passage of about 200 words. Have students read it. Next, ask five *literal*-level questions. These queries should be of sufficient difficulty to require students to look back at the text for at least some questions. When a student is "stumped," ask what should be done

Table 15–3
"Lookback" study with fourth and sixth graders

	Good Comprehenders	Poor Comprehenders
Looked back in text for unknown answers	Often	Seldom
Looked back at the right time: a) did look back when answer was in text b) did not look back if answer had to be determined from student's own background information	Good differentiation was made	Poor differentiation was made
Knew how to sample text when they looked back (i.e., they looked back to the specific area where answer could be found and did not just reread whole passage until answer appeared)	Yes	No

Source: Adapted from information in "Externalizing Question-Answering Strategies of Good and Poor Comprehenders" by R. Garner, S. Wagoner, and T. Smith, 1983, *Reading Research Quarterly 18*, 439–447.

to get the answer. Encourage the response, "Look back at the page." Praise this response and have the students *do* it. After several sessions in which lookbacks are practiced, move to phase two.

Phase 2: In this phase, students must learn to distinguish between questions for which a text lookback will help (literal-level questions), and those for which their own background information must be used. Again present 200-word passages followed by five questions—some literal, and some that require the student's prior knowledge to obtain a correct response. Through discussion, aid students in deciding which is which. Confirm their decisions by going back over the text and underlining the answers to literal-level questions, while noting the fact when there is no answer to underline for the background-dependent questions. Answer the questions. Practice these activities for several sessions before moving to phase three.

Phase 3: Follow the 200-word passages by asking only *literal*-level questions. Tell students this set of questions all can be answered by looking at the passage, and the questions should again be written at a difficulty level requiring students to engage in at least some text lookbacks. In this phase, however, before each lookback, tell students that looking through the whole passage takes too much time. They should be asked to try to remember where the answer occurred and be required to guess where they will find it (e.g., near the beginning, middle, or end; right after the part about—; in the section about—; etc.). Points should be awarded for a correct guess about where to locate the specific information needed to answer a question. Practice this strategy for several sessions.

After the direct practice of phases 1, 2, and 3, teachers must ensure that students learn to generalize the strategies across all materials and to maintain the strategies. To achieve this goal, teachers should prompt use of these strategies whenever reading with the students and must consistently remind students to employ them when reading independently.

Comprehension Monitoring. To "monitor" comprehension means to *realize* whether or not you have comprehended something and to use certain strategies to do something about it if you have not. Disabled readers and LD students often are deficient in comprehension-monitoring skills (Garner & Kraus, 1982; Kotsonis & Patterson, 1980; Wagoner, 1983).

Previous chapters of this book stressed the importance of teaching poor readers to self-monitor. To self-monitor at the word level means to ask, "Did that make sense?" when a word is miscalled. Independent self-correction of reading miscues (that is, without prompting from the teacher) is related to good comprehension (Beebe, 1982). The first task in getting students to self-monitor is to develop *awareness.* This task involves using much direct prompting by the teacher to encourage correction of obvious meaning-disrupting miscues. At the story or informational passage level, the question of whether something "made sense" should be extended to testing what has been read against prior knowledge (background information).

Two additional techniques that teachers can employ to help students gain awareness of when they have and when they have not comprehended, are to:

- Present reading goals ahead of time. For example, by saying something like, "Read the next three pages to find out (why a hippo would be friends with a bird; about the habitats of giraffes; etc.)." If students cannot determine the information specifically called for, they will (or should) realize that they have not comprehended.

Such goal-setting also compels students to focus on the important rather than the incidental ideas in a passage.

- Teach students to predict the questions that teachers will ask after a passage. For example, if the subheading of a science selection says *Insects,* by working with information found in previous sections of the same chapter the student might predict that the teacher will ask, "What are the characteristics of insects that make them different from other animals?" Give practice to students in making these predictions and in reading to see whether the answer can be determined. (Research has shown that use of a question-predicting strategy also leads to better later recall of the material.)

When good readers realize that they have not comprehended material, they reread previous material and/or continue reading to see whether subsequent information will clarify confusions. As with the strategy of using lookbacks, poor readers should be directly *taught* to use these strategies since they often do not employ them intuitively, as good readers do.

Strategies for Instruction and Practice Directly Related to Literal Comprehension

Literal level comprehension is sometimes called *reading for directly stated facts.* If the story students are reading states that "Pam was the frog in the class play," and the teacher asks the students, "What role did Pam have in the class play?" he is asking them to read for directly stated facts and to respond on a literal level. If the geography book states that corn is one of the main farm products of Nebraska and the students are asked, "What is one of the main farm products of Nebraska?" this is an example of literal level comprehension being required over content area materials. In some cases a literal level question may be answered by merely restating the exact words found in the text; in other cases the information must be paraphrased. But in both cases the information is in the book. Literal level comprehension is important because it provides the basis for higher level comprehension.

Students are exposed to and practice literal level questions and comprehension more than they practice any other type. Guszak (1967) and several other researchers have observed and tabulated teachers' questions to determine the kinds of comprehension tasks required of students. Consistently, the researchers found that about 70 percent of all questions asked by teachers address the literal content of reading assignments. Since students have much practice with this type of comprehension, the teacher should consider several questions if students persistently have difficulty comprehending directly stated facts.

The first question is, "Do the students know they are supposed to be attending to the meaning of the material?" Too many students in remedial programs look upon reading as word-calling, as in, "I said all the words right this time. You mean you wanted me to pay attention to what the words meant, too?" When students have this attitude, a teacher's effort must be aimed at getting them to understand that the purpose of reading is to gain meaning. For a time, *everything* these students read should be followed by oral questions posed by the teacher. In addition, specific activities and games aimed at comprehension of written material—not just word recognition—should be used. An example of a published game teachers can employ in their programs is "Reading For Details" (Gamco). This is a board game accompanied by 72 story cards. There are two editions of the game, one written at second grade level and one at fourth. To advance along the race track on this board, players draw a story card, read it, and answer one of four questions. The four questions require a *who, what, when* or *where* answer. A

spinner is used to determine which of the four questions a student must answer.

The second question a teacher should ask if a student is having difficulty with literal-level comprehension is, "Do I have the student placed in materials at her frustration level?" While the teacher may have administered a test and determined the student's instructional level, tests are not infallible. Even when teachers have carried out testing procedures correctly, the results may not be accurate. Try the student in material half a grade lower and see if literal comprehension is better. Incorrect placement can also be the fault of an incorrect readability level assigned to the specific material the student is reading. At best, readability formulas provide a ballpark figure of reading levels of texts. And unfortunately, some publishers use obscure formulas of questionable validity, or they simply make educated guesses about the levels of their materials. In these cases, although the instruction manual may say that a given text is a book for third-graders, in reality the reading level may be higher. If, for example, Jan's instructional level has been determined to be 4.0, but she is having difficulty comprehending directly stated facts in a given fourth grade book, try her with other materials with an assigned readability level of fourth grade. The fault may be in the material, and not in the student.

A third question the teacher should ask is, "Does the student have an unusual lack of familiarity with the topic being presented in this selection?" In order to understand what is read, students must have at least some information about the topic already stored in their heads. If difficulty is seen with literal level questions, and if lack of familiarity with the topic appears to be at the root of the problem, the implication is that the teacher must take the time to build background information before the student reads some kinds of material. This background-building can consist of discussion with the student, showing pictures, role-playing ideas, and relating examples to concepts already familiar to the student. To determine if students' problems in comprehending directly stated facts do result from lack of familiarity with the topics, they should be given other material at the same reading level, but on topics with which the teacher is certain they are familiar. Literal questions should be asked over several selections of this type to determine if there may be other causes of the difficulty.

A fourth question should be, "Does the problem lie in the form of students' written responses—and not in their actual comprehension?" If students' comprehension is evaluated based on written responses to questions (e.g., on workbook pages, to questions the teacher has written on the board, to questions found at the ends of chapters, etc.), the teacher must take care to separate their skills in *writing out a response* from their true understanding of the material. Many students typically read the questions before reading the material, search through the material until they find a sentence containing several words also found in the question, and mindlessly copy down that sentence as the answer, whether it makes any sense in answering the question or not. Suppose, for example, that the question was, "How did *the rooster get caught by the fox*?" A student may find a sentence in the story that says "*The rooster* hoped that he would not *get caught by the fox*." Note that seven words in this statement are identical to words in the question. Therefore, although this sentence does not answer the question, the student may nevertheless write it down as the answer. To help students dispense with this unproductive habit, teachers should arrange for group discussions with students, using questions and statements such as these:

A. What did Mr. Hastings do the next morning?
   1. Mr. Hastings could hardly wait for the next morning.

   2. At dawn Mr. Hastings got out his hunting dogs.

B. Describe these two kinds of stores: retail stores and wholesale stores.
   1. Retail stores sell to people like you and me, but wholesale stores sell to people who own retail stores.
   2. There are two kinds of stores: retail stores and wholesale stores.

The teacher should read the questions. Students should be asked to underline those words in each of the possible answers that are identical to words in the question. Count the number of such words for each possible answer. Point out the right answer and *discuss why the other answer does not answer the question.* Have the students note that the number of identical words is not necessarily relevant when answering a question.

A final question to ask is, "Does the student need direct instruction in how to answer a literal question?" Herber and Nelson (1975) suggest five steps to follow if the answer is "yes."

Step 1: Ask a question, *then tell students the answer.* Next, tell students where the answer may be found in the book, and have them find it. After several practice sessions of this type, proceed to Step 2.

Step 2: Ask a question, tell the answer; do *not* tell where the answer is located in the material, but have the students find it.

Step 3: Next, ask a question, but do *not* tell the answer; *do* give the location of the answer, and have the students locate it.

Step 4: Ask questions only. Students must find locations and answers.

Step 5: Finally, it is suggested that students be required to make up questions about the material themselves. This type of exercise has also been suggested by other reading authorities since it helps students predict the kinds of questions teachers may ask. This not only aids comprehension but teaches a skill to use when studying for tests.

Herber and Nelson's steps should be employed with story-type material and with content area books (such as history materials, science materials, and other informational books).

CONCLUDING STATEMENT

Comprehension is really the most important concern in reading instruction. This is why two chapters of this book are devoted to this topic. This chapter has provided background information necessary for teachers to make instructional decisions, and has offered several specific suggestions for promoting comprehension and working with problems in literal level comprehension. The next chapter is devoted to higher-level comprehension tasks.

16

Increasing Comprehension: Part 2

A recent United States National Assessment of Educational Progress (NAEP) report found that, in general, students read better in 1984 than they had when the assessment was conducted 13 years earlier. The one exception to this concerned higher order comprehension skills. In fact, each time this assessment has been conducted in recent years, this same area of weakness in reading has appeared across all age levels. Therefore, a major concern of teachers of both average and disabled readers has come to be higher-level comprehension.

Higher level comprehension involves use of interpretive thinking, and, in some cases, evaluative or creative responses. This chapter will focus on several important interpretive processes related to higher level comprehension. These processes are: a) drawing conclusions and inferences; b) determining the main ideas of passages; c) determining cause and effect relationships; d) following a sequence of events; e) using imagery; and f) using critical reading skills.

DRAWING CONCLUSIONS AND INFERENCES

The terms *drawing conclusions* and *drawing inferences* are often used to mean the same thing, but some authorities distinguish the terms in this way. *Drawing conclusions* involves use of information directly stated in a text. Although the conclusion sought is not directly stated, all information needed to reach the desired conclusion is stated in the material. In contrast, *drawing inferences* is required when part of the information needed to derive the answer is stated in the text, but part of it is not. Students must, therefore, search their background information to find the additional needed information and combine this with the information in the text to infer the correct answer. Both drawing conclusions and drawing inferences require interpretive thinking, and even if this distinction is made in defining the terms, the two strategies are closely related.

An additional distinction exists with respect to the term *inference*. On the one hand, *inference* is used to mean that *general* type of cognitive activity that permeates all reading. Thus, for example, we must use inferences even in "lower" order reading responses, such as determining the correct word to fit a context or choosing the right directly stated fact to answer a literal question. But the term *inference* is also used to refer to a *specific* type of higher level comprehension skill, whether as defined in the previous paragraph or as defined synonymously with *drawing conclusions*.

And, to add still further confusion, the process of drawing conclusions and drawing inferences forms the basis of and is interrelated with all other higher level comprehension skills. Because this is so, detailed consideration of these strategies is presented first in this chapter.

Drawing conclusions and making inferences are areas of comprehension with which many readers have difficulty. For example, in addition to the 1984 NAEP, both the 1971 and the 1975 National Assessment of Educational Progress (NAEP, 1976) showed that students in both middle school and high school produced lower scores in inferential comprehension than in literal comprehension. Further, when data in these two studies were compared, it was found that although elementary-school-age students had shown improvement in comprehension at the literal level during the intervening four years, their inferential comprehension had not increased. The problem is even greater with disabled readers. When Hansen and Lovitt (1977) examined learning disabled (LD) students' performances on literal, sequential, and inferential questions, their scores were lowest when they were required to draw inferences. Furthermore, Wilson's (1979) study indicated that the differences between average and disabled readers' performances were greater on inferential than on literal questions.

There are a number of steps and procedures a teacher can pursue to help students in

remedial programs improve their inferential comprehension.

First, teachers should ensure that students understand the task requirement. *Explain* to them that for the specific question being asked the answer is not directly stated in the book, and that they must use background information found in their heads along with the information in the text. *Specify* that the task requires being a "detective" to find and match clues to figure out the answer. Such an explanation is often an important revelation for many students who have wondered where *in the book* those other kids were finding the answers, because they had looked and looked to no avail.

Second, teachers should provide opportunities for students to practice drawing conclusions and inferences during *listening* comprehension exercises. Studies have shown that reading comprehension and listening comprehension are related (e.g., Berger & Perfetti, 1977). In listening exercises the teacher does the reading while the students devote their energies to thinking. Teachers should write or locate short passages, read them to the students, then ask them to draw an inference or conclusion. Here is one example of the type of paragraph that can be used:

> Joe's toothache was making him feel awful. He tried many times to yank the tooth out himself, but he just couldn't do it. He made a big decision. He put on his coat and walked slowly downtown. He came to a building, stopped, sighed, and bravely went up the steps. What was his purpose?

After reading the short paragraph, the teacher should ask students if the correct answer was given in the paragraph, have them name all clues in the text that helped them get the answer, and ask them to tell things from their own experiences (i.e., background information) that helped them determine the answer. This type of practice may be used even with very young students. Pictures can also be used to give young students practice with inferring and drawing conclusions. See the example in Figure 16–1. In this example, the student is to draw a picture in the empty box depicting what occurred between pictures 1 and 3. Experiences with this type of comprehension should occur in first grade, if not earlier, and continue consistently through all grade levels.

Third, teachers need to draw upon recent research findings for effective instructional practices in this area. Hansen (1981) developed two procedures that significantly improved the inferential comprehension of average readers. These procedures were also tested with remedial readers by McCormick and Hill (1984) with the same positive results. The first procedure was called the Question Technique. This technique was based on the hypothesis that students typically do poorly in drawing inferences primarily because they get very little practice with this type of comprehension. (Recall that in the previous chapter it was noted that Guszak (1967) and others found that 70 percent of the questions that teachers ask students are at the literal level.) Throughout the several weeks these research projects were being conducted with the Question Technique, students in the experimental

group were asked *only inference questions* after they read stories in their daily lessons. In contrast, students in a control group were asked only one inference question for every five literal questions asked, which is typical practice in many classrooms. In weekly comprehension tests, the students in the experimental group scored significantly higher on inferential comprehension than did the control group. An implication for remedial teachers is that they must give their students *much more practice* in drawing inferences than is usually given. For students who have a weakness in this area, teachers should select only those questions from commercial materials that require students to infer, and should write their own inference questions to supplement these materials.

The second effective procedure in the Hansen study and the McCormick and Hill research was called the Strategy Procedure. For the experimental student group, this procedure required that the teacher select three main ideas from each story and write two questions about each idea. One of these two questions always required the students to relate something in the story they were going to read to their own background experiences. The second of the two questions always required the students to make a prediction about what might happen in the story. For example, if a story concerned two boys who were such good friends that they decided to change

Figure 16–1
Preliminary practice in drawing inferences or conclusions can employ pictures: What happened between pictures 1 and 3?

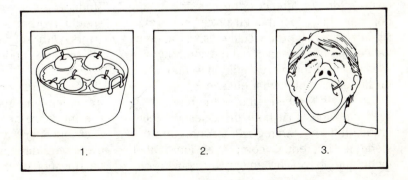

1.   2.   3.

places for a few days, one of the main ideas the teacher might wish the students to infer might be:

> Things aren't always as good for another person as they may seem.

In this case, the background question might be:

> Have you ever wished or pretended you were someone else? Who? Why?

And the prediction question could be:

> If two boys changed places, do you think anything might happen that they would think was good? Do you think anything might happen that would be bad? What?

The three main ideas were never shown or stated directly to the students, but each of the two questions written for each main idea was thoroughly discussed by the group prior to reading the story. Group discussion of the questions was considered critical because: students who at first could think of no responses often were able to respond after hearing other students' comments; students sometimes modified their original responses after hearing other students' answers, and after thinking about those answers; and students could use many persons' ideas—not just their own—to draw inferences during reading. Students in this experimental group performed significantly better on weekly tests of inferential comprehension than did the control group who received the more traditional ratio of 5:1 for literal and inferential questions.

Based on the results of the research, it seems obvious that both the Question Technique and the Strategy Procedure improve students' inferential comprehension. Other techniques for practice in drawing conclusions

and inferences are available, and several of them are discussed on the following pages.

Generic board games may be devised for use with any story to provide practice with higher level comprehension tasks. Figure 16–2 shows one example of such a game. To play this game, students use a spinner with 1, 2, and 3 on its face. After spinning, the student moves his game piece according to the number of spaces indicated by the spinner. The square on which a student lands directs him to draw from one of three piles of cards. *Question cards*—indicated on the board by the question mark—contain only questions that require a conclusion or an inference to be drawn. *Creativity cards* require a creative response, and *Evaluation cards* require an evaluative response. Sample questions for each set of cards are shown in Figure 16–2. Students attempt to answer the question on each card they draw, then the next student takes a turn.

Teachers also can use a variety of commercially available materials, such as the Specific Skills Series (Barnell Loft). One set of booklets in this series is titled *Drawing Conclusions*. Exercises in this series are available for reading levels 1 through 12.

Some activities, such as making judgments about character traits or giving and defending an opinion about what was the most important event in a story, are often referred to as evaluative responses. In fact, however, they involve inferencing and drawing conclusions. Teachers should initiate discussion with their students about these kinds of topics, and should require students to defend their answers with sound reasoning based on text information and/or their own background knowledge.

One reason students may be exposed infrequently to questions that require them to use inference or to draw a conclusion is that such questions are often hard to write! It is even more difficult to think of a good inferential question on the spur of the moment to ask

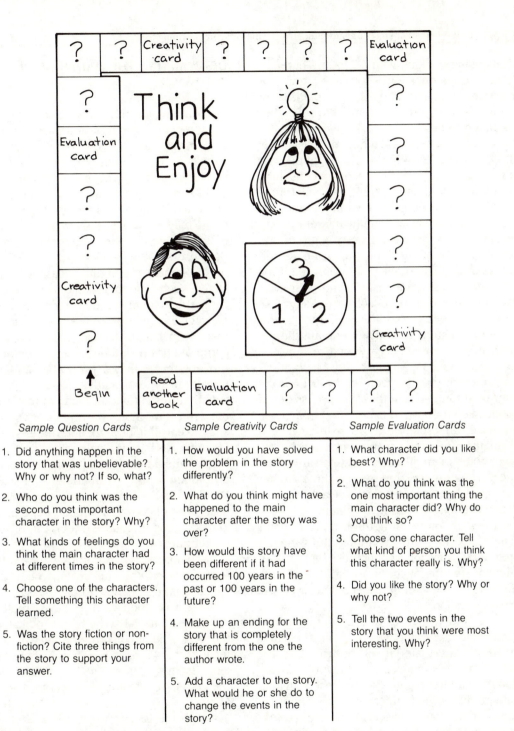

Board game labels:

Top row: ? | ? | Creativity card | ? | ? | ? | ? | Evaluation card

Center: **Think and Enjoy**

Spinner: 3 / 1 / 2

Left column (top to bottom): ? | Evaluation card | ? | ? | Creativity card | ? | Begin

Right column (top to bottom): ? | ? | ? | ? | ? | Creativity card

Bottom row: Read another book | Evaluation card | ? | ? | ? | ?

Sample Question Cards

1. Did anything happen in the story that was unbelievable? Why or why not? If so, what?

2. Who do you think was the second most important character in the story? Why?

3. What kinds of feelings do you think the main character had at different times in the story?

4. Choose one of the characters. Tell something this character learned.

5. Was the story fiction or non-fiction? Cite three things from the story to support your answer.

Sample Creativity Cards

1. How would you have solved the problem in the story differently?

2. What do you think might have happened to the main character after the story was over?

3. How would this story have been different if it had occurred 100 years in the past or 100 years in the future?

4. Make up an ending for the story that is completely different from the one the author wrote.

5. Add a character to the story. What would he or she do to change the events in the story?

Sample Evaluation Cards

1. What character did you like best? Why?

2. What do you think was the one most important thing the main character did? Why do you think so?

3. Choose one character. Tell what kind of person you think this character really is. Why?

4. Did you like the story? Why or why not?

5. Tell the two events in the story that you think were most interesting. Why?

Figure 16–2
Sample questions and a board game that can be used with any story to encourage higher level comprehension

orally while working with a group. Therefore, these types of questions should be planned in advance, as a part of the lesson plan, to be ready for use after students have finished reading a selection.

Another reason teachers may ask fewer of these higher level questions is that eliciting appropriate answers often takes up considerably more time than does eliciting answers to literal-level questions. When a literal question is asked, students can usually answer quickly. Even when an incorrect answer is given, students do not need much time to locate the correct answer in the text. Questions requiring students to draw conclusions and inferences usually are not disposed of so quickly. Students may need to be directed rather laboriously in the strategy of how to obtain the answer. In addition, when a wrong response is given, it is not so easily resolved. Much attention and time may be required to sort out the relevant information in the text, discussions of applicable background experiences may have to ensue, and so forth. As a result, while a given time period may permit a teacher to cover 10 or so literal questions, the same time interval may allow only two or three higher level questions to be discussed. Teachers must recognize that this time problem is *not* a valid reason for avoiding these more difficult tasks. Spending time in thoughtful—though prolonged—development of these higher level questions is one of the most valuable things teachers can do to help students improve their comprehension.

Any activities or questions that cause students to go beyond what is explicitly stated in the reading material will be useful in improving their strategies for drawing conclusions and inferences, including those activities that are discussed in the following sections on determining main ideas, sequences of events, cause and effect relationships, and using critical reading skills.

DETERMINING THE MAIN IDEA OF A PASSAGE

Determining the main idea is also called finding the central thought of a passage. It is the process of deciding on the general significance of the material.

Single paragraphs in informational material almost always have a main idea. On the other hand, single paragraphs in narrative material may not have a main idea because it may run across several sequential paragraphs (Robinson, 1983).

Sometimes main ideas are directly stated, such as in topic sentences, but in other cases the main idea must be inferred from the facts given. In either case, determining the main idea can be considered a higher level comprehension skill because a generalization must be made; that is, even when a topic sentence states the main idea the reader must decide that this statement, and not the others, is the central thought.

Learning how to determine the main idea of a passage is a valuable skill because it helps remedial readers identify what is important to know and to remember in a selection. Details are also more easily remembered if they are related to a major generalization. This skill is particularly important for reading content area material.

Poor readers sometimes have difficulty understanding the concept of "main idea." If asked what the main idea of a passage is they will often respond with a single small detail from the material. When it is indicated that the response is incorrect they will tell the teacher that "It *does* say that in there." Direct teaching is necessary to help them see that they must decide what the whole selection is about.

In the *beginning* phase of teaching the main idea, teachers should select paragraphs in which the topic sentence is clearly stated.

Since authors may place a topic sentence in any of three different locations in a paragraph, students should be given practice in identifying the topic sentence in each of these positions: at the beginning of the paragraph, at the end, or somewhere in the middle. Students can be asked to underline the topic sentence with a colored pen. At this stage teachers should be actively involved to give students immediate feedback about the correctness of responses and to provide direct assistance in deciding why an answer is right or wrong.

In the *second* phase of teaching the main idea, students should work with paragraphs in which the main idea is not explicitly stated. Direct teaching and group work and discussion are important at this stage. Many published activities designed for practicing the skill of determining the main idea actually test rather than teach if students work the exercises by themselves. For example, in a typical exercise, students read single paragraphs and then answer multiple-choice questions that are later marked right or wrong by the teacher. This is a test and does not teach students *how* to determine the central thought of a passage.

Here are more appropriate activities.

1. Have students work together to outline several single paragraphs to recognize the relationships between main ideas and the details that support them. First, have students read a paragraph; then, through group discussion decide on the main idea (remember that at this stage paragraphs should be used in which the main idea is *not* directly stated). Next, write a Roman numeral I on the board (using typical outlining format), followed by the statement selected as the main idea, and then ask for the details that prove or support the main idea. Finally, list these below the main idea and after capital letters (A., B.,

C., etc., again in typical outlining format). Follow this procedure for several paragraphs. This helps students distinguish between what constitutes the whole passage, and what constitutes statements that are merely details.

2. Use a visual demonstration. Demonstrate visually the relationship between the main idea and supporting details by drawing a tree with trunk and branches on a transparency for an overhead projector. After students have read a paragraph, they are asked to offer suggestions for the main idea and details. The teacher writes the main idea on the trunk and the details on the branches. Try different writing arrangements on the tree to determine which one makes sense. (Use a water-based felt tip pen for marking on the transparency; when answers are to be changed, dip a tissue in water and erase the previously written answer.)

3. Have students summarize a paragraph in *one* sentence.

4. Before students read a paragraph, write the main idea and the supporting details each on separate oaktag strips. After they read the paragraph, students arrange the strips in outline fashion to show the main idea and the details.

Measles are unpleasant and should be prevented.

- Measles cause funny-looking spots on your body.
- Measles make you itch.
- Measles make you feel as if you have a rash.
- Measles are contagious.

If a card holder is available it works well for arranging the strips. Or a feltboard can be used if small pieces of felt are glued to the backs of the strips.

5. Yet another approach is to have students read a paragraph, then draw a picture of the main idea (a quick sketch with stick figures will do), and write a caption at the bottom of the picture stating the main idea. The teacher then compares students' pictures and captions to decide if the main idea was depicted or only one of the details. Discussion follows to resolve any differences of opinion.

6. A related approach is to provide paragraphs with no title, then have students write a title, telling them that it must reflect the main idea of the paragraph and not just be an interest grabber.

7. In teaching the main idea, teachers should use the *Who?*, *What?*, *When,?* and *Why?* questions employed so often in literal comprehension exercises. If a short phrase is written to answer each such question, these often can be combined into one statement that reflects the main idea of paragraphs in which the main idea is not explicitly stated. For example,

> Steven was planning to run away from home. He had decided that if on this birthday his parents didn't get him the dog he had asked for year after year, that night he would take the Greyhound bus from the station downtown and go off to live on his own.

Who: a boy, Steven

What: planning to run away

When: on his birthday

Why: if his parents didn't get him a dog

Main idea statement: A boy, Steven, was planning to run away on his birthday if his parents didn't get him a dog.

Up to this point the discussion has centered on finding the main idea in single paragraphs. Of course the *third* phase in the program should be designed to promote transfer of this skill to longer pieces of discourse, that is, material longer than one paragraph. All of the activities suggested for phase two of the program may be used in phase three. For some of the activities, slight adaptations may help students make the transfer more readily. For example, when using outlines, the teacher may wish to print partially completed outlines on the board with the details already given for each paragraph and only the main idea slot for each one left blank. The blank slots are to be filled by the students after group discussion. When asking students to select titles for passages, teachers can cut the headlines off newspaper articles and have them write their own headlines. If students are unable to read the regular community newspaper, any of the easy-to-read newspapers or new magazines now available, such as *Know Your World* (Xerox), may be used. Also, students should receive practice in orally summarizing longer pieces of discourse. Summarization is one of the most important strategies for developing the ability to pick out what is significant in written material.

FOLLOWING A SEQUENCE OF EVENTS AND FOLLOWING WRITTEN DIRECTIONS

Following a sequence of events is important for understanding the relationships of events and characters in a story and particularly important for reading some types of content area material, such as history and science. It is also an important aid to recall.

The inability to follow a sequence and its effects often becomes apparent when a teacher asks students to retell a story or selection they have read. Some readers will choose an event that occurs anywhere in the material and begin their retelling there—not because it is the beginning of the important information, but because the event is of interest to them. Then, they may return to an earlier portion of the selection, jump ahead to a later event, and then swing back again to an earlier one. Often they begin to make comments like, "No, he really did that before she said . . . ," or, "No, that's not right, I think maybe he was the one who. . . ." As the mixed-up retelling progresses, the student forgets more and more of the relationships, causes, and correct actors in an event. Inability to follow a sequence can be detrimental when reading informational material as well; for example, when following the explanation of a scientific process or directions for carrying out a math problem.

One step in working with students who have this difficulty is to help them realize the importance of correct sequencing, as well as giving them practice with this skill. Have students talk through common events and what would happen if they follow an incorrect sequence. Ask them, for example, "What would happen if you put on your shoes and then put on your socks?" or "What would happen if your mother went to the stove to fix your breakfast, broke an egg over the burner, then put on the pan?" You might have students act out several of these mixed-up types of sequences so they can see or experience the results. After engaging in a few of these activities to instill the im-

portance of following a sequence of events, give students—in a random order—the sections of a cartoon strip you have cut apart. (See Figure 16–3.) Ask them to read each section and then place them in the right order.

Before students read a content area selection (for example, from a history book), list the important events in single sentences on a dittomaster, but list them in a mixed-up order. Reproduce a list for each student. After students have read the material, they are to cut the list apart and re-arrange the sentences on their desk tops to conform to the order of events in the selection. This type of activity gives the teacher the opportunity to provide immediate feedback and corrective suggestions because she can walk around the classroom and see who has produced an incorrect listing. Making comments while students are working on an activity is more helpful than assigning a grade on a completed worksheet and returning it later in the day or even the next day. (This latter type of activity is testing, not teaching.) Comments such as these can promote learning: "Chad, think about it. Does it make sense for this to have happened before that?" or, "Holly, I think you need to reread paragraph three. Then re-arrange your sequence and raise your hand so I can check it again."

Closely related to following a sequence of events is being able to follow written directions. This is an important academic skill, but

Figure 16–3
Learning to identify the proper sequence of events is a skill students need to understand causes and effects and to follow explanations and directions in informational material.

also one used in daily life. When instructing students in this area, it is wise to kill two birds with one stone: many instructional materials should be directions students are really going to be required to follow. Select the directions they will have to read in their spelling book next week, or choose a science experiment they must complete in an upcoming chapter in their regular classroom. What follows is a prototypical activity for practicing following directions:

1. Copy a science experiment on chart paper. Post it where it can be seen by the whole group. (See Figure 16–4.)
2. Read the first sentence aloud to the students and ask, "Does that statement give us a direction to follow?" If the students decide that it does, use a colored marking pen to write a large "1" in front of the sentence.
3. Read the next statement and ask the same question. If so, number it "2." Continue through the selection; number sentences that give a specific direction, but do not number filler statements often found intermingled with directions. Have students note the many other statements mixed in

with the directions; this type of writing style, in which narrative material is interspersed among directions (frequently found in textbooks) is difficult for poor comprehenders.

4. Encourage students to find and number (lightly with a pencil so the marks can be erased) specific direction statements in their own textbooks when they must follow written directions of any kind.

Practice may also be given in following directions by having students actually construct or assemble something in the classroom. (Figure 16–5 illustrates one activity of this type.) Invest in some inexpensive paperbacks designed to involve students in "making and doing," such as these from Scholastic:

• *Easy Costumes You Don't Have to Sew*: how to make a dragon and other nifty costumes
• *Easy to Make—Good to Eat*: easy-to-follow recipes
• *Ed Emberley's Drawing Book of Animals*: step-by-step directions for making animals from various shapes
• *Fun and Easy Things to Make*: directions for using household objects to make puppets, bookmarks, and other items

---

① Take a pan of water. ② Dip an empty bottle into the pan. You will see bubbles rising from the bottle. These are bubbles of air. Air is all around us and fills any empty space—like an empty bottle. When the water goes into the bottle it pushes the air out. ③ Take the bottle from the water and ④ turn it upside down; ⑤ let all of the water run out. What is in the bottle now. Right— air. ⑥ Repeat the experiment by pushing the bottle back into the pan of water.

Figure 16–4
Give students practice following written directions with exercises similar to tasks they can expect to do in their regular classroom.

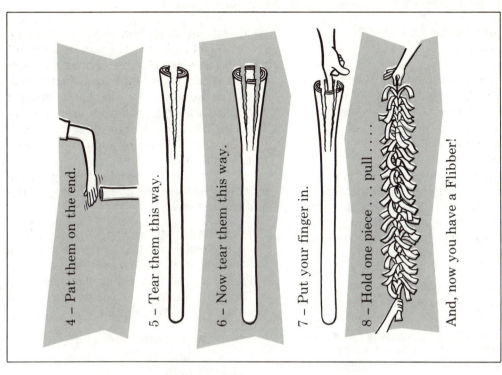

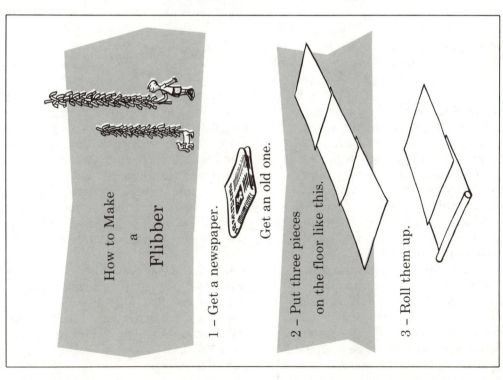

Figure 16–5
Have students make something when they are learning to follow written directions!
(*Source:* From *The Beginner Book of Things to Make*, by Robert Lapshire. Copyright ©
1964 by Random House. Reprinted by permission of the publisher.)

DETERMINING CAUSE AND EFFECT RELATIONSHIPS

The strategy of determining causes and effects involves understanding the "why" in relationships, and the results of actions and events. In some cases, the significant thing to determine is the cause, in others it is the effect, and in still others it is both.

Ascertaining causes and effects can be difficult because a number of other higher level comprehension skills underlie this process; for example, being able to draw a conclusion, infer, determine the main idea, predict outcomes, and/or follow a sequence of events. To complicate matters, sometimes a passage may relate a single outcome that has more than one cause or a single cause that results in more than one effect. Or, sometimes a chain reaction is described in which a cause produces an effect, but that effect in turn becomes a cause resulting in another effect, and so forth.

$$Cause \rightarrow Effect$$
$$(cause) \rightarrow Effect$$
$$(cause) \rightarrow Effect$$

In longer pieces of discourse, the cause may be stated in one paragraph and the effect or effects in another.

Authors often use signal words to alert the reader to cause and effect relationships; words such as *because, if, therefore, so, so that, since, then, as a result of, as, unless, hence, in order that,* and *for* can help students see the tie between causes and effects. But, sometimes no signal words are used.

Pearson and Johnson (1978) give additional reasons why this comprehension skill is complicated. Sometimes both the cause and the effect are directly stated; but sometimes although they are both stated, the relationship between the two is not, and, therefore, readers must find the relationship themselves; and finally, there are times when either the cause *or* the effect is stated, but the other is only im-

plicit and, therefore, must be inferred by the reader. Practice is necessary in dealing with passages in which all three of these situations exist. It is also important to use informational as well as story-type material in this practice. The cause and effect pattern is seen more often in social studies material than in any other type; it is also frequently found in science texts (Smith, 1967).

Some specific instructional suggestions for providing practice in recognizing causes and effects follow.

1. Begin with causes and effects students will already know in order to promote awareness of the "cause/effect" concept. Write several "causes" on the chalkboard and have students tell you the effects. List these effects. For example, you may write:

   Water spills in your lap.
   A car runs out of gas.

   Your students may suggest such effects as:

   Your clothes get wet.
   The car stops.

   Then, reverse the process, write a series of effects on the board, and have students suggest causes.

2. Have students read paragraphs that contain causes and effects. As with the blackboard exercises, these should be *familiar* experiences. Have students locate the statements of cause and underline these in red. Have them do the same with statements telling effects, underlining these in blue.

3. Follow the suggestion in item 2, but this time give paragraphs in which only a cause is specified. After they have underlined the cause in red, have students write the effect on a line below the paragraph. Next, do this when only an effect is given.

4. Follow the suggestions in items 1 and 2, using topics in which causes or effects are *unfamiliar* to students. Have your stu-

dents discover and then relate these causes and effects from the passage.

5. Use exercises like the one in Figure 16–6.

6. The Neighborhood Stories series (Jamestown) separates exercises for inferring causes from those for inferring effects. This gives students practice for those situations in which only the cause or the effect is given and they must infer the other. Reading levels of these materials range from third through fourth grade, but the selections are written to appeal to remedial readers in grades four through six. Other reading strategies treated in this series include recalling details, sequencing, drawing conclusions, predicting, and finding main ideas.

7. Use commercial board games to practice determining cause and effect. For example, one from Gamco comes in second- or fourth-grade editions. It includes 96 story cards and 24 cause-and-effect cards.

8. Interactive stories such as shown in Figure 16–7 can be used to help students perceive cause-and-effect relationships.

9. Adams and Harrison (1975) suggest using commercial television programs students watch at home to develop strategy lessons. For instance, for cause-and-effect relationships they provide this idea:

List words used in ads that show a cause and effect. For example, "congested nasal passages due to cold" (cause); "headache, sinus pain, etc." (effect); or note situation in a TV show that indicates a cause and effect. (p. 51)

10. Write cards with causes on some and effects on others. Mix them up. Have students place the appropriate cards under a label that says *causes*, then have them match the correct effect card to each, placing these under a label that says *effects*. For example,

Causes	*Effects*
forest fires	destroy thousands of trees in a short time
meat kept in warm places	often spoils

The library opens at 10:00. When the clock on the wall said ⊙, the doors were opened and the children came in. Brian went to the picture book section, while Kerry looked through magazines. Brian found two books that he took to the table. He looked through these. He liked the second one better than the first, so he put the first book back on the shelf. He took the second one to the librarian and asked to check it out.

A. 1. The library opens at 10:00.
   2. When the clock says ⊙ the doors are opened and the children come in.

                  Yes   No
   Does #1 *cause* #2? ☐ ☐

B. 1. Brian went to the picture book section.
   2. He only checked out one of the two books he looked at.

                  Yes   No
   Does #1 *cause* #2? ☐ ☐

Figure 16–6
Teachers can make simple exercises that help students learn to distinguish between cause and effect.

giant crickets. Earth crickets were noisy enough, thought Hal. But these giant insects could make sounds that would break his eardrums. Lynn waved her arms at them and mouthed the words, "Stop. Quiet! Please." At once they stopped.

Then, as Hal gazed at the giant crickets, he seemed to hear a voice. But it wasn't really a voice. It was more like someone thinking inside his mind.

Welcome to the Land of the Insects. We are sorry our greeting was too loud for you. Were you sent to help us with our problem?

Hal glanced at Lynn. "Are you getting their message too?"

She nodded, wide-eyed. "Let's beam our thoughts back to them and ask what their problem is."

Our problem is our growth. Each time we double in size, our mass becomes greater but our strength does not increase. So we can barely carry our weight. You are from a planet where insects live. Can you help us? We can no longer move as fast as we need to.

Hal frowned. "That's quite a problem. We haven't come up against that one on Earth. All our insects are small."

"But maybe we can still help," said Lynn. She aimed her thought question at the nearest cricket. "Do you have termites here?"

Yes.

"And do you have trees?" Lynn went on.

Yes.

Lynn clapped her hands. "Then maybe we can help you invent the wheel."

Hal stared at her for a moment, puzzled. Then he broke into a big smile. "Now I get it. Termites can chew through wood. Maybe tree trunks can be chewed into wheels. And insects that are too heavy to carry themselves can ride. It's a long shot, but . . ."

The cricket leader broke in and finished Hal's thought.

It's worth a try. Thank you. You helped us, so you are welcome to come out and explore our land.

Lynn and Hal climbed out of their spaceship as the giant crickets hopped away. Soon they were approached by . . . .

A GREEN MONSTER	FLYING CIRCLES	STATUES ON THE MARCH
continued on page 17	continued on page 19	continued on page 21

TAKE YOUR CHOICE

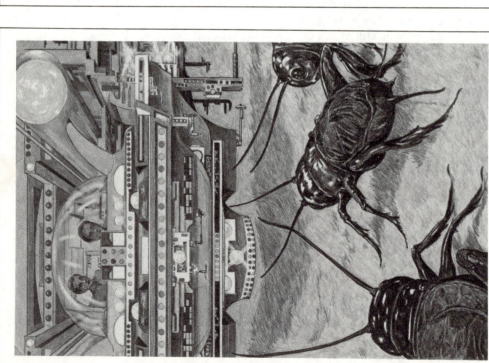

GIANT CRICKETS

Figure 16–7
Interactive stories enhance students' understanding of cause and effect. (*Source:* From "Star Trip," in *Attention Span Stories* (pp. 10–11) by Lee Mountain. © 1978 by Jamestown Publishers, Providence, Rhode Island. Reprinted

11. Display cause and effect relationships by cutting arrows from oaktag strips and affixing arrows to the chalkboard. After reading a selection, print causes on each arrow and have students write corresponding effects directly on the chalkboard next to the arrow.

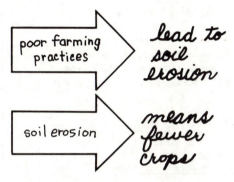

12. Give students practice with signal words that indicate a cause and effect relationship. A sample exercise of this type is seen in Figure 16–8. The Reading Spectrum series (Macmillan) also has excellent exercises for this practice in their vocabulary books.
13. Provide students with opportunities to predict outcomes. Predicting outcomes will sharpen students' thinking skills and help students infer indirectly stated causes and effects.
14. Microcomputer simulations can help students understand the concept of cause and effect and learn about story structure. Simulations allow students to manipulate story events, thus changing causes and consequences. Students make the decisions that determine the direction in which the plot evolves. One such computer program is EAMON (Kuchinskas, 1983). If a microcomputer is available for the remedial classroom or clinic, investigate other story-environment simulations to employ in your program. Information on computer use in reading classes may be found in the journal *Computers, Read-*

ing, and Language Arts; in the monthly section of *The Reading Teacher* titled "The Printout"; and in other journals.

USING VISUAL IMAGERY

When most people read a story they are likely to "see" pictures in their minds of the occurrences they are reading about as they progress through a text. Some poor readers, however, report that they do not see images as they read —perhaps because of exaggerated concern with pronunciation of words, or lack of interest in reading. Several studies have shown that when students do form mental pictures of the message in a text, both comprehension and recall are aided (Levin, 1973; Linden & Wittrock, 1981; Sadoski, 1983).

In Sadoski's (1983) study, for example, the role of imagery was shown to be related to higher level comprehension, which requires deeper levels of the processing of meaning than is required by literal level comprehension. In this study, fifth graders who reported forming a visual image of a critical part of a story scored better on higher level comprehension tasks, such as telling the theme of the story, than did students who did not report visual imagery.

It has also been suggested that visual imagery is particularly helpful when students are reading about situations that are new to them. Forming images in these cases serves as a problem-solving strategy to comprehend the unfamiliar event or information (Sadoski, 1983).

It would appear, therefore, that imagery training helps some poor readers increase their higher level comprehension achievement. Several suggestions for this training follow.

1. *Tell* students to try to form pictures in their minds or try to "see" the objects and

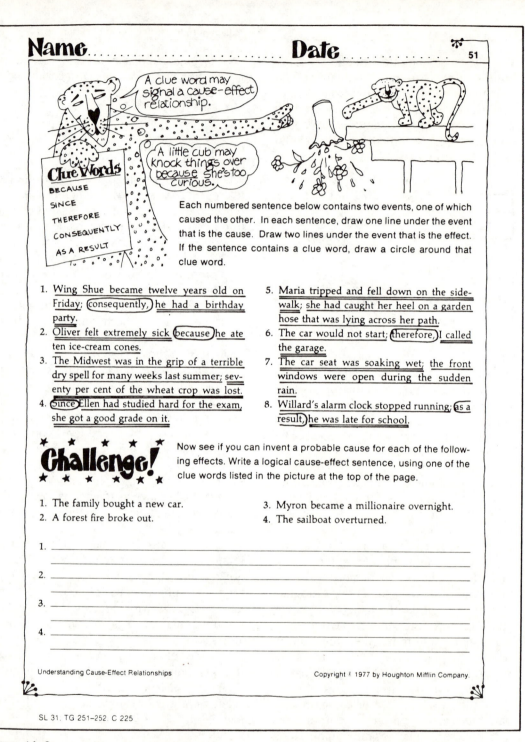

Name .... Date 51

A clue word may signal a cause-effect relationship.

Clue Words

BECAUSE
SINCE
THEREFORE
CONSEQUENTLY
AS A RESULT

A little cub may knock things over because she's too curious.

Each numbered sentence below contains two events, one of which caused the other. In each sentence, draw one line under the event that is the cause. Draw two lines under the event that is the effect. If the sentence contains a clue word, draw a circle around that clue word.

1. Wing Shue became twelve years old on Friday; (consequently,) he had a birthday party.
2. Oliver felt extremely sick (because) he ate ten ice-cream cones.
3. The Midwest was in the grip of a terrible dry spell for many weeks last summer; seventy per cent of the wheat crop was lost.
4. (Since) Ellen had studied hard for the exam, she got a good grade on it.

5. Maria tripped and fell down on the sidewalk; she had caught her heel on a garden hose that was lying across her path.
6. The car would not start; (therefore,) I called the garage.
7. The car seat was soaking wet; the front windows were open during the sudden rain.
8. Willard's alarm clock stopped running; (as a result,) he was late for school.

Challenge!

Now see if you can invent a probable cause for each of the following effects. Write a logical cause-effect sentence, using one of the clue words listed in the picture at the top of the page.

1. The family bought a new car.
2. A forest fire broke out.

3. Myron became a millionaire overnight.
4. The sailboat overturned.

1. _____

2. _____

3. _____

4. _____

Understanding Cause-Effect Relationships

Copyright ℰ 1977 by Houghton Mifflin Company.

SL 31. TG 251–252. C 225

Figure 16–8

Signal words help students understand cause and effect relationships. (Source: From *Reading Bonus Duplicating Masters Level L* (p. 51), 1977, New York: Houghton Mifflin. Reproduced by permission.)

events they are reading about because it will help them understand and remember what they read.

2. Read a paragraph *to* students. Before you begin to read, ask them to close their eyes and try to form a mental picture of what they hear as you read. Afterward, discuss these images. Poetry is often a good choice for this purpose.

3. Read a paragraph to students, again asking them to form a mental image of what they are about to hear. Afterward, ask the students to draw pictures of what they saw. *Compare and discuss the pictures.* Lesgold, McCormick and Golinkoff (1975) reported a study in which third and fourth graders were trained for four weeks to draw cartoons of selections they read; after the training period students recalled more of the stories as a result of this imagery practice.

4. Have students read a paragraph silently. Proceed as in item 2.

5. Have students read a paragraph silently. Proceed as in item 3.

6. Have students carry out suggestions 2 through 5, but with selections longer than a paragraph.

7. Ask students to act out a story they have read. Engaging in short dramatizations necessarily induces "seeing" what must be acted out. Henderson and Shanker's (1978) study showed that this type of activity improved primary grade students' comprehension more than workbook exercises designed to aid comprehension. Of course students cannot act out everything they read, but they can "act it out" in their heads.

USING CRITICAL READING SKILLS

Critical reading is defined as "the process of making judgments in reading" or "an act of reading in which a questioning attitude, logical analysis, and inference are used to judge the worth of what is read according to an established standard." (Harris & Hodges, 1981, p. 74.) Some people suppose that work with critical reading skills is far down in a priority list of needs and that critical reading skills may be too difficult for poor readers to master. Quite the opposite is true, however. Poor readers need to work with these critical skills even more than good readers. Poor readers are often the ones who believe anything in print is true or correct. As adults they are frequently bilked or misled by the vague or sensational language found in some advertising and news articles. They are often influenced adversely or make wrong decisions because they do not trust their own judgments if contrary assertions are found *in print*. In addition, these skills are no more difficult to master than other higher level comprehension skills. And the reasoning and thinking exercises employed to teach critical reading may positively affect other types of comprehension tasks.

Many teachers begin a program of teaching critical reading skills by providing practice in recognizing the seven propaganda techniques identified by the Institute of Propaganda Analysis (Robinson, 1967). These are:

1. *Bad names*—name calling designed to cause dislike. ("Americans are capitalist imperialists.")

2. *Glad names*—using "names" or descriptions of people to generate positive feelings. ("The candidate can be trusted. He was a Boy Scout in his youth.")

3. *Transfer*—suggesting approval because other people purportedly approve. ("Use Acid-O Aspirin. Nine out of ten doctors do.")

4. *Testimonial*—using public figures to endorse ideas or products. ("Melvin Mish, pole vaulting champion in the Olympics, drives the new Olds Cutlass.")

5. *Plain folks*—suggesting that an important person is just like the average person, and, therefore, can be trusted; or indicating that average folks (just like you) prefer a certain product or idea. ("Senator Kitten's campaign manager says he spent Sunday at the family farm where he ate a fried chicken dinner and played with the dog.")

6. *Stacking the cards*—not giving the full truth by omitting details or focusing attention on one detail. (The Russian press reports the American system is on the verge of collapse because unemployment is high.)

7. *The band wagon*—suggesting that since "everybody" is doing something you should too. ("Over 1½ million people have bought the Higglely Pigglely screw driver.")

Work on critical reading skills should not be limited to practice in recognizing propaganda techniques, however. Other important abilities and skills include the following.

- understanding that just because something is found in print it is not necessarily true. (Practice in recognizing propaganda devices is a beginning, but developing this understanding should be carried further—for example, by examining several newspaper accounts of the same incident or by reviewing several different reports of an event in history, such as might be found in an encyclopedia or textbook in contrast to a work of historical fiction.)
- identifying fact versus opinion
- detecting faulty generalizations
- detecting overgeneralizations
- identifying the effects of quoting out of context
- detecting false causality
- discerning writers' purposes—and bias (Do they want to inform—or influence?)

To teach critical reading skills, have students read several newspaper accounts of the same incident and contrast the details reported.

- asking questions about the writer's qualifications (Does the author of an article about learning disabilities in a women's magazine have the background and expertise for his or her statements to be believable?)
- learning to ask: Where's the proof? What facts support this? What data back this up?

Because there is some debate about whether critical reading skills can be *taught* or are a result of natural reasoning powers, one group of researchers set out to determine if critical reading skills could be improved through direct instruction (Patching, Kameenui, Carnine, Gersten, & Colvin, 1983). They compared two instructional approaches. Fifth graders in one group received a *workbook method* in which workbooks containing lessons for learning three critical reading skills were used. After students completed the exercises these were submitted to the teacher who marked right and wrong answers and gave them back to the students. This method was chosen because it is fairly consistent with the type of comprehension practice found in typical classrooms. The workbook method did not prove to be very effective in teaching critical reading skills.

The second approach, the *systematic instruction method,* did prove effective, however. What made systematic instruction so effective? In the first place, teachers worked directly with the students during each lesson. Secondly, teachers employed principles of active teaching:

- Lessons were conducted at a brisk pace.
- The teacher provided immediate correction after each error.
- The teacher immediately praised correct responses.
- Learning to mastery was required. (Students had to perform one lesson correctly without teacher help before going on to the next lesson.)
- There was much teacher-prompting to assist students in discovering the correct responses.

At the end of the program, students who engaged in the systematic instruction method scored significantly higher on a critical reading test than did the group using the workbook method.

Furthermore, the systematic instruction method was most effective with the poorer readers in the group. The important implication of this study for the remedial teacher is that students (including poor readers) *can* develop critical reading skills through direct instruction, but the specific method chosen may well determine success or failure.

CONCLUDING STATEMENT

Comprehension is the aim of everything else teachers do in reading instruction. Although admittedly the comprehension process is not entirely understood, teachers do have an immediate need to provide assistance to their students. The information in this chapter reflects the current understanding of how to go about that task. Because educators are continually expanding their understanding of and developing their ideas about how to assist students with comprehension problems, teachers need to read their professional journals to stay abreast of new findings.

UNIT FIVE

Remedial Procedures for Students Having Difficulty Reading to Learn

17

Helping Readers With Inefficient Rates of Reading and Poor Study Skills

It is unusual for elementary school students to be referred to a remedial or clinical reading program (or LD class) simply because they are using inappropriate reading rates or study skills. If, on the other hand, teachers are working with middle school or senior high school students, referrals to a remedial program are somewhat more likely, especially for inefficient rates of reading. Most often, however, the remedial teacher deals with these problems as one of several problems experienced by a student already enrolled in a special program for other reading-related reasons.

RATES OF READING

A first question teachers may have in regard to the issue of reading rates and the poor reader is, "What is an appropriate rate for reading?" The answer is, "This varies." A number of researchers have attempted to determine the rate at which the average individual reads with comprehension. Table 17–1 shows the results of several studies of reading rate for students who had received no special rate training and also shows that the average rate may vary with grade level. It also suggests that, although some variance certainly would exist among individuals within groups, a great deal of similarity exists among students at given grade levels, for example, college-age readers.

Several researchers have found that reading rate is related to listening and thinking rates (Buswell, 1951; Carver, 1983; Sticht, Beck, Hauke, Kleiman, & James, 1974). It appears that the optimum rate for reading is no faster than the rate at which a specific individual can think or listen with understanding. This means that comprehension must always be taken into account when considering rate. *An increase in rate without understanding is pointless.* In addition, it should be pointed out that the lower the IQ of the student the more likely slow reading is needed for good comprehension (Carlson, 1946; Shores & Hubbard, 1950).

343

Table 17–1
Results of selected studies on reading rates

Researcher	Grade Level of Students	Average Reading Rate
Carver (1983)	College	300 words per minute (w.p.m.)
Himelstein & Greenberg (1974)	College	283 w.p.m.
Pauk (1964)	College	250 w.p.m.
Brown (1976)	College	252 w.p.m.
Harris & Sipay (1980)	12	251 w.p.m.
Harris & Sipay (1980)	8	237 w.p.m.
Harris & Sipay (1980)	6	206 w.p.m.
Harris & Sipay (1980)	4	155 w.p.m.
Hoffman et al. (1984)	3	100 w.p.m.

The appropriate rate of reading also varies according to the *material* read and the *purpose* for reading a specific text. Narrative material may often be read at a fairly fast rate, while expository material such as social studies or science books should usually be read much more slowly. A rather rapid rate may also be appropriate when reading material on familiar topics, but a slow and careful rate is necessary when reading about new subjects containing unfamiliar concepts and terminology. Likewise, when the purpose for reading differs, rate should vary. For example, skimming (i.e., using a very rapid rate) is appropriate when the purpose is reading an encyclopedia article to determine if it contains information needed for a report, but would be inappropriate when studying a geography book chapter for the first time. Morasky (1972) found that the type of material and the task requirement affect the number of visual fixations made during reading, which in turn affects reading speed. Adapting one's rate according to the material or purpose is referred to as having *flexibility* in reading rate.

Numerous studies have shown that rate can be increased through instruction (e.g., Braam & Berger, 1968; Cason, 1943; Himelstein & Greenberg, 1974; Sailor & Ball, 1975; Westover, 1946), but some, especially advocates of certain commercial programs, have made questionable claims about the rates individuals can attain. Tinker (1958), who conducted much research on eye movements and reading rates, says that 800 words per minute is the maximum speed that can be achieved for "true reading" and that rates beyond this are really skimming or scanning. (In regard to reading rate, the terms *skimming* and *scanning* are usually considered synonymous. They mean, *to read rapidly, but selectively and purposefully.*) In a study with superior readers at the college level, Spache (1962) found that after training in a commercial speed reading program, these students did attain rates of 1800–2400 words per minute using the techniques they had been taught to use, but they comprehended only 50 percent of the material—a comprehension level unacceptable in most types of reading.

Reading rate, then, normally varies with grade level and rate of thinking ability, and it should vary according to material being read and purpose for reading. Taking into account these normal variations, teachers may still find students in their remedial classes whose rates are inappropriate. In these cases, a student's reading rate may be too slow, too fast, or inflexible. Any of these tendencies can detrimentally affect comprehension. Chapter

8 includes a section titled "Assessing Reading Rate" that offers suggestions for measuring students' rates of reading.

Reading Rates that Are Too Slow

Grob (1970) has pointed out that work-time demands for students can cause academic difficulties if reading rates are unusually slow. See Table 17–2 for estimated study times for different reading rates when completing typical assignments in secondary school. Because both elementary and secondary students may have assignments for several different subject areas, the aggregate work-time demands for all of them often make completion of the assigned tasks impossible for the excessively slow reader. In addition, Smith (1973) has suggested that a rate of at least 200 words per minute is necessary to assimilate ideas when reading material above the intermediate level. With rates slower than this, so much attention is focused on individual words that the general significance of the ideas may be lost. However, before deciding whether to include rate training in a poor reader's instructional program (and, if so, what type of training), teachers must determine *why* the student is reading too slowly.

Causes of Excessively Slow Reading. Several possible causes should be considered if a student is reading at an excessively slow rate. First, the teacher must ascertain whether this student is being asked to read material at his or her frustration level. Such mismatches often occur for poor readers when they are asked to read the same textbooks in their regular classrooms as are being read by other members of the class.

A second cause of an unacceptably slow reading rate is the lack of a sufficiently large sight vocabulary. *Sight vocabulary* in this case is defined as those words a reader can recognize instantly. When Samuels,

Table 17–2

Total work times for typical high school assignments in relation to variable reading rates

Assignment	Rate (words per minute)	Total Work Time (hours:minutes)
Selection from *Huckleberry Finn*	600	3:08
	300	6:15
	150	12:30
	75	25:00
One chapter of American history	300	0:34
	250	0:40
	200	0:50
	150	1:42
	100	1:40
	50	3:20
Preparation for chapter test in American history	300	1:42
	250	2:00
	200	2:30
	150	3:21
	100	5:00
	50	10:00

(*Source:* From "Reading Rate and Study-Time Demands on Secondary Students," by James Grob, 1970, *Journal of Reading,* January, pp. 286–288. Reprinted by permission of James Grob and The International Reading Association.)

Begy, and Chen (1975–76) compared the word recognition abilities of highly skilled readers and less skilled readers who could recognize the same words, significant differences were seen in their speed of recognition. That is, although the less skilled readers accurately pronounced the words, the more skilled readers recognized them faster. If a reader must pause to remember a large number of words in a passage or must apply word identification strategies to many of them, rate of reading will certainly be reduced. A reader must be able to instantly recognize most words in a selection in order to read at a normal rate, and to be able to adequately comprehend the material.

A third reason for excessively slow reading is related to the strategies students use to identify unknown words. In some cases students simply do not know the strategies that could help them and, therefore, sit and ponder each unknown word. In other cases they use one strategy only, or always select a less efficient one than is appropriate. "Sounding out" each unknown word letter by letter and insufficient use of context clues often characterize these latter cases.

When students read silently, a fourth cause of a slow rate can occur: lack of attention to the task. If the reader requires a longer time to read material silently than orally, poor concentration and mind-wandering may be the reason.

Finally, for some students who have a past history of a reading disability, slow rates may be the result of never having been told or required to read more rapidly or fluently. Because they have struggled with the basic requirements of word identification (often for years), the detrimental habit of very slow reading may persist even when they have learned those word identification skills and no longer need to read at a snail's pace. Students with this problem need directed prac-

tice with the more rapid rates they are now able to attain.

Remediation of Slow Reading Rates. Chapter 11 presented suggestions for instructing severely disabled readers whose reading is excessively nonfluent and "word-by-word." (See the section of that chapter titled *Improving Nonfluent, Word-by-Word Reading*.) Several of the causes of slow reading described here are also linked to lack of basic skills and strategies. Obviously, if a student lacks sufficient sight vocabulary or uses inefficient strategies for identifying unknown words, remediation should be concerned with these areas rather than with directly treating the inappropriate rate. When these basic requirements for good reading have been met, however, direct instruction for improving reading rate can be helpful.

A number of *appropriate* instructional techniques can be used to increase reading rates. In some cases, a combination of these techniques may be useful. In others, a specific technique should be selected to address the specific cause of a student's slow rate.

1. Use very easy material. Easy material allows students to read more rapidly than they usually do. To begin this activity, students should be asked to read easy-to-read, high interest material several grade levels below their instructional level. For example, a student reading at sixth-grade level may be given second-grade material at the outset. Students should be told that the text they are being asked to read is much easier than they can read, and that the purpose is to increase their fluency and rate. After several sessions of practice at this level, the text selection should be moved up to the next level. For example, after reading a second-grade selection for four or five sessions, a student would be

asked to read a 2.5-level text for several lessons; subsequently the level would be moved up to 3.0, and so forth. As the student progresses to higher levels more sessions at each level are usually needed before progression to the next level. This type of instructional activity can help students break out of the confines of a slow rate they may have "practiced" for years.

2. Timed exercises are available from commercial publishers. Some of these follow. *Timed Readings* (Jamestown) consist of 400-word selections followed by 10 multiple-choice comprehension questions. Reading passages are available for levels four through college. SRA Rate Builders (Science Research Associates) are found in several of the various SRA kits. Each rate builder is a card with a short selection followed by questions. The rate for each card is charted. The Be-A-Better-Reader Series (Prentice-Hall) contains articles with the number of words listed for each and a place to compute words read per minute. *Reading Drills* (Jamestown) are timed passages for building both speed and comprehension. The text/workbooks designated as "middle level" are for reading levels 4 through 6, while those designated "advanced level" are for reading levels 7 through 10. When selecting published rate-training activities, the teacher should be certain that all exercises are followed by a comprehension check. One set of materials that does not include any measure of comprehension is *A Fast Course in Speed Reading* (Educulture); therefore, it is not recommended. As Bond, Tinker, and Wasson (1979) say, "Put plainly, 'reading' without comprehension is not reading" (p. 382).

3. Grob (1968) has described a method used successfully with middle school remedial readers who exhibited reading behaviors typified by excessively slow speed, many hesitations, and lack of attention to the task. The following steps are taken in this individualized-instruction method. Using books at students' instructional levels, each student is told to read loudly, clearly, and as fast as possible. As the student reads, the teacher moves a pencil under the line to assist in the pacing. The rate at which the pencil-pacer is moved varies as the teacher makes judgments about when it is necessary to slow down a bit or when the student can be helped to move faster. For this specific purpose (and during this activity only), when a student has difficulty with a word the teacher immediately says the word and moves the pacer on. Grob found that not only did reading rates increase for remedial readers using this technique, but their interest in the content also improved because their reading sounded more coherent and, therefore, made more sense to them. In addition, because of the insistence that they move forward as rapidly as possible, their attention was focused and they made fewer miscues on words they actually knew than had previously been observed in their reading. The purpose of this method is to generate an immediate change in the student's approach to reading; it has some similarities to the "neurological impress method" described in Chapter 11.

4. Teach skimming. Flynn (1977) describes a successful use of this approach for increasing general reading rate. She used this technique with older, poor readers who had been locked into excessively slow rates (an average of 150 w.p.m.) because they were afraid they might miss something if they read faster. Students were told that when skimming, not only did they not have to read every word, but that it was "positively against the rules."

They were also told that *skimming* is not the same as *reading,* which is a more exacting process. To skim they were directed to read rapidly, noting only important ideas. Skimming rates gradually reached about 500 to 1000 words per minute. These increased rates also transferred to a general rate increase; when students returned to more typical reading tasks they did read more slowly than when skimming, but not as slowly as before. After each set of skimming practice in which skimming rates continued to climb, general reading rate also showed an increase.

5. Machines and mechanical devices have been used in rate training with varying degrees of success. Table 17–3 provides a description of four categories of these machines or mechanical devices, examples of each, and an evaluation of their usefulness in rate instruction. Controlled reading, pacing devices, and motion pictures or videotapes may have some value in terms of motivation because of their

Using controlled readers often increases motivation, but rate can be increased equally well with ordinary materials.

uniqueness in contrast to more typical methods of reading instruction. However, less expensive techniques for increasing reading rate work just as well. Tachistoscopes, on the other hand, are not useful for this purpose because skills learned do not generalize to real reading situations.

6. In those cases where an excessively slow rate is caused by lack of attention or concentration, charting progress can be a motivating technique. For the purpose of encouraging an increase in reading rate, a daily graph or chart should be kept of the number of words read per minute, along with the student's comprehension scores. Each day, students can record their own rate and score on the chart/graph and consult the previous day's records before each rate training session. The student should have performance goals in mind. The object is to increase both rate and comprehension as a student progresses through successive lessons, or at least to maintain comprehension at a stable level with no decrease as rate increases. See Figure 17–1 for an example of a dual graph of this type. By charting or graphing comprehension scores as well as rate, the student and teacher can be certain that a rate increase is not an "empty" improvement. This is necessary to ensure that comprehension is not adversely affected. If it is, rate training should be suspended until comprehension is maintained at the same level, or increases along with rate.

Several techniques that have been used to improve reading rate are *inappropriate.* For example, eye-movement training was used in the past. Several types of normal eye movements occur during reading, including

• Fixations—the pauses that last for a fraction of a second as the eyes rest on a word
• Saccadic movements—the quick, jerky

Table 17–3

Machines and mechanical devices used in rate training

Machine/Mechanical Device	Description	Evaluation

I. Controlled reading
  A. *Controlled Reader* (Educational Developmental Laboratories)
  B. *Craig Reader* (Craig)
  C. *Tachomatic X500* (Psychotechnics)
	Projector accompanied by filmstrips. The rate at which lines of print are projected onto a screen can be set at differing speeds.	Controlled reading can increase rate (Sailor & Ball, 1975), but results are no better than those obtained through the reading of high interest library books (Cason, 1943) or use of ordinary materials (Westover, 1946).

II. Pacers
  A. *Reading Accelerator* (Science Research Associates)
  B. *Reading Rateometer* (Audio-Visual Research)
	May be used with any material. A shutter moves down the page line by line.
	
	May be set at varying speeds.
		Use of mechanical pacing devices can increase rate (Sailor & Ball, 1975), but other methods requiring no mechanical devices may be more effective (Braam & Berger, 1968).

III. Motion Pictures/Videotapes
  A. *Speed Reading Course* (Time-Life Multimedia)
  B. *Harvard University Reading Films* (Harvard University Press)
	Series specifically designed for increasing reading speed. The rate or projection is increased from tape to tape or film to film.	Have been used successfully with older students (Harris & Sipay, 1980).

IV. Tachistoscopes
  A. *Tach-X* (Educational Developmental Laboratories)
  B. *Flash-Meter* (Keystone)
  C. *Flash-X* (Educational Developmental Laboratories)
  D. *AVR Eye-Span Trainer* (Audio-Visual Research)
	Projector or handheld device that gives short exposure to words or numbers so they are flashed for a brief period of time. Designed to increase rate of recognition and perceptual span.	Although rate of recognition for single words and perceptual span for series of unrelated words or phrases may be increased by tachistoscopic training, research indicates that this increase does not transfer to regular reading tasks (Anderson & Dearborn, 1952; Cleland, 1950).

movements between fixations
• Regressions—the movements of the eye back over material that was seen or missed during previous progress across the line
• Return sweeps—the movements of the eyes back and down to the next line

The time required for reading is the fixation time plus the movement time. Another term used in relation to eye movements and reading is *recognition span* (sometimes called *perceptual span*); this is the amount of written material seen in one fixation. As a result of studies with eye-movement cameras conducted near the end of the last century and the early part of this one, it was noted that poor readers appeared to employ less efficient eye movements than skilled readers (Buswell, 1922; Tinker, 1936). These findings led to the hypothesis that if eye movements of disabled readers could be trained to approximate those of proficient readers, their reading achieve-

Figure 17–1
Graphs showing rate and comprehension scores for each of 14 lessons

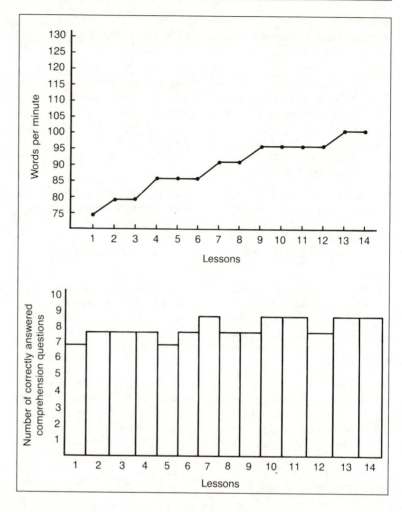

ment, as well as their reading rates, would improve. However, after years of use and research with eye-movement instruction, authorities concluded that this type of training was not helpful (Tinker, 1965). Some training for this purpose has shown that certain techniques and use of certain devices can increase recognition span, but there is no transfer of these learned responses to real, contextual reading. In fact, what has been discovered is that faulty eye movements do not cause poor reading, but rather, they are a result of it; they are symptoms, not causes. When reading

skills improve, eye-movement efficiency occurs naturally as a result of the increased reading proficiency.

Subvocalization during silent reading is also thought to be a cause of a slow reading rate. However, all silent reading is accompanied by some subvocalization. In most readers this is undetectable to the human eye or ear, but when electrodes are attached to the throat near the vocal cords, speech muscle activity can be detected even in proficient readers and even though they are engaging in "silent" reading. Subvocalization increases when the difficulty of the material is greater or when the reading ability of the individual is low (Edfelt, 1960). Several studies have shown that, in these cases, if students are required to suppress subvocal speech their comprehension decreases. Even college students may remember occasions during silent reading of difficult subject matter that they unconsciously increased their subvocalization until lip movement was evident. Some authorities have suggested that, when comprehension is poor, students should be *encouraged* to subvocalize. Like faulty eye movements, subvocalization is more often a symptom than a cause of reading difficulty. Even when it is determined that students are engaging in excessive subvocalization, instruction to reduce this habit may not be useful. Hardyck and Petrinovich (1969) found that feedback training helped students suppress unnecessary subvocalization but did not result in an increase in reading rate.

Eliminating finger-pointing, likewise, may not be helpful. This aid is sometimes necessary for poor readers to maintain their place on a line and to prevent them from losing their place in return sweeps to the next line below. Only when finger-pointing persists beyond the time when it is needed should the student be encouraged to dispense with the habit. Students who still find finger-pointing necessary are probably not candidates for rate training since more basic skills and strategies are likely needed before rate can be improved.

Reading Rates that Are Too Fast

Reading rates that are too fast occur less frequently than excessively slow rates, but are found in some disabled readers.

Causes of Excessively Fast Reading. One reason why poor readers may read too fast is that they mistakenly equate *fast* reading with *good* reading. For years they have been grouped for reading instruction with other students who plod along at a tortoise pace. They have observed, however, that the students in their classes who are considered the better readers read with fluency and at a much faster rate. After most of their word identification deficiencies have been remediated they adopt a rate of reading that they believe is of a character similar to that of their more skilled classmates. However, this can often have detrimental effects because their objective is speed rather than understanding.

Lack of interest is a second cause of reading rates that are too fast. Students may not care if they understand the material. Their sole purpose is to "get it over with," and they close their books with a clear conscience because they've "read" every word.

Remediation of Excessively Fast Reading Rates. When students believe that fast reading is good reading, the first step is to explain that this isn't necessarily so. Students should be told that during oral reading they must read at a rate that allows others to understand the information. The teacher can demonstrate reading that is too fast to permit the listener to obtain much meaning; and follow this with a demonstration of reading at a rate that sounds interesting and fully communicates. Since students tend to read too fast more frequently during silent reading, teachers can emphasize that "fast" isn't always "best," by having students read a selection silently at their present excessively fast rate, timing them, and then asking them to respond to comprehension questions. Ask them to graph their comprehension scores and rates. Next, have them read another selection at a slower pace, concentrating on the message and striving for an improved comprehension score. Again, graph the reading rate and the number of questions answered correctly. Continue this over a period of time—with the goal always being an increase in comprehension—until a comfortable rate for adequate understanding is determined and dramatized to the student.

Unfortunately, it is not unusual to find students in a remedial program who do not particularly care if they understand material they are given to read. The teacher's first task in these cases is to furnish students with highly interesting material while at the same time indicating that comprehension questions will be asked and scores recorded after the selections are read. The students should be told that the teacher hopes they will enjoy the stories or articles, but that they must slow down their rate to try to obtain the highest possible score on the comprehension exercises. Rates and scores should be graphed as in the above activity, and rewards offered for attaining scores higher than those for each previous selection. Whenever possible, teachers should underscore the evidence that slower reading produces better scores. After much success is seen with these exercises, choose reading material that more closely approximates that which they must read for normal class work, but maintain the same goals and procedures. Once improved performance has been attained, to ensure that the improvement will generalize to more typical classroom expectations (that is, good performance with no special teacher-provided external rewards), the reward system must be slowly removed and performance maintained solely by the students' self-graphing.

Inflexible Reading Rates

A skilled reader has several rates of reading. As a matter of fact, many authorities object to use of the term "reading rate" when referring to instructional objectives for increasing (or decreasing) reading speed. They suggest, instead, that the term "reading rates" always

be employed in order to highlight the importance of flexibility. The goal is to have readers change their rates according to the material they are reading and the purpose for reading this material.

To adjust rate to the material, readers must consider the type, the difficulty level, and their familiarity with the topic covered. Some types of materials commonly read by school-age individuals and the rates generally appropriate for reading each are:

narrative, story-type material	fairly fast
social studies material	average
science material	slow
mathematics texts and problems	very slow

Of course, the specific purpose for reading each of these in each given situation must also be considered. That the reading rate must be adjusted to the difficulty level of the material seems fairly obvious, but more than the needed match between the reader's instructional level and the readability level of the book is implied. Format, for example, is also a consideration. Study materials that employ subheadings, that italicize important words, and that use other organizational aids are less difficult to understand (and, consequently, may be read faster) than those in which readers must discern for themselves relationships between ideas and the relative importance of various aspects of the information. The chapter in this text on comprehension pointed out the differences in reading skills required to understand familiar versus unfamiliar material. It is possible to read selections faster when the reader already has familiarity with many of the ideas, while a slower rate is required for adequate comprehension if large numbers of unfamiliar concepts are included.

To adjust reading rate according to the purpose, students must consider which of the many possible reasons they have for reading specific material. Some of these reasons may be: reading to find the answer to a single literal question in a content-area text; reviewing familiar material; understanding the general significance of material; reading a science chapter to prepare for a test; understanding directions the reader must subsequently follow; reading a math problem that must be solved; perusing a newspaper article because of personal interest; reading a newspaper article on which an oral report must be given; reading narrative material to appreciate the beauty of language; reading critically in order to evaluate the logic of arguments; reading a letter from a friend; reading a mystery story to discover "whodunit"; reading an encyclopedia article to prepare a written report; and so on. If one takes a moment to think about each of these purposes, it will be noted that in some cases fast reading will achieve the goal, but in other cases an average or even a relatively slow rate is desirable.

Research indicates that there are more readers who are inflexible than there are those who have developed the efficiency of flexibility in their reading speeds. Carver (1983) found that individuals generally read at the same rate regardless of the difficulty of the text. For example, when college students in this study were given materials to read at first- through sixth-grade reading levels, they read all of it at a rate of about 300 words per minute. Levin (1966) found that most ninth-graders did not vary their rates either for difficulty level or for purpose. When flexibility *was* seen, good readers more often made adjustments to the purpose, while poor readers adapted their rates to accommodate the difficulty of the material. (Interestingly, Levin found that flexibility was *not* related to IQ.)

Causes of Inflexibility in Reading Rate.
The primary causes of an inflexible reading rate are lack of awareness of the need to adapt one's rate and lack of instruction regarding when and how to do so. A secondary cause is a byproduct of the first: students who have read everything at the same rate for years have essentially "practiced" inflexibility until it has become an ingrained habit.

Remediation of Inflexibility in Reading Rate. In order to gain flexibility in rate, the major task is to learn to be discriminating. This capacity can be taught by

- providing information
- having students practice making decisions about rates appropriate to the material and purpose
- having students practice reading at varying rates.

The first activity in such a program is supplying information intended to highlight the differences in materials (e.g., reading fiction versus reading math problems) and the differences in purpose (e.g., reading a sports magazine for personal pleasure versus reading three chapters in *A Tale of Two Cities* to write a character analysis). Second, group activities should be used that require students to make decisions about strategies for hypothetical reading situations. To do this, for each of several reading selections, have students respond to the following questions: a) What are you reading? b) Why are you reading? c) How should you read it? (Witty, 1953). See Figure 17–2 for a sample worksheet that might be used with this activity. Third, teachers should give students selections of various types and degrees of familiarity, and should assign various purposes for reading. Students should set a goal for the rate at which they will read each selection (fast, average, slow), and should keep records of the actual number of words read per minute.

In an earlier part of this chapter, skimming practice was advocated as one way to help students break out of an unnecessarily slow rate. Flexible readers must also know how to skim. Certain materials should not be

Selection	What Are You Reading? (And, how familiar are you with the topic?)	Why Are You Reading It?	How Fast Should You Read?
1.	Encyclopedia article on cougars (I know very little about this topic.)	To prepare a written report	slowly and carefully with note taking
2.	Article from _Sports Afield_ about a bass fishing tournament (a topic about which I know a lot.)	Just for pleasure	Fast
3.	Chapter from health textbook on communicable diseases (I know something about this topic, but I probably don't know all the information in the chapter.)	To answer questions for an assignment	moderate to slow pace (more slowly when I come to information that is new to me and for information that is probably important)

Figure 17–2
A sample worksheet to be completed by students to highlight appropriate reading rates for different materials and different purposes

read at an average rate, nor is an average rate appropriate for many reading purposes. What is often required is the very fast, albeit purposeful, rate of skimming. Schachter (1978) suggests several materials and purposes for practicing this flexibility skill; here are a few (paraphrased from pp. 150–151):

Material	Purpose (or question)
White pages of the phone book	Find the phone number of the fire department.
Yellow pages of phone book	Find the phone number of a tattoo parlor.
Classified ads in newspaper	Where can you call to buy a horse trailer?
News articles in a newspaper	Who protested at the Carbondale board meeting?
Table of contents	How many stories are in this book?
Content area textbooks	Skim to find out which president had to decide whether or not to use the atomic bomb.
A menu	What main dish is accompanied by rice?

Braam and Berger (1968) studied the effects of four different rate-training methods on flexibility. Students who practiced scanning text in paperbacks developed the greatest degree of flexibility. Those who used controlled readers or controlled pacing devices also learned to vary their reading rates. Tachistoscopic training did not help students achieve flexibility.

STUDY SKILLS

Although deficiency in knowledge of study skills is seldom the reason students are re-

ferred to a remedial reading program, some direct instruction in this area may help disabled readers exist more comfortably in their regular classrooms. During the years in which these students have had difficulty with reading, it is likely that teachers have concentrated instruction on the skills students need to *learn to read* (word recognition, comprehension strategies, etc.). Therefore, the students may have missed basic instruction on how to deal with tasks necessary when *reading to learn.*

In many cases disabled readers do not even possess certain very simple skills that are quite easy to understand and require very little instructional time to practice. One example of this is how to use a table of contents. Practice with this locational skill need not add more than a minute or two to instructional time in any given session since students can learn the helpfulness of this organizational aid if they are simply asked to use it each time they read. For instance, instead of saying, "Turn to page 28 for today's story," the teacher should direct the students by stating something like, "Turn to the table of contents. We're going to read the story titled 'A Zebra in My Bed.' Raise your hand when you can tell the rest of the group the page on which the story begins." Using this kind of brief activity each time an assigned book has a table of contents will probably be the only instruction needed for acquisition of this study skill.

What is suggested is that spending some instructional time on strategies for dealing with reading-related study tasks can be very helpful—even though the majority of time in a remedial or clinical program will be devoted to other, more basic, reading areas. If students attend the special class 40 minutes per day five times a week, for example, out of this total time of 200 minutes (approximately 3½ hours), only a small portion (e.g., 5 minutes to ½ hour) may be devoted to study skills. The amount of time devoted should vary with the age and reading level of the student.

For instance, primary-age students and very poor readers will probably benefit more from a program that emphasizes the foundations for learning to read, while secondary students and somewhat better readers should have at least some instruction on study strategies even though they are in a "remedial" program.

Although a teacher may devote the majority of instructional time to other reading areas, for students to survive the rigors of instructional activities in the regular classroom, homework assignments, assignments to be completed in study halls, and test taking, a bare-bones list of essential study skills includes a generic, independent study system, simple locational skills, a few basic test-taking techniques and strategies for organizing to study.

A Generic Independent Study System

A *generic study system* is one that may be applied to most types of content area study assignments (e.g., studying science, history, or geography texts). An *independent system* is one the student can use when working independently.

One popular generic, independent study system is SQ3R (or SQRRR), which stands for *Survey, Question, Read, Recite,* and *Review.*

Surveying a Text. To *survey* a text assignment means to scan titles, subtitles, and illustrative material (e.g., maps, pictures, graphs, etc.). Surveying provides readers with a mental set to prepare them for the information to be read. After surveying, the student should also make predictions about the kind of content that will be found in the passage.

Questioning. To *question,* in this case, refers to mentally changing titles and subtitles into questions. This conversion should be ac-

complished by the student, not by the teacher. For example, if a subheading says "Farm Products of Nebraska," students might ask themselves the question, "What are the farm products of Nebraska?"

Reading. To *read* means just what is always does, but because of the two former steps and because the student is anticipating the next *R* coming up, reading should be a more active process than is often found when students are studying expository material.

Reciting. To *recite* simply indicates that the student is to answer the questions posed in step 2. This can be accomplished either through silent mental rehearsal or by writing the answers.

Reviewing. To *review* the material means to answer the questions again after an appropriate lapse of time. The review step is important since spaced practice promotes retention.

Developed in 1941 by Robinson, SQ3R has been widely advocated by psychologists and reading authorities. Although Tadlock (1978) has given a rationale for each step of SQ3R based on an information-processing theory of learning, some educators have questioned whether this technique does have real value. Harris (1968), for example, pointed out that although "this system seems to be well grounded in the experimental psychology of learning, . . . [it] has not been subjected to much experimentation" (p. 209). Until recently what little research that did exist was conflicting and, in most cases, had serious methodological flaws. With the publication of a study conducted by Adams, Carnine, and Gersten (1982), however—a study in which the tenets of sound research were followed—the conviction of educators that SQ3R is a sound technique was upheld. In this study, fifth-graders who had deficient study skills performed significantly better on questions about social studies material after training with SQ3R. Two other recent studies, conducted by Ferrante-Alexander (1983) and Douge (1983), support the findings of Adams, et al.: in both of these methodologically sound research efforts, highly positive results were seen with intermediate grade LD students when SQ3R was used.

Another independent strategy students may apply is a *self-questioning study technique.* To use this procedure students are taught to make up their own questions based on the main idea of each paragraph they have read in a text selection. André and Anderson's (1978–79) research showed that students who employed this technique did better on tests than those who merely reread the material. Furthermore, the technique was most effective for students with lower verbal ability.

Although reading disabled students, like other students, are required to study, they are seldom taught how to do so. Direct instruction in the SQ3R or self-questioning procedures is an important step to help students gain the reading skills needed to study.

Simple Locational Skills

Few intermediate grade or secondary level students can meet the study requirements of their regular classes without having to locate information independent of the teacher's assistance. In the introduction to this section, a simple application exercise for tables of contents was suggested. Minimally, the other locational skills needed by a student are: how to use an index; how to select an appropriate reference book for needed information (plus practice with each type); and how to use a card catalog.

Using an Index. The format of an index is generally more difficult for students to understand than the more clearly written format of a table of contents. To introduce this locational skill, reproduce a section from a textbook index in a form large enough to be viewed by the whole group with whom you are working. For example, the index section in Figure 17–3 might be copied onto chart paper and posted on the chalkboard for group discussion. The advantage of a large reproduction of the index section is that the teacher can point to or underline phrases, abbreviations, and other information pertinent to understanding index use.

If the large-sized reproduction of the index is taken directly from one of the students' own textbooks, the second step is to locate the same section of the index in that text, this time actually looking up and verifying the information. Third, select other sections of the index and practice in the same manner, omitting use of the group chart.

Some real-life activities for practice with an index are exercises with those found in the classified sections of telephone books or those designed to help readers locate information in newspapers.

Quakers, 59, 257, 259

Quebec (kwē · bĕk´), 219, 225, 282, 396, m. 226

Railroads: American, 398; development of, 452–454, ill. 452; in Canada, 399; and Civil War, 367, 384, 385, ill. 386.

Recreation: in Canada, 349; colonial, 268, 269, 273, ill. 268; museums, 32.

Republican party, 247, 250, 253, 263.

Figure 17–3
Section from a typical index

Knowledge of Reference Books and Their Uses. A section titled "Use of the Dictionary" in Chapter 14 suggests a number of activities for developing dictionary skills. Proficiency in using an encyclopedia is equally important.

To take advantage of an encyclopedia's resources a student first needs familiarity with the types of information found there. As a small-group activity, teachers should have students skim through one or two volumes of an encyclopedia, noting topics, charts, illustrations, and so forth that could be useful in gathering information for various assignments. Students must also be taught the basic principles for locating information in these reference books, that is: a) information is listed in alphabetical order; b) in some cases the alphabetizing is not based on the first word (e.g., information on Sir Walter Raleigh is located in the *R* volume, not the *S* or *W* volume); and c), some thought about how topics might be cross-referenced is necessary. For teaching the latter, an exercise such as that seen in Figure 17–4 can be helpful.

Using a Card Catalog. When students have mastered alphabetizing, introduce them to the three types of cards found in the catalog: the author card, the title card, and the subject card. Begin by preparing a reproduction of an author card on an overhead transparency. See Figure 17–5. Because the transparency may be projected for everyone to see, it is easy to point to and describe the significance of the information as all students focus on the same item. This makes the learn-

---

Sometimes when you are looking up a topic in the encyclopedia, you cannot find it. Then you should ask yourself, "Is there somewhere else in the encyclopedia where I could look?" (Here is an example: Perhaps you were looking up *beavers* and looked in the *B* encyclopedia, but it was not there. You could look in the *A* encyclopedia next, under the topic *animals*—or perhaps, you would find something about beavers in the *M* encyclopedia under the topic *mammals,* since a beaver is a mammal.)

Topic	The letter you would look under first	Another place where you might find your topic
1. Saturn	S	S (Solar System)
2. Baseball's History		
3. San Francisco		
4. Ice Cream		
5. Bears		
6. Robots		
7. How Shoes Are Made		
8. Violins		
9. Cowboys		
10. Log Cabins		

Figure 17–4
An activity for helping students understand the cross-referencing system of encyclopedias

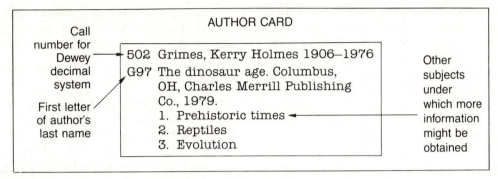

Figure 17–5
An example of an author card with explanatory labels

ing task easier for poor readers. After each portion of information is explained, ask questions such as a) What is this author's last name?, b) How does the number 502 G97 help you?, or c) If the information you need is not in this book, under what other subjects might you look in the card catalog?

Next, follow a similar procedure with reproductions of a title card and a subject card. When students have been exposed to all three types, ask questions such as these: a) If you know only the title of the book you have been assigned to read for English class, what are each of the steps you would use to find this book? b) If you must report on aeronautics for a science class project, what are some subjects you could look under?

The simulated practice described above should be followed by applying the information to the real card catalog in the school library. Give students cards with some information missing; ask them to locate the real card and fill in the missing information. Finally, have a "Book Hunt." Ask students to find and check out books from a list on which only the author, title, or subject is given.

Test-Taking Principles and Techniques

Entire books for students at all levels have been written about test-taking skills. The dis-

cussion here is not intended to be a comprehensive treatment of the topic but describes a few essential skills that poor readers need to learn.

Selecting the Significant Information to Study. One important test-taking skill is knowing how to select the important information to study. Outlining material is an important way to improve this skill, especially if students are introduced to outlining through a group process. Let us look at how this activity might be conducted.

The teacher works with the students in reading a selection of content material from one of their regular classrooms. Next, a group outline is developed on the board with the teacher doing the writing while the students suggest information to go into the outline. It is important, however, that the teacher monitor what is ultimately included. For example, suppose the students are studying a selection on Alaska from a geography book and are attempting to outline the passage shown here.

Alaska. One of our newest states to the far north is Alaska. It has an area of 589,757 square miles. It is the largest state in the United States. . . .

If a student says that an important point is

that Alaska has an area of 589,757 square miles, the teacher would probably reject that idea and say the more important point (i.e., the one they should remember) is that Alaska is the largest state in the United States—and this latter point would be placed in the outline on the board.

The objective of this exercise is to produce the outline as a group, allowing students to hash over why some points are important and others are not and letting them see why the teacher selects or rejects an idea as being important to remember for a test.

Specific Test-Taking Strategies. There are some general strategies that help poor readers when taking any test. Students should learn:

- to *ask* the teacher ahead of time about the format of the test (multiple-choice, short answer, etc.).
- never to leave an item unanswered; tell them that if they guess, they may get it right or get some points for partial information, but when an item is left blank they know they will score zero on that question.
- to read every word in the general test directions word by word (i.e., very carefully).
- to read every word in every question word by word (i.e., very carefully).

Millman and Pauk (1969) offer the following suggestions as ways for students to deal with specific types of tests.

Essay Tests

1. Read all questions on the test before beginning. *Briefly* jot down any thoughts that come to you immediately.
2. If you can't seem to begin, make your first sentence a statement that is a rewriting of the question.
3. Organize your answer before writing (e.g., jot down a *brief* outline). Work fast; do not

spend time making your outline elaborate —write down just a word or two for each point.

Objective Tests (matching, multiple-choice, true-false)

1. Read *all* options even if you think you spot the correct answer right away.
2. Look for specific determiners. (For example, terms such as *rarely, usually,* etc., are qualifiers that often signal that an answer is true; the terms *always, never,* etc., mean 100 percent of the time.)
3. Mark statements as "true" only if they are always true, i.e., there are no exceptions.
4. When two possible answers seem very much alike, study them to see what makes them different.

Other excellent suggestions may be found in *How to Take Tests* (Millman & Pauk, 1969).

Strategies for Organizing to Study

Organizing to study is a skill, and most poor readers benefit greatly from assistance in how to organize and use study time. As with many other skills, the teacher has two major teaching responsibilities. One responsibility is to provide direct instruction in how to organize to study. Teachers often give students assignments and expect that they will complete them, even though they have had no instruction on a) how to find time to complete the assignments, b) when it would be best to do them, c) how to remember exact instructions for assignments, d) how to find the best place to complete them, e) how to avoid misplacing them, f) what materials to use to do them well, g) under what conditions the assignments can best be completed, h) who may help and how, and i) why it is important to do them at all. Nothing in students' genetic codes tells them how to get their assignments done—anymore than it's in their genetic codes to know without direct instruction how to do improper fractions. While some students figure out how to study well on their own, remedial students often do not. They need direct instruction, not only in how to do a science assignment, for example, but also in how to get it done.

A second teacher responsibility is to provide opportunity for practice in organizing to study. Remedial students generally require much practice in order to learn; this includes practice in learning how to cope appropriately with the task of getting an assignment done. Beginning at least by fourth grade, even poor readers should be given opportunities for *independent* study (in other words, practice in completing assignments in a situation where they are not under the eyes of the teacher). Usually this means homework. Remedial students need opportunities to practice homework in small increments; the amount of time required for independent study should be gradually increased to ease students into the more demanding requirements for study found at the middle school and senior high school levels. For remedial fourth-graders, for example, this means beginning at a minimal level of approximately 15 minutes of homework per night. Fifteen minutes is enough time to give students an introduction to practicing skills needed for organizing to study without the length of the task being aversive. This brief interval will also get them into the good habit of getting *all* the homework done.

In addition, it is helpful to give students (and their parents) a list of materials they will need to get organized for studying: a three-ring notebook with subject-area dividers; an assignment book, pocket calendar, and wall calendar; lots of notebook paper, pencils, and pens; a dictionary and a thesaurus; phone numbers for at least one student in each of their classes; a library card; a watch and an alarm clock; a tape recorder; and earplugs (adapted from *Scholastic's A⁺ Guide to Good Grades* [Colligan & Colligan, 1979]).

CONCLUDING STATEMENT

This chapter is not intended as a source for a complete listing of study skills and related instructional activities, but rather as a basic survival list with accompanying suggestions for poor readers. For additional ideas applicable to all students, teachers can refer to the *Study Skills Handbook: A Guide for All Teachers* (Graham & Robinson, 1984).

A variety of commercial materials is also available for students' use. One attractive set is the "Learning to Study" program (Jamestown) consisting of a single colorful workbook for each grade, three through eight. Seven topics are introduced at the appropriate grade levels in this series: interpretive skills (for interpreting maps, time lines, etc.), locational skills, organizational skills (for outlining, writing reports, etc.), reading rate skills, retention skills (giving memory plans and mnemonic aids), study strategies (including SQ3R), and test-taking skills.

Another booklet, *Stop Studying, Start Learning: Or How to Jump-Start Your Brain* (Research Press) is oriented to senior high and college-age learning problems. With chapter titles like, "Two Brains Are Better than One (Especially if They're Packed in the Same Skull)," cartoons, and a humorous writing style, the research-grounded techniques presented in this booklet are highly appealing to the targeted age group. For additional materials, see the Teachers' Store in Appendix C.

18

Helping Disabled Readers With Content Area Reading

In the fourth grade, or sometimes before, students begin to receive daily assignments in history, geography, science, health, or social studies. Reading expository materials will continue to comprise much of their future in school and in life. But many students find these materials particularly demanding. One reason is that they cannot understand the words—words not in their present oral language vocabularies. For example, Harris and Smith (1976), reporting that a fifth grade science book contained words such as *esophagus, particles, valve, pancreas, glands, molecules, capillaries,* and *gristle,* all in one paragraph, point out that although these words were essential to understanding the passage, they probably would be unfamiliar to the majority of fifth-graders. Unfortunately, the problem illustrated is a common one. New words are not introduced at the moderate pace to which students are accustomed in basic reading instruction and, in addition, the words more often represent difficult concepts.

To complicate matters, students not only are required to comprehend these materials, but also to retain more of the specific facts than is generally necessary in story-type selections. Most text books have high density; *density* refers to the number of facts given in a specific amount of text. *Density* is also referred to as *proposition density, compactness,* or *concept load.* It may be necessary for students reading high-density materials to understand and remember the facts presented in every sentence so they can comprehend each subsequent sentence and, therefore, understand a paragraph. In addition, the significance of each preceding paragraph must be comprehended to understand the next one. As Goodman (1970) summarizes, "Textbooks . . . use language in special ways which vary from common language use" (p. 23).

These problems exist for all students but are particularly vexing for poor readers. In addition, the complexities inherent in reading expository materials are exacerbated by the high readability levels of some content area texts. Sometimes, unfortunately, content books are written at levels higher than the grade for which they are used. In these cases, a good deal of students' reading problems may be due to the *material,* and not to the students.

There are, then, three major reasons why disabled readers in particular have difficulty reading content area books.

- The reading level of poor readers is much lower than the level required to read assigned materials, even when the content of the text is at an appropriate level. In these cases, the reading teacher's principal responsibility is to help them develop the basic strategies and skills needed for literacy. The reading teacher may, however, also work with the regular classroom teacher to assist in putting together *circumventive strategies* that will enable the students to participate adequately in content area learning.
- The readability level of the content area text may be unrealistically high for any student, particularly poor readers. Teachers should be aware of how to judge *readability levels* to avoid this problem. Also, circumventive strategies may be appropriate.
- A disabled reader may be making progress in strategies for reading story-type materials, but he may not yet be applying these newly acquired skills to expository texts. Or the *specific skills needed for content area reading* may not have been mastered. If this is the case, specific strategies for reading content area materials may be taught by the reading teacher.

CIRCUMVENTIVE STRATEGIES

In successful reading programs, the classroom teacher and the reading or learning disabilities teacher work together toward the same literacy goals for students. Aid in content area reading affords an opportunity for cooperation between these professionals, particularly when the need for circumventive strategies is indicated.

Circumventive strategies are ways to adapt or adjust the demands of reading. For example, one circumventive strategy involves tape-recording lessons. The classroom teacher (or another student) reads a text selection (a chapter, for example) into a tape recorder. Students who are unable to read the material listen to the tape, using earphones if these are available. They may or may not follow the book as they listen, depending on the severity of their reading difficulty.

Another approach requires asking classroom teachers to provide verbal as well as written instructions for tasks. For example, although directions may be clearly written at the top of an assignment sheet or test, knowing that a disabled reader is in the class, the teacher will also go over the directions orally. This task takes little additional time. In addition, tests over material can often be given orally. The teacher's questions may be taped, or the student's answers may be taped, or both.

Check audiovisual catalogs to find audiotapes related to topics students must study. Have these purchased and placed in the library-learning center for regular classroom teachers to select for a poor reader as substitutes for the text.

Students who are having difficulty reading a content area book can, in conjunction with the teacher, study and discuss all the chapter's pictures, charts, graphs, and diagrams. Students are to read only the captions and labels that go with these visuals, and none of the text. As a group, all students then attempt to answer questions about the chapter. Teachers may be pleasantly surprised at how much students can learn from this limited amount of reading if discussions of the illustrative material are thorough.

Teachers often use movies and film-strips during the study of a topic or at the end of a unit to serve as a culminating activity. With disabled readers it is more effective to allow them to view these audiovisuals *before* they read any of the written text. This can be accomplished by having these special students use the filmstrips or movies independently in the library-learning center or in the reading teacher's room. However, the regular classroom teacher might choose to adopt this procedure for the whole class since it gives everyone a preview of the subject (thus aiding comprehension) and introduces new vocabulary. This strategy is most likely to aid the poor reader whose difficulties lie in the area of comprehension. However, it can also provide some help to those who have word recognition deficits. These students can *hear* vocabulary associated with information they are viewing and, in the case of filmstrips with captions, *see* the printed form of these words; thus they are more likely to recognize the words when they read the text. Thus filmstrips with captions are always a good idea.

Because such students also may have difficulty writing, they may be allowed to report information in alternative ways, such as by taping their reports or drawing a concept.

If students have trouble spelling certain words for written assignments, index cards may be placed on their desks. A permanent file of these problem words can be developed for remedial work, using a file box and alphabetized file-card dividers.

If students are able to identify most words in their texts, but have difficulty comprehending the material, Herber (1970, pp. 90–92) suggests a procedure that the regular classroom teacher may employ. This procedure is useful if multilevel texts are not available—in other words, it may be used as a whole-class activity while still meeting the needs of poor readers.

1. All students read the same material.

2. Questions for students should be differentiated in this way:

   a. Students who have difficulty comprehending directly stated facts are given *literal* questions to answer. They are also given the page number and paragraph where the answers can be found.

   b. Students with average comprehension abilities, or those needing practice with inferential comprehension, are given *interpretive* questions to answer. Numbers of the pages on which the facts necessary for inferring the answer can be found are given to the students.

   c. Students with superior comprehension abilities are asked to answer *application* questions. When responding to this type of question, the reader combines information derived at the interpretive level with background information in order to perceive new relationships.

3. All students' questions may be listed on the same worksheet if a key is used to indicate each type. For example, one asterisk can indicate literal questions, two asterisks can indicate interpretive questions, and three can indicate application questions:

   *What town became the county seat of Franklin County? (Page 78, paragraph 1.)

   **Tell the problems faced by the people of Franklinton at the time it became a county seat. (Pages 78, 79, and 82.)

   ***When people live together, why do they need rules?

4. The teacher assigns certain students to

answer all those questions preceded by one asterisk, others to answer all those with two asterisks, and so forth.

5. After completion of the assignment, all answers are discussed in a whole-group session so that all students hear answers to all questions, including those they did not answer themselves.

Another circumventive strategy is to place checkmarks by the portions of text in students' assigned readings that portray the most important concepts. Regular teachers should be asked to adjust the requirement for these students so that they are assigned a lesser amount of reading than is normally required; that is, they should be assigned only marked passages. In this way, poor readers can contribute to class discussions and can learn from listening to the comments and answers of others.

Moorehead, Meeth, and Simpson (undated) suggest that peer tutors can help disabled learners in the following ways:

a. helping them understand directions for assignments
b. reading important material and essential directions to them
c. helping them practice orally what they are learning
d. summarizing important text selections for them
e. writing down answers the reading disabled student presents orally
f. working with them in joint assignments
g. offering constructive criticism of the disabled readers' work and making suggestions for improvement (p. 38)

Finally, reading teachers should locate easy-to-read, high interest, *content area* materials through the school or the public library, or have them purchased. The Teachers' Store in Appendix C provides a partial list of some currently available materials. These books should be selected so that they address the same topics as assigned to the class but can be read by remedial readers because they are written at a lower level. A suggested interest level (I.L.) is given for each item listed in Appendix C, as is an approximate reading level (R.L.).

READABILITY

Reading teachers should be familiar with the issues and the processes related to determining the reading levels of text materials. It is in relation to content textbooks that readability levels are most often a concern.

What do we mean by "checking readability"? We mean that we are analyzing certain aspects of the text material, such as difficulty of words, sentence length, word length, number of syllables, and so forth, to determine an *estimate* of the grade equivalence of the material.

The most common method for assessing readability is to use a formula. These formulae generally depend on *word frequency* and *sentence length*. Analyzing these two factors is based on studies demonstrating that words that occur infrequently in language are recognized less quickly than those that occur more frequently (e.g., Soloman & Postman, 1952; Stanners, Jastrzembski, & Westbrook, 1975), as well as on studies indicating that longer sentences are more difficult to process, comprehend, and retain (e.g., Coleman, 1965; Savin & Perchonock, 1965). Formulae based on these text characteristics have limitations, however, because they do not measure certain other factors that make material difficult. For example, they do not account for the following important variables.

Background of Students. A student who has had many experiences related to the text information is able to learn new concepts about the topic more easily. However, as Standal (1978) states:

No one has devised a formula that includes components for measuring individual interest and experience. If such a formula did exist or could be constructed, it would probably prove to be so unwieldy as to be useless. (p. 642)

Interest or Motivation.   If students are interested in a subject, they may know the vocabulary and basic ideas already. Likewise, if students are motivated to read about a topic or are motivated to do well on a given reading task, this interest can override the obstacle of a high readability level; in such cases comprehension will be adequate (Klare, 1976). For example, McLaughlin (1966) presented easier and harder versions of a pamphlet to subjects. He found that subjects comprehended the easier version better if they were not highly motivated. But when they were highly motivated there was no significant difference between their comprehension scores on the easy versus the difficult version.

Abstractness of Concepts.   Consider Hamlet's famous question, "To be or not to be." Using a readability formula, this phrase would be deemed very easy because each word is simple and the phrase is short. But the idea the author wished to convey is complex, and the preprimer readability level this sentence would probably be assigned using a standard formula would certainly not be justified.

Density.   Although density adds to the difficulty of material, it cannot be measured with traditional formulae.

Meanings of Words.   Many readability formulae ignore the meanings of words. To compute a readability level with these formulae, one must determine whether words are "easy" by checking them against a prepared list. *Run,* for example, would be found on the list of easy words. But that doesn't tell

the whole story. If the word *run* in the passage being evaluated means "to move rapidly," it is likely that it would, indeed, be an easy word for students. On the other hand, if it refers to "a channel through which something flows" (e.g., *a mill run*), "to sail or steer" (e.g., *to run before the wind*), or "a trend" (e.g., *the run of events*), then the meaning might not be known by many students and, in reality, *run* in these cases would add to the difficulty of the passage.

Other factors contributing to reading ease or difficulty, and which are not measured by conventional formulae are coherence and sequence of ideas, intricacy of punctuation, length of paragraphs, and page format (Cullinan & Fitzgerald, 1984–85).

For these and other reasons authorities have differing points of view about the analysis of readability levels of materials. Some say such an analysis simply cannot be done because each reader is different and it is not possible to know all of these differences. In addition, these authorities contend that because all factors that contribute to text difficulty cannot be analyzed, levels obtained from any analysis are meaningless. At the other extreme, there are those who accept formulae results as gospel. For example, they might suggest that if a readability level of 6.0 was obtained for a textbook, it should not be used with a student for whom an instructional level of 5.7 had been indicated by a standardized test.

Others feel there is truth on both sides. They suggest that while these formulae do not (and probably never will) provide exact results, these methods can supply helpful information for matching students and materials if the scores are regarded as a good *estimate,* and if readability formulae *alone* are not used to determine which materials are readable for specific students. The implication is that use of some standard measure of readability combined with good teacher judgment is the best course to follow. This moderate approach can be implemented in combination with teacher judgment, or by using the cloze technique, rapid-calculation formulae, or in-depth formulae.

The Cloze Technique

Two specific uses of the cloze technique have been described in previous chapters: to assess students' instructional levels, and to practice use of context to predict unknown words. It can also be used to determine the degree to which specific materials are readable for specific students. The cloze technique can be thought of as a "pupil-oriented" approach to analyzing readability. Developed by Taylor (1953), but popularized by Bormuth (1966), the procedure is essentially the same as that employed for assessment purposes: words are deleted from passages at specified intervals and the student is to supply each deleted word.

Suppose it is September of a new school year. Mrs. Carmine, a middle school teacher, wants to determine which students in her new classes will have problems with the geography book adopted by the school system. To accomplish this task, she first selects two 300-word passages from different places in the book. She then follows the same procedures as those outlined on pp. 113, 116 to prepare, administer, and score the test. To determine the degree to which the geography book is readable for each student, she uses the following criteria to evaluate scores (validated by Bormuth, 1968, and others):

57 percent or higher =
the material is at this student's independent level

44 to 56 percent =
the material is at this student's instructional level

43 percent or lower =
the material is at this student's frustration level

Users of the cloze technique should realize that if the deletions are content words (adjectives, nouns, verbs) rather than structure words (prepositions, conjunctions), the missing words will be harder to supply (Hittleman, 1973). The best bet, then, is to exercise moderation: Use the results, but when it seems appropriate, temper them with judgment.

Rapid-Calculation Formulae

Using formulae to assess readability can be thought of as using a "materials-oriented" approach. Some formulae are much better than others in predicting the degree to which students reading at a specific level can handle specified material. Correlations of the scores obtained from formulae with students' actual abilities to read, comprehend, and retain the material range from .45 to .95 (Klare, 1976). Of the many methods available, rapid-calculation formulae are not the most reliable. One reason why calculations may be more "rapid" when using these formulae is that fewer samples of text are analyzed from each given set of material (that is, from a book, a story, an article, etc.) than is done with the more in-depth formula discussed later in this chapter. The small number of samples in this method increases the chance of error.

One rapid-calculation formula that has been found to produce generally valid results is the Fry Readability Formula. It measures *sentence length* and *number of syllables* in words. As stated earlier, sentence length appears to be a good measure of readability and is used in most in-depth formulae as well. There is also a sound basis for including number of syllables in the assessment. For example, Coleman (1971) showed that the number of morphemes in a passage has a correlation

Figure 18–1 Fry's graph for estimating readability—extended. (*Source:* "Fry's readability graph: Clarifications, validity, and extension to level 17," by E. Fry, 1977, *Journal of Reading, 21,* pp. 242–252. Reproduction permitted, no copyright.)

Average number of syllables per 100 words

Average number of sentences per 100 words

APPROXIMATE GRADE LEVEL

DIRECTIONS: Randomly select 3 one hundred word passages from a book or an article. Plot average number of syllables and average number of sentences per 100 words on graph to determine the grade level of the material. Choose more passages per book if great variability is observed and conclude that the book has uneven readability. Few books will fall in gray area but when they do grade level scores are invalid.

Count proper nouns, numerals and initializations as words. Count a syllable for each symbol. For example, "1945" is 1 word and 4 syllables and "IRA" is 1 word and 3 syllables.

EXAMPLE:

	SYLLABLES	SENTENCES
1st Hundred Words	124	6.6
2nd Hundred Words	141	5.5
3rd Hundred Words	158	6.8
AVERAGE	141	6.3

READABILITY 7th GRADE (see dot plotted on graph)

EXPANDED DIRECTIONS FOR WORKING READABILITY GRAPH

1. Randomly select three (3) sample passages and count out exactly 100 words beginning with the beginning of a sentence. Do count proper nouns, initializations, and numerals.
2. Count the number of sentences in the hundred words estimating length of the fraction of the last sentence to the nearest 1/10th.
3. Count the total number of syllables in the 100-word passage. If you don't have a hand counter available, an easy way is to simply put a mark above every syllable over one in each word, then when you get to the end of the passage, count the number of marks and add 100. Small calculators can also be used as counters by pushing numeral "1", then push the "+" sign for each word or syllable when counting.
4. Enter graph with average sentence length and average number of syllables; plot dot where the two lines intersect. Area where dot is plotted will give you the approximate grade level.
5. If a great deal of variability is found in syllable count or sentence count, putting more samples into the average is desirable.
6. A word is defined as a group of symbols with a space on either side; thus, "Joe," "IRA," "1945," and "&" are each one word.
7. A syllable is defined as a phonetic syllable. Generally, there are as many syllables as vowel sounds. For example, "stopped" is one syllable and "wanted" is two syllables. When counting syllables for numerals and initializations, count one syllable for each symbol. For example, "1945" is 4 syllables and "IRA" is 3 syllables, and "&" is 1 syllable.

as high as .88 with comprehension, and that the number of syllables correlates .95 with the number of morphemes.

To use the Fry Formula, consult Figure 18–1. It should take about 30 minutes to use this formula the first time to conduct an analysis; thereafter it should take about 20 minutes to complete one.

Of the other available rapid-calculation formulae, some are slightly less reliable than others, and for others the developers have failed to provide any development, validation, or cross-validation data (Klare, 1974–1975).

In-Depth Formulae

In-depth formulae are more time consuming. For example, the Dale-Chall Readability Formula (Dale & Chall, 1986) requires computations for each 100-word passage taken from every 10th page throughout an entire book (as opposed to a total of three passages in the Fry Formula). But because these formulae are more comprehensive they are often more accurate. While the cloze technique and rapid-calculation formulae are good for a single teacher to use to determine readability levels for students in a particular class, in-depth formulae are a better choice when a textbook is being considered for adoption by an entire school district.

Some in-depth formulae you may wish to investigate are

- The Spache Readability Formula (for primary grades). The revised formula is found in the ninth edition of *Good Reading for Poor Readers* (Spache, 1974).
- The Dale-Chall Formula (for intermediate grades and junior high/middle school). The revised edition of this formula is found in *Readability Revisited* (Dale & Chall, 1986).
- The Flesch Readability Formula (for senior high and adult levels). This formula is found in *How to Test Readability* (Flesch, 1951).

Other in-depth formulae are available. Recently, some computer disks have become available that shorten the analysis time. The usefulness of these computer programs varies and information about each should be carefully considered before purchasing a program to assess the readability of your textbooks.

SPECIFIC SKILLS NEEDED FOR CONTENT AREA READING

The kinds of writing found in different subject-area materials have been analyzed. The results of these investigations (Table 18–1) provide clues about the specific skills needed for content area reading.

COLLEGE-BOUND READING DISABLED STUDENTS

Some reading disabled students plan to attend college. These students do have the potential to succeed if they continue to receive support before college and during their college years.

Reading teachers need to consider specific ways to aid such students, gaining the cooperation of teachers of college preparatory courses, remedial teachers, and other professionals, possibly along with volunteer tutors. Some college-preparatory skills and information can be conveyed in regular classroom settings through listening, use of media, and adaptations of reading assignments. Other skills can be obtained in daily work with the reading or learning disabilities teacher. A volunteer tutor can provide ancillary skills work to supplement and extend the teacher's programs.

Box 18–1 (p. 373) lists basic skills most colleges consider necessary for success. This list can be used to assess students' present strengths and weaknesses. It can be used as a

Table 18–1
Content area texts: Characteristics and teaching implications

Social Studies	1. *Embedded directions*. Texts often have directions to follow within a paragraph (e.g., "The Amazon is the longest river in South America. *Turn now to page 67 and trace the Amazon's route through Brazil.*")

Teaching implications: Ask disabled readers to follow these directions rather than ignore them. Carrying out the tasks specified by the direction will help students visualize, conceptualize, and remember text information.

2. Pictures, graphs, and maps.

Teaching implications: Show students *how* to use these illustrative materials. Graphs are relatively easy to read, but many students overlook this source of information. Don't assume that students know how to use map legends or how to learn from maps—teach them how.

3. Specialized vocabulary.

Teaching implications: Encourage classroom teachers to select some words for preteaching before the selection is read. In addition, teach students how to use context clues, both for word identification and for determining the meanings of words.

4. Cause and effect patterns.

Teaching implications: Smith (1967) found that this pattern occurred more frequently in social studies than in other subject areas. Students may already have the skill to deal with this pattern in narrative material; help them transfer this skill to expository text. (See Chapter 16 for additional ideas.)

5. Comparative data (e.g., the text may ask students to compare the climate, amount of population, and major sources of income in two countries, such as Canada and Mexico).

Teaching implications: To aid *recall,* show students how to prepare charts on "likenesses and differences." To aid *interpretative comprehension,* involve students in a discussion on implications of the similarities and contrasts. Have them show their charts and provide their background information.

6. Time sequences.

Teaching implications: Encourage classroom teachers to have students develop a time line throughout the year in conjunction with their study of topics such as American or world history. Displaying the time line prominently in the classroom will help students gain a perspective about time sequences. As an individual rather than class activity, poor readers can be shown how to develop time lines to be kept in their notebooks.

Science

1. Specialized vocabulary.

Teaching implications: See the suggestion in this table under "Social Studies." Also, have students in your remedial class keep a vocabulary notebook of content-related words, divided by topics such as science or social studies. The reading teacher can obtain textbooks from regular classroom teachers and help students select words from upcoming lessons to discuss, list, briefly define, and (when appropriate) illustrate words in this notebook.

2. Broad, abstract concepts.

Teaching implications: Writers of science texts sometimes incorrectly assume students have more background information than they do. In addition, abstract ideas often are presented without sufficient concrete examples. Alert the classroom teachers to these problems and suggest that films and other audiovisuals be used to supplement existing background knowledge and provide actual, specific instances of generalized topics.

3. Density.

Teaching implications: Science material is noted for its density—more facts line for line than in other texts. Since comprehension requires understanding of the most important statement as well as each idea that supports this statement, teach poor readers how to prepare simple outlines after reading.

4. Explanations of technical processes (e.g., the workings of an internal combustion engine are explained).

Teaching implications: Students should be told that technical information must be read slowly. (Reading rates used for story-type reading are definitely not appropriate.) Since these texts often have diagrams, help students develop the habit of studying these diagrams before, during, and after reading the explanatory passage.

5. Cause and effect patterns.

Teaching implications: This pattern, found most often in social studies texts, is also found in science material. Again, use the suggestions found in this table under "Social Studies." Working *with* students to help them conduct experiments suggested in science books not only concretely illustrates cause/effect relationships but also gives practice in following directions, a skill needed for science reading.

6. Classification.

Teaching implications: This writing pattern categorizes information, such as dividing animals into mammals, birds, amphibians, etc. Teach students the concept of categorization; that is, how some ideas or facts can be subgroups of others. Outlining is also helpful.

Table 18–1 (Continued)
Content area texts: Characteristics and teaching implications

Mathe-matics	1. Specialized vocabulary.

Teaching implications: Specialized vocabulary is a characteristic of all three types of texts discussed. The most prevalent difficulty for poor readers within all content areas is that of dealing with difficult or unusual vocabulary. In math, however, the vocabulary is even more specialized. How often, for example, do students use words such as *minuend* and *subtrahend* in their everyday oral language, or find such words in anything else they read? Context clues don't help much in identifying vocabulary in math texts. All of this implies that direct teaching of mathematics vocabulary is needed, in terms of both word identification and meaning. If the classroom teacher does not do this, the reading teacher can assume this responsibility.

2. Symbols and abbreviations.

Teaching implications: Disabled readers must be taught to read symbols and abbreviations embedded in text. For example, "Solve this problem: $3 + 4 = \Delta$" is read, "Solve this problem: Three *plus* four *equals what;*" "3% of $39.14 is _____" is read, "Three *percent* of thirty-nine *dollars and* fourteen *cents* is *what;*" and "$A = \pi r^2$" is read, *"The area equals pi times the radius squared."* In addition, abbreviations such as *in., ft., rd.,* and *yd.* must be read in problems such as "How many feet of fencing are needed to enclose a garden that is 48 ft. 3 in. long and 28 ft. 7 in. wide?" or, "What is the perimeter of a rectangle having the following dimensions: Length $= 236$ rd., width $= 87$ rd.?" While these reading tasks may seem quite obvious to most, for students who think reading is what they do in the basal reader, such tasks may be quite difficult.

3. Density.

Teaching implications: Like science texts, math material is characterized by density. Readers cannot skip unknown words and still obtain meaning, as is often possible with narrative writing. In addition, the reading rate must be slow.

4. Unusual writing style.

Teaching implications: Vos (cited in Ferguson & Fairburn, 1985) suggested that one language-related factor affecting performance on math story problems (sometimes called *thought* or *word* problems) is that their writing styles are different from other prose. He pointed out that story problems lack the continuity of ideas from paragraph to paragraph found in other writing. Practice can be given to familiarize students with this writing style. In Botel and Wirtz's research (cited in Kahn & Wirtz, 1982), students who practiced making up their own story problems did significantly better on these types of math applications than did those who lacked such practice.

(*Source:* Compiled from information in Smith, 1967; Santeusanio, 1983; Piercey, 1976; Kahn & Wirtz, 1982; Ferguson & Fairburn, 1985; and McCormick, unpublished materials.)

Box 18–1
Basic Skills Needed for College

I. English/Language Arts Instruction
   A. Reading
      1. vocabulary development
      2. comprehension
      3. speed reading
      4. survey of literature/drama
      5. reading for specific information
   B. Written Communication
      1. term papers
      2. themes
      3. grammar review and reinforcement
      4. survival skills related to writing
         a. resumes
         b. applications
         c. business letters
   C. Oral Communication
      1. public speaking
      2. oral reporting
II. Social Studies
   A. Current Events
      1. newspaper/newsmagazine information
      2. television/radio news
   B. Arts
      1. integration of art/music/literature
   C. Travel (including means of transportation, hotels, motels, reading schedules, ticketing, credit cards)
III. Clerical "Helps"
   A. Personal Typing

B. Notehand (A brief writing system based on shorthand. Included, too, is instruction in how to take notes on a reading and listening basis and how to organize notes for further reference. Even if it is not used as a complete program, it is still excellent for learning symbols for common words, abbreviations, etc., to expedite note taking.)
IV. Study Skills
   A. Library Use
      1. reference materials
      2. card catalogue
      3. use of periodicals
   B. Organizational Skills
      1. use of time
      2. organization of materials, resources
      3. structuring of activities (scheduling the day)
   C. Test Taking
      1. types of tests
      2. memory improvement
      3. note taking
      4. vocabulary related to test taking
V. Math
   A. Basic Processes
   B. Survival Skills
      1. checking accounts
      2. consumer mathematics
VI. Social Adjustment
   A. Values Clarification
   B. Coping Skills
   C. College Life

Source: Moorehead, S., Meeth, D., & Simpson, V. A Guide for College-Bound Learning Disabled Students [Child Service Demonstration Center, Title VI-G project, P.L. 91–230, OEC–0–74–8725]. Columbus, Ohio: Ohio State Department of Education, undated.)

scheduling sheet to allot responsibilities to each individual who will be working with a college-bound, reading disabled pupil.

Mangrum and Strichart (1984) make the following recommendations for working with learning disabled students who will be attending college:

1. Enroll these students in college preparatory courses (i.e., avoid placing them in courses that do not provide prerequisite information for college success).
2. Provide content area instruction by specialists.
3. Give assignments like those they will encounter in college (e.g., reading novels, writing research papers).
4. Teach them how to read textbooks (use of SQ3R is particularly recommended).
5. Show them how to use graphic aids (e.g., graphs, diagrams).
6. Teach students the major study skills.
7. Show them how to organize time and space for study.
8. Teach them to function independently.
9. Show students how to use auxiliary aids (e.g., using tapes to record lectures).
10. Teach them how to take the SAT or ACT tests.
11. Obtain help for them in functional writing skills.
12. Provide heavy attention to development of meaning vocabulary.
13. Continue to emphasize basic skills development (pp. 157–160).

Since a team effort is obviously needed to develop an adequate program, involve the school principal as the leader of this effort. The school guidance counselor is also an important team member, who can gather and provide information about colleges with special programs for learning and reading disa-

Some colleges make special provisions for bright reading disabled students, such as providing clinic services and tutoring.

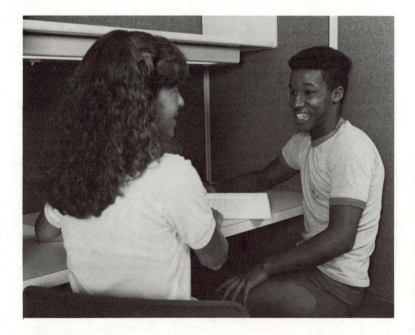

bled students (such as College of the Ozarks in Clarksville, Ark.; Johns Hopkins University in Baltimore, Md.; the University of Wisconsin at Oshkosh; Southern Illinois University at Carbondale; and Wright State University in Dayton, Oh.) Other colleges make special accommodations (such as providing clinics or learning centers that serve the college population, making provisions for oral rather than written exams, providing free tutoring services, and having reading rooms with tapes of textbooks). The guidance counselor can also lead discussions on coping skills related to pre-college and in-college experiences for reading disabled individuals.

Students with reading disabilities should not be denied the opportunity to realize their potentials. Recognize their existence; then initiate school-wide efforts to provide for their needs.

CONCLUDING STATEMENT

For *all* content area learning, some background experience about the topic is essential. If students lack this background, the reading teacher can help them (and their classroom teachers) by initiating opportunities for exposure to subject-area concepts. Articles on the subject can be used as a focus for working on literal or interpretive comprehension, and simultaneously help build background knowledge in the content area.

Many textbooks have been written about content area reading strategies for average readers. These and other similar texts can offer ideas for working with disabled readers. Also some instructional materials are available that are specifically designed for teaching students the strategies of content area reading. (See the Teachers' Store in Appendix C.)

UNIT SIX

Reading Instruction for Special Populations

19

Illiteracy and Functional Illiteracy in Older Youths and Adults

Catherine Gillie, Columbus, Ohio, wife of a judge, mother of four, part-time nurse, heard a radio commercial.

"It said seventy-seven thousand persons in central Ohio did not know how to read. I didn't believe there was anyone like that."

She and the judge took the four Saturday morning training sessions offered by the Columbus Literacy Council.

Mrs. Gillie: "Then I was assigned a student, and I called her. Her voice was so soft I could hardly hear her. It was obvious that I had awakened her, but when I said, 'I've been assigned to be your tutor,' a shriek of joy came over that telephone.

"She was so delighted. Several times before, she had tried to get help. Once she even telephoned the Columbus Board of Education to say she couldn't read, and the secretary there wouldn't believe her. Because of her use of language and the way she presented her ideas so well, the secretary was sure she was a college graduate playing a prank."

The student was Betty Elliott, something over thirty years old (she isn't sure because there are no records), who was orphaned at three weeks and taken to New York City by a woman who wanted her to help around the house. She remembers having to stand on a chair to wash dishes and diapers. Whenever the truant officer came around, the woman would say, "Don't bother with her; she's not right, you know."

Never a day in school and not able to read a word. She recalls: "I get surprised when I think back to when I had to memorize things and wasn't able to put them down on paper."

What she did was fake it a lot. She "wrote" her name—but actually she drew the letters. She made reports at the end of her night shift as a cottage mother at Franklin Village, a children's home, by calling a friend and telling her what she wanted to say. Slowly the friend would spell out the letters, and laboriously Betty would print them in capitals.

"I had no idea you could picture letters

because I didn't know what reading and writing were all about. Now I can close my eyes and see that a and b and you know, that's marvelous."

Mrs. Gillie would go to the Elliott home for lessons: "We both cried a great deal at the beginning. We spent many sessions with not too much time reading but with her telling about her life. Never before, she said, had any individual been personally interested in her. Many friends, because she's a very friendly person, but never anyone that interested."

Elliott: "People think if you can't read or write, you're stupid."

To cover up, she learned numbers. She counted on her fingers and found how to make change. She couldn't read labels at the grocery, but she knew how to shake the cans. If the contents rattled, they were peas. If the can was heavy, it was fruit. She even could tell pears from peaches without pictures.

Gillie: "It's fascinating, the extent to which people learn to cope and work around the printed word. It takes immeasurable use of energy and brainpower and time and money, but to a small extent, it can be done.

"After two months, I asked her whether she was able to see any difference at work or anywhere else because she could begin to read. Betty answered: 'I notice now that when I look in the mirror, I'm smiling.'"

Over about three years, there were some eighty tutoring sessions, ninety or so minutes each, sometimes twice a week, sometimes only once a month when both were very busy.

Elliott: "Another surprise, when you see on paper the word that you have been holding up here in your mind and rattling it around, then you see it there and begin to make some sense out of it. It's surprise; it's happiness.

"The first day I was able to do one word, one word as I have in my book, to know that I could spell it out; it stood out so much for me, just to know I could spell it and hear it. That was so neat, the way the sounds came together. I can see it; I can hear the letters."

(The word was s-p-y.)

Gillie: "She's such an intelligent person, with such compassion, such wisdom. She could write a psychology book about working with children. And she accomplished all this with no models. A very wise, very smart person."

Elliott: "If I could just tell it all, if people only knew exactly how I felt then and also bring it up to now, it would be some story. It would be like—like it's not the truth. I have all intentions some day to write that for others to know."

Gillie: "I've been involved in all the things you do as your children are growing up, and I've thought they were good causes, and you put your shoulder to the wheel, and that's fine.

"But this is different, seeing a whole world open up to one person who had been seeing the world through a long tube without much light at the end. That's the most exciting thing that can happen."

Betty Elliott's book: the one from which she read her very first word, The New Streamlined English Series: In the Valley.

Happy ending: She won a prize for reading the most books of any student in the literacy program her first year. (Sabine & Sabine, 1983, pp. 49–51.)

DEFINITIONS

This real-life story provides a poignant example of illiteracy and the effect it had on one life. An illiterate individual is one who lacks the ability to read and/or write, resulting from having had little or no instruction or from not having learned from instruction that has been provided. The term usually refers to older individuals rather than school-age pupils.

Functional illiterates, on the other hand, are older youths and adults who can read, but to such a limited extent that they cannot understand basic written information needed to function in adult daily life. They may, for example, be able to read primary-level stories, but be unable to cope with letters, traffic signs, writing found on packages, medicine bottle labels, bank statements, application forms, advertisements, bills, maps, telephone books, recipes, or newspapers. Job-related reading, which was found by Sharon (1973–74) to constitute a large part of all reading done by adults, offers another functional literacy problem. Literacy demands in some workplaces may actually be greater than those required in the daily reading of students in school. Mikulecky (1982) determined that pupils read less often in school than workers do on the job and that school reading involves easier material that can be read with less depth than that required of many workers. In addition, those jobs requiring few reading skills are diminishing in availability. The U.S. Department of Labor estimates a considerable decline in opportunities for farm workers, household help, and laborers, but a projected growth for clerical workers, managers, nonhousehold service workers, and technicians—occupations requiring a considerable degree of literacy (Mikulecky, 1984), and obviously not open to either illiterate or functionally illiterate persons. Probably because the effects are similar, a review of the literature reveals that the terms "illiterate" and "functional illiterate" are used interchangeably by many writers.

NUMBERS OF ILLITERATE AND FUNCTIONALLY ILLITERATE PERSONS IN THE UNITED STATES

Most estimates of illiterate and functionally illiterate persons in the United States range from 18 million to 31 million. An often-cited figure for functional illiterates is 23 million, based on the Adult Performance Level Assessment (Northcutt, 1975). Some estimates seem quite out of line with others, such as Fitzger-ald's (1984) figure of 64 million functionally illiterate adults. The exact number of these individuals is difficult to determine because the criteria on which statements about literacy are based have been different for various organizations and authorities.

Reading Level

Some definitions merely assume that there is a reading level one must attain to read everyday printed matter successfully, but opinions vary about just what this level is. It has been commonly reported as fifth-grade level (Smith 1977), fourth-grade level (Ahmann, 1975), sixth-grade level (Bureau of Census, 1971), and eighth-grade level (Miller, 1973). Fisher (1978) says that about 45 million adults in the U.S. score below eighth-grade level on reading tests. Obviously, if sixth or fifth or fourth grade were chosen as the reading level indicating adequate literacy, the number of illiterates or functional illiterates cited would be lower.

Grade Completed

An even more questionable criterion for defining literacy is the number of years of schooling completed by an individual. For example, in Canada literacy is assumed if a person has completed eighth grade (Rigg & Kazemek, 1985), and UNESCO believes that 4 years of schooling is the necessary requisite (Smith, 1977). However, as any reading teacher knows, the fact that students have completed a particular grade is not necessarily an indicator that they are reading at that grade level.

Skills Mastered

Others define literacy in terms of the ability to perform reading tasks related to real world experiences. Kirsch and Gutherie (1977–78), for example, say that functional literacy skills are those "required to realize outcomes with respect to job, transportation, and economic necessities" (p. 490). To determine just which skills these are, a number of studies have been conducted. The Adult Functional Reading Study (Murphy, 1973) surveyed individuals age 16 and older to develop categories of reading typically encountered by older youths and adults, and then prepared an "importance" index based on these. Most needed for understanding information were: a) reading accounting statements, forms, and invoices; b) reading letters, memos, and notes; c) reading newspapers; d) reading manuals and instructions at work; e) reading information while shopping; f) reading signs when traveling; and g) reading school assignments.

Another study, the Adult Performance Level Project (Northcutt, 1975), developed a two-way scale to examine competencies needed to function successfully both educationally and economically. The scale includes both content and skill areas. (See Figure 19–1.)

According to Northcutt, the degree to which one has skills in each of the scale's intersecting areas is a measure of competency for functional living. As can be seen, many—but not all—of these areas are directly related to literacy. The Adult Performance Level Project criteria are used in many literacy programs to plan instructional goals for clients.

Other studies to ascertain needs of adults in literacy education and to determine the extent to which U.S. citizens are functionally literate include the Survival Literacy Study (Harris, 1970) and the National Assessment of Educational Progress Mini-Assessment of Functional Literacy (NAEP, 1975). Most of these studies have made some contributions to our understanding, but most also have limitations in terms of defining the full or actual

		Content Areas			
		Occupational knowledge	Health	Community resources	Government and law
	Reading				
	Writing				
	Computation skills				
Skill	Problem-solving skills				
Areas	Speaking				
	Listening				
	Interpersonal relation skills				

Figure 19–1
A scale for measuring competency for functional living (*Source:* Based on the taxonomy developed in N. Northcutt [1975] and described in *Reading Research Quarterly, 13,* [1977–1978].)

Box 19–1

Functional Literacy Skills

1. Forms and Applications:
   a. Checks
   b. Bank forms
   c. Income tax forms
   d. Employment applications
   e. Charge account forms
   f. Social Security card application
   g. Apartment rental
   h. Change of address
   i. Unemployment insurance
   j. Voter-registration
   k. Library card
2. Advertisements:
   a. Classified ads—employment and other advertisements
   b. Specific products
3. Pictorial Materials (any information presented graphically):
   a. Maps—highway
            street
            area code
            weather
   b. Charts—bus, plane, and train schedules
            calorie chart
            employee information and pay grade chart
            tabulated results
   c. TV guide schedule

   d. Bills—bank statements, cash register receipts
   e. Road signs
4. Consumer Information and Directions:
   a. Nutritional information—products
   b. Washing instructions
   c. Medicine directions
   d. Cautions—dangerous products or conditions
   e. Directions—care of household appliances
   f. Recipes
   g. Warranties and guarantees
   h. Loan agreements
5. Information and Information Sources:
   a. Short newspaper articles
   b. Newspaper editorials
   c. Requirements—registration—voter, school, etc.
   d. Penalties
   e. Laws
   f. Constitution
   g. Policies
   h. Notices and announcements
   i. Information for driver's license, tax deductions, etc.
   j. Yellow pages
   k. Index
   l. Table of contents
   m. College catalog
   n. Dictionary

Source: From "Coping with minimal reading requirements: Suggestions for the reading teacher" by J. E. Readence and D. Moore, 1979, *Reading World,* 19 (2), pp. 139–148. Reprinted by permission.

---

spectrum of real-life reading tasks. Box 19–1 is a list of basic items for which reading is needed in everyday life.

TESTS TO DETERMINE LITERACY LEVELS

A number of tests have been developed to assess adult literacy. These are sometimes comprised of items similar to reading tasks required to function minimally in daily life. One such test is R/EAL (Reading/Everyday Activities in Life). R/EAL (Lichtman, 1974) is a criterion-referenced test which measures nine areas including reading applications, directions, and maps. The Adult Performance Level Program (American College Testing Program) is also an assessment program that focuses on basic tasks relevant to everyday living. Figure 19–2 is a sample item from one test used to assess functional literacy.

Two tests which assess more general lit-

> **Look at the instructions. Circle the statements that tell all the names you should get if you are involved in an accident.**
>
> What to Do at Time of Accident
>
> 1. Do not admit responsibility and make no statement regarding the accident except to the police or claims representatives.
> 2. Do not reveal the amount or limits of your liability coverage to anyone.
> 3. Obtain names and addresses of all occupants of other car involved.
> 4. Obtain names and addresses of all witnesses.
> 5. Report all accidents immediately.
> 6. Consult your claim representatives for complete claim reporting instructions.

Figure 19–2
A sample item from one test of functional literacy (*Source:*   From *Adult functional reading study* (PR 75–2) by R. T. Murphy, 1975, Princeton, NJ: Educational Testing Service. Reprinted by permission.)

eracy skills are the Adult Basic Learning Examination (Psychological Corporation) and Reading Evaluation: Adult Diagnosis, 2nd edition (Literacy Volunteers of America). The Adult Basic Learning Examination is a battery of tests to measure literacy skills and arithmetic. Reading Evaluation: Adult Diagnosis is designed for adults from nonreaders through fifth-grade reading level. The content of the latter test is written to appeal to adult maturity levels with three subtests: sight words, word analysis skills, and reading/listening inventory.

Reviews of adult literacy tests can be obtained from the Northwest Regional Educational Laboratory. These reviews supply information on measurement issues related to content, reliability, and validity of the tests.

SCHOOL BASED AND NONSCHOOL BASED PROGRAMS

Some reading teachers may be interested in working in school-based adult literacy programs. Others may wish to begin nonschool-based programs in their communities.

School-based programs designed to fight illiteracy and functional illiteracy, usually in the form of adult basic education (ABE) classes, are administered by local school systems, state departments of education, or other organizations. Classes may be held not only in public or private school buildings but also in other locations because of space availability or to lessen older students' adverse feelings about school. The *Journal of Reading* (Staff, 1985; Staff, 1984) has reported that about 2.3 million individuals were enrolled in these programs, with 42 percent of the participants being out-of-school older youths and adults ages 16–24. One-fifth of the clients were age 45 or over and the majority were female and white. Adult basic education programs have been authorized by the U.S. Adult Education Act, Public Law 91–230. Each year about 2 million more people are added to the number of functional illiterates in this country through refugee and immigration policies and through school dropouts. Considering these figures, the number of participants in these classes is strikingly few.

Although most *nonschool-based* literacy programs use paid staff, sometimes consisting

Reading teachers may be interested in working in school-based adult literacy programs; others may wish to begin nonschool-based programs in their communities.

of professionals with backgrounds in reading disabilities or learning disabilities, these programs rely heavily on volunteers. Clients enrolled in literacy programs usually consist of both illiterate and functionally illiterate persons, and tutors are required (professional or volunteer) who can work with reading, spelling, writing, and math. Individuals wishing to initiate such programs must take a number of administrative and instructional concerns into consideration.

Administrative Concerns

1. Can a *combined* staff of paid teachers and volunteers be used to coordinate and conduct the program?
2. What sources of funding are there for this literacy program?
3. Where can volunteers be obtained?
4. How should volunteers be assigned?
5. How should the program's budget (if any) be allotted and managed?
6. What types of publicity will help illiterate individuals learn of the services?
7. What types of publicity can be used for fund raising?

8. What types of administrative forms are needed?
9. What established programs can be contacted for advice on how to avoid stumbling blocks and growing pains?

Instructional Concerns

1. What types of training (both preservice and inservice) can be provided for teachers and volunteers?
2. What audiovisual materials are available for training workers?
3. What testing practices are best for adult learners?
4. Which teaching methods are best?
5. What reference materials can volunteers use for ideas for instruction?
6. What reading strategy sequence is most appropriate for each client's needs?
7. What types of lesson plans most facilitate the teaching sessions?
8. Where can low readability materials be obtained?
9. How can instructional materials be catalogued so they can be used to best advantage?

10. How can the public library help?
11. What special considerations (psychological, occupational, etc.) must be taken into account for adult learners?
12. What counseling services for older youths and adults are available in the community to supplement the literacy services you are providing?

Regardless of the type of program (school-based or nonschool-based), it is important for educators to realize that successful programs are *not* short term. Those that promise quick results simply raise false hopes that rapidly develop into frustrations and frequently program drop out. Promises of unrealistically rapid acquisition of literacy are fostered by uninformed literacy program workers, materials developers, and the media. Kazemek (1985) says, for example

> The 1984 television movie *The Pride of Jessee Hallam* depicted a man who went from being unable to read a single word to reading *The Old Man and the Sea* after 2 months of instruction. When such expectations are not immediately realized in their own lives adults often stop trying. (p. 333)

The most successful programs are gradual and long term.

Working with Illiterate Older Youths and Adults

Because of age, geographic isolation, unusual economic factors, immigration from an underdeveloped nation, or other reasons, illiterate older individuals have often been denied the intensive schooling enjoyed today by most youths in our society. When illiteracy results from limited educational experience, reading instruction at the acquisition or very early stages is called for.

Use of "organic primers" is one way to provide early-level reading instruction in a nonpatronizing manner to adults (Amoroso, 1985). *Organic primers* are collections of stories written by the teacher that reflect the experiences and concerns of the students in the literacy class. To prepare organic primers, teachers write simple stories, using natural language structures, about basic themes of adult interest such as marriage or job-related concerns. Each story is slightly longer than the preceding one. After students have been in the classes a few days, stories are prepared so they are based on discussions with that specific group of clients. To use the primers, the following steps are undertaken.

1. The story content is discussed prior to reading it.
2. The teacher reads the story aloud to the students.
3. The teacher and students read and reread the story in unison until students are able to read it alone.
4. Students read the story individually.
5. Practice activities are employed to ensure that word recognition will generalize to other reading materials and to emphasize meaning-related word identification strategies such as use of context clues.

This technique has some similarities to language immersion techniques described in Chapter 11, the chapter on the severely disabled reader. Amoroso (1985) points out that it has been used successfully in literacy programs in developing countries such as Brazil (Freire, 1973) and Nicaragua (Cardenal & Miller, 1981).

Others have used the language experience approach (LEA) in literacy programs because adults have a wealth of background experiences and often highly developed oral-language proficiency that can be capitalized on in story or passage dictations. A variation of the LEA (using microcomputers) has been employed in the Adult Literacy Project at the University of New Orleans (Wangberg, Thompson, & Levitov, 1984). After choosing a topic, adults in this program write their own stories on the computer, assisted by prompts programmed into it to encourage students to express their thoughts and refine their written text. After the computer lesson, the student takes the story to a teacher station for help in editing. The edited story is also entered into the microcomputer and a resulting printout displays the original story, the refined story, a list of words used by the student, and a set of follow-up activities. A composite list of words these adults have used most frequently when writing language experience stories on topics important to their lives is seen in Box 19–2. It was developed as a spelling reference since looking up spellings in a dictionary is an unwieldy process for students at beginning literacy levels (Wangberg, Thompson, & Levitov, 1984). Another helpful reference list for literacy programs is The Functional Reading Word List for Adults (Mitzel, 1966).

Kazemek (1985) and others have used song lyrics in adult reading programs, and poetry has also proved to be particularly motivating to many adult clients because such language forms often have less negative association than does typical school-type reading instructional material.

Reading strategies advocated throughout this book are appropriate for adult clients. *Materials* used with adults may be different in format (e.g., no child-like pictures) and content (e.g., passages at higher maturity and interest levels), but nonreaders must still learn to identify unknown words and comprehend the message. Many published instructional materials are currently available to use in literacy programs of this nature. (See Figure 19–3, for example.) These introduce word rec-

ognition and other basic reading strategies in formats suitable for the adult student. Some helpful programs, activities, and materials have been cited in previous chapters, others are listed in the Teachers' Store in Appendix C.

Working with Functionally Illiterate Older Youths and Adults

Functional literacy programs are appropriate for individuals who have mastered the rudiments of beginning reading strategies but who, because they are older, must be helped with reading tasks they encounter in their everyday environments—tasks that require decidedly more reading skill than they have attained. Functional literacy programs may also be more suitable than basic beginning reading programs if the individual has had years of traditional instruction with only limited success. These programs relate reading to its social uses. They emphasize direct instruction of the specific reading task that is needed.

An example of direct instruction of a specific functional literacy skill is shown in a program developed to teach reading disabled and mildly retarded students to read and complete job applications (Joynes, McCormick, & Heward, 1980; Heward, McCormick, and Joynes, 1980). As a preliminary step to this program, a Master Employment Application was developed by collecting real applications from employers who might hire functionally illiterate youths. The real applications were analyzed to determine what types of items occurred in what form. *Form* referred to instances where an item might be written in various ways on different applications, for example, "Social Security Number," "Soc. Sec. No.," or "Social Security #." The items occurring with highest frequency and the forms of these items most often seen on real applications were selected to be placed on the Master Employment Application used in the training program. The Master Employment Application is

Box 19–2
Adult Basic Word List

*a	care	*for	*it	name	sitting	too
*about	chance	forget	it's	need	skating	top
after	child	friend	job	needs	sky	trip
again	children	friends	joy	neighborhood	small	trouble
airplane	Christmas	from	July	neighbors	*so	true
*all	church	fun	just	never	soccer	try
alone	city	gave	keep	new	*some	two
along	close	G.E.D.	kind	next	someday	until
also	color	*get	*know	nice	someone	up
always	come	getting	ladies	night	something	us
*am	coming	girl	land	no	sometimes	used
an	cook	girls	last	not	song	vacation
*and	cooks	give	late	now	soon	very
any	could	*go	later	*of	special	wait
anything	country	God	learn	off	sports	*want
*are	daddy	*going	leave	old	start	wanted
around	dancing	*good	let	*on	stay	wants
as	*day	goodbye	life	*one	still	*was
ask	days	got	*like	only	stop	watch
at	dead	grade	likes	open	story	watching
away	did	great	little	or	study	water
baby	didn't	had	live	other	summer	way
back	dinner	happiness	long	our	Sunday	*we
bad	*do	happy	look	out	supper	week
ball	does	hard	looking	over	swimming	weekend
baseball	doesn't	has	Lord	own	take	well
basketball	dog	*have	lot	parents	talk	went
*be	doing	having	lots	party	talking	were
beach	*don't	*he	*love	people	teacher	*people
beat	down	head	made	person	team	when
beautiful	dream	heart	make	picnic	tell	where
*because	dreams	help	mama	plan	than	which
bed	drive	her	man	play	thanks	while
been	each	here	married	played	*that	white
before	easy	high	math	playing	that's	who
being	eat	him	may	pretty	*the	why
best	end	his	*me	put	their	*will
better	enjoy	hobbies	mean	reach	them	wish
Bible	enjoyed	hobby	meeting	read	then	*with
big	every	holiday	memories	reading	there	women
bike	everything	holidays	met	ready	these	won't
blue	family	home	mind	really	*they	words
boy	fast	*hope	miss	red	*thing	work
boyfriend	favor	hopes	money	relatives	things	working
bring	favorite	house	more	rich	think	world
brothers	feel	houses	morning	ride	thinking	worries
bus	feeling	how	most	right	this	worry
*but	few	hurt	mother	running	those	worst
buy	fire	husband	mother's	safe	three	*would
by	first	*I	mountain	said	*time	wouldn't
call	fishing	I'm	move	say	tired	write
came	flowers	if	mrs.	*school	*to	year
*can	flying	*in	much	see	today	years
can't	food	into	*my	*she	together	*you
car	football	*is	myself	sister	told	your

Words preceded by an asterisk (*) appeared 50 or more times. Words in boldface type appeared 10 or more times. All other words were used 5–9 times. (*Source:* From "First Steps Toward an Adult Basic Word List" by Elaine Wangberg, Bruce Thompson, and Justin Levitov, 1984 (December), *Journal of Reading,* pp. 246–247. Reprinted by permission of the authors and the International Reading Association.)

Figure 19–3
Published literacy
materials have
reading selections of
interest to adults.
(*Source:* From *Steck-
Vaughn Adult Reading
Program*—1300,
p. 11. Reprinted with
permission.)

IS SCHOOL FOR ME?

Should I go back to school? Mr. Night asked himself. That thought was always going through his mind. Why should I go back to school? What would other people think if I did? Am I too old to go back? Mr. Night asked himself these things over and over again.

One day Mr. Night had to face himself. He looked at himself a long time. He didn't like what he saw. Here I am now in the same place that I have been in for years, he thought. I have done nothing to better my mind. I must get back in school. I could get better work. Mr. Night knew he should go to a school for adults. He knew it well, but he didn't like the thought of it at all.

Direct attention to the picture. Have students predict what the story may be about. Read the title and the story while students read along silently.

seen in Figure 19–4. This job application was divided into four sections to teach students to read a few items at a time and to teach them to correctly fill in the requested information.

To ensure that all students had the opportunity to respond to all questions during instruction, every student had an overhead projector at his desk along with transparencies for answering

MASTER EMPLOYMENT APPLICATION

Please print

PERSONAL

Name	Last	First	Middle		Date
Date of Birth	Age	Social Security Number			Sex ☐ M ☐ F
Married ☐ Yes ☐ No	No. of Dependents	Weight		Height	

Are you a citizen of the U.S.? ☐ Yes ☐ No   Phone No.

Present Address   No.   Street   City   State   Zip Code

Previous Address   No.   Street   City   State   Zip Code

PHYSICAL

Do you have any physical disabilities? _____ If yes, describe.

Have you had any major illness in the past 5 years? _____
If yes, describe.

In case of an emergency, notify, Name _____   Address _____   Phone No. _____

EDUCATION

	Name of School	Attended From - To	Did you graduate?
Elementary			
High School			
College or University			
Other			
Other			

Do you plan to continue your education? _____

Last grade completed _____   Grade point average _____

Extracurricular activities _____

List any special office skills that you have. _____

EMPLOYMENT HISTORY

List below your last three employers:

Name and Address	Salary	Position	Date From - To
1.			
2.			
3.			

MILITARY

Have you ever served in the U.S. armed forces? ☐ Yes ☐ No

If yes, what branch? _____

Dates of Duty: From _____ To _____

Rank at Discharge _____

REFERENCES

List below three names of people not related to you, whom you have known at least one year.

Name	Address	Phone No.	Years Acquainted
1.			
2.			
3.			

Do you have any relatives in this company? _____

JOB PREFERENCE

Type of work desired _____

Date available _____   Hours available _____

Starting expected salary _____

Why do you want this job? _____

GENERAL INFORMATION

Have you committed any felonies or violations? _____
If yes, explain. _____

Are you a licensed driver? ☐ Yes ☐ No

List here any additional comments that you think are important to us in considering you for employment: _____

SIGNATURE

To the best of my knowledge the above statements are complete and are true. False statements may be cause for dismissal.

Date _____   Signature _____

Figure 19–4

Master employment application using terms that most often appear on actual application forms. (*Source:* From "Teaching Reading Disabled Students to Read and Complete Employment Applications," 1980 (May), *Journal of Reading,* pp. 712–713. Reprinted by permission of the International Reading Association.)

the teacher's questions. Their answers were projected on screens behind the pupils' desks so the teacher could give immediate corrective feedback. The instructional program required 11 class periods and had several steps.

1. The teacher showed individual items from the job application, pronounced each, and explained what each meant. Students found identical items in their sets of pre-printed transparencies and placed these on their overhead projectors so they showed on the screen.

2. The teacher showed an application item and students had to find a preprinted transparency showing the statements that would be used to fill in the required information.

3. The teacher showed an application item and students had to print the required information on a blank transparency.

4. Students filled in a transparency that depicted the entire master application.

Before the program, students were able to read and complete an average of 13 of the 35 items on the master application form. Afterward, correct reading and completion of items ranged from 29 to 35.

Abbass (1977) analyzed 50 commonly used forms and found that many of the words on them are not on high frequency word lists used in basic reading programs and that the readability of the forms ranged from 8.0 to above college level. When the NAEP Assessment of Functional Literacy examined the performances of 17-year-olds, they scored more poorly on the reading of forms than on any other area except reading reference material. Programs such as the one developed by Joynes, McCormick, and Heward (1980) for reading job applications can also be used to train functionally illiterate individuals to complete other types of forms requiring bio-graphic information, such as credit applications, Medicaid applications, and income tax forms. A circumventive strategy used with very low functioning individuals is to write basic information on the front and back sides of a small index card, such as the correct spellings of the individual's street address, the social security number, and so forth. The card is then laminated and carried in a billfold for aid in filling out forms.

Another direct instruction program was reported by Murph and McCormick (1985) when they taught low literacy clients to read road signs. Students were pretested on this task using the state driver's license manual. Signs that were unknown were placed in two groups. One of these groups was *worded signs* such as WRONG WAY or ROAD CONSTRUCTION AHEAD. The second group was comprised of *combination signs* on which pictorial information appeared along with words, such as SCHOOL CROSSING or MERGE LEFT. Students learned words on the signs using the following materials and procedures for *each* word on a sign.

1. *Use of cards with a single word printed on each:* The students were told the word, required to repeat it, and asked to use it orally in a sentence. If students could not use the word in a sentence, the teacher provided a sentence.

2. *Use of word strips on which the target word was printed along with two similar words:* Students selected the target word. If they were unable to do this, the teacher indicated the correct word and pointed out its distinguishing features.

3. *Use of sentence strips on which three different sentences were printed, each containing the same target word:* Students read all sentences. If unable to pronounce words other than the target word they were told these, then reread the sentence orally.

4. *Use of cardboard road signs:* Representations of signs constructed in the shape and color used in the students' home state were shown and students read each one orally.

Road signs were taught to students on a one-to-one basis and in sets of three; they were not allowed to move to the next set until they had performed all tasks correctly. No student was able to read any of the signs prior to the instructional program. After the program, all students read all signs correctly when post-tested with the driver's manual.

The major characteristic of the programs described here is that the necessary reading tasks were taught specifically and directly, rather than providing more generalized instruction, such as instruction in phonic analysis, for example. Direct instruction, use of mini-steps, careful sequencing of steps, and a moderately slow progression through those steps are important factors when teaching minimally literate individuals. Box 19–3 lists other functional words that could be taught in a similar manner. Adults want to learn the words that have practical meaning for their everyday lives.

The U.S. Armed Forces are using several computer programs to combat functional literacy problems within their ranks. These include programs for sentence construction, vocabulary learning, problem-solving, learning reading skills through job-related lessons, using the cloze procedure, study skills, and paragraph organization. Research on one series of computer programs used by the Navy indicates that reading skill increased about as much as with noncomputer programs, but in about half the time (Blanchard, 1984).

Ideas for teacher-made activities for functional literacy programs can be found in *Survival Learning Materials: Suggestions for Developing* (Strine Publishing). Some published materials suitable for functional literacy classes are listed in the Teachers' Store in Appendix C. (See Figure 19–5 for one example.)

One of the issues in the field of adult education is the debate about whether the "functional literacy" approach is too narrow, since literacy has a much broader scope than does reading for these specific kinds of tasks. The U.S. Armed Forces, in fact, have attempted two different approaches in their efforts with low literacy enlistees—one that deals with general literacy and the other with on-the-job literacy (Blanchard, 1984). They have found that students in general-reading programs retain 40 percent of the material learned, while those in the job-related literacy courses maintain 80 percent of their gains (Sticht, 1981).

The goals of functional literacy programs are necessarily to develop reading skills to deal with immediate tasks; once these goals have been realized, students can be encouraged to participate in wider literacy goals to improve their overall abilities to deal with all dimensions of reading experience.

Box 19–3

Twenty-five Words and Phrases Relating to Household Appliances

Switch	Instructions	Blade	Immerse	Filter
Turn	Avoid	Locked	Dial	Press button
High/low	Disconnect	Manual/automatic	Cord	Close door
Remove	Attachments	control	Plug	Empty
Caution	Left/right/rear/front	Temperature	Position	Fuses
		Cycle		

Figure 19–5
Literacy programs teach functional, as well as basic, reading skills. (*Source:* From *Steck-Vaughn Adult Reading Program*—2700, p. 66. Reprinted with permission.)

66   Schedules

This section of the book will help you learn to read schedules. Bus companies, railroads, and airlines all use schedules to show where they go and when. Schedules show a lot of information in a small area, so it is important to pay close attention to everything.

Study the schedule below. Then use it and the information in the questions to fill in the blanks.

Bus Schedule

CITIES	ARRIVALS and DEPARTURES	
Plains	Ar.	6:50a
	Lv.	7:00a
Largo	Ar.	7:32a
	Lv.	7:45a
Deton	Ar.	8:15a
	Lv.	8:30a
River City	Ar.	9:10a
	Lv.	9:25a

1. Some of the cities served by the bus company are given in a column on the left side of the schedule. What are they? ....

2. Look at the row for Largo. It is divided into two parts. The *Ar* means "arrive." the *Lv* means "leave." The *a* stands for "A.M.," or morning. At what time does the bus leave Largo? ....

3. Look at the row for River City. It shows the times of arrival and departure. The bus arrives at .... The bus leaves at ....

4. The bus from Plains to River City also stops in Largo and Deton. At what time does the bus arrive in Largo? ....

5. At what time does the bus arrive in Deton? ....

6. If you boarded the bus in Plains, at what time should you arrive in River City? ....

7. How long should the trip between Plains and Deton take?

....

**Sources of Information About
Established Literacy Programs**

Contact Literacy Center
P.O. Box 81826
Lincoln, NE 68501–1826

Literacy Volunteers of America, Inc.
404 Oak St.
Syracuse, NY 13203

CONCLUDING STATEMENT

The problems of illiteracy and functional illiteracy and issues surrounding these have become widely discussed topics among educators and lay persons. They are, indeed, topics about which all secondary teachers as well as reading and learning disabilities teachers at every level should be fully informed.

The harmful effects of nonliterate portions of our population on *society* as a whole are summarized in a report presented by Robert Orr and Harold Negley (cited in Fitzgerald, 1984) on the Indiana Adult Literacy Initiative.

At the national level, according to the National Coalition for Literacy, "functional literacy now exacts a measurable toll in crime, unemployment, poverty and human suffering. The national bill exceeds $225 billion annually for lost industrial productivity, unrealized tax revenues, remedial reading training in business and the military, and illiteracy related to crime and welfare cost." (p. 198)

The detrimental effects on the *individual* illiterate are well known; it is almost impossible in our society to lead a life of self-satisfaction and productivity if one cannot read.

Enrollment in adult literacy programs needs to be dramatically increased for society's welfare and the welfare of low literacy individuals.

20

Reading Instruction for Exceptional Children and Youth

Educators in the United States have always been concerned about the education of handicapped students, now commonly called exceptional children and youth. This concern has been heightened by the passage of a federal law, Public Law 94–142, The Education for All Handicapped Children Act.

P.L. 94–142 specifies that all handicapped children receive a free, appropriate education; all handicapped children and their parents have a right to due process to prevent abuses in carrying out this law; all handicapped children be educated in the least restrictive environment in which they can receive an *appropriate* education; an individualized education program (IEP) be written for each handicapped student specifying test results, instructional needs based on these results, and a plan for implementing instruction; parents be allowed to assist in educational decisions regarding their child; and all handicapped students receive a full and nondiscriminatory assessment before placement in a special education program.

P.L. 94–142 applies to individuals who are: mentally retarded, hard of hearing, deaf, speech impaired, visually handicapped, seriously emotionally disturbed, orthopedically impaired, deaf-blind, multihandicapped, learning disabled, and seriously health impaired.

This chapter discusses reading instruction for exceptional children and youth for several reasons. Because of the regulations related to education in the least restrictive environment, many special education students are now mainstreamed for part of their school day. *Mainstreaming* means that, when appropriate, special education students are to receive instruction in one or more subject areas in regular classrooms with other students. For certain subgroups of exceptional students, particularly learning disabled, educable mentally retarded (often called developmentally handicapped), and hearing handicapped students, a major educational problem is their difficulty with learning to read well. For another group of exceptional children and youth —visually handicapped students—although there are no major problems specifically related to their handicap that cause difficulties in learning to read, there are *teaching* adaptations which must be made. If any of these students are receiving reading instruction in regular classroom settings, teachers may require assistance from the reading teacher, as well as the special education teacher, to meet their needs. Treblas, McCormick, and Cooper (1982) point out that in these cases "the special educators' workload involves continued assistance, program planning, and evaluation of the mainstreamed student" (p. 17). Reading teachers can serve as strong support personnel for these efforts. Even if students with these handicapping conditions have reading classes within the special education room, because reading is a primary problem, the reading teacher and special education teacher may work together to solve some of the students' learning difficulties.

A second reason why this subject is pertinent pertains to the section of P.L. 94–142 that specifies development of an IEP for each handicapped student. (See Figure 20–1 for one example.) The IEP is a written plan that must provide specific information about the student's current level of functioning in all sub-areas of each academic subject area of concern. It must also relate the exact instructional plan for alleviating each area of weakness and furnish a timeline pinpointing when activities to meet these goals will be undertaken. The regulations of P.L. 94–142 require that the IEP be developed by a *team* of educators, including the individual who has tested the student, the student's present and future teachers, and any specialist whose knowledge would have a bearing on the case. Therefore, reading teachers may, and should, be included on the IEP committee for many students.

An additional reason for treating information about exceptional students is that many colleges and universities are now requiring prospective special education teachers to enroll in a course in remedial reading because of the high prevalence of reading problems among students they will teach.

Terms to describe subgroups of the total group of 11 handicapping types described in this section are the mildly handicapped population and the low incidence handicapped population. *Mildly handicapped* students are also labeled as learning disabled, educable mentally retarded, and emotionally disturbed (Heward, Cooper, Heron, Hill, McCormick, Porter, Stephens, & Sutherland, 1981); students with mild communication (speech) disorders are included in this group as well. The *low incidence handicapped* population comprises the more severe handicapping conditions, such as blind, deaf, or orthopedically handicapped students; they represent a lower *incidence,* or percentage, of the general population than do mildly handicapped individuals.

The remainder of this chapter will give teachers information and suggestions for working with those exceptional students for whom it is most likely that reading instruction will be a major concern.

MILDLY HANDICAPPED STUDENTS

While it is difficult to determine the exact number of individuals within each handicapped group, estimates of the number of mildly handicapped students within the general population are: learning disabled, 3 percent; educable mentally retarded, 3 percent; emotionally disturbed (sometimes referred to as *behaviorally disordered*), 2 percent; and speech impaired, 3.5 percent.

Learning Disabled Students

The learning disabilities (LD) field has its roots in the work of many groups of professionals dating back to the 19th century. A great impetus to the LD movement was derived from work conducted in an institution for the *mentally retarded* in the 1930s and 40s (e.g., Werner & Strauss, 1940). After a series of experi-

Part A: IEP

Yearly Class Schedule

Identification Information

Name __John Doe__
School __Beecher Sixth Grade Center__
Birthdate __5-15-73__ Grade __6__
Parents' Name __Mr. & Mrs. William Doe__
Address __1300 Johnson Street__
__Raleigh, N.C.__
Phone: Home __none__ Office __932-816__

Continuum of Services

	Hours Per Week
Regular class	20 hrs.
Resource teacher in regular classroom	6 hrs.
Resource room	
Reading specialist	
Speech/language therapist	4 hrs.
Counselor	
Special class	
Transition class	
Others:	

Yearly Class Schedule

	Time	Subject	Teacher
1st semester	8:30 - 9:20	math	Franks
	9:30 - 10:20	language arts	Bambara (Resource)
	10:30 - 11:20	social studies	Bambara
	11:20 - 12:20	science	Franks
		lunch	
	1:10 - 2:00	art	Shaw
	2:10 - 3:00	P.E.	King
2nd semester	8:30 - 9:20	math	Franks
	9:30 - 10:20	language arts	Bambara (Resource)
	10:30 - 11:20	social studies	Bambara
	11:30 - 12:20	science	Franks
		lunch	
	1:10 - 2:00	art	Shaw
	2:10 - 3:00	P.E.	King

Testing Information

Test Name	Date Admin.	Interpretation
PIAT	9-10-85	Spell - 1.7 Read comp. - 2A math - 5.7 gen. inf. - 6.3 read recog. 1.2 total - 2.0
tests of initial consonants (cat)	9-11-85	Knows 8 out of 21 initial consonant sounds
CAT		oral comprehension - 6th grade
Reading Checklist	9-12-85	reading skills - primary level
Oregon Diagnostic Reading Inventory	9-4-85	low ratios on probes of vowel & consonant sounds, irregular words and oral reading

Checklist

9-3-85	Referral by Louise Borden
9-6-85	Parents informed of rights; permission obtained for evaluation
9-17-85	Evaluation compiled
9-18-95	Parents contacted
9-19-95	Total committee meets and subcommittee assigned
9-26-85	IEP developed by subcommittee
9-27-85	IEP approved by total committee

Committee Members

Teacher __Mrs. Louise Borden__
Other LEA representative __Mrs. John Thomas__
Parents __Mrs. William Doe__
__Mrs. Mary Franks__
__Mrs. Joan Bambara__
__Mrs. Alice King__
Date IEP initially approved __9-27-85__

Health Information

Vision: __good__
Hearing: __excellent__
Physical: __good__
Other:

(continued)

Figure 20-1
A typical IEP form. (*Source:* From *Teaching Students with Learning Problems* (p. 16) by
C. D. Mercer and A. R. Mercer, 1985, Columbus, OH: Charles E. Merrill. Adapted from
Developing and Implementing Individualized Education Programs (pp. 18, 23-25) by A. P.
Turnbull, B. B. Strickland, and J. C. Brantley, 1978, Columbus, OH: Charles E. Merrill.
Copyright 1978 by Bell & Howell Company. Reprinted by permission.

Part B. I.: IEP (Complete for each subject area)

Student's Name __John Doe__   Subject Area __Reading__

Level of Performance __can identify 8 of 21 initial consonants & 1 of 5 short vowels__   Teacher __Mrs. Bambara – Resource Teacher__
__can identify few words at primer level.__
__can orally com./read stories from 6th grade books__

Annual Goals:
1. John will successfully complete the primer level of the Bank Street Reading Series.
2. John will recognize and correctly say 180 new sight words.
3. John will master 14 initial consonants and 4 short vowels.

	First Grading Period Sept.—Oct.	Second Grading Period Oct.—Nov.	Third Grading Period Nov.—Dec.	Fourth Grading Period Jan.—Feb.	Fifth Grading Period Feb.—Apr.	Sixth Grading Period Apr.—June
Objectives	Referred	1. Recognize and correctly state the sounds of the initial consonant phonemes "b," "f," "s," and "m" 100% of the time. 2. Recognize and correctly say 40 new sight words 100% of the time. 3. Complete the first six stories in the primer, reading at a rate of 90 words per minute correct.	1. Correctly recognize and state the sound of the initial consonant phonemes "h" and "g" 100% of the time. 2. Recognize and correctly say 10 new sight words 100% of the time. 3. Complete the next story in the primer, reading at a rate of 90 words per minute correct.	1. Review and correctly state the phonemes "b," "f," "s," "m," "g," "h," and short e 100% of the time. 2. Review and correctly recognize 50 previously learned sight words 100% of the time. 3. Recognize and correctly say 10 new sight words 100% of the time. 4. Review the previously read stories in the primer, reading at a rate of 90 words per minute correct.	1. Recognize and correctly state the phonemes "l," "d," "r," "w," short e, short i, and short u 100% of the time. 2. Recognize and correctly say 60 new sight words 100% of the time. 3. Complete the next 6 stories in the primer, reading at a rate of 90 words per minute correct.	1. Recognize and correctly state the phonemes "c," "t," "n," and "y" 100% of the time. 2. Recognize and correctly say 60 new sight words 100% of the time. 3. Complete the next 6 stories in the primer, reading at a rate of 90 words per minute correct. Evaluation
Evaluation-Agent		Resource teacher – 1,2 Regular classroom teacher 2,3 1. informal assessment, including probes 2. Criterion Referenced Test (CRT)	Resource teacher – 1,2 Regular classroom teacher – 2,3 1. informal assessment, including probes 2. CRT	Resource teacher – 1,2,3 Regular classroom teacher – 3,4 1. informal assessment, including probes 2. CRT	Resource teacher – 1,2 Regular classroom teacher– 2,3 1. informal assessment, including probes 2. CRT	Resource teacher – 1,2 Regular classroom teacher–2,3 1. informal assessment, including probes 2. CRT

Figure 20–1 (Continued)

Part B. II.: IEP (Complete for each subject area)

Student's Name _____ Subject Area _____

Level of Performance _____ Teacher _____

Annual Goals: 1. _____

2. _____

3. _____

Date Initiated	Objectives	Materials	Evaluation	Date Achieved	Person Responsible

399

ments, Strauss, a psychologist, and Werner, a neuropsychiatrist, noted that some retarded individuals appeared to have perceptual problems (although some did not). Some of these "perceptually handicapped" persons also had evidence of brain damage. The two researchers concluded that, even for those with no identifiable brain injury, brain damage could be presumed. They also noted that the brain-damaged clients showed characteristics of distractibility and motor dysfunction, such as awkwardness and hyperactivity. These findings, along with a study published earlier by Goldstein describing characteristics of brain damage in World War I veterans, led them to conclude that learning difficulties in some individuals were a consequence of brain injury resulting in perceptual-motor disabilities. A number of professionals working with Strauss and Werner, such as Kirk, Lehtinen, Kephart, and Cruickshank, began to test these theories and devise programs based on these hypotheses. What emerged were educational interventions that were prescribed for any children evidencing learning problems, whether they were diagnosed as brain-damaged or not. The programs emphasized training of the sensory-motor system to remedy academic difficulties. Goldstein's earlier work had also noted that brain-damaged soldiers often lost the ability for abstract thinking, which affected symbolic learning and caused language deficits. His ideas influenced the work of Myklebust, who advanced the premise that although there are verbal and nonverbal learning disabilities, those of importance to school learning result from language disorders. Myklebust also believed that these students have modality strengths and weaknesses. This latter idea further influenced Wepman, Kirk, and others to devise programs to match instructional activities with the presumed modality strength. Orton, Monroe, Fernald, and Gillingham, on the other hand, have disagreed with the premise of teaching to a preferred modality and

have contended that a multisensory approach is best in treating learning problems.

Along with supporting the notion of a preferred learning modality, Kirk (1962) also became the principal advocate of the psycholinguistic approach to remediating learning disabilities. The term *psycholinguistic* is used quite differently in this respect than it is currently used in the reading field; Kirk uses the term to refer to the ability to receive and express information and believes these skills must be taught before instituting programs for academic learning. Along with Winifred Kirk, he developed a controversial test, the Illinois Test of Psycholinguistic Abilities, to test these skills. Goldstein's earlier study also noted that his brain-damaged patients became upset by changes in daily routine and physical environment. This led to the emphasis in Cruickshank's early programs upon a highly structured environment when teaching LD students. Although historically there had always been a debate over whether a central nervous system disorder (or brain damage) was the root of learning problems, those who believed that it was had the greatest impact on early LD programming.

In the 1940s and 50s diverse professional groups introduced a number of special terms to describe individuals with learning difficulties. Psychologists, for example, described these students as *perceptually handicapped* and *emotionally labile;* members of the medical profession used the term *neurologically impaired;* and language specialists adopted a label dating back to the 1800s, *dyslexic.* Although sometimes still used, today these designations are considered questionable. Terms used prior to 1963 include brain-injured, childhood aphasics, children with cerebral dysfunctions, children with chronic brain dysfunctions, congenitally word-blind, developmentally dyslexic, dyslexic, disgraphic, minimally brain-damaged, children with minimal brain dysfunctions, minimally brain-injured, neurologically disordered, neurologically impaired, perceptually disabled, perceptually handicapped, children with perceptual-motor handicaps, psychoneurologically disabled, Strauss-syndrome children, and children with strephosymbolia.

To clear up the confusion caused by this myriad of labels, in 1963, at the Conference on Exploration into the Perceptually Handicapped Child, the term *learning disability* was proposed and soon adopted as a generic designation for all these categories. Although definitions of a learning disability vary, the description that appears with greatest consistency in current literature is

A disorder in one or more of the basic psychological processes which manifests itself in an imperfect ability to listen, think, speak, read, write, spell, or do mathematical calculations.

Since the term learning disability (LD) was first adopted, about three fourths of those served in LD programs have been students with moderate or severe reading problems. Although LD classroom and resource-room teachers may devote a portion of their class sessions to other learning difficulties, the majority of their time is spent in reading instruction.

As a result of the influence of the pioneers in the LD movement, instruction in LD classes was at one time based on a process-training philosophy (use of perceptual exercises, body management activities, and training of deficit processing functions). This approach was adopted because it was believed that LD students have intrinsic developmental dysfunctions that must be eliminated or improved *before* they could benefit from reading instruction (Kirk & Gallagher, 1979). Some programs used in the early days of the LD movement were Barsch's movigenic approach, the Delacato program, the Fitzhugh

visual-perceptual emphasis, the Frostig visual-perception program, Getman's visuomotor approach, the Kephart program, the Strauss-Lehtinen program, and the Cruickshank perceptual-motor approach. Because of a large body of research, conducted primarily in the 1970s, these types of programs are no longer favored by many professionals in the LD field.

Research that has Led to Changes in Programming for LD Students. Most of the programs described in the previous section are based on perceptual, motor, or a combination of perceptual and motor training tactics. It was not until after these programs were instituted in LD classes, however, that the efficacy of their training exercises was subjected to research. Goodman and Hammill (1973), for example, studied the Getman and Kephart approaches and reported that results showed them to be unrewarding: there was no evidence that perceptual or motor performance was improved, nor was change in academic achievement demonstrated. Hallahan and Kauffman (1978) also point out that the Kephart program was based on the hypothesis that motor development occurs before visual development, but that this hypothesis conflicts with the work of recent developmental psychologists. Research by Buckland (1970) and others on the Frostig program has failed to show that program's effectiveness for improving reading skill, and the Delacato program has produced no academic gains (Cohen, Birch, & Taft, 1970; Zigler & Seitz, 1975). General reviews of the research report that development of perceptual-motor skills is unnecessary for reading proficiency in learning disabled or reading disabled students (Balow, 1971; Hallahan & Cruickshank, 1973; Hammill, Goodman, & Wiederholt, 1974). Likewise, research on training students in auditory and visual processing skills, such as visual closure training or training of auditory sequential memory, as advocated by LD professionals with a "psycholinguistic" orientation, indicates that this training does not promote academic learning (Hammill & Larsen, 1974a).

Because it was once believed that distractibility was a syndrome found in all LD students, reduction of environmental stimulation was a common feature in past LD programs. Students worked in individual cubicles, windows were covered, and dull colors such as beige and gray were used in classrooms. Research on stimulus reduction, however, has shown that it has no effect on academic gains (Cruickshank, 1975; Sommervil, Warnberg, & Bost, 1973). In addition, the assumption that all LD students are distractible is incorrect (Cruse, 1961).

The notion that all LD students are neurologically impaired is also highly controversial, but even for those students who may have neurological problems, research indicates that the proposition that these students learn in some different and unusual manner is erroneous, and therefore, that nonacademically oriented learning tasks are not only unnecessary but unhelpful (Barnett, Ellis, & Pryor, 1960; Reed, Rabe, & Mankinen, 1970).

LD Programs Based on Current Research. The focus of reading instruction has shifted so that, in LD programs based on current research, assessment and instruction are identical to that found in any good remedial reading program. The point of view in these contemporary classrooms is that reading success depends on provision of appropriate learning experiences, not on altering students' developmental processes (Little, 1978). Kirk and Gallagher (1979), for example, now suggest these diagnostic steps for a student suspected of having a learning disability.

1. Determine whether the learning problem is specific, general, or spurious. (E.g., is the problem only in the area of reading? Are problems in general intelligence causing learning difficulties in all areas? Although suspected, is the learning problem actually nonexistent?)
2. Analyze the behavior manifestations descriptive of the specific problem. (E.g., which words are unknown? What word identification strategies are lacking?)
3. Determine possible physical, environmental, or psychological correlates. (E.g., are there hearing problems? Is school attendance poor? Are severe emotional disturbances interfering with academic progress?)

(paraphrased from pp. 305–308)

It is also now recognized that LD students' presumed reading difficulties are at times a result of a mismatch between the child's oral language and the written language of tests or texts (McCormick & Moe, 1982). Consequently, methods of assessment have changed; the Reading Miscue Inventory and other testing tools are now used to take into account natural language production and reading behaviors necessary in real reading situations. These are the same types of procedures outlined in this book for use with students designated as reading disabled.

After a review of research on learning disabilities, Little (1978), in "The Learning Disabled," pointed out two major generalizations: First, there is no single cause of learning disabilities, and second, remedial training of processes measured by psychometric tests may produce slight improvement of the processes as measured by these tests, but there is no transfer to reading ability. He says, "If you want a child to learn how to read, teach him *reading,* not visual or auditory exercises to improve processes that supposedly underlie reading" (p. 292). This view, of course, is entirely consistent with that held in effective remedial reading programs.

No special techniques are applicable to "learning disabled" students that are not also applicable to "reading disabled" students. All information and teaching strategies presented in this book pertain to those designated as learning disabled, if their learning disability involves problems with reading.

Educable Mentally Retarded (Developmentally Handicapped) Students

Levels of mental retardation are specified approximately as follows.

Level of Retardation	Intelligence Quotient
Mild	52–69
Moderate	36–51
Severe	20–35
Profound	19 or below

Mildly retarded students are those most often seen in public schools, but now because of P.L. 94–142, *moderately* retarded students are more often placed in some regular school settings; about one third of this latter group are children with Down's syndrome. P.L. 94–142 mandates that *severely and profoundly* retarded individuals also be provided with educational services, but because their training programs emphasize self-care skills rather than more typical academic learning, they are usually taught in other than public school settings.

Characteristics of Mildly Retarded Students in Relation to Reading Instruction. The overall reading performance of mildly retarded students is significantly lower than that of average readers. However, the differences in ability between these two groups are greater in the intermediate than the primary grades because of the more complex cognitive skills that necessarily come into play when students must read at higher levels.

Reading skills of the retarded should be examined from the perspective of mental age (MA). Retarded pupils have lower MAs than students of average intelligence at the same age. If retarded students are reading at levels commensurate with their own MAs then they are considered to be adequate readers; if not, their skill is considered inadequate. Another way to explain this is in relation to learning expectancy level (LEL); that is, reading disability is defined in relation to pupils' potentials, not their grade levels. From this perspective, educable mentally retarded (EMR) students may be reading below the grade level in which they would normally be placed, but they would still not be considered disabled readers if reading up to their own LELs.

Although reading difficulty is a recurring correlate of retardation, there is no single characteristic of EMR students that is the basis of all their reading deficits. Some learning characteristics of EMR students are similar to those of reading disabled students of average intelligence, but some are not. Although retarded individuals have a slower rate of language development, they nevertheless do progress through the same sequence as other children at early ages. At older ages, however, qualitative differences are also seen. EMR students generally do not reach what Piaget has called the stage of concrete operations until a later time than their intellectually average peers, and throughout life they may have difficulty with symbolic thought, imaginative concepts, critical and abstract thinking, and problem-solving (see Furth, 1970 and Piaget & Inhelder, 1973). Deficits in reading skill are generally related to this slower and less advanced language development, and to difficulties using complex rules and efficient processing skills for organizing and understanding information. Some mildly retarded pupils have problems attending to relevant stimuli in reading tasks and some may have short-term memory deficits, although differences in long-term memory of retarded versus nonretarded persons have not been found (Belmont, 1966). Formation of learning sets develops more slowly, rehearsal strategies are inadequately used to store important information, and transfer of learned information to new materials and situations presents a problem. Lack of motivation to learn is frequently apparent and is primarily linked to previous failure. Some of these deficiencies can be remediated.

Reading Instruction Programs for Mildly Retarded Students. Despite these difficulties, educable retarded students can learn. They can make progress with good instruction, although they generally progress more slowly than nonretarded pupils. In general, educators today are optimistic about the learning potential of retarded individuals. This optimism reflects a quite different point of view from attitudes in the past. Table 20–1 traces the history of treatment of retarded persons and shows the changes in attitude that have occurred. Certainly, today, it is believed that mildly retarded individuals can benefit from academic instruction and eventually become contributing members of society.

Reading ability is a basic foundation for leading this normal type of existence, and instruction in reading is of major concern to teachers of EMR pupils. Research consequently has been conducted with a variety of reading-instruction approaches to determine which might be most advantageous for EMR students. The effects of basal reading programs, the initial teaching alphabet (ITA), the language experience approach (LEA), use of programmed texts, stories printed with rebus pictures interspersed within the print, teaching machines, and the Words in Color program, for example, have been investigated (Dunn, Neville, Bailey, Pochanart, & Pfost, 1967; Haring, 1971; Woodcock & Dunn, 1967). As with programs for the nonretarded, research has shown that no one method is superior to another.

Like effective reading instruction for LD students, effective reading instruction for mildly retarded students is generally no different from that for other reading disabled individuals. Ideas presented throughout this book are valid for teaching the retarded, but some additional suggestions—which are often applicable to other reading disability cases, as well—follow here.

1. Help students organize written information so they can remember it more readily. Helping them organize can also aid language and cognitive strategies. When conducting reading instruction or constructing reading material, give students opportunities to classify, categorize, label, and match concepts. Ask questions that will require prediction and that will relate information to be read to students' background information.
2. Present tasks in smaller increments than those assigned to more capable pupils; assigning short stories, short exercises to be completed, and so forth, gives opportunity for success before attention falters.
3. Remember that meaningful material is easier to remember. Stories using natural language patterns and information

that *means* something are learned and retained better than small bits of fragmented information.

4. Work on students' selection skills. Draw attention to appropriate cues in reading; teach them how to select cues them-

Table 20–1
Historical Periods in the Treatment of Retarded Persons

Period	Social-Political Emphasis	Treatment of Retarded Persons
Antiquity to 1700 Neglect and Superstition	Varied considerably depending upon the specific historical period.	Characterized by neglect, superstition, harsh and cruel treatment. Little systematic attention given to retarded people. Occasional, infrequent humane attempts at providing care.
1700–1800 Awakening Scientific and Humanitarian Interest	Dominated by political and social idealism, with an optimistic view regarding the malleability of intelligence and the importance of assuring equality of people, freedom of thought, and democratic forms of government.	Focus on improvement of the situation of retarded persons with the hope that they could achieve normal functioning and integration into society. Generally small treatment programs located in community settings.
1880–1925 Era of Pessimism and Eugenic Alarms	Emphasis on application of genetic discoveries and the theory of evolution to understanding social issues; intense economic competition and industrial development. Assumption was that mental retardation resulted from genetic influences and that retarded persons represented a threat to society and social order.	Restrictive treatment with emphasis on protecting society from retarded persons (White and Wolfensberger, 1969). Sterilization laws, isolated institutions in remote areas, and other restrictive measures prevailed. Habilitation and community integration were given much less emphasis than during the preceding period.
1930–1965 Increased Responsibility by Government	Realization, largely resulting from the Depression, that government must assume some responsibility for the welfare of less advantaged persons.	Legislation and services expanded but often were based upon restrictive forms of treatment (e.g., special settings, remotely located institutions, large facilities).
1965–present Individual and Human Rights	Growing emphasis on the rights of individuals, along with development of treatment ideologies which deemphasize effects of labeling and provide treatment through generic services and alternative service models in settings that minimize the separateness of retarded from nonhandicapped persons.	Greatly expanded services, but under conditions of increased self-criticism and experimentation. Models of service stressing integration, individualized planning and treatment, advocacy, and accountability for decisions and programs.

(*Source:* From "The Mentally Retarded" by R. H. Bruininks & G. Warfield in *Exceptional Children and Youth: An Introduction* (pp. 189–190), ed. E. L. Meyen, 1978, Denver: Love Publishing. Reprinted by permission.)

selves. Retarded pupils usually do not develop these skills intuitively.

5. Information presented in a multisensory mode is helpful. Seeing, hearing, and tracing words calls students' attention to their distinguishing features.

6. Research has shown that mildly retarded students learn more words when teachers stress letter and language cues rather than shapes and configurations of words (Vandever & Neville, 1974a).

7. Help students train their rehearsal strategies. *Rehearsal strategies* help one remember something. For example, after looking up a telephone number, a rehearsal strategy you may use is to repeat the number to yourself mentally once or twice until you pick up the receiver and begin to dial. Most persons develop rehearsal strategies intuitively and use them automatically, but retarded individuals need to, in effect, learn the "tricks" for remembering that they have not developed themselves.

8. Mildly retarded students learn by doing. Concrete experiences and examples are more helpful than abstractions in the initial stages of learning.

9. Some retarded students, however, are capable of higher levels of thinking than was once believed if they are given opportunities to practice thinking skills. Belch (1974) studied questioning strategies with secondary-level EMR students. One group was asked no questions after reading; the second group was asked literal questions; and the third was asked higher level questions. At the end of the program, the third group performed best on a posttest of reading comprehension.

10. Using information frequently after it has been taught and using overlearning techniques (teaching of the same bit of information in a variety of ways) are im-

portant in good reading instruction programs for mildly retarded pupils.

Payne, Polloway, Smith, and Payne (1981) also advise reading teachers to reduce tension by instructing through games; praise frequently; diagnose continually to determine whether students have learned what has been taught; begin each session with a short activity related to something already known so students can experience success; use materials at the students' instructional or independent levels rather than frustration levels; use progress charts to visually demonstrate progress; involve parents in the child's learning; and give homework (if assigned) for practice (i.e., maintenance) of learned skills, not for initial learning.

Frequent review and overlearning techniques are important features in good reading programs for retarded students.

LOW INCIDENCE HANDICAPPED STUDENTS

Estimates of the number of low incidence handicapped individuals within the general population are: hearing impaired, 2 percent; severely visually impaired, 0.1 percent; orthopedically handicapped and other health impaired, 0.5 percent. In addition, although estimates differ, it is believed that a combined total of about 41,000 children in the deaf-blind and other multihandicapped categories exists in the United States today.

Hearing Handicapped Students[1]

Degree of hearing impairment varies. Students with hearing *losses within the normal range* in the better ear (25 decibels—dB—or less), those with a *slight loss* (26–40 dB), and those with a *mild loss* (41–55 dB) are more likely to be found in regular classrooms, either for all of the day or for part of the day as a result of mainstreaming practices. Those with *marked (56–70 dB)*, *severe* (71-90 dB), and *profound losses* (91 dB or more)[2] more often receive reading instruction in special classes or special schools. The following section presents information on typical characteristics of and instructional implications for those whose hearing loss is within the normal range and those who have a slight or mild loss. For these students there is a greater likelihood that regular classroom teachers and, when necessary, reading specialists will provide a reading program.

---

[1]This section was written with the assistance of Dr. Peter Paul, Assistant Professor in the teacher education program for the hearing handicapped at The Ohio State University.

[2]Decibels are discussed with respect to a standard. The numbers used here are based on ISO standards, *International Standards Organization*. A different set of numbers for decibels is used in relation to different sets of standards, for example, ASA, *American Standards Association*.

Reasons for Reading Difficulties. Students with hearing impairments often have deficits in learning to read. The severity of these difficulties is usually directly related to the *extent* of the hearing loss and can be attributed to one or a combination of factors.

Most children learn language by hearing it. Hearing-handicapped students have heard the language of others less, and less clearly. Hence they often do not have as complete a knowledge of the basic syntactic structures of language as normally hearing students.

Because they have been deprived of complete language input, they lack concepts expected of their normally hearing peers, and are, therefore, less able to acquire related concepts.

In previous reading instruction, hearing impaired students may have been taught by conventional methods that required the same sort of sensory processing expected of students without an impairment (e.g., auditory methods such as work with phonics as a word identification strategy).

Hearing impaired students are often deficient in understanding and producing complex sentences. Because they have not clearly heard the responses of others as they were developing their own sense of language structure and processes, their language may reflect short sentences, omissions of words, omissions of word endings, and atypical word order.

Hearing handicapped students have difficulty discriminating high frequency sounds (such as certain consonants) and words with minimal differences in sound (such as *sit/set*).

Because of delays in concept development, they also have difficulty understanding the idiomatic expressions found in many stories.

Hearing impaired students are often unable to learn as much from class discussions as other pupils and consequently have problems with concept development.

A weakness in knowledge of multiple meanings of words is often evident—again, resulting from delay in concept development.

Function words (e.g., *of, from, for, at,* etc.) and word endings (e.g., *-ed, -est, -ing,* etc.) are unaccented, and therefore are not heard clearly. Hence they are often misunderstood, and concepts they represent are not grasped (Degler & Risko, 1979).

Hearing impaired students may find it necessary to concentrate intensely to understand oral presentations in class; therefore, they become tired more quickly and often attend to lessons for only short periods of time.

Because of previous failure, they may be initially unmotivated to try, even when appropriate instruction is provided.

General Suggestions for Working with Hearing Impaired Students. A prerequisite to classroom learning for hearing impaired students is assigning them to advantageous seating so they will be in the best possible position to benefit from teacher presentations and class discussions. If the student has a hearing aid he should be required to wear it. When there is difficulty understanding directions, the teacher may model the task and then have the student follow through with the assignment. In addition, a quiet work atmosphere is imperative so that extraneous classroom noise does not interfere with the hearing impaired student's ability to understand instructionally relevant oral information.

Instruction should be organized so short periods of listening are interspersed with learning through other sensory modes (e.g., through the visual sense). Plans should also be made for time to engage in conversation on a one-to-one basis; peers and parent volunteers can help the teacher carry out this activity. This latter participation is important for improving oral language development.

Reading Instruction Suggestions for Hearing Impaired Students. Reading methods for hearing impaired students have many similarities to high quality instruction provided to other students. A basic tenet, however, is that techniques emphasize the visual as well as the auditory mode. While it is true that phonic analysis has been included in some programs for the hearing handicapped, the limitations of using only sound-based strategies for word identification are obvious.

King and Quigley (1985) have reviewed the limited amount of available research evidence and have concluded that no statement can presently be made regarding the best method of reading instruction for students with severe and profound hearing impairments. In addition, very little data exist on reading methods for students with lesser impairments. The language experience approach (LEA) is an appropriate method for initiating reading acquisition with normally-hearing students and can be employed with most hearing impaired students since the developmental strategies and stages of the two groups are essentially similar. In addition, since this approach uses the child's own language as the language of instruction, differences in language development of hearing handicapped children and their hearing age-mates are not a limiting factor.

It is also important to introduce new words in context so that students can use as much language information as possible. In addition to the aid to meaning that context provides for students with underdeveloped concepts, words and sounds in context are easier to discriminate auditorily than those in isolation. Students should also be required to use these new words orally in context. During initial instruction teachers should read aloud to hearing handicapped children since this may promote familiarity with the more complex syntactic structures of written language with which they will ultimately have to contend. After reading stories, teacher and students should discuss them. When the student is ready to move from the student-dictated material of the language experience approach, the teacher needs to select published materials that use language familiar to the child and avoid material with a high percentage of words for which there are undeveloped concepts.

Reading teachers need to undertake an intensive program of concept and vocabulary building. In the initial stages, they need to emphasize concrete experiences and words that describe these experiences. All students need prior concepts to relate to print in order to progress in reading, but because of limited concept development, activities that build background information are especially critical for hearing impaired students. Writing activities that develop knowledge of synonyms are also important since knowledge of multiple word meanings is a particular weakness of many hearing handicapped individuals.

Previews have been suggested elsewhere in this book for increasing comprehension (see Chapter 16). Graves, Cooke, and Laberge (1983) have shown that previews substantially increase the understanding of less skilled readers when they are reading either narrative or expository materials. Because previews are designed to enable students to share their background information

with each other, and because they allow teachers to present some preliminary information to provide a bridge to the material students will subsequently read, they provide important assistance for hearing impaired students.

Teachers should also keep in mind that hearing handicapped students' miscues should be evaluated; that is, a distinction should be made between meaningful and nonmeaningful miscues. Because there may be some differences in the oral language production of these students, oral reading miscues that do not affect meaning should be ignored. As with other students, hearing impaired students should also be given many opportunities to read whole stories silently without interruption so they can begin to internalize their own strategies for using contextual information to aid word identification and meaning.

Because oral language is the basis for reading written language, hearing impaired students should be taught to pay careful attention to spoken language. They should also be enrolled in an auditory training program (often provided by speech and hearing specialists in a school district) to increase their discrimination and recognition of sounds and words. A systematic program of listening and speaking activities should be incorporated into language arts instruction. Including sentence expansion and combining activities will also aid understanding in reading. Sentence expansion and combining should include both oral and written instruction. *Sentence expansion* means adding words to make a simple sentence more descriptive. For example,

> The man had a horse.
> The man had a brown horse.
> The old man had a brown horse.
> The old man had a small, brown horse.

Sentence combining produces longer, more complex sentences from several short ones.

> The boat was blue.
>
> The boat was a sailboat.
>
> The boat was on the bay.
>
> There was a storm.
>
> The blue sailboat was on the bay during a storm.

Both sentence expansion and sentence combining assist oral and written language production and understanding.

Degler and Risko (1979) suggest additional activities for increasing language competence, including choral reading, dramatization, composing stories, playing language games, using wordless picture books to tell stories, and using predictable books.

An important source of information for educators interested in further study of reading instruction for the hearing handicapped is the Language, Reading, and Deafness Collection. This is a recent series of over 3,000 microfiche documents compiled by leaders in the field and made available from the Alvina Treut Burrows Institute.[3] Check with your college library to see if these are available to you.

Although hearing impaired students come to school programs with a physical handicap that makes learning to read well a more difficult accomplishment than it is for many other students, teachers can provide appropriate instructional adaptations so that a mild or moderate hearing loss does not contribute to a reading disability.

Visually Handicapped Students

The term *visually handicapped* is the generic label to describe all children with severe vision

[3]Alvina Treut Burrows Institute, Inc.
Box 49
Manhasset, New York 11030

problems. *Blind* students are those with no useful vision, while students with *low vision* can perform visual tasks with some specialized aids.

Because of the current emphasis on mainstreaming, intervention programs have been conducted to prepare visually handicapped students for instruction in regular classrooms. These programs include instruction in areas directly related to coping with regular classroom placement despite one's handicap, and have dealt with development of residual vision, orientation and mobility, and social skills (Mosely, 1974). For preschool children there has also been an emphasis on readiness for reading. All of this presupposes that at some time during their school careers these students will obtain at least part of their instruction for reading in regular classroom settings.

Classroom teachers and reading teachers who lack training in working with the visually handicapped are often concerned about their competency to teach these students. Some differences in reading instruction for the visually impaired do exist, but there are also many similarities to teaching sighted students.

Visually handicapped students may be taught reading through the same approaches as those employed with other children. While individualized reading and techniques based on psycholinguistic research have been used to teach both blind and low vision students successfully, Nolan and Kederis (1969) report that the most common approach is use of basal readers. Kirk (1970) contends that because low vision "children must depend a great deal upon auditory perception, phonics are an indispensable aid to word recognition" (p. 199). Others, however, suggest that an LEA is especially advantageous for blind students because LEA allows these students to learn to read words that have meaning for them. This is not necessarily true in basal readers originally designed for sighted children since these employ descriptions and concepts outside of the blind child's experience (Curry, 1975). In addition, since these students do not differ from others in their control of oral language structures, LEA builds on one of their strengths. Although most reading approaches can be used with visually impaired students, some adaptations within the methods must be implemented.

Adaptations for Prior Information.   As has been repeatedly emphasized, background information is crucial to understanding printed text. Special consideration should be made for visually handicapped students in this regard because they have a more limited range of experiences from which to draw; colors, for example, are nonexistent concepts for blind children. Even low vision students—because they are unable to see things distinctly—do not have sharply defined understandings about some conceptual information. Cutsforth (1951) describes this as a problem of "verbal unreality." Curry (1975) points out that text descriptions of "clouds, stars, giraffes, mountains and the like [are] all things which are impossible or difficult to apprehend by touch alone" (p. 273). For this reason, Bleiberg (1970) has suggested that a specially designed reading series is needed for the blind. Teachers who provide verbal descriptions of activities when visually handicapped students are in their classrooms help greatly with this problem since hearing verbal descriptions will lead to more accurate interpretations. Focusing on the other senses (hearing, feeling, smelling, tasting) also allows visually handicapped students to use concepts they *have* developed. In addition, tactual examination of objects in the classroom or of objects associated with other learning experiences lets blind and low vision students link sounds and descriptions with shapes, textures, and sizes. For example, Ward and McCormick (1981) suggest that

On a class trip to the farm, while the other children may only look at and perhaps pat a baby pig, the visually handicapped children should be helped to feel the pig's body from snout to curly tail, all the while being provided with a verbal description and asked to describe in their own words what they are feeling and other animals that are similar or different. (p. 439)

Adaptations of Materials.   Materials must also be adapted. This does not, however, mean that reading teachers are responsible for preparing special materials; indeed, they may not have the skills to do so. Many large-print materials (for low vision students) and braille materials (for blind students) are readily available. Most basal reading books, many easy-to-read high interest materials, and many content area texts can be obtained free of charge from the American Printing House for the Blind.[4]

Certain specialized aids will allow some low vision students to read regular print materials. Magnifiers can be purchased which are hand held, attached to eye glasses, or set on a desk over the printed text.

For testing blind students there are special standardized tests such as the Stanford Achievement Test in Braille, intelligence tests such as the Perkins-Binet Tests of Intelligence for the Blind, and a Braille Informal Reading Inventory with test passages for reading levels primer through grade 9. Berger and Kautz (1967) describe the latter test and say that it may be used to assess comprehension, knowledge of braille contractions (common ways of spelling many English words in the braille code), students' use of their fingers to move to the next line, student skill in reading in a meaningful manner rather than word by word, and rate of reading.

---

[4]American Printing House for the Blind
1839 Frankfort Avenue
Louisville, Kentucky 40206

Adaptations in Instructional Techniques. For low vision children, most standard word identification strategies may be employed, but use of context clues should be stressed (as is true with sighted readers, also). A very slow reading pace is a problem for most low vision students; using context to predict unknown words increases their reading speed. Instructional procedures that combine sound with visual tasks are also helpful, such as use of tape recordings, records, and mechanical equipment like a Language Master (Bell & Howell).

Phonic and structural analysis as word identification strategies are only partially helpful for blind children because of the nature of the braille code. For example, short forms are used in braille, such as *immly* which stands for *immediately,* or *b* which stands for *but.* Asking a reader to "sound out" such a form or find known word parts would not make much sense (Ward & McCormick, 1981).

Adaptations in Expectations. Teachers may find it necessary to adjust the length of assignments for visually handicapped students because of low reading speeds. Adaptations in mode of presentation may also be required (a student may need to have a test read orally by the teacher or fellow pupil, for instance). But in all cases, the quality of the performance expected of these students should not be adjusted. Lowering of standards is not beneficial to the student and is also unnecessary.

CONCLUDING STATEMENT

Working with exceptional children and youth provides an interesting and exciting challenge for reading teachers. Success in these efforts is best obtained through cooperation with special education teachers. In this team approach, the reading teacher can contribute expertise about reading instruction, while the special education teacher can provide insights about specific problems and characteristics of the handicapped population for which there is concern.

21

Remedial Instruction for Students with Linguistic and Cultural Differences

Today's teacher often provides reading instruction to students from culturally and linguistically different backgrounds. These culturally different students include those who speak Standard English, those who speak nonstandard English, those who are bilingual, and those who do not speak English at all. Culturally different students can come from any socioeconomic background, but many of those who speak nonstandard English, who are bilingual, or who speak no English also come from low income homes. Some may have "true" remedial reading problems; others may read well in another language, but not in English.

Some students for whom there may be special linguistic and cultural considerations are rural, Black, Appalachian, migrant, native American (Indian and Eskimo), Hispanic (Puerto Rican, Cuban, Mexican-American), and new Asian immigrant (Vietnamese, Laotian, Cambodian) students. In addition, in Hawaii many different dialects may be found in single classrooms as well as a rich and diverse cultural heritage among the pupils. And there are, of course, other, smaller groups of foreign-born individuals who now make their homes in this country and who may require special attention from the reading teacher because of their linguistic and cultural backgrounds.

LINGUISTIC CONSIDERATIONS

Because reading is language-based, when reading problems have arisen among pupils whose linguistic patterns are different from those of students from the mainstream culture, it has often been suggested that the language differences may be at the root of the problem. In some cases this may be true, but in others it is not.

Nonstandard Dialects

Nonstandard dialects may be used by students whose only language is English and by bilingual students. Standard English is also a

413

Figure 21–1
Because of the multi-cultural nature of American society and the yearly influx of immigrants, migrant workers, and refugees, reading teachers often work with culturally and linguistically different students.

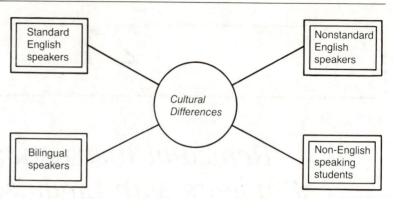

dialect, but since it is the dialect used by educated members of society it is the one valued by most Americans.

Variations in the *phonological* aspects of language production are heard quite often throughout this country (e.g., the differences in the pronunciation of certain vowels in the Southeast, Northeast, or Midwest may be referred to as a Southern "accent," Boston "accent," or Midwestern "accent"). Vocabulary (*semantic*) variations are also prevalent; for example, speakers from different parts of the country may refer to the same beverage as "pop," "soda," or "a soft drink." These variations are not considered renditions of nonstandard English, but rather, regional dialect variations. Although there are some semantic and sound considerations, a nonstandard English dialect is most often perceived in terms of *grammatical* variation. When a student drops or adds morphological units (e.g., "He land on his feets" as opposed to "He landed on his feet"), uses archaic language forms (e.g., the Elizabethan English *ain't* instead of the modern English *isn't,* and multiple negatives such as, "We *don't* have *no* more of them" instead of "We *don't* have *any* more of them"), or produces lack of subject-verb agreement ("Charles *like* it" instead of "Charles *likes* it"), the student is usually tagged as a nonstandard dialect speaker.

Most people have a positive attitude to-

ward regional dialect differences, viewing them as interesting products of our diverse heritage ("You say *to-mā-to,* I say *to-mah-to;*" "What a charming Southern accent she has."). But, many standard English speakers have decidedly negative feelings about the grammatical (and sometimes semantic and sound) variations of nonstandard American dialects, probably because these are frequently associated with low socioeconomic levels. The attitude is that these dialects should be changed (although this is considered unnecessary for regional dialect variations).

Pressure to adopt the standard dialect comes not only from speakers of standard English, but also from many nonstandard dialect speakers, for example, the parents in homes where a nonstandard dialect is spoken who believe an important role of the school is to teach their children the "standard" manner of speaking as a prerequisite to job attainment and upward social mobility. This attitude indicates dual goals for teachers in relation to the *oral* language of nonstandard dialect speakers: although one purpose may be to help these students add a second dialect (standard English) for social reasons, the second purpose—of more importance to reading teachers—is to understand how nonstandard dialect should be handled so it does not adversely affect reading achievement.

Much research has been conducted in

the area of nonstandard dialect production since the 1960s. What this research shows is that these dialects are viable language forms in their own right with their own rules and complexities, just as in the dialect known as standard English. They also communicate equally well. These dialects are not a deficient or substandard language form; they are only different. (See Box 21-1.)

There is no exact match between any oral dialect, including standard English, and the written language. Therefore, it is not surprising that research has also shown that the lack of an exact match between the language forms of nonstandard dialects and the printed language found in reading material does not affect reading achievement, if handled appropriately by the teacher. Attempts to change written materials to match students' dialect productions also have made no differences. For example, writing instructional materials such as basal readers in one or more of the various Black dialects used in this country failed to produce changes in reading ability of Black dialect-speaking students (and also caused waves of protest from Black parents who wanted their children's school exposure to language to be consistent with that of the mainstream culture.) Likewise, rewriting standardized reading tests in Black dialect has made no difference in scores obtained. Attempts to change the oral language of pupils to standard English have also failed to promote *reading* growth.

Nonstandard dialect speakers understand standard English even if they don't always produce it. They understand television. They understand their teachers and others who speak standard English. They can also understand printed English as can standard English speakers, even though there are differences between their respective printed language forms. In fact, when students orally read a printed form so that it conforms to their own oral language this is a clear indication

that they *do* understand the author's message. Doing this is referred to as a *dialect translation*. For example, if the text reads, "she isn't at home," and a rural Appalachian student reads, "she ain't at home," the student has had to understand the printed sentence to translate its meaning to the spoken form of her own oral language.

The major implication of research is that teachers must distinguish between language differences and reading errors. Research shows that teachers require students to correct meaningful miscues (those that do *not* affect the meaning gained from the page) more often when those miscues represent a dialect variation than when they do not. In these cases, teachers are confusing goals. In a language arts lesson designed to aid students in adding a second dialect to their language repertoires, discussing alternative ways to express meaning may be appropriate (e.g., pointing out that another way to make the statement is, "She *isn't* at home"). But in the case of reading, the nonstandard English performance does not affect the major purpose—getting meaning. When oral reading during instructional lessons and on tests is evaluated, dialect renditions must be assessed for what they are—simply variations of the most common dialect—and not as mistakes. Dialect alternatives are not reading errors.

Language Interference

Language interference is the phenomenon of sounds, syntax, and vocabulary of two languages intruding on each other as they come into contact in the learner's oral language learning and reading experiences. Some educators have suggested that language interference is detrimental to the reading growth of nonEnglish-speaking students as they learn a second language. This has also been suggested as a problem for nonstandard English speakers and bilingual students.

At the phonological (sound) level, Eng-

Box 21–1

Phonological and Grammatical Variations between Standard English and Certain Black Vernacular English Dialects

Sociolinguists generally suggest that there are more similarities than differences between Black English and standard English. Among the differences, some are more relevant to reading problems than others. The following have been found by Labov, Wolfram, and Shuy to be some of the phonological and grammatical interferences which may affect reading:

1. r-lessness. Black English has a rather high degree of r-lessness. The *r* becomes a schwa or simply disappears before vowels as well as before consonants or pauses: *r* is never pronounced in four, Paris becomes Pass, carrot becomes cat.

2. l-lessness. Dropping of the liquid *l* is similar to that of dropping *r* except that the former is often replaced by a back unrounded glide (u) instead of the center glide for *r*. Or the *l* disappears completely, especially after the backrounded vowels. Examples: help = hep, tool = too, all = awe, fault = fought.

3. Simplification of consonant clusters at the end of words. There is a general tendency to reduce end consonant clusters to single consonants, particularly those ending in /t/, /d/, /s/, or /z/. In approximate order of frequency, the /t,d/ clusters affected are -st, -ft, -nt, -nd, -ld, -zd, -md, thus generating homonyms such as past = pass, meant = men, rift = riff, mend = men, wind = wine, hold = hole. The /s,z/ cluster simplification results in these homonyms: six = sick, box = bock, Max = Mack, mix = mick. Labov found that the simplification of the /s,z/ clusters is much more characteristic of Black speakers than of White speakers.

4. Weakening of final consonants. This is another example of a general tendency to produce less information after stressed vowels, so that the endings of words (be they consonants, unstressed final vowels, or weak syllables) are devoiced or dropped entirely. Children who possess this characteristic seem to have the most serious reading problems. Most affected by this are the following: boot = boo, road = row, feed = feet, seat = seed = see, poor = poke = pope, bit = bid = big.

Labov and Wolfram, from their respective studies in Harlem and Detroit, contributed significant data on Black English grammatical rules which may be sources of reading problems.

5. Possessive deletion. The absence of /-s/ inflection results in: John's cousin = John cousin, whoever's book = whoever book. Deletion of /-r/ makes two possessive pronouns identical to personal pronouns: their book = they book, your = you = you-all.

6. Verb suffix. Labov believes that the third person singular was not present in Black English but imported from standard English in view of the low percentage of use (only 5-15 percent in some cases) and the sharp class stratification between middle and working classes. Some illustrations of the use of the verb suffix in Black English are: Somebody get hurts. He can goes out. He always bes on the beach mosta de time. All our men ares each on side. We goes to church on Sunday. Judy go to school today.

7. Be$_2$ form. There are two forms of "do" and two forms of "have" in English as in "Does he do it?" and "Has he had any?" In the first question, they could be called Do$_1$ and Do$_2$. The second form in each class is a normal main verb. *Be* has a main verb Be$_2$ which is like other main verbs. The meaning of Be$_2$ is so versatile that in some instances standard English has no equivalents:

   a) Habitual rather than a temporal or short occurrence. From now on, I don't be playing. He be sad. I be crying. She always be happy. Guys that bes with us.

   b) Repeated occurrence. Wolfram found between 11 to 16 percent of frequency adverbs with Be$_2$, such as hardly, usually, sometimes, always, mostly, all the time.

   c) Single nonrepeated activity in the future. This practice is used in all cases where *will* is possible or where an underlying *will* could be elicited in tag questions or in negatives:

Sometime he don't be busy. He be in in a few minutes. I know he will. Sometime he be busy. I know he do.

d) Deletion of "would." She just be talking, and I wouldn't listen. If he didn't have to go away, he be home.

8. Copulation. Copula deletion is considered basically a phonological process, but it also has strong grammatical constraints which are not random. Deletion may occur with verb following, no vowel preceding, but pronoun preceding. Semantically, deletion occurs most often on short active utterances: Riff eatin. He going. Ricky too old. Jim goin. She real tired. Carol chairman.

9. Person-number agreement.

a) In Black English, there is person-number agreement for I am, you are, and he is.

b) There is no third person singular marker, as in most languages around the world. The preferred forms are: He don't. He do. He have. *Does, has,* and *says* are used infrequently.

c) *Was* is the preferred form for past tense of *be.*

10. Past tense. Phonological conditioning weakens the regular past tense, as in the reduction of /t,d/ inflection: passed = pass, missed = miss, fined = fine, picked = pick, loaned = loan, raised = raise.

11. Negative forms and negation. A study of these forms should convince anyone that Black English has rules as other dialects do. In Black English, *ain't* is used as past negative; for example, I told im I ain't pull it; He didn't do nothing much, and I ain't neither. Adults used *didn't* more often than *ain't.* Preteens use *ain't* less often than teenagers. *Ain't* is a stigmatized form but has special social meaning to teenagers.

In negation, Black English seems to carry negative concord principles further than nonstandard Anglo English. Examples: Nobody had no bloody nose or nosebleed. I am no strong drinker. She didn't play with none of us. Down there nobody don't know about no club.

This brief summary concerning Black English is by no means complete but should give the classroom teacher an introduction to variations between Black English and standard English that may affect children's learning to read.

(*Source:* From *Reading and the Bilingual Child* by Doris Ching, 1976, pp. 15-17. Newark, DE: International Reading Association. Reprinted with permission of Doris Ching and the International Reading Association.)

---

lish sounds may be perceived in terms of the sound system of the pupil's first language or dialect. In Spanish, for example, there are only five variations in vowel sounds, while in English there are many. Therefore, a Spanish-speaking student may pronounce some English vowel sounds to make them sound like one of the vowel sounds of Spanish. Likewise, some Black vernacular dialects employ other sound substitutions (e.g, /d/ for initial /th/ as in *dem* instead of *them,* and /f/ for final /th/ as in *wreaf* instead of *wreath*). During *oral* English instruction it is appropriate to teach students to hear these differences, but the differences have little importance in understanding what is *read.* If a Black student reads, "Tiny Tim hung the Christmas *wreaf*" (instead of *wreath*), or a Chicano student reads, "Goldilocks tried to *set* [instead of *sit*] on Papa Bear's huge chair," these pronunciations do not change the author's intended meaning. If a teacher asks, "Did that make sense?" the student can rightfully say, "Yes." Teachers must maintain the attitude that there is more than one acceptable enunciation of a word. It is important, however, to be sensitive to the phonological differences in the student's primary language. This means that a heavily phonetic program of reading instruction is inappropriate. Even when a more moderate application of phonic analysis is used, certain activities of "sounding out" words, marking vowel sounds, or finding letters that sound alike may have no real application to word identification in relation to the pupil's oral language. Primary-grade reading tests that require these tasks also lack utility for students with linguistic differences.

At the syntactic level, nonEnglish-speaking students may face a special learning task as they attempt to gain control of English sentence structure because syntactic rules vary across languages. Spanish syntax, for example, is quite different from English. In addition, the order in which English syntactic and morphological rules become a part of the student's oral English varies according to the first language of the pupil and it often differs from the order of acquisition by native English speakers. Special attention to English syntactic form is often necessary in oral language instruction for nonEnglish-speaking students. Bilingual students may read more slowly in their weaker language because of the need to mentally reorganize syntactic forms to obtain their meanings (Kolers, 1966). However, when the second language is fully developed (i.e., is not weaker than the first) this finding does not hold true (Garcia, 1974).

Concerns of language interference at the semantic level are related to vocabulary. Bilingual speakers frequently intermingle English expressions with vocabulary from their primary language, resulting in polylinguistic expressions when *speaking* in either of their languages. Ziros (1976) gives the examples, *Vamos pa la dance* in which the English word *dance* was adopted into Spanish, and *Your mother is planching* in which the Spanish word *planchando,* which means *ironing,* was anglicized to fit into an English sentence. However, Garcia (1974) and Ziros point out that vocabulary switching in oral language

does not hamper students' cognitive activities and is not detrimental to reading growth.

Lack of Oral English

Current opinion about the best approach to reading instruction for nonEnglish-speaking students is that beginning instruction should occur in materials using the pupil's first language, while the second language is gradually introduced. This necessitates a teacher who is bilingual for that student's language. In some situations no such person is available in the regular school setting. Therefore, initial reading instruction in these cases will usually have to occur in the second language. In either case, introduction to reading in the second language may occur in two ways: a) after a year or so of oral language instruction, reading in that language is introduced, or b) learning of oral vocabulary and learning to read those words occur concurrently.

To develop *oral* English, teachers use concrete objects and pictures to teach vocabulary for nouns, and use role-playing to develop knowledge of action words. Games can be employed in which printed words are matched to pictures. Sentence scrambling and cloze activities are also helpful to assist students in gaining control of English syntax. In order to have good retention of new vocabulary and forms, these must be used frequently; some teachers use songs to promote retention. Teaching pupils songs and having them sing these every day provides repeated exposures to the second language. Richards (1975) suggests a step-by-step procedure for using singing as a route to second language learning. Puppets are helpful if young nonEnglish-speaking students are shy about practicing their new language learning. Tape recorders are useful with both younger and older pupils. Many states now have laws that make oral English instruction mandatory for non-English-speaking and bilingual students. For example, Alaska requires that any school system with eight or more pupils whose first language is not English must provide special language programs (Johnson, 1975).

The language experience approach has been widely adopted by teachers of English as a second language (ESL) to use when students are ready to make the switch from reading their first language to reading English. This approach is facilitative because student-dictated stories or informational passages reflect the oral vocabulary students have mastered. Moustafa and Penrose (1985) suggest that teachers prepare limited English-speaking students for a LEA lesson by adding new oral vocabulary and giving practice with sentence structure through discussions of pictures prior to each dictation. To do this, the teacher is to point to people, objects, places, and actions in the picture and ask that they be named. To reinforce the oral language development, questions about the pictures should be repeated so that students in the group produce names and answers to questions several times during the course of the lesson. To transfer these oral English words to print, key words about the picture are printed on cards and matched to that portion of the picture. Finally, students dictate information about the picture, and their statements are printed for a) the teacher to read *to* them; b) the teacher and pupils to read in unison; c) the pupils to read as a group without the teacher; and d) the pupils to read individually. Moustafa and Penrose found that LEA stories were longer and contained more appropriate English syntax when dictation was preceded by picture discussion.

It is also important to tie reading lessons to other language arts activities in order to reinforce new learning. After students have learned to read their own dictated stories successfully in English, then listening, reading, speaking, and writing may be developed simultaneously. Correlation of these language activities will support a smoother transition into the reading of published materials.

Some special considerations for teach-

ing reading to students who are only beginning to learn English, are the following.

- Take special care to explain English idioms. Confusions result from literal interpretation of phrases like *she came out smelling like a rose, he escaped by the skin of his teeth, he bit her head off,* or *she had a bitter pill to swallow.* When idioms such as these appear in published reading material, discuss them.
- After the common meanings of English words are learned, attention should be given to multiple meanings ("there are leaves under the tree"; "she put the leaves in the table").
- Homonyms may also cause problems (hair/hare; hole/whole). Explain the differences when they occur in oral language or reading instruction.

The Teachers' Store in Appendix C lists some materials that may be used with students when teaching reading through their first language and some for students who are in the stage where they are making a transition to reading in English.

CULTURAL CONSIDERATIONS

Considerations related to differences in cultural backgrounds of students that are relevant to reading instruction are diversities in value systems and differences in concept development based on experiences.

Value Systems

Mores[1] or value systems of individuals can affect how they learn best and how they perform in relation to school expectations. Earlier in this book studies were cited that showed that some Hawaiian children learned best when verbal interactions during reading lessons

---

[1]Mores (more–āz) are accepted traditional customs and beliefs of cultural groups.

were like those of their oral language traditions; that certain American Indian students participated in group activities more readily than in individual activities because of their value systems; and that some Spanish-surnamed pupils fall afoul of school expectations because of values about time, timidity, and cooperative action that differ from those of the mainstream culture.

Most schools promote value systems consistent with the middle-class American mores of hard work, delayed gratification, achievement orientation, and meeting one's responsibilities on time. These values contrast with those of some other cultures whose children are educated in American schools. Culturally instilled beliefs of some of these groups, for example, are to maintain the occupational positions of one's parents rather than to strive for higher socioeconomic status; to value anonymity rather than recognition; to experience the joys of life each day rather than work to experience them at some later time; to work for the good of the group rather than strive for individual attainment; and to adopt an unhurried approach to meeting commitments rather than a time-scheduled approach to punctuality and making every minute productive. Careful consideration of some of these values by harried, stress-ridden middle-class Americans should cause one to see the good sense of many of these points of view. But because these values are different from those of most professionals in the education system, problems can arise if teachers are insensitive to the traditions of the students they teach.

To help students have successful learning experiences, teachers need to respect differences in value systems, understand the specific values of the groups of students within an individual class, help students acculturate to mainstream values within the school setting when their own values are detrimental to learning, and adapt teaching proc-esses to the pupil's belief system when this facilitates learning. When attempting to adapt to pupils' cultural differences, teachers should remember that there are also differences among members of the same group or subgroup as well, for example, between urban and rural low socioeconomic status (SES) Blacks, or among different American Indian tribes, or among various Asiatic or Hispanic groups.

While they are selecting books for reading instruction with bilingual or bicultural students, teachers may also wish to select some books to introduce their mainstream-culture pupils to a realistic understanding of the culture of these classmates. Books can help pupils avoid misleading overgeneralizations and distorted views. Aoki (1981) suggests several criteria for book selection. First, books should realistically reflect the way of life of the cultural group represented and avoid stereotypes. Secondly, they should seek to rectify historical omissions and distortions. Finally, they should contain illustrations that accurately reflect the racial diversity of the group. (paraphrased from p. 384)

One helpful resource for the teacher selecting these types of books is *Reading for Young People: The Southwest* (American Library Association). This is an annotated bibliography of books for students in grades K–12 about the Anglo, Indian, and Spanish cultures of the American Southwest. A list of books recommended by the Asian American Children's Book Project Committee is shown in Box 21–2. Other annotated bibliographies of book titles for young people are *Shadow and Substance: Afro-American Experience in Contemporary Children's Fiction* (National Council of Teachers of English) and *Reading Ladders for Human Relations* (National Council of Teachers of English).

Concept Development

Knowledge of concepts and related word

Box 21–2
Good Asian American Children's Fiction

Aruego, Jose. *A Crocodile's Tale*. New York, N.Y.: Scribner's, 1972. (Primary)
Coutant, Helen, and Vo-Dinh. *First Snow*. New York, N.Y.: Knopf, 1974. (Primary)
Sone, Monica. *Nisei Daughter*. Boston, Mass.: Little, Brown, 1953. Seattle, Wash.: University of Washington Press, 1979. (Intermediate and up)
Uchida, Yoshiko. *Journey to Topaz*. New York, N.Y.: Scribner's, 1974. (Intermediate)
Uchida, Yoshiko. *The Rooster Who Understood Japanese*. New York, N.Y.: Scribner's, 1976. (Primary)
Uchida, Yoshiko. *Samurai of Gold Hill*. New York, N.Y.: Scribner's, 1972. (Intermediate)
Yashima, Taro. *Umbrella*. New York, N.Y.: Viking Press, 1958. (Primary)
Yep, Laurence. *Child of the Owl*. New York, N.Y.: Harper and Row, 1977. (Intermediate and up)
Yep, Laurence. *Dragonwings*. New York, N.Y.: Harper and Row, 1975. (Intermediate and up)
Yep, Laurence. *Sea Glass*. New York, N.Y.: Harper and Row, 1979. (Intermediate and up)

(*Source:* From "Are You Chinese? Are You Japanese? Or Are You Just a Mixed-Up Kid? Using Asian American Children's Literature" by Elaine Aoki, 1981, (January) *The Reading Teacher,* p. 384. Reprinted with permission of the author and the International Reading Association.)

---

meanings depends on both direct and vicarious experiences. When their experiences differ from those expected by the teacher, students may not understand concepts presumed to be commonly known. For culturally different students who have always lived in this country, television has certainly filled in some of the background gaps that might otherwise exist. Nevertheless, other subtleties, in differences of vocabulary and concept knowledge, often prevail. Pupils who have only recently moved to this country show even greater disparities between their vocabulary and background knowledge and that of the majority of students in their schools. This is not to say that either of these groups has a deficiency of experience. Indeed, they have rich backgrounds and vocabulary development specific to their own cultures that middle-class American pupils lack. But some of their concepts may be different. The list here illustrates selected concepts or vocabulary that are common to certain cultural/regional groups within this country but less familiar to others.

Concept/(Vocabulary) / Culture

chitterlings / Black or Caucasian southern rural
divan / eastern rural
egg cream / northeastern urban
hawk (not the bird) / Black
lava tube / Hawaiian
poke salad / Appalachian
pollo / southwestern Hispanic
salted soybeans / Hawaiian
scrapple / eastern rural
volunteer corn / rural

The teacher's task in dealing with these differences is fairly simple. During reading instruction the teacher should be alert to vocabulary and concepts that are based on experiences that may be unfamiliar to students who are not from the mainstream culture. The teacher should explain these, provide experiences, provide for wide reading, and furnish vocabulary development activities. At the same time he should capitalize on the vocabulary and concepts culturally different students bring to the classroom by including these in reading lessons and activities. This latter strategy also allows mainstream-culture students to broaden their horizons.

SPECIAL CONSIDERATIONS FOR STUDENTS FROM LOW SOCIOECONOMIC HOMES

Special considerations may be needed when providing remedial or clinical reading instruction for students from low socioeconomic status (SES) backgrounds because of a lack of intellectual stimulation found in some of their homes. In many cases, though not all, the parents themselves may have a low educational attainment and consequently neither model nor purposely expose their children to experiences that enhance school learning. Sometimes life styles appear to be disorganized in terms of middle-class perceptions, resulting in poor health habits and lack of self-discipline that can also adversely affect the child's education. Children from low SES homes may come to school with fewer of the advantages that promote rapid reading growth, and may lack helpful support throughout their school years. In many instances low SES parents care deeply about their children, but simply do not know the kinds of things they should be doing to enhance school achievement. In other cases the family may be unable to handle the child's educational needs because of other severe problems in their own lives.

Problems in low SES students' learning can also be caused by attitudes of educational personnel. Unfortunately, some teachers and administrators hold lower expectations for these pupils than for their middle- and upper-class counterparts. Low expectations lead to low achievement. In contrast, Durkin (1982) reported in a study of poor Black children who became successful readers that minority students from low-income homes were most likely to read at or above grade level when the school gave special attention to reading and math, and when it maintained high expectations for pupils.

Problems that May Originate from the Home Environment

A dual approach can be taken to help low-income students overcome limitations that have originated in the home environment: educate parents and compensate at school.

Parent Education. Some parents from low-income homes are willing participants in programs to learn how to help their children have school success. Some may wish to do so, but have difficulty adding this responsibility to the intricate mix of other duties and problems they must contend with; efforts can be made by school professionals to help this latter group of parents find at least limited ways to be of assistance. A few impoverished parents may be unreceptive to school suggestions.

Chapter 22 provides many ideas for eliciting parental involvement. Additionally, teachers may find it helpful to visit low SES parents in their homes and work with them individually. Providing low-income parents with information about home behaviors that have helped other disadvantaged children and telling parents about low SES children who are good readers helps establish a positive rapport. Parents need to know that successful students:

- are read aloud to by older brothers and sisters
- come from homes where discipline is evident, but fair
- come from homes rich in books
- come from organized homes
- have parents who are aware of local, national, and world events (and presumably

model an interest in these for their children)

- have parents who read a lot themselves
- have parents who show an interest in each of their children's needs and interests
- have parents who understand the value of education to their own lives and the lives of their children
(Durkin, 1966; Durkin, 1982; Greenberg & Davidson, 1972).

Compensation at School. Some myths have arisen about the causes for reading failure in low SES children. Teachers should be aware of these. For example, research has shown that factors unrelated to success or failure include absent fathers, the size of the family, attendance at many schools, a work-

ing mother (Greenberg & Davidson, 1972). Not only does the school lack control over these conditions, but the data point out that school attempts to compensate for home-originated limitations can concentrate directly on educationally-related variables. Some suggestions for compensating within the school setting follow.

1. Have a classroom rich in books. There should be many books, a wide variety of types, and books of high appeal, including fiction and nonfiction books that are easy, short, funny, colorful, scary, and so on. Ascertain students' interests and be sure there are books related to these.
2. Structure your program so that independent-activity time and free time

Reading to low SES students every day provides a good introduction to high quality literature and book language.

is spent in reading (or even just looking at) books.

3. Set up learning centers with listening stations so students can hear taped books read to them as they look at the books.

4. Take students to the school library regularly to check out books (even if the books are sometimes lost).

5. Help students acquire and own books. Use school or PTA/PTO funds to purchase inexpensive books and give them to pupils.

6. Have magazines in your room intended for both young people and adults. Bring in your own discarded magazines and give them to students to take home.

7. During sustained silent reading (SSR), read so students see an adult reading. Talk to students about books you loved as a child; have them available for your pupils to read. Tell them about books you are reading and enjoying now.

8. Read aloud to them—every day. Choose books of high quality children's or adolescent literature.

9. Have an organized classroom; have set procedures and no wasted time; let every minute of the school day include interesting intellectual stimulation.

10. Help students learn self-discipline and organize their tasks and time.

11. Try to understand students' problems, but remember that the kindest thing you can do for low SES students is to help them obtain a first-rate education. You do have control over what happens in your classroom and education is the business of schools.

12. If disruptive behavior occurs, be firm, consistent, and fair about refusing to accept those behaviors in an educational setting.

13. Ask successful individuals who have come from low-income backgrounds to talk to your students to provide inspiration and models.

14. Expand students' interests. Try to get them interested in things outside their own homes or neighborhoods.

15. Capitalize on the rich (although sometimes different) backgrounds these students bring to school. Use these as an impetus to read, write, share, and then compare with the experiences of others.

Problems that Originate at School

In discussing programs for low-income students, Durkin (1982) states that "children achieve what they are expected to achieve." Although teachers may find it necessary to provide compensatory and remedial activities for poverty students, their ultimate expectations for these pupils should equal those for others. A watered-down program or a willingness to adapt to a lower set of standards does an injustice to low SES children. Understanding cultural predilections and maintaining an appropriate attitude toward dialect differences can also provide a basis for learning so students rise to meet your expectations.

In schools where large numbers of students come from low-income homes, reading teachers can take a leadership role in assessing the school reading program and teachers' attitudes and background information. School-wide efforts to adopt a goal of high achievement for all, and to provide a careful, systematic, and rich reading program in every classroom have proven successful in low-income areas.

CONCLUDING STATEMENT

This chapter has discussed issues that are fundamental to working with students with ethnic, language, and social class differences. Remedial teachers must be as prepared to understand students' conceptions of language and culture as they are to understand the reading process. This necessitates a strong inclination on the part of the teacher to be concerned with the affective as well as academic nature of the learning environment.

UNIT SEVEN

Ancillary Roles for Reading Teachers

22

Enlisting Parental Involvement to Increase Reading Achievement

The parent-teacher partnership—how do you achieve it? Teachers who instruct remedial readers can use all the support they can get. Parents are ideal partners for working to accomplish the many tasks necessary for students to increase their reading proficiency. This chapter suggests tactics parents can execute effectively, as well as strategies for getting parents to work consistently with their children. One role of the reading teacher is working to establish this parent-teacher partnership.

SUGGESTIONS AND INFORMATION FOR PARENTS

Often when parents first learn their child is having difficulty with reading they attempt to alleviate the problem based on what they remember about their own reading instruction as a child or on commonly held notions about how one learns to read. Parents may have their child read aloud to them and make the child "sound out" each unknown word, make flashcards and drill the child on words in isolation, or purchase phonics workbooks. All too often these exercises lead to frustration for both parent and child. At this point, the parents may seek a teacher's advice, asking, "What can I do to help with my child's reading problem?" Teachers can offer a variety of useful suggestions to parents who want to help their children but don't know how.

"Read Aloud *to* Your Child"
The *best* way parents can help their children read is by reading aloud, every day if possible.

Reading aloud by the parent to the child provides a nonthreatening, easy-to-accomplish activity that introduces important print information to remedial readers. It also helps the student view reading as a pleasurable activity, increases attention span, and motivates the desire to read.

Because reading to their child is such a simple activity, parents are often skeptical about its value. For this reason, teachers should explain why they are asking parents to engage in read-aloud experiences. The research specifying the positive effects of this activity, which have been discussed in this book, should be cited in an understandable manner, and the need to read daily, even if briefly, should be stressed.

It is also helpful to suggest books and other materials that are good choices for reading, and to suggest places where these may be obtained easily. Since many books are expensive, the library is one obvious place for getting books free of charge. If parents are reluctant to use library services because returning books on time is inconvenient, tell them where they can buy books cheaply and easily (e.g., at the grocery or drug store). McCormick (1977a) found that syntactic complexity and vocabulary diversity in "grocery store" books were no different from those found in books that authorities recommended for reading aloud. "Grocery store" books are small, inexpensive books, such as "Little Golden Books,"[1] "Wonder Books,"[2] and other series found in grocery stores, drug stores, and discount stores. Though they may lack the literary merit of books considered the best in children's literature they can still acquaint students with syntactic patterns found in "book

language," broaden their vocabularies, and increase their knowledge of word meanings. Parents with low incomes and those unwilling to make trips to the library should be encouraged to buy these inexpensive, readily accessible books. Leland Jacobs (personal communication, September 26, 1975) states

> The "grocery store" book . . . has certainly served a purpose by making it possible for young children particularly to go home carrying a book while mother or father carries the cornflakes, soap, brown sugar, or liver. To *own* books is important.

You may also suggest that parents read material already in the home, such as comic strips in the newspaper. And, in addition, you can send home books from school to be read.

"Have Your Child Read Something Orally to Someone Every Day"

After getting parents to read aloud to their child each day, the next step is to encourage the student to read at home. Although hearing someone else read stories and informational material provides excellent support for learning vocabulary, concepts, and written language structures, remedial students also need to process an enormous amount of print themselves.

Oral reading is often the best way to initiate at-home reading because when students are reading aloud, parents can be sure reading is going on. Students who are simply told to go sit down and read a book may actually be daydreaming or merely looking at pictures. If they are by themselves, they may play or engage in any number of activities other than read. Oral reading makes it evident when students get off task. The sounds of their voices stop or they begin talking about something else—signals to the parent to prompt the resumption of the reading activity.

Material for the student to read at home should be short, easy, and highly appealing.

---

[1] "Little Golden Books" is a registered trademark of Western Publishing Co., Racine, Wis.

[2] "Wonder Books, Inc." is a division of Grosset & Dunlap, Inc., New York.

Remedial readers may be reluctant to read orally at home because reading is not easy for them and therefore not as interesting as many other at-home activities. In addition, parents may dismiss the oral reading suggestion because of their own busy lives: they wonder when they will find time to sit with their child to listen. Keeping the reading selection *short* will increase the likelihood that it will be read. Suggest that parents begin with 5 minutes a day and eventually increase this to 10. In the long run many parents and children sustain the activity for longer periods of time, once it becomes part of their established routines.

Encourage parents to allow the child to read *easy* material. When you send books home from school, remember to select those at the student's independent rather than instructional level. Oral reading at home should not be an onerous task. The intent is that students be exposed to many and varied language structures, that they internalize some word identification strategies, learn some new words from context, and gain confidence in their ability to handle print. Permitting students to do their at-home oral reading in easy material accomplishes all these purposes without the pressures of an instructional-level lesson. Because students are less likely to make errors in easy material, parents are less likely to become impatient and the lesson is less likely to disintegrate into tension and frustration between parent and child.

Students should also be encouraged to read *highly appealing* books during these oral reading sessions. *Good* children's and adolescent literature *is* highly appealing. Of course, the first choice is to expose students to fine books while they are sharpening their reading skills, but if students prefer reading magazines or newspapers or books on a topic of interest to them, they should be allowed to do so. The goal of reading aloud is to have students engage in these daily sessions eagerly, viewing them as a pleasant part of their day.

Teachers can pass along several other hints to parents for making at-home oral reading work. If parents say it is difficult to find time to listen to their child read, suggest that the child read to them while Mom or Dad works on another job. For example, Jim can pull a kitchen stool up to the sink as Mom is preparing dinner. His mother can listen and pause in her task to give a little assistance when she hears him fumbling with a word. Also, remind parents that children's minds are as important as their bodies. Few parents would say they were too busy to provide their children with food; point out that it is also important that they nourish their children's intellectual growth. Then too, an older brother or sister can also listen to a younger remedial reader during at-home oral reading. Or suggest that family members take turns. And, of course, encourage parents to be positive, to use praise, and to remain patient during these short sessions.

"Try Assisted Reading"

When oral at-home reading is initiated, parents should just listen and do what comes naturally as their child reads to them, as long as they can maintain a pleasant attitude throughout the activity. After oral reading has become an established habit, they may want suggestions for providing more active assistance to the student. Hoskisson, Sherman, and Smith (1974) suggest assisted reading as one way to help youngsters overcome reading difficulties through parent involvement.

Assisted reading is conducted differently according to the ability of the student. With severely disabled readers, parents read to the student, having the child read each sentence immediately afterward; in some cases the youngster reads each word after the parent, rather than a whole sentence. This is repeated until a whole book is read. After several books have been completed, students have often acquired a sight vocabulary large enough to read beginning books. Hoskisson et al. report that after one year of parent participation in assisted reading, one nonreader scored at a high second-grade level on a standardized test.

For somewhat better readers, assisted reading is easier for parents to conduct. The parents listen to their youngsters read, and *tell* them any word they do not know, then the children get on with their reading. Parents are asked to avoid criticism and to plan the oral reading time so that it will not interfere with other favored pastimes. They are also asked to deliver praise immediately after a good performance.

Before this easy parent procedure was conducted, students in the study by Hoskisson et al. (1974) expressed dislike for reading and were uncooperative during school reading instruction. After the 4-month study in which parents used assisted reading for 15 to 20 minutes three to five times each week, students self-corrected more miscues, made fewer meaningless miscues, made fewer miscues of all types, read more grammatically correct sentences, increased their reading rate, and scored higher on subtests of a standardized test that measured word recognition, paragraph meaning, and vocabulary. They also voluntarily checked out library books, participated willingly in reading classes, and no longer said they did not like to read.

Assisted reading is basically a language immersion technique. Although no specific help is given on word identification strategies, these strategies generalize somewhat from the large amount of connected text youngsters process. They actually read more words because they are not slowed down to figure out unknown words. Granted, some more-specialized instruction in word identification is necessary for times when students are reading independently, but this instruction can be accomplished at school. The assisted reading technique is effective in meeting some impor-

tant reading goals and is a simple means by which parents can be active participants in their child's learning.

"Engage the Whole Family in Sustained Silent Reading"

This suggestion is for parents who are really committed to doing all they can to help with their child's reading. While easy to carry out and fun to do once it is underway, getting everyone in a family to agree to participate in sustained silent reading (SSR) can tax parents' ingenuity and organizational skills. But it is worth it.

SSR at home is conducted in much the same way as at school. A specific time is set aside and *everyone* agrees to read. Be sure to explain to parents the critical factors: all family members read anything they wish to read, and the process must start slowly (5 minutes initially, with gradual increase to longer time spans).

No special knowledge of reading instruction techniques is needed for SSR at home. This fact makes it an ideal way for parents to provide reading benefits and enjoyment for their remedial reader. And since parents are reading, too, this demonstrates the value of reading and helps to develop good reading habits.

STRATEGIES FOR OBTAINING CONSISTENT PARENT HELP

Research has shown that sustained parent cooperation provides the favorable conditions that help schools do their jobs better. Contemporary schools advocate parent involvement, but encouragement is not enough. Parents' good intentions to supply a helping hand can go awry after initial enthusiasm has diminished and when other life requirements interfere. This section suggests ways to remedy the "parent drop-out" problem and to encourage a comprehensive parent role in the remedial student's reading education.

Establish a Communication System ①

If you and a parent have agreed on a task or two that the parent is to attempt at home, establish a communication system to ensure that these will be implemented. The communication system should serve as a prompt and reinforcer for both parent and child. Suppose, for example, that Mrs. Adkins has agreed to read aloud to her son Mark every night for 10 minutes after supper. The teacher can provide a form (like the one in Figure 22–1) that Mark delivers back and forth between the school and Mrs. Adkins. Mrs. Adkins writes in the date and the name of the book each evening and Mark returns it to school the next day. The teacher then uses the column at the right to deliver some sort of reinforcer. For example, she may place a sticker there, or draw a happy face, or simply mark it with a red check. The form can also be used to signal when it is time to send home more books. Similar communication systems can be adapted to the tasks parents are conducting.

Send Home a Newsletter ②

This should be done often and regularly. The newsletter does not have to be long. On the contrary, it is more likely to be read if it is not long. Nor does it have to be typed; parents may be more attentive to a handwritten message from their child's teacher than to a more formal, typed communication, especially if the teacher signs her name. A simple way to prepare a newsletter is to write out the message on a ditto master and reproduce copies for all students in the class.

If some children tend to lose school communications before they ever reach home, a space should be left on the newsletter for each child to draw a picture. Young students will take the newsletter to their parents so they can see the drawing. For older students, a place may be designated on the newsletter for parents to sign indicating that they have seen and read it.

What should be written in newsletters? Specific information about what the class is working on is helpful, but suggestions for at-home activities should be emphasized. A journal, *The Reading Teacher,* often includes a feature called, "Copy This for Parents." It is designed for just this purpose—to send information home. This can be combined with handwritten suggestions. A sample of such a newsletter is seen in Figure 22–2. Following are some suggestions for items to include in a newsletter; but don't send them all at once. Good ideas embedded in a long list are easily

Date	Name of Book Read	
3-15-87	*Amigo*	
3-16-87	*The Murder of Hound Dog Bates*	
3-17-87	*Emma's Dragon Hunt*	
3-18-87	*Alistair in Outer Space*	

Figure 22–1
A typical form for reinforcing parent-child activities at home

Dear Parents,   Dec. 6

For this week's newsletter I have copied some information for you that I found in a teachers' magazine. It has several good ideas in it, so I hope you will read it.

By the way, on Saturday I saw copies of a

Copy this for parents

Gerald A. Jennings, *Mars and Sylvester Elementary Schools, Berrien Springs, Michigan*

Adults can influence children's reading habits

Adults can help children learn to read by providing them with a home that is rich in books, words, and language. It doesn't take money to develop this kind of atmosphere, but it does take time and effort.

First, talk to your children about everything from sports to current events. Use new words, discuss their meanings, and play word games. Don't let words go by if you don't understand them; stop and ask for an explanation.

This interest in words will help children build a number of habits—reading to get the message so you can talk about it later, reading with a purpose, and reading without missing the meaning of a lot of words.

You also need to have books, newspapers, and magazines in your home. However, you don't have to buy reading material if you have a library near your home. Everyone in the family should check books out regularly, and then be sure to read them. You can read anywhere—under a tree, in the bathtub, on the floor, while waiting at the doctor's office. Having reading material around and then reading it goes a long way toward establishing good reading habits. Home has an enormous impact on how children do in school—make it a positive impact.

832   The Reading Teacher   April 1985

book at Wiedner's Drug Store that you might be interested in for reading aloud to your child if he/she is in the primary grades. It's the classic Little Red Hen story, and although it's quite inexpensive (79¢), the pictures are well done and the story nicely written.

                              Happy Reading! Mrs. Allen

Figure 22–2

Newsletters to parents can incorporate interesting and topical items from professional sources. (*Source:*   From "Copy This for Parents" by Gerald Jennings, from the Classroom Reading Teacher section of *The Reading Teacher,* April 1985 (p. 832). Reprinted with permission of the International Reading Association.)

forgotten. Send one each week. Suggest these to parents.

1. If children want to hear the same book more than once, *do* be willing to read it aloud repeatedly.
2. Read poetry to children. Help children learn to recite short poems from memory.
3. Facilitate interesting experiences. Take children on trips; go to fairs; visit sites of interest in the community; help them make or grow things; or talk about things in the immediate environment (e.g., birds or plants in your own yard). These experiences build background information, which in turn helps reading comprehension.
4. Write simple directions for making something. Have your child read the directions and then actually make the product.
5. Help your child count *all* the books in your home—children's books, adult books, everything. Try to increase the number and variety of books you own.
6. Help your child to obtain a library card. Use it regularly, together.
7. "Have you had your child's hearing and vision checked this year?" (Provide information on local resources.)
8. When you buy books or go to the library, select some books about things you know your child is already interested in. But, in addition, ask the librarian for recommendations, and occasionally select these books to extend your child's interests to new areas.
9. Subscribe to a magazine for children or teenagers. (Give parents the names of some of these, along with addresses for subscribing.)
10. Read the comic strips in your daily newspaper to your child; or role-play: you read one character's part, your child reads another.
11. Talk to your child. But do not limit this to

Parents should help children choose books that will extend their interests, as well as books on topics for which the child already shows an interest.

conversations about everyday matters. Ask provocative questions. Listen. Give interesting responses. Ask your child questions like these: Who would you rather be, President of the United States or an astronaut? Why? Suppose you had a magic carpet, where would you go? Why?
12. Help your child write a "book." Help send the story to a grandparent.
13. Write messages to your child for reading and writing a response back to you. See how long you can keep the messages going back and forth.
14. When you are driving, have your child read aloud as many passing signs and billboards as possible. Help with the reading of others.
15. At breakfast, help your child read the

sides of cereal boxes to you.

16. Cut a short article from a newspaper. Have your child circle words he knows. Help him learn three others from the same article.

17. Have your child read a recipe and help you prepare a dish.

18. Use reading materials you already have in your home, not only books, but magazines, junk mail, grocery ads, the telephone book, catalogs, and pamphlets as well. Use inexpensive materials and valuable junk to help your child read, read, read—all the time.

19. Use television to your child's advantage. Limit the number of viewing hours so there is time left for reading. Ask the school for a list of educational programs, then watch and discuss these with your child. Have your child read the TV program listings to you. Select books on topics identical to those of TV programs that interest your child. During commercials, ask your child to predict what will happen next (a good skill for reading comprehension).

20. Avoid comparing any child to siblings or peers. Each child is unique; although your child may be having reading problems at the present time, he undoubtedly has strengths that other children your child knows do not have. Make a list of your child's strengths and add to the list each time that you think of another one. (Does your child: have a lovely smile that brightens your day? excel in math? draw well? have patience with a younger brother or sister? try hard even though reading is difficult? help you around the house? have good mechanical skills?) At least once a week emphasize one of your child's strengths and compliment him in front of someone else.

Distribute Pamphlets, Booklets, and Book Lists; Recommend Books to Parents

Occasionally teachers may wish to supplement their newsletter by sending home *short* pamphlets, booklets, or book lists that are obtained free or inexpensively from a variety of educational organizations. A note about these materials within the newsletter urging parents to read them (and explaining why the ideas they provide are important for their children) is helpful. Sometimes parents will request more in-depth information about reading, and you can recommend a book to them. Listed in the Teachers' Store are several items that suggest ways parents can support reading at home using easily obtained materials and everyday activities.

Have a Make and Take Workshop for Parents

One type of inservice meeting popular with teachers is the *make-and-take workshop.* In these meetings teachers make materials they can use in their own classrooms. At the first session of the workshop the organizer presents ideas for instructional games and activities. In the second session, materials and equipment are made available, and teachers spend the entire meeting cutting, pasting, drawing, writing, typing, and so forth; and they leave with one or more finished products to use with their students.

Make-and-take workshops can be organized for parents as well. If parents are actively involved in preparing games and materials for their children, they will certainly use these at home to practice reading strategies. To conduct a parent make-and-take workshop, teachers should do the following.

1. List students by groups according to reading needs they have in common. For instance, one group may be students need-

ing practice with sight vocabulary, another may need work on simple literal-level comprehension. Students should also be grouped by age levels, for example, by placing primary children together, with intermediate students in another group.

2. Decide on one to three game-like activities that could be used to practice needed skills for each age group according to their needs.

3. Write out directions for preparing activities and gather materials necessary for making each one.

4. Invite parents to participate in the workshops by groups: all parents of intermediate students who need work on literal comprehension are invited to one session; all parents of primary children who need work on sight vocabulary are invited to another; and so on.

5. At the workshop, demonstrate how the games are made and used, tell how the activity can help students' reading, and have parents make one or more items during the session. Provide refreshments such as coffee, soft drinks, and light snacks. Keep the atmosphere informal so parents can chat as they cut, write, and prepare. Move among the group talking with them and helping with game preparation.

6. Be sure that parents make a commitment about how they will use the materials they have made. ("My husband and I will play this game with Becky until she knows the words." "I'll get Jeremy's older sister to play this with him.")

Few parents will expend the time and energy to make instructional materials and then fail to use them. A make-and-take workshop is one more way to obtain parental help.

Help Parents Understand Test Results

Learning that their child is not performing as well as others in reading is stressful to parents. Interpreting test results, putting scores in perspective, pointing out the positive value of tests (to provide guidance regarding areas where the child can be helped), and emphasizing gains over past performances are important.

Some teachers hold small-group parent meetings to describe tests used in their programs, to explain the purpose of each test, and to make the results intelligible. This can also be accomplished in individual parent conferences.

When test results are merely sent home to parents without explanation, they often fail to understand, or they misunderstand, information the tests convey. Better reporting will improve parents' attitudes and willingness to assist with the problems indicated by the tests. Dreher and Singer (1985) surveyed parents to determine the type of test report they preferred after their child had taken a standardized test. Most preferred was a report that gave norm comparisons, self-comparisons, and a sample of the most difficult item their child had passed. *Norm comparisons,* of course, report in terms of percentiles or grade scores how a given child fares in comparison with others. *Self-comparisons* show how the child improved from the previous test. A sample of the *most difficult item passed* also gives parents a clearer picture of what their child can do. Dreher and Singer suggest that since preparing such a report for each child is time consuming, the school district's computer could be programmed to generate the reports.

CONCLUDING STATEMENT

The home environment during preschool years influences later classroom learning.

Likewise, the amount of teacher-parent contact has been shown to correlate with the extent to which underachievers are able to make gains in reading ability during their school years. Reading teachers, then, should expand their roles to include more than the provision of instruction in their own classrooms. They should also contact, communicate to, and work with parents to increase reading growth of remedial students.

23

The Reading Teacher as Consultant

In addition to working directly with students, reading teachers often serve as resource persons to other teachers who need help planning and implementing exemplary instructional programs in reading that improve the learning climate for *all* pupils. Reading teachers provide support to strengthen programs for average readers so they do not develop reading problems because of an inadequate curriculum or faulty teaching strategies. Reading teachers can also provide suggestions for corrective reading instruction for pupils who have mild reading difficulties and who usually receive the additional needed instruction within the regular classroom setting. Finally, reading teachers help classroom teachers coordinate the reading programs of students with moderate or severe reading problems with their remedial class or clinical reading programs.

Heron and Harris (1982) distinguish between developmental consultation and problem-centered consultation. *Developmental consultation* focuses on long range goals,

while *problem-centered consultation* is aimed at solving specific and immediate problems. A trend exists today for the reading teacher to devote a portion of his day to both of these roles. This trend is supported by many reading authorities (e.g., Bean & Eichelberger, 1985). In schools where the roles have not been formally defined, reading teachers frequently undertake this responsibility in informal ways.

Wylie (1969) surveyed both classroom teachers and reading teachers to determine the types of assistance preferred when a reading teacher serves as a consultant. Table 23–1 indicates the percentage of teachers who said they valued various types of assistance. Although there are some similarities between what classroom teachers and reading teachers thought was helpful, it is important to note that there are also differences. In Adams' (1964) study, 90 percent of classroom teachers expressed a need to know more about corrective or remedial reading techniques.

Teachers in Wylie's (1969) study liked reading consultants who had in-depth knowl-

Table 23–1
Comparison of classroom teachers' and reading teachers' views on ways the reading teacher can assist when serving in a consultant's role

Teacher	Percent	Consultant	Percent
Materials	85	Materials	86
Demonstrations	81	Time allotments	81
Diagnostic & corrective procedures	81	Grouping	76
		Scope of total program	75
Grouping	74	Interpretation of test results	75
Interpretation of test results	73		
Inservice education; small groups, grade level meetings	94	Inservice education; grade level meetings	94
Demonstration teaching	90	Orientation program early in year	88
Free time to visit other classrooms—schools	86	Bulletins or letters to teachers	83
Frequent meetings with reading specialists	79	Suggestions of courses to take	73
Workshops	56	Workshops	60
Materials to vary program	96	Show new materials, devices and games	94
Meaningful seatwork	94	Classroom management	93
New materials	85	Meaningful seatwork	88
		Special services available	83

(*Source:* Adapted from Tables 2, 3, and 4 in "Diversified Concepts of the Role of the Reading Consultant" by Richard Wylie, 1969 (March), *The Reading Teacher*, pp. 520–521. Reprinted with permission of the International Reading Association.)

edge of reading, had regular classroom teaching experience, and provided criticisms that were constructive.

FACILITATING COOPERATIVE EFFORTS

Initially, reading teachers may feel shy about assuming a consultant's role with their fellow teachers, and classroom teachers may be wary about asking for help. Although the pattern can vary, reading teachers who have worked as consultants with other teachers say that it is typical for about 3 years to elapse before all teachers to whom the reading teacher has an obligation are willing to engage in such cooperative efforts.

In the first year, reading teachers offer *any* kind of assistance related to reading to develop good working relationships with all of their peers. This means they often volunteer for jobs that really may not require much expertise about reading instruction, but merely assist the overburdened classroom teacher in getting things done (e.g., helping teachers make reading materials they need or monitoring classrooms during administration of standardized reading tests).

During the second year, some teachers begin to ask for assistance in making their already good reading programs better. Good teachers sometimes feel more confident about sharing their concerns than average teachers because they know they have already instituted many high quality activities for promoting reading achievement. They are, therefore, less reluctant to admit that there are areas where they do not have solutions.

By the third year, other teachers have begun to see the advantages enjoyed by teachers who obtain assistance from the reading teacher. Workloads are being shared, problem readers have become less of a problem, and exciting new activities are occurring in their classrooms. At this time, reading teachers find they are kept very busy with requests from many classroom teachers and long range, school-wide cooperative efforts can be initiated.

To hasten the process of getting teachers to accept help from the reading teacher, or at least to ensure that they do accept the reading teacher, the reading teacher should follow several principles: a) seek the support of the school administrator and suggest the benefits that can be derived if reading teachers work with other teachers as well as with students; b) maintain an attitude of mutually solving problems—that is, the classroom teacher and reading teacher should work together rather than reading teachers attempting to impose their attitudes and ideas;

c) ask what teachers need to know *now*—help with immediate problems will set the groundwork for instituting long range goals; d) do not make assumptions about what teachers perceive as their most important problems; when Treblas, McCormick, and Cooper (1982) surveyed teachers who were going to have learning and behaviorally disordered students mainstreamed into their classes, it was predicted that concerns about discipline (or social behavior) would predominate; however, among the five concerns listed by teachers as most important, discipline was considered the least pressing, with communication, scheduling, curriculum, and teacher attitudes (in that order) taking precedence; e) do what *classroom teachers want* first, then suggest other ways you can help; f) understand that cooperative efforts work best when classroom teachers want to change a teaching behavior rather than when they are forced to do so; help teachers see how certain changes will benefit them and their students; g) highlight good things classroom teachers are doing in reading instruction; tell them so, tell other teachers about these, and ask the school principal to allow the ideas to be shared in a staff meeting.

Reading teachers often serve as resource persons to other teachers who need assistance in planning and implementing good reading programs.

SPECIFIC SUGGESTIONS FOR WORKING WITH CLASSROOM TEACHERS

McCormick (1975) reported consulting activities in one school district by remedial reading teachers who spent part of each day working with students and part of the day working with teachers. Some of these activities are reported here.

1. Reading teachers taught demonstration lessons in classrooms while classroom teachers observed.
2. Classroom teachers asked for suggestions for working with children who were low achievers in reading. Reading teachers went into the classrooms and taught these children in small groups for three days. They were then able to make suggestions from direct experience and observation. They also marked pages and suggestions in *Locating and Correcting Reading Difficulties* (Ekwall, 1985) and gave copies of this paperback book to classroom teachers. The marked pages applied to the problems of specific children or to general problems of a group.
3. In one school, the principal declared the first month of school to be "Diagnostic Testing Month," with the reading teacher as coordinator of this project. The reading teacher taught classroom teachers how to determine the learning expectancy level for each child in their classrooms and taught them how to administer a phonics test and a group survey test in reading. She set up the scheduling for the tests and did all computations that did not involve teacher judgment. Afterward she helped teachers group their children using the scores obtained. This included setting up skills groups. The reading teacher had individual conferences with classroom teachers about those children needing special help and provided suggestions and materials to use with these students. Finally, after seeing reading scores and a list of skills deficiencies for children in their classrooms, classroom teachers met with the school principal to state their goals for teaching reading in their classrooms for the year.
4. Reading teachers set up listening stations in every first grade room in selected schools and then made tapes and accompanying worksheets of reading related exercises which were given to classroom teachers to use for independent activities.
5. Some reading teachers taught reading in the regular classroom in a team-teaching arrangement with classroom teachers. This was done in several different ways. Sometimes both teachers worked with a different group simultaneously in two different areas of the classroom. Sometimes one teacher taught a lesson to the whole group, while the other teacher moved about the room making sure children were following directions, understanding what was being taught, and so forth. This worked especially well in primary grades. Sometimes the teachers planned a reading related teaching unit together, such as "Reading Content Area Materials," and then divided the teaching duties. Other plans were also used.
6. At the request of classroom teachers, a number of reading teachers trained older children to tutor younger children. They also scheduled and provided some supervision for this activity.
7. Reading teachers conducted building level workshops. Sometimes these workshops were held after school. Other times released time during the school day was provided for classroom teachers by utilizing student teachers and substitutes to teach classes. Some topics covered in workshops were: Diagnostic Testing, Using Audio-Visual Equipment to Enhance Your Reading Program, Grouping, How to Teach a Reading Group, Providing for Individual Differences, Word Analysis Skills, Increasing Meaning Vocabulary, Comprehension Skills, Critical Reading, Reading Content Area Materials, Children's Literature in Your Reading Program, Make-and-Take Workshops, and others.
8. Adult volunteer tutors were trained by reading teachers. These tutors then worked with children who had been suggested by classroom teachers. Videotapes were made of selected sessions of the tutor training program. These tapes were used for training tutors who began

working in the schools after the original training sessions had been completed. Reading teachers also provided some supervision of the volunteers and served as resource persons to them.

9. Reading teachers taught classroom teachers to use audiovisual equipment, such as controlled readers, that could be used as additions to their reading programs.

10. The necessary arrangements to set up materials displays were made by reading teachers. This came about as the result of classroom teachers requesting to have the opportunity to see a large variety of newly published materials that could be used to complement their reading programs. Sales representatives then set up displays in four areas of the city on four different afternoons. This made it possible for classroom teachers from different parts of the city to attend the materials displays after the school day with the minimum amount of inconvenience.

11. When the school system adopted a new reading series for primary grades, reading teachers were given the responsibility of seeing that it was assimilated into the instructional program with as little difficulty as possible. They met with classroom teachers several months before the use of the series was to begin to explain the program and to demonstrate materials. This gave classroom teachers an opportunity to plan ahead. After the series was in use, classroom teachers and principals called upon reading teachers to help them work out any problems that developed.

12. Ideas and information gained at monthly inservice meetings for reading teachers were reported to classroom teachers. They were also given copies of handouts and other materials received there.

13. Reading teachers compiled idea booklets to give to classroom teachers. Some of these contained ideas for card games for practicing reading skills, ideas for reading related bulletin boards, and lists of supplementary reading materials.

14. Reading teachers taught school aides how to make reading games and independent activities that can be used by classroom teachers. In a series of workshops each aide was taught how to make a different activity. The aide then produced several copies of this, so that multiple copies of every activity were available to classroom teachers.

15. Principals, classroom teachers, and reading teachers worked together to develop a checklist for evaluating the total school reading program. Areas evaluated included the availability of resources, the quality of assistance given by the principal and the reading teacher, and the instructional program in classrooms.

16. In some schools where no school aides were employed, reading teachers made reading games that were kept in the school's library or instructional materials center. These could be checked out by classroom teachers on a monthly basis for use as independent activities.

17. Make-and-Take workshops are always popular with teachers. Reading teachers sponsored Make-and-Take workshops with a difference. They were for children. Classroom teachers supplied the names of children plus a list of each child's skills deficiencies. Reading teachers grouped the children according to the area in which they needed to practice a reading skill. Children were then brought in according to these groups to make games they could take home to use for practice in this area.

This list of activities only begins to convey the possibilities of what can be accomplished when the reading teacher and the classroom teacher work together to plan an effective reading program. (pp. 361–363; 369)

Special Considerations for Inservice Sessions

One way to elicit confidence from classroom teachers and to let them know that the reading teacher does have in-depth knowledge about reading (and is therefore a resource person whose suggestions can be relied upon) is for the reading teacher to conduct periodic inservice meetings or workshops. Inservice activities are a major way of informing teachers of current instructional strategies and adding new ideas to their teaching repertoires.

A first consideration for effective in-service meetings is the selection of a *time* for conducting the sessions. Ideally, teachers should have released time for attending these meetings, with the school system providing substitute teachers for their classrooms. Too often, however, school district budgets preclude this. Some districts set aside one or two days a year for teachers to devote to professional growth activities. If neither of these options is available, an alternative is to arrange with the school principal for some of the regularly scheduled staff meeting times to be devoted to inservice sessions. Although *other* after-school days may also be selected, this is likely to be viewed with disfavor by many teachers, and Saturday meetings are sparsely attended unless teachers are paid for participating in them.

A second consideration is *method of presentation*. If after-school sessions are necessary, remember that at the end of the school day most teachers are tired, hungry, and preoccupied with jobs they need to be doing in their own classrooms. Provide food (apples, cookies, coffee, soft drinks). Keep the after-school session short. One hour is the maximum before most of the audience begins to tune out; a shorter presentation time is probably better. Keep the session upbeat: present information in a lively fashion, elicit occasional audience involvement, use audiovisuals, and frequently change the *mode* of presentation. For example, if the presenter has been talking for several minutes, a switch to showing information with an overhead projector or on a chalkboard is in order. At another time in the same session the audience can be asked to contribute ideas orally, or to write out a brief practice activity. Short films or filmstrips can also be interspersed through the presentation.

A third consideration is *content* for the meeting. Initially, the best approach is to ask the regular classroom teachers to pick the top-ics themselves. If the content is unrelated to their needs, after all, the session will be ineffective. Remember: begin with what they need to know now. After teachers have become aware of the value of the inservice meetings, the reading teacher can select some topics based on needs he has observed, but which may have gone unnoticed by others.

A final consideration for inservice sessions is the *number of meetings* to be held. Occasional or sporadic attempts at inservice education are not as effective as regularly scheduled sessions. Trione (1967) found that *repeated* inservice/consultation efforts resulted in increased teacher knowledge of reading principles, greater confidence in using reading techniques, and higher student achievement in these teachers' classes. To accomplish the goal of regularly scheduled inservice, the reading teacher in one school, which held a compulsory faculty meeting every Monday after school, convinced the principal to turn the weekly meeting over to her once a month for presentations on reading instruction (and convinced the principal to attend these sessions to show support for them.) The first year, teachers filled out forms indicating topics they wanted covered. These were tabulated by category and those subjects for which the most teachers expressed an interest constituted the year's inservice program. The following year, the reading teacher selected the topics, and took responsibility for the presentations at every other meeting, while guest "experts" were invited to present at the alternate sessions. The experts were faculty from a local university, a head librarian noted for her skill in working with children and books, and others who had special knowledge or experience related to problems the reading teacher had observed in the school program. In some sessions, case studies of pupils in the school were analyzed and solutions to their reading problems discussed. In other sessions: teachers actually made materials they wanted for use with their classes; slides were shown of pictures that the reading teacher had taken to demonstrate good ideas and activities in classrooms throughout the building; classroom teachers were asked to present during portions of a meeting to share their ideas; and educational materials that teachers had made were displayed for others in the building to see.

When these specific considerations for effective inservice sessions are taken into account, inservice meetings provide a viable and ongoing method of informing teachers, keeping enthusiasm for reading instruction high, and solving problems specific to individual school programs.

Working toward Program Congruence

In most cases, students with moderate or severe reading problems receive reading instruction in their regular classrooms *and* in a remedial or clinical reading program, or a learning disabilities class. Instruction has more impact if there is congruence between the two programs. The remedial teacher has the responsibility to consult with the regular classroom teacher to plan the pupil's program.

At the beginning of the year the two teachers should go over test results together, discuss where they think they should place the major emphasis of instruction, and determine what each teacher will do initially to meet these instructional objectives.

Throughout the year, the remedial teacher should send brief notes to classroom teachers to keep them posted on what has been done in the student's remedial program each day. (See an example of one such note in Figure 23–1.) And at least once a week, the remedial teacher should talk to classroom teachers to find out if students are *using* in the regular classroom what they have learned during remedial lessons; to determine what the classroom teacher is doing to meet the student's reading instructional goals; and, finally, to find out whether problems have cropped up for which the reading teacher can furnish as-

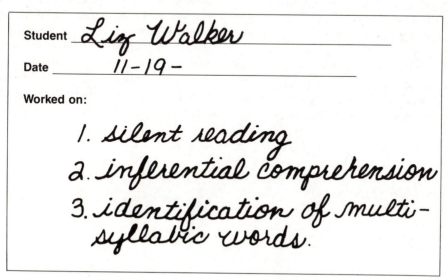

Student *Liz Walker*

Date *11-19-*

Worked on:

1. silent reading
2. inferential comprehension
3. identification of multi-syllabic words.

Figure 23–2
Example of a daily report sent by a reading teacher to a student's classroom teacher

sistance to the classroom teacher or directly to the student in the remedial class.

CONCLUDING STATEMENT

With the amount of attention that must be given to careful planning of students' remedial programs, it is not surprising that reading teachers often wonder when they'll find time to carry out the tasks specified for a consulting role. Ideally, each school should have the services of a reading teacher who works directly with students and another whose time is devoted solely to working with teachers. This arrangement is seldom found, however. Usually, the one reading teacher assigned to a building is called upon to provide both services.

School staff must consider their own program and their students, and must then develop and implement a realistic plan that will serve students in the best way. In buildings where a small number of students need remedial services, reading teachers have often been assigned to work with the children during half of the day, and with teachers during the other half. Or, when there is an average number of pupils with moderate to severe reading problems, the reading teacher is asked to spend four days a week working with the students and one day working with teachers. In schools where the number of reading

teachers is not adequate for the large numbers of pupils in need of specialized help with reading, there is no question but that the consulting role of the reading teacher is necessarily more limited and usually conducted only in relatively informal ways. In these latter cases, there must at the very least be consultation with classroom teachers to promote congruence between students' regular class programs and remedial programs. Other ways by which reading teachers can assist teachers in these latter cases are to simply answer questions about reading when they come up, to place pertinent materials in teachers' mailboxes, to discuss reading problems and questions over lunch and during planning periods, and to pass along information relevant to a classroom teacher's needs. Reflection upon the ideas found in this chapter will show other methods that do not require large amounts of teacher time.

When school system budgets provide a proper balance among often-competing elements of education, such as instructional needs, building requirements, equipment demands, and other concerns of sometimes dubious relevance to academic learning, then greater attention can be given to providing services for teacher-learning as well as student-learning. The teacher is the crucial variable in the success or failure of reading instruction.

Appendix A

Test Bank

Information in this Appendix was obtained from The Ninth Mental Measurements Yearbook (MMY) and Tests in Print III. Teachers are strongly urged to examine the 9th MMY and to use criteria discussed in this text to make decisions about the suitability of any test for a given purpose and to determine its strengths and weaknesses. Tests listed in this appendix are new tests on the market, recent revisions of older tests, and/or tests used often in American reading programs.

Table A–1
Intelligence Tests

Name	For Ages	Type of Administration	Time for Administration	Publisher
Kaufman Assessment Battery for Children (K–ABC). Also available for hearing impaired and non-English-speaking children	2.5–12.5	Individual	35–85 minutes	American Guidance Service
Slosson Intelligence Test for Children and Adults (SIT)	2 weeks and up	Individual	10–30 minutes	Slosson Educational Publications
Stanford-Binet Intelligence Scale, Fourth Edition (S–B)	2 and up	Individual	30–90 minutes	Riverside
Wechsler Adult Intelligence Scale— Revised (WAIS–R)	16 and up	Individual	60–90 minutes	Psychological Corporation
Wechsler Intelligence Scale for Children— Revised (WISC–R). Spanish edition available	6–16	Individual	50–75 minutes	Psychological Corporation

Table A–2
Norm Referenced Survey Tests

Name	For Grades	Type of Administration	Time for Administration	Publisher
California Achievement Tests— Forms C & D (CAT)	K–9	Group	Varies by level	CTB/McGraw-Hill
CAP Achievement Series	Preschool–12	Group	Varies by level	American Testronics
*Comprehensive Tests of Basic Skills—*Forms U & V (CTBS). Spanish edition available	K–9	Group	Varies by level	CTB/McGraw-Hill
Curriculum Referenced Tests of Mastery. Also provides criterion-referenced scores	1–12	Group	Varies by level	Psychological Corporation
Educational Development Series—1984 Edition (EDS)	K–12	Group	Varies by level	Scholastic Testing Service
Gates-MacGinitie Reading Tests	1–12	Group	Varies by level	Riverside
Iowa Silent Reading Tests (ISRT)	6–16	Group	Varies by level	Psychological Corporation
Iowa Tests of Basic Skills (ITBS)	K–9	Group	Varies by level	Riverside
Metropolitan Achievement Tests—5th Edition (MAT). A "Survey Battery" and "Reading Instructional Tests" are available; the latter are used most often in reading programs.	K–12	Group	Varies by level	Psychological Corporation
Nelson-Denny Reading Tests (NDRT)	9–12, plus adults	Group	50 minutes	Riverside
*Nelson Reading Skills Test—*Forms 3 & 4 (RST)	3–9	Group	Varies by level	Riverside

SRA Achievement Series	K–12	Group	Varies by level	Science Research Associates
Stanford Achievement Test: Reading Tests— 1982 Edition	1–9	Group	Varies by level	Psychological Corporation
Stanford Test of Academic Skills— 1982 Edition	8–13	Group	Varies according to subtests used	Psychological Corporation
Tests of Achievement and Proficiency. This test battery includes subtests on using sources of information as well as on reading comprehension.	9–12	Group	Varies according to subtests used	Riverside

Table A–3
Informal Reading Inventories

See Table 6–3 for comprehensive information about many published informal reading inventories. Other IRIs are listed here.

Name	For Grades	Type of Administration	Time for Administration	Publisher
Advanced Reading Inventory (ARI)	7 through college	Group	Varies according to subtests used	Wm. C. Brown
McCarthy Individualized Diagnostic Reading Inventory—Revised Edition	K–12	Individual	35–60 minutes	Educators Publishing Service
Pupil Placement Tests	1–9	Individual	20 minutes	Houghton Mifflin

Table A–4
Early Detection of Reading Difficulties

Name	For Ages	Type of Administration	Time for Administration	Publisher
Croft Readiness Assessment in Comprehension Kit (CRAC–Kit)	Students for whom early diagnostic information is needed	Individual	Varies according to subtests used	Croft
Sand: Concepts About Print Test	5–7	Individual	5–10 minutes	Heinemann Educational Books
Stones: Concepts About Print Test	5–7	Individual	5–10 minutes	Heinemann Educational Books
The Test of Early Reading Ability	3–8	Individual	15–30 minutes	Pro-Ed

Table A–5
Norm Referenced Diagnostic Test Batteries

Name	For Grades	Type of Administration	Time for Administration	Publisher
Basic Skills Assessment (BSA)	7 and up	Group	40–60 minutes	CTB/McGraw-Hill
Basic Skills Inventory. The reading subtest of this battery may be ordered separately.	K–12	Group	45 minutes per subtest	Los Angeles County Office of Education
Biemiller Test of Reading Processes (BTORP)	2–6	Individual	Varies according to subtests used	Guidance Centre, University of Toronto
CIRCUS	Nursery school–3	Group	30–40 minutes per subtest	CTB/McGraw-Hill
Diagnostic Achievement Battery (DAB)	Ages 6–14	Individual	Varies according to subtests used	Pro-Ed
Diagnostic Reading Scales (DRS)	1–7 and disabled readers in grades 8–12	Individual	60 minutes	CTB/McGraw-Hill

Diagnostic Screening Test: Reading—3rd Edition. For preliminary screening, not in-depth diagnosis	1–12	Individual	5–10 minutes	Facilitation House
Durrell Analysis of Reading Difficulty—3rd Edition	1–6	Individual	Varies according to subtests used	Psychological Corporation
ERB Comprehensive Testing Program II	1–12	Group	Varies by level	Educational Testing Service
Gates-McKillop-Horowitz Reading Diagnostic Test—2nd Edition	1–6	Individual	Varies according to subtests used	Teachers College Press
Iowa Tests of Educational Development—7th Edition. This battery measures a broad area of achievement and includes a subtest on general vocabulary.	9–12	Group	Varies according to subtests used	Science Research Associates
Primary Reading Profiles	1–3	Group	95–100 minutes	Riverside
Sequential Tests of Educational Progress, Series III (STEP). Includes tests of listening and study skills	3–12	Group	Varies by level	CTB/McGraw-Hill
Stanford Diagnostic Reading Test—1976 Edition (SDRT)	1–13	Group	Varies by level	Psychological Corporation
Test of Individual Needs in Reading (and Red Fox Supplement). The three forms of this test were designed for students in the Western United States and Canada, American Indians, and Western Australians.	1–6 and older poor readers	Individual (Red Fox Supplement is group-administered)	25–50 minutes	Council for Indian Education
The 3–Rs Test	K–12	Group	Varies by level	Riverside
Woodcock-Johnson Psycho-Educational Battery	Ages 3–80	Individual	Varies according to subtests used	Developmental Learning Materials

Table A–6
Norm Referenced Diagnostic Tests of Specific Skills

Name	For Grades	Type of Administration	Time for Administration	Publisher
Assessment of Reading Growth. Consists of tests of literal and inferential comprehension	Ages 9, 13, or 17	Group	42–50 minutes	Jamestown
Degrees of Reading Power. Assesses comprehension	3–14	Group	Varies by level	The College Board
McCullough Word Analysis Tests	4–6	Group or individual	70 minutes in 7 sessions	Chapman, Brook, & Kent
Standardized Oral Reading Check Tests	1–8	Individual	1–30 minutes	Pro-Ed
Stanford Achievement Test: Listening Comprehension Tests	1–9	Group	25–35 minutes	Psychological Corporation
The Test of Reading Comprehension: A Method for Assessing the Understanding of Written Language (TORC)	Ages 6–14	Group	90–180 minutes	Pro-Ed

Table A–7
Criterion Referenced Diagnostic Test Batteries

Name	For Grades	Type of Administration	Time for Administration	Publisher
Achievement Tests	1–8	Group	Varies according to subtests used	Macmillan
Assessment of Basic Competencies (ABC)	Ages 3–15	Individual	120 minutes; given over 3 or 4 sessions	Scholastic Testing Service
Basic Achievement Skills Individual Screener	1–post high school	Individual	50–60 minutes	Psychological Corporation
Bench Mark Measures	Ungraded	Some parts group; some parts individual	30–60 minutes	Educators Publishing Service
Botel Reading Inventory (BRI)	1–12	Individual and group	Varies according to subtests used	Follett
Brigance Diagnostic Comprehensive Inventory of Basic Skills	K–9	Individual	Varies according to subtests used	Curriculum Associates
Brigance Diagnostic Inventory of Essential Skills	4–12	Individual and group	Varies according to subtests used	Curriculum Associates
Clarke Reading Self-Assessment Survey. Self-administered and self-scored	11–college	Individual	60 minutes	Academic Therapy Publications
Corrective Reading Mastery Tests	4–adult	Group	Varies according to subtests used	Science Research Associates
Criterion Test of Basic Skills	K–8	Individual	10–15 minutes per subtest	Academic Therapy Publications
Diagnostic Skills Battery. Also provides norm-referenced information	1–8	Group	150–200 minutes	Scholastic Testing Service
Distar Mastery Tests (DMT)	Preschool–3	Group	30–60 minutes per subtest	Science Research Associates

Table A–7 (Continued)

Name	For Grades	Type of Administration	Time for Administration	Publisher
IOX Basic Skill System	5 and 6, and 9–12	Group	40–50 minutes	IOX Assessment Associates
Multilevel Academic Skills Inventory: Reading and Language Arts	1–8	Individual	Varies according to subtests used	Psychological Corporation
Pope Inventory of Basic Reading Skills	Reading levels 4 and below	Individual	Varies according to subtests used	Book-Lab
Prescriptive Reading Performance Test	1–12, and adults	Individual	Varies according to subtests used	Western Psychological Services
PRI Reading Systems (PRI/RS)	K–9	Group	Varies according to subtests used	CTB/McGraw-Hill
Reading Skills Diagnostic Test III	2–12	Group	40–60 minutes	Brador Publications
Reading Yardsticks	K-8	Group	Varies by level	Riverside
Roswell-Chall Diagnostic Reading Test of Word Analysis Skills, Revised and Extended. Also includes tests of high frequency words, letter naming, and spelling	1–4	Individual	10–15 minutes	Essay Press
Spadafore Diagnostic Reading Test	1–12	Individual	30–60 minutes	Academic Therapy Publications
Task Assessment for Prescriptive Teaching (TAPT)	Ages 6 and up	Individual and group	20–40 minutes per subtest	Scholastic Testing Service
Test Lessons in Primary Reading, Second Enlarged and Revised Edition	Reading levels 1–3	Group	Varies according to subtests used	Teachers College Press
Zip Scale for Determining Independent Reading Level	6–12	Group	Varies according to subtest used	J. Weston Walch

Table A–8
Criterion Referenced Diagnostic Tests of Specific Skills

Name	For Grades	Type of Administration	Time for Administration	Publisher
Alphabet Mastery	K and up	Group	Varies by age level	Ann Arbor Publishers
Cooper-McGuire Diagnostic Word-Analysis Test	1 and up	Group	Varies according to subtests used	Croft
Decoding Inventory (DI)	1 and up	Individual	Varies according to subtests used	Kendall/Hunt
Diagnostic Word Patterns Test	3 and up	Group	15–30 minutes	Educators Publishing Service
Doren Diagnostic Reading Test of Word Recognition Skills	1–4	Group	60–180 minutes	American Guidance Service
Group Phonics Analysis	Reading levels 1–3	Group	10–15 minutes	Jamestown
Informal Evaluation of Oral Reading Grade Level	Ages 5–11, plus older individuals with reading problems	Individual	Varies by level	Book-Lab
The Instant Words Criterion Test. Measures sight-word knowledge	1–6	Individual	15–20 minutes	Jamestown
The Instant Words Recognition Test	1–3, plus poor readers	Group or individual	10 minutes	Jamestown
The IOX Basic Skills Word Lists. Teachers devise their own tests from these word lists.	1–12	Individual	Varies according to student's ability level	IOX Assessment Associates
Listening Comprehension. Uses game format for testing	1–3	Group	Varies according to subtests used	Educators Publishing Service
The McGuire-Bumpus Diagnostic Comprehension Test	1–6	Group	30–40 minutes	Croft

Table A–8 (Continued)

Name	For Grades	Type of Administration	Time for Administration	Publisher
McLeod Phonic Worksheets	3 and below	Individual	Varies with student	Educators Publishing Service
Phonovisual Diagnostic Tests—1975 Revision. Assesses phonics skills	3–12	Group	Varies according to subtests used	Phonovisual Products
Signals Listening Tests	3 and 5	By tape recording	35 minutes	Project SPOKE
Sipay Word Analysis Tests	1–adult	Individual	Varies according to subtests used	Educators Publishing Service
Wisconsin Tests of Reading Skill Development: Comprehension	K–6	Group	Varies by level	NCS Interpretive Scoring Systems
Wisconsin Tests of Reading Skill Development: Study Skills	K–6	Group	Varies by level	NCS Interpretive Scoring Systems
Wisconsin Tests of Reading Skill Development: Word Attack	K–6	Group	Varies by level	NCS Interpretive Scoring Systems

Table A–9
Test of Reading Strategies

Name	For Grades	Type of Administration	Time for Administration	Publisher
Reading Miscue Inventory (RMI)	1–8	Individual	45 minutes	Richard C. Owen

Table A–10
Tests of Study Skills

Name	For Grades	Type of Administration	Time for Administration	Publisher
CAI Study Skills Test (SST). Microcomputer edition also available	College-bound students	Group	55 minutes	Effective Study Materials
Diagnostic Test of Library Skills	5–9	Group	30 minutes	Learnco
Survey of Study Habits and Attitudes. Spanish edition available	7–14	Group	20–25 minutes	Psychological Corporation

Table A–11
Measures of Attitude

Name	For Grades	Type of Administration	Time for Administration	Publisher
Estes Attitude Scales: Measures of Attitudes Toward School Subjects (EAS)	2–12	Group	20–30 minutes	Pro-Ed

Table A–12
Tests of Functional Literacy

Name	For Grades	Type of Administration	Time for Administration	Publisher
Life Skills— Forms 1 and 2	9–12, and adults	Group	80–100 minutes	Riverside
Minimum Essentials Test	8–12, and adults	Group	45–50 minutes per subtest	American Testronics
Performance Assessment in Reading	6–9	Group	100 minutes	CTB/McGraw-Hill
Reading/Everyday Activities in Life (REAL)	Age 10 and up	Individually by tape recording	50–90 minutes	Westwood Press
Senior High Assessment of Reading Performance (SHARP)	9–12	Group	120–150 minutes	CTB/McGraw-Hill
SRA Survival Skills in Reading and Mathematics	7–12	Group	60 minutes	Science Research Associates

Appendix B

Addresses of Publishers

This appendix lists addresses of many publishers of tests and teaching materials. All addresses were current at time of publication. For change of addresses or for publishers not listed in this appendix, you may refer to one of the following reference books, available in most libraries: *El-Hi Textbooks in Print; Books in Print; Small Presses Directory;* or *Literary Marketplace.*

Academic Therapy Publications
20 Commercial Blvd.
Novato, CA 94947

Ace Books
1120 Ave. of the Americas
New York, NY 10036

ACI Films
35 W. 45th St.
New York, NY 10036

Addison-Wesley Publishing
2725 Sand Hill Rd.
Menlo Park, CA 94025

Allyn & Bacon
College Division
7 Wells Ave.
Newton, MA 02159

Allyn & Bacon
El-Hi Division
7 Wells Ave.
Newton, MA 02159

Ambassador Publishing
Box 3524
St. Paul, MN 55165

American College Testing
 Program
P.O. Box 168
Iowa City, IA 52243

American Educational Computer
2450 Embarcadero
Palo Alto, CA 94303

American Guidance Service
Publishers' Building
Circle Pines, MN 55014

American Library Association
50 East Huron St.
Chicago, IL 60611

American Printing House
 for the Blind
1839 Frankfort Ave.
Louisville, KY 40206

American Testronics
Box 2270
Iowa City, IA 52244

Amidon Publications
1966 Benson Ave.
St. Paul, MN 55116

Amsco School Publications
315 Hudson St.
New York, NY 10013

Ann Arbor Publishers
P.O. Box 7249
Naples, FL 33940

Apple Computer
20525 Miriana Ave.
Cupertino, CA 95014

Arista Publishing
2 Park Ave.
New York, NY 10016

A. S. Barnes & Co.
Forsgate Dr. P.O. Box 421
Cranbury, NJ 08512

The Associated Press
50 Rockefeller Plaza
New York, NY 10020

Association of American
 Publishers
One Park Ave.
New York, NY 10016

ATC Publishing
P.O. Box 5588
Lakeland, FL 33803

Atheneum Publishers
115 Fifth Ave.
New York, NY 10003

Atlantic Monthly Press
8 Arlington St.
Boston, MA 02116

Audiotronics
7428 Bellaire Ave.
No. Hollywood, CA 91609

Avon Books
Educational Dept.
1790 Broadway
New York, NY 10019

AVR Audio-Visual Research
1509 8th St., S.E.
Waseca, MN 56093

Baker Street Productions
502 Range St.
Box 3610
Mankato, MN 56001

Ballantine/Fawcett Books
201 E. 50th St.
New York, NY 10022

Bantam Books
666 Fifth Ave.
New York, NY 10103

Barnell Loft
958 Church St.
Baldwin, NY 11510

Barry Instrument
1156 North Batavia Avenue
Orange, CA 92667

Bell & Howell
7100 McCormick Rd.
Chicago, IL 60645

Benefic Press
1900 N. Narragansett
Chicago, IL 60639

Bloomfield Learning Programs
P.O. Box 769
Bloomfield Hills, MI 48303

B.M.I. Educational Services
Hay Press Rd.
Dayton, NJ 08810

Boise State University Press
Boise, ID 83725

Book-Lab
1449 37th St.
Brooklyn, NY 11218

Booklist
50 East Huron St.
Chicago, IL 60611

Borg-Warner Educational
   Systems
600 West University Dr.
Arlington Heights, IL 60004

Bowmar/Noble Publishers
P.O. Box 25308
Oklahoma City, OK 73125

Boynton/Cook Publishers
Hunting Ridge Rd.
Sharon, CT 06069

Bradbury Press
866 Third Ave.
New York, NY 10022

Brador Publications
Education Division
36 Main St.
Livonia, NY 14487

Wm. C. Brown
2460 Kerper Blvd.
Dubuque, IA 52001

Burgess Publishing
426 S. 6th St.
Minneapolis, MN 55415

Buros Institute of Mental
   Measurements
University of Nebraska—
   Lincoln
Lincoln, NE 68588

Burr Oak Press
Rt. 3, Box 193
Platteville, WI 53818

The Alvina Treut Burrows
   Institute
49 Rolling Hill Rd.
Manhasset, NY 11030

Caedmon
1995 Broadway
New York, NY 10023

Cambridge Book
488 Madison Ave.
New York, NY 10022

Cambridge University Press
32 East 57th St.
New York, NY 10022

Carolrhoda Books
241 First Ave. North
Minneapolis, MN 55401

Carson-Dellosa Publishing
207 Creek Ridge Rd.
P.O. Drawer 16327
Greensboro, NC 27416

C. C. Publications
P.O. Box 23699
Tigard, OR 97223

Center for Applied Linguistics
1611 N. Kent St.
Arlington, VA 22209

Center for Applied Research
   in Education
521 Fifth Ave.
New York, NY 10017

Chapman, Brook, & Kent
1215 DeLeVina
Suite F
Santa Barbara, CA 93101

Childrens Book Council
67 Irving Place
New York, NY 10003

Childrens Press
1224 West Van Buren St.
Chicago, IL 60607

Churchill Films
662 N. Robertson Blvd.
Los Angeles, CA 90069

Clarion Books
52 Vanderbilt Ave.
New York, NY 10017

Classroom World Productions
P.O. Box 2090
Raleigh, NC 27602

Cobblestone Publishing
20 Grove St.
Peterborough, NH 03458

The College Board
888 Seventh Ave.
Box 886
New York, NY 10101

Comprehension Games
200 South Service Rd.
Roslyn Heights, NY 11577

Computer Advanced Ideas
1442–A Walnut St.
Berkeley, CA 94709

Computers, Reading, and
  Language Arts
Dept. M
P.O. Box 13247
Oakland, CA 94661–0247

Conference Book Service
80 South Early St.
Alexandria, VA 22304

The Continental Press
520 East Bainbridge St.
Elizabethtown, PA 17022

Coronado Publishers
1250 6th Ave.
San Diego, CA 92101

Council for Indian Education
517 Rimrock Rd.
Billings, MT 59102

Crane Publishing
P.O. Box 3713
Trenton, NJ 08629

Creative Classroom
866 Third Ave.
New York, NY 10022

Creative Education
P.O. Box 227
Mankato, MN 56001

Creative Publications
1101 N. San Antonio Rd.
Suite 101
Mountain View, CA 94043

Crestwood House
P.O. Box 3427
Mankato, MN 56002

Croft
4601 York Rd.
Baltimore, MD 21212

CTB/McGraw-Hill
Del Monte Research Park
2500 Garden Rd.
Monterey, CA 93940

Curriculum Associates
5 Esquire Rd.
N. Billerica, MA 01862

Curriculum Innovations Group
  of General Learning Corp.
3500 Western Ave.
Highland Park, IL 60035

Curriculum Review
517 South Jefferson
Chicago, IL 60607

John Day Jr. Books
A Division of Harper & Row
10 E. 53rd
New York, NY 10022

Delacorte Press
245 East 47th St.
New York, NY 10017

Demco
P.O. Box 7488
Madison, WI 53707

Developmental Learning
  Materials
P.O. Box 4000
One DLM Park
Allen, TX 75002

Developmental Reading
  Distributors
P.O. Box 1451
Cape Coral, FL 33910

Didax Educational Resources
6 Doulton Place
Peabody, MA 01960

Walt Disney Educational Media
500 S. Buena Vista St.
Burbank, CA 91521

Dodd, Mead & Company
79 Madison Ave.
New York, NY 10016

Dormac
P.O. Box 1699
Beaverton, OR 97075–1699

Doubleday & Company
501 Franklin Ave.
Garden City, NY 11530

Dreier Educational Systems
Box 1291
Highland Park, NJ 08904

Dura-Clad Books
P.O. Box 82
LaBelle, MO 63447

E. P. Dutton/Dial Books for
  Young Readers/Lodestar
  Books
2 Park Ave.
New York, NY 10016

Early Years/K–8
11 Hale Lane
Box 1266
Darien, CT 06820

EBSCO Curriculum Materials
Div. EBSCO Industries, Inc.
Box 11542
Birmingham, AL 35202

The Economy Company
P.O. Box 25308
Oklahoma City, OK 73125

Education Systems Technology
  Corporation
5230 Carroll Canyon Rd.
Suite 300
San Diego, CA 92121

Education Today Company/
  Pitman Learning
6 Davis Dr.
Belmont, CA 94002

Educational Activities
1937 Grand Ave.
Baldwin, NY 11510

Educational Developmental
  Laboratories (EDL)
1221 Avenue of the Americas
New York, NY 10020

Educational Insights
20435 South Tillman Ave.
Carson, CA 90746

Educational Press Association
of America (EDPRESS)
Glassboro State College
Glassboro, NJ 08028

Educational Progress
8538 E. 41st St.
Tulsa, OK 74145

Educational Publishers'
Center (EPC)
432 Park Ave. South
New York, NY 10016

Educational Reading Services
320 Rt. 17
Mahwah, NJ 07430

Educational Record Sales
157 Chambers St.
New York, NY 10007

Educational Service
P.O. Box 219
Stevensville, MI 49127

Educational Teaching Aids
199 Carpenter Ave.
Wheeling, IL 60090

Educational Testing Service
Rosedale Rd.
Princeton, NJ 08541

Educators Publishing Service
75 Moulton St.
Cambridge, MA 02238

Effective Study Materials
Box 603
San Marcos, TX 78667

Ellison Educational Equipment
P.O. Box 7986
Newport Beach, CA 92660

E.M.C. Corporation
180 East 6th St.
St. Paul, MN 55101

Encyclopaedia Britannica
Educational Corporation
425 North Michigan Ave.
Chicago, IL 60611

English-Vietnamese Bilingual
Program
San Diego City Schools
Programs Division
Education Center
4100 Normal St.
San Diego, CA 92103

Enrich Corporation
2325 Paragon Dr.
San Jose, CA 95131

ERA/CCR Corporation
P.O. Box 650
Nyack, NY 10960

ERIC Clearinghouse on Reading
and Communication Skills
1111 Kenyon Rd.
Urbana, IL 61801

ESP, Inc.
P.O. Drawer 5037
Jonesboro, AR 72403

Essay Press
Box 2323
La Jolla, CA 92037

Facilitation House
Box 611
Ottawa, IL 61350

Faculty Press
1449 37th St.
Brooklyn, NY 10036

Farrar, Straus & Giroux
19 Union Square West
New York, NY 10003

Fearon Education/Fearon-Pitman
19 Davis Dr.
Belmont, CA 94002

Field Publications
245 Long Hill Rd.
Middletown, CT 06457

Films
733 Green Bay Rd.
Wilmette, IL 60091

Follett Publishing
1010 W. Washington Blvd.
Chicago, IL 60607

Follette Microcomputer Division
4506 Northwest Highway
Crystal Lake, IL 60014

Gallaudet College
Kendall Green
Washington, D.C. 20002

Gamco Industries
Box 1862–B
Big Spring, TX 79720

Garrard Publishing
1670 N. Market St.
Champaign, IL 61820

Ginn and Company
191 Spring St.
Lexington, MA 02173

Globe Book Company
50 West 23rd St.
New York, NY 10010

Golden Books/Western
Publishing
850 Third Ave.
New York, NY 10022

Goldencraft
1224 West Van Buren St.
Chicago, IL 60607

Good Apple
P.O. Box 299
Chicago, IL 62321

Good Year Books
1900 E. Lake Ave.
Glenview, IL 60025

Gorsuch Scarisbrick
576 Central
Dubuque, IA 52001

Gralan Distributors
P.O. Box 45134
Baton Rouge, LA 70895

Guidance Associates of
Delaware
1526 Gilpin Avenue
Wilmington, DE 19806

Guidance Centre
Faculty of Education
University of Toronto
10 Alcorn Ave.
Toronto, Ontario, Canada
M4V 2Z8

J. L. Hammett Company
Braintree, MA
Lynchburg, VA
Lyons, NY
Union, NJ

Hammond Incorporated
515 Valley St.
Maplewood, NJ 07040

Harcourt Brace Jovanovich
School Division
Orlando, FL 32887

Harcourt Brace Jovanovich
Trade Children's Books
1250 Sixth Ave.
San Diego, CA 92101

Harper & Row Publishers
Junior Books Group
10 East 53rd St.
New York, NY 10022

Hartley Courseware
2023 Aspen Glade
Kingwood, TX 77339

Harvard University Press
79 Garden St.
Cambridge, MA 02138

D.C. Heath and Company
125 Spring St.
Lexington, MA 02173

Heinemann Educational Books
70 Court St.
Portsmouth, NH 03801

High Interest Teaching System
P.O. Box 3178
Mission Viejo, CA 92690

Highlights for Children
2300 West 5th Ave.
P.O. Box 269
Columbus, OH 43216

Holcombs Education Materials
  Mart
3000 Quigley Rd.
Cleveland, OH 44113

Holiday House
18 East 53rd St.
New York, NY 10022

Holt, Rinehart & Winston,
  CBS
383 Madison Ave.
New York, NY 10017

Hopewell Books
1670 Sturbridge Drive Rd. #1
Sewickley, PA 15143

The Horn Book
31 St. James Ave.
Boston, MA 02116–4167

Houghton Mifflin
One Beacon St.
Boston, MA 02108

Houghton Mifflin
Educational Software Division
P.O. Box 683
Hanover, NH 03755

Houghton Mifflin
Trade Division
2 Park St.
Boston, MA 02108

Ideal School Supply
11000 S. Lavergne Ave.
Oak Lawn, IL 60453

Imperial International
  Learning Corp.
Box 548
Kankakee, IL 60901

Incentive Publications
3835 Cleghorn Ave.
Nashville, TN 37215

Innovative Sciences
300 Broad St.
Stamford, CT 06901

Instructional/Communications
  Technology
10 Stepar Pl.
Huntington Station, NY 11746

Instructional Fair
P.O. Box 1650
Grand Rapids, MI 49501

The Instructor Publications
545 Fifth Ave.
New York, NY 10017

International Reading
  Association
800 Barksdale Rd., Box 8139
Newark, DE 19714–8139

IOX Assessment Associates
Box 24095–W
Los Angeles, CA 90024–0095

Jamestown Publishers
P.O. Box 9168
Providence, RI 02940

January Productions
249 Goffle Rd.
P.O. Box 66
Hawthorne, NJ 07507

Janus Book Publishers
2501 Industrial Parkway W.
Hayward, CA 94545

Jostens Learning Systems
800 East Business Center Dr.
Mt. Prospect, IL 60056

Joyce Motion Picture
8613 Yolanda Ave.
Northridge, CA 91324

Judy/Instructo
4325 Hiawatha Ave. So.
Minneapolis, MN 55406

Kendall/Hunt Publishing
2460 Kerper Blvd.
Dubuque, IA 52001

Kenworthy Educational Service
Box 60
138 Allen St.
Buffalo, NY 14205

Keystone View
2212 E. 12th St.
Davenport, IA 52803

Kids and Co.
P.O. Box 49034B
Los Angeles, CA 90049

Kidstamps
P.O. Box 18699
Cleveland Heights, OH 44118

Klamath Printing
628 Oak St.
Klamath Falls, OR 97601-2280

H. P. Kopplemann
P.O. Box 145
Hartford, CT 06141

L & S Computerware
1589 Fraser Dr.
Sunnyvale, CA 94087

Ladybird Books
Chestnut St.
Lewiston, ME 04240

Laidlaw Educational Publishers
(Spanish Language Publications)
Thatcher & Madison
River Forest, IL 60305

Lakeshore Curriculum Materials
P.O. Box 6261
Carson, CO 90749

Landmark Editions
1420 Kansas Ave.
Kansas City, MO 64127

Laubach Literacy Council
Box 131
1320 Jamesville Ave.
Syracuse, NY 13210

Learnco
128 High St.
Greenland, NH 03840

Learned and Tested
The Education Company
1627 Woodland Ave.
Austin, TX 78741

Learning 86 Magazine
1111 Bethlehem Pike
Springhouse, PA 19477

The Learning Factory
P.O. Box 297
Clearwater, KS 67026

Learning Management Systems
P.O. Box 254
New Paltz, NY 12561

Learning Multi-Systems
340 Coyier Lane
Madison, WI 53713

Learning Systems
60 Connolly Pkwy.
Hamden, CT 06514

Learning Tree Publishing
P.O. Box 4116
Englewood, CO 80155

Learning Well
200 South Service Rd.
Roslyn Heights, NY 11577

The Learning Works
P.O. Box 6187
Santa Barbara, CA 93111

Lerner Publications
241 First Ave. North
Minneapolis, MN 55401

Library Professional Publications
c/o The Shoe String Press, Inc.
Hamden, CT 06514

LINK
1895 Dudley St.
Lakewood, CO 80215

J. B. Lippincott
Division of Harper & Row
E. Washington Sq.
Philadelphia, PA 19105

Listen for Pleasure Ltd.
417 Center St.
Lewiston, NY 14092

Listening Library
One Park Ave.
Old Greenwich, CT 06870

Literacy Volunteers of America
404 Oak St.
Syracuse, NY 13203

Little, Brown & Company
34 Beacon St.
Boston, MA 02106

Little Brown Bear Learning
Associates
Robert Rosche, Inc.
711 Apple Tree Lane
Glencoe, IL 60022

Longman Books
Suite 1012
19 W. 44th St.
New York, NY 10036

Los Angeles County Office
of Education
9300 East Imperial Highway
Downey, CA 90242

Love Publishing
6635 East Villanova Pl.
Denver, CO 80222

Macmillan Publishing Company
866 Third Ave.
New York, NY 10022

Marie's Educational Materials
P.O. Box 60694
Sunnyvale, CA 94088

Mastery Education Corporation
85 Main St.
Watertown, MA 02172

McCarthy-McCormack
1440 Oak Hills Dr.
Colorado Springs, CO 80919

McDonald Publishing
925 Demun Ave.
St. Louis, MO 63105

McDougal, Littell & Co.
P.O. Box 1667
Evanston, IL 60204

MCE Inc.
157 S. Kalamazoo Mall
Kalamazoo, MI 49007

McGraw-Hill
1221 Avenue of the Americas
New York, NY 10020

Media Materials
2936 Remington Ave.
Baltimore, MD 21211

Merrill Publishing
1300 Alum Creek Dr.
Columbus, OH 43216

Midwest Publications
P.O. Box 448
Pacific Grove, CA 93950–0448

Milliken Publishing
1100 Research Blvd.
St. Louis, MO 63132

Milton Bradley
443 Shaker Rd.
East Longmeadow, MA 01028

Modern Curriculum Press
13900 Prospect Rd.
Cleveland, OH 44136

Moffett/Seifert
1201 Claridge Rd.
Wyndmoor, PA 19118

Monarch Press
c/o Simon and Schuster
630 Fifth Ave.
New York, NY 10020

The Monkey Sisters
22971 Via Cruz
Laguna Niguel, CA 92677

Montessori Matters and
E–Z Learning Materials
701 E. Columbia Ave.
Cincinnati, OH 45215

William Morrow & Co.
105 Madison Ave.
New York, NY 10016

The Moving Picture Company
2507 Thornwood Ave.
Wilmette, IL 60091

National Council of Teachers of
English
1111 Kenyon Rd.
Urbana, IL 61801

National Textbook
4255 W. Touhy Ave.
Lincolnwood, IL 60646

NCS Interpretive Scoring System
P.O. Box 1416
Minneapolis, MN 55440

New American Library
1633 Broadway
New York, NY 10019

New Dimensions in Education
160 Dupont St.
Plainview, NY 11803

New Readers Press
Division of Laubach Literacy,
Inc.
P.O. Box 131
Syracuse, NY 13210

Newsweek
444 Madison Ave.
New York, NY 10022

Noble & Noble Publishers
1 Dag Hammarskjold Plaza
New York, NY 10017

Northwest Regional Education
Laboratory
300 S. W. Sixth Ave.
Portland, OR 97204

Oceana Educational
Communications
40 Cedar St.
Dobbs Ferry, NY 10520

Open Court Publishing
P.O. Box 599
LaSalle, IL 61301

Opportunities for Learning
8950 Turline Ave.
Chatsworth, CA 91311

William Orr
111 Roe Blvd. East
Patchogue, NY 11772

Richard C. Owen Publishers
Rockefeller Center
Box 819
New York, NY 10185

OWL/TV
56 The Esplanade
Suite 302
Toronto, Ontario M5E 1A7
Canada

Oxford Book Company
11 Park Place
New York, NY 10007

Pacific Books
P.O. Box 558
Palo Alto, CA 94302

Palisades Educational Films
132 Lasky Dr.
Beverly Hills, CA 90212

Pantheon Books
201 E. 50th St.
New York, NY 10022

Paradox Press
P.O. Box 1438
Los Gatos, CA 95030

Partners in Publishing
P.O. Box 50347
Tulsa, OK 74150

Pendulum Press
The Academic Bldg.
237 Saw Mill Rd.
West Haven, CT 06516

Perma-Bound Books
E. Vandalia Rd.
Jacksonville, IL 62650

Philomel Books
51 Madison Ave.
New York, NY 10010

Phonovisual Products
12216 Parklawn Dr.
P.O. Box 2007
Rockville, MD 20852

Plays
8 Arlington St.
Boston, MA 02116

Pocket Books
Div. of Simon & Schuster
1230 Ave. of the Americas
New York, NY 10020

Polaroid Corporation
575 Technology Square
Cambridge, MA 02139

Prentice-Hall
Educational Books Division
Englewood Cliffs, NJ 07632

Price, Stern, Sloan, Publishers
410 N. La Cienega Blvd.
Los Angeles, CA 90048

PRO-ED
5341 Industrial Oaks Blvd.
Austin, TX 78735

Professional Educators
  Publications
P.O. Box 80728
Lincoln, NE 68501

Project LEARN
2238 Euclid Ave.
Cleveland, OH 44118

Project SPOKE
315 W. Main St.
Norton, MA 02766

Proyecto LEER
Library Development Program
Organization of American States
Washington, D.C. 20006

The Psychological Corporation
555 Academic Court
San Antonio, TX 78204–0952

Publishers' Showcase
P.O. Box 158
Great Neck, NY 11022

The Putnam Publishing Group
  (Coward-McCann, Inc.,
  G. P. Putnam's Sons, Philomel
  Books, Grosset & Dunlap)
51 Madison Ave.
New York, NY 10010

Quercus
2768 Pineridge Rd.
Castro Valley, CA 94546

Radio Shack
1400 One Tandy Center
Fort Worth, TX 76102

Raintree Publishers
330 East Kilbourn Ave.
Milwaukee, WI 53202

Rand McNally & Company
Box 7600
Chicago, IL 60680

Random House/Knopf/Pantheon/
  Villard/Times Books
201 East 50th St.
New York, NY 10022

Random House School Division
201 E. 50th St.
New York, NY 10022

Reader's Digest Association
Pleasantville, NY 10570

Reading Joy
P.O. Box 404
Naperville, IL 60540

Reading Resources
401 East Wilson Bridge Rd.
Worthington, OH 43085

Regents Publishing
2 Park Ave.
New York, NY 10016

Remedia Publications
P.O. Box 1174
Scottsdale, AZ 85252

Remedial Education Press
Kingsbury Center
2138 Bancroft Place, N. W.
Washington, D.C. 20008

Research Press
2612 N. Mattis Ave.
Champaign, IL 61821

Frank E. Richards Publishing
P.O. Box 66
Phoenix, NY 13135

The Riverside Publishing
  Company
8420 Bryn Mawr Ave.
Chicago, IL 60631

Robert Rosche
711 Apple Tree Lane
Glencoe, IL 60022

Santillana Publishing
257 Union St.
Northvale, NJ 07647

Scan Tron Corporation
3345 Duke St.
Alexandria, VA 22314

Frank Schaffer Publications
19771 Magellan Dr.
Torrance, CA 90502

Scholastic
730 Broadway
New York, NY 10003

Scholastic Testing Service
480 Meyer Rd.
P.O. Box 1056
Bensenville, IL 60106

Schoolhouse Press
4700 Rockside Rd.
Independence, OH 44131

SRA-Science Research
  Associates
155 North Wacker Dr.
Chicago, IL 60606

Scott Education Division
Scott Graphics, Inc.
Holyoke, MA 01040

Scott, Foresman & Company
1900 East Lake Ave.
Glenview, IL 60025

Scribner Educational Publishers
866 Third Ave.
New York, NY 10022

Charles Scribner's Sons
115 Fifth Ave.
New York, NY 10003

Dale Seymour Publications
P.O. Box 10888
Palo Alto, CA 94303

Shakean Stations
P.O. Box 68
Farley, IA 52046

Shoe String Press
995 Sherman Ave.
Hamden, CT 06514

Signet
The New American Library, Inc.
1301 Ave. of the Americas
New York, NY 10019

Silver Burdett
250 James St.
Morristown, NJ 07960

The Simon & Schuster Juvenile
  Publishing Division (Archway
  Paperbacks, Julian Messner,
  Little Simon and Wanderer
  Books)
1230 Avenue of the Americas
New York, NY 10020

Skillcorp Publishers
2300 W. 5th Ave.
Columbus, OH 43216

Slosson Educational
   Publications
P.O. Box 280
East Aurora, NY 14052

Small Fry Originals
2700 S. Westmoreland
Dallas, TX 75233

The SMART ALEX Press
P.O. Box 7192
Quincy, MA 02169

Society for Visual Education
1345 Diversey Pkwy.
Chicago, IL 60614

Stampede
4938 Bruges
Woodland Hills, CA 91364

Stanwix House
3020 Charters Ave.
Pittsburgh, PA 15204

Steck-Vaughn Company
P.O. Box 2028
Austin, TX 78767

STEP
P.O. Box 887
Mukilteo, WA 98275

Story House Corporation
Bindery Lane
Charlotteville, NY 12036

Strine Publishing
P.O. Box 149
York, PA 17405

Sundance Publishers &
   Distributors
Newtown Rd.
Littleton, MA 01460

Sylvan Learning Corporation
1407–116th Ave., NE
Suite 200
Bellevue, WA 98004

Teacher Created Materials
5251 McFadden
Huntington Beach, CA 92649

Teacher Support Software
P.O. Box 7125
Gainesville, FL 32605

Teachers College Press
1234 Amsterdam Ave.
New York, NY 10027

Teachers Exchange of San
   Francisco
600–35th Ave.
San Francisco, CA 94121

Teachers Practical Press
Englewood Cliffs, NJ 07632

Teaching Exceptional Children
Council for Exceptional Children
1920 Association Drive
Reston, VA 22091

Teaching Resources Corporation
50 Pond Park Rd.
Hingham, MA 02043

Time-Life Books
777 Duke St.
Alexandria, VA 22314

Time-Life Multimedia
Time & Life Building
New York, NY 10020

Treetop Publishing
220 Virginia St.
Racine, WI 53405

TREND Enterprises
300 9th Ave., S. W.
New Brighton, MN 55112

Trillium Press
P.O. Box 921
Madison Square Station
New York, NY 10159

Troll Associates
320 Route 17
Mahwah, NJ 07430

Turman Publishing
200 West Mercer, Suite 508
Seattle, WA 98119

Mark Twain Media
Dura-Clad Books
Box 82
LaBelle, MO 63447

United Learning
6633 W. Howard St.
Niles, IL 60648

U.S. Government Printing Office
Center for Systems and Program
   Development
1511 K Street, NW
Suite 740
Washington, D.C. 20005

USA Today
1000 Wilson Blvd.
Arlington, VA 22209

VALIC
2929 Allen Parkway
Houston, TX 77019

Viking Penguin
40 West 23rd St.
New York, NY 10010

Voxcom
P.O. Box 2520
Peachtree City, GA 30269

J. Weston Walch
P.O. Box 658
321 Valley St.
Portland, ME 04104–0658

Warner Books
666 5th Ave.
New York, NY 10103

Weekly Reader Secondary
   Periodicals
245 Long Hill Rd.
Middletown, CT 06457

Wendy Watson Productions
222 South Linton Rd.
Columbus, GA 31904

Western Psychological Services
12031 Wilshire Blvd.
Los Angeles, CA 90025

Western Publishing
Education Division
850 Third Ave.
New York, NY 10022

Westwood Press
770 Broadway, 3rd floor
New York, NY 10003

Albert Whitman & Co.
5747 W. Howard St.
Niles, IL 60648

Woodbury Software
127 White Oak Lane
Old Bridge, NJ 08857

World Almanac Education
1278 West Ninth St.
Cleveland, OH 44113

World Book
Merchandise Mart Plaza
Chicago, IL 60654

The Wright Group
7620 Miramar Rd.
Suite 4100
San Diego, CA 92126

Xerox Education Publications
4343 Equity Dr.
Columbus, OH 43228

Zaner-Bloser
2300 W. Fifth Ave.
P.O. Box 16764
Columbus, OH 43216

Appendix C

Teachers' Store

Materials helpful to teaching reading have been discussed throughout this text. Others, organized by general topic, are listed here. In parentheses beside each listed item is the publisher's name. To learn more about the material, write to the publisher and ask for a catalog (catalogs are sent to teachers free of charge). Addresses for publishers are found in Appendix B.

SIGHT VOCABULARY

1. *ETA Language Arts Program: Basic Vocabulary Kit* (Educational Teaching Aids)
2. *Reading Reinforcement Skill Text Series* (Charles E. Merrill)
3. *Filmstrips: Read On! Series II* (ACI Films)
4. *Common Words* (Charles E. Merrill)
5. *Vocabulary Laboratories* (Holt, Rinehart & Winston
6. *LEIR—Language Experiences in Reading, Levels I, II, and III* (Encyclopaedia Britannica Educational Corporation)
7. *Supermarket Recall Program* (William Orr)
8. *Sight Words for Survival* (Lakeshore Curriculum Materials)
9. *Reading Joy Gameboard Kits* (Reading Joy)
10. *Sight Word Labs: Set 1 and Set 2* (Developmental Learning Materials)
11. *Breakthrough to Literacy* (Longman)
12. *Cove School Reading Program* (Developmental Learning Materials)
13. *Sight Words* (ESP)
14. *Reading Cartoons* (Frank Schaffer)
15. *Picture Word Program* (Amidon)
16. *Dolch Puzzle Books* (Garrard)
17. *Word Cover* (Houghton Mifflin)
18. *Play 'N Read* (Little Brown Bear Learning Associates)
19. *High Action Reading for Vocabulary* (Modern Curriculum Press)
20. *The Little Big Box of Books* (Fearon-Pitman Learning Inc.)
21. *Dolch Phrase Card Game* (Garrard)
22. *Sight Words for Beginning Readers* (Audiotronics)
23. *The Monster Series* (Bowmar/Noble)
24. *Sight Word Memory Match* (Developmental Learning Materials)
25. *Ladder Games: Sight Word Builders* (Developmental Learning Materials)
26. *Strange and Silly Stories* (Frank Schaffer)
27. *Basic Word Skills* (Frank Schaffer)

WORD IDENTIFICATION STRATEGIES

1. *Consonant Soup Cans* (Gamco)
2. *Group Word Teaching Game* (Garrard)

468

3. *Corrective Reading* (SRA)

4. *Rainbow Word Builders* (Kenworthy)

5. *Jumbo Phonics Cassette Program* (EBSCO)

6. *Phonic Rummy Card Games* (Kenworthy)

7. *Building Words* (Lakeshore Curriculum Materials)

8. *Programmed Phonics, Books 1 and 2* (Educators Publishing Service)

9. *Lessons in Vowel and Consonant Sounds* (Curriculum Associates)

10. *Individualized Reading Skills Program* (Science Research Associates)

11. *Sounds, Words, and Meanings* (Steck-Vaughn)

12. *Creature Teachers* (Bowmar/Noble)

13. *Language Lollipop* (Kids & Co.)

14. *Go Fish* (Remedial Education Press)

15. *Sound and Symbol Puzzles* (Developmental Learning Materials)

16. *Blank Gameboards* (Developmental Learning Materials)

17. *The College Reading Skills Series* (Jamestown)—the *Olive* set of this series is written at 6th through 8th grade reading levels and is suitable for use with high school students.

18. *Turn and Read* (Childcraft)

19. *Doghouse Game* (Kenworthy)

20. *Blend and Build* (Robert Rosche)

21. *Consonant Flip Book* (Developmental Learning Materials)

22. *Game Tree Kits* (Xerox)

23. *Reading Spectrum: Word Analysis* (Macmillan)

24. *HITS* (High Interest Teaching System)

25. *Sound Phonics* (Borg-Warner)

26. *Learning with Laughter* (Prentice-Hall)

27. *A Word Recognition Program* (Barnell Loft)

28. *System 80* (Borg-Warner)

29. *Help Your Child Learn Phonics: Consonants* (Frank Schaffer)

30. *Whatchamacallit* (Gamco)

31. The filmstrip "Suffixes" in the set, *What's the Word*, from the Reading-for-Meaning Series (Houghton Mifflin)

32. *Tutorgrams* (Gamco)

33. *The Frank Schaffer Gameboards* (Frank Schaffer)

MEANING VOCABULARY

1. *Vocabulary Building* (Zaner-Bloser)

2. *Words Are Important* (Hammond)

3. *SRA: Structural Analysis* (Science Research Associates)

4. *Prefix Puzzles* (Developmental Learning Materials)

5. *Suffix Puzzles* (Developmental Learning Materials)

6. *Cloze Practice Sheets* (Opportunities for Learning)

7. *Developing Structural Analysis Skills* (Educational Record Sales)

8. *Verbal Classifications* (Midwest Publications)

9. *Words in Context* (Opportunities for Learning)

10. *Be a Better Reader* (Prentice-Hall)

11. *The Vocabulary Development Series* (Macmillan)

12. *Vocabulary Drills* (Jamestown)

13. *Vocabulary Building Exercises for Young Adults* (Dormac)

14. *Idioms* (Dormac)

15. *Many Meanings* (Dormac)

16. *Word Power* (Developmental Learning Materials)

17. *Vocabulary Development* (Frank Schaffer)

18. *Vocabulary Building: A Process Approach* (Zaner-Bloser). (Professional material for teaching meaning vocabulary)

COMPREHENSION

1. *Adult Learner Series* (Jamestown)

2. *Accent on Reading Skills* (Holt, Rinehart & Winston)

3. *Attention Span Stories* (Jamestown)

4. *A Need to Read* (Globe)

5. *Best Selling Chapters* (Jamestown)
6. *Comprehension Through Active Involvement* (Developmental Learning Materials)
7. *Best Short Stories* (Jamestown)
8. *Clues for Better Reading* (Curriculum Associates)
9. *Word Attack and Comprehension* (Developmental Learning Materials)
10. *Computer-Based CLOZE-PLUS Program* (Instructional/Communications Technology)
11. *Test Lessons in Primary Reading* (Slosson Educational Publications)
12. *Test Lessons in Reading and Reasoning* (Slosson Educational Publications)
13. *Cloze Connections* (Barnell Loft)
14. *The Follett Adult Basic Reading Comprehension Program* (Follett)
15. *Clues for Better Reading* (Curriculum Associates)
16. *Comprehension Packet* (Burr Oak Press)
17. *Gates-Peardon-LaClain Reading Exercises* (Teachers College Press)
18. *The Comprehension Carnival* (The Learning Works)
19. *Tutorial Comprehension Courseware PLUS* (Random House)
20. *Catching On* (Open Court)
21. *Six-Way Paragraphs* (Jamestown)
22. *Comprehension Skills Series* (Jamestown)
23. *TR Reading Comprehension Series* (Developmental Learning Materials)
24. *Pirates Scramble* (Developmental Learning Materials)
25. *Cartoon Comprehension* (Frank Schaffer)
26. *Sequencing* (Frank Schaffer)
27. *Getting the Main Idea* (Frank Schaffer)
28. *Drawing Conclusions* (Frank Schaffer)
29. *Specific Skills Series* (Barnell Loft)
30. *Reading for Concepts* (McGraw-Hill)

ORAL READING FLUENCY

1. *Favorite Plays for Classroom Reading* (Plays, Inc.)

2. *Your First Adventure* (Bantam Books)
3. *Invitations to Read, A Read-Along Listening Program* (Noble & Noble)
4. *SCORE Reading Improvement Series* (Prentice-Hall Media, Inc.)
5. *Film Ways to Reading* (Palisades Educational Films)
6. *Voycom Card Reader* (American Guidance Service)
7. *Read-A-Part* (Houghton Mifflin)
8. *Language Master* (Bell & Howell)
9. *Double Play Reading Series* (Bowmar/Noble)
10. *Sounds of Language Readers* (Holt, Rinehart & Winston)
11. *Cassette/Book Combinations* (Scholastic)
12. *Read-Along Libraries* (Random House)

BOOKS AND MATERIALS TO MOTIVATE SECONDARY STUDENTS

1. *All for Love* by Tasha Tudor (Philomel Books)
2. *The Mysteries of Harris Burdick* by Chris Van Allsburg (Houghton Mifflin)
3. *Fastback Romance* and *Fastback Mystery* (Fearon/Pitman)
4. *Perspectives II* (Academic Therapy Publications)
5. *Comprehension Crosswords* (Jamestown)
6. *Story Starters* (Steck-Vaughn)
7. *Poetry for People Who Hate Poetry* (Churchill); a film
8. *The Six-Million-Dollar Cucumber* (Laurel-Leaf Books)
9. *Fourteen Language Arts Lessons for Students Who Like Math* (Educators Publishing Service)
10. *Weird and Mysterious* (Globe)
11. *Journeys to Fame* (Globe)
12. *Real Stories* (Globe)
13. Scholastic Magazines (Scholastic): *Sprint, Action, Scope, Scholastic News*
14. *Disasters!* (Jamestown)

MORE MATERIALS ESPECIALLY FOR SECONDARY LEVEL DISABLED READERS

1. *New Beginnings in Reading: A Program for Adolescents and Adults* (Teachers College Press)
2. *Jamestown Classics* (Jamestown)
3. *Words Are Important* (Hammond)
4. *How to Read in Content Areas* (Educational Activities)
5. Hi-Lo Books (Dell) stories and nonfiction; the following titles:
   (RL indicates Reading Level; IL indicates Interest Level)
   Bewitched and Bewildered (RL 2; IL 7–11)
   Breakaway (RL 4; IL 7–12)
   I Gotta Be Free (RL 2; IL 7–11)
   Rescue Chopper (RL 3; IL 7–11)
   A Winning Position (RL 2; IL 7–12)
   Dracula Go Home (RL 2.5; IL 7–12)
   Run for Your Life (RL 2.2; IL 7–12)
   World War II Resistance Stories (RL 3.5; IL 7–12)
   Kidnap in San Juan (RL 2; IL 7–12)
   Trading Secrets (RL 4.5; IL 7–12)
6. *Quest Reading Program* (Scholastic)
7. *Essential Skills Series* (Jamestown)
8. *Reading the Content Fields* (Jamestown)
9. *Myths* (Dormac)
10. *Simple English Classics Series* (Dormac)

Professional Resources for Secondary Reading Teachers

1. *Games for Language Learning* (Cambridge University Press)
2. *Reading Comprehension: New Directions for Classroom Practice* (Scott Foresman)
3. *To Help Them Learn* (Churchill); a film demonstrating classrooms where excitement, learning, and motivation occur.
4. *Thinking Thursdays* (International Reading Association)
5. *Student-Centered Language Arts and Reading, K–13* (Houghton Mifflin)

6. *Careers in Fact and Fiction* (American Library Association)
7. *Exciting, Funny, Scary, Short, Different, and Sad Books Kids Like About Animals, Science, Sports, Families, Songs, and Other Things* (American Library Association)

STUDY SKILLS

1. *Card-o-Log* (Scott Foresman)
2. *Don't Be Afraid, It's Only a Test* (Churchill Films)
3. *Individualized Reading Skills Program* (Houghton Mifflin)
4. *Skimming and Scanning* (Jamestown)
5. *Newslab* (Science Research Associates)
6. *Dictionary Drills* (Jamestown)
7. *Researchlab* (Science Research Associates)
8. *Graphical Comprehension: How to Read and Make Graphs* (Jamestown)
9. *30 Lessons in Outlining* (Curriculum Associates)
10. *30 Lessons in Notetaking* (Curriculum Associates)
11. *Timed Readings* (Jamestown)
12. *Library Skills* (Xerox)

MATERIALS FOR USE IN PROGRAMS FOR COLLEGE-BOUND READING DISABLED STUDENTS

1. *Better Writing Through Applied Grammar: Sentence Combining* (Hammond)
2. *College "Helps" Newsletter: College Handicapped and Exceptional Learner Programs and Services* (Partners in Publishing)
3. *Creative Communication* (Steck-Vaughn)
4. *The Five Hundred Word Theme* (Prentice-Hall)
5. *Gregg Notehand* (McGraw-Hill)
6. *The College Student* (Jamestown)
7. *How To Study in High School* (Pacific Books)

8. *Language Arts Skillcenter* (Random House)
9. *Language Skill Books* (Steck-Vaughn)
10. *The Paragraph* (Educators Publishing Service)
11. *Prep for Better Reading* (Holt, Rinehart & Winston)
12. *Reading and Learning Power,* 2nd ed. (Macmillan)
13. *Read, Write, React Series* (Oxford Book Company)
14. *The Tuned-In, Turned-On Book about Learning Problems* (Academic Therapy)
15. *Vocabulary for the College-Bound Student* (Amsco)
16. *The Writing Clinic* (Prentice-Hall)
17. *Word Power* (Developmental Learning Materials)
18. *Your Library: A Reference Guide* (Holt, Rinehart & Winston)
19. *Films:* (All from Churchill Films)
    The Voyage of Odysseus
    Be Prepared for the S.A.T.
    Be Prepared for the A.C.T.
    About Words
    e.e. cummings
    Shakespeare
    Robert Frost's New England
    The Tell-Tale Heart

6. *Prueba del Desarrollo Inicial del Lenguaje* (PRO-ED)—the Spanish version of The Test of Early Language Development (TELD).
7. *El Gran Cesar* (Education Consulting Association)
8. *Primeros Pasos Para Prepararse A Leer* (Highlights for Children); the Spanish version of *First Steps in Getting Ready to Read.*
9. *Maria Luisa* (Lippincott)
10. *Reading Adventures in Spanish and English* (Highlights for Children)
11. *I Am Here. Yo Estoy Aquí* (Franklin Watts Co.)
12. *Spanish-language audiovisual materials* (Proyecto LEER)
13. *Navajo and Zuni bilingual publications* (Gallup-McKinley County Public Schools, Gallup, New Mexico)
14. *Multilingual books and audiotapes in Vietnamese, Spanish, Korean, Cantonese, Mandarin, and Japanese* (Los Angeles City Schools, California)
15. *The Monster Series I and II* (Bowmar/Noble); Spanish version
16. *A test for determining language dominance in Indochinese students* (English/Vietnamese Bilingual Program)

MATERIALS FOR TEACHING LINGUISTICALLY AND CULTURALLY DIFFERENT STUDENTS

1. *Vietnamese/English Bilingual Readers* (National Textbook)
2. *The Spanish Oral Reading Test* (Paradox Press)
3. *Miami Linguistic Readers Series* (D. C. Heath)
4. *Bilingual Syntax Measure* (Harcourt Brace Jovanovich)
5. *Spanish Reading Charts* (Dissemination Center for Bilingual-Bicultural Education)

Professional Resources for Teaching Linguistically and Culturally Different Students

Books

1. *Reading and the Bilingual Child* (International Reading Association)
2. *Literacy for America's Spanish Speaking Children* (International Reading Association)
3. *When You Teach English as a Second Language* (Book-Lab)
4. *Hints for Dealing with Cultural Differences in Schools: A Handbook for Teachers Who*

Have Vietnamese Students in Their Classrooms (Center for Applied Linguistics)

5. *Migrant Education* (International Reading Association)
6. *Reading and the Black English Speaking Child* (International Reading Association)
7. *Dialects and Educational Equity* (Center for Applied Linguistics)

Articles

1. "A Spanish Readability Formula" (by Spaulding, *Modern Language Journal,* Dec. 1956)
2. "Considerations for the Development of a Reading Program for Puerto Rican Bilingual Students" (by Diaz, *Reading Improvement,* Winter 1981)
3. "Promoting Language and Reading Development for Two Vietnamese Children" (by Weaver and Sawyer, *Reading Horizons,* Winter 1984)
4. "Oral Vocabulary and Beginning Reading in Disadvantaged Black Children" (by Cohen and Kornfeld, *The Reading Teacher,* October 1970)
5. "Reading in Appalachia" (by Anderson, *The Reading Teacher,* January 1967)
6. "Mexican-American Reading Habits and Their Cultural Basis" (by Justin, *Journal of Reading,* March 1973)
7. "The Migrant Child in the Elementary Classroom" (by Read, *The Reading Teacher,* March 1978)

ERIC Documents

1. "A Reading and Writing Program Using Language-Experience Methodology Among Adult ESL Students in a Basic Education Program" (ED 213 915)
2. "Providing Effective Reading Instruction for Refugee Students" (ED 217 373)
3. "A Haitian-Spanish Bilingual Program" (ED 200 696)
4. "The Challenge of the Multicultural Classroom" (ED 207 023)

5. "The Use of Games in Teaching a Second Language in the Classroom" (ED 225 357)
6. "Language Arts for Native Indian Students" (ED 238 630)
7. "A Review of Research on the Teaching of Reading in Bilingual Education" (ED 210 903)
8. "Chinese/Korean Bilingual Language Arts Resource Center" (ED 201 687)
9. "A Handbook for Teaching Vietnamese-Speaking Students" (ED 228 335)
10. "The Rock Point Experience: A Navajo School Program" (ED 195 363)
11. "Adult ESL Suggested Materials List" (ED 233 610)
12. "Language and Literacy Learning in Bilingual Instruction: Cantonese/English" (ED 245 572)

Audiovisual

The Children of Akiachak (Bureau of Indian Affairs, Fairbanks, Alaska); a film showing training techniques in bilingual education with young children.

ILLITERACY AND FUNCTIONAL ILLITERACY

For Use With Illiterate Individuals

1. *The Steck-Vaughn Adult Reading Program* (Steck-Vaughn)
2. *Adult Reading Improvement Series* (Monarch)
3. *Survival Vocabularies* (Janus)
4. *Programmed Reading Comprehension, Level I* (National Tutoring Institute)
5. *The Work Series; The Health Series; The Money Series* (Hopewell Books)
6. *Pacemaker Vocational Readers* (Fearon)
7. *Basic Education: Reading Book I* (Follett)
8. *News for You* (Laubach Literacy Council)
9. *Communications* (Follett)

For Use With Functionally Illiterate Individuals

1. *Practical Skills in Reading* (National Textbook)
2. *I Can Make It On My Own* (Good Year)
3. *Recipes for Learning* (Good Year)
4. *Survival Guides* (Janus)
5. *BesTeller Magazines* (Fearon)
6. *Essential Life Skills Series* (National Textbook)
7. *Cambridge Pre-GED Program, Introduction to Reading* (Cambridge Book Co.)
8. *Scope/Consumer Skills, Dollars and Sense* (Scholastic)
9. *Forms in Your Future* (Globe)

Professional Resources for Teaching Illiterate and Functionally Illiterate Older Youths and Adults

1. *Teaching and Learning Basic Skills: A Guide for Adult Basic Education and Developmental Education Programs* (Teachers College Press)
2. *Books for Adult New Readers*, 2nd Edition (Project LEARN)
3. *Teaching Reading in Adult Basic Education* (Wm. C. Brown)
4. *The Illiterate Adult Speaks Out* (National Institute of Education)
5. *Challenging Adult Illiteracy* (Teachers College Press)
6. *Adult Literacy* (International Reading Association)
7. *Adult Education* (a journal)
8. *Lifelong Learning* (a journal)
9. *TUTOR* (Literacy Volunteers of America)
10. *Tutor's Sampler* (Faculty Press)

MATERIALS TO RECOMMEND TO PARENTS

1. *Choosing a Child's Book* (Children's Book Council)
2. *Summer Reading is Important* (International Reading Association)
3. *Getting Involved: Your Child and Reading* (U.S. Government Printing Office)
4. *How Can I Help My Child Read English as a Second Language?* (International Reading Association)
5. *Children's Classics* (The Horn Book)
6. *Books and the Teenage Reader* (Harper & Row)
7. *Babies Need Books* (Atheneum)
8. *The Read-Aloud Handbook* (Viking Penguin)

TEACHER IDEA RESOURCE BOOKS

1. *Enriching Your Reading Program* (Fearon)
2. *77 Games for Reading Groups* (Fearon)
3. *Reading Games that Teach* (Creative Teaching Press)
4. *Reading Skills: Simple Games, Aids and Devices to Stimulate Reading Skills in the Classroom* (Fearon)
5. *Reading Games in the Classroom* (Jamestown)
6. *The Reading Box: 150 Reading Games and Activities* (Educational Insights, Inc.)
7. *rēadíng gāmes* (Macmillan)
8. *Managing Your Classroom!* (Frank Schaffer)

Appendix D

Easy-to-read, High-interest, Content-area Books

Many lists of easy-to-read, high-interest story books are available to help remedial teachers. However, most reading teachers believe their responsibilities to disabled readers extend beyond the remedial classroom, resource room, or clinic. The books in this list will make poor readers more comfortable in their regular classes and better able to learn. Share this information about easy-to-read, high-interest, content-area books with other teachers. Some books listed here are suitable for upper elementary-level students, but most are intended for students in middle school or senior high school.

Table D–1
English

Title and Publisher	Instructional Level	Reading Level
Get It Down in Writing (Xerox)	7–12	2.5–4.5
The Learning Language Skills Series: Language Arts (McGraw-Hill)	7 and up	1.5
Learning our Language, Books One and Two (Follett)	7–Adult	5
Guidebook to Better English (Economy)	7–Adult	4.7
Getting Help (Skill area: language arts) (Xerox)	9–12	3.5–4.5
Write for the Job (Xerox)	9–12	3.5–4.5
Read It Right (Using reference materials) (Xerox)	7–12	2.5–4.5
Language Workshop: A Guide to Better English (Globe)	7–12	4–5
The World of Vocabulary Series (Globe)	8–12	2–7
Everyday English (Globe)	7–12	3–4
Writing Sense (Globe)	7–12	5–6
Writing a Research Paper (Globe)	7–12	5–6

Table D–1 (Continued)

Title and Publisher	Instructional Level	Reading Level
Using Spelling, Capitalization & Punctuation Performance Packs (Holcombs)	7–12	2.5–3.5
The Business of Basic English (Holcombs)	7–12	4.5–5.5
English for Everyday Living (Holcombs)	7–12	3.0–4.0
Language Drills, Book 1–52 Duplicating Masters (Holcombs)	7–12	3.0–4.0
Language Drills, Book 2–50 Duplicating Masters (Holcombs)	7–12	3.5–4.5
Big Time Comics—Complete Collection (Written Expression: Paragraphs & Sentences) (Holcombs)	7–12	2.0–6.0
Letter Writing Learning Lab (Holcombs)	7–12	3.0–4.0
Writing Skills for Everyday Life—A Multimedia Program (Holcombs)	8–12	5.0–7.0
Spotlight on Writing (reproducible activities) (Holcombs)	7–12	2.0–4.0
Letter Writing Skills (reproducible activities) (Holcombs)	7–12	3.5–4.5
Writing to Others Program (Holcombs)	8–12	3.0–4.0
English for Employment (Holcombs)	8–12	4.0–5.0
English for Everyday (Holcombs)	7–12	3.0–4.0
How Do I Fill Out A Form? Duplicating Masters (Holcombs)	9–12	3.5–4.5
Basic Writing Skills: The Freddy Klinker Skill-Box Series (Holcombs)	7–12	3.0–5.5
Improve Your Writing for Job Success (handwriting kit) (Holcombs)	7–12	3.0–4.0
Handwriting Legibility Kit (Holcombs)	7–12	2.5–3.5
Webster's Alphabetical Thesaurus (Holcombs)	7–12	5.5–6.5
Super Dictionary Activity Unit (Holcombs)	7–12	4.0–5.0
Using a Dictionary Duplicating Masters (Holcombs)	7–12	4.5–5.5
Library Strategies Learning Lab (Holcombs)	7–12	3.0–4.0
Libraries Are For Finding Out: Using the Encyclopedia (Holcombs)	7–12	3.5–4.5
Libraries Are For Finding Out: Using the Card Catalog (Holcombs)	7–12	3.5–4.5
Using Reference Skills Performance Pack (Holcombs)	7–12	3.5–5.0
Language Skills Crossword Puzzles Duplicating Masters (Holcombs)	7–12	3.0–5.0
Grammar for Adult Living (Holcombs)	9–12	3.0–4.0
English Exercises Duplicating Masters (Holcombs)	7–12	2.0–3.0
Spinning Grammar Game Set (Holcombs)	7–12	3.0–4.0
Spelling Rules & Problem Areas Learning Lab (Holcombs)	7–12	2.0–3.0
Spell Stumpers Duplicating Masters (Holcombs)	7–12	2.5–3.5
Basic Writing Game Module (Holcombs)	7–12	3.0–4.0
Right Your Writing Performance Pack (Holcombs)	7–12	3.5–4.5
Spotlight on Sentences (Holcombs)	7–10	2.5–3.5
Sentence Writing Learning Lab (Holcombs)	7–12	3.0–4.0
Paragraph Writing Learning Lab (Holcombs)	7–12	3.5–4.5

Title and Publisher	Instructional Level	Reading Level
Descriptive Writing: Using Nouns and Verbs (Holcombs)	7–12	3.0–4.0
Sentences and Paragraphs Workshop (Holcombs)	7–12	3.0–4.0
Activities for Writing and Rewriting (Holcombs)	7–12	3.5–4.5
Outlining Skills Duplicating Masters (Holcombs)	7–12	4.5–5.5
Flub Stubs (Composition) (Holcombs)	7–12	2.5–3.5
Everyday Reading & Writing (New Reader's Press)	7–12	5–6
From A to Z (Handwriting) (Steck-Vaughn)	7–Adult	1
Using English (Steck-Vaughn)	10–Adult	3–4
Everyday English (Steck-Vaughn)	10–Adult	4–5
Learning Our Language Revised Books 1 & 2 (Steck-Vaughn)	7–Adult	6–8
English Essentials: A Refresher Course Revised (Steck-Vaughn)	11–Adult	8–10
Fundamental English Review (Steck-Vaughn)	11–Adult	8–12

Table D–2
History

Title and Publisher	Instructional Level	Reading Level
The New Exploring World History (Globe)	7–12	5–6
Exploring American Citizenship (Globe)	7–12	5–6
Cultures in Conflict (Globe)	7–12	5–6
Our Nation of Immigrants (Globe)	7–12	5–6
Inquiry: Western Civilization (Globe)	7–12	5–7
The Afro-American in the United States History (Globe)	7–12	5–6
Pollution of the Environment (Globe)	9–12	8
The New Exploring Our Nation's History (Globe)	7–12	6–7
United States Government (Bowmar/Noble)	7–12	4–6
The War Between the States (Educational Insights)	7–12	4
Frontiers West (Educational Insights)	7–12	4
American History Study Lessons Units 1–9 (Follett)	7–12	5
Study Lessons in Our Nation's History (Follett)	7–12	5
World History Study Lessons Units 1–9 (Follett)	7–12	5
Study Lessons in Civics (Follett)	7–12	6–9
The New Exploring American History (Globe)	7–12	5–6
Civilizations of the Past: Peoples and Cultures (Globe)	7–9	6
The United States: Its People and Leaders (Globe)	7–9	4
The Story of William Penn (Prentice-Hall)	7–12	3

Table D–2 (Continued)

Title and Publisher	Instructional Level	Reading Level
William Penn: Founder of Pennsylvania (Wm. Morrow)	7	4–5
Human Cargo: The Story of the Atlantic Slave Trade (Garrard)	7	6
North to Liberty: The Story of the Underground Railroad (Garrard)	7–9	6
The American Revolution (Educational Insights)	7–12	4
Our Indian Heritage (Xerox)	7–9	4–5
Women in American Life (Xerox)	7–9	4–5
Youth Crime and Punishment (Xerox)	7–9	4–5
America Moves West (Xerox)	7–9	4–5
The Great Depression (Xerox)	7–9	4–5
Juveniles and the Law (Xerox)	7–9	4–5
The Labor Movement (Xerox)	7–9	4–5
Land of Immigrants (Xerox)	7–9	4–5
A Nation in Rebellion (Xerox)	7–9	4–5
Exploring Civilizations: A Discovery Approach (Globe)	7–12	5–6
The United States in the Making (Globe)	7–12	5–6
Our American Minorities (Globe)	7–12	3–4
(Benjamin) Franklin/(Martin Luther) King (Pendulum)	7–12	4–6
We Honor Them, Vols. 1, 2, 3, (Short biographies of Blacks in America) (New Readers Press)	7–12	3–5
Insights About America (Educational Insights)	7–12	4
The Police and Us (New Readers Press)	7–12	3–4
Claiming a Right (Biography of 24 Indians) (New Readers Press)	7–12	3–4
Our United States (New Readers Press)	7–12	3–4
Government by the People (New Readers Press)	7–12	4–5
The Peoples' Power (New Readers Press)	7–12	4–5
Blacks in Time (New Readers Press)	7–12	4–5
I Am One of These (Real life stories of Blacks, Whites, Mexican-American, American Indian, Cuban, foreign-born citizens) (New Readers Press)	7–12	3–4
Martin Luther King (New Readers Press)	7–12	4–5
The Men Who Won the West (Scholastic)	7–12	4–7
Lincoln/Roosevelt (Pendulum)	7–12	4–6
Washington/Jefferson (Pendulum)	7–12	4–6
Crockett/Boone (Pendulum)	7–12	4–6
Lindbergh/Earhart (Pendulum)	7–12	4–6
Forts in the Wilderness (Children's Press)	7–12	4
Explorers in a New World (Children's Press)	7–12	4

Title and Publisher	Instructional Level	Reading Level
Men on Iron Horses (Children's Press)	7–12	4
Pioneering on the Plains (Children's Press)	7–12	4
Settlers on a Strange Shore (Children's Press)	7–12	4

Table D–3
Math

Title and Publisher	Instructional Level	Reading Level
Daily Math Application Program (Holcombs)	10–12	4.5–5.5
Real-Life Math Program (Holcombs)	8–12	4.5–5.5
Using Checks and Charge Cards Learning Lab (Holcombs)	8–12	3.0–4.0
Survival Math Skills Program (Holcombs)	9–12	4.0–5.0
Using Money Wisely (Xerox)	9–12	3.5–4.5
Math For the Road (Xerox)	9–12	3.5–4.5
Checking Account: A Multimedia Kit (Holcombs)	9–12	5.5–6.5
Lakeshore Math Competency Performance Packs (Holcombs)	9–12	3.0–4.5
Math in the Marketplace Filmstrip Activity Library (Holcombs)	8–12	2.5–4.0
Basic Skills in Using Money (Holcombs)	9–12	4.0–5.0
Money Management Duplicating Masters (Holcombs)	8–12	4.5–5.5
Job Simulations Using Math (Holcombs)	9–12	4.0–5.0
Math For Employment 1 Skillbook (Holcombs)	9–12	4.5–5.5
Math For Employment 2 Skillbook (Holcombs)	9–12	4.5–5.5
Math for the Worker Skillbook (Holcombs)	9–12	4.5–5.5
Payroll Deductions Activity Unit (Holcombs)	9–12	5.5–6.5
Basic Buying Skills Duplicating Masters (Holcombs)	7–12	2.5–4.0
Using Consumer Math Competency Lab (Holcombs)	7–12	3.5–4.5
Consumer Math for Self Defense (Holcombs)	7–12	5.0–6.0
Grocery Bills Skillbook (Holcombs)	7–12	2.5–3.5
Arithmetic for Grocery Shopping (Holcombs)	7–12	2.0–3.0
Consumer Math Strategies (Holcombs)	7–12	4.5–5.5
Newspaper Math Tasks (Holcombs)	7–10	4.5–5.5
Using Dollars & Sense Activity Book (Holcombs)	7–12	2.5–3.5
Everyday Math Survival Skills (Holcombs)	7–12	3.5–4.5
Mathematics & You: A Hands-On Approach (Holcombs)	7–12	4.5
Your Daily Math Skills Books 1 & 2 (Holcombs)	7–12	4.5–5.5
Math Marathon (Holcombs)	7–12	2.5–3.5

Table D-3 (Continued)

Title and Publisher	Instructional Level	Reading Level
Math Puzzlers (Holcombs)	7–12	4.5–5.5
Metric Football (Holcombs)	7–12	4.0–5.0
Metric Puzzles Duplicating Module (Holcombs)	7–12	5.0–6.0
Measurement Learning Labs (Holcombs)	7–12	2.8–3.8
Money Makes Sense Activity Book (Holcombs)	7–12	2.0–3.0
Multi-Step Math Drill Cassettes (Holcombs)	7–12	2.5–3.5
Basic Math Facts Competency Lab (Holcombs)	7–12	2.0–4.0
Number Power Skillbook (Holcombs)	7–12	2.0–4.0
Back to Basics From Addition to Division (Holcombs)	7–12	2.5–4.5
Lifeskills Math Activity Book (Holcombs)	7–12	3.2–4.5
Veri-Tech: A Self-Check Basic Math System (Holcombs)	7–12	3.0–4.0
Sports Cards Math Kit (Holcombs)	7–12	3.0–4.0
Making Basic Math Easy (Holcombs)	7–12	4.2–5.5
Single Topic Math Duplicating Series (Holcombs)	7–12	4.5–5.5
Fractions Sequential Activity Card Set (Holcombs)	7–12	3.5–4.5
Lakeshore Learning Lab (Fractions & decimals) (Holcombs)	7–12	3.0–4.5
Decimals Sports Cards (Holcombs)	7–12	4.5–5.5
Figure It Out (Xerox)	5–9	2.5–3.5
The Learning Skills Series Arithmetic, 2/e (McGraw-Hill)	6–up	2–3
Understanding Word Problems Multimedia Kit (Holcombs)	7–12	4.5–5.5
How to Solve Word Problems Practice Cards (Holcombs)	7–12	3.5–4.5
Solving Word Problems Duplicating Masters (Holcombs)	7–12	4.5–5.5
High Interest Math Duplicating Library (Holcombs)	7–12	3.0–3.5
Basic Math Operations (Holcombs)	7–12	2.5–3.5
Whole Number Operations (Holcombs)	7–12	3.5–4.5
Captain Quotient (Holcombs)	7–12	3.0–4.0
Mysteries of History (Multiplication) (Holcombs)	7–12	3.0–4.0
Arithmetic Drills Review (Holcombs)	7–10	2.5–4.5

Table D-4
Science

Title and Publisher	Instructional Level	Reading Level
Spaceship Earth/Life Science (Houghton Mifflin)	8–12	7
Spaceship Earth/Physical Science (Houghton Mifflin)	8–12	6–7
Spaceship Earth/Earth Science (Houghton Mifflin)	9–12	7–8

Title and Publisher	Instructional Level	Reading Level
Edison/Bell (Pendulum)	7–12	4–6
Curie/Einstein (Pendulum)	9–12	4–6
Biology Workshop 1: Understanding Living Things (Globe)	9–12	4–5
Earth Science Workshop 1: Understanding the Earth's Surface (Globe)	9–12	4–5
Chemistry Workshop 1: Understanding Matter (Globe)	9–12	4–5
Physics Workshop 1: Understanding Energy (Globe)	9–12	4–5
Biology Workshop 2: Understanding the Human Body (Globe)	9–12	4–5
Earth Science Workshop 2: Understanding the Atmosphere and Oceans (Globe)	9–12	4–5
Chemistry Workshop 2: Understanding Mixtures (Globe)	9–12	4–5
Physics Workshop 2: Understanding Forces (Globe)	9–12	4–5
Biology Workshop 3: Understanding Reproduction (Globe)	9–12	4–5
Earth Science Workshop 3: Understanding Space (Globe)	9–12	4–5
Chemistry Workshop 3: Understanding the Chemistry of Metals (Globe)	9–12	4–5
Physics Workshop 3: Understanding Light and Sound (Globe)	9–12	4–5
What is an Atom? (Benefic)	7–8	4
What is a Cell? (Benefic)	7–8	4
What is Energy? (Benefic)	7–8	4
What is Gravity? (Benefic)	7–8	4
What is Heat? (Benefic)	7–8	4
What is an Insect? (Benefic)	7–8	4
What is a Machine? (Benefic)	7–8	4
What is a Magnet? (Benefic)	7–8	4
What is Matter? (Benefic)	7–8	4
What is a Solar System? (Benefic)	7–8	4
What is Sound? (Benefic)	7–8	4
What is Space? (Benefic)	7–8	4
What is Weather? (Benefic)	7–8	4
What Makes a Light Go On? (Little, Brown)	7–up	3
The Bug Club Book: A Handbook for Young Bug Collectors (Holiday House)	7	4
What Colonel Glenn Did All Day (John Day)	7–up	4
Magic With Chemistry (Grosset & Dunlap)	7–up	4
This is Cape Kennedy (Macmillan)	7–up	3
Experiments for Young Scientists (Little, Brown)	7–up	3

Table D–5
Health

Title and Publisher	Instructional Level	Reading Level
Keeping Fit! (Xerox)	9–12	3.5–4.5
Health & Safety: Keeping Fit Multimedia Kit (Holcombs)	7–12	5.0–6.0
Human Body Activity Cards (Holcombs)	7–12	3.5–4.5
Your Life in Your Hands (Holcombs)	7–12	4.0–5.0
Health Resource Cards (Holcombs)	7–12	5.0–6.0
First Aid: Newest Techniques Multimedia Program (Holcombs)	7–12	3.0–4.0
Health Survival Skills Multimedia Kit (Holcombs)	7–12	3.0–4.0
Sigh of Relief: First Aid Guide for the Classroom (Holcombs)	7–12	3.0–4.5
Having a Baby Series (New Readers Press)	7–12	4
Be Informed on Drugs (New Readers Press)	7–12	4–5
Contemporary Reading Series (7 books on topics such as drugs, alcohol, V.D., pregnancy) (Educational Activities)	7–12	4–5
Emergency Medical Care Worktext (Holcombs)	7–12	5.0–6.5
Health & Nutrition Reference Library (Holcombs)	8–12	5.0–7.5
Is It Safe to Eat Anything Anymore? (Holcombs)	7–12	3.0–5.0
The Basics of Nutrition, A Multimedia Program (Holcombs)	7–12	4.0–5.0
Nutrition Survival Kit (Holcombs)	7–12	4.5–6.0
Nutrition: Food vs. Health (Holcombs)	7–12	3.0–4.0
You & Food Additives Activity Unit (Holcombs)	7–12	5.0–6.0
Label Literacy: How to Read Food Packages (Holcombs)	7–12	2.0–3.0
Modern Human Sexuality (Houghton Mifflin)	7–9	4–5
The Body Machine: Parts and Functions (Xerox)	7–9	4.0–6.0
The Body Machine: Care and Maintenance (Xerox)	7–9	4.0–6.0

Table D–6
Careers

Title and Publisher	Instructional Level	Reading Level
Survival Skills for Work (Holcombs)	9–12	4.5–5.5
The Very Basics of Work Reading Series (Holcombs)	9–12	1.5–2.5
The Job Hunt Cassette Activity Program (Holcombs)	9–12	5.0–6.0
The Job Hunting Game (Holcombs)	9–12	3.5–4.5
Don't Get Fired Activity Book (Holcombs)	9–12	2.0–3.0
Job Applications Activity Book (Holcombs)	8–12	2.5–3.5
Job Interview Worktext (Holcombs)	8–12	2.5–3.5
You & Others on the Job Reading Series (Holcombs)	8–12	3.5–4.5
Janus Job Interview Guide (Janus)	7–12	2.5
Janus Job Planner (Janus)	7–12	2.8

Title and Publisher	Instructional Level	Reading Level
People Working Today (10 books about teenage workers) (Janus)	7–12	1.9
Get Hired! 13 Ways to Get Your Job (Janus)	7–12	2.5
Don't Get Fired! 13 Ways to Hold Your Job (Janus)	7–12	2.5
First Jobs Multimedia Program (Holcombs)	7–12	3.0–4.0
Your First Job Reading Series (Holcombs)	7–12	2.0–3.0
Career Exploration Resource Library (Holcombs)	7–12	5.5–6.5
The Info-Job Resource Center (Holcombs)	7–12	4.5–5.5
Real People at Work Library 1 (Holcombs)	7–12	2.0–4.0
Real People at Work Library 2 (Holcombs)	7–12	4.0–5.0

Table D–7
Geography

Title and Publisher	Instructional Level	Reading Level
The Earth: Regions and Peoples (Globe)	7–8	3
Homelands of the World: Resources and Cultures (Globe)	7	5
Exploring the Western World (Globe)	7	5
The New Exploring the Non-Western World (Globe)	7–12	5–6
Exploring the Urban World (Globe)	7–12	5–6
The Congo: River into Central Africa (Garrard)	7	5
The Niger: Africa's River of Mystery (Garrard)	7	5
The Nile: Lifeline of Egypt (Garrard)	7	5
The Ganges: Sacred River of India (Garrard)	7	5
The Indus: South Asia's Highway of History (Garrard)	7	5
The Yangtze: China's River Highway (Garrard)	7	5
The Rhone: River of Contrasts (Garrard)	7	5
The Seine: River of Paris (Garrard)	7	5
The Shannon: River of Loughs and Legends (Garrard)	7	5
The Thames: London's River (Garrard)	7	5
The Tiber: The Roman River (Garrard)	7	5
The Volga: Russia's River of Five Seas (Garrard)	7	5
The Amazon: River Sea of Brazil (Garrard)	7	5
The Mississippi: Giant at Work (Garrard)	7	5
The St. Lawrence: Seaway of North America (Garrard)	7	5
The Jordan: River of the Promised Land (Garrard)	7	5
The Colorado: Mover of Mountains (Garrard)	7	5
The Rio Grande: Life for the Desert (Garrard)	7	5
A World Explorer: Roald Amundsen (Garrard)	7	4

Table D–8
Literature

Title and Publisher	Instructional Level	Reading Level
Great American Library—Biography (Junior A + B, Senior A + B) (Scholastic)	7–12	3–7 4–8
House of the Seven Gables (Globe)	8–12	6–7
An O. Henry Reader (Globe)	9–12	7–8
Short World Biographies (Globe)	9–12	5–6
Profiles: A Collection of Short Biographies (Globe)	9–12	5–6
A Tale of Two Cities (Globe)	9–12	5–6
Moby Dick (Globe)	9–12	5–6
Jane Eyre (Globe)	8–12	4–5
An Edgar Allen Poe Reader (Globe)	8–12	6–7
Turning Point: A Selection of Short Biographies (Globe)	8–12	3
Lorna Doone (Globe)	8–12	5–6
Journeys to Fame (A series of short biographies) (Globe)	7–12	2–3
Modern Short Biographies (Globe)	7–12	5–6
Tales Worth Retelling (Rudyard Kipling) (Globe)	7–12	5–6
The Adventures of Sherlock Holmes (Globe)	8–12	6–7
Tom Sawyer (Globe)	7–12	3–4
Chitty Chitty Bang Bang (Scholastic)	7–12	6
Kidnapped (Globe)	7–12	5–6
The Odyssey (Globe)	7–12	5–6
Twenty Thousand Leagues Under the Sea (Globe)	7–12	4–5
Treasure Island (Globe)	7–12	5–6
American Folklore and Legends (Globe)	7–12	4
Legends for Everyone (Globe)	7–12	3
Myths and Folk Tales Around the World (Globe)	7–12	4
The Magnificent Myths of Man (Globe)	7–12	4–5
Scholastic Reluctant Reader Libraries (Junior A + B, Senior A + B) (Scholastic)	7–12	4–8
Their Eyes on the Stars: Four Black Writers (Garrard)	7–9	6

References

A

Aaron, R. L., & Muench, S. (1974–75). Behaviorally disordered adolescents' perceptions of adult authority figures after treatment using a taxonomy of comprehensions skills. *Reading Research Quarterly, 10*, 228–243.

Abbass, M. (1977). The language of fifty commonly used forms. *Dissertation Abstracts International, 37*, 5655A. (University Microfilms No. 77–6197, 520)

Abelson, W. D., Zigler, E., & Deblasi, C. (1974). Effects of a four year Follow Through program on economically disadvantaged children. *Journal of Educational Psychology, 66*, 756–771.

Abrahms, J. C. (1968). *Dyslexia—single or plural.* Los Angeles: National Reading Conference. (ERIC Document Reproduction Service No. ED 028 048)

Ackerly, S. S., & Benton, A. L. (1947). Report of a case of bilateral frontal lobe defect. *Proceedings, Association for Research on Nervous and Mental Disease, 27*, 479–504.

Adams, A., Carnine, D., & Gersten, R. (1982). Instructional strategies for studying content area texts in the intermediate grades. *Reading Research Quarterly, 18*, 27–55.

Adams, A. H., & Harrison, C. B. (1975). Using television to teach specific reading skills. *The Reading Teacher, 29*, 45–51.

Adams, M. L. (1964). Teachers' instructional needs in teaching reading. *The Reading Teacher, 17*, 260–264.

Ahmann, J. S. (1975). An exploration of survival levels of achievement by means of assessment techniques. In D. M. Nielsen & H. F. Hjelm (Eds.), *Reading and career education.* Newark, DE: International Reading Association.

Allen, R., & Allen, C. (1966). *Language experiences in reading.* Chicago: Encyclopedia Britannica Press.

Allington, R. (1984). Content coverage and contextual reading in reading groups. *Journal of Reading Behavior, 16*, 85–96.

Altus, G. T. (1956). A WISC profile for retarded readers. *Journal of Consulting Psychology, 20*, 155–157.

Amoroso, H. C. (1985). Organic primers for basic literacy instruction. *Journal of Reading, 28*, 398–401.

Anderson, I. H., & Dearborn, W. F. (1952). *The psychology of teaching reading.* New York: Ronald Press.

Anderson, R. C. (1977). *Schema-directed processes in language comprehension.* (Report No. 50). Urbana: University of Illinois, Center for the Study of Reading. (ERIC Document Reproduction Service No. ED 142 977)

Anderson, R. C., Hiebert, E. H., Scott, J. A. & Wilkinson, I. A. G. (1985). *Becoming a nation of readers.* Washington, D.C.: National Institute of Education.

Anderson, R. W. (1965). Effects of neuropsychological techniques on reading achievement. Unpublished doctoral dissertation, Colorado State College, Boulder.

Anderson, R. W. (1966). Effects of neuro-psychological techniques on reading achievement. *Dissertation Abstracts International, 26*, 5216A. (University Microfilms No. 65–14, 796)

Andre, M. E. D. A., & Anderson, T. H. (1978–79). The development and evaluation of a self-questioning study technique. *Reading Research Quarterly, 14*, 605–623.

Andrews, J. F. & Mason, J. M. (1984). *How do young deaf children learn to read? A proposed model of deaf children's emergent reading behaviors.* (Tech. Rep. No. 329). Champaign: University of Illinois, Center for the Study of Reading.

Aoki, E. M. (1981). "Are you Chinese? Are you Japanese? Or are you just a mixed-up kid?" Using Asian American children's literature. *The Reading Teacher, 34,* 382–385.

Are computers in the classroom here to stay? (1982, September). *Newsline,* p. 6.

Arlin, M., Scott, M., & Webster, J. (1978–79). The effects of pictures on rate of learning sight words. *Reading Research Quarterly, 14,* 645–660.

Au, K. H., & Mason, J. M. (1981). Social organizational factors in learning to read: The balance of rights hypothesis. *Reading Research Quarterly, 17,* 115–152.

Ausubel, D. P. (1960). The use of advance organizers in learning and retention of meaningful material. *Journal of Educational Psychology, 51,* 267–272.

Auten, A. (1985). Small group instruction: Effective classroom management? *Journal of Reading, 28,* 460–462.

Ayres, A. J. (1972). *Sensory integration and learning disorders.* Los Angeles: Western Psychological Services.

B

Bader, L. A., & Wiesendanger, K. D. (1986). University based reading clinics: Practices and procedures. *The Reading Teacher, 39,* 698–702.

Bailey, E. J. (1975). *Academic activities for adolescents with learning disabilities.* Evergreen, CO: Learning Pathways.

Bailey, M. H. (1967). The utility of phonics generalizations in grades one through six. *The Reading Teacher, 20,* 413–418.

Bailey, M. H. (1971). Utility of vowel digraph generalizations in grades one through six. In M. A. Dawson (Ed.), *Teaching word recognition*

skills. Newark, DE: International Reading Association.

Bakwin, H. (1973). Reading disability in twins. *Developmental Medicine and Child Neurology, 15,* 184–187.

Balow, B. (1965). The long-term effect of remedial reading instruction. *The Reading Teacher, 18,* 581–591.

Balow, B. (1971). Perceptual-motor activities in the treatment of severe reading disability. *The Reading Teacher, 24,* 513–525; 542.

Balow, B., Rubin, R., & Rosen, M. J. (1975–76). Perinatal events as precursors of reading disability. *Reading Research Quarterly, 11,* 36–71.

Balow, I. H. (1963). Sex differences in first grade reading. *Elementary English, 40,* 303–306; 320.

Balow, I. H., & Balow, B. (1964). Lateral dominance and reading achievement. *American Educational Research Journal, 1,* 139–143.

Barbe, W. B., & Swassing, R. H. (1979). *Teaching through modality strengths: Concepts and practice.* Columbus, OH: Zaner-Bloser.

Bargantz, J. C., & Dulin, K. L. (1970). Readability levels of selected mass magazines from 1925 to 1965. In G. B. Schick & M. M. May (Eds.), *Reading: Process and pedagogy, (Nineteenth Yearbook of the National Reading Conference),* 2 (26–30). Washington, D.C.: National Reading Conference.

Barnett, C. D., Ellis, N. R., & Pryor, M. (1960). Learning in familial and brain-injured defectives. *American Journal of Mental Deficiency, 64,* 894–897.

Barrett, T. C. (1965). The relationship between measures of prereading visual discrimination and first grade reading achievement: A review of the literature. *Reading Research Quarterly, 1,* 51–76.

Barrett, T. C. (1967). The evaluation of children's reading achievement. *Perspectives in reading, No. 8.* Newark, DE: International Reading Association.

Barrett, T. C. (1979). A taxonomy of reading comprehension. In R. Smith & T. C. Barrett (Eds.), *Teaching read-*

ing in the middle grades (2nd ed.). Reading, MA: Addison-Wesley.

Barron, R. C. (1969). The use of vocabulary as an advance organizer. In H. Herber & P. L. Sanders (Eds.), *Research in reading in the content areas: First year report.* Syracuse: Syracuse University Reading and Language Arts Center.

Bartlett, F. C. (1932). *Remembering.* Cambridge, MA: Harvard University Press.

Bateman, B. (1971). The role of individual diagnosis in remedial planning for reading disorders. *Reading Forum,* NINDS Monograph II. Bethesda, MD: National Institute of Neurological Diseases and Stroke.

Bates, G. W. (1984). Profile of university-based reading clinics: Results of a U.S. survey. *Journal of Reading, 27,* 524–529.

Bean, R. M., & Eichelberger, R. T. (1985). Changing the role of reading specialists: From pull-out to in-class programs. *The Reading Teacher, 38,* 648–653.

Beck, I. L., Omanson, R. C., & McKeown, M. G. (1982). An instructional redesign of reading lessons: Effects on comprehension. *Reading Research Quarterly, 17,* 462–481.

Becker, J. T. (1970). Language experience approach in a Job Corps reading lab. *Journal of Reading, 13,* 281–284; 319–321.

Beebe, M. J. (1982). The effect of different types of substitution miscues on reading. *Reading Research Quarterly, 15,* 324–336.

Beery, K. E., & Butenica, N. A. (1967). *Developmental Test of Visual-Motor Integration.* Chicago: Follett.

Belch, P. J. (1974). An investigation of the effect of different questioning strategies on the reading comprehension scores of secondary level educable mentally retarded students. *Dissertation Abstracts International, 35,* 2077A–2078A. (University Microfilms No. 74–820, 820)

Belloni, L. F., & Jongsma, E. A. (1978). The effects of interest on reading comprehension of low-achieving students. *Journal of Reading, 22,* 106–109.

Belmont, J. M. (1966). Long-term memory in mental retardation. In N. R. Ellis (Ed.), *International review of research in mental retardation, Vol. I.* New York: Academic Press.

Belmont, L., & Birch, H. G. (1965). Lateral dominance, lateral awareness, and reading disability. *Child Development, 36,* 57–71.

Benton, C. D., & McCann, J. W. (1969). Dyslexia and dominance: Some second thoughts. *Journal of Pediatric Ophthalmology, 6,* 220–222.

Berber, E. S., & Romanczyk, R. G. (1980). Assessment of the learning disabled and hyperactive child: An analysis and critique. *Journal of Learning Disabilities, 13,* 531–538.

Berger, A., & Kautz, C. (1967). The braille informal reading inventory. *The Reading Teacher, 21,* 149–152.

Berger, N. S., & Perfetti, C. A. (1977). Reading skill and memory for spoken and written discourse. *Journal of Reading Behavior, 9,* 7–16.

Bernstein, M. R. (1955). Relationship between interest and reading comprehension. *Journal of Educational Research, 49,* 283–288.

Bettman, J. W., Stern, E. L., & Gofman, H. F. (1967). Cerebral dominance in developmental dyslexia. *Archives of Ophthalmology, 78,* 722–729.

Betts, E. A. (1940). Reading problems at the intermediate grade level. *Elementary School Journal, 15,* 737–746.

Biemiller, A. (1970). The development of the use of graphic and contextual information as children learn to read. *Reading Research Quarterly, 6,* 75–96.

Bittner, J. R., & Shamo, G. W. (1976). Readability of the 'Mini Page'. *Journalism Quarterly, 53,* 740–743.

Bjork, R. A., & Whitten, W. B. (1974). Recency-sensitive retrieval processes. *Cognitive Psychology, 6,* 173–189.

Blachowicz, C. L. Z. (1977). Cloze activities for primary readers. *The Reading Teacher, 31,* 300–302.

Black, W. F. (1974). Achievement test performance of high and low perceiving learning disabled children. *Journal of Learning Disabilities, 7,* 178–182.

Blackman, L. S., & Capobianco, R. J. (1965). An evaluation of programmed instruction with the mentally retarded utilizing teaching machines. *American Journal of Mental Deficiency, 70,* 262–269.

Blanchard, J. S. (1984). U.S. Armed Services computer assisted literacy efforts. *Journal of Reading, 28,* 262–265.

Blanchard, J. S., & Mason, G. E. (1985). Using computers in content area reading instruction. *Journal of Reading, 29,* 112–117.

Bleiberg, R. (1970). Is there a need for a specially designed reading series for beginning blind readers? *The New Outlook for the Blind, 64,* 135–138.

Bliesmer, E. T. (1962). Evaluating progress in remedial reading programs. *The Reading Teacher, 15,* 344–350.

Blom, G. E., Waite, R. R., & Zimet, S. G. (1970). A motivational content analysis of children's primers. In H. Levin & J. Williams (Eds.), *Basic studies on reading.* New York: Basic Books.

Bloom, B. S. (Ed.). (1956). *Taxonomy of educational objectives.* New York: Longman.

Boag, A. K., & Neild, M. (1962). The influence of the time factor on the scores of the Triggs Diagnostic Reading Test as reflected in the performance of secondary school pupils grouped according to ability. *Journal of Educational Research, 55,* 181–183.

Boder, E. (1973). Developmental dyslexia: A diagnostic approach based on three typical reading-spelling patterns. *Developmental Medicine and Child Neurology, 15,* 663–687.

Bohac, C. A. (1976). *Improving Reading Skills: A Learning Module Based on the South Carolina Driver's Handbook.* Columbia, SC: Wil Lou Grey Adult Reading Council of the International Reading Association, Midlands Technical College.

Bond, G. L., & Dykstra, R. (1967). The cooperative research program in first grade reading. *Reading Research Quarterly, 2,* entire issue.

Bond, G. L., & Fay, L. C. (1950). A comparison of the performance of good and poor readers on the individual items of the Stanford-Binet scale. *Journal of Educational Research, 43,* 475–479.

Bond, G. L., & Tinker, M. A. (1957). *Reading difficulties: Their diagnosis and correction.* New York: Appleton-Century-Crofts.

Bond, G. L., & Tinker, M. A. (1967). *Reading difficulties: Their diagnosis and correction* (2nd ed.). New York: Appleton-Century-Crofts.

Bond, G. L., & Tinker, M. A. (1973). *Reading difficulties: Their diagnosis and correction* (3rd ed.). New York: Appleton-Century-Crofts.

Bond, G. L., Tinker, M. A., & Wasson, B. B. (1979). *Reading difficulties: Their diagnosis and correction* (4th ed.). Englewood Cliffs, N. J.: Prentice-Hall.

Borko, H., Shavelson, R. J., & Stern, P. (1981). Teacher decisions in the planning of reading instruction. *Reading Research Quarterly, 16,* 449–466.

Bormuth, J. R. (1966). Readability: A new approach. *Reading Research Quarterly, 1,* 79–132.

Bormuth, J. R. (1968). The cloze readability procedure. In J. R. Bormuth (Ed.), *Readability in 1968.* Champaign, IL: National Council of Teachers of English.

Bormuth, J. R. (1973–74). Reading literacy: Its definition and assessment. *Reading Research Quarterly, 9,* 7–66.

Boyle, R. C. (1959). *How can reading be taught to educable adolescents who have not learned to read?* (Project No. 162.) Washington, D.C.: U.S. Office of Education.

Braam, L. S., & Berger, A. (1968). Effectiveness of four methods of increasing reading rate, comprehension, and flexibility. *Journal of Reading, 11,* 346–352.

Bradley, J. M. (1976). Evaluating reading achievement for placement in special education. *Journal of Special Education, 10,* 239–245.

Brophy, J. E. (1983). Classroom organization and management. *Elementary School Journal, 83,* 265–285.

Brown, D. A. (1970). Measuring the reading ability and potential of adult illiterates. In R. Farr (Ed.), *Measure-*

ment and evaluation of reading. New York: Harcourt, Brace, Jovanovich.

Brown, D. A. (1982). *Reading diagnosis and remediation.* Englewood Cliffs, NJ: Prentice-Hall.

Brown, J. I. (1976). Techniques for increasing reading rate. In J. E. Merritt (Ed.), *New horizons in reading.* Newark, DE: International Reading Association.

Bruininks, R. H., & Warfield, G. (1978). The mentally retarded. In E. L. Meyen (Ed.), *Exceptional children and youth: An introduction* (pp. 189–190). Denver: Love.

Bryan, T. H. (1974). Learning disabilities: A new stereotype. *Journal of Learning Disabilities, 7,* 304–309.

Buckland, P. (1970). The effect of visual perception training on reading achievement of low readiness first grade pupils. *Dissertation Abstracts International, 31,* 1613A. (University Microfilms No. 70–15, 707)

Bureau of Census, Department of Commerce. (1971, March). Illiteracy in the United States: November 1969. *Current Population Reports.* (Series P–20, No. 217)

Burnett, S. M. (1890). A case of alexia (dysanagnosia). *Archives of Ophthalmology, 19,* 86–90.

Burns, E. (1982). Linear regression and simplified reading expectancy formulas. *Reading Research Quarterly, 17,* 446–453.

Bush, W. J., & Waugh, K. W. (1982). *Diagnosing learning problems* (3rd ed.). Columbus, OH: Merrill.

Buswell, G. T. (1922). Fundamental reading habits: A study of their development. *Supplementary Educational Monographs, 21.* Chicago: University of Chicago Press.

Buswell, G. T. (1951). Relationship between rate of thinking and rate of reading. *School Review, 49,* 339–346.

Byers, R. K., & Lord, E. E. (1943). Late effects of lead poisoning on mental development. *American Journal of Diseases of Children, 66,* 471–493.

C

Calkins, E. (1972). Free to learn. In Smith, B. K. (1972). *American Education, 8,* 11–16.

Capobianco, R. J. (1966). Ocular-manual laterality and reading in adolescent mental retardates. *American Journal of Mental Deficiency, 70,* 781–785.

Capobianco, R. J. (1967). Ocular-manual laterality and reading achievement in children with special learning disabilities. *American Educational Research Journal, 2,* 133–137.

Cardenal, F., & Miller, V. (1981). Nicaragua 1980: The battle of the ABCs. *Harvard Educational Review, 51,* 1–26.

Carlson, T. R. (1946). *The relationship between speed and accuracy of comprehension of reading.* Unpublished doctoral dissertation. University of Minnesota, Minneapolis.

Carroll, J. B., Davies, P., & Richman, B. (1971). *American Heritage word frequency book.* Boston: Houghton Mifflin.

Cartwright, C. A., & Cartwright, G. P. (1984). *Developing observation skills* (2nd ed.). New York: McGraw-Hill.

Carver, R. P. (1982). Optimal rate of reading prose. *Reading Research Quarterly, 18,* 56–88.

Carver, R. P. (1983). Is reading rate constant or flexible? *Reading Research Quarterly, 18,* 190–215.

Cason, E. B. (1943). *Mechanical methods for increasing the speed of reading.* New York: Bureau of Publications, Teacher's College, Columbia University.

Cegelka, P. A., & Cegelka, W. J. (1970). A review of research: Reading and the educable mentally handicapped. *Exceptional Children, 23,* 187–200.

Ceprano, M. A. (1981). A review of selected research on methods of teaching sight words. *The Reading Teacher, 35,* 314–322.

Chall, J. (1978). A decade of research on reading and learning disabilities. In S. J. Samuels (Ed.), *What research has to say about reading instruction.* Newark, DE: International Reading Association.

Chan, J. M. T. (1985). Computer software. *The Reading Teacher, 39,* 99–101.

Chandler, T. A. (1966). Reading disability and socio-economic status. *Journal of Reading, 10,* 5–21.

Chang, T., & Chang, V. (1967). Relation of visual-motor skills and reading achievement in primary grade pupils of superior ability. *Perceptual and Motor Skills, 24,* 51–53.

Chase, A. (1977). *The legacy of Malthus: The social costs of the new scientific racism.* New York: Knopf.

Chomsky, C. (1976). After decoding: What? *Language Arts, 53,* 288–296; 314.

Clark, N. L. (1972). *Hierarchical structure of comprehension skills.* A. C. E. R.: Victoria, Australia: A. C. E. R.

Clay, M. M. (1967). The reading behavior of five-year-old children: A research report. *New Zealand Journal of Educational Studies, 2,* 11–31.

Clay, M. M. (1979). *Reading: The patterning of complex behavior* (2nd ed.). Auckland, New Zealand: Heinemann.

Claycomb, M. (1978). *Brain research and learning.* Washington, D.C.: National Education Association.

Cleary, D. M. (1978). *Thinking Thursdays: Language arts in the reading lab.* Newark, DE: International Reading Association.

Cleland, D. L. (1950). *An experimental study of tachistoscopic training as it relates to speed and comprehension in reading.* Unpublished doctoral dissertation. University of Pittsburgh, Pittsburgh.

Cleland, D. L. (1964). Clinical materials for appraising disabilities in reading. *The Reading Teacher, 17,* 428.

Clymer, T. (1963). The utility of phonics generalizations in the primary grades. *The Reading Teacher, 16,* 252–258.

Cohen, D. (1968). Effect of literature on vocabulary and reading. *Elementary English, 45,* 209–213.

Cohen, D. K. (1972). *The effects of the Michigan Tracking Program on gains in reading.* New Brunswick, NJ: Rutgers University. (ERIC Document Reproduction Service No. ED 064 700)

Cohen, H. J., Birch, H. G., & Taft, E. T. (1970). Some considerations for evaluating the Doman-Delacato "patterning" method. *Pediatrics, 45,* 302–314.

Cohen, M. L. (1968). Field dependence-independence and reading comprehension. *Dissertation Abstracts International, 29,* 476A–477A. (University Microfilms No. 68–11, 783)

Cohen, S. A. (1969). Dyslexia. *Encyclopedia Americana, 9,* 516.

Cohen, S. A., & Kornfeld, G. (1970). *Oral vocabulary and beginning reading in disadvantaged children.* New York: Reading and Language Arts Center, Yeshiva University.

Coleman, E. B. (1965). Learning of prose written in four grammatical transformations. *Journal of Applied Psychology, 49,* 332–341.

Coleman, E. B. (1971). Developing a technology of written instruction: Some determiners of the complexity of prose. In E. Z. Rothkopf & P. E. Johnson (Eds.), *Verbal learning research and the technology of written instruction.* New York: Teachers College Press, Columbia University.

Coleman, R. I., & Deutsch, C. P. (1964). Lateral dominance and right-left discrimination: A comparison of normal and retarded readers. *Perceptual Motor Skills, 19,* 43–50.

Coles, G. S. (1980). Evaluation of genetic explanations of reading and learning problems. *The Journal of Special Education, 14,* 365–383.

Colligan, L., & Colligan, D. (1979). *Scholastic's A⁺ guide to good grades.* New York: Scholastic.

Comfort, A. (1967). *The anxiety makers: Some curious preoccupations of the medical profession.* New York: Dell.

Committee on Nutrition, American Academy of Pediatrics (1976). Megavitamin therapy for childhood psychoses and learning disabilities. *Pediatrics, 58,* 910–912.

Conley, M. W. (1986). Test review: Basic Achievement Skills Individual Screener. *The Reading Teacher, 39,* 418–420.

Cook, D. L. (1957). A comparison of reading comprehension scores obtained before and after timed announcement. *Journal of Educational Psychology, 48,* 440–446.

Cook, W. D. (1977). *Adult literacy education in the United States.* Newark, DE: International Reading Association.

Cooper, H. M., Baron, R. M., & Love, C. A. (1975). The importance of race and social class information in the formation of expectancies about academic performance. *Journal of Educational Psychology, 67,* 312–319.

Craik, F. I. M., & Lockhart, R. S. (1972). Levels of processing: A framework for memory research. *Journal of Verbal Learning and Verbal Behavior, 11,* 671–684.

Critchley, M. (1964). *Developmental dyslexia.* London: William Heinemann.

Critchley, M. (1970). *The dyslexic child* (2nd ed.). London, England: Heinemann Medical Books.

Croft, J. (1951). A teacher's survey of his backward class in a secondary modern school. *British Journal of Educational Psychology, 21,* 135–144.

Cruickshank, W. M. (1966). *The teacher of brain-injured children: A discussion of bases for competency.* Syracuse: Syracuse University Press.

Cruickshank, W. M. (1975). The learning environment. In W. M. Cruickshank & D. P. Hallahan (Eds.), *Perceptual and learning disabilities in children, Vol. 1: Psychoeducational practices.* Syracuse: Syracuse University Press.

Cruse, D. B. (1961). Effects of distraction upon the performance of brain-injured and familial retarded children. *American Journal of Mental Deficiency, 66,* 86–90.

Cullinan, B., & Fitzgerald, S. (1984, December/1985, January). Background information bulletin on the use of readability formulae. *Reading Today,* p. 1.

Culyer, R. C. (1978). Guidelines for skill development: Vocabulary. *The Reading Teacher, 32,* 316–322.

Cunningham, P. M. (1976–77). Teachers' correction responses to black-dialect miscues which are non-meaning-changing. *Reading Research Quarterly, 12,* 637–653.

Cunningham, P. M. (1977). Investigating the role of meaning in mediated word identification. In P. D. Pearson & J. Hansen (Eds.), *Reading: Theory, research, and practice.* Clemson, SC: National Reading Conference.

Cunningham, P. M., Moore, S. A., Cunningham, J. W., & Moore, D. W. (1983). *Reading in elementary classrooms.* New York: Longman.

Curry, R. G. (1975). Using LEA to teach blind children to read. *The Reading Teacher, 29,* 272–279.

Cutsforth, T. D. (1951). *The blind in school and society.* New York: American Foundation for the Blind.

D

Dale, E. (1965). Vocabulary measurement: Techniques and major findings. *Elementary English, 42,* 895–901; 948.

Dale, E., & Chall, J. (1986). *Readability revisited: The new Dale-Chall formula.* New York: McGraw-Hill.

Dale, E., & O'Rourke, J. (1971). *Techniques of teaching vocabulary.* Palo Alto, CA: Field Educational Publications.

Dale, E., & O'Rourke, J. (1976). *The living word vocabulary.* Elgin, IL: Dome.

Daneman, M., & Carpenter, P. A. (1980). Individual differences in working memory and reading. *Journal of Verbal Learning and Verbal Behavior, 19,* 450–466.

Davidson, J. L. (1982). The group mapping activity for instruction in reading and thinking. *Journal of Reading, 27,* 52–56.

Davis, F. B. (1944). Fundamental factors of comprehension in reading. *Psychometrika, 9,* 185–197.

Davis, F. B. (1968). Psychometric research on comprehension in reading. *Reading Research Quarterly, 3,* 339–345.

Davis, H., & Silverman, S. (Eds.). (1970). *Hearing and deafness.* New York: Holt, Rinehart & Winston.

Davis, N. (1967). *Vocabulary improvement.* New York: McGraw-Hill.

Davis, W. D. (1954). Possible organic basis for a syndrome: Reading disability, hyperactivity, and behavior problems in boys. *Delaware State Medical Journal, 26,* 199–201.

Dearborn, W. F., & Anderson, I. H. (1938). Aniseikonia as related to disability in reading. *Journal of Experimental Psychology, 23,* 559–577.

Dechant, E. (1976). Reading: Psychological bases. In P. Lamb & R. Arnold (Eds.), *Reading: Foundations and instructional strategies.* Belmont, CA: Wadsworth.

Dechant, E. V., & Smith, H. P. (1977). *Psychology in teaching reading* (2nd ed.). Englewood Cliffs, NJ: Prentice-Hall.

Degler, L. S., & Risko, V. J. (1979). Teaching reading to mainstreamed sensory impaired children. *The Reading Teacher, 32,* 921–925.

DeHirsch, K. (1971). Are hyperlexics dyslexics? *Journal of Special Education, 5,* 243–245.

DeHirsch, K., Jansky, J., & Langford, W. (1966). *Predicting reading failure: A preliminary study.* New York: Harper & Row.

Delacato, C. H. (1963). *The diagnosis and treatment of speech and reading problems.* Springfield, IL: Charles C. Thomas.

Denny, D. R. (1974). Relationships of three cognitive style dimensions to elementary reading ability. *Journal of Educational Psychology, 66,* 702–709.

Diehl, W. (1978). A critical summary of Rumelhart's interactive model of reading. In W. Diehl (Ed.), *Secondary reading: Theory and application.* Bloomington, IN: Indiana University School of Education.

Dolch, E. W. (1936). A basic sight vocabulary. *The Elementary School Journal, 36,* 456–460.

Douge, J. S. (1983). *The effect of study skill training on the retelling of small groups of fourth, fifth, and sixth grade learning disabled students.* Unpublished master's thesis, The Ohio State University, Columbus, OH.

Downing, J. (1974). Some curious paradoxes in reading research. *Reading, 8,* 2–10.

Dramer, D. (1977). Interchange. *The Reading Teacher, 30,* 666.

Dreher, M. J., & Singer, H. (1985). Parents' attitudes toward reports of standardized reading test results. *The Reading Teacher, 38,* 624–632.

Dreyer, L. G., Futtersak, K. R., & Boehm, A. E. (1985). Sight words in the computer age: An essential list. *The Reading Teacher, 39,* 12–15.

Drew, A. L. (1955). Familial reading disability, *University of Michigan Medical Bulletin, 21,* 245–253.

DuBois, J. J. (1977). I'm sorry I asked. *Language Arts, 54,* 898–901.

Dunn, L. M. Neville, D., Bailey, C. F., Pochanart, P., & Pfost, P. (1967). The effectiveness of three reading approaches and an oral language stimulation program with disadvantaged children in the primary grades. *IMRID Behavioral Science Monograph, 7,* (George Peabody College for Teachers).

Dunn, R. S., & Dunn, K. J. (1975). *Learning style inventory.* Lawrence, KS: Price Systems.

Durkin, D. (1966). *Children who read early.* New York: Columbia University Teachers College Press.

Durkin, D. (1975). The little things make a difference: Part V. *The Reading Teacher, 28,* 473–477.

Durkin, D. (1976). *Strategies for identifying words.* Boston: Allyn & Bacon.

Durkin, D. (1978–79). What classroom observations reveal about reading comprehension instruction. *Reading Research Quarterly, 14,* 481–533.

Durkin, D. (1982). *A study of poor Black children who are successful readers.* (Reading Education Report No. 33). Urbana: University of Illinois, Center for the Study of Reading.

Durr, W. K. (1973). Computer study of high frequency words in popular trade juveniles. *The Reading Teacher, 27,* 37–42.

Durrell, D., Nicholson, A., Olson, A., Ganel, S., & Lineham, E. (1958). Success in first grade reading. *Boston University Journal of Education, 140,* entire issue.

Durrell, D. D. (1940). *Improvement of basic reading abilities.* New York: World Book.

Dykstra, R. (1966). Auditory discrimination abilities and beginning reading achievement. *Reading Research Quarterly, 1,* 5–34.

Dykstra, R. (1967). The use of readiness tests for prediction and diagnosis: A critique. In T. Barrett (Ed.), *Evaluation of children's reading achievement.* Newark, DE: International Reading Association.

Dykstra, R. (1968). Summary of the second grade phase of the Cooperative Research Program in primary reading instruction. *Reading Research Quarterly, 4,* 49–70.

E

Eames, T. H. (1932). A comparison of ocular characteristics of unselected and reading disability groups. *Journal of Educational Research, 25,* 211–215.

Eames, T. H. (1948). Comparison of eye conditions among 1000 reading failures, 500 ophthalmic patients, and 150 unselected children. *American Journal of Ophthalmology, 31,* 713–717.

Eames, T. H. (1951). Visual handicaps to reading. *Journal of Education, 141,* 2–35.

Eamon, D. B. (1978–79). Selection and recall of topical information in prose by better and poorer readers. *Reading Research Quarterly, 14,* 244–257.

Earle, R. A., & Sanders, P. L. (1977). Individualizing reading assignments. In W. J. Harker (Ed.), *Classroom strategies for secondary reading.* Newark, DE: International Reading Association.

Edfelt, A. W. (1960). *Silent speech and silent reading.* Chicago: University of Chicago Press.

Edson, W. H., Bond, G. L., & Cook, W. W. (1953). Relationships between visual characteristics and specific silent reading abilities. *Journal of Educational Research, 46,* 451–457.

Edwards, T. L. (1965). The language-experience attack on cultural deprivation. *The Reading Teacher, 18,* 546–551, 556.

Ehri, L. C. (1976). Word learning in beginning readers: Effects of form class and defining contexts. *Journal of Educational Psychology, 68,* 832–842.

Ekwall, E. E. (1975). *Corrective reading system.* Glenview, IL: Psychotechnics.

Ekwall, E. E. (1976). *Diagnosis and remediation of the disabled reader.* Boston: Allyn & Bacon.

Ekwall, E. E. (1980). *Locating and correcting reading difficulties.* Columbus, OH: Charles Merrill.

Ekwall, E. E., & Shanker, J. L. (1983). *Diagnosis and remediation of the disabled reader.* Boston: Allyn & Bacon.

Eller, W., & Attea, M. (1966). Three diagnostic tests: Some comparisons. In J. A. Figurel (Ed.), *Vistas in reading* (pp. 562–566). Newark, DE: International Reading Association.

Elliott, M. M., & Washburn, W. V. (1977). *Small group talk and reading comprehension.* Calgary, Alberta: Calgary University Faculty of Education. (ERIC Document Reproduction Service No. ED 173 810)

Ellis, N. R. (1970). Memory processes in retardates and normals. In N. R. Ellis (Ed.), *International review of research in mental retardation,* Vol. 4. New York: Academic Press.

Emans, R. (1967). The usefulness of phonic generalizations above the primary grades. *The Reading Teacher, 20,* 419–425.

Erickson, F., & Mohatt, G. (1977, April). *The social organization of participation structures in two classrooms of bilingual children.* Paper presented at the meeting of the American Educational Research Association, New York.

Estes, T., & Vaughan, J. (1973). Reading interest and comprehension: Implications. *The Reading Teacher, 27,* 149–153.

Estes, T. H. (1971). A scale to measure attitudes toward reading. *Journal of Reading, 15,* 135–138.

Evans, J. R., & Smith, L. J. (1976). Psycholinguistic skills of early readers. *The Reading Teacher, 30,* 39–43.

Evans, M. M. (1982). *Dyslexia: An annotated bibliography.* Westport, CT: Greenwood Press.

Ewoldt, C. (1981). A psycholinguistic description of selected deaf children reading in sign language. *Reading Research Quarterly, 17,* 58–89.

"Executive Summary" (1984). Sixth annual report to Congress on the implementation of Public Law 94–142: The Education for All Handicapped Children Act. *Exceptional Children, 51,* 199–202.

F

Farr, R. (1969). *Reading: What can be measured?* Newark, DE: International Reading Association.

Farr, R., & Carey, R. F. (1986). *Reading: What can be measured?* (2nd ed.). Newark, DE: International Reading Association.

Fearn, L. (1971). The oral model as a strategy in developmental reading instruction. *The Reading Teacher, 25,* 205.

Feingold, B. F. (1975). *Why your child is hyperactive.* New York: Random House.

Felton, G. S., & Felton, L. S. (1973). From ivory tower to the people: Shifts in readability estimates of American presidential inaugural addresses. *Reading Improvement, 10,* 40–44.

Ferguson, A. M., & Fairburn, J. (1985). Language experience for problem solving in mathematics. *The Reading Teacher, 38,* 504–507.

Ferrante-Alexander, D. J. (1983). The effect of study skill training on the reading and retelling of fourth, fifth, and sixth grade learning disabled students. (Doctoral dissertation, Ohio State University, 1983). *Dissertation Abstracts International, 44,* 1042A.

Finucci, J. M., Gutherie, J. T., Childs, A. L., Abbey, H., & Childs, B. (1976). The genetics of specific reading disability. *Annals of Human Genetics, 40,* 1–23.

Fisher, D. L. (1978). *Functional literacy and the schools.* Washington, D.C.: National Institute of Education. (ERIC Document Reproduction Service No. ED 151 760)

Fisher, J. A. (1962). The use of out-of-grade tests with retarded and accelerated readers. *Dissertation Abstracts International,* 1962, *22,* 2683A. (University Microfilms No. 61–5564).

Fitzgerald, G. G. (1984). Functional literacy: Right or obligation? *Journal of Reading, 28,* 196–199.

Flesch, R. (1948). A new readability yardstick. *Journal of Applied Psychology, 32,* 221–233.

Flynn, P. (1977). Speed is the carrot. *Journal of Reading, 20,* 683–687.

Foch, T. T., DeFries, J. C., McClearn, G. E., & Singer, S. M. (1977). Familial patterns of impairment in reading disability. *Journal of Educational Psychology, 69,* 316–329.

Foster, J. M. (1966). Effects of mobility training upon reading achievement and intelligence. *Dissertation Abstracts International, 26,* 3779A. (University Microfilms No. 66–00, 336)

Fox, B., & Routh, D. K. (1976). Phonemic analysis and synthesis as word-attack skills. *Journal of Educational Psychology, 68,* 70–74.

Freedman, G., & Reynolds, E. G. (1980). Enriching basal reader lessons with semantic webbing. *The Reading Teacher, 33,* 677–684.

Freire, P. (1973). *Education for critical consciousness.* New York: Seabury Press.

Frostig, M. (1966). *Marianne Frostig Developmental Test of Visual Perception, Third Edition.* Palo Alto, CA: Consulting Psychologists Press.

Fry, E. B. (1980). The new instant word list. *The Reading Teacher, 34,* 284–289.

Fuchs, L. S., Fuchs, D., & Deno, S. L. (1982). Reliability and validity of curriculum-based informal reading inventories. *Reading Research Quarterly, 17,* 6–25.

Furth, H. G. (1966). A comparison of reading test norms of deaf and hearing children. *American Annals of the Deaf, 111,* 461–462.

Furth, H. G. (1970). *Piaget for teachers.* Englewood Cliffs, NJ: Prentice-Hall.

G

Gambrell, L. B. (1984). How much time do children spend reading during teacher-directed reading instruction? In J. A. Niles & L. A. Harris (Eds.), *Changing perspectives on research in reading/language processing instruction.* Rochester, NY: National Reading Conference.

Ganschow, L., Weber, D. B., & Suelter, S. K. (1984). To remediate reading-like behavior, teach a beginner to self-monitor. *The Reading Teacher, 37,* 718–721.

Garcia, R. L. (1974). Mexican American bilingualism and English language development. *Journal of Reading, 17,* 467–473.

Gardner, H. (1975, August). Brain damage: A window on the mind. *Saturday Review,* pp. 26–29.

Garner, R., & Kraus, C. (1982). Monitoring of understanding among seventh graders: An investigation of good-comprehender–poor-comprehender differences in knowing and regulating reading behaviors. *Educational Research Quarterly, 6,* 5–12.

Garner, R., Wagoner, S., & Smith, T. (1983). Externalizing question-answering strategies of good and poor comprehenders. *Reading Research Quarterly, 18,* 439–447.

Garrigan, J. J., Kender, J. P., & Heydenberk, W. R. (1980). Reading disability and family dynamics. In D. J. Sawyer, (Ed.), *Disabled readers: Insight, assessment, instruction.* Newark, DE: International Reading Association.

Gates, A. I. (1926). A study of the role of visual perception, intelligence and certain associative processes in reading and spelling. *Journal of Educational Psychology, 17,* 433–445.

Gates, A. I. (1931). *Interest and ability in reading.* New York: Macmillan.

Gates, A. I. (1940). A further evaluation of reading readiness tests. *Elementary School Journal, 40,* 577–591.

Gates, A. I. (1941). The role of personality maladjustment in reading disability. *Pedagogical Seminary and Journal of Genetic Psychology, 59,* 77–83.

Gates, A. I., & Bennett, C. C. (1933). *Reversal tendencies in reading: Causes, diagnosis, prevention and correction.* New York: Bureau of Publica-

tions, Teachers College, Columbia University.

Geva, E. (1983). Facilitating reading comprehension through flow charting. *Reading Research Quarterly, 18,* 384–405.

Gibson, E. J., & Levin, H. (1975). *The psychology of reading.* Cambridge, MA: MIT Press.

Giordano, G. (1978). "Congenital verbal deficiency" in Navajo children—more on testing. *The Reading Teacher, 32,* 132-134.

Gipe, J. (1978–79). Investigating techniques for teaching word meanings. *Reading Research Quarterly, 14,* 624–644.

Glaser, N. A. (1965). A comparison of specific reading skills of advanced and retarded readers of fifth grade reading achievement. *Dissertation Abstracts International, 25,* 5785A–5786A. (University Microfilms No. 65–2467).

Glass, G. G., & Burton, E. H. (1973). How do they decode? Verbalizations and observed behaviors of successful decoders. *Education, 94,* 58–64.

Goldstein, K. (1936). The modifications of behavior consequent to cerebral lesions. *Psychiatric Quarterly, 10,* 586–610.

Goodman, K. S. (1965). A linguistic study of cues and miscues in reading. *Elementary English, 42,* 639–643.

Goodman, K. S. (1967). Reading: A psycholinguistic guessing game: *Journal of the Reading Specialist, 6,* 126–135.

Goodman, K. S. (1970). Behind the eye: What happens in reading. In K. S. Goodman & O. S. Niles (Eds.), *Reading: Process and Program.* Champaign, IL: National Council of Teachers of English.

Goodman, L., & Hammill, D. (1973). The effectiveness of the Kephart-Getman activities in developing perceptual-motor and cognitive skills. *Focus on Exceptional Children, 4,* 1–9.

Goodman, Y. M., & Burke, C. L. (1972). *Reading miscue inventory manual.* New York: Macmillan.

Graham, K. G., & Robinson, H. A. (1984). *Study skills handbook: A guide for all teachers.* Newark, DE: International Reading Association.

Grassi, J. R. (1973, Summer). Prevention of learning disabilities by the Scoptec method. *Academy News* (Gables Academy, Miami, FL), *4,* 2–5.

Graves, M. F., & Cooke, C. L. (1980). Effects of previewing difficult short stories for high school students. *Research on Reading in Secondary Schools, 6,* 38–54.

Graves, M. F., Cooke, C., & Laberge, M. J. (1983). Effects of previewing difficult short stories on low ability junior high school students' comprehension, recall, and attitudes. *Reading Research Quarterly, 18,* 262–276.

Graves, M. F., & Palmer, R. J. (1981). Validating previewing as a method of improving fifth and sixth grade students' comprehension of short stories. *Michigan Reading Journal, 15,* 1–3.

Gray, L., & Reesi, D. (1957). *Teaching children to read.* New York: Ronald Press.

Gray, W. S. (1960). The major aspects of reading. In H. M. Robinson (Ed.), *Sequential development of reading abilities.* Chicago: University of Chicago Press.

Greenberg, D. (1983). *Slugs.* Boston: Little, Brown.

Greenberg, J. W., & Davidson, H. H. (1972). Home background and school achievement of black urban ghetto children. *American Journal of Orthopsychiatry, 42,* 803–810.

Greenwood, C. R., Delquadri, J. C., & Hall, R. V. (1984). Opportunity to respond and student academic performance. In Heward, Heron, Hill, & Trap-Porter (Eds.), *Focus on behavior.* Columbus, OH: Merrill.

Greenwood, S. C. (1985). Use contracts to motivate and manage your secondary reading class. *Journal of Reading, 28,* 487–491.

Grob, J. A. (1968). Forcing speed in oral reading. *Journal of Reading, 11,* 621–624.

Grob, J. A. (1970). Reading rate and study-time demands on secondary students. *Journal of Reading, 13,* 285–288; 316.

Guszak, F. J. (1967). Teacher questioning and reading. *The Reading Teacher, 21,* 227–234.

Guszak, F. J. (1972). *Diagnostic reading instruction in the elementary school.* New York: Harper & Row.

Gutherie, J. (1973). Models of reading and reading disability. *Journal of Educational Psychology, 65,* 9–18.

Gutherie, J., Seifert, M., Burnham, N. A., & Caplan, R. I. (1974). The maze technique to assess, monitor reading comprehension. *The Reading Teacher, 28,* 161–168.

Gutherie, J. T. (1982). Reading in New Zealand: Achievement and volume. *Reading Research Quarterly, 17,* 6–27.

H

Haggard, M. R. (1985). An interactive strategies approach to content area reading. *Journal of Reading, 29,* 204–210.

Hagin, R. A., Silver, A. A., & Corwin, C. G. (1971). Clinical-diagnostic use of the WIPPSI in predicting learning disabilities in grade 1. *Journal of Special Education, 5,* 221–232.

Hallahan, D. P., & Cruickshank, W. M. (1973). *Psychoeducational foundations of learning disabilities.* Englewood Cliffs, NJ: Prentice-Hall.

Hallahan, D. P., & Kauffman, J. (1978). *Exceptional children: Introduction to special education.* Englewood Cliffs, NJ: Prentice-Hall.

Hallgren, B. (1950). Specific dyslexia: A clinical and genetic study. *Acta Psychiatrica et Neurologica,* Suppl. No. 65, Copenhagen.

Hammill, D. D., Goodman, L., & Wiederholt, J. L. (1974). Visual-motor processes: Can we train them? *The Reading Teacher, 27,* 469–478.

Hammill, D. D., & Larsen, S. C. (1974a). The effectiveness of psycholinguistic training. *Exceptional Children, 41,* 5–15.

Hammill, D. D., & Larsen, S. C. (1974b). The relationship of selected auditory perceptual skills and reading ability. *Journal of Learning Disabilities, 7,* 429–435.

Hansen, C., & Lovitt, T. (1977). An applied behavior analysis approach to reading comprehension. In J. T. Gutherie (Ed.), *Cognition, curriculum, and comprehension.* Newark, DE: International Reading Association.

Hansen, J. (1981). The effects of inference training and practice on young children's reading comprehension. *Reading Research Quarterly, 16,* 391–417.

Hardyck, C. D., & Petrinovich, L. F. (1969). Treatment of subvocal speech during reading. *Journal of Reading, 12,* 361–368, 419–422.

Haring, N. G. (1971). *Investigation of systematic instructional procedures to facilitate academic achievement in mentally retarded disadvantaged children: Final Report.* Seattle; University of Washington, Child Development and Health Retardation Center.

Harris, A. J. (1968). Research on some aspects of comprehension: Rate, flexibility, and study skills. *Journal of Reading, 12,* 205–210, 258–260.

Harris, A. J. (1970). *How to increase reading ability* (5th ed.). New York: David McKay.

Harris, A. J., & Jacobson, M. D. (1972). *Basic elementary reading vocabularies.* New York: Macmillan.

Harris, A. J., Morrison, C., Serwer, B. L., & Gold, L. A. (1968). *A continuation of the CRAFT project: Comparing reading approaches with disadvantaged Negro children in primary grades.* (Project No. 5, 0570, 2, 12, 1; Division of Teacher Education). New York: The City University of New York.

Harris, A. J., & Serwer, B. L. (1966). The CRAFT Project: Instructional time in reading research. *Reading Research Quarterly, 2,* 27–56.

Harris, A. J., & Sipay, E. (1980). *How to increase reading ability.* New York: Longman.

Harris, C. W. (1967). *Problems in measuring change.* Milwaukee: University of Wisconsin Press.

Harris, L. (1970, November 18). *Survival literacy study.* (Conducted by National Reading Council, September 1970; discussed by Hon. Margaret Heckler of Massachusetts in U.S. House of Representatives). *Congressional Record,* 38036–38040.

Harris, L., & Associates. (1970). *Survival literacy study.* (Congressional Record, Nov. 18, 38036–38040). Washington, D.C.: U.S. Government Printing Office.

Harris, L., & Smith, C. (1976). *Reading instruction: Diagnostic teaching in the classroom.* New York: Holt, Rinehart & Winston.

Harris, T. L., & Hodges, R. E. (Eds.). (1981). *A dictionary of reading and related terms.* Newark, DE: International Reading Association.

Hartlage, L. C., & Hartlage, P. L. (1973). Comparison of hyperlexic and dyslexic children. *Neurology, 23,* 436–437.

Hayes, C. S., Prinz, R. J., & Siders, C. (1976). Reflection-impulsivity and reading recognition ability among mildly retarded children. *American Journal of mental Deficiency, 81,* 94.

Healy, J. M. (1982). The enigma of hyperlexia. *Reading Research Quarterly, 17,* 319–338.

Heathington, B. S., & Alexander, J. E. (1978). A child-based observation checklist to assess attitudes toward reading. *The Reading Teacher, 31,* 769–771.

Heinrich, J. S. (1976). Elementary oral reading: Methods and materials. *The Reading Teacher, 30,* 10–15.

Henderson, E. H., Estes, T. H., & Stonecash, S. (1971–1972). An exploratory study of word acquisition among first-graders at midyear in a language-experience approach. *Journal of Reading Behavior, 4,* 21–31.

Henderson, L. C., & Shanker, J. L. (1978). The use of interpretive dramatics versus basal reader workbooks for developing comprehension skills. *Reading World, 17,* 239–243.

Herber, H. L. (1970). *Teaching reading in content areas.* Englewood Cliffs, NJ: Prentice-Hall.

Herber, H. L. (1978). *Teaching reading in content areas* (2nd ed.). Englewood Cliffs, NJ: Prentice-Hall.

Herber, H. L. & Nelson, J. (1975). Questioning is not the answer. *Journal of Reading, 18,* 512–517.

Heron, T. E., & Harris, K. C. (1982). *The educational consultant.* Boston: Allyn & Bacon.

Heward, W. L., Cooper, J. O., Heron, T. E., McCormick, S., Porter, J. T., Stephens, T. M., & Sutherland, H. A. (1981). Noncategorical teacher training in a state with categorical certification requirements. *Exceptional Children, 48,* 206–212.

Heward, W. L., McCormick, S., Joynes, Y. (1980). Completing job applications: Evaluation of an instructional program for mildly retarded juvenile delinquents. *Behavioral Disorders, 5,* 223–234.

Hillerich, R. L. (1967). Vowel generalizations and first grade reading achievement. *Elementary School Journal, 67,* 246–250.

Himelstein, H. C., & Greenberg, G. (1974). The effect of increasing reading rate on comprehension. *The Journal of Psychology, 86,* 251–259.

Hinshelwood, J. (1896). A case of dyslexia: A peculiar form of word-blindness. *Lancet, 2,* 1451–1454.

Hinshelwood, J. (1917). *Congenital word blindness.* London: H. K. Lewis.

Hirshoren, A., Hunt, J. T., & Davis, C. (1974). Classified ads as reading materials for the educable retarded. *Exceptional Children, 41,* 45–47.

Hittleman, D. R. (1973). Seeking a psycholinguistic definition of readability. *The Reading Teacher, 26,* 783–789.

Hittleman, D. R. (1978). *Developmental reading: A psycholinguistic perspective.* Chicago: Rand McNally.

Hittleman, D. R. (1983). *Developmental reading, K–8: Teaching from a psycholinguistic perspective* (2nd ed.). Boston: Houghton Mifflin.

Hockman, C. H. (1973). Black dialect reading tests in the urban elementary school. *The Reading Teacher, 26,* 581–583.

Hoffman, J. V. (1980). The disabled reader: Forgive us our regressions and lead us not into expectations. *Journal of Learning Disabilities, 13,* 8–11.

Hoffman, J. V., O'Neal, S. F., Kastler, L. A., Clements, R. O., Segel, K. W., & Nash, M. F. (1984). Guided oral reading and miscue focused verbal feedback in second-grade classrooms. *Reading Research Quarterly, 19,* 367–384.

Holmes, J. A. (1953). *The substrata-factor theory of reading.* Berkeley: California Book.

Hood, J. (1977). Sight words are not going out of style. *Reading Teacher, 30,* 378–382.

Hood, J., & Kendall, J. R. (1975). A qualitative analysis of oral reading errors of reflective and impulsive second graders: A follow-up study. *Journal of Reading Behavior, 7,* 269–281.

Hoover, M. R. (1978). Characteristics of Black schools at grade level: A description. *The Reading Teacher, 31,* 757–762.

Horn, A. (1941). The uneven distribution of the effects of special factors. *Southern California Education Monograph,* (No. 12).

Hoskins, R. L. (1973). A readability study of AP and UPI wire copy. *Journalism Quarterly, 50,* 360–363.

Hoskisson, K., Sherman, T. M., & Smith, L. L. (1974). Assisted reading and parent involvement. *The Reading Teacher, 27,* 710–714.

Hunt, B. C. (1974–75). Black dialect and third and fourth graders' performance on the Gray Oral Reading Test. *Reading Research Quarterly, 10,* 103–123.

Hunt, L. (1957). Can we measure specific factors associated with reading comprehension? *Journal of Educational Research, 51,* 161–172.

Hunt, L. (1970). The effect of self-selection, interest, and motivation upon independent, instructional, and frustrational levels. *The Reading Teacher, 24,* 146–151.

Hutchinson, J. O. (1972). Reading tests and nonstandard language. *The Reading Teacher, 25,* 430–437.

Huttenlocher, R. R., & Huttenlocher, J. (1973). A study of children with hyperlexia. *Neurology, 23,* 1107–1116.

Hynd, G. W. (1986, April). *Neurophysiological basis of developmental dyslexia.* Paper presented at the meeting of the International Reading Association, Philadelphia, PA.

Hynd, G. W., & Hynd, C. R. (1984). Dyslexia: Neuroanatomical/neurolinguistic perspectives. *Reading Research Quarterly, 29,* 482–498.

I

Ilg, F., & Ames, L. B. (1950). Developmental trends in reading behavior. *Journal of Genetic Psychology, 76,* 291.

Inouye, R. (1981). *Dyslexia.* Unpublished manuscript.

Irwin, D. M., & Bushnell, M. M. (1980). *Observational studies for child study.* New York: Holt, Rinehart & Winston.

Irwin, T. (1969, May). Helping children overcome learning disabilities. *Todays Health,* pp. 20–25, 70.

Iverson, B. K., Brownlee, G. D., & Walberg, H. J. (1981). Parent-teacher contacts and student learning. *Journal of Educational Research, 74,* 394–396.

J

Jackson, M., & McClelland, J. (1979). Processing determinants of reading speed. *Journal of Experimental Psychology, 108,* 151–181.

Jackson, M. D. (1980). Further evidence for a relationship between memory access and reading ability. *Journal of Verbal Learning and Verbal Behavior, 19,* 683–694.

Jacobs, J. N., Wirthlin, L. D., & Miller, C. B. (1968). A follow-up evaluation of the Frostig visual-perception training program. *Educational Leadership Research Supplement, 26,* 169–175.

Jarvis, O. T. (1962). *Time allotments and pupil achievement in the intermediate elementary grades.* A Texas Gulf Coast Study. (ERIC Document Reproduction Service No. ED 035 063)

Johns, J. L. (1982). The dimensions and uses of informal reading assessment. In J. L. Pikulski & T. Shanahan (Eds.), *Approaches to the informal evaluation of reading.* Newark, DE: International Reading Association.

Johnson, D., & Pearson, P. D. (1978). *Teaching reading vocabulary.* New York: Holt, Rinehart & Winston.

Johnson, D. D. (1971). A basic vocabulary for beginning readers. *Elementary School Journal, 72,* 31–33.

Johnson, D. D. (1973–74). Sex differences in reading across cultures. *Reading Research Quarterly, 9,* 67–86.

Johnson, D. D. (1984, May). Two important approaches to vocabulary development: Semantic mapping and semantic feature analysis. Paper presented at the meeting of the International Reading Association, Atlanta.

Johnson, L. R., & Platts, D. (1962). A summary of a study of the reading ages of children who had been given remedial teaching. *British Journal of Educational Psychology, 32,* 66–71.

Johnson, L. S. (1975). Bilingual bicultural education: A two-way street. *The Reading Teacher, 29,* 231–239.

Johnson, R. (1969). The validity of the Clymer-Barrett Prereading Battery. *The Reading Teacher, 22,* 609–614.

Johnston, P. H. (1983). *Reading comprehension assessment: A cognitive basis.* Newark, DE: International Reading Association.

Jones, M. B., & Pikulski, E. C. (1974). Cloze for the classroom. *The Reading Teacher, 17,* 432–438.

Joynes, Y. D., McCormick, S., & Heward, W. L. (1980). Teaching reading disabled students to read and complete employment applications. *Journal of Reading, 23,* 709–714.

K

Kagan, J. (1965). Reflection, impulsivity, and reading ability in primary grade children. *Child Development, 36,* 609–628.

Kahn, E., & Wirtz, R. W. (1982). Another look at applications in elementary school mathematics. *Arithmetic Teacher, 30,* 21–25.

Kameenui, E. J., Carnine, D. W., & Freschi, R. (1982). Effects of text construction and instructional procedures for teaching word meanings on comprehension and recall. *Reading Research Quarterly, 17,* 367–388.

Kamin, L. J. (1974). *The science and politics of I.Q.* New York: Wiley.

Kastelen, L., Nickel, M., & McLaughlin, T. F. (1984). A performance feedback system: Generalization of effects across tasks and time with eighth-grade English students. *Education and Treatment of Children, 7,* 141–155.

Kaufman, A. S., & Kaufman, N. L. (1983). *Kaufman assessment battery for children.* Minneapolis: American Guidance Service.

Kazemek, F. E. (1985). Functional literacy is not enough: Adult literacy as a developmental process. *Journal of Reading, 28,* 332–335.

Kiesling, H. (1977–78). Productivity of instructional time by mode of instruction for students at varying levels of reading skill. *Reading Research Quarterly, 13,* 554–582.

Keister, B. V. (1941). Reading skills acquired by five-year-old children. *Elementary School Journal, 41,* 587–596.

Keogh, B. K. (1971). Hyperactivity and learning problems: Implications for teachers. *Academic Therapy, 7,* 47–58.

Keogh, B. K. (1974). Optometric vision training programs for children with learning disabilities: Review of issues and research. *Journal of Learning Disabilities, 7,* 219–231.

Keogh, B. K., & Donlon, G. M. (1972). Field dependence, impulsivity and learning disabilities. *Journal of Learning Disabilities, 5,* 331–336.

Kephart, N. C. (1960). *The slow learner in the classroom.* Columbus, OH: Charles E. Merrill.

Killgallon, P. A. (1942). *A study of relationships among certain pupil adjustments in language situations.* Unpublished doctoral dissertation, Pennsylvania State University, University Park.

Kilty, T. K. (1976, March 17). Many are found unable to comprehend instructions on grocery store package. *The New York Times,* p. 49.

King, C., & Quigley, S. (1985). *Reading and deafness.* San Diego, CA: College-Hill.

Kintsch, W. (1979). On modeling comprehension. *Educational Psychologist, 14,* 3–14.

Kirk, E. C. (1970). The future of reading for partially seeing children. *The Reading Teacher, 24,* 195–202, 220.

Kirk, S., & Gallagher, J. (1979). *Educating exceptional children* (3rd ed.). Boston: Houghton Mifflin.

Kirk, S. A. (1962). *Educating exceptional children.* Boston: Houghton Mifflin.

Kirsch, I., & Gutherie, J. T. (1977–78). The concept and measurement of functional literacy. *Reading Research Quarterly, 13,* 485–507.

Klare, G. R. (1974–75). Assessing readability. *Reading Research Quarterly, 10,* 62–102.

Klare, G. R. (1976). A second look at the validity of readability formulas. *Journal of Reading Behavior, 8,* 129–152.

Klasky, C. (1979). Some funny business in your reading class. *Journal of Reading, 22,* 731–733.

Klausmeir, H. J., Feldhusen, J., & Check, J. (1959). *An analysis of learning efficiency in arithmetic of mentally retarded children in comparison with children of average and high intelligence.* Madison: University of Wisconsin Press.

Kolers, P. A. (1966). Reading and talking bilingually. *American Journal of Psychology, 79,* 357–376.

Kotsonis, M. E., & Patterson, C. F. (1980). Comprehension-monitoring skills in learning disabled children. *Developmental Psychology, 16,* 541–542.

Kroll, N. E. A., Parks, T., Parkinson, S. R., Bieber, S. L., & Johnson, A. L. (1970). Short-term memory while shadowing: Recall of visually and aurally presented letters. *Journal of Experimental Psychology, 85,* 220–224.

Kuchinskas, G. (1983). 22 ways to use a microcomputer in reading and language arts classes. *Computers, Reading, and Language Arts, 1,* 11–16.

Kwolek, W. F. (1973). A readability survey of technical and popular literature. *Journalism Quarterly, 50,* 255–264.

L

LaBerge, D., & Samuels, S. J. (1974). Toward a theory of automatic information processing in reading. *Cognitive Psychology, 6,* 293–323.

Labov, W., Cohen, P., Robbins, C., & Lewis, J. (1968). *A study of the nonstandard English of Negro and Puerto Rican speakers in New York City.* (Cooperative Research Project #3288). New York: Columbia University.

Lahaderne, H. M. (1976). Feminized schools—Unpromising myth to explain boys' reading problems. *Reading Teacher, 29,* 776–786.

Lange, R. (1978). Flipping the coin: From text anxiety to test wiseness. *Journal of Reading, 22,* 274–277.

Lanier, R. J., & Davis, A. P. (1972). Developing comprehension through teacher-made questions. *The Reading Teacher, 26,* 153–157.

Larrick, N. (Ed.). (1968). *Piping down the valleys wild.* New York: Dell.

Leong, C. K., & Haines, C. F. (1978). Beginning readers' analysis of words and sentences. *Journal of Reading Behavior, 10,* 393–407.

Lerner, J. (1981). *Learning disabilities* (3rd ed.). Boston: Houghton Mifflin.

Lesgold, A. M., McCormick, C., & Golinkoff, R. M. (1975). Imagery training and children's prose learning. *Journal of Educational Psychology, 67,* 663–667.

Leu, D. J. (1982). Oral reading error analysis: A critical review of research and application. *Reading Research Quarterly, 17,* 420–437.

Levin, B. J. (1966). An investigation of the flexibility of reading rate. *Dissertation Abstracts International, 27,* 959A. (University Microfilms No. 66–9215)

Levin, J. R. (1973). Inducing comprehension in poor readers: A test of a recent model. *Journal of Educational Psychology, 65,* 19–24.

Lichtman, M. (1974). The development and validation of R/EAL, an instrument to assess functional literacy. *Journal of Reading Behavior, 2,* 168–181.

Linden, M., & Wittrock, M. C. (1981). The teaching of reading comprehension. *Reading Research Quarterly, 17,* 44–57.

Little, L. J. (1978). The learning disabled. In E. R. Meyen (Ed.), *Exceptional children and youth: An introduction.* Denver: Love.

Long, J. V., Schaffran, J. A., & Kellog, T. M. (1977). Effects of out-of-level survey testing on reading achievement scores of Title I, ESEA students. *Journal of Educational Measurement, 14,* 203–213.

Lorenz, L., & Vockell, E. (1979). Using the neurological impress method with learning disabled students. *Journal of Learning Disabilities, 12,* 420–422.

Lowell, R. (1971). Reading readiness factors as predictors of success in first grade reading. *Journal of Learning Disabilities, 4,* 563–567.

M

MacGinitie, W. H. (1973a). An introduction to some measurement problems in reading. In W. H. MacGinitie (Ed.), *Assessment problems in reading.* Newark, DE: International Reading Association.

MacGinitie, W. H. (1973b). Testing reading achievement in urban schools. *The Reading Teacher, 27,* 13–21.

Maddux, C. D. (1986). Microcomputers in education and counseling: Problems and cautions. *Techniques: A Journal for Remedial Education and Counseling, 2,* 9–14.

Mallett, G. (1977). Using language experience with junior high Native Indian students. *Journal of Reading, 21,* 25–28.

Malmquist, E. (1958). *Factors relating to reading disabilities in the first grade of the elementary school.* Stockholm, Sweden: Almquist & Wiksell.

Mandel, R. G., & Johnson, N. S. (1984). A developmental analysis of story recall and comprehension in adulthood. *Journal of Verbal Learning and Verbal Behavior, 23,* 643–659.

Mangieri, J. N., & Kahn, M. S. (1977). Is the Dolch Test of 220 Basic Sight Words irrelevant? *The Reading Teacher, 30,* 649–651.

Mangrum, C. T., & Strichart, S. S. (1984). *College and the learning disabled student.* Orlando, FL: Grune & Stratton.

Marks, C. B., Doctorow, M. J., & Wittrock, M. C. (1974). Word frequency and reading comprehension. *The Journal of Educational Research, 67,* 259–262.

Marzano, R. J., Larson, J., Tish, G., Vodehnal, S. (1978). The graded word list is not a shortcut to an IRI. *The Reading Teacher, 31,* 647–653.

Masland, R. L., & Cratty, B. J. (1971). *The nature of the reading process, the rationale of noneducational remedial methods: Reading Forum* (NINDS Monograph No. 11). Bethesda, MD: National Institute of Neurological Disease and Stroke.

Matějček, Z. (1977). Specific learning disabilities. *Bulletin of the Orton Society, 27,* 7–25.

Matheny, A. P., Dolan, J. B., & Wilson, R. S. (1976). Twins with academic learning problems: Antecedent characteristics. *American Journal of Orthopsychiatry, 46,* 464–469.

Mavrogenes, N. A. (1975). Using psycholinguistic knowledge to improve secondary reading. *Journal of Reading, 18,* 280–286.

Mavrogenes, N. A., Winkley, C. K., Hanson, E., & Vacca, R. T. (1974). Concise guide to standardized secondary and college reading tests. *Journal of Reading, 18,* 12–22.

May, R. B., & Ollila, L. O. (1981). Reading sex-role attitudes in preschoolers. *Reading Research Quarterly, 16,* 583–595.

McClean, T. K. (1968). *A comparison of the sub-test performance of two groups of retarded readers with like groups of non-retarded readers on the Wechsler Intelligence Scale for Children.* Unpublished doctoral dissertation, University of Oregon, Eugene.

McCormick, S. (1975). Alternative roles for reading teachers. *Elementary English, 52,* 361–363, 369.

McCormick, S. (1977a). Choosing books to read to preschool children. *Language Arts, 54,* 543–548.

McCormick, S. (1977b). Should you read aloud *to* your children? *Language Arts, 54,* 139–143, 163.

McCormick, S. (1980). A month of fun: Spelling practice for elementary school students. *Exceptional Teacher, 1,* 6–9, 15–16.

McCormick, S. (1981). Assessment and the beginning reader: Using student dictated stories. *Reading World, 21*, 29–39.

McCormick, S. (1983). Reading aloud to preschoolers aged 3–6: A review of the research. *Reading Horizons, 24*, 7–12.

McCormick, S., & Collins, B (1981). A potpourri of game-making ideas for the reading teacher. *The Reading Teacher, 34*, 692–696.

McCormick, S., & Hill, D. S. (1984). An analysis of the effects of two procedures for increasiing disabled readers' inferencing skills. *Journal of Educational Research, 77*, 219–226.

McCormick, S., & Moe, A. J. (1982). The language of instructional materials: A source of reading problems. *Exceptional Children, 49*, 48–53.

McCracken, R. A. (1962). Standardized reading tests and informal reading inventories. *Education, 82*, 366–369.

McCrossan, J. (1966). *The reading of the culturally disadvantaged.* Urbana, IL: University of Illinois. (ERIC Document Reproduction Service No. ED 010 755)

McDonald, A. S. (1960). Factors affecting reading test performance. In O. S. Causey & E. P. Bliesmer (Eds.), Yearbook of the National Reading Conference. *Research and evaluation in college reading.* National Reading Conference.

McLaughlin, G. H. (1966). Comparing styles of presenting technical information. *Ergonomics, 9*, 257–259.

McNaughton, S., & Glynn, T. (1981). Delayed versus immediate attention to oral reading errors' effects on accuracy and self-correction. *Educational Psychology, 1*, 57–65.

Measurement and training of perceptual-motor functions. (1986). *Learning Disabilities Quarterly, 9*, 247.

Mehegan, C. C., & Dreifus, R. E. (1972). Hyperlexia—exceptional reading ability in brain damaged children. *Neurology, 22*, 1105–1111.

Mikulecky, L. (1982). Job literacy: The relationship between school preparation and workplace actuality. *Reading Research Quarterly, 17*, 400–419.

Mikulecky, L. (1984). Preparing students for workplace literacy demands. *Journal of Reading, 28*, 253–257.

Miller, G. A. (1973). *Linguistic communications: Perspectives for research.* Newark, DE: International Reading Association.

Millman, J., & Pauk, W. (1969). *How to take tests.* New York: McGraw-Hill.

Mills, R. E. (1970). *The teaching of word recognition.* Ft. Lauderdale: The Mills School.

Mitchell, J. V. Jr. (Ed.). (1985). *The ninth mental measurements yearbook.* Lincoln, NE: The Buros Institute of Mental Measurements.

Mitzel, M. A. (1966). The functional reading word list for adults. *Adult Education, 2*, 67–69.

Moe, A. J. (1972). Methods of increasing student participation in the classroom. *Elementary English, 49*, 1112–1116.

Monroe, M. (1932). *Children who cannot read.* Chicago: University of Chicago Press.

Moorehead, S., Meeth, D., & Simpson, V. (Undated). *A handbook of circumventive strategies.* (Child Service Demonstration Center—Project Expand [P.L. 91–230, OEC–0–74–8725]. Worthington, OH: Ohio Department of Education, Division of Special Education.)

Morasky, R. L. (1972). Eye movements as a function of adjunct question placement. *American Educational Research Journal, 9*, 251–261.

Morris, J. M. (1959). *Reading in the primary school: An investigation into standards of reading and their association with primary school characteristics.* Sevenoaks, Kent, Great Britain: Newnes Educational Publishing.

Morrison, V. B. (1968). Teacher-pupil interaction in three types of elementary classroom reading situations. *The Reading Teacher, 22*, 271–275.

Moseley, P. F. (1974). *Visually handicapped young children: An early intervention study.* Lafayette, LA: Lafayette Parish School Board. (ERIC Document Reproduction Service No. ED 122 577)

Moustafa, M., & Penrose, J. (1985). Comprehensible input PLUS the language experience approach. *The Reading Teacher, 38*, 640–647.

Moyer, S., & Newcomer, P. (1977). Reversals in reading: Diagnosis and remediation. *Exceptional Children, 43*, 424–429.

Murph, D., & McCormick, S. (1985). Evaluation of an instructional program designed to teach minimally literate juvenile delinquents to read road signs. *Education and Treatment of Children, 8*, 133–155.

Murphy, R. T. (1973). *Adult functional reading study.* (Research Rep. No. 09004, PR 73–48). Princeton, NJ: Educational Testing Service.

Myklebust, H. R. (1954). *Auditory disorders in children.* New York: Grune & Stratton.

Myklebust, H. R. (1968). Learning disabilities: Definition and overview. In H. R. Myklebust (Ed.), *Progress in learning disabilities, Vol. 1.* New York: Grune & Stratton.

Myklebust, H. R. (1968). *Progress in learning disabilities* (Vol. 1). New York: Grune & Stratton.

N

NAEP. (1975). *Functional literacy: Basic reading performance.* (Technical summary of an assessment of in-school 17-year-olds in 1974). Denver: National Assessment of Educational Progress.

NAEP. (1976). *Reading in America: A perspective on two assessments.* (Reading Report No. 06–R–01). Denver: National Assessment of Educational Progress.

NAEP data on reading comprehension released. (1982, August). *Reading Today*, p. 5.

Nassi, A. J., & Abramowitz, S. I. (1976). From phrenology to psychosurgery and back again: Biological studies of criminals. *American Journal of Orthopsychiatry, 46*, 591–606.

National Advisory Committee on Hyperkinesis and Food Additives (1975). *Report to the Nutrition Foundation.* New York: The Nutrition Foundation.

Newcomer, P. L., & Hammill, D. D. (1975). ITPA and academic achievement: A survey. *The Reading Teacher, 28,* 731–741.

Newsome, G. L. (1986). The effects of reader perspective and cognitive style on remembering important information from texts. *Journal of Reading Behavior, 18,* 117–133.

Nicholson, T. (1984). Experts and novices: A study of reading in the high school classroom. *Reading Research Quarterly, 19,* 436–451.

Nicholson, T. (1985). The confusing world of high school reading. *Journal of Reading, 28,* 514–526.

Nolan, C. Y., & Kederis, C. J. (1969). *Perceptual factors in braille word recognition.* New York: American Foundation for the Blind.

Norman, D. A. (1984). Theories and models in cognitive psychology. In E. Donchin (Ed.), *Cognitive psychophysiology.* Hillsdale, NJ: Erlbaum.

Northcutt, N. (1975). *The adult performance level project (APL): Adult functional competency* (Report to the Office of Education dissemination review panel). Austin: University of Texas.

O

O'Donnell, P. A., & Eisenson, J. (1969). Delacato training for reading achievement and visual-motor integration. *Journal of Learning Disabilities, 2,* 441–447.

Otto, W. (1986). Peter Johnston, we salute you. *Journal of Reading, 29,* 700–703.

P

Pachtman, A. B., & Riley, J. D. (1978). Teaching vocabulary of mathematics through interaction, exposure, and structure. *Journal of Reading, 22,* 240–244.

Pany, D., & Jenkins, J. R. (1977). *Learning word meanings: A comparison of instructional procedures and effects on measures of reading comprehension with learning disabled students.* (Tech. Rep. No. 25). Champaign, IL: University of Illinois, Center for the Study of Reading.

Paradis, E., Tierney, R., & Peterson, J. (1975). A systematic examination of the reliability of the cloze procedure. In G. H. McNinch & W. D. Miller (Eds.), Yearbook of the National Reading Conference. *Reading: Convention and inquiry.* National Reading Conference.

Park, G. E., & Burri, C. (1943). The relation of various eye conditions and reading achievement. *Journal of Educational Psychology, 34,* 290–299.

Parker, S. W. (1917). Pseudo-talent for words. *Psychology Clinics, 11,* 1–7.

Patching, W., Kameenui, E., Carnine, D., Gersten, R., & Colvin, G. (1983). Direct instruction in critical reading skills. *Reading Research Quarterly, 18,* 406–418.

Patterson, G. R., (1965). An application of conditioning techniques to the control of a hyperactive child. In L. P. Ullman & L. Krasner (Eds.), *Case studies in behavior modification.* New York: Holt.

Pauk, W. (1964). Speed reading? *Journal of the Reading Specialist, 4,* 18–19.

Pauk, W. (1973). The interest level— That's the thing. *Journal of Reading, 16,* 459–461.

Payne, J. S., Polloway, E. A., Smith, J. E., & Payne, R. A. (1981). *Strategies for teaching the mentally retarded* (2nd ed.). Columbus, OH: Merrill.

Pearson, P. D. (1982). *Asking questions about stories.* Occasional Paper No. 15. Columbus, OH: Ginn.

Pearson, P. D., & Johnson, D. (1978). *Teaching reading comprehension.* New York: Holt, Rinehart & Winston.

Peck, C. V., & Kling, M. (1977). Adult literacy in the seventies: Its definition and measurement. *Journal of Reading, 20,* 677–682.

Petre, R. M. (1972). Pupil response in open structured and close structured reading activities. In H. A. Klein (Ed.), *The quest for competency in teaching reading.* Newark, DE: International Reading Association.

Pflaum, S., & Pascarella, E. (1980). Interactive effects of prior reading achievement and training in context on the reading of learning disabled

children. *Reading Research Quarterly, 16,* 138–158.

Phillips, S. U. (1972). Participant structures and communicative competence: Warm Springs children in community and classroom. In C. Cazden, V. John, & D. Hymes (Eds.), *Functions of language in the classroom.* New York: Teachers College Press.

Piaget, J., & Inhelder, B. (1973). *Memory and intelligence.* New York: Basic Books.

Piercey, D. (1976). *Reading activities in content areas.* Boston: Allyn & Bacon.

Powell, W. R. (1971). Validity of the IRI reading levels. *Elementary English, 48,* 637–642.

Pressley, G. M. (1976). Mental imagery helps eight-year-olds remember what they read. *Journal of Educational Psychology, 68,* 355–359.

Pugh, R. C., & Brunza, J. J. (1975). Effects of a confidence weighted scoring system on measures of test reliability and validity. *Educational and Psychological Measurement, 35,* 73–78.

Purves, A. C. (1979). *Achievement in reading and literature in secondary schools: New Zealand in an international perspective.* Wellington, New Zealand: New Zealand Council for Educational Research

Pyrczak, F. (1976). Readability of instructions for Form 1040. *Journal of Reading, 20,* 121–127.

R

Rankin, E. F. (1978). Characteristics of the cloze procedure as a research tool in the study of language. In P. D. Pearson & J. Hansen (Eds.), Yearbook of the National Reading Conference. *Reading: Disciplined inquiry in process and practice.* National Reading Conference.

Ransom, P. (1968). Determining reading levels of elementary school children by cloze testing. In J. A. Figurel (Ed.), *Forging ahead in reading.* Newark, DE: International Reading Association.

Ratekin, N. (1978). A comparison of reading achievement among three racial groups using standard reading materials. In D. Feitelson (Ed.), *Cross-cultural perspectives on reading and reading research*. Newark, DE: International Reading Association.

Razik, T. A. (1969). A study of American newspaper readability. *The Journal of Communication, 19*, 317–324.

Readence, J. E., & Moore, D. (1979). Coping with minimal reading requirements: Suggestions for the reading teacher. *Reading World, 19* (2), 139–148.

Recht, D. R. (1976). The self-correction process in reading. *The Reading Teacher, 29*, 632–636.

Reed, J. C., Rabe, E. F., & Mankinen, M. (1970). Teaching reading to brain-damaged children: A review. *Reading Research Quarterly, 6*, 379–401.

Rees, N. S. (1973). Auditory processing factors in language disorders: A view from Procrustes' bed. *Journal of Speech and Hearing Disorders, 38*, 304–315.

Resnick, D. P. (1981). Testing in America: A supportive environment. *Phi Delta Kappan, 62*, 625–628.

Rhodes, L. K., & Hill, M. W. (1985). Supporting reading at home—naturally: Selected materials for parents. *The Reading Teacher, 38*, 619–623.

Ribovich, J. K. (1978). Teaching reading fifty years ago. *The Reading Teacher, 31*, 371–375.

Richards, R. G. (1975). Singing: A fun route to a second language. *The Reading Teacher, 29*, 283–285.

Richek, M. A., List, L. K., & Lerner, J. W. (1983). *Reading problems: Diagnosis and remediation*. Englewood Cliff, NJ: Prentice-Hall.

Richmond, J. (1970). *Learning disorders in children*. (Report of the Sixty-First Ross Conference on Pediatric Research). Columbus, OH: Ross Laboratories.

Rigg, P., & Kazemek, F. E. (1985). Professional books. *Journal of Reading, 28*, 569–571.

Ringler, L. H., & Smith, I. L. (1973). Learning modality and word recognition of first grade children. *Journal of Learning Disabilities, 6*, 307–312.

Robbins, M. P. (1966). A study of the validity of Delacato's theory of neurological organization and reading. *Exceptional Children, 32*, 517–523.

Roberts, T. (1975). Skills of analysis and synthesis in the early stages of reading. *British Journal of Educational Psychology, 45*, 3–9.

Robinson, H. A. (1983). *Teaching reading, writing and study strategies: The content areas* (3rd ed.). Boston: Allyn & Bacon.

Robinson, H. M. (1946). *Why pupils fail in reading*. Chicago: University of Chicago Press.

Robinson, H. M. (1966). The major aspects of reading. In H. A. Robinson (Ed.), *Reading: Seventy-five years of progress*. Chicago: University of Chicago Press.

Robinson, H. M. (1967). Developing critical readers. In M. L. King, B. D. Ellinger, & W. Wolf (Eds.), *Critical reading*. Philadelphia: Lippincott.

Robinson, H. M. (1972). Visual and auditory modalities related to methods for beginning reading. *Reading Research Quarterly, 8*, 7–39.

Robinson, H. M., & Huelsman, C. B. (1953). *Clinical studies in reading, II*. (Supplemental Educational Monographs, No. 77). Chicago: University of Chicago Press.

Robinson, M. E., & Schwartz, L. B. (1973). Visuo-motor skills and reading ability: A longitudinal study. *Developmental Medicine and Child Neurology, 15*, 281–286.

Rodenborn, L. (1974). Determining, using expectancy formulas. *The Reading Teacher, 28*, 286–291.

Roelke, P. L. (1969). Reading comprehension as a function of three dimensions of word meaning. *Dissertation Abstracts International, 30*, 5300A–5301A. (University Microfilms No. 70–10, 275)

Rosen, C. L. (1966). A study of visual perception capabilities of first grade pupils and the relationship between visual perception training and reading achievement. *Dissertation Abstracts, 26*, 5247A. (University Microfilms No. 65–15, 287)

Rosen, C. L., & Ortega, P. D. (1969). *Issues in language and reading instruction of Spanish speaking children: An annotated bibliography*. Newark, DE: International Reading Association.

Rosenshine, B. V. (1980). How time is spent in elementary classrooms. In C. Dunham & A. Lieberman (Eds.), *Time to learn* (Publication No. 695–717). Washington, D.C.: U.S. Government Printing Office.

Rosenshine, B., & Stevens, R. (1984). Classroom instruction in reading. In P. D. Pearson (Ed.), *Handbook of reading research*. New York: Longman.

Rothman, J., Palacios, A., & Ruben, P. (1979). *This can lick a lollipop*. Garden City, NY: Doubleday.

Rowell, C. G. (1972). An attitude scale for reading. *The Reading Teacher, 25*, 442–447.

Ruddell, R. B. (1978). Developing comprehension abilities: Implications from research for an instructional framework. In S. J. Samuels (Ed.), *What research has to say about reading instruction*. Newark, DE: International Reading Association.

Ruddell, R. B., & Boyle, O. (1984). A study of the effects of cognitive mapping on reading comprehension and written protocols (Tech. Rep. No. 7). Riverside, CA: University of California, Learning from Text Project.

Rumelhart, D. E. (1976). Toward an interactive model of reading. In S. Dornic (Ed.), *Attention and performance, VI*. Hillsdale, NJ: Erlbaum.

Rumelhart, D. E. (1981). Schemata: The building blocks of cognition. In J. T. Gutherie (Ed.), *Comprehension and reading*. Newark, DE: International Reading Association.

Rupley, W. H., & Blair, T. R. (1979). *Reading diagnosis and remediation: A primer for classroom and clinic*. Chicago: Rand McNally.

Ruppert, E. T. (1976). The effect of the synthetic-multisensory method of language instruction upon psycholinguistic abilities and reading achievement. *Dissertation Abstracts International, 37*, 920A–921A. (University Microfilms No. 76–18, 223)

Rystrom, R. (1970). Negro speech and others: A reply. *Reading Research Quarterly, 6*, 123–125.

S

Sabatino, D. A., Ysseldyke, J. E., & Woolston, J. (1973). Diagnostic-prescriptive perceptual training with mentally retarded children. *American Journal of Mental Deficiency, 78,* 7–14.

Sabine, G., & Sabine, P. (1983). *Books that made the difference: What people told us.* Hamden, CT: Library Professional Publications.

Sadoski, M. (1983). An exploratory study of the relationships between reported imagery and the comprehension and recall of a story. *Reading Research Quarterly, 19,* 110–123.

Sailor, A. L., & Ball, S. E. (1975). Peripheral vision training in reading speed and comprehension. *Perceptual and Motor Skills, 41,* 761–762.

Salmon-Cox, L. (1981). Teachers and standardized achievement tests: What's really happening? *Phi Delta Kappan, 62,* 631–634.

Salvia, J., & Ysseldyke, J. E. (1982). *Assessment in special and remedial education* (2nd ed.). Boston: Houghton Mifflin.

Samuels, S. J. (1972). The effect of letter name knowledge on learning to read. *American Educational Research Journal, 9,* 65–74.

Samuels, S. J. (1977). Introduction to theoretical models of reading. In W. Otto, C. Peters, & N. Peters (Eds.), *Reading problems: A multidisciplinary perspective.* Reading, MA: Addison-Wesley.

Samuels, S. J. (1981). Characteristics of exemplary reading programs. In J. Gutherie (Ed.), *Comprehension and teaching: Reviews of the research.* Newark, DE: International Reading Association.

Samuels, S. J., Begy, G., & Chen, C. C. (1975–76). Comparison of word recognition speed and strategies of less skilled and more highly skilled readers. *Reading Research Quarterly, 11,* 72–86.

Samuels, S. J., & Dahl, P. R. (1975). Relationships among I.Q., learning ability, and reading achievement. In J. Johns (Ed.), *Literacy for diverse learners.* Newark, DE: International Reading Association.

Samuels, S. J., & Turnure, J. E. (1974). Attention and reading achievement in first grade boys and girls. *Journal of Educational Psychology, 66,* 29–32.

Sanders, N. M. (1966). *Classroom questions: What kinds?* New York: Harper & Row.

Santeusanio, R. P. (1983). *A practical approach to content area reading.* Reading, MA: Addison-Wesley.

Santostefano, S., Rutledge, L., & Randall, D. (1965). Cognitive styles and reading disabilities. *Psychology in the Schools, 2,* 57–63.

Saphier, J. D. (1973). The relation of perceptual-motor skills to learning and school success. *Journal of Learning Disabilities, 6,* 583–591.

Sardy, S. J. (1970). Dialect, auditory discrimination and phonics skills. *Dissertation Abstracts International, 30,* 2914–A. (University Microfilms No. 69–21, 022)

Savin, H. B., & Perchonock, E. (1965). Grammatical structure and the immediate recall of English sentences. *Journal of Verbal Learning and Verbal Behavior, 4,* 348–353.

Sawyer, D. J. (1974). The diagnostic mystique—A point of view. *The Reading Teacher, 27,* 555–561.

Schachter, S. W. (1978). Developing flexible reading habits. *Journal of Reading, 22,* 149–152.

Schain, R. J. (1971–72). Neurological diagnosis in children with learning disabilities. *Academic Therapy, 7,* 139–147.

Schell, L. M. (1984a). Test review: Comprehensive Tests of Basic Skills (CTBS, Form U, Levels A–J). *Journal of Reading, 27,* 586–589.

Schell, L. M. (1984b). Test review: Reading Yardsticks. *The Reading Teacher, 38,* 318–321.

Schmeck, R. R., Ribich, F., & Ramanaiah, N. (1977). Development of a self-report inventory for assessing individual differences in learning processes. *Applied Psychological Measurements, 1,* 413–431.

Scott, K. G., & Scott, M. S. (1968). Research and theory in short-term memory. In N. R. Ellis (Ed.), *International review of research in mental re-*tardation, Vol. 3. New York: Academic Press.

Sears, P. S. (1963). *The effect of classroom conditions on the strength of achievement motive and work output on elementary school children.* (Report of Cooperative Research Project No. 873). Washington, D.C.: U.S. Office of Education.

Senf, G. M. (1969). Development of immediate memory for bisensory stimuli in normal children and children with learning disorders. *Dissertation Abstracts International, 29,* 3517B. (University Microfilms No. 69-5351).

Serafica, F. C., & Sigel, J. E. (1970). Styles of categorization and reading disability. *Journal of Reading Behavior, 2,* 105–115.

Shannon, D. (1985). Use of top-level structure in expository text: An open letter to a high school teacher. *Journal of Reading, 28,* 426–431.

Sharon, A. (1973–74). What do adults read? *Reading Research Quarterly, 9,* 148–169.

Sheldon, W. D., & Carrillo, L. (1952). Relation of parents, home, and certain developmental characteristics to children's reading ability. *Elementary School Journal, 52,* 262–270.

Shores, H. J., & Hubbard, K. L. (1950). Are fast readers the best readers? *Elementary English, 27,* 52–57.

Sieben, R. L. (1977). Controversial medical treatments of learning disabilities. *Academic Therapy, 13,* 133–147.

Silberberg, N., & Silberberg, M. (1967). Hyperlexia: Specific word recognition skills in young children. *Exceptional Children, 34,* 41–42.

Silvaroli, N. (1965). Factors in predicting children's success in first grade reading. In J. A. Figurel (Ed.), *Reading and inquiry.* Newark, DE: International Reading Association.

Silver, A. A., & Hagin, R. (1960). Specific reading disability: A delineation of the syndrome and relationship to cerebral dominance. *Comprehensive Psychiatry, 1,* 126–134.

Simmons, G. A., & Shapiro, B. J. (1968). Reading expectancy formulas: A warning note. *Journal of Reading, 11,* 625–629.

Simon, H. (1980). Verbal reports as data. *Psychological Review, 87,* 215–249.

Sindelar, P. T., & Wilson, R. J. (1982, October). *Application of academic skills as a function of teacher-directed instruction and seatwork.* Paper presented at the meeting of the Applied Behavior Analysis in Education Conference, Columbus, OH.

Singer, H. (1969). Theoretical models of reading. *Journal of Communication, 19,* 134–156.

Singer, H. (1978). Active comprehension: From answering to asking questions. *The Reading Teacher, 31,* 901–908.

Sipay, E. R. (1964). A comparison of standardized reading scores and functional reading levels. *The Reading Teacher, 17,* 265–268.

Smith, F. (1971). *Understanding reading.* New York: Holt, Rinehart & Winston.

Smith, F. (1973). *Psycholinguistics and reading.* New York: Holt, Rinehart & Winston.

Smith, F. (1978). *Understanding reading* (2nd ed.). New York: Holt, Rinehart & Winston.

Smith, F. (1982). *Understanding reading* (3rd ed.). New York: Holt, Rinehart & Winston.

Smith, H. P., & Dechant, E. V. (1961). *Psychology in teaching reading.* Englewood Cliffs, NJ: Prentice-Hall.

Smith, I. L., Ringler, L. H., & Cullinan, B. L. (1968). *New York University Learning Modality Test.* New York: New York University.

Smith, L. (1977). Literacy: Definitions and implications. *Language Arts, 54,* 135–138.

Smith, N. B. (1965). *American reading instruction.* Newark, DE: International Reading Association.

Smith, N. B. (1967). Patterns of writing in different subject areas. In M. L. King, B. D. Ellinger, & W. Wolf (Eds.), *Critical reading.* Philadelphia: Lippincott.

Smith, R. J., & Barrett, T. C. (1974). *Teaching reading in the middle grades.* Reading, MA: Addison-Wesley.

Soloman, R., & Postman, L. (1952). Frequency of usage as a determinant of recognition thresholds for words. *Journal of Experimental Psychology, 43,* 195–201.

Sommervil, J. W., Warnberg, L. S., & Bost, D. E. (1973). Effects of cubicles versus increased stimulation on task performance by first grade males perceived as distractible and nondistractible. *The Journal of Special Education, 7,* 169–185.

Spache, G. D. (1962). Is this a breakthrough in reading? *The Reading Teacher, 15,* 258–263.

Spache, G. D. (1974). *Good reading for poor readers.* Champaign, IL: Garrard.

Spache, G. D. (1976). *Investigating the issues of reading disability.* Boston: Allyn & Bacon.

Spache, G. D. (1981). *Diagnosing and correcting reading disabilities* (2nd ed.). Boston: Allyn & Bacon.

Spache, G. D., & Tillman, C. E. (1962). A comparison of the visual profiles of retarded and non-retarded readers. *Journal of Developmental Reading, 5,* 101–109.

Spaulding, R. L. (1963). *Achievement, creativity, and self-concept correlates of teacher-pupil transactions in elementary school classrooms.* (Report of Cooperative Research Project No. 1352). Washington, D.C.: U.S. Office of Education.

Spearitt, D. (1972). Identification of subskills of reading comprehension by maximum likelihood factor analysis. *Reading Research Quarterly, 8,* 92–111.

Sperry, R. W. (1975, August 9). Left-brain, right-brain. *Saturday Review,* pp. 30–33.

Spiegel, D. L., & Rogers, C. (1980). Teacher responses to miscues during oral reading by second-grade students. *Journal of Educational Research, 74,* 8–12.

Staff. (1984). Who takes adult education in U.S.? *Journal of Reading, 28,* 267.

Staff. (1985). Who's taking adult basic education classes? *Journal of Reading, 28,* 364.

Stallings, J. A. (1980). Allocated academic learning time revisited, or beyond time on task. *Educational Researcher, 9* (11), 11–16.

Stallings, J. A. (1986). Using time effectively: A self-analytic approach. In K. K. Zumwalt (Ed.), *Improving teaching.* Alexandria, Virginia: Association for Supervision and Curriculum Development.

Standal, T. C. (1978). Readability formulas: What's out, what's in? *The Reading Teacher, 31,* 642–646.

Stanners, R. F., Jastrzembski, J. E., & Westbrook, A. (1975). Frequency and visual quality in a word-nonword classification task. *Journal of Verbal Learning and Verbal Behavior, 1,* 259–264.

Stauffer, R. G. (1969). *Teaching reading as a thinking process.* New York: Harper & Row.

Stauffer, R. G. (1970). *The language experience approach to the teaching of reading.* New York: Harper & Row.

Stauffer, R. G. (1975). *Directing the reading—thinking process.* New York: Harper & Row.

Stein, N., & Prindaville, P. (1976). Discrimination learning and stimulus generalization by impulsive and reflective children. *Journal of Experimental Child Psychology, 21,* 25–39.

Sticht, T. G. (Ed.). (1975). *Reading for working: A functional literacy anthology.* Alexandria, VA: Human Resources Research Organization.

Sticht, T. G. (1981). *Basic skills in defense.* Alexandria, VA: Human Resources Research Organization.

Sticht, T. G., Beck, L. J., Hauke, R. N., Kleiman, G. M., & James, J. H. (1974). *Auding and reading: A developmental model.* Alexandria, VA: Human Resources Research Organization.

Stolurow, L. M. (1964). Social impact on programmed instruction: Aptitudes and abilities revisited. In J. P. DeCecco (Ed.), *Educational technology.* New York: Holt.

Strang, R., McCullough, C. M., & Traxler, A. E. (1967). *The improvement of reading* (4th ed.). New York: McGraw-Hill.

Stromer, R. (1977). Remediating academic deficiencies in learning disabled children. *Exceptional Children, 43,* 432–440.

Sulzer-Azaroff, B., & Mayer, R. G. (1977). *Applying behavior-analysis procedures with children and youth.* New York: Holt, Rinehart & Winston.

Suran, B., & Rizzo, J. (1979). *Special children: An integrative approach.* Glenville, IL: Scott, Foresman & Co.

Swalm, J. E. (1972). A comparison of oral reading, silent reading, and listening. *Education, 92,* 111–115.

Swartz, S. (1979). *The writing and teaching of adolescent literature.* San Diego, CA: Paper presented at the California Association of Teachers of English annual meeting. (ERIC Document Reproduction Service No. ED 170 770)

Swartz, R. M., & Raphael, T. E. (1985). Concept of definition: A key to improving students' vocabulary. *The Reading Teacher, 39,* 198–205.

Swassing, R. H., & Barbe, W. B. (1979). *The Swassing Barbe Modality Index.* Columbus, OH: Zaner-Bloser.

Szasz, T. S. (1970). *The manufacture of madness: A comparative study of the inquisition and the mental health movement.* New York: Dell.

T

Tadlock, D. F. (1978). SQ3R—Why it works, based on an information processing theory of learning. *Journal of Reading, 22,* 110–112.

Tapia, F. (1968). Girls with conditions seen mostly in boys. *Diseases of the Nervous System, 29,* 323–326.

Tarver, S. G., & Dawson, M. M. (1978). Modality preference and the teaching of reading. *Journal of Learning Disabilities, 11,* 5–29.

Taylor, B. M., & Beach, R. W. (1984). The effects of text structure instruction on middle-grade students' comprehension and production of expository text. *Reading Research Quarterly, 19,* 134–146.

Taylor, E. A. (1937). *Controlled reading.* Chicago: University of Chicago Press.

Taylor, W. L. (1953). Cloze procedure: A new tool for measuring readability. *Journalism Quarterly, 30,* 415–433.

Thompson, B. B. (1963). A longitudinal study of auditory discrimination. *The Journal of Educational Research, 56,* 376–378.

Thonis, E. W. (1976). *Literacy for America's Spanish speaking children.* Newark, DE: International Reading Association.

Thorndike, E. L. (1917). Reading as reasoning: A study of mistakes in paragraph reading. *Journal of Educational Psychology, 8,* 323–332.

Thorndike, E. L., & Lorge, I. (1944). *The teacher's word book of 30,000 words.* New York: Columbia University Teacher's College.

Thorndike, R. L. (1973). *Reading comprehension education in fifteen countries.* New York: Wiley.

Thorndike, R. L. (1974). Reading as reasoning. *Reading Research Quarterly, 9,* 137–147.

Tien, H. C. (1971). Hyperlexia, hypolexia, or dyslexia. *Journal of Special Education, 5,* 257–259.

Timian, J., & Santeusanio, R. (1974). Context clues: An informal reading inventory. *The Reading Teacher, 27,* 706–709.

Tinker, M. A. (1936). Eye movements in reading. *Journal of Educational Research, 30,* 241–277.

Tinker, M. A. (1958). Recent studies of eye movements in reading. *Psychological Bulletin, 55,* 4.

Tinker, M. A. (1965). *Bases for effective reading.* Minneapolis: University of Minnesota Press.

Torgerson, T. L., & Adams, G. S. (1954). *Measurement and evaluation for the elementary school teacher.* New York: Holt, Rinehart & Winston.

Torgesen, J., & Goldman, T. (1977). Verbal rehearsal and short-term memory in reading-disabled children. *Child Development, 48,* 56–60.

Travers, R. (1967). Perceptual learning. *Review of Educational Research, 5,* 599–619.

Treblas, P. V., McCormick, S., & Cooper, J. O. (1982). Problems in mainstreaming at the grassroots. *The Directive Teacher, 4,* 14–18.

Trione, V. (1967). The school psychologist, teacher change, and fourth grade reading achievement. *California Journal of Educational Research, 18,* 194–200.

Two million micros in public schools by 1988. (1983, October). *Teaching and Computers,* p. 8.

U

Ullmann, C. A. (1969). Prevalence of reading disability as a function of the measure used. *Journal of Learning Disabilities, 2,* 556–558.

V

Vacca, R. (1981). *Content area reading.* Boston: Little, Brown.

Valmont, W. J. (1983). Cloze deletion patterns: How deletions are made makes a big difference. *The Reading Teacher, 37,* 172–175.

Vandever, T. R., & Neville, D. D. (1974a). Letter cues vs. configuration cues as aids to word recognition in retarded and nonretarded children. *American Journal of Mental Deficiency, 79,* 210–213.

Vandever, T. R., & Neville, D. D. (1974b). Modality aptitude and word recognition. *Journal of Reading Behavior, 6,* 195–201.

Van Houten, R., & McKillop, C. (1977). An extension of the effects of the performance feedback: Secondary school students. *Psychology in the Schools, 14,* 480-484.

Van Houten, R., & Van Houten, J. (1977). The performance feedback system in the special education classroom: An analysis of public posting and peer comments. *Behavior Therapy, 8,* 366–376.

Venezsky, R. L. (1970). Regularity in reading and spelling. In H. Levin & J. Williams (Eds.), *Basic studies on reading.* New York: Basic Books.

Venezsky, R. L. (1975). The curious role of letter names in reading instruction. *Visible Language, 9,* 7–23.

Veron, M. D. (1971). *Reading and its difficulties.* London, England: Cambridge University.

Vernon, P. E. (1962). The determinants of reading comprehension. *Educational and Psychological Measurement, 22,* 269–286.

Voight, S. (1978). It's all Greek to me. *The Reading Teacher, 31,* 420-422.

W

Wachs, T. D., Uzgiris, I. C., & Hunt, J. McV. (1971). Cognitive development in infants of different age levels and from different environmental backgrounds: An exploratory investigation. *Merrill-Palmer Quarterly, 17,* 283–317.

Wade, E. W. (1961). The construction and validation of a test of ten teacher skills used in reading instruction, grades two to five. *Dissertation Abstracts, 22,* 167A. (University Microfilms No. 60–6071)

Wagoner, S. A. (1983). Comprehension monitoring: What it is and what we know about it. *Reading Research Quarterly, 18,* 328–346.

Wallen, N. E., & Wodtke, K. H. (1963). *Relationships between teacher characteristics and student behavior—Part I* (Report of Project No. 1217). Washington, D.C.: U.S. Office of Education.

Wangberg, E. G., Thompson, B., & Levitov, J. E. (1984). First steps toward an adult basic word list. *Journal of Reading, 28,* 244–247.

Ward, M., & McCormick, S. (1981). Reading instruction for blind and low vision children in the regular classroom. *The Reading Teacher, 34,* 434–444.

Warwick, B. E. (1978). Cloze procedures (Ebbinghaus completion method) as applied to reading. In O. K. Buros (Ed.), *Eighth mental measurements yearbook, Vol. II.* Highland Park, NJ: Gryphon Press.

Weber, G. (1971). *Inner-city children can be taught to read.* Washington, D.C.: Council for Basic Education.

Weber, R. (1970). Some reservations on the significance of dialect in the acquisition of reading. In J. A. Figurel (Ed.), *Reading goals for the disadvantaged.* Newark, DE: International Reading Association.

Weinstein, R. S. (1976). Reading group membership in first grade, teacher behaviors, and pupil experience over time. *Journal of Educational Psychology, 88,* 103–116.

Werner, E. E., Simonian, K., Smith, R. S. (1967). Reading achievement, language functioning and perceptual-motor development of 10- and 11-year-olds. *Perceptual Motor Skills, 25,* 409–420.

Werner, H. & Strauss, A. A. (1940). Causal factors in low performance. *American Journal of Mental Deficiency, 45,* 213–218.

West, R. F., Stanovich, K. E., Feeman, D. J., & Cunningham, A. E. (1983). The effect of sentence context on word recognition in second- and sixth-grade children. *Reading Research Quarterly, 19,* 6–15.

Westover, F. L. (1946). *Controlled eye movements versus practice exercises in reading.* New York: Bureau of Publications, Teachers College, Columbia University.

Williams, J. L. (1964). A comparison of standardized reading test scores and informal reading inventory scores. *Dissertation Abstracts International, 24,* 5262A. (University Microfilms No. 64–4485)

Willows, D. M., & Ryan, E. B. (1986). The development of grammatical sensitivity and its relationship to early reading achievement. *Reading Research Quarterly, 21,* 253–266.

Wilson, M. M. (1979). The processing strategies of average and below average readers answering factual and inferential questions on three equivalent passages. *Journal of Reading Behavior, 11,* 235–245.

Wilson, R. M., & Barnes, M. M. (1974). *Survival learning materials.* York, PA: Strine Publishing.

Witty, P. (1953). *How to become a better reader.* Chicago: Science Research Associates.

Woodcock, R. W. (1967). The Nashville-Chicago-Detroit reading program: Report of the second year results. *Institute on Mental Retardation and Intellectual Development, 4,* 155.

Woodcock, R. W., & Dunn, L. M. (1967). *Efficacy of several approaches for teaching reading to the educable mentally retarded.* (U.S. Office of Education Project). Nashville, TN: George Peabody College for Teachers.

Worthington, J. S. (1977). The readability of footnotes to financial statements and how to improve them. *Journal of Reading, 20,* 469–478.

Wrightstone, J. W., Aaronow, M. S., & Moskowitz, S. (1963). Developing reading test norms for deaf children. *American Annals of the Deaf, 108,* 314–316.

Wylie, R. E. (1969). Diversified concepts of the role of the reading consultant. *The Reading Teacher, 22,* 519–522.

Y

Young, B. (1976). A simple formula for predicting reading potential. *The Reading Teacher, 29,* 659–661.

Ysseldyke, J. E., & Algozzine, B. (1982). *Critical issues in special and remedial education.* Boston: Houghton Mifflin.

Yukish, J. F. (1976–77). Do letter reversals imply a reading disability? *Ohio Reading Teacher, 11,* 6–12.

Z

Zigler, E., & Seitz, V. (1975). On an experimental evaluation of sensorimotor patterning: A critique. *American Journal of Mental Deficiency, 79,* 483–492.

Zintz, M. A. (1972). *Corrective reading* (2nd ed.). Dubuque, IA: W. C. Brown.

Ziros, G. I. (1976). Language interference and teaching the Chicano to read. *Journal of Reading, 19,* 284–288.

Zutell, J. (1985). Linguistic and psycholinguistic perspectives on brain mechanisms and language. In Rental, V., Corson, S., & Dunn, B. (Eds.), *Psychophysiological aspects of reading and learning.* New York: Gordon & Breach.

Index

WE VALUE YOUR OPINION—PLEASE SHARE IT WITH US

Merrill Publishing and our authors are most interested in your reactions to this textbook. Did it serve you well in the course? If it did, what aspects of the text were most helpful? If not, what didn't you like about it? Your comments will help us to write and develop better textbooks. We value your opinions and thank you for your help.

Text Title _____ Edition _____

Author(s) _____

Your Name (optional) _____

Address _____

City _____ State _____ Zip _____

School _____

Course Title _____

Instructor's Name _____

Your Major _____

Your Class Rank _____ Freshman _____ Sophomore _____Junior _____ Senior

_____ Graduate Student

Were you required to take this course? _____ Required _____Elective

Length of Course? _____ Quarter _____ Semester

1. Overall, how does this text compare to other texts you've used?

_____ Superior _____Better Than Most _____ Average _____Poor

2. Please rate the text in the following areas:

	Superior	Better Than Most	Average	Poor
Author's Writing Style	_____	_____	_____	_____
Readability	_____	_____	_____	_____
Organization	_____	_____	_____	_____
Accuracy	_____	_____	_____	_____
Layout and Design	_____	_____	_____	_____
Illustrations/Photos/Tables	_____	_____	_____	_____
Examples	_____	_____	_____	_____
Problems/Exercises	_____	_____	_____	_____
Topic Selection	_____	_____	_____	_____
Currentness of Coverage	_____	_____	_____	_____
Explanation of Difficult Concepts	_____	_____	_____	_____
Match-up with Course Coverage	_____	_____	_____	_____
Applications to Real Life	_____	_____	_____	_____

3. Circle those chapters you especially liked:
   1   2   3   4   5   6   7   8   9   10   11   12   13   14   15   16   17   18   19   20
   What was your favorite chapter? _____
   Comments:

4. Circle those chapters you liked least:
   1   2   3   4   5   6   7   8   9   10   11   12   13   14   15   16   17   18   19   20
   What was your least favorite chapter? _____
   Comments:

5. List any chapters your instructor did not assign. _____

6. What topics did your instructor discuss that were not covered in the text?_____

   _____

7. Were you required to buy this book? _____ Yes _____ No

   Did you buy this book new or used? _____ New _____ Used

   If used, how much did you pay? _____

   Do you plan to keep or sell this book? _____ Keep _____ Sell

   If you plan to sell the book, how much do you expect to receive? _____

   Should the instructor continue to assign this book? _____ Yes _____ No

8. Please list any other learning materials you purchased to help you in this course (e.g., study guide, lab manual).

   _____

9. What did you like most about this text? _____

   _____

10. What did you like least about this text? _____

    _____

11. General comments:

    May we quote you in our advertising? _____ Yes _____ No

    Please mail to: Boyd Lane
                      College Division, Research Department
                      Box 508
                      1300 Alum Creek Drive
                      Columbus, Ohio 43216

    Thank you!